FAMILY PLANNING
AND
POPULATION PROGRAMS

FAMILY PLANNING

AND

POPULATION

PROGRAMS

A Review
of World Developments

THE UNIVERSITY OF CHICAGO PRESS
CHICAGO AND LONDON

Standard Book Number: 226-04347-9
Library of Congress Catalog Card Number: 66-20575

THE UNIVERSITY OF CHICAGO PRESS, CHICAGO 60637
The University of Chicago Press, Ltd., London

To

Our Colleague

MARSHALL C. BALFOUR, M.D.

On the Occasion of His Retirement

THE ROCKEFELLER FOUNDATION, 1926–1960
THE POPULATION COUNCIL, 1958–1965

FOREWORD

The International Conference on Family Planning Programs, the first of its character ever to be held, met at Geneva, Switzerland, on August 23–27, 1965. It was sponsored by the Ford Foundation and the Population Council, with additional support from the Rockefeller Foundation. The Conference was attended by nearly two hundred participants from thirty-six countries on every continent: obstetricians and gynecologists, public health administrators, health educators, media specialists, educators, demographers, economists, and behavioral scientists; from governmental health offices, medical schools, university departments, national aid and technical assistance programs, planned parenthood centers, international organizations, and private foundations.

This is not the place to stress the importance of the world's population problem. That has been fully documented elsewhere and is becoming increasingly recognized and attacked throughout the world. Indeed, a major *raison d'être* for the Conference was precisely that developments in this field had been so numerous and rapid in recent months that some review and consolidation was needed. Consider, for example, how much has happened in the course of the past few years.

Family planning programs are successfully underway in South Korea, Taiwan, and Tunisia, and are currently in process of major expansion and intensification in India and Pakistan. Turkey, Malaysia, Singapore, Ceylon, and Egypt are embarking upon national efforts. A high-level seminar on population policy in Thailand was followed by a successful pilot project and that in turn by a seminar to consider extension of the program there. In the Philippines, the Health Department of Manila and a major university are beginning experimental efforts. In Latin America, the first Pan-American Assembly on Population Problems was held in summer, 1965; Peru and Venezuela have established population units within their Ministries of Health, and Colombia within its Association of Medical Faculties;

and a national program is being established in Chile. The government of Mauritius is supporting family planning efforts there, and a technical assistance mission submitted its report to the government of Kenya in the summer of 1965, the first such mission to a country in sub-Saharan Africa.

Within the United Nations, the World Health Organization in May, 1965, authorized the development of an advisory program; the UNICEF Governing Council in June instructed the Director to prepare a statement on possible activities in the field; and the Economic and Social Council in July unanimously recommended "advisory services and training on action programs in population." Moreover, the United Nations sent an expert mission to India in the spring of 1965 to advise on that country's family planning program, and so did the World Bank.

The Roman Catholic Church became engaged in a "wide and profound" study of its position on this matter, including the establishment of a Papal Commission. Several high prelates in the Ecumenical Council called for a searching re-examination of Church teachings.

A major advance in contraceptive technology, the intra-uterine device, was developed and came into widespread use.

In the United States, the Agency for International Development extended its policy in the spring of 1965 to include the provision of technical assistance on family planning. Several universities have established centers for population study, typically in their schools of public health. Two great American foundations have included population studies prominently among their programs. The American Medical Association reversed a neutral policy dating from the 1930's; the National Academy of Sciences issued reports on world and United States population problems; the Supreme Court voided a state law against contraception on grounds of the right to personal privacy; federal, state, and local governmental agencies expanded their activities in family planning; and the President of the United States spoke out about the urgency of dealing with population problems.

All these developments occurred not in the past twenty years, or even ten, but in the past three years, many of them within the past twelve months. As someone has said, nothing is so powerful as an idea that has come of age.

So one of the tasks of the Conference was to guide and expedite subsequent efforts by spreading information about family planning programs from one geographic area to another and from one specialization to another. This volume is the outcome—a volume containing papers on the major family planning programs underway throughout the world in mid-1965 and on the major substantive problems confronting the specialists involved.

The Conference was administered by a Planning Committee whose members are listed facing the title page. That Committee not only made all the arrangements for the Conference and issued invitations to the participants, but organized the final program and selected authors for both the background papers (distributed in advance) and the papers presented at the several sessions, all of which were held before the entire membership. This volume follows the Conference organization.

The Planning Committee and the supporting organizations are indebted to all the people who contributed to the success of the Conference. It is no easy task to take care of the numerous arrangements that need to be made for such a meeting, especially one of an international character. Mrs. Catherine Gallaway of the Population Council handled such matters with her customary competence and good humor. She was assisted at Geneva by Miss Joyce Tait of the Council staff. Miss Martha Dalrymple and Mr. Clarkson Hill, also of the Council, took good care of informational and administrative matters, respectively. The staff of the Hotel Intercontinental, the site of the Conference, was most helpful in enabling the sessions to run smoothly and comfortably.

In view of the rapid developments characterizing this field, the Planning Committee has made every effort to bring these proceedings out at the earliest possible moment. In this endeavor we have been greatly aided by the skill and speed with which the papers were edited for publication by Mrs. Gallaway, Dudley Kirk, Mrs. Raymond Lamontagne, Mrs. Dorothy Nortman, John A. Ross, Lyle Saunders, Miss Kathleen Shafer, Mrs. Robert Spelleri, and Dr. and Mrs. Christopher Tietze, as well as by some members of the Planning Committee.

Mainly, however, we are indebted to the authors of papers and the participants themselves. As was said at the opening of the Conference: "It is not given to many men to be at the right place at the right time doing the right thing. The population problem is among the world's great problems. Whether it will be attacked soon enough, well enough, hard enough, depends upon the people in this room. That sobering yet simple fact bears repetition: one of the world's greatest problems rests mainly on the people in this room. If the problem is to be attacked in a major way in the next five to ten years, you will do the job. If you do not, the job will not be done. There is no sharper way to commend to you—and to the world outside that depends on you—the importance of this meeting: an importance that justifies the term historic. We are all engaged in an historic undertaking and we of the Planning Committee trust that this Conference will prove to be an historic milestone along the way." It is in that spirit that we offer this volume.

BERNARD BERELSON
Chairman, The Planning Committee

CONTENTS

---

xi

PART TWO

Organization and Administration of Programs

PART THREE

Contraceptive Methods: Programmatic Implications

PART FOUR

Research and Evaluation

OPENING REMARKS

JOHN D. ROCKEFELLER 3RD
Chairman of the Board of Trustees, The Population Council

In 1960 the Milbank Fund and the Population Council co-sponsored a conference in New York on Research in Family Planning. The seventy participants came from ten countries, and although they represented different aspects of work in family planning, most of them were oriented toward research. Here, only five years later, are nearly two hundred participants from over thirty-five countries, and the emphasis has shifted from research to action.

The main objectives of this Conference are to assess the status of family planning programs throughout the world, to enable you to pool your experiences, to exchange information and ideas, and to discuss your methods, your problems, your failures and your successes. It is important to realize that the papers to be presented here will contain the major part of all that is known about organizing, conducting, and evaluating programs of family planning.

Since 1960, the population problem and the initiation of action toward its solution have become matters of increasing public interest. Several countries have embarked on national family planning programs. Others have undertaken pilot projects and are developing national policies on population. Such progress is encouraging, but far from enough to cope with what President Johnson recently described as "the multiplying problems of our multiplying populations."

In the past few years, I have taken several trips to different parts of the world and have had the opportunity to talk about population with numerous government officials and private citizens. These trips, and my association with the Population Council since its founding thirteen years ago, have led me to certain conclusions, which I would like to mention briefly.

The first is that, today, no problem is more urgently important to the well-being of mankind than the limitation of population growth. It is a world problem demanding the attention of all nations, East and West, large and small, developed and developing. In many parts of the world it obstructs much needed economic growth even as it fosters social unrest and political instability.

In a recent statement before the United Nations Population Commission, the Director General of the Food and Agriculture Organization, Dr. B. R. Sen, described the seriousness of the problem as he sees it from his vantage point. He said:

> ... it has been recognized that there will be no lasting peace or security in the world until hunger and want can be eliminated. In fact what is in danger is not merely the health and happiness of individuals but the very basis of free and democratic society. The next 35 years, till the end of the century, will be, as I have said, a most critical period in man's history. Either we take the fullest measures both to raise productivity and to stabilize population growth, or we will face disaster of an unprecedented magnitude. We must be warned that in the present situation lie the seeds of unlimited progress or unlimited disaster, not only for individual nations but for the whole world. I myself feel optimistic that mankind will not stand aloof from the drama of life and death that is unfolding before our eyes but will come forward to achieve that miracle of organized will which seems too distant today. This indeed must happen if freedom and dignity are to survive.

This forthright statement expresses the urgency of the population problem far better than I could.

My second conclusion is that world leaders must recognize, without further delay, the gravity of the population problem and act now to resolve it, political sensitivities notwithstanding.

I recognize that it is sometimes difficult for government to take initiative on questions which are considered politically sensitive. Government moves most effectively when need has been demonstrated, when public opinion has begun to form, when history is on the march. In my opinion, we have reached this point in regard to the population problem.

The subject of population limitation is losing the aura of sensitivity which for so long forestalled action or even reasonable discussion. However, most top government officials still seem to consider the matter too controversial to risk taking responsibility for bold and imaginative leadership in effective programs of population limitation. Consequently, the relatively few action programs have, for the most part, been initiated and supported by private individuals, private organizations, and a small number of concerned government officials with little more than acquiescence from top-level leaders.

The reluctance to act of world leaders adds to the difficulties of your work, but it adds also to the challenge. Your knowledge can influence, your experiences can provide a rational basis upon which governments can formulate policies and programs. The success of your pilot projects has demonstrated that the desire for family planning far exceeds the estimates of government leaders. Moreover, your work is heartening evidence that the intelligence and ingenuity of man can resolve the population problem—and soon enough to avert the worst of its consequences, granted always that leadership is found equal to the challenge.

My third conclusion is that if the population problem is to be resolved, government organization must be strengthened and developed so that it can effectively provide the family planning information and services people want and need.

It might be said that a successful program of family planning has three basic ingredients: practical contraceptives, public acceptance, and effective organization. The development of the intra-uterine device and the success of recent pilot projects are solid indications that the first two ingredients are no longer the primary problem, although work in technology and motivation must continue. But the lack of the third ingredient—adequate government organization—will hamper and may ultimately frustrate all our efforts.

Private groups like those sponsoring this Conference have played and will continue to play a significant role in the solution of the population problem, but only government can provide the organization to deal effectively with the problem on the scale required. Only government has the resources and the capacity for the sustained and concerted effort needed to make voluntary family planning a fact throughout the world. Only government can assure that the myriads of individual decisions, which are the very substance of the population problem, can be made in the light of knowledge rather than in the darkness of ignorance.

My final conclusion is that the ultimate objective of our work in family planning is not the restriction of human life, but rather its enrichment.

To me, it is disturbing that so many people think of the population problem only as numbers of people versus available food. This seems to equate man with animal, and food with fodder. The question, as I see it, has, in fact, three dimensions. It is numbers of people versus material resources—but also cultural resources. This third dimension of the population problem is society's ability to satisfy man's mental, emotional, and spiritual needs and aspirations, what every man needs in addition to bare necessities and creature comforts, to lead a life of satisfaction and purpose, to achieve in life more than mere existence.

Those who are concerned with the *quality* of life have no choice but to be concerned as well with the *quantity* of life. Even if science by some magic could show the way to feed new billions of people, we still would not have solved the population problem. The moral, spiritual, and intellectual aspects of life cannot be omitted from the solution. Indeed there can be no true solution until society can offer every individual an opportunity to live—in the fullest sense—as well as to survive.

John Kenneth Galbraith recently wrote that in every country there are two classes of people: those who see the ultimate problem and warn, and those who see the immediate problem and act. The former are the prophets and philosophers; the latter are the operators. He maintains that family planning is still in the hands of the philosophers and prophets. The important thing, he points out, is that the population problem must now be put into the hands of those who act.

You are the relative few who have acted—or are preparing to act. You have recognized that it is no longer enough merely to call attention to the ultimate problem and warn. You know that the problem is immediate, and that the time for action is now. The hopes of many countries for the well-being of their people rest heavily upon the success of family planning. I believe it is reasonable to say that your work will be the major factor in determining that success, and therefore that you carry the key to the resolution of the world's most important problem.

On behalf of my friends at the Ford Foundation and my associates in the Population Council and the Rockefeller Foundation, I hope this conference serves you well. May you leave strengthened by a constructive exchange of information and by an increased awareness of the importance of your work; and, thus, even better prepared to fulfill your basic mission: the enrichment of human life and the enhancement of individual dignity.

PART ONE

National Programs: Achievements and Problems

1

JAPAN

MINORU MURAMATSU, M.D.
Institute of Public Health

ORIGINS AND OPERATIONS OF FAMILY PLANNING PROGRAMS

Japan experienced a sudden population increase immediately after the last war. The population of Japan as a whole in 1945 was estimated to be 72 million. Three years later it had risen to a level of 80 million, according to the census taken in 1948. This sudden jump in population was due partly to large-scale repatriation and demobilization, but as a more persistent cause the postwar baby boom exerted a significant influence. The crude birth rate for 1948, for example, was recorded as 33.5, which means a total of about 2.7 million births.

Defeat in the war meant an extremely difficult time for the general public. Daily life, especially in large cities, suffered tremendously. Faced with adverse economic conditions people did not take long to recognize the necessity of birth limitation in order not to lower further their level of living. Thus concern over the country's overpopulation and its inevitable relation to the nation's economic future came to the fore, and awareness of the need for birth limitation rose spontaneously among the people.

In 1946 and 1947 a number of newspapers and radio programs took the lead in discussions about population problems. A minor protest against birth control as a solution was raised from time to time in these discussions for ideological or religious reasons, but the general trend was represented by a group of strong proponents of fertility limitation. It is believed that mass communication of this kind acted powerfully to encourage and endorse the general feeling of the need for fertility control both as national policy and as the practice within individual families.

In the meantime, the primary method to which people began to

7

resort for the purpose of birth control was induced abortion. Despite the fact that the old National Eugenic Law of 1940 was still alive, with its highly restrictive attitude toward induced abortion, the illegal performance of induced abortion showed an upward trend. Concerned with this, a number of leading gynecologists of the Japanese Medical Association met in 1947 for preliminary discussions on possible repeal or amendment of the law, which seemed to have become so inappropriate. This movement proceeded further, and in the following year a new legal basis for the performance of induced abortion was established which has since been known as the Eugenic Protection Law. The new enactment was first introduced to the Diet by a number of medical representatives and was passed by both Houses without serious objections. According to the original proposal, the objective of the Eugenic Protection Law was twofold: first, it aimed at eliminating as far as possible the undesirable effects of criminal, clandestinely performed induced abortion by according more liberal indications for its legal performance, and, second, it implied a hope that induced abortion would help ameliorate the grave problem of rapid population growth.

In 1949 and later, vigorous discussions of Japan's overpopulation continued. The Population Association of Japan, the Population Problem Council established by the government, and other official organizations all favored the adoption of fertility regulation as a necessary population policy. However, the administrative units of the government never explicitly adopted these recommendations and resolutions. That the population phenomenon itself was serious enough was obvious to many, but nevertheless the actual adoption of a government policy to advocate openly a negative check on population growth was still highly debatable. On the other hand, the government did take a positive step forward in 1949 by authorizing the sale of some sixty brands of contraceptive chemicals. In a word, population was talked about in many quarters of society in those years, but the government purposely refrained from taking a definite stand because of the highly complicated nature of the topic, though it initiated a preliminary step to meet the people's demand for contraceptive materials.

In October, 1951, the government leaders met in a cabinet conference to discuss the increase in induced abortions. They were cognizant of an acute demand by the people for fertility control but rather seriously concerned about the many induced abortions. They decided to indicate officially their preference for "conception control" over induced abortion as a means to regulate fertility and issued a cabinet decision which contained the following statement: "The number of induced abortions is increasing each year. These are often necessary to protect the life and health of the mother. Occasional damage to the mother's health, however, makes the dissemination of the knowledge of contraception desirable to eliminate the bad influence of abortions on the mother's health. . . ." A possible interpretation of this move would be that here again a certain demographic consideration was involved behind the scenes but that the stated aim of switching from induced abortion to contraception provided an immediate and rational motive for the official promotion of family planning practice. To put it somewhat differently, motivation toward family limitation was already sufficient; the leaders did not have to enter into an embarrassing discussion of population. What concerned government people most were the methods through which people tried to accomplish their purpose. Once it became a matter of choice of methods, it could legitimately be handled as a health question. Hence there is no direct allusion to population in the statement, and the responsibility for administrative operations was assigned to the Ministry of Health and Welfare.

In 1952 the Eugenic Protection Law underwent a radical amendment. With this amendment, a consultation on the part of physicians with a local official committee as to the legality of a proposed performance of induced abortion was no longer required. The judgment in each case was to be made entirely at the discretion of the physician concerned. Even today not a few have serious doubt whether a physician can make an objective judgment when a woman asks for an abortion mainly on economic grounds. In any event, the number of induced abortions maintained its steady rise until 1955, when a total of 1.17 million abortions were reported.

Meanwhile, also in 1952, the Ministry of Health and Welfare introduced for the first time government programs explicitly designed for the promotion of family planning. The Bureau of Public Health of the Ministry assumed the administrative responsibility. In the directives issued, three levels of family planning education of the general public were indicated: "general education" in the principles of family planning to be administered mainly by the central and prefectural governments; "group education" designed for small groups of people to learn about various techniques of contraception, to be carried out mainly by local health centers and family planning instructors; and finally "individual education," which provides an opportunity for a detailed personal consultation about contraception with family planning instructors. The programs aimed to cover the nation as a whole, the target group being all married persons desiring to practice family planning. Although there were some fluctuations in the actual amount from year to year, certain budgetary appropriations were provided by the central government for these programs, usually in the form of grants-in-aid (Table 1). It is to be noted that these subsidies were given to all prefectures at a rate of one-half to one-third the expected expenditures—in other words, the actual sum spent on official family planning programs in those years in Japan

TABLE 1

FAMILY PLANNING BUDGET, 1952–65,
PROVIDED BY THE JAPANESE MINISTRY
OF HEALTH AND WELFARE

Year	Yen (millions)	U.S. $ (thousands)
1952[a]	21.2	59
1953	39.3	109
1954	28.9	80
1955	58.7	163
1956	58.5	163
1957	71.8	199
1958	72.5	201
1959	54.1	150
1960	47.7	133
1961	53.8	149
1962	55.9	155
1963	62.7	174
1964	66.4	184
1965[b]		

[a] From 1952 through 1964, the budget shown in this table was compiled as federal grants-in-aid to prefectures at a rate of one-half to one-third the actual expenditure. The total amount spent on family planning in Japan as a whole was therefore two to three times the amount given.

[b] In 1965 a change was made in the over-all policy regarding family planning. Instead of central and prefectural governments, local community authorities are to be directly responsible for the administration of family planning programs. The central government urged all community administrators to carry on the programs, using roughly the same budget as that of 1964, but only a small number of local communities will actually carry out the programs, it is anticipated.

as a whole was two to three times as high as the amount shown here. A certain proportion of the budget was earmarked for preparing audiovisual materials for family planning education, such as leaflets, pamphlets, and slides, but the major portion was for administrative expenses. Until 1954 there were no provisions for the government to subsidize the purchase of contraceptive materials; the main sources of supply were commercial channels, predominantly local drugstores, though in some cases local midwives and women's groups took the initiative in their distribution.

In the actual execution of the programs the question of personnel naturally came up. Medical doctors, public health nurses, and midwives alike were all regarded as important, especially in relation to the personal consultation on family planning techniques. Viewed from the practical standpoint, however, and particularly from the standpoint of their wide geographical distribution, the government decided to rely heavily on midwives. In order to make village midwives familiar with the principles and techniques of modern family planning, and also to overcome the inherent feeling among some of them that birth control runs counter to their primary mission of helping mothers through childbirth, a number of refresher training courses were initiated throughout the country. A curriculum of 33 hours, including some practical experience in the fitting of the diaphragm in addition to formal didactic lectures, was set up. In the teaching of methods, the general pattern indicated to the trainees was to let the client choose whatever method she liked after an over-all explanation of all methods that the instructor thought appropriate to that particular case. The methods thus advocated included such traditional methods as condoms, diaphragms, tablets, jellies, and the safe period. Upon completion of this official training, graduates were awarded the title of "family planning instructor," which authorized the handling and even the sale of contraceptive materials. The instructors were encouraged to seek, on their own, possible clients of family planning in their villages, but no honorarium or the like was provided by the government, at least for the first three years after the initiation of the programs.

In this initial step of the government-sponsored family planning programs in Japan, one may note that the administrative scheme put the task of family planning teaching upon health center personnel, who had already been occupied with routine health activities. No specific category of personnel exclusively devoted to family planning was created at the local level; the health officers in charge of maternal and child health at local health centers were in function also for family planning. Thus, through lack of time and personnel, health centers mostly turned to midwives for their active participation in individual education. The midwives, on the other hand, certainly did take interest in their own training so as to obtain the official title of "family planning instructor." They soon realized, however, that family planning teaching was time-consuming and painstaking but not necessarily gainful economically. In consequence, family planning clinics held at health centers were not active, and the home visits to be carried out by the instructors were infrequent.

Against these administrative problems of family planning, however, the practice of contraception among the general public made steady progress (Table 2). Women's magazines and word-of-mouth communication apparently provided major sources of information. At the same time the number of women visiting doctors for induced abortion was still on the rise.

In 1955, the government introduced a second step in its official programs for the promotion of family planning in Japan. The emphasis in the revised approach was mainly on two points: (1) since there was a strong demand for more practical information about techniques of family planning, not for preaching the advantages of a planned family, it was felt necessary to strengthen the technical information service; and (2) a number of couples, though not many,

TABLE 2

PROPORTION OF CURRENT CONTRACEPTORS AMONG WIVES
UNDER 50 YEARS OF AGE, 1950–65, JAPAN

Year	Source	Per Cent
1950........	Mainichi Newspapers	19.5
1951........	National Opinion Survey Institute	19.0
1952........	Institute of Population Problems	21.7
1954........	Ministry of Health and Welfare	33.2
1955........	Mainichi Newspapers	33.6
1957........	Mainichi Newspapers	39.2
1959........	Mainichi Newspapers	42.5
1961........	Mainichi Newspapers	42.3
1963........	Mainichi Newspapers	44.0
1965........	Mainichi Newspapers	51.9

could not afford to purchase contraceptive materials themselves. The government saw fit to correct the situation by providing a subsidy from public funds whereby the necessary materials could be obtained either free of charge or at half the usual cost.

As a result of this policy decision, since 1955 the family planning promotion service for the economically disadvantaged has become a major component of the programs. The total budgetary allocation increased considerably because of this addition of direct service for the indigent. The training of midwives was expanded to produce more family planning instructors, so that intimate consultations about contraceptive practice could be held without difficulty in towns and villages. Also, a special item was added to the budget which allowed some remuneration for those midwives who had participated in the teaching of family planning for the economically less advantaged.

Since it was generally recognized that there were no particular difficulties for the general public in their purchase of contraceptive materials except for the economically handicapped, and that the new scheme would offer a substantial help to such underprivileged couples financially, this modification in the programs was welcomed in many quarters. As time went on, and as the scheme was put into effect, however, a number of new administrative problems arose. In the first place, the definition of the indigent who were entitled to receive contraceptives at reduced cost was hard to determine. Also, not a few rejected the service when they learned that it was specifically designed for the poor. The family planning instructors found it too laborious to seek out the widely scattered, relatively few indigent clients. Even when they succeeded in reaching them by home visits, a personal consultation was hardly possible because of their housing and other conditions. Moreover, the remuneration which the government provided for the instructors, though raised frequently year after year, was not considered adequate. As a result, the scheme had to be revised in small details from time to time. The immediate objective, the reduction of induced abortions, was accomplished to some extent, as indicated by the downward trend in reported abortions since 1955, but not to the significant extent the government had hoped.

On the other hand the nation's birth rate declined rapidly to a level below 20, indicating that in fertility regulation people were far ahead of the official programs. According to a 1953 report, some 320,000 families were covered by the family planning program for the indigent. Thus, the government-sponsored programs had done something, but in general it may be said that this low level of fertility had been brought about by the people themselves.

In any event, since 1957 the crude birth rate in Japan has continued at the low level of about 17. Gradually there arose an opinion that the government need not play a large part in the promotion of family planning any longer, except for an effort to reduce further the number of induced abortions, since the understanding of family planning was already well ingrained among the masses. This opinion, coupled with the shortage of young workers in the labor force, tended to lead many national leaders to believe that family planning was no longer a matter of paramount importance. It was felt that quantitative considerations about population should now give way to the qualitative aspects of it. Some went further to raise a serious question of whether it was advantageous for the national development of Japan to continue such a low level of fertility.

In the face of these changes in the political and ideological atmosphere, the central government in Japan accordingly changed its family planning programs in 1965. The central government now has no specific budget allocation for family planning. Decisions on the necessity of family planning education programs are left entirely in the hands of village administrators. If the headman of a village believes it is still important, he will do it; if he does not, he does not have to implement any special programs. The future course of official family planning programs will, therefore, depend on the personal interest of each local administrator. It may well be said that family planning in Japan has now come to a turning point, a critical stage for the future development in this field.

So far this review has been focused entirely on the official family planning programs administered by the central and local governments and their subordinate organizations. Aside from these official programs, there are certain other aspects of family planning programs in Japan which might well be summarized briefly.

In 1951 the Institute of Public Health initiated a series of field studies in family planning. At first, three typical rural villages were selected for the studies and later a population on public relief and a group of coal miners were added. The main purpose of the studies was to offer concrete data about family planning to the government as a possible guide for future administration of their programs. Through these pilot projects it was demonstrated that even in populations that seem resistant to family planning teaching the program can be conducted with success. Also, they revealed a possibility of reducing induced abortions while the birth rate continued to decline. The most popular method among these groups was found to be condoms. The over-all results were highly encouraging.

One of the criticisms against this type of test project is based on an argument that a pilot project always remains an ideal operation and that replication of the same results elsewhere is hardly possible. On the other hand, however, one has to note an indirect merit of such an undertaking in creating a favorable stimulus to many other communities. In Japan a number of similar pilot programs have been operated, and they helped a great deal in fostering a general opinion favoring family planning throughout the nation.

Since 1953, family planning education has gradually become an integral part of the health and welfare services offered by large industrial establishments to their employees. At first a few establishments instituted the programs experimentally. They hired a small number of family planning instructors who, through frequent home visits, soon established a favorable rapport with their clients. Elaborate teaching in the techniques of contraception was conducted. Contraceptive materials were provided at a reduced price. The programs were accepted by the employees, and the rate of family planning practice picked up sharply.

In the past ten years many other establishments have started similar activities. It is reported that 68 of them are now rendering this kind of service as an organized effort, covering a total of 410,000 families. This figure slightly exceeds the number of families which have been directly served under the official family planning programs described above. Though privately conducted, the total influence of the programs has obviously been great.

The programs undertaken by private industry had an administrative advantage over those carried out by the government. They provided their own budgets, which could be freely spent according to their own decisions. No red tape was attached to their administrative system, which enabled them to hire, train and use the best qualified personnel in a most efficient manner. They were already familiar with business administration, and the same principles could easily be applied to family planning administration. Thus, many experts today maintain that the family planning activities performed by these enterprises have been far more successful than any others, including those conducted by the government.

Under circumstances where the government and large industrial establishments are engaged in family planning movements on a large scale, the position of voluntary family planning organizations is necessarily limited to some extent. The Family Planning Federation of Japan, a national organization representing all voluntary family planning groups in Japan, does not operate planned parenthood clinics of its own. Instead, it has concentrated its efforts mainly on publicity and education. In the past several years it has been particularly helpful in conducting a series of basic and refresher training courses for medical and paramedical personnel. Furthermore, a most significant value of this organization perhaps lies in the fact that it is the only organized body in Japan that takes part in international co-operation in the field of population and family planning.

Last but not least, a further word about the role played by mass communication might be in order. The influence of mass communication in the promotion of family planning has been really great in Japan. Whenever a question has been asked in a survey as to the source of information about family planning, the majority of respondents have never failed to give such sources as women's magazines, newspapers, and weekly magazines. In fact, one of the leading newspapers has conducted a long series of opinion polls about birth control, the results of which have been published in the paper from time to time. The high degree of literacy among the Japanese people is undoubtedly an important factor which makes it possible for these media to function in this way, but at the same time one must remember that they have given so much space and attention to family planning primarily because they are aware of their audience's keen interest in family planning and the resultant great demand for articles about family planning.

EVALUATION OF RESULTS TO DATE

An evaluation of the family planning programs conducted in Japan after the war can be made in various ways depending on the different standpoints from which the data can be viewed.

Viewed from the standpoint of reducing the birth rate, Japan certainly offers a unique example of how rapidly the birth rate can be brought down. The birth rates recorded for the immediate postwar years were abnormal because of unusual conditions associated with the war, but even compared with the prewar level of fertility the decline is significant. The present birth rate is one of the lowest in the world. Since 1956 the net reproduction rate has always been below unity and is still falling. In some quarters there is grave concern about this "too low level" of fertility. It is to be admitted that the decrease in the birth rate was mainly brought about by induced abortion, though recent trends are beginning to favor contraceptive practice. As was repeatedly mentioned in the foregoing, the low birth rate today reflects mainly the spontaneous effort on the part of the general public in fertility regulation.

If viewed from the standpoint of contraceptive practice, the conclusion would be that it has spread fairly quickly and successfully. As indicated in Table 2, progress in this regard has been steady and is still going on. Not a few observers remark that there are no other national programs in public health that have shown so much progress in such a short span of time and with so little budget available. Though there has been little over-all evaluation of the official family planning programs carried out by public health personnel and midwives for the general population, it is recognized that the progress here again has been made possible mainly by the people themselves; in view of the considerable difficulties and problems involved in the administration of such official family planning programs, it can be reasonably assumed that the role of the official programs must have been limited.

If the same family planning programs are viewed from the standpoint of lowering induced abortions, which has been one of their most important objectives, it must be admitted that not so much has been achieved. Since 1955 the reported numbers of abortions have in fact declined, but not to the degree desired by the governmental authorities. The trend will probably go on to show a further decline, but at the same time it will not be an easy task to achieve a significant reduction in the near future, while certain factors that favor induced abortions continue, such as the inexpensiveness of the operation, the relative ease with which it can be procured, and a human tendency to resort to an *ex post facto* method to "liquidate" the failure in contraception.

In contrast to the lack of over-all evaluation of official family planning programs for the general population, there have been some attempts to review the results obtained in the "special" program for the indigent and also those conducted by industrial groups. One of the prefectures that made an evaluation of its "special" program published the results some time ago, indicating that, among those poor groups receiving family planning education, the pregnancy rate fell by 57% in the course of five years of operation. It may be questioned how much of this decline can actually be attributed to the "special" program, and also to what extent this particular prefecture is representative. In any event, the "special" program for the economically underprivileged in general has not been one hundred per cent successful, but it has undoubtly contributed something.

On the other hand, family planning education undertaken by industry has been most gratifying. In the course of three years after the initiation of the programs, the prevalence of contraceptive practice has risen from 40% to about 70%. Not only have they made progress in quantitative terms but a steady qualitative improvement has also been observed—there has been a constant shift from less reliable methods, such as foam tablets and the safe period, to more effective means such as condoms, diaphragms, or the use of basal body temperature. The pregnancy rate has fallen to less than one-third the pre-program level in three years and to less than one-fourth in five years of operation. By and large, the family planning programs of industrial groups have shown the most successful operation.

SOME LESSONS TO BE LEARNED FROM THE JAPANESE EXPERIENCE

Generally speaking, the past experience of Japan in the decline in fertility has followed the classic pattern of the demographic transition which the West experienced in the nineteenth century. Japan belongs to the East by geographic location, religion, culture, ethnology, and so on. Nevertheless, the basic social and economic changes which were conducive to Japan's demographic transition were similar to those occurring in many European countries and the U.S.A. Differences in religion, in culture, or in language did not much alter the course of events, but basic common factors were just as effective in the Japanese experience as in others. The decline in the birth rate in the past one or two decades is certainly conspicuous, but the preparatory stage necessary for such transition in Japan was already set as early as the 1920's. The secular trend in fertility since then has apparently been downward; the postwar experience is nothing but the manifestation of this trend in its extreme form. Thus Japan is rather close to the West in the fundamentals of demographic transition, though her experience came about much later.

If the above interpretation is accepted, one may then question to what extent the Japanese experience in this field can be helpful in other countries. The question becomes even more serious when countries with totally different basic factors are considered. Japan is significant in the sense that it has offered a factual example of the possibility of reducing the birth rate sharply, but the significance fades when the detailed causes of fertility decline are examined in the hope of finding possible relevance elsewhere. People in Japan already knew much about family planning and indeed were already taking definite action when family planning programs were introduced by the government and other interested organizations. The task was not to indoctrinate people in family planning; the real requirement was only to encourage practice and to improve techniques.

On the other hand, there is one condition to be considered in relation to the whole question of whether the Japanese experience could be useful elsewhere. None of the family planning programs in Japan has ever tried to push forward the use of intra-uterine devices (IUD's), but it is believed that a great number of women have depended on devices of one type or another. But the general policy toward this method so far has been more negative than positive. It is possible, or even probable, that family planning in the developing countries would succeed in the near future regardless of similarities or dissimilarities in the basic social factors, if their programs were heavily dependent on the use of the IUD.

Aside from the discussion of the relevance of Japanese experience under different conditions, a few practical lessons worth consideration may be mentioned.

In the first place, teaching in the practical and technical aspects of family planning is more rewarding than preaching its principles. When family planning teachers spend an unnecessarily large amount of time on principles, the clientele easily gets bored and dissatisfied. What they want is service to accommodate their immediate needs.

Perhaps one of the errors of the Japanese programs was a policy of adding family planning to the duties of health officers who were already busy with other matters. It seems important to provide a certain number of family planning workers as such, who can devote their full efforts to this specific assignment.

As mentioned before, the use of the IUD has not been given outright sanction in Japan. Though there were certain reasons for this, a result was a general tendency among medical doctors to be unwilling to co-operate with the official programs. The same difficulty would not arise in other countries, with different views on the devices; nevertheless a general lesson might be learned that a government is handicapped if it attempts to act in the face of hostility on the part of the medical profession.

MAJOR UNSOLVED PROBLEMS

Many of the major problems encountered in the Japanese family planning programs have been mentioned in this chapter. Almost all of them have been administrative problems. As described earlier, with a change in the policy at the government level, local family planning programs in Japan are now undergoing major changes. Future problems and difficulties will become more diverse and manifold. At any rate, an immediate question for Japan to consider is how to enlighten local administrators so that they take interest in the family planning service within their communities.

Another of the important unsolved problems is undoubtedly the one related to induced abortion. Induced abortions are decreasing, but slowly, and it seems necessary to try a new approach if a substantial decrease is desired. In view of the facts that abortions have not decreased markedly even after ten years of family planning programs and that a considerable proportion of the abortions are performed because of failure in contraceptive methods employed, the need for a new approach is particularly great. The attitude toward new methods, orals and IUD's, is gradually shifting. It remains to be seen, however, whether the IUD, if generally approved, would be able to solve this long-standing question of induced abortion under the conditions peculiar to Japan.[1]

[1] Accounts given in this paper are based on the state of affairs as of mid-1965. Later, the basic policy of family planning programs was considerably changed again. It is likely that the central and prefectural governments will continue to maintain a major responsibility in the programs as they used to, at least for the few years to come.

2

SOUTH KOREA

YOUN KEUN CHA, M.D., M.P.H.
Director, Bureau of Public Health
Ministry of Health and Social Affairs

BACKGROUND

The Republic of Korea, comprising about 42% of the Korean peninsula, has a population of approximately 28 million. With crude birth and death rates estimated at 40 and 11, respectively, the annual rate of natural increase is about 2.9%, a rate at which numbers double in 24 years. More than half the population (54%) is under age 20, about a third (31%) is aged 20 to 44, and 15% is aged 45 or over.

Korea, an agricultural nation, has a population density of about 280 per square kilometer. Although 70% of the people live in rural areas and most of them earn their living from the soil, less than 22% of Korea's mountainous countryside is arable. Thus the average farm has about two acres to support the average rural family of six persons. Surplus production, if any, is meager and funds for land improvement or support of community enterprises are extremely limited. Crowded living conditions—five or six persons to the average dwelling of two rooms—also testify to the need for a new reproduction-production balance. Present requirements for adequate living space are estimated at two million more homes.

Closely linked with the problem of food and housing is the scarcity of jobs. Out of a total labor force of 10.5 million (age group 14–60), 2.75 million are unemployed or underemployed. Per capita national income is about $70 to $80 per year. The problems of economic and social development are further aggravated by the division of the industrial north from the agricultural south after World War II, and by the Korean conflict in 1950–53, which created a tremendous rehabilitation burden and an abnormal demographic picture following mass emigration from the north. Also, as did other countries, Korea experienced a "baby boom" immediately following the war. By 1960, the need for family planning in Korea was recognized as critical.

Origin and Objective of the Program

The military revolution of May, 1961, brought to authority a group of modern-thinking leaders dedicated to economic progress and improvement in levels of living. The Supreme Council for National Reconstruction, the agency established to achieve these ends, reviewed and approved the plan developed by the Ministry of Health and Social Affairs to provide nationwide family planning services. The Council announced the plan as a policy, allocated development funds from the investment budget, and adopted its targets as a priority goal of the five-year economic development plan. Simultaneously the Council repealed a law prohibiting the import of contraceptives.

The objective of the program is to reduce the annual rate of natural increase to about 2% by the end of 1971. To achieve this goal, it is estimated that the program must enlist 1.5 million participants, or about one-third of the eligible couples in the 20–44 year age group. Specific targets have been tentatively set at 300,000 regular users of traditional contraceptives; 200,000 vasectomies; and 1,000,000 IUD insertions.

Organization and Development

Responsibility for the program was assigned to the Ministry of Health and Social Affairs, which created a new family planning section in June, 1963. Following this action, most of the provincial governments established family planning subsections during the first half of 1964. To bring the program to the public, and to integrate it with the maternal and child health services, family planning field workers were added to the regular staff of the 189 nationwide health centers. By April, 1965, 2,207 field workers had been assigned to the nationwide family planning organization, plus 11 field supervisors, 723 senior field workers, and 1,473 assistant field workers. A summary of major developments and achievements is presented in Table 1.

Operationally, the basic aim of the program is to contact all eligible couples and to make available contraceptive information, supplies, and clinic services. Although the program places great reliance on vasectomies and the new IUD, traditional methods will be retained, first because they are a bridge to the new device, and, second, because an estimated 20% of Korean women cannot retain or accept the loop.

TABLE 1

SUMMARY OF MAJOR DEVELOPMENTS AND ACHIEVEMENTS IN FAMILY PLANNING PROGRAM OF KOREA

Item	1962	1963	1964	1965 (First 4 months)
1. Budget allocated	$328,357	$593,337	$1,357,900	$997,571 (25% from local govts.)
2. Personnel	183 nurse-midwives trained, 1 per health center	Add'l 183 nurse-midwives trained	Field staff: 2,060 Local level: 1,473	Field staff, 2,207; trained: 193 nurse-midwives, 744 local workers, and 400 physicians for IUD insertions
Voluntary leaders			28,713	17,917
Population per worker	142,000		13,287	
3. Program participants (couples registered)	328,514	1,005,511	965,717	161,353
Vasectomies (60% aged 35–44)	3,413	19,559	26,105	4,969
IUD's inserted (68% aged 30–39)	1,493 (research)		111,883	82,951
Couples receiving free supplies (per month)	59,352	129,804	156,301	
Per cent receiving: condom	28	31	64	Not certain. Survey shows 37% of condom users and 41% of foam users switched to IUD
foam tablet	26	58	29	
jelly	46	10	7	
Monthly number of clinic consultations	16,195	34,117	78,954	
home visits	18,832	38,088	170,898	
group meetings	2,801	3,549	16,021	
4. Local production of supplies	Foam tablets started	80,000 loops 4,000 inserters	Condoms and jellies started	

TABLE 1—*Continued*

Item	1962	1963	1964	1965 (First 4 months)
5. Clinics in operation	....	....	IUD, 842 Vasectomy, 683	....
6. Publicity	Nationwide information program	....	May designated "Family Planning Month"	....
7. Research, pilot projects	Yonsei Univ. rural project to test acceptability of traditional contraceptives	24 field research clinics to study acceptability and effectiveness of Lippes loop (IUD)	Urban project to study effectiveness of communication methods in enlisting participants	National family planning evaluation team established
8. Government agencies and interest	Family planning advisory committee to Ministry of Health and Social Affairs established	Family planning advisory committee co-ordinated with maternal and child health program. Prime Minister outlines role of other government agencies in the program	Family planning subsections established in all 11 states and special city health sections	....
9. Technical assistance	Population Council (of New York) mission	....	Population Council full time adviser appointed, plus financial and other assistance	Continued Population Council support

The records indicate that the program appeals mainly to women in the 30–39 year age bracket who have four or more children, including at least two sons. Studies indicate that the "ideal" family size is four children.

Services and supplies are free for those couples unable to meet the fees ($1.20 for IUD insertion, $2.00 for vasectomy). The three traditional contraceptives offered are condom, spermicidal foam tablets, and jelly.

TRAINING

The preparation given field workers is both academic and practical. The training covers all family planning aspects plus related public health topics to increase the worker's ability to meet the public and provide simple health information and referral services during home visits and group meetings.

Instruction is given in lectures, workshops, and demonstrations. "Learn by doing" is the keynote of all training programs, with students serving as "eligibles" and "critics." In simulated field situations, acquired knowledge is applied and the various program aids are demonstrated. Emphasis is on what to do and how to do it. Trainees receive manuals containing outlines of the subjects covered and of the workshop programs in which they are to participate during the course. At the end of the training program, an examination is given, followed by an evaluation session.

Responsibility for training has been delegated to the Planned Parenthood Federation, an organization rich in leadership, with representatives of all the professions necessary to teach the required specialties, including public relations. Courses vary in length from two to four weeks depending upon the background and experience of the participants. The training is given in four provincial centers in addition to the national public health training institute in Seoul.

PROGRAM AIDS

Every effort has been made to develop and provide simple and practical program aids for family planning workers. Emphasis in the audio-visual and mass media programs is informative rather than persuasive. These programs illustrate the reproductive process and contraceptive methods, and state where services are available. The public information program provides the press with articles, conducts radio and television programs, prepares exhibits, and during May, 1964, which was officially proclaimed "Family Planning Month," carried on mass enlightenment activities of all types. Also, three movies have been produced.

A potent supplementary force in all these efforts is the wholehearted co-operation of the Planned Parenthood Federation, the Office of Public Information, the National Reconstruction Movement, and the Office of Rural Development Workers, as well as the publishers of numerous magazines and professional journals. These efforts are meaningful because of the relatively high literacy rate in Korea, about 72%, and because religious opposition involves less than 1% of the population.

SUPPLIES AND COSTS

A major development was the undertaking of local manufacture of supplies. This has expedited supply procurement, reduced foreign exchange requirements, and, most important, increased the availability of contraceptives, particularly condoms, through commercial channels. About 40% of the traditional contraceptives available in the country during 1962 and 1963 were distributed free through governmental supply depots. The practice is to distribute a one month's supply: one vial of 16 foam tablets, one package of 6 condoms, or 15 grams of spermicidal jelly packed in three plastic containers. Loops of all sizes (including a sufficient supply of the 27.5 mm. to meet all requirements) plus 20 inserters per clinic have also been distributed, to "charge" as well as "free" clinics. Other necessary equipment and expendables, such as antiseptics and cotton, are not furnished.

The wholesale cost of locally manufactured condoms is about 8 cents per dozen; foam tablets, 8.6 cents per vial; jelly, 17.6 cents for 30 grams; loop materials and processing, about 2 cents per loop; loop inserters, about 27 cents each.

The total cost of the program during the three-year period from 1962 through 1964 has been $1,823,000, or an average of $0.022 per capita per year (see Table 3, below). On an annual basis the per capita costs were $0.012 for 1962, $0.022 for 1963, and $0.032 for 1964. At present operational costs, it is estimated that program goals can be achieved at an annual per capita expenditure of about $0.05. On this basis, $10 million will have been invested in the next seven years to attain the ten-year goal of 1.5 million participants.

SURVEY RESULTS

In April, 1964, and again in April, 1965, a nationwide survey on knowledge, attitudes, and practices was conducted among some 3,500 couples with the wife under 44 years of age. The results, presented in

Table 2, indicate almost universal approval of contraceptive use, in rural as well as urban areas; widespread knowledge of the existence of the family planning program; substantial increase in the proportion of respondents who knew the condom method (from 51% in April, 1964, to 81% in April, 1965); a jump from 11% to 71% in the proportion who had heard of the IUD; and an increase from 13% in the earlier survey to 23% in the later survey in the proportion who had ever practiced some method.

MAJOR ACHIEVEMENTS

The outstanding characteristic of the Korean Family Planning Program is the scope of its objective and its rapid development to meet its

TABLE 2

PERCENTAGE OF RESPONDENTS BY KNOWLEDGE, ATTITUDE AND PRACTICE, APRIL, 1964, AND APRIL, 1965, SURVEYS

ITEM	1964	1965		
		Total	Urban	Rural
1. Knowledge:				
Heard of program	74	84		
Knew condom method	51	81		
Knew IUD method	11	71		
2. Major source of knowledge:				
Neighbors		64		
Health centers		51		
Radio		46		
Rhee-Dong chiefs		35		
Relatives		34		
Newspapers		24		
3. Attitude toward contraception:				
Approve		89	91	87
Oppose		4	3	5
Don't know		7	6	8
4. Practice:				
Currently practicing	9.9	16.2	21.0	14.1
Stopped practicing	3.1	6.4	9.2	5.1
Ever practiced (CP+SP)	13.0	22.6	30.2	19.2
Never practiced	41.4	40.9	35.8	43.2
Don't know any method	45.4	36.5	34.0	37.6
No response	0.2	0.0	0.0	0.0
5. Method(s) of those who ever practiced:				
Condom		54		
Foam tablets		38		
Jelly		12		
Loop		24		
Total number of respondents	3,591	3,421	2,060	2,361

goals. From the public, the program has helped to elicit an ever increasing demand for contraceptive information, supplies, and clinic services. Administratively, the program has shown much ingenuity and can point to considerable progress in the yearly increase in staff, facilities, clinics, and services rendered. Moreover, the experience of the program has clearly demonstrated the realism of its long-range goal to reduce the rate of natural increase to a suitable level in the not too distant future. Evidence for this appraisal rests on the following considerations:

1. Readiness of the Korean people to limit their families to the number of children they feel they can afford to raise and educate in a proper manner.
2. High acceptability of the highly effective loop by Korean wives.
3. Ease of integration of family planning with maternal and child health services.
4. Effectiveness of the mass media in stimulating discussion and readiness of eligible couples to seek information and services.
5. Growing awareness of the potential of family planning programs to reduce the number of induced abortions.

In sum, it now seems clear that the official goals of the Korean Family Planning Program are also the desire and will of the people.

Major Problems Still Ahead

While on the one hand the rapidity with which the program has developed can be regarded as a major achievement, on the other hand, it has inevitably produced certain disequilibria. The immediate principal needs of the program can be summed up as follows:

1. To establish a referral system for IUD acceptors and vasectomy patients who develop difficulties that require extra medical treatment or hospital care. About one case per thousand requires such referral.
2. To establish an in-service IUD and vasectomy training program for physicians with limited preservice training or experience in obstetrics and gynecology or urology. This involves sending mobile training teams of qualified physicians into the rural areas and scheduling instruction in the medical schools and provincial hospitals.
3. To extend family planning information and services more effectively into the rural areas. This involves redistribution as well as recruitment of personnel. Mobile teams, too, will be relied on to perform IUD and vasectomy services and train rural physicians.
4. To improve methods of evaluation in order to assess the effectiveness of the program. This involves a well-conceived, uniform, and statistically correct system of records and reports for which co-operation of

the Bureau of Statistics will be enlisted. The result should also provide better nationwide reporting of vital events.

The above does not pretend to exhaust the list of problems. Indeed, in the course of solving old ones, new ones can be expected to arise. On the whole, as readers of this report are well aware, the problems stem from the difficulties that attend any program under government sponsorship, particularly those that operate through non-revenue service

TABLE 3

PROGRAM EXPENDITURES, BY ITEM AND YEAR

Item	1962	1963	1964	1965
A. Central government (million won)	42.7	77.1	158.2	195.4
Distribution (per cent):				
1. Operation	25.8%	28.7%	38.1%	33.8%
2. Publicity and education	5.0	28.5	12.6	3.4
3. Contraceptives	63.7	25.3	19.2	22.6
4. Vasectomy	5.5	15.0	14.3	5.3
5. IUD		2.5	15.8	32.8
6. Research and evaluation				1.1
7. Assistance to PPFK				1.0
B. Local government (million won)			58.3	64.0
C. Grand total (million won)	42.7	77.1	216.5	259.4
U.S. dollars (thousands)[a]	328	593	902	998
D. Per capita in U.S. dollars[a]	0.012	0.022	0.032	0.034

[a] Exchange rate was $1.00 to 130 won up to May, 1964, and $1.00 to 260 thereafter. These rates are used in the conversions, with 1964 prorated.

agencies. Long-time health projects that involve an augmented staff and distribution of free supplies are particularly prone to problems of securing adequate funds and trained personnel. That the program also involves the active co-operation of its participants, in a sensitive and intimate area that is bound up with tradition, creates unprecedented difficulties.

Fortunately for Korea, the Family Planning Program has progressed at a rapid pace. For this it is indebted not only to its own efforts, but to the financial and technical assistance received from abroad, and to the efforts of many local groups, particularly the Planned Parenthood Federation of Korea.

IUD AND VASECTOMY ACCEPTORS
BY AGE GROUP (1964)

Age Group	IUD (per cent)	Vasectomy (per cent)
−24..............	2.2	0.1
25–29..............	20.3	5.1
30–34..............	38.0	23.2
35–39..............	30.0	35.3
40–44..............	8.4	25.2
45–49..............	1.0	8.5
50–..............	....	2.6
Total number......	89,013	25,362

ORGANIZATION OF KOREAN FAMILY PLANNING PROGRAM

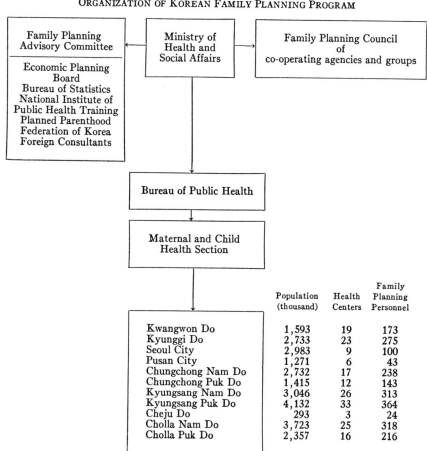

	Population (thousand)	Health Centers	Family Planning Personnel
Kwangwon Do	1,593	19	173
Kyunggi Do	2,733	23	275
Seoul City	2,983	9	100
Pusan City	1,271	6	43
Chungchong Nam Do	2,732	17	238
Chungchong Puk Do	1,415	12	143
Kyungsang Nam Do	3,046	26	313
Kyungsang Puk Do	4,132	33	364
Cheju Do	293	3	24
Cholla Nam Do	3,723	25	318
Cholla Puk Do	2,357	16	216

3

MAINLAND CHINA

IRENE B. TAEUBER
Princeton University

and

LEO A. ORLEANS
National Science Foundation

The demographic dilemma of modernization is most awesome in mainland China. In 1953, population was less than 600 million. In 1965, it numbered perhaps three-quarters of a billion. If births and deaths continue at levels estimated for 1957, with only the deviations associated with the difficult years from 1959 to 1961, population would be more than 1 billion by 1980.

The vastness and diversity of China's area, the increase and dispersion of the population, the depth and pervasiveness of the initial backwardness, and the revolutionary shifts from the traditional ways of a disintegrating order to the compulsive reorientations of evangelical communism suggest an immensity and an intensity of the problems of population growth unmatched elsewhere on earth. This, however, is a limited assessment. The basic Chinese culture remains as the strength of a continuing population. Industrialization and urbanization are in process. The changing social and economic organization of the rural population, the crusading health activities, and the struggles for education are components in modernization as well as factors in the generation of population growth and its associated problems.

Many of the driving reforms of the Peoples Republic of China alter the conventional roles of the sexes and the generations and thus im-

This paper is a condensed and therefore often oversimplified summary of the massive materials available in late June, 1965. The co-operation of Warren K. Guinn and Pearl Ouyang of the Reference Department of the Library of Congress in the exploration and interpretation of sources is gratefully acknowledged.

31

pinge on value structures and reproductive mores. There is de-emphasis of marriage, childbearing, and domesticity, along with emphasis on personal development and service to the larger society. The ideological momentum of party and state requires the dedication of the individual to the goals of polity and power.

The demographic relevance of the politically motivated shifts is major. Over the millenniums, cultural cohesion and conformity perpetuated Confucian relationships and a sufficient if not overabundant reproduction. Now, however, loyalty and conformity to the new order require the postponement of marriage and initial childbearing, along with rigid limitation on total childbearing. The ideologies and motivations may be political and economic but, to the extent that transformations accord with ideals, the consequences will also be demographic.

Data are limited for a thorough demographic approach to planning. Neither its predecessor nor the Peoples Republic published in detail even the largely traditional types of data from investigations and registrations. Research was not and is not precluded thereby. Events relevant to demographic processes are reported, however defective the numerical bases. Moreover, there is increasing knowledge of demographic processes among other peoples in monsoon Asia, including the Chinese or Chinese-related cultures of Japan, the Ryukyus, Korea, Taiwan, Hong Kong, Singapore, and Malaysia.

Present barriers to research on the population of mainland China are not likely to be enduring. The government will have to assess population dynamics more intensively as population becomes an increasingly critical component in development planning and progress. Hence the evaluation, estimation, and model construction that are now possible may be preparatory to more intricate analyses in the future.

The intricacies of decision, publicity, advocacy, and denunciation in the move toward policy and program in birth control need not be resummarized here.[1] We shall argue, rather, that the cumulative dynamics of the formative years of the Peoples Republic are approaching a phase in which the economic impacts of population growth and receptivity to reproductive change are alike accentuated. There is or

[1] John S. Aird, "Population Policy in Mainland China," *Population Studies* 16 (1): 38–57 (July, 1962); Michael Freeberne, "Birth Control in China," *ibid.*, 18 (1): 5–16 (July, 1964); Leo A. Orleans, "Birth Control: Reversal or Postponement?" *China Quarterly*, No. 3, pp. 59–73 (July–September, 1960). Also: "A New Birth Control Campaign?" *China Quarterly*, No. 12, pp. 207–10 (October–December, 1962); H. Yuan Tien, "Birth Control in Mainland China? Ideology and Politics," *Milbank Memorial Fund Quarterly*, 41 (3): 269–90 (July, 1963); Roland Pressat, "La population de la Chine et son économie," *Population* (Paris), 13 (4): 569–89 (October–December, 1958); Alfred Sauvy, *Fertility and Survival: Population Problems from Malthus to Mao Tse-tung* (New York: Criterion Books, 1961).

soon will be an inherent necessity of response by government to the demographic processes that are generating increasing pressures, not alone on levels of living, but also on economic and political viability. The approaching crisis and the increasing amenability to resolution are argued on the basis of cohort transformations in growth, modernization, and indoctrination.

Laws, regulations, policy statements, education, and propaganda are verbal, without essential or proportionate relations to the reproductive behavior of the people. The reduction of birth rates in the national population, and particularly the rural sector, has three distinctive but interrelated operational requirements: (1) means acceptable to and effective for Chinese women, produced in China in sufficient quantities and at low cost; (2) channels of organization that reach from the center to the individuals in the appropriate ages throughout China, with competence in service personnel; (3) strengthened receptivity and response in the younger and maturing generations, with whatever commendations and sanctions are necessary to overcome lethargy and resistance and to move the vaguely and erratically motivated into the category of those who limit fertility rigidly.

Given the requisite decisions, sufficient priorities in finance and in the allocation of personnel, and the operational requirements in means, channels, and response, what is the future path of the population? What would be the demographic and associated consequences of a precipitant move to a one- or two-child family with a greatly lengthened separation of the generations?

POLICIES, MEANS, AND PROGRAMS

The leaders of the Peoples Republic of China work enthusiastically to generate growth among minority peoples or to populate the peripheral regions of the country.[2] They shrink from the knowledge that the future of the economy and therefore the political structure and na-

---

[2] Solomon I. Bruk, *Naseleniye Kitaia, MNR i Korei* [Population of China, the Mongolian Peoples Republic, and Korea] (Moscow: Academy of Sciences of the USSR, Institute of Ethnography, 1959), editorial notes translated, *Joint Publications Research Service* 3710 (New York) (hereafter cited as *JPRS*), Aug. 16, 1960; Chih-yüan Kao [The huge change from feudal serfdom to socialism—in commemoration of the 10th anniversary of the founding of Apa Tibetan Autonomous Chou, Szechwan Province], *Min-tsu t'uan-chieh*, No. 12 (December, 1962), and No. 8 (August, 1963), *Survey of China Mainland Magazines* 351: 35–39 (Feb. 11, 1963) (hereafter cited as *SCMM*); Correspondent [The sound of footsteps in Tibet's historic progress], *Jen-min jih-pao*, Dec. 17, 1964, *JPRS* 28348, Jan. 19, 1965. Also: [Nomadic people must settle down], *Jen-min jih-pao*, Dec. 14, 1959, translated, *Communist China Digest*, No. 14 (May 2, 1960); T'an Feng and Lu Hung-hsiang [Tears and laughs of the Kazakh people], *Kuang-ming jih-pao*, Oct. 27, 1964, *JPRS* 27833, Dec. 14, 1964.

tional power of the government depend directly on the immediacy and the rapidity of the reduction of the birth rate in China as a whole, including that 85% of the population that is rural. Actions to reduce birth rates have been or are now being evaluated as national programs. The evidence available to us suggests that experimentation in an expansion of operational programs may be underway. We argue that a major factor in the move to action is the existence of means to secure rapid reduction in childbearing among today's young people.

The timing of the Chinese revolution in the mid-twentieth rather than the mid-nineteenth century assured its communist character and so structured both the form and the dynamism of the changes that are related to the birth, the maturing, and the passing of the generations. The timing of the new order in turn permits direct manipulation not only of mortality but also of fertility. The technologies and administrative models for the reduction of death rates have long been available to developing countries. These have been and are being utilized in China. A coincidental by-product was, of course, the generation of a population growth that outpaced political anticipations and threatened both economic productivity and social aspirations.[3] This occurred before the scientific and technical advances essential to the manipulation of birth rates across the regional and developmental spectrum of a country such as China. Hence in China, as elsewhere, the experiences in the diffusion of birth control in the past are not directly relevant to the assessment of the future.

The policies and programs of the fifties had minimal impact on birth rates at provincial or national levels, for the means to limit births remained those indigenous to Chinese culture or conventional in the West.[4] Techniques of and facilities for induced abortion were highly

[3] John Aird, *The Size, Composition, and Growth of the Population of Mainland China*, U.S. Bureau of the Census, International Population Statistics Reports, Ser. P-90, No. 15, 1961; China, Peoples Republic, State Statistical Bureau, *Ten Great Years: Statistics of the Economic and Cultural Achievements of the Peoples Republic of China* (Peking: Foreign Language Press, 1960); Chen Ta, "New China's Population Census of 1953 and Its Relations to National Reconstruction and Demographic Research," *Bulletin de l'Institut international de statistique*, 36: 255–71 (1958); "Ch'uan kuo jen k'ou shu mu cheng chai chu p'u tseng chia" [Steady increase of the population of China], *Jen-min jih-pao*, Nov. 3, 1954; Leo A. Orleans, "The 1953 Chinese Census in Perspective," *Journal of Asian Studies*, 16 (4): 565–73 (August, 1957); Roland Pressat, "La révolution démographique en Chine," *Economie appliquée*, 13: 445–60 (July–September, 1960); S. K. Tai, *1953 Population Census of China* (Calcutta: Indian Statistical Institute, 1956).

[4] Chinese medicine and birth control: Wang Yuan, in *Chung kuo ch'ing nien-pao*, Aug. 10, 1956, p. 2; Chou Ngo-fang, in *Chung kuo fu nü*, No. 9 (September, 1956), p. 30; Feng Han-yung, in *Shanghai chung i yo tsa chih*, No. 3 (March, 1957), p. 33; Li Hêng-yu et al., in *Kiangsi chung i k'an*, No. 48 (September, 1957), p. 43; Wang Pê-yüeh, in *Chien kang-pao*, Nov. 27, 1956, p. 3. Concerning the prescription for the

developed in Japan, but China lacked the needed facilities for nation-wide programs. Moreover, Western-trained physicians saw abortion as repugnant. Intra-uterine rings were known and occasionally used, but the major potentialities of the intra-uterine devices were not recognized.[5]

Thus the Chinese, as other peoples, learned through experience that rhythm, tablets, and other means that offer statistical probabilities of reduced conception are not acceptable to rural women; that diaphragms and other sophisticated gadgetry are appropriate for the educated and the highly motivated; that the use of condoms diffuses slowly outside the metropolitan context; that the use of traditional means is not transformed easily into the achievement of effective and acceptable means; that sterilization of those with many children is not a major deterrent to rising growth curves; that the crisis of ascending numbers can be alleviated and then resolved only through the incisive use of techniques that are not dependent on the deep motivations and continuing cautions of the people who constitute the core population, as well as the population problems, of China.[6]

Until quite recently, the limiting problem in the reduction of a national birth rate in a developing country was not so much the motivation or the decision of government as the availability of appropriate means.[7] Today China's problems are not so much motivation and means as decisions of government. Induced abortions and the intra-

swallowing of the embryo tadpole: *Chien kang pao*, Aug. 28, 1956, p. 1; Chang Tsun-shih and Chêng Fêng, in *Jen-min jih-pao*, Aug. 28, 1956, p. 7; Ch'üan I-mao, in *Wen hui pao*, Oct. 22, 1956, p. 2.

[5] Chang Tieh-min et al., [An introduction to the "contraceptive ring": a speech of the Japanese Medical Delegation to China], *Chung hua fu chan k'o tsa chih*, 6 (1): 100 (February, 1958); Liu Wei-ya, [T'ai-tien's contraceptive ring], *Chien kang pao*, Apr. 19, 1957, p. 2; Shanghai Municipal Bureau of Health, [The experience of the utilization of the contraceptive ring], *Shanghai wei shêng ch'u pan shê*, March, 1958.

[6] Chia Wei-lien, [The safety period for use in the rural areas], *Chien kang-pao*, Feb. 22, 1957, p. 3, and Mar. 29, 1957, p. 3; Shu Ming-yen, [Several contraceptives recommended for general use], *Survey of China Mainland Press*, 2795, July 24, 1962 (hereafter cited as *SCMP*); [The plan for the use of rhythm by the Japanese medical experts], *Wên hui pao*, Apr. 7, 1957, p. 3.

[7] Publications were widespread: Harbin Municipal Association for the Diffusion of Scientific Technology, *Heilungkiang jen-min ch'u pan shê*, January, 1958; *Hopeh jên-min ch'u pan shê*, June, 1958; *Hunan jên-min ch'u pan shê*, February, 1957, April, 1958; *Hupeh jên-min ch'u pan shê*, June, 1958; *Kansu jên-min ch'u pan shê*, June, 1958; *Liaoning hua pao shê*, May, 1958, reprinted June, 1958. Also, *Liaoning jên-min ch'u pan shê*, November, 1958; *Peking ch'u pan shê*, December, 1957, reprinted March, 1958, May, 1958; *Shantung jên-min ch'e pan shê*, September, 1958; *Shanghai wei shêng ch'u pan shê*, April, 1958, reprinted May, 1958; *Shensi jih pao*, Mar. 21, 1957; *Szechwan jên-min ch'u pan shê*, March, 1958, reprinted April, 1958; *Yünnan jên-min ch'u pan shê*, June, 1957.

uterine devices are acceptable and effective to developing peoples of Chinese or Chinese-related cultures outside mainland China.[8] They should also be acceptable and effective within mainland China.

The statement that the problems of means of family limitation are not the major ones for China may be questioned, but it is quite plausible.[9] The Chinese obtain medical literature and equipment from other areas. There is advanced training and research in medical fields. Health personnel from other countries visit China; Chinese health personnel go abroad, either directly or as delegations of the Chinese Red Cross.[10] Hence modern approaches to the control of births are available as components in the drives toward health, social transformation, and party dedication.[11] Reliance is now placed on the IUD's, induced abortion, and sterilization as associated means for precluding specific births and preventing future births.[12] The concentrated push for induced abortion is surprising even to Japanese gynecologists. Major emphasis is placed on the suction technique, which is reputedly simpler, quicker, less hazardous, and leaves the patient ambulatory. Indigenous production and local adaptations have been reported both for the IUD's and the instruments for induced abortion. Experiments in methods, procedures, rewards, and sanctions seem to be widespread.

Thus the critical questions with reference to the future of the Chinese birth rate and therefore of the Chinese population are no longer those of technological advances in means of birth limitation. They are, rather, the extent of the compulsions of party and planners to reduce rates of population growth, the availability of a health network to reach the people with appropriate and sufficient services, and the receptivity of the generations now maturing to the adjurations to

[8] Induced abortion is prevalent in Eastern Europe and the USSR as well as Japan.

[9] The arguments of associations between oscillations in government policy and propaganda concerning birth control and the feasibility of reducing birth rates are conjectural. Past analyses of Chinese demographic developments have been made by sociologists and economists. In the present, questions pertain to birth control activities and facilities in the health and related services; medical involvement in research is essential.

[10] Ken Majima, [The birth control controversy in China. Induced abortion is coming into the foreground], *Bungei Shun-ju*, February, 1965, pp. 144–48.

[11] Limitations of means alone would have been sufficient to negate the earlier efforts to achieve measurable reductions in fertility. As indicative: Speeches to the 1957 session of the Chinese People's Consultative Conference (CPPCC), Section VI, "Birth Control and Population Problems," in *Jen-min Jih-pao*, Mar. 8, 9, 16, 17, 20, 1957, translated and abridged in *Current Background*, No. 445, Apr. 5, 1957 (hereafter cited as *CB*).

[12] Tameyoshi Katagiri, Report on Family Planning in China, by the Regional Secretary, IPFF Western Pacific Region, May, 1964; Edgar Snow, "Halte aux naissances," *Les dossiers de candide*, No. 209, pp. 19–22 (1965).

postpone marriage, postpone the first birth, and limit later births, if indeed later births are to be envisioned in the ideal.

POPULATION DYNAMICS AND COHORT TRANSFORMATIONS

In the shift from slow and erratic growth to continuing increase at accelerating rates, the impacts of the increases in births and the higher survival rates of the living are concentrated initially among the very young. Gradually they move upward to successively higher ages as the cohorts of the new order advance to later ages. Infants consume relatively little and do not participate in productive activities, but the needs of growing children soon involve the educational and other institutions of the community.

The oncoming and ever larger cohorts seem a tidal wave threatening institutional facilities and the depletion of productive potential. In mainland China, verbal reactions to increasing numbers are or soon will be replaced by the inescapable difficulties of increasing man power. The waves of youth now push against the society and the economy of the adults.

The earliest of the enlarged birth cohorts that survived in higher proportions is now aged 15–19. The problem is a manifold one. It is entrants to the labor force and claimants to employment. It is now additive consumption units; soon it will be new families with their pyramiding requirements. Soon there will be the secondary waves of even larger birth cohorts as the increasing numbers of women reaching childbearing ages themselves bear children. Thus in mainland China there is a coincidence of demographic and economic pressures on resources and development potential with technical advances in means of population control. The reduction of rates of population growth should become a priority goal in planning and administration.

Again there is the duality of increasing problems and increasing possibilities for resolution. The dynamics of transitional growth are responsible for an escalating school population during the years when the extension of education is critical to transformation. It is also this natural process of population change that permits swift demographic transformations if the training and conditioning of the successive birth cohorts have been pervasive in cities and rural areas alike and intensive in dispersed leadership groups.

Since these conclusions are basic to the evaluation of the developmental prospects of mainland China, it is necessary to sketch the numerical arguments that underlie them.

Reconstruction of the growth of the population of the Peoples Republic of China in the years before 1965 is similar in all estimates linked to the official count of the census-registration of 1953 and the official statements on rates of growth and total numbers from 1953 to 1957 (see Table 2, at end of chapter). Given a pre-Communist birth rate somewhat above 40 per 1,000 total population and continuity or some increase in that rate under communism, combined with an initial death rate above 30 and continuing but hard-won declines in that rate under communism, the range of the estimated populations as of 1965 cannot be great. It is on these assumptions that we state with reasonable probability, though not surety, that the population as of 1965 was approximately 750 million.

The developments of the decade from 1965 to 1975 are less predict-

TABLE 1

PEOPLES REPUBLIC OF CHINA: ESTIMATED AND PROJECTED CHANGE BY AGE, 1955–65 AND 1965–75, ON ASSUMPTIONS OF CONTINUITY IN VITAL RATES

AGE	POPULATION (millions)			CHANGE			
				Amount (millions)		Per Cent	
	1955	1965	1975	1955–65	1965–75	1955–65	1965–75
Total........	603	746	933	143	187	23.7	25.1
0– 4.......	103	120	154	17	34	16.5	28.3
5–14.......	140	197	234	57	37	40.7	18.8
15–24.......	110	133	186	23	53	20.9	39.8
25–44.......	152	178	213	26	35	17.1	19.7
45–64.......	78	95	114	17	19	21.8	20.0
65 and over..	19	25	13	6	8	31.6	32.0

SOURCE: U.S. Bureau of the Census, *Explanation and Citations*, Appendix Table 2.

able and the range of the hypothetical estimates is wide (see Tables 2 and 4). Barring war or famine, the critical questions concern the stability or the decline of the birth rate. Since later sections will consider the problems and probabilities of widespread and effective birth control, we shall consider here the dynamics of the past and the coming decade on the standstill assumptions of a model constructed by the United States Bureau of the Census (see Table 3). We use this projection because it presents what the population would be if vital rates did not change. Since vital rates neither will nor indeed could remain unchanging for a decade in the on-going setting of the Peoples Republic of China, the numbers, rates, and ratios for the next decade are obviously conjectures.

In the years from 1955 to 1965, the increase of the population alone amounted to 143 million (Table 1). More than half of this increase consisted of children below age 15. The percentage increase, 23.7% for the total population, was above 40% for children aged 5–14. The pressures of increase were greatest in the years when elementary schooling should have been the major activity. In the period from 1965 to 1975, the school-age population as of 1965 will age ten years. The increase of 40% in the next decade will characterize youth aged 15–24. This push of youth into adult status is the major and largely immutable demographic fact of the next decade.

The alternate projections shown in Tables 2 and 4 permit exploration of the immediate and longer-run impact of various hypothetical changes in the fertility of the population in the years from 1955 to 1980. Space precludes further argument here except to note that the past dynamics of the population necessitate extraordinary expansions in productivity and employment if the society and the economy are even to remain as they now are for another decade. The urgency of slowing the increase of the oncoming cohorts is apparent. This slowing of growth through reduced rates of childbearing would seem to require the availability of modern means of limitation along with the social and economic opportunities that only a rapidly expanding industrial economy can provide.

The functional allocation of the increasing man power is difficult to envision. Relatively small portions can be involved in movements to the border regions. The urban absorption of any substantial portion of the rural increase does not seem feasible. The government has struggled against the "blind infiltration" of rural migrants with the associated problems of housing and employment. The emphasis on agriculture since the Ninth Plenum of the Communist Party in 1961 includes continuing efforts to control and reduce the urban population. The general principles governing the relations of the rural and urban sectors merit statement.[13] First, industrial productivity must increase faster than the industrial labor force. Second, "the movement to cities of people who do not belong to the labor force must be subjected to appropriate control." Third, the labor force engaged in "non-material production" must increase only as productive capabilities increase. Fourth, the labor needed by the cities should come primarily from the labor resources of the cities themselves. Finally, the size of the urban population depends on "the development of agricultural production and the productivity of agricultural labor."

[13] Ernest Ni, *Distribution of Urban and Rural Population of Mainland China, 1953 and 1958*, U.S. Bureau of the Census, International Population Reports, Ser. P-95, No. 56 (October, 1960); Leo A. Orleans, "The Recent Growth of China's Urban Population," *Geographical Review*, 49 (1): 43–57 (January, 1959); Morris B. Ullman, *Cities of Mainland China, 1953 and 1958*, U.S. Bureau of the Census, International Population Reports, Ser. P-95, No. 59 (August, 1961).

The economic arguments for the concentration on agriculture are doubtless conclusive. It is also plausible to plan for that 15% of the total population that is now urban to provide the natural increase needed in the urban population. Two questions arise immediately. First, what is to be the economic activity of that 85% or more of China's annual increase that occurs in rural areas? Second, can even the fostered if not forced movement of urban residents for periods of work in rural areas prevent a widening gap between developing urban populations and rural populations that already have too much man power for labor needs and productive capacity?

The relevance of this acute and central problem to the success of programs of family planning is obvious. However, there is a high potential for change in the increasing predominance of youth. In modernization, each maturing cohort is more educated, more conditioned to the new order, and more adaptable to its possibilities and its hazards than the preceding one. Demographic, economic, and social modernization is an associated complex. In China, the continuity of the values and the folkways of the ancient order occurred as transmission from generation to generation. The current transformations are designed to break this transmission. Those who will be aged 15–24 in 1975 will all have been born under the new order; those now aged 15–24 have only childhood memories of another order.

Thus, that which presents the major challenge to the economy may be the major opportunity for the permanent demographic resolution of precipitant decline to truly low levels of fertility.

OPERATIONAL FEASIBILITIES

Today, reductions in birth rates involve so many new factors that the experiences of the past have only limited relevance. These new factors concern means, requirements for implementation, time dimensions, and receptivities. They are so interrelated that they will be discussed in two groupings: means and implementation; time dimensions and receptivities.

The earlier discussion of the problems of population growth and the feasibility of resolutions involved the pressures to seek solutions, the newly available means, and the conjectural responses of the younger women. These were abstractions at the all-China level. Intra-uterine devices, induced abortions, and sterilization are medical means in the sense that practitioners of some as yet unspecified level of medical training must provide personal service to each woman whose fertility is to be limited. Propaganda and the distribution of supplies of conventional contraceptives, talks, exhibits, manuals, and do-it-yourself kits are no longer sufficient. The problems of administrative organization, personnel, and training are largely those of the health services. Thus general administrative systems, party sanctions and controls, and choices among alternate goals within and outside the health field are all involved. We shall limit our exploration to the organization of the health services, and we shall be concerned primarily with one question. Given a drive to do so, with appropriate priorities in personnel, training, and finance, are there channels that reach directly from the central health ministry to the production brigade and the production team levels? If so, is the present activity in or related to obstetrical and gynecological fields such that present or added personnel could provide the necessary services in the insertion of intra-uterine devices and the performance of induced abortions and sterilizations?

The organization and channels of control of the health system parallel those of the general administrative structure. There are 26 provinces and autonomous regions in mainland China, plus the cities of Peking and Shanghai. The provincial capitals control most of the *shih* (large urban areas) and about 2,000 *hsien* (counties). Since 1958 *hsien* have been divided into communes, presently numbering about 70,000.[14] Communes are divided into production brigades that include one or two villages; these in turn are divided into production teams.

The Ministry of Health of the central government transmits decisions to public health departments in the provincial capitals. Controls extend downward to the medical bureaus in cities and in *hsien* centers. The urban medical bureaus control all the hospitals, clinics, and other medical facilities in the cities.[15] In the rural areas, control extends from the health bureau at the *hsien* center to the communes under its jurisdiction, and from these down through the production brigades to the production teams.

In 1958, the last year for which integrated health statistics are available, medical personnel were sparse in relation to the needs of a population of perhaps 650 million.[16] At that time, there were 75,000 West-

14 The communes have varied in number, administration, and responsibility. Today they have limited economic and political significance, in effect exercising the administrative power of the former *hsiang*.

15 In the late fifties, the rural areas with 85% of the population had two-thirds of the hospitals (loosely defined), but only one-third of the hospital beds, including "simple beds." There are also inequities in medical workers, many of whom are "intoxicated with work in large cities, in large hospitals, and in laboratories" (*Hung-ch'i*, No. 18, Sept. 16, 1960). The continuing efforts to achieve a more appropriate balance of urban and rural services does not seem to have been successful. The problem was stated in the headline of a Canton newspaper, "Stop Concentrating Health Work on Show-Case Big Cities," *Nan-fang jih-pao*, Sept. 28, 1960.

16 *Ten Great Years* (see n. 3 above). Quantitative information on public health and medicine is defective and deficient. In addition to the general problems of statistics in

ern-trained doctors, 131,000 medical assistants, 138,000 nurses, 35,000 midwives, and 1,781,000 other personnel. The last mentioned are largely responsible for the health care of the peasants; they include practitioners of traditional medicine,[17] midwives with little formal training, other paramedical and often part-time personnel, and the graduates of secondary medical schools.

Although higher education has expanded rapidly, the proportion of graduates in medicine remains only about 10%. Even this small percentage includes both the graduates of two-year medical schools and those of the few large centers that have four- or five-year curriculums. China's needs have been so critical that emphasis has been placed on the two-year medical schools and secondary medical education. The graduates of secondary medical schools practice in most of the urban medical centers and fill key positions at the *hsien* level. Some may work at the commune level, but it is unlikely that any are stationed with production brigades.

Estimates of present medical and related personnel are difficult because of the limitations on publication and the diversities of the people involved. There are reported to have been 110,000 graduates from higher medical institutions between 1949 and 1963. Additions for the survivors of medical personnel trained before 1949 and for the graduates of 1964 suggest some 135,000 persons with higher medical education at the beginning of 1965.[18] This number includes medical doctors, pharmacists, and dentists. Graduates with secondary medical education may have reached 350,000 by 1965.[19]

---

the Peoples Republic of China, there are no adequate and uniform definitions. Figures on health personnel may include only those completing formal training at specified levels of university or secondary school, or they may include part-time midwives with little or no training or even workers in other activities with a few days of instruction in first aid. Or, again, data may refer to the health industry and include janitors along with administrators. Data on health are often combined with those on education and cultural affairs. Health statistics were disrupted during the "great leap" and not restored thereafter. See Cho-ming Li, *The Statistical System of Communist China* (Berkeley: University of California Press, 1962); Leo A. Orleans, "Troubles with Statistics," *Problems of Communism*, January–February, 1965.

[17] In November, 1958, the 500,000 doctors of native medicine were given equal status with Western doctors and all medical schools were required to offer courses in traditional medicine.

[18] *New China News Agency*, Aug. 17, 1963 (hereafter cited as *NCNA*). It was estimated that there were 6,400 persons with higher medical degrees received prior to 1949 (Leo A. Orleans, *Professional Manpower and Education in Communist China*, Washington, D.C., 1961). The number of graduates reported in 1963 was 25,000 (*NCNA*, Aug. 17, 1963). An estimate of 25,000 was used as maximal for 1964, since there was a decrease in the total number of graduates in this year.

[19] A member of the board of directors of the Chinese Medical Association, Hung K'ai-yun, stated in Japan in 1963 that there were 290,000 persons with completed sec-

The health facilities in urban areas are relatively adequate to implement birth control programs.[20] There are municipal hospitals, clinics, maternity homes, and other centers along with factory clinics that sometimes include hospital beds. The problem in family planning services, as in other health activities, is the rural public health network that serves or fails to serve some 85% of the total population of China.

Several recent or current developments should contribute to the efficiency of birth control activities, particularly in the rural areas. Half the graduates of medical schools are now women.[21] Medical personnel are transferred from urban to rural health facilities, either permanently or for periods of time. Increasing emphasis is placed on mobile medical teams, particularly urban groups serving rural areas.[22] The vice-minister of health, Chang K'ai, states that each of the *hsien* towns has its own hospital, generally with sections for obstetrics and pediatrics and capable of handling abdominal operations and difficult cases of childbirth.[23] Moreover, "each commune has its own health center or clinic, some production brigades have their own health centers or health production stations, while production teams are provided with health personnel and midwifery assistants who are not divorced from production."

Closer assessment of the health services that reach the people directly may be secured from descriptions of health organizations in specific communes.[24] The approach is admittedly hazardous, for there are variations and selectivity among communes, and available reports per-

---

ondary medical education (*Ajiva keizai jumpo* [Asian Economic Report], July, 1963, *JPRS* 21834, Nov. 13, 1963). Vice-Minister of Health Tsui Yi-tien stated at the end of 1962 that China had qualified 450,000 nurses, technicians, midwives, pharmacists, and others (*Science*, Sept. 20, 1963). According to a report of early 1965, from 1949 to 1964 more than 450,000 medical workers were trained, including doctors and nurses; of these, 120,000 were graduates of medical colleges, the rest graduates of vocational medical schools. All provinces and autonomous regions except Tibet were said to have one or more "medical schools" (*NCNA*, Jan. 16, 1965).

20 According to *NCNA*, Mar. 3, 1962, "In Peking, almost every street has its own maternity and child-care center. They maintain regular contact with ten maternity and children's hospitals for technical guidance. . . ."

21 The proportion of women in total college enrollment increased from 20% in 1949 to 25% in 1963. However, proportions of women were higher in medicine and public health. In Peking, 60%–70% of the students enrolled in the medical schools were women (*Chung-kuo hsin-wen*, Oct. 11, 1963, JPRS 22990, Jan. 30, 1964).

22 *Jen-min jih-pao*, Feb. 26, 1965, had two news reports (pp. 1 and 2) and an editorial (*JPRS* 29516, Mar. 29, 1965).

23 Chang K'ai [Health work makes big strides in the service of industrial and agricultural production], *Kuang-ming jih-pao*, JPRS 28543, Jan. 29, 1965.

24 Unless otherwise indicated, the sources are *Jen-min pao-chien* [Peoples Health], 1959, issues 1, 3, 5, 6, 8, 11, 12.

tain to the years 1958–60. This is the only approach possible, though, for administrative and statistical reports are not published, at least for distribution.

The Department of Health, Education, and Culture, under the Administrative Committee of the People's Commune, was the executive organization. Each commune center had a hospital that also functioned as a center for all public health work. The ideal staff varied from five to twenty, depending on the size of the commune and the source of the information. Since these numbers probably included some administrative and service personnel, it may be assumed that the average commune hospital and center had ten persons in full-time medical work. If so, there were about 260,000 medical and health personnel in the commune services.[25]

The production brigades were supposed to have health centers with simple beds and staffs of three to seven full- or part-time health workers. Some centers served two or three brigades; there were one million health workers at this level in all China. If it is further assumed that each production brigade had two part-time health workers, another million persons must be added to those who had some limited training in public health or first aid.

The services in the production units were given by "part-time health workers, midwives, and nurses working under the direction of brigade health centers." Only the most basic health needs were met at this level. However, if the three million production teams had an average of two part-time health workers, an additional six million persons were utilized within the health system.

The sum of these estimates indicates that as of 1959 there may have been one and a quarter million full-time and seven million part-time health workers at the commune level and below.[26] If this is so, there was one health worker for each seventy persons in the rural areas of China.

The discussion of commune health services places major emphasis on facilities for the care of mothers and children. Some of these facilities parallel the basic health organization with independent lines of command. Possibly because of the shortage of personnel, however, most of the maternity clinics are under the medical center and attached to the existing plant. Although two or more production brigades may have to share one health center, there is at least one "maternity hos-

[25] Although there are now 74,000 communes, in the period of these reports there were only 26,000.

[26] This total is consistent with reports. "By 1959 over one million were serving in the hospitals, clinics, and health protection centers. In addition, there were millions of spare-time participants in health work" (Peking Review, No. 16 [Apr. 21, 1961]).

pital" for each brigade, even though this "hospital" may be only lying-in beds in the home of a part-time midwife. Though few of the production brigades and none of the production teams have full-time health personnel in permanent maternity facilities, women are encouraged to give birth under the care of trained midwives and in maternity homes.[27]

Is it possible to estimate the changes in the rural health facilities since 1958–60? During the economic disruptions and the near-famine conditions of the early sixties, there can have been only minor improvements. There may also have been adverse effects. In the past two or three years, there should have been improvements in the numbers and qualifications of personnel. Since most of the rural public health people are trained in *hsien* or commune hospitals, national assessment is difficult.

What was the spatial distribution of these public health workers? Communes vary greatly in size. In the central agricultural regions they are small and densely populated. In the sparsely settled provinces along the periphery of China the areas are very large and the inhabited places may be many miles apart.[28] It is probable, however, that the greatest difference between the central and outer provinces lies in the quality of the public health staffs. Most of the modern medical schools and hospitals are in the coastal provinces where the need for medical people is almost limitless. Only special pressures can force graduates to migrate westward, even to cities.

Thus there are many deficiencies in the medical services of rural China. However, the medical organization has many features favorable to the assumption of responsibilities for birth control. The lines of command run directly downward, including both permanent staff and part-time workers. There are direct communications between the various levels in the rural areas as well as in the cities. Moreover, at each level the medical organizations are under the jurisdiction of a member of the Communist Party.[29] Lines of command thus go down

[27] For example: "Statistical data gathered from 23 provinces revealed that 60.7 per cent of all childbirths were attended by new-method midwifery, while in bigger cities the percentage was over 95 per cent" (*T'ung chi yen-chiu* [Statistical Research], May 23, 1958, *URS*, Vol. 11, No. 25, June 24, 1958). According to another report, "in Honan Province over 80 per cent of the pregnant women were delivered in maternity homes in 1958." It should be noted that "new-method midwifery" presumes recent training, and that "maternity homes" include the two or three lying-in beds in the home of a part-time midwife.

[28] Numerous reports indicate that there are medical teams or individual health workers who travel to villages lacking medical personnel, especially in more remote areas.

[29] There are presently about 19 million Communist Party members in China; roughly three-fourths are in the rural areas.

through the public health system and the party structure. At each level, lines extend laterally to the hospital, clinic and other medical facilities.

It should also be noted that, despite the low level of competence of many of the health workers, there is respect by the peasants. "The peasants' idea about a doctor, either Western or Chinese, is very simple and also very practical. They are not interested in the difference between a doctor and a nurse. They want to have someone cure their diseases with little or no charge. . . . So long as one knows something about medicine, he is very much respected by the peasants."[30]

There is an additional resource and line of communication in the Chinese Medical Association, a powerful auxiliary of the Ministry of Health with a membership of more than 19,000 and branches in all the provinces, autonomous regions, and municipalities. The Association publishes fourteen medical journals that receive considerable distribution throughout China. It also publicizes health techniques through radio and television, press and periodicals.[31]

Thus there is already a health service that reaches from center to production brigade and team levels. Immense training would be required to make intra-uterine devices and induced abortions available in rural as well as urban areas.[32] However, massive training and nationwide campaigns in general or limited health fields are not novelties in the Peoples Republic.[33] Responsibilities in birth control were allocated to the health services as early as August, 1956, and there have been arrangements for giving basic knowledge of birth control to health workers who in turn transmit it to the women.[34] The training for induced abortion is already widespread in urban areas; presumably more extended training in the various medical means is now underway. There are few evidences of this in press or broadcast. It is possible, though, that mass communication media continue along accepted lines while preparatory measures for new lines or new specificities are being made.

30 *Jen-min pao-chien* [Peoples Health], No. 8, 1959, *JPRS* 5484, Sept. 2, 1960.

31 *NCNA*, Sept. 22, 1963.

32 The problem of what health personnel at what levels of education could be trained to the requisite tasks under varying assumptions as to the availability of more highly trained personnel and more adequate medical facilities requires research and experimentation in countries considering programs to control births, including mainland China.

33 Robert M. Worth, "Health in Rural China: From Village to Commune," *American Journal of Hygiene*, 77:228–39 (1963); "Health Trends in China since the 'Great Leap Forward,' " *ibid.*, 78:349–57 (1963).

34 *JPRS* 225, Feb. 11, 1958; *JPRS* 96, Jan. 8, 1957.

Heritage, Change, and the Future

Persistence and adaptation, stability and change, were alike characteristic of what we refer to as traditional China. These were the Confucian ideas and pervasive values of large multigeneration families. Or, phrased more precisely, these are the ideals and values attributed to the Chinese by those who have studied the literature and talked with the elite. In fact, the imperatives of subsistence and the hazards to life dictated small, co-living households and few surviving sons. Reproductive and familial behavior were alike pragmatic. Lower order sons might be adopted within the larger family, while daughters might be placed for adoption outside the family. In difficult conditions, boys had priority over girls, while those already maturing had priority over the newly born.

There are other aspects of the behavior of the Chinese within China in the past and outside China today that are directly relevant to the assessment of the future of mainland China. These include the dedication of men to their familiies, even when economic contributions require long absences and hence interrupt reproduction; the achievement orientations with visions long in years and even in generations; the adaptability to altered conditions of working and living; and the upward mobility in developing and developed economic systems.

Behavior in traditional settings and under conditions of comprehensive modernization permits plausible inferences concerning the future of fertility. Increasingly strong motivations to limit childbearing in accord with the desires of the leaders and in relation to the mobility of the individual would be anticipated among those perceptive of the new opportunities for service and status. Postponement of marriage would be a component in new adaptabilities as in old, for appreciable proportions of the men of the old China never married and appreciable proportions of those who did were absent from wives and families for long periods of time.

In mainland China, the arguments, the strategies, and the plans for change and action leading to reduction in childbearing are proper to revolutionary communism, but the people who formulate programs and those who respond are both Chinese. Delay in marriage until a late age and rigid limitation of childbearing are required for continuing and increasing service to Chairman Mao and the party.[35] Alternatively, family planning is essential to health and a better life for mothers and children.

[35] For selections from the literature on preferable ages at marriage, see U.S. American Consulate General, Hong Kong, *SCMP* 2745, May 24, 1962; 2757, June 13, 1962; 2871, Dec. 3, 1962. Also: *Extracts from China Mainland Magazines* (hereafter cited as *ECMM*), 65, Sept. 11, 1963.

Economic conditions must be assuming primacy in the control of population growth.[36] There are the grim figures of per capita food production. The surging youth of the countryside push against the system of rural enclosure, but urban employment and facilities are not conceivable for other than a small portion of those who wish them. Economic arguments for the reduction of rates of growth are dangerous, though, for Malthusianism remains a viable villain. This intellectual barrier to comprehension may be an asset in the implementation of programs. Persuasion must be impeccable in its concern with the individual and the high values of group identifications and service to the millennial process.

Prestige, leadership groups, and achievement drives are all involved in the creation and diffusion of new life patterns for the oncoming generations. Even today, codes are firm and discipline hard among the cadre, the university students, and other elite groups. The ideal and largely the requirement are late marriage and the one- or two-child family. Induced abortions are reported to be obligatory for those who would avert the penalties of accidental pregnancies.[37]

What, then, are the probabilities for a rapid extension of the goals of the elite to the general population of the rural areas? The initial and perhaps most fundamental assessment is a repudiation of this phrasing of the question. The activities do not involve general diffusion but the conversion and the dedicated practice of youth.[38] Educational, motivational, and increasingly compulsive campaigns proceed through the

[36] The anti-economic reaction was severe in 1958. In later years, Premier Chou En-lai is cited somewhat ambiguously. In 1961, in a television interview with Felix Greene, he stated: "Education on planned parenthood was and continues to be carried on in China mainly to protect the health of the mothers and provide favorable conditions for bringing up children, not because of so-called 'population pressure'" (*Communist China Digest*, No. 32, Feb. 14, 1961, *JPRS* 6751). In 1965, according to Edgar Snow in the *Washington Post*, Feb. 26, "China's leaders are clearly aware that a substantial gain in living standards can only come about through a reduction in birth rates." Perhaps mounting evidence of the magnitude of the growth is involved in changing economic assessments. There are reports of an investigation and registration of the population in mid-1964. See *Manchester Guardian*, July 30, 1964, p. 7, cols. 1–3, and *The Times* (London), July 10, 1964. The economic capacities to produce contraceptives of various types are already developed. See, for example, [Comparatively complete plastic industry department established in Peking], *Jen-min jih-pao*, Sept. 3, 1964; [Rapidly developing rubber industry in China], *Chung-kuo hsin-wen* (Canton), July 17, 1964; Wang Hung-ch'en, [Five years' progress in pharmaceutics in China], *Yao-hsueh t'ung-pao*, 10 (10): 456–59 (1964).

[37] Majima, [The birth control controversy in China]. Journalist and refugee reports are numerous. As indicative of the latter, see Tung Chi-ping, "Red China," *Look Magazine*, Dec. 1, 1964.

[38] [Is contraception still necessary? ... reply to a reader's query], *Chung-kuo fu-nü*, No. 14, July 16, 1959, *ECMM*, 184, Sept. 21, 1959, pp. 18–20; Sung Hung-tsao, [Will vasectomy affect health?]; Lu Ta-ch'uan, [Before and after I had my vasectomy]; Lin Ch'iao-chih, [Can late marriage cause difficult labor?]; and Fu Lien-chang, [The

women's organizations and the Communist Youth League. Women's groups afford widespread publicity; their activities may reach some of the middle-aged and older women in the villages with the word that late marriage and few children are now proper for their daughters and their granddaughters. Changes are unlikely in the reproductive performance of the older women, whose behavior is conditioned so deeply by the ancient codes. The key organization is the Communist Youth League.[39] These young people, numbering some 50 million, are components in the power structure of the present; they will be the power structure of tomorrow.

This approach to the reduction of the rate of population growth through late marriage and limited childbearing among young people is probably unique to Communist China. It certainly has possibilities for major reductions in birth rates. The reasons are twofold. The first is obvious. Long postponement of first and second births minimizes if it does not bar births of higher orders. It also lengthens the time between generations. The second is less obvious to non-demographers, and so will be elaborated in more detail.

In a country such as China, traditional patterns of marriage and childbearing are such that some three of each four babies are born to mothers below age 35. Thus women aged 15–34 should be the target group in any campaign to reduce births. There is the further fact that, given high fertility and recent declines in mortality, youth are a relatively large and increasing proportion of the population. In 1965, almost one-third of all the women of mainland China were in the ages from 15 to 34.[40] The oncoming generations of girls below age 15 were one-third again as numerous as the total number of women in the

positive significance of planned family] in *Chung-kuo fu-nü*, No. 4, Apr. 1, 1963, *SCMM* 364, May 13, 1963, pp. 32–39. Also, in the same source, [I do not want to get married early], Editorial, August, 1963, *SCMM* 384, Sept. 30, 1963; [Reader's opinion on the consequences of "love at first sight"], No. 2, February, 1963, *SCMM* 357, Mar. 25, 1963; [Treat the relationship between work, children, and household chores in a revolutionary spirit], No. 11, November, 1963, *SCMM* 394, Dec. 9, 1963; [How I fight for freedom of marriage], No. 10, October, 1963, *SCMM* 392, Nov. 25, 1963; [Advantages of birth control to newly-wed], Letters to the editor, No. 9, Sept. 1, 1964, *JPRS* 27122, Oct. 28, 1964.

39 From *Chung-kuo ch'ing-nien* [China Youth]: [For late marriage], by Yang Hsiu, No. 11, June 1, 1962, *SCMM* 322, July 16, 1962; [How can family relations be handled properly?] No. 14–15, July 28, 1963, *SCMM* 383, Sept. 23, 1963. Also: Huang Yu-ho, [Is it right not to unite, educate married young women?], Letter to the editor by the Secretary of the Ho-nan-wu-ts'un Production Brigade Communist Youth League Branch, Sun-yu Commune, Hsiang-ho Hsien, Hopei Province, *JPRS* 28061, Dec. 30, 1964; Yen Ch'ien, [She insists on late marriage], *Chung-kuo ch'ing-nien*, Aug. 15, 1964, *SCMM*, 440, October, 1964; [How should young workers look at the question of love and marriage?], *Ta kung-pao*, Sept. 12, 1964, *JPRS* 27895, Dec. 17, 1964.

40 Projections and estimates, U.S. Bureau of the Census; see source note and citation, Table 3.

twenty-year span from 15 to 34. The high proportions and the rapidly increasing numbers of women in the young ages of maximum reproductive potential may be illustrated in comparisons of the populations projected for China in 1965 and in 1975. Barring changes in mortality, women aged 15–34 in 1975 will be one-third more numerous than those in the same age group in 1965. Thus, roughly, one-third reduction in age-specific fertility within a single decade would be required simply to keep the number of births from increasing. Drastic reductions concentrated among women in the young ages seem clearly indicated if the goals of policy and program are to be achieved.

Space precludes other than notation of the arguments concerning the receptivity of youth to the altered marriage and reproductive patterns. These arguments, discussions of population policy, are prevalent in the literature.[41] The tenets of communism elevate the status of women and condemn those aspects of the old order that lowered it. These tenets also deny the validity of the loyalties, responsibilities, obligations, and attachments of the traditional family and proclaim duties to party and leader.[42] The affirmative crusades, partially realized, include education and extra-family roles for women, along with community responsibilities for the socialization and education of children. The preconditions for demographic modernization in the altered values, motivations, and capabilities of women are aspects of the revolution itself. The extent to which the ideals of the revolution have become the views and practices of the people will remain conjectural as long as statistics are concealed and objective observations barred.

The major question, of course, is that of the correspondence between ideals and the realities of village life. The one thing that can be stated definitively is that the ancient ways and the traditional values are not living experiences for today's young people. They are, rather, the reminiscences of the elders. Girls aged 15–19 in 1965 were all less

[41] Hsu Chia-tun, [Make up your mind to be the first generation of new peasants— discussing the question of revolutionary ambitions with young intellectuals going to work in the countryside], *Chung-kuo ch'ing-nien*, No. 12, June 16, 1963, *SCMM* 373, July 15, 1963; Kan Feng, [Steer clear from the bourgeois idea of pleasure-seeking], *ibid.*, No. 16, Aug. 16, 1963, *SCMM* 385, Oct. 7, 1963; Li Ch'i-t'ao, [Persist in instilling the Communist spirit in our new generation], *ibid.*, No. 1, January, 1963, *SCMM* 352, Feb. 18, 1963; Lo Jui-ch'ing, [Learn from Lei Feng], *ibid.*, No. 5–6, Mar. 2, 1963, *SCMM* 358, Apr. 1, 1963; Wu Yü-chang, [Be successors to the revolution], *ibid.*, No. 1, Jan. 1, 1963, *SCMM* 351, Feb. 11, 1963. Yang Hsiu, [Inherit the traditions of the revolution, carry the burden of the times—on the question of ideological training for the children of revolutionary cadres], *ibid.*, No. 16, Aug. 16, 1963, *SCMM* 389, Nov. 4, 1963. See also the series of articles by Mark Gayn of the *Toronto Daily Star* in the *New York Times*, June 7–12, 1965.

[42] Yen Chang-kuei, [Let us discard filial piety and family loyalty], *Che-hsueh yen-chiu* [Philosophical research], No. 6, Nov. 25, 1963, *JPRS* 25108, June 16, 1964.

than 5 years of age when the new regime was established. Those aged 30–34 now were less than 5 years of age when the Japanese invaded China and effectively ended what had been assumed to be the enduring life of the old China. In another five years, youth aged 15–19 will all have been born under communism. Since parents, community leaders, and teachers all had traditional backgrounds, knowledge, and values, however, the basic conditioning of this first new generation reared under communism may be more that of the continuing rather than of the new China.

TABLE 2

PEOPLES REPUBLIC OF CHINA: ESTIMATES AND PROJECTIONS
OF THE POPULATION, 1955–80 AND 1953–78

(In Millions)

PROJECTION	YEAR					
	1955 (1953)	1960 (1958)	1965 (1963)	1970 (1968)	1975 (1973)	1980 (1978)
United Nations, as of 1963[a]						
Officially based:						
Low mortality, late fertility decline...............	608.2	686.4	764.0	843.0	930.7	1,032.3
High mortality, earlier fertility decline...........	608.2	675.7	740.6	815.5	902.7	1,001.9
Estimated base:						
Continued trends.........	599.7	648.1	703.5	767.4	842.2	932.7
Low mortality, late fertility declines...............	599.7	648.1	703.5	767.4	839.8	916.8
High mortality, late fertility declines...............	599.7	641.7	684.2	735.3	794.8	857.8
Low mortality, early fertility declines............	599.7	645.8	691.5	734.4	774.1	811.9
High mortality, early fertility declines............	599.7	639.4	672.7	704.3	735.1	762.2
U.S. Bureau of the Census[b]						
Model projection...........	603.2	680.5	746.4	833.3	933.0	1,048.9
R. Pressat[c]						
Fertility unchanged:						
Marriage unchanged......	(583)	(651)	(729)	(824)	(944)	(1,098)
Marriage changed........	(583)	(651)	(729)	(823)	(937)	(1,072)
Fertility changed:						
Marriage unchanged......	(583)	(651)	(729)	(798)	(845)	(885)
Marriage changed........	(583)	(651)	(729)	(797)	(837)	(865)

[a] United Nations, Department of Economic and Social Affairs, *Provisional Report on World Population Prospects as Assessed in 1963*, ST/SOA/Ser. R/7 (New York, 1964), pp. 81–96, 118–19. Assumptions: Low mortality, expectation of life at birth: 42.5 years in 1955–60, 45.0 years in 1960–65, rising to 63.2 years in 1955–2000. High mortality expectation of life at birth: 42.5 years in 1955–2000, 52.5 years in 1975–80. Low fertility: Age-sex adjusted birth rate of 37.91, with a thirty-year reduction of 50% beginning in 1955. High fertility: Age-sex adjusted birth rate of 37.91, with a thirty-year reduction of 50% beginning in 1970. Estimated base: Age distribution in 1953 appropriate to a pre-Communist birth rate of 37.91 per 1,000 total population, with an expectation of life at birth of 30 years; age distribution in 1955 appropriate to a birth rate of the same level but an expectation of life at birth risen to 40 years for the period 1950–55.

[b] For source and explanations, see Table 3, source note.

[c] Roland Pressat, "Etat présent et avenir de la population chinoise," United Nations World Population Conference, Belgrade, Yugoslavia, August 30 to September 10, 1965, WPC/WP/90. Assumptions: Cohort births as in a rural region of Taiwan, 1900–1937, for 1958 and 1963; fertility unchanged or moving toward a generalized level of two births; marriage ages as in Taiwan, 1935 (19.7 years), moving to France, generation of 1871–75 (24.3 years).

TABLE 3

PEOPLES REPUBLIC OF CHINA: ESTIMATED AND PROJECTED POPULATION, BY AGE, 1955–80, ON ASSUMPTIONS OF CONTINUITY, 1964–80

AGE	YEAR					
	1955	1960	1965	1970	1975	1980
Numbers (in millions)						
Total.......	602	680	746	833	933	1049
0 to 4...	103	115	120	136	154	177
5 to 14...	140	171	197	212	234	266
15 to 24...	110	119	133	161	186	201
25 to 44...	152	167	178	193	213	246
45 to 64...	78	88	95	104	114	124
65 and over	19	23	25	29	33	36
Per Cent Change						
Total.......	....	13.0	9.7	11.7	12.0	12.4
0 to 14...	....	17.7	10.8	9.8	11.5	14.2
15 to 24...	....	8.2	11.8	21.1	15.5	8.1
25 to 44...	....	9.9	6.6	8.4	10.4	15.5
45 to 64...	....	12.8	8.0	9.5	9.6	8.8
Per Cent Age Structure of Change						
Total.......	....	100.0	100.0	100.0	100.0	100.0
0 to 14...	....	53.1	47.7	35.6	40.4	47.4
15 to 24...	....	11.1	21.5	32.2	25.3	12.9
25 to 44...	....	18.5	16.9	17.2	20.2	28.4
45 to 64...	....	12.3	10.8	10.3	10.1	8.6
65 and over	....	4.9	3.1	4.6	4.0	2.6
Per Cent Age Structure of Population						
Total.......	100.0	100.0	100.0	100.0	100.0	100.0
0 to 14...	40.4	41.9	42.4	41.7	41.5	42.2
15 to 24...	18.3	17.4	17.8	19.3	19.9	19.1
25 to 44...	25.2	24.5	23.8	23.1	22.8	23.4
45 to 64...	13.0	12.9	12.7	12.5	12.5	11.8
65 and over	3.2	3.4	3.3	3.5	3.5	3.4

SOURCE: U.S. Bureau of the Census, Foreign Demographic Analysis Division, *Mainland China*, Model II, January 1, 1953 to 1981 (Washington, D.C., 1965), manuscript tables.

Assumptions: Base, numbers from census-registration of 1953, age and sex structure consistent with assumed demographic history. Birth rates, 45.0 in 1953; gross reproduction rate 312.7 in 1953, 315.8 in 1964, constant thereafter; expectation of life at birth, men, 41.2 in 1953, 45.3 in 1958, dropping to 34.8 in 1961, rising to 42.7 in 1964, constant thereafter. Annual figures as of January 1.

COMMENTS

If the government of the Peoples Republic of China bases its decisions on analyses of the dynamics of its population, programs to reduce birth rates will have increasing priority among the drives toward economic advance and political stability. There are mounting indications that population fields are becoming areas for firm decisions and decisive actions rather than arguments on ideology and discussions of

TABLE 4

PEOPLES REPUBLIC OF CHINA: ESTIMATES AND PROJECTIONS OF THE
UNITED NATIONS AS OF 1957, BY AGE, 1953–78

(In Millions)

AGE	YEAR					
	1953	1958	1963	1968	1973	1978
High Estimate						
Total.......	582.5	647.8	732.9	837.0	960.6	1,112.7
0 to 14...	213.9	253.1	304.9	355.3	414.7	485.8
15 to 29...	146.4	154.5	166.6	196.5	236.3	287.4
30 to 44...	110.1	116.7	124.1	132.0	141.7	154.5
45 to 59...	72.8	78.9	86.1	93.5	101.3	109.4
60 and over	39.3	44.6	51.2	58.7	66.6	75.6
Low Estimate						
Total.......	582.5	635.6	688.2	721.8	744.6	770.6
0 to 14...	206.9	233.2	251.9	241.9	211.4	187.3
15 to 29...	149.2	157.5	169.8	190.3	217.7	237.7
30 to 44...	112.2	118.8	126.6	134.5	144.4	157.4
45 to 59...	74.2	80.5	87.7	95.3	103.2	111.4
60 and over	40.0	45.6	52.2	59.8	67.9	76.8

SOURCE: United Nations, Department of Economic and Social Affairs, *Future Population Estimates by Sex and Age*, Report IV, *The Population of Asia and the Far East, 1950–1980*, Population Studies No. 31, ST/SOA/Ser. A 31 (New York, 1959), pp. 24–30, 94–99.
Assumptions: High estimate, birth rate, 41.6, constant 1953 to 1983. Low estimate, birth rate 37.0, declining to half the initial level in the decade from 1958 to 1968. Expectation of life at birth assumed to be 40 years in 1948–53, 60.4 years in 1978–83. Initial age distributions appropriate to the selected vital rates.

policy.[43] The medical means of the intra-uterine devices, induced abortion, and sterilization permit effective programs. These means are ac-

[43] [Kwangtung Province convenes conferences on planned childbirth, Apr. 5–8], *Nan-fang jih-pao, Kuang-chou*, Apr. 11, 1965, JPRS 31265, July 27, 1965, p. 104. The speech was given by Yin Lin-p'ing, chairman of the Kwangtung Province Provincial Guidance Committee for Planned Childbirth *and* Secretary of the Secretariat of the CCP Kwangtung Provincial Committee.

ceptable to the Chinese. They are also suitable for use in programs where ideological pressures and material sanctions reinforce the normal aspirations of women to space their pregnancies and to limit the number of their children.

Perhaps the dynamics of the Communist system itself have already transformed youth so deeply that acceptance of delayed marriage and the family of only one or two children present few problems. This may be true for the youths of the cities. It is not likely to be true for the great majority of youths living in the rural areas remote from great metropolitan centers. Paradoxical as it may seem, the success of programs to secure the postponement of marriage and the limitation of childbearing among the oncoming generations of the Communist-born and the Communist-reared will provide an objective measure of the extent to which the Peoples Republic of China has achieved those fundamental transformations of person and personality that are its goals.

4

TAIWAN, REPUBLIC OF CHINA

T. C. HSU, M.D., M.P.H., Sc.D.
Commissioner of Health, Taiwan Provincial Health Department
Director, Taiwan Population Studies Center

and

L. P. CHOW, M.D., ScD., Dr.P.H.
Senior Specialist, Joint Commission on Rural Reconstruction
Associate Director, Taiwan Population Studies Center

ORIGIN AND OPERATION

BACKGROUND INFORMATION

Demographic situation in Taiwan.—Taiwan, one of the 35 provinces of the Republic of China, had, at the end of 1964, a total of 12,256,682 people living on its 14,047 square miles of land. The density of population, therefore, was 873 persons per square mile.

Although fertility in Taiwan has declined slightly, it still remains rather high. In 1964 the crude birth rate was 34.5, decreased from 38.3 in 1947; the crude death rate, 5.7, declined from 18.1 in 1947; and the rate of natural increase, 28.8, increased from 20.2 in 1947. The general fertility rate was 162, the total fertility rate 5,100, and the gross reproduction rate 2,480, all per 1,000, in 1964.

Including migration from the mainland, the population of Taiwan doubled in the past 18 years, or increased at an average annual rate of 4%.

The present paper summarizes the efforts and contributions made by many persons on the program staff including the field workers. Thanks are particularly due to Dr. S. C. Hsu, Chief, Rural Health Division, JCRR, and Mr. S. M. Keeny, Representative for East Asia, the Population Council, for their leadership and guidance. The staff of the Taiwan Population Studies Center helped analyze the data upon which this paper has been prepared. Dr. and Mrs. Christopher Tietze, Dr. John Y. Takeshita, and Mr. Keeny kindly reviewed and edited the manuscript.

High fertility in Taiwan has resulted in a young population. In 1964, 54.2% of the total population was less than 20 years old, 43.3% was 20–64, and only 2.6% was 65 years of age and older. The dependency burden has therefore been heavy—a ratio of 132 to 100.

Family planning movement in the past.—Until quite recently, family planning had long been taboo in Taiwan. The recent family planning movement owes its advocacy to the late Dr. Chiang Mon-lin, former chairman of the Sino-American Joint Commission on Rural Reconstruction.

In 1954, the Family Planning Association of China was organized and chartered by the Ministry of the Interior. The Association has been engaged in publicity and educational activities and in implementing programs involving mainly the traditional methods in several areas of the province. The total number of cases recruited by the Association was reported to have exceeded 100,000, but most of them never returned.

Government participation in family planning.—Government participation in family planning started in 1959, when family planning was included as an integral part of the maternal and child health program. The program has since been designated as the "Pre-pregnancy Health (PPH) Program," which implies maternal care before pregnancy.

The PPH clinics were established in all of the thirteen government general and maternity hospitals, and PPH workers were employed at the eight township health stations, one in each township, in Nantou County. The number of PPH workers was increased to 120 in 1964. The PPH workers make home visits and conduct group meetings to educate and motivate women toward family planning. By the end of 1964, PPH workers recruited 69,715 cases, equivalent to 5.3% of all married women 20–39 years of age in the province. About 60% of these cases are reported to be "active."

Despite its moral support and participation through the maternal and child health (MCH) program, the government so far has no formal policy with regard to family planning.

DEVELOPMENT OF THE FAMILY PLANNING HEALTH PROGRAM

Taiwan Population Studies Center.—The Taiwan Population Studies Center (TPSC) was established in 1962 with a first grant of $60,000 from the Population Council (New York). The objectives of the TPSC were to make studies and surveys to find out the determinants and consequences of population growth and its impact on the health of the people and on the economic development of the country. By presenting facts to the public, the TPSC also hoped to elicit greater understanding and to enlist more support from the people for family planning.

Immediately after its establishment and until July, 1964, when the Michigan contract expired, the TPSC was affiliated with the Michigan Population Studies Center (MPSC). Drs. Ronald Freedman and John Y. Takeshita of the MPSC still serve as its consultants.

Since 1962, the TPSC has undertaken two comprehensive fertility surveys in Taichung City and in other areas, supervised the statistical aspects of the Taichung action program, conducted a series of field experiments to get more loop insertions with less cost, prepared two sets of population projections for the use of the national economic planning body in drafting the ten-year economic development plan, projected future school populations, and published a monthly review of the current population of Taiwan for distribution to interested organizations and individuals.

Taichung pilot action program.—In 1962, the new intra-uterine devices (IUD's), the Lippes loop and Margulies coil, were first introduced into Taiwan and created a new era for the family planning program.

A pilot program was implemented in Taichung City to measure the acceptability, effectiveness, and side effects of the new devices. A total of 4,155 cases was recruited in nine months, of which three-fourths elected to use the new devices when offered a choice of all methods. These IUD cases are being examined every six months by specialists in obstetrics and gynecology (OBG) through a grant made by the Population Council.

Medical advisory board.—For the Taichung action program, a medical advisory board, composed of eleven leading OBG specialists, in Taiwan was organized. The board carefully studied the new IUD's and gave its approval for their use in Taichung as a pilot study.

Later, before the extension of the IUD program, the board again gave its approval, based upon the favorable results obtained through the Taichung studies.

Once the loop was accepted by the leading medical authorities, distribution to medical practitioners under a mass program could be started.

The expanded action program—family planning health program.— In view of the encouraging results of the Taichung pilot action program, an extension program was started in January, 1964, using mainly Lippes loops in areas beyond Taichung. The program now covers the whole province and, by the end of May, 1965, a total of 95,487 women in the province had accepted the device.

The program has been most carefully planned on the basis of various surveys, studies, and pilot programs, and so designed as to permit continuous evaluation to ensure that money and effort are efficiently utilized.

Evaluation.—The family planning health program is unique in having an evaluation unit to guide program operations. The responsibility now rests with the Taiwan Population Studies Center.

THE FAMILY PLANNING HEALTH PROGRAM

Organization.—To implement the program more effectively, a Committee on Family Planning Health (CFPH) has been organized within the provincial department of health. It is the responsibility of this organization to decide on policy matters and to supervise technically the related activities of the voluntary organizations. The government health authorities so far assume responsibility only for the education and motivation of the people. Actual service to those who desire it is provided by the Maternal and Child Health Association (MCHA), a voluntary organization. The MCHA provides supplies, including loops, inserters, and record forms to medical practitioners, and pays half the cost of insertion.

The committee is composed of nine members, three of whom are standing members, with the senior author of this chapter, Dr. T. C. Hsu, Commissioner of Health, as the ex-officio chairman. Dr. S. C. Hsu, Chief, Rural Health Division of the Joint Commission on Rural Reconstruction (JCRR), and Mr. S. M. Keeny, Representative for East Asia, The Population Council, are the two other standing members.

The executive body of the committee is represented by the junior author, Dr. L. P. Chow, Associate Director of the Taiwan Population Studies Center, who is the executive secretary of the committee. Under his supervision are four divisions: medical, urban program, rural program, and the secretariat. The MCHA is guided by a board of directors, chaired by Mrs. S. T. Hsu-Wong, elected by the members for a term of three years. Dr. L. P. Chow concurrently supervises the execution of the program of the Association, which has twenty-two regional representatives, one in each county and city.

Field workers.—There are two types of field workers employed by the Department of Health: (1) the pre-pregnancy health workers (PPHW's), who had been employed originally to promote traditional contraceptive methods; (2) the village health education nurses (VHEN's), who had been employed to teach people personal hygiene and sanitation.

The former, numbering 200 at present, are stationed in the assigned townships, usually one in each. The latter, numbering 100, integrate the subject of family planning into their health education activities and move monthly from one village to another in teams of three. An additional 60 PPHW's will be recruited to bring total workers to 360, including supervisors. The VHEN's are all graduates of senior vocational nursing schools, but only one-third of the PPHW's are professional. The rest are high school graduates with two years' experience in various kinds of social work.

Workers are usually recruited through advertisements in newspapers. Competitive examinations are given to the applicants. Ability to get along with people and to make a speech fluently in a local dialect are essential requirements.

Pre-employment training comprises 100 hours of both theory and field practice. The curriculum includes the following:

1. Orientation to the program—objectives, target, work procedures of the program, population of Taiwan, common demographic terms, and other related common sense factors (30 hours).
2. Medical knowledge about contraception—simple anatomy of female sexual organs, physiology of reproduction, induced abortion, traditional contraceptive methods, IUD's, oral pills, sterilization, including demonstration and practice (25 hours).
3. Health education—principles, educational media, interview and group meeting techniques, public speech, including practice in the classroom (20 hours).
4. Field practice—home visits and group meetings including evening meetings (25 hours).

A final evaluation is made at the end of the course: by the trainees to evaluate the course, and by the instructors to evaluate the trainees.

The workers are usually brought back for two days of in-service training twice a year.

Supervisors.—There are twenty-one supervisors, fifteen for the PPH workers and six for the VHEN's. Supervisors are selected from workers who show good performance and leadership qualities. Each is assigned to an area with ten to fifteen workers.

A two-week intensive course is offered to prospective supervisors. A final examination is also conducted at the end of the course.

Work procedures.—Home visits and small group meetings have been the two major approaches of the field workers. Coupons are issued to women who show interest in the IUD. The coupon entitles the holder to a discount of 50% in the cost of insertion, which has been fixed by the MCHA at NT$60 (US$1.50), including after-care.

In addition, health and medical organizations at all levels have been mobilized to support the program and to refer cases.

Based upon the findings of the Taichung pilot action program, the field workers have been instructed to:

1. Go to the township registration offices to copy the names of all married women 20–44 years of age living in the township.
2. Make home visits or conduct small group meetings at every fifth *lin* (neighborhood of about twenty families). One-fifth of the married women in the area will thus be contacted.
3. In making home visits, first approach only those with at least three children and at least one son.
4. Recruit volunteers from among satisfied users of the IUD in particular, to facilitate the spread of information.
5. Make only one follow-up visit about six to eight weeks after the first visit. Explore new areas rather than spend time on the old.

The field workers also carry samples of supplies for the traditional methods, such as condoms and foam tablets. In cities where such materials are easily obtainable, motivated women are advised to buy the supplies from nearby drugstores. In rural areas, supplies may be sold at a reduced price if women desire to buy them from the workers.

Training of doctors for the IUD program.—During the first year's operation, only specialists in obstetrics and gynecology (OBG's) were allowed to insert loops. There are about 500 OBG's in Taiwan, 376 of whom have already had one day's training.

The OBG's in a county or city were invited by local health directors to attend the training courses. About 80% of the doctors invited actually attended.

The training includes explanation of the objectives and work procedures of the program and knowledge about the new IUD's. Cases are usually prepared for the trainees to practice at least one insertion. Since most of the OBG's in Taiwan have had a great deal of experience with the Ota ring, a brief orientation is considered quite adequate.

After the training, contracts are signed by these doctors with the MCHA.

The OBG's are usually available only in cities or larger towns. The 376 trained OBG's are distributed in about 120 out of the 361 townships. It was felt necessary to train the general practitioners (GP's), and this year a program to train them has been started.

The GP's require longer training—a minimum of three days. The curriculum includes the following major items:

1. Introduction to the program, including objective, procedures, record forms, and the expected role of practitioners.
2. Brief historical review of the IUD's and the recent development of the new IUD's.
3. Summary finding of the Taichung Medical Studies Program.

4. Anatomy and physiology of female reproductive organs.
5. Gynecological diagnostic technique.
6. Sterilization technique of instruments and supplies.
7. Clinical demonstration and practice of insertion. Ten insertions are usually required to qualify a GP for the program.
8. Discussions, questions, and answers on medical problems. Selection of size of loops, medical contra-indications to IUD insertion, accidental pregnancy with the device in place, side reactions, expulsion, ectopic pregnancy, etc., are of major interest to the practitioners.

By the end of July, 1965, a total of 200 GP's had been trained.

Publicity and health education.—Because there is still no official policy, publicity for the program has been restricted. The unwritten "line" is: "Do it, but don't talk about it publicly." This principle is

TABLE 1

PROPOSED REDUCTION OF NATURAL INCREASE RATE, 1963–73

Rate	1963	1973	Decline (per cent) 1963–73
Crude birth rate..................	36.3	24.1	33.6
Natural increase................	30.2	18.7	38.1
Total fertility....................	5,220	2,935	43.8
General fertility................	170	98	42.4

easily said but difficult to follow, because, if indeed nothing had been publicized, nothing would have happened.

In the past, the Taiwan Population Studies Center has been most careful in issuing news releases on various studies and survey results of public interest. If a news release on an action program is required, the MCHA has always been the sponsor. The MCHA, being a voluntary agency, enjoys more freedom in publicity.

The health educational media prepared and distributed to the field workers include film strips, flip charts, leaflets, and flyers. Posters of various kinds have been prepared for the Taichung action program but have seldom been used.

Objectives, goals, and targets of the program.—The principal objective of the program is to reduce the natural increase rate from 30.2 per 1,000 in 1963 to 19.7 in 1968 and to 18.7 in 1973 as shown in Table 1.

Based upon the age distribution of loop acceptors in the past, the marriage fertility rates of women in Taiwan in 1963, and the continuation rate and effectiveness of the loops, it has been estimated roughly that about five insertions are required to reduce one annual live birth. To attain the objective above, it has, therefore, been estimated that approximately 600,000 loops will have to be inserted in six years: 50,000 in 1964, 100,000 in 1965, 150,000 each in 1966 and 1967, 100,-000 in 1968, and 50,000 in 1969.

In the first year, 46,600 loops, 93% of the annual target, were actually inserted.

Budget for the program.—For the six-year plan, the Council for International Economic Cooperation and Development (CIECD) has approved NT$60 million (US$1.5 million) out of the interest on the counterpart funds, which are no longer under United States jurisdiction.

The Population Council provides dollars for equipment that is procured outside of Taiwan and pays for items which cannot be borne by local funds. It also appropriated US$50,000 for the medical follow-up studies of the new IUD's.

MAJOR ACHIEVEMENTS OF THE PROGRAM

Loop Acceptors

Before the inception of the extended action program, there were 3,650 cases registered by the Taichung pilot program. During 1964, a total of 46,600 cases was recruited, 93% of the annual target of 50,000. In 1965, from January to the end of August, 67,198 acceptors were recruited, making the total in the province 95,487, or 7.4% of the married women aged 20–39.

What Has Been Learned from the Program

Attitude of people toward family planning.—The fertility surveys undertaken before the expanded action program revealed that the traditional concept favoring large families is undergoing a rapid change. Although most women (85%) wanted less than four children, they had actually had more than five. The overwhelming majority of women (92%) are in favor of family planning and are eager to learn how to do it. A carefully planned program on family limitation will meet their need and will be accepted by these women.

A survey undertaken in 1964 by the VHEN's in 82 townships, with 14,189 respondents, married women 20–39 years old, revealed that 10.1% of the respondents had experienced at least one induced abortion, 15.0% were currently using contraceptive methods, 5.6% of the wives and 0.4% of their husbands had been sterilized, 14.8% were currently pregnant, 22.9% wanted no more children yet were not practicing fertility control methods of any kind, and 24.9% of the respondents indicated their desire to accept loops.

Acceptability, effectiveness, and side effects of the loops.—The medical follow-up studies indicated that the new IUD's are highly acceptable to women in Taiwan. Three out of every four women who accepted any method elected to use the new IUD's when offered all methods through a "cafeteria" type of offer.

Long previous exposure to the Ota ring in Taiwan no doubt was one reason that accounted for the popularity. The following additional factors may also account for this result:

1. The IUD, once inserted, requires no co-operation of couples.
2. The effectiveness is reasonably high (pregnancy rate 3–4), and side effects, although not absent, occur to only a minor proportion of the users. About 80% of the acceptors can wear the device without trouble.
3. The first cost is cheap and there is no recurrent cost.
4. The devices are particularly suitable under the local housing conditions, where methods requiring elaborate procedures are not practical.
5. The simplicity of insertion and removal is another advantage of the new device over the Ota ring.
6. The IUD's, unlike sterilization, are reversible.

TABLE 2

PERCENTAGE OF ACCEPTANCE OF THE IUD

TREATMENT	DENSITY OF HOME VISITS (per cent)			
	20	33	50	Total
Nothing...............	5	5	7	5
Mail.................	6	5	7	6
Mail plus home visits:				
Wives only...........	11	13	16	14
Wives and husbands...	12	10	18	15
All treatments......	7	7	12	9

Health education methods.—Through a study on the methods of health education in Taichung, the percentages of acceptance shown in Table 2 were recruited in eleven months. The figures show the acceptors as a per cent of the married women aged 20–39 by "treatment" and density sector.

Person most influential in acceptance of loops.—Another study of 602 acceptors revealed that satisfied users are the most influential persons to motivate other women to accept loops. Of the respondents 22.6% said that they had been influenced by their neighbors or friends who had had loops inserted and were happy about the device; 17.1% said that either their husbands convinced them or they made up their minds themselves; 16.2% were influenced by the VHEN's; 15.8% by the OBG's; 14.3% by the PPH workers; 7.0% by the health personnel; 5.8% by neighbors who had not worn the device and 1.2% by private midwives.

Instruction has been given to the field workers to enlist the cooperation of the satisfied users in their own areas to distribute flyers, give testimonials at the group meetings, or tell their experience with the device to their neighbors, relatives, and friends. A volunteers' program to organize the satisfied users for the IUD program is being planned.

The workers and OBG's.—The best workers seem to be married women, aged 30–40, having a few children of their own, with vocational training in nursing or midwifery, or with senior high school education.

An analysis shows that unmarried young workers have definite disadvantages. While 116 married workers on the average recruited 23.9 cases in April, 91 unmarried recruited an average of only 16.6 cases.

The efficiency of workers is also positively correlated with their ages, up to 39 years old. Among the married workers, while those less than 24 years old on the average recruited 16.5 cases, those 35–39 years of age recruited an average of 26.7 cases per month.

The PPH workers who are assigned to the various townships have a definite advantage over the VHEN's, who move monthly from village to village in groups of three. A recent analysis showed that a PPH worker on the average recruited 20.1 cases per month of work, compared with 12.2 cases by a VHEN.

Cases are also more easily recruited from an area with a larger population. In a township with more than 60,000 people, the average monthly acceptors exceeded 30 cases per person-month of work. In a township with 25,000–60,000 people, the monthly acceptors averaged 20, and with less than 25,000 population, averaged only around 15 cases.

Availability of OBG doctors for the insertion has a great deal to do with the number of acceptances. In an area without OBG's the average monthly acceptors were only 19.4, which increased to 22.0 in areas with one to three OBG's and 39.4 in areas with more than four OBG's.

Field experiments on loop costs.—A series of field experiments has been undertaken by the Taiwan Population Studies Center to find out methods to get loops at the least cost.

A group meeting study showed that it is cheaper to hold meetings in every other *lin*, rather than in every *lin*. The cost to recruit a case was NT$38 (US$0.95) for the former compared with NT$65 (US$1.40) for the latter.

Another study to measure the impact of an offer of free insertion of loops for a limited period through home visit resulted in 12.4% of the married women aged 20–39 in the area accepting loops. Since they usually must pay NT$30, an offer of free insertion for a limited time will stimulate acceptance.

A study on the type of supply depot for the traditional methods indicated that health stations, private midwives, and farmers' associations are three places women are most willing to go to get supplies. Places where women are used to going, such as the beauty parlor, may also be utilized.

Inasmuch as the traditional methods and oral contraceptives are heavily dependent on a simple and acceptable supply system, a study has just been implemented by the TPSC to measure the practicability of mail order pills. The initial response was favorable, and the rate of continuation is being observed.

A study on use of a mobile clinic for the insertion of loops is also underway. The first result seems to be quite favorable.

In Taichung City, where the program started earliest and the rate of acceptance reached 13%, an intensive campaign has begun to try to double the rate by the end of 1965. Experience gained through the foregoing experiments is being vigorously utilized to recruit cases.

EVALUATION OF THE PROGRAM

ACCEPTORS BY ADMINISTRATIVE UNIT

By the end of May, 1965, a total of 95,487 married women in Taiwan had accepted the device, the rate of acceptance to the total married women aged 20–39 being 7.4%. This figure includes acceptors before January, 1964, mainly in Taichung City.

The rate of acceptance at the city and county level was highest in Taichung City (16.5%), where the first action program was started in February, 1963, and was lowest in Penghu County (2.2%).

ACCEPTORS BY SOURCES OF REFERRAL

From the 46,600 coupons returned during 1964 we learn that the PPH workers were the most important source of referral. They contributed 37.1% of the total acceptors, followed by the OBG doctors themselves (31.5%), health personnel (17.8%), and VHEN's (7.0%). The contribution from other sources was rather insignificant.

CHARACTERISTICS OF THE ACCEPTORS

From the coupons we learn also that the modal age group of acceptance in 1964 was 30–34 (34.4%), followed by the age groups of

25–29 (25.4%), 35–39 (25.0%), 40–44 (8.4%), and 20–24 (6.1%). The acceptors aged 45–49 comprised 0.7% of the total.

The rate of acceptance was also highest among women aged 30–34. Taking the rate of acceptance of all ages as 100, the indices were 37 (20–24), 114 (25–29), 168 (30–34), 145 (35–39), 63 (40–44), and 6 (45–49) for the respective ages.

The rate of acceptance increased with parity. Taking the rate of acceptance of all ages as 100, the indices were 2 for women without a child, 13 for those with one, 57 for two, 111 for three, 132 for four, and 156 for five or more children.

The new IUD seems to be particularly acceptable to the higher

TABLE 3

RATE OF EXPULSION, REMOVAL, AND CONTINUOUS USERS

CONDITION	NUMBER OF CASES	PER CENT	MEDICAL FOLLOW-UP (%)	
			6 Months[a]	12 Months[b]
Loop in place at time of interview..	869	84.0	79.4	70.0
Never expelled or removed...........	855	82.5	75.6	66.5
Expelled.........................	44[c]	4.4	8.4	11.3
Removed..........................	135	13.1	16.0	22.2
Reinserted........................	17	1.6	3.8	3.5
Total interviewed................	1,034	100.0	100.0	100.0

[a] 1,222 cases.
[b] 1,440 cases.
[c] Including 8 "uncertain."

educated groups. Taking the rate of acceptance of women of all ages as 100, the indices are 99 for those with no formal education, 89 with primary school education, 149 for those with junior high training, and 191 for the senior high education and above. This might be due to the fact that information reaches the educated groups faster.

FOLLOW-UP INTERVIEW OF ACCEPTORS

A total of 1,034 samples of acceptors were interviewed by public health nurses of the TPSC in 1964 for evaluation. The average period of use was 4.3 months. The results are shown in Table 3. For comparison, some findings of the medical follow-up studies are included.

In general, 78.5% of the users were satisfied with the loop, although they had had some mild side effects.

A total of 211 complaints were made by 118 women who had had the loops removed because of side effects. Of the 211 complaints made by these 118 women, 46.4% were very mild and 40.3% moderate, severe complaints accounting for only 13.3%.

The pregnancy rate per 100 woman-years, as determined through the follow-up interview, was 3.8 after an average of 4.3 months of use. The rates were 2.5 at the 6-month and 5.3 at the 12-month medical follow-up studies.

FOLLOW-UP INTERVIEW OF COUPON-HOLDERS

A total of 275 coupon-holders was sampled and interviewed to find out why they had not taken action to insert the device.

Coupons had been given to women who really did not mean to use them (42.5%). Hesitation or lack of confidence in the device and the desire to see the result in others was the second major reason given (27.5%). The influence of others, including family members, husbands, and medical practitioners, accounted for 17.4% of the non-responses. Other miscellaneous reasons accounted for 12.6%.

Through these follow-up interviews, the administrative and educational barriers of the program are discovered. Improvement has been made by informing the workers of these findings and instructing them how to overcome the barriers.

EFFECT OF THE PROGRAM

Obviously, it is still premature to discuss the effect of a program less than two years old. However, somewhat unorganized efforts to control fertility, made by various groups before January, 1964, have shown some results. In 1963, the crude birth rate of the province was 36.3 per 1,000. It decreased to 34.5 in 1964, a reduction of 5%. In Taichung City, where the IUD program was started in 1963, the reduction in the crude birth rate between 1963 and 1964 was 6.3%, the greatest decline among the five major cities in the province.

With a larger number of IUD acceptors in 1964, a more significant reduction in the birth rate is in sight.

PERSPECTIVE OF THE PROGRAM

The target for 1965, insertion of 100,000 loops, seems within reach. The program is expected to encounter more difficulty after 1966, when high-parity women will be largely reached and loops will have to be used not only for stopping but for spacing births. Some new ideas are essential to make a "breakthrough" when this plateau is reached.

It is, nevertheless, to be hoped that Taiwan may be the first area in the world to show that fertility of a sufficiently large population can be significantly brought down by planned contraceptive efforts. A 5% reduction in the crude birth rate had already occurred in Taiwan between 1963 and 1964. The total annual live births registered in 1964 (416,927) were 7,323 less than those in 1963, the first such experience in the past twelve years.

MAJOR UNSOLVED PROBLEMS

NATIONAL POLICY

The government takes the attitude that in a democratic country it is for the people themselves to decide how many children they should have. Although the overwhelming majority of the people approve of the program, some opposition is bound to come. The health authorities have to be cautious in promoting the program.

Despite this disadvantage, the program has progressed rapidly, indicating that a national policy is not an absolute "must" if the program leaders have enough drive and imagination.

PUBLICITY AND HEALTH EDUCATION

Because of the reasons above, the program has had limited publicity through mass media. Except for the results of some scientific studies, surveys, or analyses of demographic situations, which have been tactfully released to newspapers, there has been little publicity on the action program itself. The program is making its own news, however, and articles now appear in the newspapers rather frequently.

PARTICIPATION OF GOVERNMENT DOCTORS

Again because of the lack of government policy, only private practitioners have so far been utilized for the program. The uneven distribution of OBG doctors is a bottleneck. Should government doctors be allowed to participate, the program will progress much faster, since there is one health station in each of the 361 townships in the province.

ORGANIZATION FOR THE EXECUTION OF THE PROGRAM

The participation of government health organizations started as an integral part of the maternal and child health program. Although this was a wise approach, the regular activities of MCH were too diluted. Complaints have been received that the family planning program hampered the regular MCH work.

Later, the Health Education Division of the Provincial Health Department started to participate in the program in the name of village health education. The latter activities again considerably diverted the regular health education program.

The establishment of the Taiwan Population Studies Center greatly facilitated the program, particularly for planning and evaluation. Unfortunately, the TPSC is a temporary group and not a statutory organization of the government.

Realizing that the responsibility to implement the program rests with various organizations, and co-ordination is important, the Committee on Family Planning Health has been organized.

To promote the program more efficiently and effectively, an independent organization should be set up in the health department and be solely responsible for the implementation of the program.

Type of Workers

It has now become obvious that the PPH type of workers have definite advantage over the VHEN's as far as the family planning program is concerned.

The ideal age, background, marital status of the workers are also known. Since the program expanded rather rapidly, it has not been always possible to recruit the ideal type of workers. The new workers recruited are rather young, mostly unmarried, and non-professional. Recruitment through competitive examination, although it is a fair method and avoids unnecessary criticism, often fails to get ideal persons for the work.

Users of Other Methods

The program emphasizes the new IUD's—the Lippes loop in particular, because it seems to be a most suitable and acceptable method under local circumstances. There are, however, from 20% to 30% of acceptors for whom the loop is not suitable. Moreover, there are others who prefer to use other methods. For these women, provision should be made for easy access to supplies for traditional methods and oral contraceptives.

To a special group of people, sterilization may offer an effective solution, although it is curative rather than preventive in nature.

It is felt that a program should not be dependent on a single method. There are four reasons for this: (1) 25% prefer traditional methods; (2) another 20% will drop out of the IUD programs; (3) traditional methods are the steppingstone to permanent and semi-permanent methods; (4) traditional methods are preferred by women who wish to space births. More studies should be made to remove the barriers to the acceptance of traditional methods, such as cost and bad supply channels.

KEY PROGRAM STAFF

Budget, personnel, and organization are three major factors in a program. Utmost emphasis should be given to recruiting and training a group of key personnel. More incentive should be given to a nucleus of people by offering decent pay and granting opportunity for advanced training. The program, although it has progressed smoothly in the past, has been handicapped by scarcity of trained personnel.

SUMMARY AND CONCLUSION

This paper briefly describes the development and achievements of a family planning health program in an area where there is no national policy.

Despite the traditional concept favoring larger family size and the disadvantage of having no national policy, the family planning health program implemented in Taiwan, Republic of China, in 1964 has progressed smoothly and rapidly. Imaginative and energetic leadership, careful planning, and tactful approaches have helped make significant achievements possible.

The program also owes its success to a series of pilot undertakings, basic studies, and surveys. Experience obtained through these studies has been quickly applied in the actual operation. Having a unit to evaluate the operation continuously has proved most useful.

Although some unsolved problems still remain, the program staff is confident that Taiwan may be the first area in the world to show that fertility of a sufficiently large population can be significantly reduced by planned contraceptive efforts. A reduction of 5% in the crude birth rate had already occurred between 1963 and 1964, and the total annual live births registered in 1964 were 7,323 fewer than those in 1963, the first such experience in the past twelve years. This drop, however, cannot be attributed solely to the loops, which were inserted in quantity only after 1964 and the results of which should become evident after 1965.

5

HONG KONG

DAPHNE CHUN, M.D.
President, Family Planning Association

Hong Kong is a British Crown Colony. It consists of the Island of Hong Kong together with a number of scattered islands, a portion of the adjacent mainland known as the Kowloon Peninsula, and the 365.5 square miles of leased territory known as the New Territories including more than thirty small islands. The total land area is 398.25 square miles of which only 62 are inhabitable. Yet the total population at the end of 1964 was estimated to be almost 3.75 million and the density was therefore almost 9,400 per square mile. The need to decrease or at least to stabilize the population by reducing the birth rate in the face of such overcrowding is our ever present challenge.

The Family Planning Association of Hong Kong was first known as the Hong Kong Eugenics League, founded in 1936. In 1950, however, it was felt that "Family Planning" more accurately expressed the organization's aim and was more in conformity with the names of similar organizations in other parts of the world. The Association, under its present name, HKFPA, was reorganized in September, 1950.

HONG KONG'S FAMILY PLANNING PROGRAMS

Origin and Operation

Little approach to the problem of planned parenthood was made before 1936, when the Hong Kong Eugenics League was founded. The population was then about 900,000. The League had no offices, and the group of enthusiastic family planners met occasionally in such places as homes of members, private offices, hospitals, and even restaurants.

Starting with one clinic and an attendance of 135 patients during the first year, the activities of the League progressed steadily until the year 1940–41, when it operated five clinics and had an annual attendance of 1,823. The chief method used was the diaphragm and jelly, but the results were not evaluated. The patients who received assistance were usually about 31 years of age and had had six children. The work of the League was disrupted by the outbreak of the Pacific War toward the end of 1941.

The postwar revival of the work of the League, under the name of the Family Planning Association, received its initial stimulus from members of the Hong Kong Council of Women, who in November, 1948, strongly advocated that the work of the League be resumed. Eventually, on September 20, 1950, the Family Planning Association of Hong Kong was founded and preparations made to embark on a twofold program of (1) providing facilities for married people to space or limit their families and (2) assisting childless couples to attain their ambition of becoming parents. Before the war the Eugenics League had been under fairly heavy criticism from a particular religious group and it was felt, therefore, that a good deal of this criticism could be prevented by simultaneously placing a proper emphasis on the positive phase of family planning. There was an immediate and encouraging response to an appeal for funds, and the Association soon received a sum of HK$10,000 (US$1,724) and recruited nearly 250 members and subscribers contributing HK$8,222 (US$1,417).

With the co-operation of the government medical department, which made available fully equipped premises, the Association started its activities in March, 1951, with two clinics, the first of which was opened at a health center on the Island and the other at an infant and maternity welfare center in Kowloon. The demand for advice was so great that it soon became necessary to open three additional clinics within a few months; so a third was opened in May, 1951, in the Dockyard Welfare Center. A clinic for wives of service personnel in the Colony was started in December, 1951, and yet another was opened before the end of the year in a refugee camp housing over 10,000 Chinese refugees. Sub-fertile cases were referred to the gynecological unit of the University of Hong Kong.

That the services offered by the Association were much needed in Hong Kong can be seen readily from the steady increase in attendance at the clinics, which rose from 2,971 during 1951 to 138,195 (Table 1) in 1964. This called for almost continuous expansion, resulting in the opening of more clinics until by the end of 1964, the number of clinics reached 51 (Table 2) with a substantial increase in personnel (Table 3).

The Association is a non-profit, voluntary organization financed by donations, membership subscriptions, and patients' registration fees (Table 4) until 1955, when the government, realizing the importance of the work for the community, gave an initial subsidy of HK$5,000 (US$862) for the year. In the same year, the Hong Kong Jockey Club (which promotes horse racing and is noted for its philanthropy) donated the sum of HK$10,000 (US$1,724) and another HK$125,000 (US$21,552) for the building of a headquarters on land provided by the government. From 1950 to 1956 the headquarters of the Association were located in a spacious room provided rent free and furnished by one of its patrons, the late Mr. J. H. Ruttonjee, C.B.E.

The need for the Association's services in Kowloon became greater

TABLE 1

BIRTH CONTROL CLINIC

YEAR	FEMALE				MALE		GRAND TOTAL ATTENDANCE
	New Cases		Total	Revisits	Over-fertile		
	Over-fertile	Sub-fertile			New Cases	Revisits and Old Cases	
1951	1,508	147	1,655	1,316			2,971
1952	2,893	150	3,104	3,810			6,914
1953	3,386	58	3,504	5,161			8,665
1954	3,798	134	3,932	6,974			10,906
1955	4,608	116	4,724	10,768			15,492
1956	5,182	51	5,233	12,847			18,080
1957	6,579	271	6,850	19,089			25,939
1958	8,903	441	9,344	28,284			37,628
1959	9,633	331	10,014	39,801			49,910
1960	10,181	311	10,492	46,589	150		57,231
1961	11,734	397	12,131	53,533	535	318	66,517
1962	12,581	527	13,108	62,534	548	552	76,742
1963	14,861	594	15,455	77,041	427	466	93,389
1964	21,060	438	21,498	116,070	309	318	138,195

TABLE 2

NUMBER OF CLINIC CENTERS

Year	Number	Year	Number
1951	3	1958	20
1952	5	1959	26
1953	7	1960	28
1954	8	1961	36
1955	10	1962	43
1956	10	1963	50
1957	14	1964	51

as the population there increased to about twice that of Hong Kong. Again, the Hong Kong Jockey Club generously contributed the sum of HK\$200,000 (US\$34,483) and the Kowloon Center came into being in 1960, built on land provided free by the government. Thus, with two of its own buildings, one in Hong Kong and another in

TABLE 3

CLINIC PERSONNEL

Year	Doctors			Nurses			Clerks/Field and Social Workers		
	Full-time	Part-time	Volun-tary	Full-time	Part-time	Volun-tary	Full-time	Part-time	Volun-tary
1951	....	2	6	1	....	2	......	......	12
1952	....	3	9	1	....	4	......	1	25
1953	....	6	7	1	5	4	1	....	30
1954	....	7	9	1	5	3	1	....	35
1955	....	9	12	1	5	3	1	2	65
1956	....	....	18	2	5	3	1	3	49
1957	....	....	18	4	6	3	2	11	65
1958	....	3	17	5	7	4	2	9	57
1959	2	4	15	6	7	....	2	13	58
1960	4	4	11	7	7	....	3	11	47
1961	4	6	5	7	5	1	3	10	47
1962	4	4	7	9	4	....	9	7	47
1963	4	5	9	10	4	2	5	8	57
1964[a]	1	12	9	15	7	2	51	2	27

[a] Plus 4 family advisers.

TABLE 4

FINANCE—SOURCE OF INCOME

(Hong Kong \$)

Year	Government Subvention	Jockey Club	Foreign Grants	Sales of Appliances	Patients' Registration Fees	Membership Fees	Miscellaneous Donations
1951	....	....	....	2,285[a]	1,524	2,185	18,222
1952	....	....	....	6,546	3,020	1,615	22,462
1953	....	....	....	5,772	3,260	3,390	17,477
1954	....	....	....	7,690	3,803	3,610	17,223
1955	5,000	10,000	....	8,932	4,604	3,610	11,784
1956	20,000	10,000	....	4,251	5,583	3,655	10,913
1957	57,500	20,000	10,000	5,226	9,175	3,110	15,636
1958	120,000	20,000	10,000	15,467	12,691	2,145	27,105
1959	200,000	30,000	5,000	17,784	12,364	1,995	66,671
1960	200,000	30,000	8,000	62,599	15,645	3,165	76,033
1961	240,000	30,000	....	32,664	13,627	3,394	21,845
1962	240,000	30,000	....	37,196	9,229	5,190	43,285
1963	300,000	50,000	16,650	63,517	17,412	4,280	150,825
1964	400,000	50,000	86,031	254,000	31,100	5,820	84,503

[a] Loss on sales of appliances.

Kowloon, the Association was able to operate twenty-two clinic sessions per week where patients could come daily from Monday to Friday and on Saturday morning.

With the steady increase in population by natural increase as well as by influx of refugees, the need for more clinics—especially in the resettlement and squatter areas where population was most dense and also in rural areas—became even greater. The government has been very helpful and although monetary contribution was meager in the beginning it provided facilities without charge in its maternity and child health centers after their regular office hours. Since 1964, the Association has been allowed to run its clinics simultaneously with theirs; this means that their patients may avail themselves of the Association's services at the same time—a great convenience. In some congested areas where there are no maternal and child health centers in operation, the Association has been fortunate in obtaining the loan of clinic premises from charity and religious welfare organizations. It has also been able to rent quarters in the resettlement areas or estates for its work.

At the end of 1964 the Association operated 50 clinic centers (10 for IUD) and provided 85 weekly birth control sessions (24 for IUD). By June, 1965, the IUD clinics increased to 20 with 90 birth control sessions (47 for IUD) per week. These clinic centers are scattered over the island of Hong Kong, Kowloon Peninsula, and the rural districts of the New Territories, in the congested tenement areas, villages, resettlement estates, and industrial and squatter areas.

The initial aim of the Association was to lower or at least stabilize the population of Hong Kong by reducing its birth rate through providing facilities for married people to space or limit their families, thus improving the health of the mothers and welfare of the family and raising the living standards and, in addition, assisting childless couples to become parents. The following services are provided: birth control (including clinic for males), sub-fertility, and marriage guidance.

The Association's work since the beginning of 1964 covers a substantial area in Hong Kong, including Kowloon Peninsula, the New Territories, and the many islands, although it still needs many more clinics to cover the entire area effectively. The pilot program on the use of the IUD in 1,600 cases was carried out in 1963. It started with two clinic sessions per week but within a month long queues of patients were waiting for appointments. This pilot study showed that IUD was up to that time, and still is, the most popular method of contraception and is, in addition, more reliable than all other temporary contraceptive methods. The average attendance was 3,000 new patients every month.

The activities of the Association and the services offered are prominently publicized through radio broadcasts, newspapers, pamphlets, posters, and exhibitions. Contraceptive information, materials, and services, however, are not normally available outside the program except from medical doctors, although many contraceptives are obtainable commercially.

The program is operated solely by the Association. Although no other government or private agencies operate such a program, much help and co-operation have been given to the Association. For example, the government Medical and Health Department provides facilities at their MCH centers to run our clinic sessions; the government Social Welfare Department helps to publicize our work through social workers and refers cases to our clinics; the government Labor, Information, Resettlement and Housing Departments and the Kai Fong Associations (private welfare organizations for the districts) provide clinic premises, publicize the Association's work and refer cases to it; the armed forces, various charity and private hospitals, business firms, religious institutions, and foreign organizations provide premises, grants and other forms of assistance.

The administration of the Association is vested in the president and twenty-six executive committee members who also sit on six sub-committees (medical, clinic, education and social work, personnel, finance, and fund-raising); these are all voluntary workers. The committee is also served by paid workers—the executive, deputy, and assistant secretaries, and two clerks. Under the executive secretaries are the clinic supervisor, the doctors, the publicity officer and the senior social worker. The clerks, nurses, social workers and field workers are on the next scale. The doctors, both paid and voluntary, are under the direction of the honorary medical supervisor (the president). The Association employs altogether seventy-nine full and part-time staff members who are assisted by thirty-nine voluntary non-medical workers and six voluntary doctors.

Administrative staff.—(*a*) Voluntary committee members invited because of the interest they have taken in social welfare work in the Colony, and (*b*) executive secretary (a university graduate, who holds a diploma in social work), deputy and assistant secretaries, publicity officer, and clerical staff.

Medical staff.—(*a*) Doctors who are fully qualified and registered, and (*b*) family planning advisers—these are doctors trained and qualified in mainland China but with degrees not registerable in Hong Kong. They are trained by the Association's doctors and work under their supervision for varying periods of time before working in a clinic.

Clinic staff.—(*a*) Nurses—non-registerable in Hong Kong—who work under the supervision of the clinic doctors, and (*b*) clerks who keep case histories and other records.

Social workers and field workers.—These work under the senior social worker and are trained by her. Most of the social workers hold certificates of social work studies. The field workers have school-leaving certificates and are mostly young married women chosen for their awareness and their pleasant personality, which enable them to speak convincingly to the women they visit.

Voluntary workers.—These are women who give their time and services voluntarily and assist in the registration of patients and the taking and keeping of case histories and other records.

The Association has a training program of two weeks for field workers. This was started in February, 1965, under the sponsorship of the American Friends Service Committee. The course includes lectures on the principles and practice of family planning, physiology, psychology, maternal and child welfare, birth, nutrition, and health; visits to clinics and hospitals; home visits; and film shows. Each day the organizer meets the field workers in the morning and goes over the day's program and in the late afternoon she meets them again and answers their questions and discusses the work they have done.

No specific course of training is offered to other members of the staff. Doctors, however, are required to work under a senior member until they have acquired the technique. Family planning advisers are trained individually in the assigned clinics by doctors experienced in family planning and work under their supervision for periods ranging from three to six months. Nurses receive training on family planning from clinic doctors. Lectures on family planning and the IUD are given from time to time by the president to doctors in private practice and midwives.

The Association's program is not aimed toward any specific group, since there is a general need for its services and with its limited resources it can barely cope with the demand. As it was felt, however, that the Association should first concentrate on the highly congested resettlement estates and squatter areas, factories and villages, its social and field workers have been working in these areas. They interview and give lectures about the services available in the clinics. The most favorable response so far is from the lower-income groups, from which there is a marked increase in attendance.

The Association's program is financed mainly by the government, which gives us a gradually increasing yearly subsidy, covering slightly more than one-half of the total expenditure, with the rest derived from donations from local and foreign organizations, institutions, well-wishers, patients' registration fees, sales of appliances, and membership subscriptions (see Table 4).

The total expenditure for the year 1964 was about HK$700,000 (US$120,000). The average outlay for each case calculated on the expenditure against the number of patients treated (46,038; see Table 5) comes to about HK$15 (US$2.60) per year. The low cost of the service was due mainly to the number of voluntary workers, including doctors, who gave their time and experience without charge. Without this, the expenditure on salaries would have been almost double. It was estimated that the Association would need HK$900,000 (US$155,-172) during 1965. The government subsidy is HK$450,000 (US-$77,586 and the rest is to be raised from other sources. It is anticipated that many more patients will be treated, as the cost will be drastically reduced with the introduction of the IUD to about HK$5 (US$0.86) per patient each year.

TABLE 5

THE FAMILY PLANNING ASSOCIATION OF HONG KONG: ANNUAL REPORT ON DIFFERENT CONTRACEPTIVE METHODS, 1964

Method	New Cases	Current Cases	Total Cases	Per Cent	Revisits	Total Attendance
Female						
Diaphragm	1,750	11,864	13,614	30.07	....	....
Condom	3,042	3,519	6,561	14.49	....	....
Foaming tablets	4,925	3,761	8,686	19.18	.....	....
Oral pill	935	1,495	2,430	5.37	....	....
Applicator and jelly	670	644	1,314	2.90	....	....
Emko	197	204	401	0.89	....	....
No appliance	267	530	797	1.76	....	....
Change to IUD	370	1,413	1,783	3.94	....	....
Total	12,156	23,430	35,586	....	57,273	92,859
Male						
Condom	83	92	175	0.39	....	....
Wants vasectomy	226	11	237	0.52	....	....
Total	309	103	412	....	215	627
IUD	8,904	376	9,280	20.49	11,875	21,155
Birth control total	21,369	23,909	45,278	100.00	69,363	114,641
Sub-fertility total	438	209	647	....	1,296	1,943
Marriage guidance total	113	....	113	....	9	122
Grand total	21,920	24,118	46,038	....	70,668	116,706

There is no charge for services in birth control clinics apart from a registration fee of HK$1 (US$0.17), and even this fee is waived in many cases. There are six clinics where no fee is charged. A small sum is charged for supplies of oral pills, diaphragms, and condoms, but the IUD is given free. The charge depends on the patient's financial circumstances and may be waived altogether.

At the clinics for English-speaking women and wives of service personnel a registration fee of HK$1 (US$0.17) is also charged and supplies are generally provided at less than cost.

Non-Chinese patients are charged HK$5 (US$0.86) for each insertion of IUD, but it is free for Chinese patients because those who can afford to pay usually go to their private doctors.

Post-partum sterilization or vasectomy is done without charge by government and charity hospitals.

At the sub-fertility clinic the registration fee is HK$10 (US$1.72) and the charge for treatment varies from HK$5 to HK$25 (US$0.86–US$4.31).

Papanicolaou smear when requested by the patient may be made at cost to all patients, both Chinese and non-Chinese, at HK$25 (US$4.31) per smear, except for 1,600 IUD cases selected for research.

Consultation at the marriage guidance clinic is free.

Methods Used for Disseminating Information

Because the literacy rate among native women in Hong Kong is rather low, any attempt to impart information on family planning to them must take this fact into consideration. Emphasis has therefore been put on door-to-door visits by social workers and field workers. The following publicity methods are used simultaneously:

Written information.—This consists of nine different kinds of publications on family planning, besides leaflets, advertisements, and news releases. The press, especially the Chinese papers, have included many articles on family planning.

Visual information.—Apart from colorful posters, illustrated pamphlets, cartoons, and slides, a short film entitled "A Story of Two Families" is shown to women's clubs, groups of interested people, industrial workers, and at village fairs and meetings organized by social workers. On such occasions, it is the usual practice for a social worker to be in attendance to supplement the film with a talk on family planning and to answer questions from the audience. A short film strip lasting one minute has recently been made. Five cinemas have agreed to show it without charge, and it is hoped that others will follow.

Radio and television.—At least twenty radio interviews were given and a 30-minute documentary program with pictures was shown on the Chinese television channel last year about family planning in Hong Kong.

Lectures.—Talks were frequently given on the principles of family planning to members of Rotary Clubs and young women's organizations as well as to youth groups and post-secondary schools by executive members or social workers of the Association.

Exhibitions.—A large proportion of the public is also reached through two annual public exhibitions: the Health Education Exhibition organized by the Kaifong (neighborhood) Welfare Associations held in July and the Chinese Manufacturers Exposition held annually in December. More than one million people visited the exhibits on these two occasions, when the film "A Story of Two Families" was shown every night and the social workers handed out literature and answered questions on family planning.

SERVICES OFFERED (WHAT, WHERE, AND HOW?)

The services offered include the following:

Birth control.—The methods of contraception used to bring about temporary sterility include the IUD, oral pills, condoms, diaphragm and jelly, foaming cream, foaming tablets, and applicator and cream. With the exception of the IUD which is presently only available in eighteen specialized clinics, all the other methods are offered in the Association's fifty-one clinics located in its own centers, in government MCH centers, and in rented premises.

There has been a decrease over the past year in the number of applicants—both male and female—registering for sterilization. This may be a sign of the growing popularity and success of the different methods of birth control providing temporary sterility, against permanent sterility provided by post-partum sterilization and vasectomy. Permanent sterilization by bilateral salpingectomy in women who have had many children is done only in exceptional cases to those who do not wish other methods of birth control. This operation is performed in government and public charity hospitals free of charge.

Sub-fertility.—The sub-fertility clinic is held twice weekly at the Hong Kong headquarters. The attendance at these clinics has been small—most women who want this advice go direct to their own doctor or to a hospital.

Marriage guidance.—There are two marriage guidance clinics, one at the Hong Kong headquarters and another in Kowloon. It is the practice of the marriage guidance clinic to send pamphlets to those couples who have registered to marry.

Male birth control.–The two weekly male clinics were established in 1960 to make available family planning advice to the male population.

CHOICE OF METHODS

Although the Association's doctors recommend the type of method most suited to each case, patients are at liberty to make their own choice. The popularity of the diaphragm and jelly method has rapidly decreased in recent years as it is regarded as troublesome and not practical to those living in congested slum areas and squatter huts with no privacy and limited cleaning facilities. There has been some increase in popularity of foaming tablets and of the condom for the husbands, but the demand for the IUD is phenomenal and the number of insertions averaged 3,000 per month in 1965. The demand for oral contraceptive pills is on the increase but the prices remain prohibitive for most of the patients.

HANDLING OF SUPPLIES

All orders for supplies, including the IUD, which are manufactured by the Association's makers in Hong Kong, are placed by the executive secretary on the recommendation of the doctor in charge. These are kept at headquarters under the control of the storekeeper and issued to clinics against requisition made by clinic doctors.

RECORDS

Records are kept for both patients and supplies as follows:

Patients.–Detailed case histories are taken on registration of each patient, covering age, address, general health, family income, husband's occupation, patient's occupation if any, number of previous pregnancies, number of children living, and previous experience in family planning. These particulars are revised and brought up to date on subsequent visits when necessary.

Supplies.–Comprehensive stock lists are kept for the separate types of supplies, and entries are made covering date of order and arrival, quantity ordered, cost, expiration date if applicable, quantity issued, and finally balance on hand to ensure that stocks are promptly replenished. Any supplies which have deteriorated or are returned to manufacturers for replacement are also entered.

EVALUATION OF RESULTS TO DATE

Religion does not seriously complicate the Association's task, since 98% of the people in Hong Kong are Chinese the majority of whom believe in ancestral worship or Buddhism, and only 5% of the population are Roman Catholic. In certain areas where Catholics predominate, some hesitate to visit the clinics for fear they may be barred from receiving food parcels. The fact that most of the people are Chinese contributes favorably to the work, as most patients come to know about it from those who have previously received treatment in the clinics. Because the total land area of Hong Kong is so small, it is not

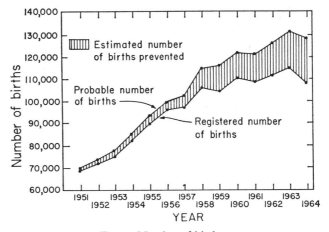

Fig. 1.—Number of births

difficult for service to be extended to everyone everywhere, but for this the Association needs more clinics and more social workers. This extension is being implemented gradually whenever additional funds are available.

Hong Kong's small area and consequent high population density can be considered an advantage, for when people are so closely packed the Association's message can reach many of them simultaneously. That most of the people are poor is also advantageous in fostering its work as poverty leads them to seek services for family planning.

Since family planning work in Hong Kong was revived in 1951 with the establishment of two clinics, the number of clinics had increased to fifty-one by the end of 1964. The increase in the attendance from about 3,000 at the commencement to almost 120,000 is gratifying (see Table 1). The Association projects that out of the estimated 500,000 child-bearing women in Hong Kong, more than 50,000 will attend its clinics in 1965. In 1964 alone, there were 46,038

(21,920 new, 24,118 current) patients with a total of over 116,706 visits. A conservative estimate that more than 20,717 births (Fig. 1) were prevented in 1964 alone was based on the fact that 45% of the fertile women attending the clinics probably would have conceived within the year if family planning had not been practiced. The estimated number of births prevented yearly for the past decade is also shown in Figure 1.

The birth rate for Hong Kong was very high up to 1960 (Fig. 2) ranging between 34 per thousand in 1951 and 39.7 in 1956 against an average of 24 for advanced Western countries. The efforts made by the Association have finally proved effective, as the birth rate began to drop in 1961 to 32 per 1,000 and it was down to 29 in 1964, the

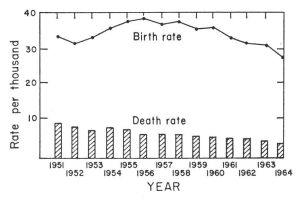

FIG. 2.—Birth and death rates

lowest recorded for Hong Kong, with 6,744 fewer births than the previous year.

The Association is confident that taking into consideration the number of births and making a comparison of the birth rate for various years is a reliable method for evaluating its work, since over 95% of deliveries are performed either in hospitals or maternity homes by doctors or midwives. These figures are fairly accurate, for all births are required by law to be reported and parents must register with the government births and deaths registry for issuance of a birth certificate. Even the illiterate people are well aware of this.

The main goal is to reduce the birth rate to about 20 per 1,000 in five to ten years' time. Prospects for attaining this goal look promising since the introduction of the simple and cheap IUD. The Association's most important project for 1965 is to make the IUD available in all its centers and to do 30,000 insertions this year. Judging from results so far—an average of 3,000 insertions in new patients per month for the first quarter—this goal is likely to be achieved, if not exceeded.

84 / NATIONAL PROGRAMS

Another objective is to train more social and field workers for carrying the education program on family planning by person-to-person contact to the vast number of women with no education and with low intelligence.

The continuation and expansion of the programs are of vital importance and changes, if any, will be to promote more family planning by all means available.

MAJOR ACHIEVEMENTS

1. The Association considers its major achievement the unexpectedly great demand for the IUD as the contraceptive chosen by Hong Kong people—simple, cheap, and well received. In addition, the patients seldom have to revisit except for follow-ups at yearly intervals. Further, the phenomenal increase in clinic attendance proves that more people are becoming aware of the need for planned parenthood. The Association strongly recommends to other countries its IUD program as a means of helping to solve their population problems.

2. Fewer births and in 1964 the lowest birth rate ever recorded have already been mentioned.

3. The constant and close co-operation of the Hong Kong government is evidenced by the increasing yearly subsidy and the free loan of clinic premises.

UNSOLVED PROBLEMS

Despite what has been achieved, many barriers still have to be overcome. These include resistance by traditionalists, who still think of a large family as a symbol of prosperity; by the ignorant, who still have the impression that harm or injury may be caused by appliances or pills; by some religious bodies, e.g., Roman Catholics, who still oppose almost all contraceptive methods, and by the government, which still hesitates to take over the entire responsibility of family planning.

The Association has not encountered any administrative or informational problems. Its programs are operated solely by its executives. The valuable co-operation extended by many organizations throughout the world has provided up-to-date information and data on the latest developments of all phases of family planning. The Association is gratified with the results of its present program but constantly keeps in mind that further progress can be made as simpler methods become available.

Finally, if it were to start all over again, it would press for more government support and try to eliminate more thoroughly superstition and religious beliefs against birth control.

6

MALAYSIA AND SINGAPORE

MAGGIE LIM, M.R.C.S.
Medical Representative, Southeast Asia and Oceania Region
International Planned Parenthood Federation, Singapore

MALAYSIA

The eleven states of mainland Malaysia have a combined population (1965) of around eight million. The population has been growing rapidly for some time. Since 1952 the growth rate has consistently been above 3% a year, although a slight decline has been apparent since 1957. The major ethnic groups are Malays (50% of the total population at the time of the last census in 1957), Chinese (37%) and Indians and Pakistanis (11%). More than three-fourths of the population is concentrated in a densely settled area along the western coast of the peninsula from Penang to Johore. A smaller concentration, mostly Malays, is found in the northeast, particularly around Kota Bharu in Kelantan. Somewhat more than a third of the population live in communities of 5,000 or more; this urban population is increasing at a rate of about three times that of the population as a whole.

Until the early 1950's family planning in Malaya was a sporadic activity carried on in some of the states by individual physicians and nurses in conjunction with their routine duties in offices, hospitals, or maternal and child health clinics. The first organized efforts began with the formation of a state family planning association in Selangor in July, 1953. A similar association was organized in Johore in 1954,

At the time this report was initially prepared, Singapore was part of Malaysia although the two areas had relatively separate family planning programs. Since Singapore is now independent, a separate account is now given for each country in this revision. The author is indebted to Mrs. M. K. Butcher, Honorable Field Adviser, Federation of Family Planning Associations of Malaya, for her assistance in compiling materials for this report.

85

and, shortly after, two more were formed in Perak and Malacca with the encouragement and help of the Singapore Family Planning Association (SFPA). With small financial assistance from the International Planned Parenthood Federation (IPPF) and the Pathfinder Fund and with the beginning of an annual subsidy from Malaya's Social Welfare Lotteries Board in 1958, interest and activity expanded until, by July 1962, there were family planning associations in all eleven states.

FEDERATION OF FAMILY PLANNING ASSOCIATIONS

A Malayan Federation of Family Planning Associations was formed in 1958 to co-ordinate the work of the, then, four state associations. With headquarters in Kuala Lumpur—but until recently without any full-time paid staff—the Federation has been concerned with over-all planning and policy-making and with giving stimulation and guidance to the state associations as their programs have developed. It has been the mechanism through which the Social Welfare Lotteries Board grant—increased to M$200,000 annually in 1962—has been distributed to the various state organizations for support of their operations. The Federation works through a slate of elected officers, a council that includes representation from all state associations, and a number of standing committees. Early in 1965 it obtained a headquarters building and employed a full-time administrator. There is a national group of patrons that includes prominent members of all three of the major ethnic groups in the country.

All states have paid employees, including at least one paid organizer, but more than half of those presently active in providing family planning services are voluntary workers. All categories of workers are used, from untrained members of the public to social workers, nurses, and physicians. Recruitment has largely been by personal invitation and persuasion, recently augmented by advertising in the press. Training has been largely provided by the SFPA, although recently the reliance has been on courses organized and offered by the Southeast Asia and Oceania regional office of the IPPF.

Educational materials for public information have been adapted from those obtained from the IPPF or the SFPA. Films, leaflets, group meetings, contact work, and home visiting are used in varying degree. Rediffusion, cinema slides, short film announcements, and both paid and unpaid notices in the press have all been used at one time or another. The extent to which various media are used is governed by the limited resources available to meet the increased demand for services that might be created by overactivity on the educational side. Focused educational activity is directed toward two target groups: post-partum and high-parity women, through contacts at MCH centers and maternity hospitals; and, to a more limited extent, males in the armed forces, in industry, and on rubber estates.

In mid-1965, the various state associations were operating in 133 clinics and hospitals, many of them government facilities in which the Federation and its affiliates are permitted to work. In addition, several different patterns of service were being offered to about 120 agricultural estates where large numbers of workers are concentrated. Services are offered in especially rented accommodations, mobile clinics that operate in several states, and armed forces medical inspection rooms, as well as in government clinics and hospitals and estate dispensaries.

The providing of contraceptive materials and advice is the main service activity. Sub-fertility cases are referred to appropriate hospital departments. A choice of contraceptive methods is offered, including oral tablets, diaphragms, condoms, foam tablets, paste and applicator. The largest group of acceptors is on oral compounds. Thus far only two small pilot studies of the IUD have been undertaken. The majority of users pay for their supplies; a minority receive them free. Two states have introduced a low registration fee. It is likely that other state associations will also require registration fees in the future.

The main source of income is the annual grant of M\$200,000 from the government-operated Social Welfare Lotteries Board. Other income is derived from profit on contraceptive supplies, grants from state governments, municipalities, and the IPPF; fees from estates, and special fund-raising efforts, donations, and subscriptions. The annual budget for family planning activity in 1963 was around M\$340,000.

It is felt that the Federation has largely achieved its first main objective, which was to create a climate in which government would be prepared to become more actively involved in family planning. Activities of the Federation and its affiliates have demonstrated that there is no strong opposition to family planning service in Malaya and that many people are eager to learn how to control the size of their family. An informed climate of opinion has been created; government interest has been stimulated to the point where there is now serious consideration being given to the possibility of incorporating family planning as part of government policy; fears of religious opposition have been allayed; and family planning has become a subject which can be freely and openly discussed.

SARAWAK

On the basis of work carried out earlier by private physicians and medical missions, and with the stimulation of the Southeast Asia and

Oceania Regional Council of the IPPF, a Sarawak Family Planning Association was formed in 1964. The Association operates mainly with voluntary workers, has one full-time paid nurse, and provides only limited service in a few major towns. The immediate target groups are patients attending MCH clinics; there has been a small amount of general publicity, using materials supplied by the IPPF, which has also provided training for six of the Association's workers. Financial support comes mainly from the IPPF. The government of Malaysia also gave M$5,000 to the Association in 1965.

GOVERNMENT OF MALAYSIA

The government of Malaysia has been subsidizing family planning in Malaya since 1958 with an annual grant to the Federation of Family Planning Associations that, since 1962, has been set at M$200,000 per year. It has also permitted the use of government clinic and health center facilities by affiliates of the Federation, first on an "after-hours" basis and more recently at the same time that government health activities are being carried on. The aid to family planning has been stimulated by an increasing concern among some government officials about the adverse effects of high fertility on the health of mothers and children and on the rate of progress toward economic development goals.

For several years there has been growing support for the idea of an official government population policy and program. Two of the major supporters of the idea have been Mohamed Khir Johari, popular Minister of Education, and Tan Siew Sin, Minister of Finance and leader of the Malayan Chinese Association. Late in 1964, following extensive discussion, particularly in the Economic Planning Unit of the Prime Minister's Department and in the cabinet, a cabinet-level subcommittee, under the chairmanship of the Minister of Education, was established and charged with exploring and recommending ways to obtain wide public and political support for family planning and with drawing up a plan for an integrated national program. A working party, headed by the Deputy Secretary for Economic Planning, was activated in January, 1965. The report of the working party was submitted to the cabinet subcommittee late in August and at the time of the Geneva Conference was awaiting formal acceptance by the entire cabinet.

The major recommendations of the working party call for a national sample survey of knowledge, attitudes, and practices relating to fertility and for the creation of a National Family Planning Board—with representation from eight ministries and various interested non-governmental institutions and organizations—that will assume responsibility for planning and operating a national program. The Ford Foundation has been asked to provide technical assistance and other support during initial phases of program development. No firm decisions have yet been taken about the nature and scope of the program to be undertaken or about the part the Federation of Family Planning Associations will be expected to play in the national effort.

SINGAPORE

Singapore is a small island at the tip of the Malay Peninsula with a largely urban population. It became an independent nation in August, 1965, when its affiliation with Malaysia was dissolved. It has a population of about 1.8 million with a recent crude death rate of 5.7 and a birth rate of 32. The birth rate has been declining since at least 1958 and, with the exception of 1963 when there was a slight upturn, the number of children born has declined in each of the past seven years. More than two-thirds of all Singapore births take place in a single hospital. Chinese make up about 78% of the total population, Malays nearly 14%, and Indians between 5% and 6%.

Singapore Family Planning Association

As in Malaya, organized family planning efforts in Singapore developed from the independent activities of isolated individuals, in this case several social workers and an MCH physician. The latter, early in 1949, obtained permission to give family planning advice in municipal infant welfare clinics, with the original effort being limited to once-a-week sessions at three clinics. Growing interest led to the formation of the SFPA which worked first in the clinics of private physicians after office hours and entirely with volunteer workers. Later, a paid staff was recruited and work was expanded to include services in the outpatient department of the maternity hospital and in a few municipal clinics. Eventually the work being done by the municipal MCH staff was turned over to the SFPA.

Up to mid-1965, the SFPA has been working through a large paid and volunteer staff that includes an administrative secretary, a full-time medical officer, four part-time physicians, a social worker, a publicity officer, a clinical supervisor, two home visitors, and eighteen qualified midwives, with supporting clerical workers. Policy determination and over-all supervision are provided by an elected executive committee.

The full-time medical officer was trained at the Margaret Sanger

Research Bureau in New York; other physicians, as they have joined, have been trained by doctors already in service. The social worker is qualified from the London School of Economics with supplementary family planning training from the IPPF regional office. IPPF training has also been provided for the publicity officer, midwives, and other service staff.

Services include the provision of contraceptive information and materials; sub-fertility investigations and advice, with difficult cases being referred to an obstetrician; and laboratory tests relating to fertility done by two technicians who are being trained at Perth University. Since 1959, the government has allowed SFPA services to be offered in twenty-seven MCH clinics run by the government as well as in the outpatient clinic of Kandang Kerbau Maternity Hospital. There are also family planning sessions in two SFPA clinics, in three IPPF clinics, in several community centers, and in clinics of private physicians. All the accepted methods of contraception are offered, with the client being given a choice. Condoms are the leading contraceptive chosen, but the demand for oral tablets is growing rapidly. IUD's have not yet become popular, but their acceptance is expected to increase rapidly as there is more experience with them and they become more readily available. A combined annual registration and clinic fee of M$4 is charged and those who can afford to pay are charged for contraceptives.

The program is aimed at all people in the fertile age groups, but especial attention is given to women patients in MCH clinics and to mothers in the lying-in beds in the maternity hospital. Health education talks, stressing the need for family planning, are given by midwives to antenatal clinic groups, and advice about family planning and the availability of service is given in post-partum visits to individual homes. Family planning workers contact mothers in the hospital, and a public address system routinely explains family planning benefits and where information and materials may be obtained. Men's clinics, including individual consultation on request, have been held since late 1963.

The service load has been steadily rising. More than 9,000 new patients were seen in 1964 and a total of more than 78,000 different women have used the service since 1949.

A variety of methods are used for disseminating public information. In 1960, with the co-operation of the SFPA, the Ministry of Health mounted an extended campaign that included a training course for lay workers; a large exhibition that was visited by from 10,000 to 12,000 persons daily for twelve days and was then sent on a tour of rural community centers; and a great amount of press and radio publicity with supporting public discussions, cinema slides, posters, and informational leaflet distribution. The publicity officer and publicity committee of the SFPA, working with the regional office of the IPPF, have been active in many areas. Large numbers of informational leaflets have been distributed in house-to-house coverage, from community centers, in offices and factories, through labor unions, and from permanent stands in the offices of the registrar of births and registry of marriage, as well as in the Maternity Hospital. Discussion meetings and seminars have been frequently sponsored; television and radio programs in appropriate languages have been prepared and broadcast; public forums have been organized; good co-operation has been obtained from the press, especially the Chinese press; cinema slides have been effectively used with the co-operation of cinema owners; contests and true life stories have been used to capture public interest.

Funds have come from a number of sources. The government, since 1959, has given an annual grant of M$100,000. This is likely to be sharply reduced after 1965. Clinic earnings have increased steadily over the years and in 1964 totaled about M$55,000 over expenditures. The SFPA has been industrious and ingenious in the development of a variety of fund-raising activities including film shows, bazaars, mahjong drives; letters of appeal to firms and individuals; persuasion of potential donors by active members of the Association; raffles and lotteries. The Asia Foundation at one stage provided funds for a social worker for one year; the IPPF has consistently contributed funds as well as services; and in 1964 the Ford Foundation made a substantial grant to help establish and house a family planning institute that will be concerned with research, training, and the development of a model clinic. The annual budget is of the order of M$160,000, excluding the fund for building the institute.

The SFPA was originally organized out of concern for the improvement of family welfare and the health of mothers and children. Recently it has also been concerned about population increase as it has become apparent that such increases affect the socioeconomic status of families and create pressures on the government for housing, schools, and medical and welfare services. SFPA has been co-operating with government in the attempt to reduce the birth rate to between 20 and 25 in the next five to ten years and to achieve a natural increase rate of 2% or less. The birth rate has dropped ten points in the past eight years, and, with the availability and acceptance of new contraceptive methods and the forthcoming increased participation by the government in direct family planning service, it is felt that the goal of an annual population increase of 2% or less can be attained.

The major achievements of the SFPA have been in motivating large numbers of people to an acceptance of family planning methods and the allaying of both public and government fears of opposition on religious, political, or traditional grounds. As might have been expected, the largest group among the acceptors have been the Chinese who constitute the bulk of the population, but there has been increasing acceptance among Malays and Indians and the latter two groups are now represented among family planning acceptors in about the same proportion as they appear in the population.

The SFPA has demonstrated that interest in family planning can be created by education and publicity; that the most successful approach is one which appeals to personal and family benefits in terms of health and welfare rather than one which emphasizes the dangers of the population explosion; that opposition based on traditional or religious views gives way before prospects of material benefits resulting from family limitation; and that sound leadership is an indispensable factor in a successful program.

Major unsolved problems relate to staffing, administration, and finance. Because of financial uncertainties, there has never been sufficient staff to cope with the increasing work load. With the popularity of the oral pill and with patients returning regularly for supplies and occasional medical check-ups, the clerical and clinical work loads have increased. With the adoption of the IUD, there may be even greater strain if any substantial percentage of patients come back complaining of side effects or to have a check to see if the device has been expelled. The staff have been so busy giving initial service that valuable follow-up services and evaluation have had to take second place.

Also because of uncertain income, it has not been possible to offer sufficiently attractive terms to employ administrative personnel. A strong administration by qualified paid staff is badly needed. Decisions at present can be made only by the executive committee, which meets only once a month. Moreover, the composition of the committee can change at any annual election, thus jeopardizing continuity of policy. The committee consists of busy business and professional people who cannot give full attention to Association problems and housewives who, though enthusiastic and dedicated, may lack experience in business and professional procedures. Delays in obtaining decisions and a reduction in reversals of decisions in subsequent meetings could be avoided if there was a full-time paid director empowered to take responsibility and of sufficient stature to negotiate directly with the government.

REGIONAL OFFICE OF IPPF

The SFPA works closely with and has an interlocking membership with the Southeast Asia and Oceania regional office of the IPPF. The IPPF maintains a headquarters staff that includes an administrative secretary, a medical consultant, a training organizer, a social worker, and a nurse, together with supporting clerical help. Administration is provided by a regional council with a small steering committee active between annual council meetings.

The IPPF operates three family planning clinics, mainly as sites for its varied training programs. It works closely with the SFPA in its service and public information programs, but its main contribution is in training, which is oriented not only to the needs of Singapore but also to those of the entire Southeast Asia and Oceania region. A full-time medical officer is in charge of the training program. Both initial and refresher courses are offered for three categories of personnel: technical staff, administrative staff, and voluntary workers. Training is oriented toward both urban and rural service programs.

Relations between the SFPA and the IPPF will be even closer in 1966 with the opening of the SFPA's new institute building which will also serve as administrative and training headquarters for the IPPF as well as a center for publicity and education.

GOVERNMENT OF SINGAPORE

Since 1959 the government of Singapore has been annually contributing M$100,000 to the SFPA and has been allowing the Association to work in its MCH centers. In March, 1965, a three-member committee, composed of representation from the SFPA, the Ministry of Health, and a neutral member, was appointed and charged with reviewing the existing arrangement and recommending desirable changes to the Minister of Health.

As a result of the committee's report, recommendations have been put forward in a "white paper" for changes in the pattern of family planning activity and responsibility in Singapore. Plans are not yet complete but it is likely that, beginning in 1966, the Ministry of Health will take on responsibility for family planning service in its MCH centers and in Kandang Kerbau Hospital and will sharply reduce the amount of its annual grant to the SFPA. The Ministry's program will rely heavily on the IUD and will operate with the advice of a Family Planning and Population Board whose members will represent the Ministry, the SFPA, the IPPF, the obstetrical profession in Singapore, the University of Singapore, and Kandang

Kerbau Hospital. It is expected that the program will operate on a fee-for-service basis, with all types of contraceptives and sterilization being offered, and with a goal of bringing the growth rate of Singapore's population down to a figure approximating that of Western countries in the next five years.

Under the new arrangement, the SFPA will continue to operate its two clinics not on government premises, will open its new institute program, and will probably offer a service complementing that given by the government. Exactly what its new program will be is not yet definite, but it is anticipated that it may include the design and operation of one or more model clinics; trials of new contraceptive methods as they become available; surveys and other evaluative activity that the government may not be able to undertake; a continuation of publicity and education programs; and co-operation with the IPPF in training programs for personnel from the Southeast Asia and Oceania region.

7

THAILAND

WINICH ASAVASENA, M.D.
Chief, Maternal and Child Health Division
Department of Health, Ministry of Public Health

and

AMOS H. HAWLEY
Demographic Adviser, The Population Council

and

J. Y. PENG, M.D.
Medical Adviser, The Population Council

It may be said that serious thought about population control in Thailand began with the National Population Seminar which was held in Bangkok in March, 1963. Thailand's very rapid population growth—around 3% per year—and its implications were examined at some length. There were mixed opinions among government officials and others at the seminar about the desirability of family planning in Thailand. Nevertheless, the majority agreed that a family planning pilot project should be initiated to discover the response of a sample of the population to family planning services. With the approval of the government, the Population Council was asked for aid in launching an exploratory demonstration project.

The Population Council responded with a grant of funds for a year's operation, and sent two technical advisers—a social scientist and a physician experienced in family planning work. Since the project was to have both research and demonstration objectives, it was placed under the joint sponsorship of the National Research Council and the Ministry of Public Health.

A further organizational step was the creation of an advisory committee composed of twelve high-ranking members of government and the two Population Council advisers. This committee has established a joint project involving the National Research Council, the Health Department of the Ministry of Public Health, and the Population Council. This project is called "The Family Health Research Project," this name being used because it is hoped that eventually this activity will be integrated into the general health services, especially as far as maternal and child health is concerned. It was also felt that this name provided some security against intervention that might jeopardize the project.

The committee decided to carry out the project in Photharam, a rural district of about 70,000 population, located some 85 kilometers west of Bangkok. Although access to this site is not easy, it was felt that a nationwide program, should one ever develop, would need information on the problems encountered in providing service to a representative sample of the population, which in Thailand is 85% rural. There were also other reasons for the selection of this site. In the district chosen, settlement is clustered in compact villages rather than spread out, and health facilities already existed in which to house clinics. And, of no small importance, local health personnel, village headmen, and others in authority were enthusiastic about the prospect of a family planning service in their area. Their co-operation has since proved to be a valuable asset to the program.

The Family Health Research Project

As a first step in the project a field survey was conducted in August, 1964, to obtain information useful to an action program and to obtain baseline data for the subsequent measurement of changes. Every fourth house in the district was visited and an interview was held in each with one married woman who was 20–45 years of age and whose husband was living.

The principal findings of the survey can be briefly summarized. The average ideal size of a family, according to the survey, is 3.8 children. Although 72% of the women wanted no more children, they had almost no knowledge of how to prevent pregnancies. Less than 1% of the women had even the vaguest knowledge of contraception. Seven out of ten women wished either to begin practicing contraception or to learn about contraceptive methods. The survey also revealed a high incidence of illiteracy and rare use of newspapers or other printed matter. It was clear that mass media would not be useful in disseminating information.

Three months after the field survey, in November, 1964, the action program was started. A core staff, comprising two lady doctors and four nurses, was assigned to the project by the Maternal and Child

Health Division of the Department of Health, which is charged with responsibility for the action program. This staff was given preliminary training by the medical adviser. They soon moved into the field and began to offer service, first at two clinics and subsequently at six clinics placed in different health installations in the district. The rush to the clinics in the first few weeks was so great that service amounted to little more than a brief talk about four contraceptive methods—the IUD, oral pill, condom, and foam tablet—followed by free distribution of supplies for methods selected. Later, after the heavy case load had subsided, it became possible to begin development of an educational program.

In the second month, seven field workers were recruited and trained by the medical adviser, who now had assistance from the medical staff of the project. After training, the field workers were sent out to visit every third house in the district. At first they were concerned only with education, with the aid of flip books and contraceptive appliances. Later, the field workers were instructed to seek out women who were due for follow-up examination. A second phase of the educational effort took the form of a series of village meetings conducted by medical personnel. While these meetings dealt mainly with family planning, they also included talks on nutrition and general health matters. The educational program has continued to expand, to include meetings with folk or granny midwives, talks by local government officials, and small group meetings in houses. All communication has necessarily been by direct oral and visual means, since neither newspapers nor radio are accessible to more than a small minority.

Description of the staff is not complete without mention of the local health personnel, who have assisted in every way possible within the limits imposed by their regular duties.

ACHIEVEMENTS OF THE PROJECT

The action program is barely six months old; therefore it should be noted that the statistics present only a preliminary picture. Nevertheless we feel that we have a tangible measure of success. Starting from almost no contraceptive practice in the district, the proportion of eligible women who now are contraceptive users is approximately 20%. Incidentally, most of these (about 60%) heard about the service and were induced to visit clinics as a result of talking with neighbors or friends. A small attitude survey conducted midway through the program revealed a general improvement of morale: women were looking forward to a more secure economic position with greater hope of providing adequately for the children they had.

Table 1 shows that out of a total of about 5,000 eligible women, the total number of contraceptive users is 1,220. Of these, 1,046 live within the Photharam district; a further 174 users are outside the district. The latter adopted the practice in spite of the absence of mass media; they did so on their own volition after verbal contact with their friends or other persons.

The IUD is the most popular contraceptive. Table 2 shows that of the 1,046 users within the Photharam district, 77% used the IUD, 13% preferred pills, and 9% chose condoms. A very few selected foam tablets. Of the users of traditional methods, 29.3% of the pill users have switched to IUD; 7% of the condom users and 21.4% of foam

TABLE 1

NUMBER OF NEW CONTRACEPTIVE USERS BY WEEKS, IN A
POPULATION OF ABOUT 5,000 ELIGIBLE WOMEN

WEEK	MONTH	TOTAL USERS				
		Number	Subtotal	Three weeks' running average	Photharam District	Outside Photharam
1......	Nov. 30, 1964	54	....	....	54	....
2......	Dec. 8	71	....	81	71	....
3......		119	....	113	119	....
4......		148	 392	105	148	....
5......		47	....	80	47	....
6......	Jan. 4, 1965	46	....	55	46	....
7......		73	....	63	73	....
8......		70	 236	66	70	....
9......		54	....	55	54	....
10......	Feb. 1	40	....	51	40	....
11......		59	....	49	59	....
12......		49	 202	54	49	....
13......		58	....	46	53	5
14......	Mar. 1	32	....	35	29	3
15......		16	....	26	7	9
16......		30	 136	26	12	18
17......		33	....	30	15	18
18......		27	....	25	11	16
19......	Apr. 5	15	....	19	10	5
20......		15	 90	27	6	9
21......		51	....	35	28	23
22......		40	....	44	18	22
23......	May 3	40	....	38	17	23
24......		33	 164	37	10	23
Total.	....	1,220	....	....	1,046	174

TABLE 2

VARIOUS CONTRACEPTIVES USED IN THE PROGRAM

WEEK PERIOD	PHOTHARAM DISTRICT					OUTSIDE PHOTHARAM				TOTAL				
	Total Users	IUD	Pill	CD	FT	Total Users	IUD	Pill	CD	Total Users	IUD	Pill	CD	FT
1– 4.......	392	322	53	9	8	.....	.....	.....	.....	392	322	53	9	8
5– 8.......	236	176	39	18	3	.....	.....	.....	.....	236	176	39	18	3
9–12.......	202	134	19	46	3	.....	.....	.....	.....	202	134	19	46	3
13–16.......	101	69	21	11	0	35	34	1	0	136	103	22	11	0
17–20.......	42	35	4	3	0	48	44	3	1	90	79	7	4	0
21–24.......	73	66	4	3	0	91	88	3	0	164	154	7	3	0
1–24.......	1,046	802	140	90	14	174	166	7	1	1,220	968	147	91	14
Per cent.....	.....	77	13	9	1	.....	96	3	1	.....	79	12	8	1

TABLE 3

FOLLOW-UP OF IUD USERS

Period (4-week)	Duration of Use (weeks)	Total Insertions	Examined at Clinics	Through Home Visits	Not Met or Not Made	Lost Case
1st..........	21–24	326	324 (99.4%)	2	0	0
2d..........	17–20	189	176 (93.1%)	5	0	8
3d..........	13–17	150	138 (92%)	7	2	3
4th..........	9–12	75	58 (77.3%)	15	1	1
5th..........	5– 8	39	30 (77%)	5	4	0
6th..........	1– 4	69	25 (36%)	2	18	1
Total......	1–24	852[a]	751 (88.1%)	36	25	13

[a] Including the cases switched over from conventional methods and oral pills.

TABLE 4

PILL USERS

Period (4-week)	Duration of Use (weeks)	Total Users	Number Followed	Lost	Discontinued	Changed to IUD	Active Users
1st.....	21–24	53	50	3	27	19 (35.8%)	4 (7.5%)
2d.....	17–20	40	34	6	17	13 (32.5%)	4 (10%)
3d.....	13–16	18	17	0	9	6 (33.3%)	3 (16.7%)
4th....	9–12	22	21	1	10	3 (13.6%)	8 (36.4%)
5th....	5– 8	4	3	0	1	0	3 (75%)
6th....	1– 4	3	1	0	0	0	3 (100%)
Total	1–24	140	126	10	64	41 (29.3%)	25 (17.9%)

tablet users have switched to IUD. (This is shown in Tables 4, 5, and 6; and Table 3 gives the follow-up rates for IUD users.)

Tables 7 and 8 show the incidence of removal and expulsion and re-insertion of IUD's. Table 7 shows that the rate of removal was 13% (111 cases) of the insertions, medical reasons accounting for 6%, psychological reasons accounting for 3.6%, and personal reasons account-

TABLE 5

CONDOM USERS

Period (4-week)	Duration of Use (weeks)	Total Users	Number Followed	Lost	Discontinued	Changed to IUD	Active Users
1st......	21–24	9	9	0	3	3 (33.3%)	2 (22.2%)
2d......	17–20	18	15	2	11	2 (11.1%)	2 (11.1%)
3d......	13–16	46	24	1	39	1 (2.1%)	3 (6.3%)
4th.....	9–12	11	4	1	10	0	0
5th.....	5– 8	3	1	0	0	0	3 (100%)
6th.....	1– 4	3	3	0	0	0	3 (100%)
Total.	1–24	90	56	4	63	6 (7%)	13 (14%)

TABLE 6

FOAM TABLET USERS

Period (4-week)	Duration of Use (weeks)	Total Users	Number Followed	Lost	Discontinued	Changed to IUD	Active Users
1st........	21–24	8	8	3	2	2 (25%)	0
2d........	17–20	3	3	0	2	1 (33%)	0
3dª........	13–16	3	0	0	3	0	0
Total....	13–24	14	11	3	7	3 (21.4%)	0

ª No foam tablet users after this period.

TABLE 7

REMOVALS OF IUD

Period (4-week)	Duration of Use (weeks)	Total Insertions	Total Removals	Medical Reasons	Psychological Reasons	Personal Reasons
1st.....	21–24	326	51 (15.6%)	25 (7.7%)	15 (4.6%)	11 (3.4%)
2d......	17–20	189	22 (11.6%)	10 (5.3%)	4 (2.1%)	8 (4.2%)
3d......	13–16	150	24 (16%)	9 (6%)	8 (5.3%)	7 (4.7%)
4th.....	9–12	75	6 (8%)	1 (1.3%)	3 (4%)	2 (2.7%)
5th.....	5– 8	39	4 (10.3%)	4 (10.3%)	....	....
6th.....	1– 4	73	4 (5.5%)	2 (2.7%)	1 (1.4%)	1 (1.4%)
Total.	1–24	852	111 (13%)	51 (6%)	31 (3.6%)	29 (3.4%)

TABLE 8

REMOVAL, EXPULSION AND REINSERTION OF IUD

Period (4-week)	Duration of Use (weeks)	Total Insertion	Total Removal	Reinsertion	Total Expulsion	Reinsertion	Lost	Active Users
1st......	21–24	326	51	9	21 (6.4%)	17	0	280 (86%)
2d......	17–20	189	22	1	14 (7.4%)	12	8	147 (78%)
3d......	13–16	150	24	1	8 (5.3%)	7	3	123 (82%)
4th.....	9–12	75	6	0	8 (10.7%)	5	1	65 (87%)
5th.....	5– 8	39	4	1	1 (2.6%)	1	0	36 (92%)
6th.....	1– 4	73	4	1	0	0	1	69 (95%)
Total.	1–24	852	111	13	52 (6%)	42 (81%)	13	720 (85%)

TABLE 9

SOURCE OF MOTIVATION FOR WOMEN REGISTERED AT CLINICS

(Nov. 30, 1964–Apr. 30, 1965)

Source of Motivation	Number of Women	Per Cent
Through users and friends.........	595	54.9
Through local health personnel.....	156	14.4
Through group meetings..........	109	10.0
Through field workers.............	93	8.6
Through district officers...........	87	8.0
Through granny midwives.........	29	2.7
Other sources...................	15	1.4
Total........................	1,084	100

TABLE 10

AGE OF WOMEN REGISTERED AT CLINICS FOR SERVICES

(Nov. 30, 1964–Apr. 30, 1965)

Age	Number of Women	Per Cent
Under 20.........	12	1.2
20–24.............	147	13.6
25–29.............	308	28.4
30–34.............	316	29.0
35–39.............	230	21.2
40 and over.......	71	6.6
Total..........	1,084	100

ing for 3.4%. Table 8 illustrates that of the 111 removals, there were 13 reinsertions. The rate of expulsion was 6%, most of which (81%) were followed by reinsertion.

Table 9 emphasizes the fact that the vast majority of users (54.9%) were motivated by verbal contact with friends and neighbors. Tables 10 and 11 show the distribution of 100 users by age and size of family. The largest number of users fall into the 25–34 age group, and women with an average of 2 to 5 children form a substantial majority.

TABLE 11

DISTRIBUTION OF WOMEN FOR SERVICES BY
NUMBER OF LIVING CHILDREN

NUMBER OF LIVING CHILDREN	REGISTRANTS FOR SERVICES		PER CENT IN TOTAL POPULATION
	Number	Per Cent	
0............	1	0.1	4.8
1............	40	3.7	11.3
2............	167	15.4	15.1
3............	233	21.5	16.3
4............	215	19.8	16.5
5............	163	15.1	13.9
6............	124	11.4	9.3
7............	72	6.6	7.2
8............	40	3.7	4.1
9............	19	1.8	1.0
10 or more....	10	0.9	0.5
Total.......	1,084	100	100

COMMENTS

Our problems lie not in the present but in the future. We think we have demonstrated the existence of a high degree of readiness to engage in family planning in Thailand. We also believe we have learned something about supplying services, though admittedly there is still much to be learned. Our questions are: Will we have a national program soon? If so, what problems will arise in operating such a program?

A first consideration in reflecting on these questions is that Thailand is a highly centralized society. Everyone looks to the central government for guidance, especially when change is imminent. Hence the opinion of the government is of vital importance in the acceptance of a national program. We are not informed about how much that opinion has shifted from its somewhat neutral position of several months ago, though we are counting on the reports on our project to convince the government of the advisability of such a program.

Whether governmental approval of a national program, should it be given, will emerge as an explicit policy or simply as acquiescence to an extension of the present mandate of the Ministry of Public Health is impossible to forecast. Experience in Taiwan indicates that a formal policy is not essential. On the other hand, without a clear affirmative high-level commitment there is bound to be a certain amount of insecurity at the base of the program. Disavowal by the government is possible at any time. Co-ordination of population control with other development programs is made haphazard in the absence of a policy.

But if we undertake a national program, we will encounter serious problems. We have less than one doctor and two nurses for 8,000 people, on the average. Two-thirds of our doctors live and practice in the Bangkok metropolitan area. Thus a national program will call for innovation of various kinds. One of these may be the development of mobile clinics operating from provincial hospitals and health centers. In this connection we may have to rely entirely on paramedical personnel for follow-up examinations. We have already concluded that field workers are a luxury. They do not seem to stimulate enough women to come to the clinics to justify the expense. We shall continue to try to anticipate problems and to seek at least tentative solutions in our demonstration project.

CONCLUSION

A pilot project, approved by the government and of six months' standing, with an objective of studying the response of the population, has recruited about 20% of the eligible women, in spite of the lack of mass media. As this is a pilot project in itself and is not representative of the nation as a whole, it is felt that further pilot projects should be carried out.

It is worth noting that conventional methods of contraception have not proved popular in our project. About 80% of the contraceptive users have chosen the IUD—the Lippes loop. Most of the rest prefer the IUD, but are denied it for medical reasons. Other methods, as the women put it, are either inconvenient to use or involve the risk of forgetting. The greatest use occurs among women whose number of children is close to the ideal family size of four. A special effort to reach high-parity women will be needed.

We are reluctant to guess how our experience might be applied to other areas in Southeast Asia. We can, however, confirm some of the experiences encountered elsewhere. First, the ideal size of a family is very similar to that reported in many other parts of Asia. Second, motivation to engage in family planning is no problem. The problem is mainly that of supplying correct information. Third, motivation is basically economic in character. That is, it is concerned with attaining or preserving a viable household economy so that existing members can enjoy a life above the minimum subsistence level. Fourth, the most effective means of communicating information about a family planning service is by word of mouth on the part of the satisfied users.

8

CEYLON

ARNE KINCH, M.D.
Director, Sweden-Ceylon Family Planning Pilot Project

POPULATION

The last Ceylon census, in July, 1963, showed that the country's population was 10.6 million. Children below the age of 15 years were estimated to be 42% and the productive age group (15–64 years) to be 54% of the total. The latest crude birth and death rates (for 1964) are 32.6 and 8.7 per thousand population, respectively. The population growth rate is estimated to be 2.8%, and if this persists the population of Ceylon will double itself in twenty-five years. In 1961 it was found that 46% of the females were in the age group of 15–44 years.

In 1958 Mr. S. Selvaratnam, of the Department of Census and Statistics, prepared three projections—high, medium, and low—covering the 25-year period 1956–81, based on the 1953 census.[1] The high projections show that by 1975 the population will surpass 15 million, and that 20 million may be attained soon after 1980.

This fast-growing population must be fed. Rice is the staple food but domestic production is insufficient and imports are necessary. It is estimated that between 1954 and 1961 Ceylon imported rice at an annual cost of Rs. 250 million. According to S. Selvaratnam:

... [since] a substantial portion of the country's limited foreign exchange resources are spent on feeding the people, Ceylon has not been in a position to accumulate badly needed savings for the capital requirements of development. Ceylon cannot continue to do this and it is very important

[1] S. Selvaratnam, "Population Projections for Ceylon, 1956–1981," Planning Secretariat, Colombo, Ceylon, May, 1959.

that this drain on scarce resources be reduced, if not completely eliminated, if the country is to achieve speedy economic development.[2]

Ceylon's fast-growing population also entails increased unemployment, shortage of housing, and educational problems, all of which the
government has to face. To quote again from the same source:

It is clear that Ceylon has to embark on a vigorous policy of industrial
development and agricultural expansion in order to provide avenues of
employment for the increasing work force and to attain self-sufficiency
in food and other consumption goods. The investments on industry and
agriculture will have to be much larger than on education, health and
housing. But the problem facing Ceylon, like other under-developed
countries, is the acute shortage of capital. The difficult question therefore
is to determine the priorities that have to be assigned to the demands of
the various competing sectors of the economy. The question becomes still
more difficult when the government is already committed to a policy of
free education and health services. The accelerated increase in population
imposes a serious strain on the limited resources of the country and prevents any substantial expansion in the economy.

Since the chief factor in the rapid increase of Ceylon's population is
fertility, any measures taken to moderate the rate of growth of the population should concern the birth rate and family size. Though there are a
number of factors outside the field of conscious decision which influence
the course of fertility, experience of other countries shows that it is the
conscious desire to limit births that has been chiefly responsible for reduction in family size. In Ceylon today, with the rapid decline in death rates
and the increasing pressure of population on land, the advantages associated with large families are fast disappearing. There is a growing awareness among the people to limit the size of their families. This awareness,
coupled with governmental effort to disseminate knowledge on family
limitation would produce the desired results. Emphasis has also been placed
in the development programs on the need for a nationwide discussion on
the whole question of population policy in all its aspects, perhaps through
the medium of a competent committee of inquiry.

Some activities related to population control are conducted in Ceylon, as reported below.

FERTILITY TRENDS

During 1963 and 1964 a study in fertility trends in Ceylon was conducted by Professor Abhayaratne and Dr. Jayewardene, supported by
grants from the Population Council. The study has revealed that:

[2] "Population Policy for Ceylon," paper presented at the Symposium on Population
Policy for Ceylon organized by the Ceylon Association for the Advancement of
Science, 1964.

1. The mean age at marriage of women in Ceylon has increased since the beginning of the century; in 1900 it was 21.0 years compared to 23.1 years during 1960. The average reproductive span of women during the first decade of this century was 24.13 years, and during the last decade 22.1 years.
2. The increase in average age of marriage does not seem to have resulted in a reduction of the average reproduction span. This can be attributed to changes in the health of women, as reflected in a decreased death rate.
3. The total fertility rate was 5.13 in 1952 and 5.07 in 1960. The highest age-specific fertility rate during 1952–60 was among the group aged 25–29 years. Women in the 65-and-over age group who completed fertility before 1926 had given birth to 6.0 children during their reproductive periods, while the 45–49 year age group who completed fertility during the years 1941–46 gave birth to only 5.62 children.

Examination of the gross reproductive rate shows that:

1. The average woman bore during her reproductive period 6 children at the end of the first quarter of this century, and 5 children at the end of the second quarter of this century.
2. Of every 100 females born, 60 survived to enter the reproductive period at age 15 at the end of the first quarter, while 80 did so at the end of the second quarter of this century.
3. Of every 100 women in the reproductive age group, 58 entered the process of reproduction at the end of the first quarter, while 65 did so at the end of the second quarter of this century.

These data reveal that for every 100 women in actual reproduction at the beginning of this century, there were 102 taking their place at the end of the first quarter and 115 doing so at the end of the second quarter of this century. The difference is due to the combined effect of a high survival rate and a higher marriage age.

THE FAMILY PLANNING ASSOCIATION OF CEYLON

Activities of the Family Planning Association, started in 1953, have increased considerably during the past few years. According to the Association's 1963 annual report, there were 63 clinics in operation, located in all parts of the island, which had received a total of 11,153 cases during the year. Colombo, the capital city, has three large clinics, which had a combined total of 4,894 cases in 1962. This left 6,259 cases treated by the other 60 clinics or an annual average of 104.3 cases per clinic in 1963.

The Family Planning Association receives annual grants from various sources, with the largest (Rs. 75,000) coming from the government of Ceylon. In addition to its work in the more urbanized areas, the Association is also very much interested in promoting family planning on the tea estates, for which purpose it has appointed a propaganda officer who co-operates with officials from the Planters' Association Health Scheme.

All birth control methods are available at the clinics and supplies are furnished at a nominal charge. A research study has been conducted regarding oral contraceptives as well as intra-uterine devices (IUD's). With regard to oral contraceptives, there are some 2,900 cases, mainly in Colombo and two or three of its suburbs. The results are favorable.

As for the IUD, a survey indicates about 1,000 cases, mainly in Colombo. Side effects are not more than are found in other countries. For its IUD program, the Association receives a grant from the Population Council of New York. House visits were necessary to initiate the IUD program, but people are now coming as a result of word-of-mouth communication. Three centers in Colombo offer training to doctors, but among medical personnel there are still some who do not consider the IUD a suitable method. Although these have had an adverse influence on the IUD program, the response among the population has nevertheless been good and the demand is increasing.

SWEDEN-CEYLON FAMILY PLANNING PILOT PROJECT

The activities of the project are based on a bilateral agreement between the government of Ceylon and the government of Sweden which was first signed on May 22, 1958, for a three-year period. In May, 1961, the agreement was renewed for another two years; and in May, 1963, it was extended for an additional two years. The present bilateral agreement is an extension of the original, which expired on May 22, 1965.

According to Article 1 of the bilateral agreement:

The Government of Ceylon and the Royal Government of Sweden agree to cooperate in order to promote and facilitate a pilot project in Community Family Planning to take place in two or more rural areas in Ceylon with the aim of extending such activities on the basis of the experience found on a nationwide scale.

Thus the project was meant to assist the government of Ceylon to institute a nationwide program on the basis of experience from pilot areas. The project works in accordance with the principle of *action-cum-research*, where *research* means collecting data from different surveys in order to reveal the most effective *action*. Article 1 of the bilateral agreement states that activities should be performed in two or more rural areas, in order to gain experience in a variety of situations.

During 1958 two pilot areas were selected: one was a rice-village area with a population of 7,000–8,000 Sinhalese Buddhists, situated 20 miles south of Colombo; the other was an up-country tea estate with 7,000–8,000 people of Indian-Tamil origin, mainly of Hindu religion.

The Public Health Service of Ceylon is regarded as one of the best in Asia, and the bilateral project has worked toward integrating family planning with maternal and child health services. If this could be done, family planning could be conducted on a nationwide scale by Ceylon's MCH services without very great increases in personnel or expenditures. In this connection the program in the village area is of particular interest because the Maternal and Child Health Service subdivision with which it works is typical of the smallest administrative unit in the Public Health Service. Having first been tested in a small unit, the project extended its activities in 1962 to a medium-sized unit (the Point Pedro MCH area, population 95,000) and in 1963 to a large unit (Polonnaruwa-Matale District, population over 300,000). During 1964 the activities of the original "Village Area" were extended to encompass the entire Horana area of the MCH, which has a population of about 185,000.

An annual census provides the basis for the research findings. Most of the data are compiled in Sweden and have yet to be published, but preliminary results show a decline in the crude birth rate for the "Village Area" from about 30 in 1958 to 20.4 in 1964. Because the most notable decline in age-specific rates is among women aged 25–35, it is reasonable to attribute the declining trend to the activities of the project. It should be noted that project personnel give advice and provide supplies but that the actual servicing is in the hands of the regular public health staff of the area concerned.

Based on the achievements of the "Village Area" project, its director is of the opinion that family planning can be successfully integrated into the nationwide MCH service. This, however, requires additional training of the public health staff; the public health midwives are regarded particularly as key personnel for family contact. Accordingly, during the past two years, the Department of Health and the project have been engaged in a joint training program, which has taken definite form in the past eight or nine months. It offers a two-week training course, one week for lectures and one week for practical field work, with board and lodging provided by the project. The trainees are public health inspectors, nurses, and midwives. In addition to these members of the public health staff, the project also gives training to public health personnel attached to family planning centers run by the Family Planning Association. The project plans to extend its training program to more centers and greater numbers of trainees.

Funds for equipment are allocated quarterly to the project and are remitted by the government of Sweden to Ceylon in English pounds sterling. Extension of the bilateral agreement in May, 1965, by the Ceylon government is the basis of the Swedish project. Some new articles were added to the effect that the government of Ceylon will take over activities area by area. The main task of the Swedish project during the next three years is to train the public health staff, train doctors, supply contraceptives of various kinds, advise on field work, and collect data to evaluate results achieved, and thus pave the way to make family welfare planning a "nationwide program."

9

INDIA

B. L. RAINA

Director, Central Family Planning Institute, New Delhi

BACKGROUND

India has about 2.4% of the total land area of the world, and has to support about 14% of the world population. The Indian setting is varied, spread over about 1.2 million square miles, with deserts, forests, endless plains, and mountains over 20,000 feet. Temperatures vary from 28° F. to 122° F., with rainfall from less than 10 inches in Rajasthan to 80 inches in Assam. Its sixteen states have populations ranging from 3.6 million to 73.7 million, with people speaking different languages and having various resources and rates of development. Cultural phases dating back to Indus Valley civilization (2400–1500 B.C.) and varied physical environments and cultural and dynastic impacts have led to development of different kinds of socioeconomic patterns. There are strong family ties and group family systems, which are now changing. There is, however, a common bond and uniformity in India of culture, tradition, and aspirations.

India is engaged in a strenuous effort to raise the standard of living of every citizen through planned development within the framework of a democratic government, elected and maintained by the will of the people. The precipitous increase in population seriously threatens the achievement of the national objective of ensuring economic and social welfare to the masses of the Indian people.

The 1961 census recorded 439.2 million (40% in age group 0–14 years) for the country. The annual growth rate has accelerated in successive decennial periods; 11.0 per 1,000 population (1921–30), 13.5 (1931–40), 14.0 (1940–50), and 21.5 (1951–60). The population of women aged 15–44 years is nearly 20%–22% of the total; 85% of them are married. Percentage of births of the sixth order and above is about 22.8%. The demographic picture varies considerably in different states.

The population growth depends upon birth rates, death rates, and migration. There is relatively little in- or out-migration. There was a net immigration for the period 1951–60, averaging about 0.8% annually. The birth rate in India was estimated to be 41.7 per 1,000 population per year for the decade 1951–60, in some parts even higher. The birth rate during 1961–65 is estimated to be 41.0. The death rate has been rapidly declining but is still high. It is estimated to be 27.4 in 1941–50, 22.8 in 1951–60, and 17.2 in 1961–65. The population in August, 1965, is estimated to be about 488 million. The increase of about 11 million people per year is a matter of most serious concern. Control of births is, therefore, a matter of great urgency not only for socioeconomic development but also to prevent the further deterioration of already low standards of living.

The governmental expert committee dealing with population has made three different projections based on three different assumptions, namely, (1) no decline in fertility, (2) moderate decline in fertility, and (3) high decline in fertility. The projection based on moderate decline in fertility assumes that the general fertility rate would decline by 5% during 1966–70, by 10% during 1971–75, and by 20% during 1976–80. The projected birth rates for different periods would then be 38.6 in 1968–69, 35.1 in 1973–74, and 28.7 in 1978–79.

EARLY EFFORTS

Although the development of an intensive family planning program in India is of recent origin, the movement to control birth has been advocated for about fifty years. In 1916, Pyare Kishan Wattal published his book *The Population Problem in India*. In 1925, Professor Raghunath Dhondo Karve opened a birth control clinic. The Neo-Malthusian League was formed in Madras a few years later. On June 11, 1930, the Mysore government issued orders to open the first government birth control clinic in the world. In 1932, the senate of Madras University, the government of Madras, and the All-India Women's Conference in its Lucknow session supported birth control. In 1935, the National Planning Committee set up by the Indian National Congress, under the chairmanship of Shri Jawaharlal Nehru, supported family planning. At the invitation of the All-India Women's Conference, Mrs. Margaret Sanger visited India in 1935–36. On December 1, 1935, the Society for the Study and Promotion of Family Hygiene was formed. Dr. A. P. Pillai, a vigorous advocate for family planning, conducted training courses in 1936. In 1939, Birth Control

World-Wide opened clinics in Uttar Pradesh and Madhya Pradesh, and Raina started Matra Sewa Sangh in Ujjain, Madhya Pradesh.

In 1940, Shri P. N. Sapru successfully moved a resolution in the Council of States for establishment of birth control clinics. About this time Mrs. Rena Dutta toured extensively on behalf of the Family Planning Association, London. By 1940 the Society for the Study and Promotion of Family Hygiene became the Family Planning Society, incorporating the Bhagini Samaj Birth Control Clinic in Bombay. The Health Survey and Development Committee appointed in 1943 by the government of India recommended provision of birth control services, but for health reasons. In 1949, the Family Planning Association of India was formed under the presidency of Shrimati Dhanvanthi Rama Rau.

On April 11, 1951, the health panel of the Planning Commission appointed a committee to report on population growth and family planning programs, with Dr. Sushila Nayar, Smt. Dhanvanthi Rama Rau, Shri R. A. Gopalaswami, Dr. Gyan Chand, and Dr. A. C. Basu as members. In the meantime, Dr. Abraham Stone visited India under the auspices of World Health Organization to advise on establishment of studies on rhythm, and the Population Council sent Dr. Frank Notestein and Dr. Leona Baumgartner to India to study population matters.

The Family Planning Research and Program Committee set up two subcommittees, one on socioeconomic and cultural studies and the other on biological and qualitative aspects of population. A number of other basic studies were undertaken. They included the study of couple fertility by the Indian Statistical Institute, Calcutta, based on the National Sample Survey Second and Fourth Rounds, the Sample Survey of Patna City by Patna University to estimate the fertility and mortality rates and the Demographic Survey of six villages by the Gokhale Institute of Politics and Economics. Pilot service programs were undertaken, and it was demonstrated that government-supported family planning programs would be welcomed by the bulk of the people.

The Family Planning Research and Program Committee in its first meeting in July, 1953, stressed that the family planning program should not be concerned in the limited sense of birth control or merely spacing of children. The purpose was ultimately to promote, as far as possible, the growth of the family as a unit of society in a manner designed to facilitate the fulfillment of those conditions necessary for welfare.

The development of a national program began to emerge with the Second Five-Year Plan. In November, 1955, at an interdepartmental meeting, the machinery for the co-ordination of population and vital statistics and demographic studies was reviewed. This led to formation of a standing committee for co-ordination of population and vital statistics, consisting of representatives of the ministries concerned and the Indian Statistical Institute. High-level family planning boards were established at the center and in the states. An officer on special duty, later designated as Director, Family Planning, was appointed, and family planning officers were placed in the states. Training centers and centrally financed field units in the states were set up. Research and training on demography, reproductive physiology, communications, and action research were established.

The national program was launched with four main components: (1) education to create the background of contraceptive acceptance; (2) service through rural and urban centers, including provision of sterilization facilities; (3) training of personnel; and (4) research. A large number of posters, pamphlets and folders, films, film strips, slides, and exhibits were produced. Public minded leaders in states and districts were appointed honorary family planning education leaders. Liberal grants were given to local bodies and voluntary organizations. Assistance was given to strengthen the staffs of a large number of health institutions and hospitals. Existing medical and health centers were utilized for distribution of contraceptives. In the beginning, it was not possible to single out distinct "targets" for sterilization or contraceptives. Some areas were still not responsive to the program. Maharashtra State (39,553,718 population) was not prepared to implement the program until 1957. (Once this state agreed to implement the program, the progress was outstanding.) At this stage, there was necessarily heavy dependence on general promotional efforts. This approach did lead to increasing awareness, acceptance, and rapid development of the program.

The training activities had long-term and short-term objectives. As a long-term objective, the Medical Council of India, Inter-University Board, and Nursing Council were requested to integrate training in family planning with normal courses of instruction. To meet immediate needs, short-term training and orientation courses were initiated. Training centers under the Ministry of Community Development developed courses in family planning, and schools of social work began taking increasing interest.

NATIONAL POLICY

National policy clearly identifies family planning to be "at the very center of planned development." This is reflected in the provision made for family planning—approximately Rs. 1.45 million in the First Five-Year Plan, Rs. 21.56 million in the Second Plan, Rs. 270 million in the Third Plan, and tentative allocation of Rs. 950 million for the Fourth Plan, to begin in 1966.

The financial assistance offered to local governmental bodies and voluntary organizations was 100%. The assistance to state governments was 100% for training, sterilization, contraceptives, education and research programs, and for the state family planning officer. For other services, 75% aid was given. The co-operation of voluntary organizations was sought on the widest scale.

THIRD FIVE-YEAR PLAN

The Third Five-Year Plan in India is considered the first phase of an intensive development period, extending over a period of fifteen years from 1961–62 to 1975–76. The basic objectives "are to lay sound foundations for self-sustaining economic growth, to provide avenues and opportunities of employment to all those who seek it and, while narrowing economic and social disparities, to ensure a minimum level of living to every family in the country." In this context, the family planning program is an essential element in the strategy of gaining the above objectives.

The immediate task of the family planning program is to reduce birth rate to 25 per 1,000 as soon as possible. General approaches to this goal include:

1. Popularizing the adoption of family planning methods, including the intra-uterine device, voluntary sterilization, condoms, chemical contraceptives, coitus interruptus, abstinence, rhythm, and such new contraceptives as are found effective and acceptable in India for mass application.
2. Stimulating social changes affecting fertility, such as raising the age of marriage of women, increasing women's status, education, and employment opportunities, old age security, education of children, and elimination of child labor.
3. Accelerating basic economic changes so as to increase per capita income in real terms.

The family planning program was critically reviewed in 1963 and a reorganized, extended program was launched in October of the same year. The extended program envisages three basic conditions necessary for fertility moderation: (1) each individual should know and feel that the immediate society or community to which he belongs has agreed as a group that having a small family size is the normal, desirable behavior for its members; (2) each individual should have knowledge that a small family is valuable to him personally and should have knowledge of contraceptive methods; and (3) each individual should have contraceptive methods readily accessible. In order to create these basic conditions for the people, the existing family planning and health organization was strengthened. Provision was made for increasing the family planning training centers to one per 10 million population.

The extended family planning program is an integrated effort aimed at establishing conditions conducive to the adoption of family planning throughout the entire population. For work in rural areas the operational unit is a community development block having about 80,000 population, and in urban areas a population unit of about 50,000. The program emphasizes community education efforts aimed at helping people to help themselves, to organize educational activities within their own groups, and to utilize local channels for supply of simple contraceptives requiring no clinical consultation. Male and female family planning leaders (*parivar kalyan sahayak* and *sahayika*) are developed from among the people, and efforts are being made to have one such male and female worker for every village or group of 1,000 population. Additional honorary family planning education leaders have also been appointed to mobilize public opinion. The basic female family planning worker at the periphery is the auxiliary nurse-midwife. Also intended in due course are one auxiliary nurse-midwife and one male basic health worker for every 10,000 population. For each 20,000 population, a family planning health assistant is being posted. At the block health unit headquarters is a male family planning educator plus medical and nursing services.

At the national level, the emerging organization includes:

1. A Cabinet Committee consisting of the Minister of Finance, Minister of Information and Broadcasting, Minister of Food and Agriculture, Minister of Labor Employment, Deputy Chairman of the Planning Commission, and Minister of Health. The Secretary of the Ministry of Health, Director General of Health Services, and Commissioner of Family Planning are advisers to the Cabinet Committee.
2. A Central Family Planning Council with the Health Minister as chairman, and a standing committee.
3. A Commissioner of Family Planning.

There are three national expert committees, namely, Demographic Advisory Committee, Communications and Action Research Advisory Committee, and Advisory Committee on Bio-Medical Aspects of Family Planning.

A Central Family Planning Institute is being developed to provide leadership in research, training, and evaluation. The basic organization envisaged includes nine technical divisions: training, program development and evaluation, administration and operational research, medical education and research, biological research, population genetics and human development, contraceptive materials, demography and statistics, social research, and information and audiovisual media.

In August, 1960, the standing committee for co-ordination of population and vital statistics was reconstituted as the National Council of Population. The Minister of Home Affairs is chairman, and the Minister of Health and the honorary statistical adviser to the Cabinet are vice-chairmen. This Council makes recommendations to the government on work during the intercensus period, especially for the improvement of vital statistics, and on the scope and purpose of demographic studies. It reviews programs already in hand, formulates work, and advises from time to time on new programs in the field of population and health statistics, man power, and demographic studies. It also serves to meet the requirements of the United Nations and the World Health Organization in the field of population and health statistics. The Demographic Advisory Committee is a subcommittee of this Council.

PROGRESS

At the outset of the program, there was practically no organizational structure. The focus was on promoting the safe period method. Then, mechanical and chemical contraceptives, especially the foam tablets, were accepted. Finally came voluntary sterilization and now the IUD. During this period, a very great deal has been learned about attitudes of the people and the program's effectiveness. Widespread awareness of family planning in rural and urban areas has been developed. By July, 1965, there were 15,808 family welfare planning units, 13,901 in rural areas. There were also 3,223 surgical sterilization units. The use of contraceptives has increased rapidly. Chemical contraceptives are now manufactured in India in both private and public sectors; manufacture of condoms in the private sector has commenced and also will be undertaken in the public sector. The extended national program has recently been reinforced by the addition of IUD services; and manufacture of IUD's in India has commenced. So far, over 400,000 have been distributed and about 60,000 have been inserted. It is hoped a million women will be using IUD's by early 1966. Sterilization has also expanded rapidly. There were about 7,000 persons sterilized in 1956. Since 1963 over 100,000 operations have been performed yearly, and the cumulative figure is expected to reach 1,000,000 soon.

The staff for the extended family planning program is being placed in position. The progress varies from state to state. In Kerala, for example, almost the entire staff is in position including women medical officers in the primary health centers. There are state family planning officers in all the sixteen states, usually at the level of assistant director or deputy director of health services. In more than half of the 320 districts, district family planning bureaus have now been established.

Over 115 persons have had advanced training in the population field, under fellowship programs in demography, bio-medical, and communication, with the assistance mainly of the Population Council and the Ford Foundation. The Demographic Training and Research Center, Bombay, has been developed as the foremost institute in Asia and the Far East in demography. The Center, set up by the government of India in collaboration with the United Nations and the Tata Trust with assistance of the Population Council, has, during the past eight years, trained over 130 students from seventeen countries. A network of special family planning training centers has been set up and is now expanding further. In 83 medical colleges and 228 nursing schools (up to the end of 1963) instruction in family planning is given.

The education materials produced number over 13,368,500 pamphlets, posters, and folders, not including films and film strips and other such material.

The expenditure has steadily increased from Rs. 14.51 lakhs on the First Plan, Rs. 215.58 lakhs in the Second Plan, to Rs. 138.35 in 1961–62, Rs. 268.46 in 1962–63, Rs. 397.52 lakhs in 1963–64, and Rs. 605.02 lakhs in 1964–65 and an estimated Rs. 1,200 lakhs in 1965–66 (one lakh = 100,000 rupees).

In the area of research, work is progressing at the Demographic Training and Research Center, Bombay, the Demographic Research Center at the Institute of Economic Growth in Delhi, the Indian Statistical Institute at Calcutta, the Department of Statistics of the government of Kerala, the Institute of Economic Research at Dharwar, the Gokhale Institute of Economics and Politics, Poona, and in Madras. A number of communications and action research projects have been carried out at the Central Family Planning Institute, Delhi; Demographic Training and Research Center, Bombay; Kerala University, Institute of Rural Health and Family Planning, Gandhigram; Planning Action and Research Institute, Lucknow; Indian Statistical Institute, Calcutta; Lady Hardinge Medical College, New Delhi; and by the New Delhi Family Planning Association. Over twenty inquiries in biomedical fields were carried out mainly at the All-India Institute of Medical Sciences, Delhi; Central Drug Research Institute, Lucknow; Zoology Department of Delhi University; and Indian Cancer Research Center, Bombay.

The proposed fertility goal has been reached by the people in the highest economic level throughout India. The goal has been nearly reached by the heterogeneous population of Bombay City, where the birth rate is reported to have gone down to 27 per thousand. In several districts in Maharashtra where the intensive sterilization program (especially vasectomy camps) was pursued, there appears to be a reduction of birth rates which is being further investigated before firm results are announced. It has been demonstrated in pilot projects like Athoor Block in Gandhigram that with the extended family planning program, birth rates can be reduced. At last we have in hand the necessary elements: (1) effective educational methods, (2) improved contraceptive methods, and (3) an organizational structure through which these can be applied. There are now reasons to believe that with the extended program, reinforced with the IUD, further progress toward goals can be achieved quickly.

TABLE 1

TARGETS FOR THE USE OF CONTRACEPTIVES
(In Millions)

Date	IUD	Sterilization	Condom
1966–67	2.33	1.38	1.83
1967–68	5.09	1.90	3.56
1968–69	8.46	2.57	4.66
1969–70	13.70	3.39	4.66
1970–71	19.69	4.51	4.66

PROGRAM TARGETS

Births are likely to decline at different rates in various districts and states owing to differences in local socioeconomic, demographic, and program factors. With the further extension of development programs there even may be a tendency toward an increase in the birth rate in some places. It is hoped that all the states will come ultimately to a fairly uniform level. However, annual targets will differ for different states and districts.

Targets of specific achievement for contraceptive use during the period through 1971 are now being considered as part of the process of over-all program planning (see Table 1). The lines of analysis are briefly sketched below.

Some tentative assumptions are:

1. The couples who will have to be covered under the IUD, sterilization, and contraceptive program constitute 17% of the population.
2. The urban and rural couples will be in ratio of 1:4.

3. The average numbers of sterilization in succeeding years may be 0.75, 1.00, 1.25, 1.50, and 2.0 per 1,000 population. (Some states have already exceeded these targets.)
4. The couples will resort to different methods in varying proportions, and preference for IUD will rapidly increase.
5. The reduction in birth rates will be possible if there are 21 IUD and sterilized couples per 1,000 in 1968–69, about 43 in 1973–74, and about 80 in 1978–79, and among the remaining couples (users and non-users), the average effectiveness may be 3%, 6%, and 15% by 1968–69, 1973–74, and 1978–79, respectively.

Is it possible to achieve the targets shown in Table 1, especially those for the IUD and sterilization? To do so will involve considerable effort in mobilizing professional personnel and solving organizational problems. If the available medical man power, including private practitioners, is mobilized, the targets can be achieved. It is estimated that there are now about 12,429 women doctors. By the end of the Fourth Plan their number may be 17,500. About 1,200 women doctors may be required for the program in 1966–67 and about 9,000 in 1970–71. Gradually, also, it is expected that male doctors will become more acceptable for IUD insertions. Twenty million loops can be inserted by the end of the Fourth Plan (1.80 million in 1966–67, 2.30 in 1967–68, 3.50 in 1968–69, 5.40 in 1969–70, and 6.00 in 1970–71). The "camp" technique for use of medical personnel on a mobile basis has proved successful in sterilization, and experience with this method for IUD insertions is encouraging.

LOOKING AHEAD

It may be emphasized that contraceptive technology is only a part of the total program. It is now even more imperative to build up basic organization, better supervision, and intensified educational activities in order to be able to apply the improved technology. Further coordination and mobilization of different resources that reach the public are required, and mobility, flexibility, and a sense of urgency are highly necessary. Financial and administrative authority at all levels must act quickly.

In order to keep close track of the effects of the program and continually to improve its efficiency, there is urgent need to improve collection of vital statistics and to develop more sensitive indicators of fertility trends and of changes in relevant social factors. We must do more, also, to share experiences within the country and with other countries.

The establishment of a small-family norm in a huge population is a tremendous and complex task. For this purpose, the forces of social policy and social legislation also remain to be fully harnessed.

We also must continue to seek much better basic understandings of human biology and behavior as they relate to reproduction. It is obvious that, although we have gone far in learning how to build practical family planning programs, our basic knowledge is still relatively scant. The problems of adjusting reproduction to resources will be with us for a long time, and it behooves us to gain better scientific understanding of this area. The fact that profound changes are and will be occurring gives an excellent opportunity to learn, at the same time, about the dynamics of such changes in different groups and under different situations.

In the present program there is still great need for administrative and operational research at all levels to clarify organizational problems and to find solutions to these. The solutions to these problems will inevitably lead also to development of a stronger base for future health programs. Efforts in these directions can lead to the achievement of the World Health Organization objective "to promote maternal and child health and welfare and to foster the ability to live harmoniously in a changing total environment."

We are dealing with a problem which dominates our time, underlying much of the world's political unrest, and frustrating man's hopes for a better life. It certainly deserves our most devoted and most imaginative efforts on a most urgent basis. As we strive to meet the immediate crisis, which is a quantitative one, it is well, also, to think now about the ultimate, qualitative goal of raising the level of the daily life of mankind, of further freeing and improving the quality of the human mind. We should begin to study more carefully the inevitable genetic effects of rapid demographic transition on selection of human traits, including psychological traits, especially the capacity for abstract thought. And we should maintain a strong concern for building the social and cultural environment which preserves and promotes the dignity of individuals. As we work on such common problems, I hope that the spirit of world neighborliness and international good will can also flourish.

With the harnessing of all available knowledge, skills, and experience, humanity can gain control over its fertility. If we proceed with objectivity, cogency, and humility, the stage is set for such control and perhaps for moving beyond to levels of civilization and concord not yet dreamed of.

10

PAKISTAN

ENVER ADIL, C.S.P.
Family Planning Commissioner

The fundamental problem that faces the world today is the present and prospective rapid increase in population. It is particularly important in Pakistan, a developing country which is striving very hard to improve the socioeconomic conditions of the masses.

Economic development in Pakistan is one of the highest among the developing countries. But the rapid increase in population is nullifying economic gains considerably. A high dependency burden, due to 44.5% of the population being under the age of 15, is adversely affecting the capital requirements for industrialization by diverting the resources to current consumption and social expenditure.

GEOGRAPHICAL AND SOCIAL BACKGROUND

To understand the factors resulting in high fertility and the difficulties in implementing a family planning program in Pakistan, it is necessary to give some geographical and social background of the country.

Pakistan has the fifth largest population in the world. It is a land with a long history, but as an independent nation it is only 18 years old. The country is divided into two parts, East and West Pakistan, by 1,100 miles of Indian territory. The two wings differ considerably in topography, climate, land use, and population distribution, but they are united politically and religiously.

The East wing is tropical delta with annual average rainfall of 100 inches; the West is largely semi-irrigated desert with a rainfall of 10 inches. While East Pakistan comprises about one-sixth of the country's total land area, it is occupied by more than half the total population and is one of the world's most crowded areas. The total area of East Pakistan is 55,126 square miles with a population of over 50 million and a density of 922 persons per square mile. Urban population is 5% and literacy 21.5%, excluding children below five years. In West Pakistan the density is 138 per square mile, the urban population is 23% and literacy 16.3%, excluding children below five years. The total area is 310,403 square miles with a population of nearly 43 million. (These figures are based on the 1961 census.)

A predominantly Muslim country (88% of the total population), Pakistan, with 84% of its people illiterate, is not only one of the underdeveloped countries having high fertility but has perhaps the highest in the Muslim world. The reasons for this very high fertility seem to be early and universal marriage (average age at marriage of females is 15.5 years and 99% of women marry before the end of the reproductive period); early motherhood; remarriage of widows; illiteracy; dependence on agriculture (87% of the population lives in the rural areas and 76% earn their livelihood from agriculture); isolation; low standards of living (average per capita annual income is less than $70); the form of family organization; the absence of economic incentive to limit the number of children and, to a certain extent, fatalistic attitudes. The practice of family limitation is almost entirely absent. Little knowledge exists about birth control, and the masses cannot afford to buy any but the most inexpensive type of contraceptives.

POPULATION TRENDS

Pakistan's population in 1901 was 46 million and it increased to 76 million in 1951 and to 94 million in 1961. While in fifty years (1901–51), population increased by 30 million, during 1951–61 alone the increase was 18 million, giving a growth rate of 2.2% per annum. According to estimates of the Planning Commission, the actual population of the country in 1961 was 102 million and reached the 115 million mark in 1965. The growth rate during 1961–65 is estimated at 2.6% per annum.

Some demographers consider that, owing to constant fertility and declining mortality, the population growth rate has now reached 3% per annum, making a net annual addition to the population of 3 million persons which thus will double the population in the next twenty-three years. This period of twenty-three years may be even shorter as the improvement in health facilities and the eradication of malaria and other communicable diseases will further reduce the death rate and increase the growth rate.

FAMILY PLANNING MOVEMENTS

In 1953, the Family Planning Association of Pakistan made a tentative beginning to popularize family planning in the country. Some clinics were opened, and some publicity and education were undertaken to emphasize the need for family limitation.

The population problem was first recognized by the government in formulating the First Five-Year Plan and a small provision was made for family planning. But practically nothing was done in the early years of the period except some pilot work by the family planning associations.

During the reform period of martial law, which was promulgated in 1958, the presidential cabinet, under the leadership of Field Marshal Ayub Khan, one of the few spokesmen on birth control in Asia, examined the population with other nation-building activities of the country. After an appraisal of the economic development in the first three years of the First Five-Year Plan, it was realized that rapid increase in population was putting a great strain on the economy. Population growth offset any effect that increased productivity under the plan might have had on the per capita level. It was clear that decreasing the population growth rate required decreasing fertility rates, since opportunities for emigration were limited and the existing health program would steadily lower the death rates. With the President's personal leadership and support from the family planning associations already at work in major cities, the government courageously faced the population problem by declaring family planning a national policy and deciding to launch a comprehensive family planning program throughout the country. This led to an interim program of the Ministry of Health in January, 1960, which was later merged with the Second Five-Year Plan (1960–65). Under this plan the government of Pakistan undertook to make family planning a government activity.

SECOND FIVE-YEAR PLAN

The objective of the Second Five-Year Plan program of family planning (1960–65) was population control through voluntary participation in limiting family sizes and spacing of children. The program was administered through the existing health services as a normal function of the government hospitals, dispensaries, and rural clinics. As this was the first major attempt in this direction by the government of Pakistan, it is dealt with in more detail in the following paragraphs. It is on the experience of this program that a new one has been devised.

The Second Five-Year Plan provided an outlay of Rs. 30.5 million

(£2.26 million) for expenditure during five years beginning in 1960. Specific targets of the program that were accepted are as follows:

1. Three hundred thousand families to be covered in the first year increasing to 1.2 million in five years. This represented 10% of women of child-bearing ages according to the 1951 census.
2. The families who were introduced to family planning to be motivated to continue.
3. Six hundred family planning centers to be opened every year in the existing hospitals and dispensaries in the country.
4. Each center to attain in one year a coverage of five hundred families and continue to give service to them uninterruptedly.
5. Sufficient number of technical personnel such as doctors, health visitors, nurses, and village aid workers, among others, to be trained to man the target number of centers per month, i.e., twenty-five in each province each month.
6. Contraceptive material to flow monthly or quarterly into family planning centers in sufficient quantity to keep pace with the target. Only simple methods, like condoms and foam tablets were advocated. Diaphragms and jellies were to be used only in urban areas. Male sterilization for which monetary incentive was introduced was also recommended.

EVALUATION OF THE FAMILY PLANNING PROGRAM
(1960–65)

ACHIEVEMENTS

Whatever the country achieved in family planning during this period was modest. A family planning directorate at the center and family planning offices in two provinces under the health organizations were established. While the central organization was responsible for policy, planning, and technical direction, execution and implementation of the program was with the provinces.

To train persons (both medical and non-medical) and to do research in family planning, one training-cum-research institute at the center and four in the provinces were established. The main functions assigned to the central institute are (a) to promote, co-ordinate, and conduct research in family planning with emphasis on a cheap, effective, and practicable type of contraceptive for the national family planning program, (b) to motivate, communicate, and educate regarding family planning, (c) to find interrelationships between demographic changes and other socioeconomic conditions, and (d) to do research on the physiology of reproduction.

Besides the above-mentioned research institute, two research projects, Public Health Education Project and Medical Social Research Project (MESOREP), were established with the help of the Population Council at the two provincial headquarters.

The government's need to discover and evaluate practical educational approaches which would be effective in family planning led to the establishment in 1961 of the Public Health Education Project in collaboration with the University of California. This project began its initial studies in the city of Dacca. Later on, the work was extended to the rural areas around the city. The primary objectives of the project are (*a*) to develop research in educational methods relating to family planning, (*b*) to assist the central government in the development of family planning educational programs, (*c*) to develop for the national program ideas or educational methods that might be of value throughout the country and especially for East Pakistan, and (*d*) to assist in the development of methods for in-service training of medical and public health personnel. This project has published an exploratory study of ligated women, and is doing an extensive urban family growth study in Dacca in addition to some rural studies.

The activities of the MESOREP are (*a*) general family planning program through the health services, (*b*) oral pills study in a rural setting using the phases of the moon as a calendar, (*c*) extension of IUD services to areas outside the reach of health centers, using mobile clinics, and (*d*) training of doctors, paramedical personnel and family planning workers. The research done by this project is discussed later in this paper. This project has been established at Lahore in collaboration with the Johns Hopkins University.

In co-operation with the royal government of Sweden, family planning centers in some of the urban areas have been established. The main objectives of these centers are (*a*) to organize and supervise model clinics, (*b*) to train medical and paramedical personnel, and (*c*) to assist the National Research Institute in conducting research and planning in family planning communication.

To motivate the people toward family planning, all publicity media such as radios, films, billboards, and bus panels were used. Some efforts were also made to use workers of established social agencies to promote family planning among the illiterate population.

LIMITATIONS

The program during the Second Plan period was limited in scope owing to clinical approach. Out of the total budgeted expenditure of Rs. 24.7 million, a sum of Rs. 9.4 million was spent during the first four years of the plan period. Foreign aid amounting to Rs. 1.2 million for 1961–64 was obtained from the Population Council and the government of Sweden. The achievements in physical terms compared to the actual utilization of allocated funds is even lower. Whereas the establishment of family planning clinics was almost 100% of the total planned target during 1960–64, the new patients visiting the clinics were 31% of the target, training of medical and paramedical personnel 42%, distribution of condoms and foam tablets, 17% and 15%, respectively.

Though the number of family planning clinics opened during 1960–65 reached the target, the program did not result in reaching the target population. The plan to cover 1.2 million women practicing some type of contraception was not achieved. The reasons for failure were lack of motivation of people, reliance on mass media for publicity, emphasis on the urban population constituting 13% of the total population, and utilization of the existing health and medical services, which, already busy with other clinical work, could not devote sufficient time to family planning.

SELECTED RESEARCH STUDIES

Various government and private research organizations conducted research studies on the knowledge, attitude, and practice of family planning. Some studies were also made for testing efficacy and applicability of different types of contraceptives among different strata of the population. These studies aimed to help the family planning administrator make necessary changes in the program without dissipating limited resources and without losing much time. Results of some studies have already been published and others are in process.

The National Intra-uterine Contraceptive Device Study was made in the calendar year of 1963. This study was made to test the advantages and disadvantages, the efficacy and safety, of the IUD so that it might be introduced in the national program. Twelve clinics in different parts of the country were associated in this program and 1,757 insertions were made. Those women who still have the device *in situ* are regularly followed up. As this study gave very encouraging results, the IUD program was extended in 1964 as a research-cum-action program.

The demographic data of this study show that women are interested in the device in proportion to the size of the family already acquired. Their objective usually seems to be to maintain their present family size rather than to space pregnancies.

The most common reason for discontinuation of the device is bleeding. Though the bleeding is usually of minor degree, often merely spotting and not greatly prolonged, it causes great concern. In a population with high illiteracy such a situation could result in failure of the program. For this reason, another more extended study is being done on needs for training and supervision and on other problems that may arise when the program is broadened to include less selective groups of people and is under varying conditions of control and medical management.

Under the Extended Intra-uterine Contraceptive Device Study, which started at the beginning of 1964, about forty clinics are working and 5,200 insertions have been made. Paramedical personnel (lady health visitors and nurses) are also associated in this study, working under the supervision of qualified medical doctors. The initial and the follow-up forms are very simple, and the study is not yet closed. Results of this study so far are very encouraging.

The above two studies show that the IUD can be very helpful for an effective and practicable birth spacing and family limitation program. More educational and motivational programs are needed to introduce the device among the younger and lower-parity women.

A study by MESOREP shows that the IUD has the greatest promise for use in rural Pakistan. It is relatively well accepted by illiterate women, and the spontaneous word-of-mouth spread of the news about the IUD has been rapid, resulting in an exponential rate of increase of IUD recipients. Oral contraceptives, although expensive and difficult to distribute, are the best alternatives for couples who do not want the IUD or sterilization. They work well for illiterate women when synchronized with the phases of the moon.

As for preference for the IUD from among a cafeteria choice of contraceptive methods, one study population was given an opportunity to change from the IUD to oral contraceptive pills and another group to do the reverse. Approximately 50% of both shifted. This demonstrates that women are not completely satisfied with any method that is as yet available to them and that a good many will experiment with almost any new method offered.

One village study in East Pakistan finds that all respondents were unaware of contraceptive methods for limiting births. Of the respondents 47% expressed their willingness to practice family planning if they knew the appropriate methods; 18% refused in spite of widespread information stating that family planning was not prohibited in Islam.

The Comilla Pilot Project administered by the East Pakistan Academy for Rural Development advocated conventional contraceptives in those villages where government modernization programs, improvement of agricultural practices, better home sanitation, women's education, and similar programs were already underway. Information was collected regarding the contraceptive adoption behavior of the rural population and the importance of local persons as diffusion leaders and sales agents. The study showed that desire for limiting family size is commonly present. However, the people lack the necessary knowledge and often live far from sources of contraceptive supplies. Most of the female adopters are in high orders of parity and middle-aged. Their average married life span is fourteen years. Local village women could be more effective agents for family planning if there were less restriction on movement outside their homes.

The Family Planning Association of Pakistan made two surveys on knowledge, attitude, and practice regarding birth control in the two urban centers of Karachi and Lahore. The survey in Lahore was systematic and detailed. It used a 10% sample (2,087) of ever-married persons in a reasonably representative area; men were interviewed by men, and women interviewed by women. Twenty per cent of the men and 8% of the women reported that they had at some time tried to space children, largely by abstinence or condom. Forty-three per cent of the men and 14% of the women were aware that it was possible to space children with normal sexual intercourse. Additional data were also obtained on actual and desired family size and on age, literacy, length of marriage, occupation, and income.

These studies show that men more than women have knowledge about family planning methods. But one study shows that husbands think women know more about contraception than the women admitted to the interviewers. This shows a feeling of shyness more in women than in men.

The communication section in co-operation with the demographic section of the National Research Institute has conducted family planning research among a sample of the Pakistan International Airlines employees. The objectives of the survey are (a) to set up a family planning service program in an industrial setting, (b) to survey knowledge and attitude in urban population in an industrial setting, (c) to do a study of contraceptive preference and effectiveness of different contraceptive methods, and (d) to try to find the diffusion process of family planning in such a setting.

The first objective has been fulfilled fairly well. The knowledge and attitude survey was completed in October, 1964. Analysis of the data will be completed soon. A family planning program has been established with the assistance of the medical section of the National Research Institute. Information regarding the third objective is being collected at the PIA clinic.

Some of the major findings of the various research projects are summarized below.

1. The need for family limitation is commonly felt. However, on account of ignorance, nothing is done by couples to limit family size.
2. When a program starts in any area, there is initial resistance, but as it progresses, the subject of family planning becomes sufficiently open for people to approach the family planning workers.
3. Individual contacts by local family planning workers can achieve success.
4. Projection of family planning in a manner acceptable in the local culture is necessary.
5. Consent of the husband is necessary before the wife will accept use of contraceptive material.
6. Local publicity is necessary.
7. The family planning workers must be trained in techniques of motivation and education.
8. Supplies of contraceptives must be available locally, easily, and from a number of distributing points.
9. The IUD has great promise of success.
10. The medical staff, overworked in clinical duties, cannot devote sufficient time to family planning. It is, therefore, necessary to have full-time medical staffs, as well as doctors working part time.

THIRD FIVE-YEAR PLAN

In his election manifesto, President Ayub incorporated family planning as a plank of his platform. Accordingly, the government is launching a comprehensive family planning program and has budgeted Rs. 280 million for the next Five-Year Plan period (1965–70). Since the success of the family planning program is vital to attain economic viability, this program has been assigned high priority by recognizing family planning as a separate sector in the plan.

The family planning program will be a movement to make planned limited families a way of life. The increasing gap between the birth and death rates will be narrowed by controlling the number of births through birth-spacing and limiting family size.

The program incorporates all the information and knowledge that was obtained during the Second Plan period. There are at present fifteen different research projects in progress in both wings. Each project uses a different approach, a different kind of personnel, and different kinds of contraceptives. It is found that the main obstacles in the path of the family planning program are ignorance and cultural inertia. The efficacy of the program is dependent on personal motivation. Great emphasis will be laid, therefore, on educational and motivational programs among the younger women and lower-parity women to popularize conventional contraceptives as well as the IUD.

Methods of the program are to associate with it professional (both medical and social) personnel and people in influential positions, to distribute supplies of conventional contraceptives at each doorstep, and to provide facilities for mechanical contraceptives at all clinics.

The salient features of the new family planning program follow.

A Central Family Planning Council with the Health Minister as its chairman has been formed. The Commissioner of Family Planning, who is responsible for the success of the program, is the secretary of the Council. He is also joint secretary to the government of Pakistan in the newly created Division of Family Planning in the Ministry of Health, Labor, and Social Welfare. The Central Family Planning Council will be responsible for policy, co-ordination, assessment, evaluation, and research and will be generally responsible for the execution of the program. Similar organizations have been created in the provinces and up to the administrative district level. The actual implementation and execution of the program is the responsibility of the provinces. The program will be treated as an administrative activity of importance, and the district officers and elected members of the union councils and the Thana councils will be closely associated with it.

The target of the program is to prevent 5–6 million births in the next five years by reducing the annual birth rate from 50 per thousand to 40 per thousand and to reduce the growth rate to 25 per thousand. The program has been phased out from 65% to 100% coverage of the population by 1970. The plan is not aimed at special groups. Rather, it will be a mass activity covering all the fertile women in Pakistan, estimated to be 20 million.

The effective annual target is based mainly on the adoption of conventional contraceptives and the introduction of clinical contraceptives (IUD and vasectomy). The methodology employed will be to (a) motivate through individual contact; (b) motivate through group discussions at village level; (c) motivate by monetary incentive; and (d) motivate by bringing supplies and services to the doorsteps of the people. Publicity will have a predominantly local tinge and will be fully decentralized down to the village level and undertaken on an extensive scale. Mass media, including films, radio, press, and television, will be utilized.

Thirty-seven full-time urban clinics will be established in towns and cities where population is more than 100,000. Rural part-time clinics for clinical contraception have also been provided. Fifty thousand village dais will be trained for five weeks and are being recruited to organize the program in each village through motivation and distribution of conventional contraceptives and to secure large-scale adoption of the IUD.

By the end of 1970, there will be 1,400 family planning supervisors —1,000 in West Pakistan and 400 in East Pakistan. These officers will be primarily responsible for the registration of village dais, agents for distribution of contraceptives, publicity group discussions, motivation, and the popularization of the IUD. They will be in close liaison with the family planning doctors and will tour all the villages in their areas at least bimonthly. They will also supervise the work of their union council secretaries.

According to the revised program which has now been started, the following personnel will be trained: doctors and paramedical personnel, family planning supervisors and union council secretaries, village dais, and family planning assistants. A special syllabus and training manuals have also been prepared.

Transport will be provided for the supervisory staff to enable them to tour, inspect, and watch the progress of this program. The district administration has been strengthened with full-time family planning staffs. The doctors of the hospitals and clinics as well as some private practitioners are associated with the program.

The revised program for the Third Five-Year Plan envisages an outlay of Rs. 284.4 million with a foreign exchange component of Rs. 71.3 million to be spent during the next five years. Money is being provided by the government of Pakistan as a part of its development project.

There will be a nominal charge for the supply of contraceptives, which will be subsidized. The charges are Rs. 0.10 per dozen condoms or foam tablets, and one rupee for contraceptive jelly, EMKO, and diaphragms. The IUD will be inserted free.

The total cost to the government for contraceptives in the next five years will be Rs. 75 million. A monetary incentive has also been introduced to make the IUD popular. Doctors, lady health visitors, and trained midwives will be paid an IUD fee. The village dais and others who refer a case for IUD insertion will also be paid a referral fee.

EVALUATION PLAN FOR THE NEW PROGRAM

The basic objective of the national family planning program is to reduce the national birth rate. Unfortunately, like other developing countries, Pakistan has no accurate measurement of its birth rate owing to the incompleteness of vital statistics. In order to demonstrate the effectiveness of the program the technique of the sample survey will be utilized in finding the fertility rate. To determine the trend in different communities, surveys will also be utilized for measuring the extent to which various contraceptive methods are used by the population and in determining the use and effectiveness of methods commonly used. For this purpose several "short-cut" methods have been selected and will be utilized periodically in evaluation of the new family planning program.[1]

In Pakistan, only few and limited studies are available regarding the knowledge, attitude, and practice of different types of contraceptives. Many surveys will be conducted among the different communities with different geographical and socioeconomic conditions to find the effectiveness of the family planning program.

[1] A paper entitled "The Use of Statistical Guides and Measures of Effectiveness in Determining Government Policy for Influencing Fertility—Pakistan" was presented to the Second World Population Conference, Belgrade, 1965.

11

TURKEY

TURGUT METINER, M.D.
Director of Family Planning

ORIGINS AND OPERATION

Turkish policy in the early 1920's was designed to increase the population at a maximum rate to offset man-power losses incurred in wars from 1911 to 1922. This prohibited importation of contraceptives, made abortion illegal, prohibited advertising and education concerning contraceptive methods and materials, and provided financial incentives for large families.

During the period 1945–60 there was a demographic change of significant proportion in the Turkish population. From 1958 to 1962 various studies revealed that the rate of increase of population was about 3% to 3.2%, the age group 15 years and younger was 41.5%, the births per 1,000 were about 45 per year, and the death rate had been reduced to about 13 per 1,000 per year. In addition, a serious and rapid increase in illegal abortions occurred. These factors have an extremely significant effect on the ability of Turkey to modernize as outlined in the three five-year plans—1962 to 1977. Therefore a reduction in the rate of increase from 3.2% to 2.0% is an integral element of these development plans.

In early 1963, the government of Turkey requested the Population Council to send a team of experts to Turkey to analyze the demographic factors, conduct a field survey to determine the feasibility of a nationwide program of family planning, and to provide recommendations for operational guidelines and costs. This was carried out; plans were made to conduct a nationwide survey, which revealed a high interest and favorable attitude; and a technical assistance project was agreed upon between the government of Turkey and the Population Council. In late 1963 a dollar budget was provided by the Population Council and a 4.5 million lira budget was provided by the Ministry of Health. In 1964 Turkish personnel were trained in various aspects of family planning in the United States and a Population Council resident representative arrived to assist in planning, initiate local training, and assist the implementation program. Provisions have been made for additional advisers, both resident and short term, when needed.

In 1964 the Ministry of Health established a Family Planning Organization, and appointed an experienced gynecologist as director. This group supported several seminars, group discussions, and instituted the preparatory phase of planning the detailed program for a nationwide effort. Throughout this period, 1960–64, the multiplicity of factors involved were managed by farsighted and enlightened Turkish members of the Ministry of Health and the State Planning Organization.

Preceding and concurrent with these preparatory steps the government of Turkey developed a new law to provide the legal framework for funding and implementing a nationwide program of family planning. This law was passed by the Assembly and the Senate and was signed by the President on April 10, 1965.

An interesting and significant footnote to the passage of the Family Planning Law is that three ministers participated and each represented a different political party.

At the present population level (30 million) there are about 5,000,000 married women in the reproductive ages of 14–45. About 1.7 million pregnancies per year can be expected. Of these, according to current estimates, approximately 1.2 million will be full-term pregnancies. This is approximately a 3% to 3.3% rate of increase. The balance of about 500,000 will be aborted, primarily under non-medical conditions. While some abortions will always be necessary, the new law provides precise instructions and conditions for adequate medical control. Furthermore, this group of women represents obviously high-parity cases who will rapidly adopt modern family planning practices. In addition, another group of high-parity cases exists. From this analysis and other considerations we have set a goal of 500,000–600,000 family planning practitioners by the end of the calendar year 1967. Each year thereafter we anticipate an annual increase of 300,000–400,000. By 1972 our goal is 2.5 to 3.0 million women practicing family planning. At this level, about 50% of the married women in the reproductive age group will be practicing family planning. This perhaps might indicate that family planning will have been incorporated solidly into the behavior patterns of the society.

Admittedly these are large goals and to date have not been achieved elsewhere. However, there are several distinct potentials in Turkey that offer great promise. No serious religious objections are apparent. The Ministry of Education plans to emphasize human reproduction in biology courses in the middle and high schools of Turkey starting in the 1965–66 school year. It will also incorporate the social, economic, and political considerations of a high rate of population increase in the social studies courses of the middle and high schools. Prototype materials are completed and available. Another strong potential for exploitation is the Turkish armed forces. Two educational programs are envisaged: one for presently married military personnel and the other for all enlisted men just before release from active duty. Since Turkey requires two years' military duty of all able-bodied males, a considerable annual turnover of men takes place. Both the Education Ministry and the Defense Ministry are assigned functions in the new law, and we plan closely co-ordinated information programs through the Ministries of Rural Affairs and Agriculture.

It should be noted that both the high-parity and the non-married elements of the population are included in order to provide penetration in depth. Many other groups are, of course, potentials. These include men's and women's associations, labor unions, large industries, university students, government employees, and so on.

Operationally, the philosophy is to utilize existing facilities and personnel of the Ministry of Health. To these will be added a small central family planning organization which will train all the public health services in modern family planning methods, provide approximately 7,500 full-time and trained family planning field technicians, conduct scientific research in evaluating program progress and in bio-medical factors, and conduct saturation education programs on the "how" of family planning. Continuous basic training and in-service training for all participating groups and concern with adequate and timely distribution of family planning supplies are other functions. This organization has been established and is an independent department of the Ministry of Health under the direct supervision of the under-secretary. It is in the process of acquiring personnel. Its policy is designed to provide mutually reinforcing family planning services from all elements of public health. To counter the inherent weakness of "part-time" and "additional duty" implementation, full-time family planning personnel will be added to the staff of all public health activities such as maternity child health centers, maternity hospitals, and nationalized health units.

At present Turkey has about 700 OB gynecologists. Of this total 50% are located in the metropolitan areas of Istanbul, Ankara, and Izmir. Obviously the remainder is much too small a number to provide the family planning services needed in the rural areas, which contain 80% of the population and which are the primary target of the family planning program. To meet this deficiency it is planned to attract two hundred medical graduates, both men and women. They will be given about three months' intensive training in the gynecological subject matter necessary to allow competent IUD insertions. These will be the nucleus of mobile service family planning teams to take the program to the people. The mobile teams (200) will work within the present public health administrative pattern.

The contraceptives and methods offered through public health will be the IUD, oral pill, aerosol foam, condom, and rhythm. Other methods will be authorized for commercial and private medical utilization as desired. The Public Health Services will offer the IUD free and the others at cost. In the interim, direct imports of various contraceptives will be made through the government of Turkey and commercial sources. Funds are available now. The government's policy on pharmaceutical materials requires local manufacture, packaging, and distribution. It is estimated that within one year most contraceptives will qualify under this policy. Quality and purity control systems exist and will be expanded as required.

It is obvious that this program is designed to hinge on an axis of integrated rural health services. This concept includes minimizing costs by preventing duplication of administrative patterns, maximum utilization of present personnel and existing facilities, and, perhaps most important, a geometric progression of coverage and impact through mutually reinforcing elements of the Ministry of Health. As a more precise example of this philosophy, the ability of a provincial team in the nationalized health services to provide effective and complete family planning service in depth will markedly increase through assignment of full-time, trained family planning personnel with sufficient vehicles to take the total health package to the people, however remote.

The new Family Planning Law stipulates the formation of a scientific board to determine the contraceptives to be utilized in the program and to make precise recommendations for medical reasons which might justify a legal abortion. The scientific board is made up of senior doctors from the universities and the Ministry of Health. The board has approved all the traditional contraceptives and decided upon a test, using controlled research methods, of the various IUD's and oral pills. These will be tested in six clinics, which include two government maternity hospitals, one military dependents hospital, and three university hospitals. In addition to testing the safety and feasibility of IUD's and oral pills for use in Turkey, various concurrent efforts will be undertaken.

1. A 1,500-family sample in the immediate vicinity of the Ankara Maternity Hospital will be selected for close examination. Follow-up of post-partum potentials, attitudes, pretesting of a wide variety of educational techniques and materials, detailed follow-up of IUD and oral pill cases are some of the elements to be examined. The entire sample consists of rural-to-urban migrants who have low incomes and low education. This work will be directly co-ordinated by the education, demographic, and bio-medical divisions of the Central Family Planning Organization.

2. Constant and close liaison with the six clinics will be a major concern of the Central Family Planning Organization staff. The goal is to ensure uniformity of operation to the extent possible, and to provide educational, demographic, bio-medical, and logistical support.

3. Special emphasis will be placed on training the employees at all levels in the Ministry of Health. The concept is to have a trained base from which to expand into a nationwide family planning operation, when the research and test phase of IUD's and oral pills are completed. Also, it is necessary to have this pretrained base ready for action when the local manufacture or import of traditional male and female contraceptives reaches the stage of nationwide distribution.

4. It can be seen that Turkey plans a phased introduction of family planning following a step-by-step procedure. To the extent possible we hope to predicate each new step on careful evaluation of preceding steps. The philosophy is to be flexible so that changes may occur smoothly as scientific scrutiny indicates a need.

5. Advanced planning will be a continuous process during the early phases. Precise descriptions of some of the future action steps cannot be given at this time. However, certain generalities can be outlined. We shall use mass media to a maximum degree, but its use will be closely co-ordinated with all other methods of education. Use of a family planning method is entirely voluntary, and this policy will be continually emphasized. Every type of contraceptive will be offered. The private medical sector of Turkey will certainly be encouraged to participate, and plans are being formulated to provide sufficient monetary inducement to attract this group.

MAJOR ACHIEVEMENTS

Turkey is at the threshold of the action program. Evaluation of past results in terms of action-program elements is therefore not possible. Some observation may be offered on obstacles that have been largely surmounted. Since there has been a period of more than thirty years without a legally established family planning activity, there still is an almost total lack of knowledge of the subject at every level. Especially was this apparent in consideration of the broad scope of family planning potential. Economic development, social pressures, political stability, and mother and child health were all common terms used by the intellectual and educated groups, but they have been looked upon as separate entities. For example, in the past several years, Turkey has had above average harvests but has found it necessary to continue to import wheat and other foods. Also, a recent study indicated a rising curve of juvenile delinquency. Insufficient and substandard housing is becoming more and more serious as urban migration continues. A much longer list could be compiled. One difficulty was in disseminating the knowledge that these multiple-problem areas were related to a very high rate of increase in the population. In addition, there was a segment of influential people who considered a rapidly increasing population to be highly desirable. This was predicated on the principle that strength lies in numbers, and the idea was fortified by Mustafa Kemal Atatürk's 1925 pronouncement that Turkey should grow to 60,000,000 as rapidly as possible. Another element in this mixture of viewpoints was the rapid increase in illegal abortion. An estimated 500,000 abortions per year, or about one-third of the annual pregnancies, was a problem paramount in the minds of the medical fraternity. Since most of these abortions were done under non-medical conditions, the incidence of female deaths was very high. The additional load resulting from serious infection and other problems caused by illegal and non-medical abortion was and is a considerable overload on hospital and medical facilities. Translated into money this additional burden assumes major proportions.

The passage of a suitable law to repeal the prior prohibitive legislation and to provide a framework for a nationwide program was a long process. It was necessary to bring out the true facts to the legislators and the influential people concerned with a major policy change of this magnitude. This effort was successful, but it was not an easy or simple task. No single person was responsible. In fact, a considerable number of enlightened and dedicated people from within the Ministry of Health, from the private medical fraternity, and the State Planning Organization were responsible. Perhaps the most important lesson to be learned is the great amount of hard work, based on very careful planning, that is needed to accomplish the task. Another lesson that seems most valid is the need for people outside government circles to participate in order for legislators to have complete authentication of the facts presented. Finally, we in Turkey are convinced of the primary need for a detailed but flexible legal framework as a basis for any nationwide program of family planning.

We think the inclusion of other government agencies in addition to the Ministry of Health in the basic law represents an innovation in national family planning legislation.

If a number of agencies are involved on a co-ordinated basis, the chances of success are considerably enhanced. Of course, the mere inclusion in the wording of a law does not guarantee wholehearted participation from agencies like the Ministries of Defense, Agriculture, Education, and Rural Affairs, to mention a few. But the inclusion does provide a very real reason for these agencies to consider carefully the scope of their logical participation and gives them the legal support on which to act. It seems to me these are the main points of our program which may be useful to other countries faced with the complex problems inherent in establishing nationwide family planning programs.

MAJOR UNSOLVED PROBLEMS

Any new family planning program has many problems. Some problems can be anticipated, others have not yet appeared, and some may never be completely solved. We do have administrative bottlenecks which, at times, seem to be major problems. Customs problems are always present, as are the normal problems associated with starting a new organization with inadequate pay scales. Training of personnel so as to upgrade them to the necessary level of competency will be a continuous problem. Distribution of supplies in sufficient depth to provide ready availability to even the most remote areas will no doubt be difficult. Our educational and informational problem is formidable in a country where only a handful of people are presently adequately informed. This problem must be surmounted at every level of the society and via many co-ordinated channels. But we are confident about the future. We look forward to meeting these problems and solving them to the satisfaction of the Turkish people.

12

UNITED ARAB REPUBLIC

HASAN M. HUSEIN
Dean, Institute of Statistics, Cairo University
Vice-Chairman, Egyptian Association for Population Studies

The present-century censuses of population of the UAR shown in Table 1 indicate continuous growth at an increasing annual rate. These findings are also supported by the annual rate of natural increase as calculated from vital statistics. Whereas the annual birth rate wavered between 40 and 45 per thousand during the course of this century, the annual death rate dropped from about 28 per thousand in the early decades to about 18 and fewer per thousand after 1945. As can be seen from Table 1, the population doubled between 1917 and 1960, i.e., in forty-three years. At the present rate of increase it would double again in less than thirty years. On the other hand the area of cultivable land has been almost constant, so that per capita share of land has dropped sharply to about half its value at the beginning of the century.

Egyptian economists and students of humanities have been aware of this unfavorable development since the early 1930's and some attempt was made to alert the authorities to these facts. Some enlightened individuals started planning their families. This was made feasible by the fact that condoms were always available in pharmacies. Diaphragms and dutch caps came later after a few progressive gynecologists started giving service in this field, including fitting rings to married women whose husbands consented. Historically women have always been known to use some non-medical contraceptives, such as foreign bodies inserted in their uteri, and to resort to illegal induced abortion, practices that occurred in rural as well as urban areas of the country.

It was not until the new government took over after the 1952 revolution, however, that the authorities began to respond seriously to the

dangers of rapid population growth. The new government immediately established two planning organizations. The first was concerned with the economic development of the country, while the
second was concerned with its social development. The latter set up
in 1953 a high-level commission to study population problems in
Egypt. This organization, the National Committee for Population
Problems, was presided over by the Minister of Social Affairs and
included the Ministers of Agriculture, Education, and Health, the
Deputy Minister of Finance, and very high caliber professors of gynecology, economics, demography, sociology, and statistics. This committee undertook research work in the demographic and other related
aspects of the population of the country with the objective of reaching any necessary definite recommendations on population policy.

TABLE 1

POPULATION OF THE UAR

Year	Population (1,000)	Average Annual Increase from Preceding Date (per cent)
1907............	11,287	....
1917............	12,751	1.3
1927............	14,218	1.1
1937............	15,933	1.2
1947............	19,022	1.9
1960............	26,085	2.7

Analytical studies comparing economic and population growth
showed an unfavorable rate in the first half of this century and gave
no encouraging indications for the near future. Results of demographic
studies clearly showed the responsible authorities the high rate at
which the population was increasing. From the very beginning it was
expected that birth control might have to be recommended as one of
the solutions. For this reason the committee immediately started planning national studies on attitudes toward birth control. Studies were
also planned to evaluate the applicability, acceptability, and efficiency
of modern methods. To provide opportunities for field studies in these
matters family planning clinics had to be established.

EARLY FAMILY PLANNING CLINICS

Toward the end of the year 1955 the National Committee for
Population Problems established eight family planning clinics. Four
of these clinics were in Cairo, the capital, with a population now
approximately 4 million, and the other four in Alexandria with a popu-

lation of approximately 2 million, the next largest city. The clinics were attached to non-governmental voluntary organizations working in the field of social service and interested in family welfare as a whole. Most of these organizations were run by boards formed mostly of women dedicated to public service. Among these were, prominently, the Mabarra Association and the Red Crescent Association, both of which run hospitals and outpatient clinics; also the Federation of Women and the Health Improvement Women's Association. One of the first clinics started in Cairo was attached to the Moslem Women's Association purposely as a practical illustration that Islam has no genuine opposition to enlightened and well-founded contraceptive activities.

EGYPTIAN ASSOCIATION FOR POPULATION STUDIES

In 1957, the National Committee for Population Problems was transferred to a non-governmental organization called "The Egyptian Association for Population Studies." The financing of the Association remained governmental, through aid from the Ministry of Social Affairs. The Association retained the responsibilities of the National Committee and followed the same procedures. These and subsequent clinics belonged to the Association. The role of each chosen organization was to single out at least two rooms in its premises, three afternoons each week, for the work of the clinic—one room for receiving the cases and the other for treating them. Competent members of the organization staff are called on for help and paid by the National Committee.

Each clinic is staffed by a physician, a nurse, a social worker, a clerk, and an odd-job man, chosen very carefully from government employees in the vicinity. Staff members are always given strong specific practical training before receiving their jobs. Almost all the doctors and nurses have been chosen from maternal and child health centers and are trained by doctors with long experience in family planning. They also receive social and demographic lectures to help them appreciate their role in a wider sense than just the medical aspect. The social workers are all females chosen from qualified workers involved in group guidance and assistance and then given specific training in interviewing cases and filling out forms about each case. They are also trained to follow up cases, to reduce drop-outs to a minimum, and to get complete information on the reaction to the treatment of each case. The clerks also receive specific training in keeping books and records in good order and making periodic statistical summaries of the activities of the clinic.

At the beginning this program was aimed toward high-parity

women or those with health indications in urban areas or women belonging to industrial groups. Clinics were instructed to give contraceptive service only to those satisfying three requisites: consent of both husband and wife, existence of at least three living children, and presence of strong health, social, or economic justifications. In time the service spread to semi-urban and then rural areas with less strict insistence on the requisites.

Besides dealing with contraception, the centers are also responsible for treating sub-fertility. This was correctly assumed useful in overcoming any sense of objection among the women toward visiting the centers, and in fact it acted as an inducement.

The Charter of the Republic announced by the President in 1962 included references to the scientific work conducted by competent

TABLE 2

NUMBER OF CLINICS FUNCTIONING EACH YEAR

Year	Urban	Rural	Total
1955.........	8	....	8
1956.........	12	....	12
1957.........	12	6	18
1958.........	12	12	24
1959.........	13	12	25
1960.........	13	13	26
1961.........	14	13	27
1962.........	14	14	28
1963.........	20	14	34
1964.........	24	14	38
1965.........	49	49	98

organizations in the field of population growth and, recognizing the possibility of the existence of a population problem, called on every citizen to consider planning his family. This enhanced the work of the Association and invited acceleration of its activities. Since then, no limitations have been set on the administration of contraceptive services to those who applied for them.

Before the charter, the centers of the Association were intended less to give service than to be fields for experimentation and sources of data and information. After the charter the centers received strong support both quantitatively and qualitatively to provide real service. Table 2 gives the numbers of family planning clinics of this Association functioning each year.

The only method used by the Association in the early stages to inform women about these clinics was by word of mouth in maternal and child health centers advising women of the existence of the clinics and their addresses. Occasionally there were public lectures on the subject, articles in the papers and some hints in other mass media such as radio or television. The partial success of these methods of attraction can be inferred from Table 3, giving numbers of new cases annually. The increased frequency and intensity of publicity that followed the reference to population and family planning in the Charter of 1962 obviously swelled the number of new clinic cases. It would be a mistake, however, to think that all opposition had disappeared.

STATISTICAL FINDINGS AND CURRENT OPERATIONS

One of the main tasks of the clinics was to assess the applicability, acceptability, and success of the various contraceptive devices by the different communities in the UAR. For this reason the clinics prescribe

TABLE 3

ANNUAL NUMBER OF NEW CASES IN URBAN BIRTH
CONTROL CLINICS SINCE 1955

Year	Number of Cases	Year	Number of Cases
1956	4,811	1961	3,506
1957	5,929	1962	4,997
1958	4,150	1963	4,880
1959	3,421	1964	13,390
1960	3,704		

all recognized medical devices except abortion and sterilization. These clinics are also participating in scientific experiments on new devices.

Past experience in these clinics yields the following results:

Vaginal diaphragm and jelly (VD and J).—This method, the most widely used in the clinics, meets with the highest success and least complaints. It is mostly used by higher-class women, whereas women of lower class prefer foam tablets because of their simplicity. A follow-up study of 474 women using VD and J in two Cairo clinics showed that among 398 who persevered for a total period of 3,206 menstrual cycles, 43 conceptions took place. This is a failure rate of 16 per 100 woman-years, a very encouraging result.

Vaginal foam tablets (VFT).—In spite of its lower rate of success than the diaphragm and jelly, this method has high demand because of its simplicity of use. It is especially favored by illiterate women, particularly in rural areas.

Preceptine jelly and Delfin cream with applicators (PJ and DC).—This method was first used by clinics of the Association on a wide basis in 1962. Its simplicity led to immediate strong acceptance. A follow-up study of 398 women in two Cairo clinics using this method for 2,824 menstrual cycles showed that 60 conceptions took place. This means a failure of 25.5 per 100 woman-years, a rate less successful than the previous two methods.

Oral contraceptive pills (OCP).—The use of these pills started recently in one clinic only on an experimental basis under the supervision of a group of professors of gynecology from Cairo University and the Association. No final results have been determined yet, especially concerning side effects; but so far the method has wide acceptability and high success.

Intra-uterine contraceptive devices (IUD's).—These were first introduced in four clinics at the beginning of August, 1964. Two hundred cases were treated in the first three months with encouraging results.

TABLE 4

RESULTS OF EXPERIENCE IN THE ASSOCIATION'S CLINICS

Method Used	Distribution of Women by Method Used (per cent)	Acceptance by Those to Whom Method Was Recommended (per cent)	Those Using Method and Going 12 Months with No Pregnancy (per cent)
VD and J............	20	90	90
VFT..............	30	90	85.
PJ or DC..........	15	85	80
OCP..............	20	80	98
IUD..............	15	95	98
	100		

Table 4 summarizes the experience up to the present in the Association's clinics in the use of the different methods.

It is well understood that however efficient and successful the methods are from a clinical point of view, decisive results are impossible without an overwhelmingly widespread belief in and acceptance of the birth control policy. To bring this about, mass media are now being employed to spread the idea of family planning and to increase awareness among the people of the great economic and social disadvantages to the family and the nation of the current high rate of population growth. Increasing education and a rise in the level of living should greatly facilitate this task.

In their early days the Association's clinics distributed contraceptives free of charge. Later it was decided to change this policy to allow the clinics to serve greater numbers of applicants within the limited means of the Association. Contraceptives are now sold mainly at cost price, while a substantial proportion is given free or sold at half price to those who need it most and cannot afford the full price.

It was decided in June, 1965, that, as of July 1, all devices should be dispensed in the clinics at a nominal price of 3 piasters each (about 7 American cents). This is in conformity with the policy followed in the health units of the government where patients receive all medicines either free or at this nominal charge of 3 piasters each.

In November, 1962, an experiment in family planning was started in Alexandria by the very capable woman Director General of Social Affairs, who believes adamantly in the necessity for a population policy. With the help of the professor of gynecology in Alexandria University, she started a limited number of family planning clinics in popular housing communities. Consisting of families coming originally from very different geographical origins, these communities vary greatly in educational, social, and economic status.

Seventeen per cent of the families were chosen for the experiment—excluding women past fertile age, divorced, separated, or widowed, sterile or newly married, as well as families with less than three children. The only contraceptive used in this experiment was the oral pill, which was supplied gratis for the experiment by some European producers and was thus distributed free to the cases. Recently a sizable number of intra-uterine devices has also been given to the director for the sake of the experiment. The general consensus is that this experiment has been handled very efficiently and thus proved a success.

Early in 1964 the Cairo Women's Club also started to show practical interest in this field. Under the able guidance of its chairman, the club first established two family planning clinics in rural areas, one in Upper Egypt and one in Lower Egypt. Her efforts have since led to the formation of the Joint Committee on Family Planning by three women's social organizations. Professors of gynecology from Cairo and Heliopolis universities have volunteered their services to the Joint Committee, and the Committee has started to receive sizable numbers of contraceptives as gifts for the project.

The Joint Committee is taking great interest in developing means of disseminating information. Its main contraceptives are the oral pills and the intra-uterine devices, which they supply to their cases free of charge. The number of clinics now operating under the Joint Committee is over ten and soon will be nearer twenty.

DEVELOPMENTS FOR THE FUTURE

Early in 1965 the Ministry of Public Health, on a recommendation by the Egyptian Association for Population Studies, started including family planning service in their maternal and child health centers. By the end of May about forty such centers were providing this service, about equally divided between urban and rural areas. During the first half of June six more MCH centers in Cairo were added. These centers are considered ideal for this service because of the availability of an experienced medical staff and the presence of post-partum women. In these centers all kinds of contraceptives are prescribed and distributed free of charge.

At present a big medical and social service project is being designed by the departments of gynecology and public health of Cairo University with the assistance of the Ford Foundation in the Governorate of Giza, the first governorate south of Cairo. Plans are to include family planning experiments. Another project is being designed by the Institute of Statistical Research and Studies of Cairo University with the help of the Population Council of New York to carry out a follow-up study on the use of intra-uterine devices on a nationwide basis.

The Parliament, at present, is taking at least as deep an interest in the subject as the government. It is considering the advisability of forming a general organization of some sort to co-ordinate all these enthusiastic but detached efforts. Although all the above-mentioned organizations dealing with family planning work in close contact with the Egyptian Association for Population Studies, no complete co-ordination exists. It is now believed that this Association should be given the responsibility and authority to co-ordinate present efforts and to provide the necessary scientific research in this field.

In the meantime it is hoped that about half a million Egyptian pounds can be allocated in the budget this year for the establishment of at least three hundred new family planning clinics to serve the rural areas, besides a few more for urban areas. This is considered the first stage of a longer-range plan to provide family planning service.

13

TUNISIA

AMOR DALY, M.D.
Le Sous-Directeur Medical
Ministry of Public Health and Social Affairs

Some time before the start of the experimental program in family planning in Tunisia, the Tunisian government had been concerned about the rapid growth of population and the imbalance between this rate of growth and the national income. In order to control the problem, the government undertook various administrative measures. Thus, a law passed on January 9, 1961, removed all restrictions on contraception and permitted the importation and sale of contraceptives to the public. In addition, a decree in December, 1960, limited the family allowance granted to commercial and industrial workers to four children only. These measures constituted a complete change from the pro-natalist policy which existed in Tunisia from the time of the Protectorate and which had been based on the French pro-natalist policy.

The measures prohibiting polygamy and postponing the age of marriage should also be considered as favoring a policy of limiting population growth.

Finally, the problem has been clearly stated in the first national Plan of Economic and Social Development.

This report contains a chapter on demographic problems and points out the fact that demographic growth must be slowed down in order to achieve the economic and social objectives of the plan. However, in the Ten-Year Perspectives (1962–71) and the Three-Year Plan, a decrease in population growth is anticipated (from 2.3% to 1.7%) due only to the economic development of the country and improved education, urban development, and industrialization.

151

THE PROGRAM

At that time (1962), meetings between the Ministry of Health and Social Affairs and representatives of the Ford Foundation and the Population Council took place. This was the first time that family planning problems were discussed officially in Tunisia and that direct action was envisaged in this area.

The discussions led to an agreement for co-operation between both organizations and the Tunisian government on a two-year experimental family planning program. Owing to our ignorance concerning these problems, this was only a modest and cautious trial.

The program approved in May, 1963, is divided into three main phases: information and preparation phase, operational phase, and evaluation at the conclusion of the program.

The information and preparation phase was facilitated by the effective co-operation of the Population Council, which through its family planning activities throughout the world and its direct co-operation with such programs in America and Asia, enabled a Tunisian delegation composed of doctors, midwives, and social workers to make a six-week study trip through the United States, Japan, and Pakistan during September–October, 1963. The reception given to the Tunisian delegation by the Population Council representatives in those countries made this an agreeable and instructive trip. By studying many family planning programs in the countries they visited and by discussion with the highest officials in this field, the Tunisian delegation was able to study many aspects of a problem which was absolutely unknown to them before.

A few months later, a four-week seminar on family planning was organized in Tunis with the assistance of consultants invited by the Population Council. Doctors, midwives, health educators, and representatives of national organizations in charge of the program took part in this seminar.

The participation of women's organizations, the political party, and the unions was of utmost importance for the operational phase to follow.

The seminar included the following subjects: demography, physiology of reproduction, and contraceptive methods. Considerable attention was given to health education and communications methods.

At the same time, the radio and the press aided the seminar by spreading information about the family planning programs studied by the Tunisian delegation during its trip. Incidentally, it should be noted that the impact of the press is limited because of the high adult illiteracy rate. The radio, on the other hand, reaches all classes of society throughout the country. It is because of the radio that family planning has become a subject of interest in rural and urban areas, in women's circles, and in the social divisions of the political party.

It is also noteworthy to point out the significant part played by political leaders, especially the President. During an important speech devoted to family planning problems, he stated:

We cannot help being apprehensive of the human tide which is rising implacably with a speed far beyond the increase in the essentials of life. What is the use of increasing our agricultural production, our raw materials ... if the population keeps increasing in an uncontrolled and maddening fashion? We would have achieved nothing, for we would find ourselves, despite all our efforts, at a level lower than our present one. Humanity, which through reason has dominated nature and progressively vanquished illness, which has invented the tool and has transformed the face of the world, humanity can restrain itself and decrease the rate of procreation.

In order to understand how the population was quickly and easily informed and its support obtained, it is important to note that Tunisia is a small country with no high mountains and good and numerous roads. Furthermore, the administrative and political organization of the country enables the population to respond quickly to its leaders in such fields as rural development, campaigns against infectious diseases, and family planning problems.

The operational phase consisted of a sample survey and the opening of family planning services in twelve maternal and child health centers. These centers were divided among urban and semirural areas and were situated throughout differing regions of the country. This economic and demographic variation attempted to provide services to characteristic samples of the whole country.

The survey was undertaken before the beginning of the clinical work by the social and health personnel attached to the family planning program and was done under the direction of Professor Jean Morsa of the Free University of Brussels (see his paper, chap. 47 in this volume.) The main objective of the survey was to inform the population surrounding the centers and to provide a basis of comparison for future program evaluation. The analysis of the survey is not yet complete.

The clinical work started in June, 1964; condoms, vaginal jellies, and aerosols were made available to the public, while intra-uterine and oral contraceptives were provided to large hospitals for experimental use. Because of widespread interest by the public, the administration decided to increase the family planning services and to make widely available intra-uterine devices long before the end of the two-year experimental period. Centers specializing in the insertion of IUD's have been started in all hospital gynecology services and in a few well-equipped family planning centers.

For this purpose, two conferences on intra-uterine contraception were held in December, 1964, and April, 1965, in order to train gynecologists and surgeons. These conferences were directed by the specialists at the hospitals where these methods were first used experimentally. During these conferences there were discussions concerning the results of experiments and clinical demonstrations in the hospitals. At the end of each conference, participants were asked to experiment with intra-uterine contraception in their own services and were supplied with IUD's. Fifteen centers for the insertion of IUD's were thus created, twelve of which were in the main hospitals. Some of the hospital personnel went as far as to create a mobile service to insert IUD's in the surrounding regional health stations. During the month of March, 1965, one regional hospital made 875 insertions. The use of this contraceptive method presents numerous advantages but raises some problems of co-ordination which are sometimes very delicate.

Although the family planning program is a governmental one, family planning services are currently offered by doctors for their private clients, as permitted by the law allowing importation and sale of contraceptives. In order to acquaint private doctors with modern contraceptive methods, they have been invited to participate in the various conferences organized by the family planning program administration. But the spread of this private activity cannot be controlled.

Furthermore, private initiative in family planning is developing. A national association of doctors, politicians, and social workers will be created shortly.

The experimental family planning program of Tunisia is administered directly by the official responsible for medical services, under the authority of the Ministry of Health. This facilitates the integration of the program into the health services.

In Tunisia, the activities of the various public services are closely meshed. The family planning program works in close collaboration with the Ministry of Planning, the Department of Statistics, and the Ministry of Justice in matters concerning the reform of statutes.

All the personnel actively involved in the program are health employees, trained and recruited according to the standards of the government health service; but before working in the framework of the family planning program the personnel receive special training, including theoretical and practical aspects, which vary for the different categories of personnel.

Doctors are familiarized with family planning through the above-mentioned conferences. The midwives, who are the senior personnel in the family planning services, undergo this training in a demonstration maternal and child health center which has a family planning service.

In this center, all the midwives who have finished their basic midwifery course are obliged to undergo a three-month complementary training period in the family planning clinic of the center, and in a hospital gynecology service. This training is under the direction of a midwife and a gynecologist experienced in family planning.

At the end of this training period, the midwife is authorized to give consultations in family planning. However, she can give advice only on contraception and distribute traditional contraceptives (condoms, vaginal jelly, etc.). She cannot prescribe oral contraception or insert IUD's. In both cases she can only direct the patients to the doctor at the clinic or hospital and keep records.

The whole population is eligible for family planning services. However, in this limited experimental project only the education program reaches all regions of the country.

The family planning clinics, whose number is still limited, receive only married women regardless of the number of children and class of society. The mother is therefore free to adopt family planning to limit childbirth or to space her children. In general, most women coming to the family planning clinics already have large numbers of children and are from the poorest classes. Women from higher socio-economic levels prefer to go to their private doctors.

Two clinics are reserved for special groups: The National Guard Clinic and the Social Security Clinic for industrial and commercial workers. For technical reasons, the program has not yet attempted to reach men with male contraceptives, though men have been given appropriate information.

Both the urban and rural populations benefit from family planning, as indicated by the geographical situation of the clinics.

The program is financed by the state budget and a grant from the Ford Foundation. The total cost for the two years is $370,000. This budget does not include the contribution of hospitals for IUD services, which cannot be estimated separately.

Family planning services include information on family planning and the provision of the chosen contraceptive method. Contraceptive methods used in the program are condoms, vaginal jellies, vaginal aerosols, oral contraceptives, intra-uterine devices, and surgical sterilization of multiparae. The Lippes loop and the Margulies spiral are the intra-uterine devices available. However, the loop is the most widely used. Family planning service as well as the contraceptives are free to all classes of the population.

The accounting for all distributed contraceptive products is similar to accounting for drugs at all public health services. In the system, a card is used for each product. Amounts received and dispersed are recorded. Every week a balance of the medical cards is made. Actually, a central accounting service receives monthly reports sent by clinics. But later, this accounting system will be decentralized and taken over by the pharmacy of the regional hospital following the system presently used for drugs.

EVALUATION OF RESULTS

This experimental program has not yet been completed. Activities started only one and a half years ago, and the clinical program has been underway only one year. It is premature therefore to give a complete evaluation of the results concerning social, demographic, and clinical aspects of the program. However, we can give some fragmentary impressions of the evolution of the program, the attitudes of the population toward family planning and contraceptive methods used, and some suggestions for future action.

It is important to note at the outset that in Tunisia conditions for developing a family planning program are most favorable. These conditions are of a demographic, psychological, and economic nature.

Psychologically, there is no religious opposition to contraception in Tunisia. Islam is not represented by a clergy and the last manifestations of Maraboutism go back forty years.

The religious laws are combined with civil law and are applied by a modern legal system. Tunisian lawmakers have shown considerable interest in limiting population growth. They even chose this topic for the opening speech of the legal year in 1963. The only protest against contraception was made by the medical profession, motivated by caution and skepticism concerning certain methods of contraception. However, these objections are disappearing as doctors become more familiar with contraceptive techniques.

The protest from the medical profession is due to the fact that it has been trained in France, where contraceptive literature and methods are not yet well known. On the other hand, English literature on this subject is not well known because of the language barrier. This should be an area of interest to international family planning organizations. The exchange of information between countries in the two or three languages most widely used should be facilitated.

Among the favorable conditions for developing a family planning program are the ethnic and linguistic homogeneity of the population, the spread of education to include almost 80% of the school-age children, urban development, and the policy of economic planning.

These special conditions justify the rapid expansion of the program. In all areas where family planning services are well underway, public attendance is excellent. The total number of women who adopted family planning from June, 1964, to May 31, 1965, was 14,112. Consultations totaled 27,898. Of the 14,112 women registered, 7,701 chose intra-uterine devices and therefore only one visit was needed. The rapid extension of the program is reflected in Table 1.

Two examples show how rapidly the program can be expanded throughout the country if the proper contraceptive device is chosen and all the necessary means of action made available.

TABLE 1

EXPANSION OF TUNISIAN FAMILY PLANNING PROGRAM

Date	First Visits	IUD's Inserted	Total Number of Family Planning Centers	Number of Centers Reporting IUD Insertions
1964				
June..........	375	11	6	1
July..........	764	103	9	2
August........	1,175	147	11	3
September......	984	167	10	3
October........	972	106	10	5
November......	735	258	10	6
December......	772	362	11	7
1965				
January........	653	417	13	11
February.......	757	663	14	12
March.........	2,561	2,053	17	13
April..........	2,030	1,555	19	15
May..........	2,334	1,859	21	19
Total.........	14,112	7,701	....	....

Two centers for inserting the loops have been created recently in two large rural regions, Le Kef and Beja. In Beja, a family planning center using traditional methods had been active since the beginning of the program. But at Le Kef, only some surgical sterilizations had been performed. In January in Beja and in February in Le Kef, the hospital staff surgeons started to insert loops on request.

Local organizations and government workers disseminated information to the public. At Le Kef, the surgeon works only at the hospital, but at Beja working sessions are organized in the rural dispensaries which are used by some 6,000 people. Table 2 shows the number of insertions made each month in each one of these centers from January to May, 1965.

Concerning the families who adopted family planning it has been stated that most of them have large families. The analysis of the records in one urban family planning center demonstrates the acceptance of contraception by the number of living children in the family (Table 3).

Intra-uterine contraception already seems to be the most popular method and the one best accepted by the medical profession. Among

TABLE 2

IUD INSERTIONS

	January	February	March	April	May
Beja.............	135	229	857	685	659
Le Kef...........	work not started	24	581	227	432

TABLE 3

WOMEN ACCEPTING CONTRACEPTIVES, BY
NUMBER OF LIVING CHILDREN

Number of Children	Traditional Contraceptives	IUD's
1................	37	3
2................	77	27
3................	113	32
4................	127	78
5................	90	45
6................	77	48
7................	36	35
8................	16	28
9................	7	13
10................	2	3
11................	1	1
12................	2	2
Total...........	585	315

the different devices the loop is most widely used. It is therefore impossible to give comparative results for the loop and the coil.

GENERAL CONCLUSIONS

At the most, this program furnishes some information on the methods of formulation for a family planning program, giving due consideration to the existing social structure and methods of utilizing existing institutions.

In the area of motivation, although technical means are often modest or non-existent, it is possible to mobilize various organizations and use them effectively by giving them general information on the subject. The Beja and Le Kef experiences are significant examples. No matter what kind of organization is involved, political parties, unions, co-operatives, or local groups can provide information via mass media or through local meetings.

In the organization and execution of the program, it appears that integration of family planning into the existing health services is an effective solution for Tunisia. Family planning is considered an aspect of preventive medicine, and therefore should not be separated technically or administratively from such programs as vaccination, for example. However, it is difficult to have medical and paramedical personnel, who have received a general medical education, do nothing

TABLE 4

CONTRACEPTIVE METHODS CHOSEN IN BEJA, 1964–65

Month	Number of Consultations	Traditional Methods Chosen	IUD's Chosen
October.........	28	17	0
November........	50	0	50
December.........	103	2	80
January..........	135	0	135
February.........	229	0	229

but family planning. This is especially true in a developing country where so much illness exists and where so many health services are needed.

It is also well known that even a person who strongly desires family planning services prefers to be discreet on the subject. A medical office or a health center assures her that her privacy is well guarded. For all these reasons, an integrated system appears to be preferable to an autonomous family planning organization.

A third lesson is that the continuity of family planning services and the availability of supplies are essential to the success of the program.

Analysis of the results in the various family planning centers shows that failure is almost always due to technical breakdown in the supply system or to shortages of personnel.

Finally, in developing countries the most effective contraceptive method is the one which requires as little action as possible on the part of the patient. In fact, the public in Beja completely abandoned the traditional contraceptive methods as soon as IUD services became available, as indicated in Table 4.

FUTURE PERSPECTIVES

In Tunisia, demographic growth is so rapid that it well may endanger the social and economic development of the country. It is therefore important that a nationwide family planning program be created in order to cope with this problem.

The demographic situation in Tunisia is demonstrated by the following data for 1964:

Crude birth rate—46 per 1,000 population
Crude death rate—23 per 1,000 population
Rate of population increase—2.3%
Population 0–19 years old—2,270,000 (more than 50% of the total population)
Female population 20–40 years—650,000
Male population 19–65 years—1,000,000

These data show that each male Tunisian of productive age has four people to feed (female employment is still very small in Tunisia). Almost half of the population is so young as to be non-productive and hence an economic, health, and educational burden on the country's resources. One woman out of three in the reproductive age has a child every year (this does not include women under 20 and over 40).

Economic planners in the first Three-Year Plan (1961–64) estimated that the rate of demographic growth would decrease from 2.3% to 1.7% between 1962 and 1971, because of economic and social development and a higher standard of living. However, the number of births registered during 1964 (206,000), at the end of the Three-Year Plan indicate that there has been no decrease. On the other hand, the death rate will go on decreasing owing to the steady improvement of public health services. It is thus necessary to change the birth rate by positive action if the plan's objectives are to be reached. Of all the methods employed in the experimental family planning program, the intra-uterine device seems to be the best method for a nationwide program. Such a plan is envisaged in the framework of the second social and economic development plan (1965–68).

A possible objective is to reduce the birth rate by 6% during this period. In terms of the female population and the number of insertions of intra-uterine devices, this means approximately 120,000 insertions would have to be performed in four years. The average number of insertions per year would be 30,000, and the program could be carried out by thirteen family planning teams working in the regional hospitals of the republic.

Each family planning team will include a gynecologist, a midwife, a medical-social assistant, and a chauffeur. The team will work full time in the regional hospital and will visit all the health centers in the region, performing IUD insertions according to a prearranged program. This mobile activity requires the transportation of the necessary equipment prepared in advance and ready to use. In certain cases it would be necessary to have complete mobile clinics in order to reach isolated populations who do not have a proper health center available. The local health center would take care of the follow-up examinations of the women wearing intra-uterine devices.

It is understood that doctors and health workers will require special training to assure that services of a high level are maintained. In addition, the Four-Year Plan (1965–68) envisages the creation of a national family planning research center to work in conjunction with the short-term action program outlined above. It will also study other contraceptive methods and their use on a large scale, and will conduct research on new techniques appropriate to the needs of the country in the light of scientific progress.

14

AFRICA

J. C. CALDWELL
Demographic Department
The Australian National University

THE DEMOGRAPHIC POSITION

In mid-1964 Africa's population was estimated to be 303 million or about one-eleventh of the human race. Approximately one-third of all Africans live in the northern part of the continent, where the crude birth and death rates were thought to average around 45 and 22 per thousand, respectively. The rest live south of the Sahara in tropical and southern Africa. There birth and death rates varied rather widely, but were believed to average about 47 and 24 per thousand, respectively.

Thus throughout the continent the rate of natural increase was estimated to be 2.3% and rising. It may have been higher, for in many countries revised estimates of birth rates have usually tended upward. Population density was the lowest of all the continents, averaging only 26 persons per square mile. From this fact some African political leaders conclude that they have little to fear from continued rapid population growth. This conclusion is almost certainly wrong. The low density of settlement is merely a reflection of limited agricultural potential, which modern technology has not as yet affected very strikingly. Africa is the driest of all major continents and contains little in the way of broad, fertile lowlands.

In this paper major attention will be paid to all of the continent except the United Arab Republic and Tunisia, which are treated separately in this volume. As the latter two countries have about 33 million inhabitants altogether, this study is confined to the 270 million who live in the other fifty countries and territories of Africa.

GOVERNMENTAL POPULATION POLICIES

In modern Africa a knowledge of governmental population policies is fundamental to any understanding of family planning programs. The relevance of government springs partly from the kinds of political philosophy that have characterized twentieth-century independence movements but partly also from the sheer poverty of the populace, which has meant in many countries that only governments have enough money to undertake such tasks as the employment of doctors, the establishment of hospitals or family planning clinics, and even the purchase of contraceptives. Technical aid also increases the importance of governments, since they are necessarily the main channel through which aid flows into their countries.

During the past three years I have been laying the foundations of a study of governmental population policies in all countries of Africa, relying mainly on published governmental statements, articles in the press, parliamentary records, and interviews with officials. More recently this has been supplemented by an attempt to obtain high-level statements on population policies from all governments. The first approaches to the governments have been through the heads of government, and these have been followed by communications with ministers and the heads of departments. The program is still in a very early stage and this is but an interim report. To date full statements have been received from twelve governments, controlling about a third of the continent's inhabitants and about two-fifths of those falling within the scope of this paper. These countries are Nigeria, Morocco, Tanzania, Madagascar, Upper Volta, Rhodesia, Malawi, Somalia, Sierra Leone, Gambia, Basutoland, and Mauritius. With the addition of four other governments who have informed me that they are preparing replies—South Africa, Kenya, Zambia, and Rio Muni—the survey will shortly include about half the population of Africa as defined here.

At the same time a study was begun of the family planning movement in Africa. This study is still at a very early stage of development. In the countries examined in this paper, detailed analyses have been received of these movements in Nigeria, Sierra Leone, and Rhodesia. Less complete information has been made available on movements in Kenya, Uganda, South Africa, Mauritius, the Seychelles, Zambia, and Liberia. Something is also known of the position in Ghana.[1]

These studies show that family planning activities and governmental population policies form a very definite pattern within the con-

[1] Information has been gathered from various sources but particular thanks must go to the International Planned Parenthood Federation for its assistance.

tinent. The major determinant of that pattern has been the distribution of colonial empires. These affected the religious composition, the legal structure, the national outlook, and the way of life of many of the newly independent countries. An important secondary determinant has been the distribution of Islamic and especially Arabic culture. One can subdivide the countries of Africa, excluding this time only the United Arab Republic, into six groups (for names of countries see lists below). In order of population size they are: (1) former British colonies, which have attained independence under indigenous

GROUP 1

Gambia	Uganda
Ghana	Zambia
Kenya	
Malawi	Basutoland
Nigeria	Bechuanaland
Sierra Leone	Mauritius
Sudan	Seychelles
Tanzania	Swaziland

GROUP 2

Cameroon	Niger
Central African Republic	Senegal
Chad	Togo
Congo (Brazzaville)	Upper Volta
Dahomey	
Gabon	Burundi
Guinea	Congo (Leopoldville)
Ivory Coast	Rwanda
Madagascar	Somalia
Mali	

governments, and a few small colonies being prepared for this (42% of the population); (2) former French, Belgian, and Italian colonies, the inhabitants of which are not Arabs (25%); (3) former French and Italian colonies with Arab populations (12%); (4) countries that have not been colonies, except for relatively short periods of occupation (8%); and (5) European-dominated areas where the dominant population is partly or wholly British (8%); and (6) Portuguese-controlled areas, together with a few territories controlled by Spain or France (5%).

In Group 1 the laws have permitted since colonial times the import or manufacture of contraceptives and their sale or distribution. Abortion on medical grounds or sterilization with safeguards have been permitted but have been performed legally only on a very limited scale. The British colonial class bought contraceptives openly at pharmacies and sought advice on the subject from their doctors. The question of family planning clinics had often been raised, unofficially but within the British community, before the achievement of independence. Neither the British administration as such nor the British establishment was much given to claiming the benefits of greater population or the need for settling sparsely populated areas. In many of these countries there has recently been a movement toward forming family planning clinics on a voluntary basis, although often with

GROUP 3

Algeria	Morocco
Libya	Tunisia
Mauritania	

GROUP 4

Ethiopia	Liberia

GROUP 5

Rhodesia	South-West Africa
South Africa	

GROUP 6

Angola	Ifni
Cape Verde Islands	Spanish North Africa
Mozambique	Spanish Sahara
Portuguese Guinea	
São Tomé and Principe	Comoro Islands
	French Somaliland
Equatorial Guinea	Réunion

the support of government medical officers and even the use of municipal medical facilities. This has been easiest in countries most favoring the open society or even the open economy and has met with some misgivings in countries where the tendency toward centralized organization or authoritarian rule have been more pronounced.

The legal background has been similar in Group 5. Indeed a considerable demand for family planning services by the European population of South Africa and Rhodesia has led to the establishment of a large number of family planning clinics, well over a hundred in South Africa alone. But the fact that Europeans could afford to pay for consultations with physicians and contraceptives at market prices long kept prices so high as to be prohibitive for much of the African population. Both countries are now developing cheap family planning services for the indigenous population, but it may prove difficult to avoid giving offense along racial lines and to achieve the full confidence of the Africans.

Most countries of Group 2 retain French laws prohibiting or greatly restricting the import, manufacture, or sale of contraceptives and the performance by doctors of operations to induce abortion or sterilization. Such laws have been much more effective in achieving their stated end in the simple economies and small urban societies of Africa than they have been in the more complex situation found in France itself. In most former French sub-Saharan countries there is little use of modern contraceptives by the African population and little talk of establishing family planning clinics. In many of them the governments are very conscious of what they regard as underpopulation. However, most administrations do regard the legal restrictions on contraception as largely a French heritage, which, in common with other elements of the French heritage, might some day be re-examined to see if they are in the best national interest.

The position is very similar in Group 6.

The most significant changes in attitudes on family planning found in the new nations of the old French Empire are occurring in the Arab north, classified above as Group 3. Winds of change have been blowing westward from the United Arab Republic and even from Asia. It is precisely for these reasons that this paper omits both the UAR and Tunisia, so that they can be given more detailed treatment elsewhere. However, it does not appear that these two countries will be unique. Morocco, in an effort to raise standards of living, is certainly considering the possibility of limiting her rate of population growth.

Group 4 contains only Ethiopia and Liberia. Although the government of the latter does not appear to favor family planning, the country contains at least one clinic and has had a family planning association.

The survey of population policies sought to link various governmental policies. At the present time migration policy and official attitudes toward immigrant groups is causing far more soul-searching in the new African governments than is the question of family planning. Of the twelve governments to give statements of policy to date, nine either stated flatly that they do not feel that their countries would benefit from a much larger population or said that such a population should only be reached over a protracted period. None seek to encourage immigration except of certain persons with skills. Some, like Sierra Leone and Mauritius, seek to discourage any immigration for permanent settlement, and others, like Rhodesia and Basutoland, seek to discourage specifically Asian immigration. One-third desire to discourage the emigration of their own nationals on the grounds that such migration mostly affects the much-needed adult labor force, although interestingly enough no government saw this as a reason for encouraging immigration. Upper Volta pointed out that it faces particular problems with the seasonal emigration of a quarter of its male labor force each year.

All governments believe in health planning and most control directly a very large proportion of the medical facilities and personnel in their countries. Many are spending around a tenth of their budgets, and often a larger proportion of foreign aid, on the reduction of mortality and morbidity. As a result, most reported evidence of continued decline in the death rate and a rise in the rate of natural increase. In spite of increasing imbalance between birth and death rates, only four of the ten governments expressed a desire for a lower birth rate; they are Morocco, Nigeria, Rhodesia, and Mauritius. On the other hand, only three wish for a higher one, largely on the grounds that their countries still had room for more people; they are Sierra Leone, Tanzania, and Somalia. Some of the countries hope to use their sparsely settled areas more effectively by also encouraging internal population redistribution.

Finally, before looking more specifically at the question of population restriction, it might be noted that African governments probably have fewer doubts on governmental intervention in the economy and society in the process of modernization than do the governments of any other continent. All governments represented in the survey gave unqualified assent to the need for economic planning. Such a consensus could not have been obtained among former Asian colonies so soon after achieving independence. There is no similar consensus on the role of population planning as an integral part of economic planning. Two countries, Madagascar and Somalia, did not believe that population growth could occur in their countries so rapidly as to jeopardize economic advance. Three more—Sierra Leone, Tanzania, and Upper Volta—stated that it was not likely to have this effect in their countries in the years immediately ahead providing measures were taken to redistribute internal population. However, over half the respondents did believe that population planning should play some role in over-all governmental planning. These countries are Nigeria, Morocco, Sierra Leone, Rhodesia, Zambia, Mauritius, and Somalia, but the last implied that planning should encourage a higher birth rate and level of natural increase. Four—Upper Volta, Tanzania, Malawi, and Basutoland—said "not at this stage," and Madagascar did not foresee governmental action at any stage.

FAMILY PLANNING PROGRAMS—ORIGINS AND OPERATIONS

With the exception of the United Arab Republic and Tunisia in the Arab north of Africa, the only family planning facilities in Africa are in countries influenced by the British tradition. There may be a parallel here with the first demographic transition, when the fertility decline in northwestern and central Europe was witnessed also among overseas Europeans in countries that had once been British colonies but not in the regions of the old Spanish and Portuguese empires. Since World War II the spread of family planning in the developing world has often been greatest where British and American influence has been most strongly felt. The Anglo-Saxon cultural tradition has had, since the days of Adam Smith and before, a cost-accounting component which has tended to affect the behavior of governments and families alike. Doubtless the Protestant influence has also played a part.

This can be seen clearly in Africa, where, apart from the UAR and Tunisia, family planning clinics have come into existence in South Africa, Rhodesia, Uganda, Kenya, Mauritius, Nigeria, Sierra Leone, Liberia, and the Seychelles. Only in South Africa do the clinics form an extensive system, but there are a considerable number in Rhodesia, Kenya, and Uganda, and they are spreading in Mauritius. The only members of the International Planned Parenthood Federation in the African region are South Africa, Kenya, Uganda, Mauritius, and the UAR. In the following analysis attention will be paid to all these areas, but at the time of writing more detailed information is available to the writer on the experience of the Rhodesian, Nigerian, and Sierra Leonean clinics and hence these will be examined more closely.

Most clinics are described as "family planning clinics," although the term "marital clinic" has also been used in Nigeria. As the program spreads, the parent body usually takes on the name of "Family Planning Association." However, in Nigeria one controlling body has called itself "The Family Planning Council of Nigeria," and the National Council of Women's Societies has formed an "Advisory Council on Family Planning."

Apart from South Africa, the first stirrings of the family planning movement occurred during the colonial period. The first successful attempts to found family planning movements or to establish clinics occurred in Rhodesia in 1955, Uganda in 1956, Kenya and Mauritius in 1957, Nigeria in 1958, and Sierra Leone in 1959.

However, a perceptible quickening of activity occurred around 1964. In that year the Family Planning Council of Nigeria was formed and began to recruit a full-time organizer and other staff for an expanded clinic program. The Kenyan and Ugandan movements began to expand and the government of Mauritius decided to encourage the setting-up of clinics. The use of IUD's was begun by many clinics.

By mid-1965 the position appeared to be this: There were 115 clinics throughout South Africa and a marked increase in the demand for services was reported. In Rhodesia there were several clinics in the capital, Salisbury, and others were to be found in major towns. Kenya had twenty-one clinics, of which fourteen were in the capital, Nairobi. Uganda had three clinics in the capital, Kampala, but these were supplemented by four African home visitors. In Nigeria there were four clinics in the capital, Lagos, and one in the second town of the country, Ibadan. In Sierra Leone there was still only one clinic, attached to the Freetown Maternity Hospital, but midwives from up-country were trained in contraceptive methods during special courses. In Liberia and Ghana the governments were not enthusiastic about family planning, but in the former a Family Planning Association was based in the Monrovia Maternity Hospital and the director of nursing provided both advice and contraceptive materials. In Ghana the government had discussed the possibility of penal sanctions against contraception, but it was quite likely that no legislative action would in fact be taken, as had been the case earlier when very strong action against the practice of abortion had been foreshadowed. At one time there had been a suggestion that the main hospital in the capital, Accra, might become a source of family planning information, and indeed contraceptives are still sold in the country. In Zambia two family planning clinics are being assisted by the Rhodesian Family Planning Association. It should also be remarked that some of the Protestant missions in tropical Africa have shown an increased interest in providing information about family planning or allowing the establishment of clinics in conjunction with missions or mission hospitals. Beyond the continental coast, numerous family planning clinics are now being opened in Mauritius, where the government has begun subsidizing two family planning organizations, and the first one was established on the Seychelles this year.

Except in South Africa and the small island of Mauritius the clinics still cater particularly to the urban population, often with by far the most provision for the inhabitants of the capital. In Kenya an interesting new rural clinic was opened in 1964 and thought is being given to the possibility of mobile rural clinics. In Uganda a pilot IUD experiment was conducted in rural areas in 1964 and two rural clinics are planned. The Uganda home visitors and Sierra Leonean midwife-training schemes previously mentioned also do something to extend assistance to rural areas.

In Nigeria pilot demonstrations are being used and more are planned.

In some areas such demonstrations have recently proved their value in introducing oral contraceptives and IUD's. Clinical trials of the former have been carried out in Rhodesia, and a rural demonstration of IUD's was held in Uganda.

Contraceptives are available through such commercial outlets as pharmacies in old British Africa, but elsewhere are unobtainable, difficult to buy, and expensive. In Ghana the types of contraceptives now available seem to be limited to foam tablets, jellies, and condoms.

In most countries with clinics these are run by some kind of family planning association. These associations are usually directed by a committee with lay and medical members. The latter are often employees of the governmental health services, which admittedly employ a very big proportion of all medical personnel in many African countries. Because of such connections the family planning associations, while remaining mostly voluntary organizations, often have the blessing and official or unofficial assistance of either health departments or municipal health services. The Nigerian government may go beyond this nearly neutral stance, and in Salisbury, Rhodesia, the family planning program has been integrated with the Salisbury Municipal Health Services since 1962. In Uganda the Family Planning Association is affiliated with the National Council of Social Services and is thus assured of some indirect governmental support and of assistance through some municipal health centers. In Nairobi, Kenya, family planning is accepted as part of the city council's health services, although the Minister of Health in the Kenyan government stated as recently as February, 1964, that the government as such cannot recognize the Family Planning Association of Kenya or give it any assistance in its work. Some governmental support is given in Mauritius, the Seychelles, and South Africa.

The clinics are staffed by doctors, nurses, and lay administrative or clerical staff. The doctors are often unpaid volunteers from the governmental health services. In one sense their recruitment is less difficult than it often is in Asian countries, in that African society, except in some parts of Arab Africa, does not find it particularly distasteful for male doctors to cater in the clinics to female patients. Most recruitment is still by personal contact with those who show some personal enthusiasm. In some countries, like Rhodesia, doctors at Protestant mission hospitals are undertaking family planning work.

The doctors, nurses, and lay assistants often supplement their previous knowledge with lectures, seminars, or demonstrations. Frequently, some of the doctors and nurses have taken overseas courses in family planning or have attended specialist conferences. However, there is a general worry about lack of training in the newest methods, especially the use of IUD's and oral contraceptives. Some family planning workers argue that the very considerable number of African students at present receiving medical training overseas should all take family planning courses. It should be noted that training at two different levels is already appearing in Africa itself. In Lagos, Nigeria, the university will give medical students family planning training and will use an adjacent family planning clinic as a demonstration center. In Sierra Leone, Africa's impressive force of village midwives is being harnessed. Seminar courses have been run at the Freetown clinic to train these women in family planning methods.

There is often wide divergence between the supposedly most desirable target groups and the majority of patients served. The greatest social worries center upon the poor and ill-educated. The majority of patients are still middle-class and economically better off. In South Africa and Rhodesia the great majority of patients are Europeans, and this group is still disproportionately represented further north in parts of East Africa. In Nigeria and Mauritius the only stated aim is to reach all classes of people. In Sierra Leone this is modified by choosing for special attention those women who have already borne many children and whose risk of pregnancy is still high. In Rhodesia the family planning system is now trying to give more attention to the African population than it has in the past, since Africans exhibit twice the birth rate of the European population and their community has an average age little more than half as great as the latter. Special interest is being shown in the lower income groups, particularly the urban poor, low-educated groups, industrial workers' wives, and more generally in women who have recently given birth.

Outside southern Africa lack of funds has been a greater limiting factor than has the pace of social change. Assistance, some of it hidden by the use of personnel and facilities, has come from health departments or municipal health services. Among the European populations of South Africa and Rhodesia the chief source of income has been the charges made to patients. This, of course, has been of some significance everywhere. External aid, critically important often in the first stages of the movement or in the establishment of new clinics, has come from the American Pathfinder Fund or the International Planned Parenthood Federation. The South African government has given direct support, as has also the Nigerian government through the Department of Public Health. Private contributions have been important in both Sierra Leone and Rhodesia, and in the latter a considerable part of these donations has come from business firms. In Kenya there has been some indirect governmental support through the National Council of Social Services. But in most of these countries the family planning associations have clear ideas about new areas of the country or society which they could invade now if only the extra money could be found.

As yet, again with the exception of southern Africa, the new family planning organizations are running on shoe-string budgets. In the first half of 1965 the Nigerian scheme was operating at an annual rate of expenditure of £3,000, and that of Sierra Leone, where almost all service is voluntary, at £400. The latter, which has applied to the IPPF for assistance, envisages a rise to about £1,700 in the near future. Expenditure was very considerably greater in Rhodesia, but in mid-1965 was climbing rapidly and extra funds were urgently needed if a substantial extension of work to the African population was to be undertaken.

Most programs charge patients something for services. In Rhodesia Europeans have to pay a full medical consultation fee and pay for contraceptives at cost plus 20%. The African patients pay no service fee and obtain contraceptives at cost price. In Sierra Leone no charge is made for services, but a small payment is asked for supplies except where the patients are unable to afford it. The Nigerian scheme is to charge all patients.

All family planning schemes in Africa attempt to secure publicity, and most lament that they have not taken this side of their work even more seriously. Posters are used, as also are pamphlets. In Rhodesia pamphlets printed in English and three African languages offer the small family the possibility of being able to afford "nice clothes, education, a nice home, good health and good food." The press is used, rather effectively in Nigeria, but there has been some opposition in Sierra Leone. In both Nigeria and Sierra Leone radio talks and discussions have been employed, but neither radio nor television can be used in Rhodesia. All organizations arrange lectures and talks to doctors, to mothers in maternity hospitals and medical clinics, and to women's groups. In Rhodesia and Zambia films shown by the family planning organizations or by other groups such as missions have proved to be particularly effective. But it has been found that such effectiveness depends almost entirely on the films being locally made. Films of clinics and people in other African countries, let alone in non-African countries, have failed either to hold attention or to get their message across. In Rhodesia too, arrangements have now been made for family planning information to be made available by government officers who come into contact with the public, especially those employed by the agricultural, information, health, and African health workers' services.

All family planning clinics offer advice and information as well as contraceptive supplies. In Sierra Leone clinic officers undertake to give advice on any family problems. Most clinics also offer advice or treatment for sterility or infertility. This service can attract people to the clinics and familiarize them with the program. So seriously is sub-fertility regarded in tropical Africa that in many places the traditional culture and religion have offered treatment for generations. In Ghana the room for treating the disorder is often one of the main sections of the traditional religious shrine. It is in this field of family planning that Ghana's health services have so far been encouraged to concentrate, and to date they have achieved considerable progress. In Rhodesia the family planning clinics refer such cases to the hospitals for treatment.

Clinics are more commonly attached to hospitals, especially maternity hospitals, and municipal health clinics than established as completely separate institutions. In Lagos, Nigeria, a new clinic has been established near the medical faculty of the university so that it can be employed in the training of medical students in family planning methods. In Sierra Leone, the clinic at the Maternity Hospital in Freetown is supplemented by the advice and services given by midwives, who received some training at the clinic but who have since returned to their home towns or villages in other parts of the country. However, many of these midwives prefer to advise patients to make the journey to the capital to consult the clinic there. In Rhodesia the system is more complex. There are private clinics as well as municipal clinics for Africans only. Clinics are attached not only to government hospitals but to four mission hospitals as well. Family planning clinics north of South Africa rarely have enough patients to warrant full-time service. Most open between once and four times weekly, and such limited hours permit the use of voluntary, part-time service by medical personnel.

All clinics have offered foam tablets and diaphragms since their inception. Most have provided oral contraceptives since the early 1960's and IUD's from 1964. The last two forms of contraception are still causing considerable excitement in the associations. It is felt that they may well revolutionize the position, but it is still too early to make clear predictions. In Rhodesia four centers are supplying IUD's and 1,150 had been fitted by early 1965. Condoms are distributed from the Nigerian clinics, but, although they are widely sold throughout former British Africa, their handling by family planning clinics is comparatively rare, largely because the clinics have specialized in female methods of contraception. The Nigerian clinics provide instruction in the rhythm method, but in Rhodesia patients requesting such advice are referred to private Catholic doctors. In most of former British Africa import duty is still paid on contraceptives, but it is not prohibitively high as has been the case in some of the former French colonies.

Contraceptive supplies are usually handled by an organizing secretary, sometimes the only salaried officer of the family planning organization. He arranges for imports, pays duty, keeps records of supplies, and distributes the contraceptives to the medical and nursing staff of individual clinics.

Two types of record are normally kept. The first are of imports, duty paid, finances, and the like, which are kept by the secretary and for which responsibility lies with the association. The second are individual clinical records, which are kept by nearly all associations for every patient. An exception here is the fairly large-scale catering to Africans by the Rhodesian municipal clinics. The clinical records are kept by the medical or nursing staff. The introduction of oral contraceptives has led the non-municipal clinics in Rhodesia to keep additional registers of patients currently being supplied with them.

Family planning in Africa is still very far from a mass movement except among the Europeans in the southern part of the continent. Thus the Sierra Leone clinic had so far treated only about 300 patients, although it is emphasized that these have been drawn from the illiterate as well as literate classes. But the expanded Nigerian system has already provided a service for over 5,000 persons. In Rhodesia the position is more complex because the municipal clinics claim that their patients are too numerous for the limited staff to attempt to record their numbers. However, a few examples may be noted of work at certain other clinics in Salisbury which are controlled by one of the six regional family planning associations of the country. At the Lister Clinic 2,880 patients, mostly European, had been seen up to early 1965. At the Harari Hospital Clinic, 1,500 Africans had been seen, while at the new Highfields Community Centre 50 IUD's had been fitted in the first two months of operation.

Three special circumstances were repeatedly mentioned. They are friction with the cultural mores of the local society, the poverty of patients, and the difficulties found in organizing enough supply points. African culture has long laid great stress on high fertility and hence organizations urging low fertility may well incur deep suspicion. However, African culture is also capable of surprisingly rapid adjustment to new situations, such as are now being created by decreasing infant mortality, by the economic pressures of urban and middle-class life, and by the great increase in the numbers of children attending school. It is interesting to note that while African suspicion in Rhodesia was once dominant, it has since waned, leaving Catholic groups as the chief sources of opposition. The poverty of a very large proportion of patients, or in some places the lack of cash in a largely subsistence economy, has meant that a very significant fraction of the patients can pay little or nothing for services and supplies. This is accentuated by the fact that the clinics necessarily must cater mostly to wives. In addition, if family planning services are offered in conjunction with governmental health services providing free medicines, there is often at the outset a suspicion that those charging for contraceptive supplies are doing so for their own personal gain. Thus the clinics will need to depend increasingly on governments or external sources for their finances. Third, Africa is a continent of vast distances with comparatively little nucleation of settlement. If an adequate provision of family planning services is to be provided, there must be a great number of service points and a complex supply network. This raises the cost of treatment per individual well above what it is in many parts of Asia.

Evaluation of Results

Most program directors regard the results achieved to date as indicating success in what some of them have described as the first stage of their activities. As yet there has been no measurable decline in the birth rate in any African country with a family planning program. But the possibility of family limitation is becoming known, at least in the major towns, and the framework for larger organizations has been established. Furthermore, the opposition to family planning activities and to publicity for such activities has significantly declined. Most programs report that their work has certainly been justified in terms of the improvement of the lives of individual patients and the situations of their families, and many of the doctors concerned, looking at the position from the point of view of a medical practitioner rather than that of a demographer or political scientist, would be prepared to argue that no further justification is needed. Most report that the extension of family planning activities has been paralleled by a marked increase in the quantity of contraceptives sold through normal commercial channels.

The weakest point in the programs is probably the evaluation of results. Most programs keep individual records, and the time has arrived when they would certainly benefit from a competent analysis of these cards. However, their own personnel usually have neither the time nor the training to allow them to do this. A general evaluation of the requirement for services and of continuing patients is certainly attempted. The Nigerian clinics report that they do this by seeing their patients at regular intervals. The Sierra Leone Family Planning Association holds quarterly meetings to which evaluation reports are presented. The Rhodesian Association has plans for a more ambitious evaluation toward the end of the present year.

Major Achievements and Problems

No program has as yet reached any of its major goals, except in the sense of the Nigerian clinics when they report that their recent expansion of services has been as rapid as had been hoped. In Sierra Leone certain goals have been reached in Freetown, but the desired expansion into other parts of the country still awaits the government's approval.

Most programs are optimistic about future prospects, for two reasons. First, there is a perceptible quickening of interest on the part of the African population in family planning, a phenomenon reported from such widely scattered places as Kenya, Nigeria, and Rhodesia. Second, there is the arrival on the scene of such new contraceptives as IUD's and oral contraceptives, especially the former. The Rhodesian clinics report that the IUD is chiefly responsible for the present upsurge of their activities among the African population. Such optimism is usually tempered by the fact that expansion depends largely on the finding of sufficient finance, either locally or abroad.

The various programs are in general agreement on three lessons which have been learned to date from their experience. The first is that governments must be converted to favor or even support them. This means publicity for what is happening elsewhere in Africa and in the world outside. It also means expert testimony on the relationship between economic change and population growth in their own countries, and advice from international organizations on attitudes and decisions on governmental population policy in other parts of the world. The second is that more publicity through the mass media is needed from the outset, irrespective of the resistances and resentments that are thus suddenly produced. It is felt that such resistances and resentments are in the long run just as great if evoked more gradually, and eventually have to be combatted. The third is that progress has been retarded by addressing argument overmuch to women and insufficiently to their husbands. The opinions of the latter necessarily count greatly within the marriage. Usually they must approve the decisions to employ family planning methods and to devote part of the family budget to meeting the costs involved. Other points put forward by the associations were the need for local training in family planning methods and the case for greater use of local films in publicity drives.

The obstacles to more rapid expansion in order of stated importance are lack of finance, shortage of trained personnel, insufficient publicity, and unsureness of governmental support. Also listed were the logistics of supplying remote and rural areas, rural illiteracy, the suspicion of those holding more traditional attitudes, and some Catholic opposition. On the last point, however, it might be pointed out that a survey among economically better-off urban families in Ghana showed little significant association between the willingness to use family planning clinics and the religion of either husband or wife.[2] Furthermore, on Mauritius the Catholic church is accepting government aid for an organization encouraging family limitation by approved methods.

When asked what they would do differently if they were to start their family planning movements over again, the most common answer received from those who had worked to establish these movements was that they would try much harder to secure governmental support at every stage of the project. In addition they stated that they would make attempts at an earlier stage to overcome each of the obstacles listed above.

THE FUTURE

Family planning is not carried out on a large scale in Africa. The demonstration in this paper that there are new family planning associations and that the first clinics have been established in widely scattered parts of Africa does not alter the facts that birth control is not yet in any sense a mass movement and that birth rates are not falling. Probably the majority of Africans know very little about the existence of modern contraception. On the other hand the foundations for family planning have already been laid. This point has not been widely appreciated and tropical Africa has frequently been omitted from outlines of family planning in the world.

The incidence of family planning has been uneven, and public interest in family planning has been evinced in only three of the six groups of countries listed earlier in this paper. In my surveys of population policies and family planning activities I received some response from both countries in Group 5 (European dominated, British traditions); twelve out of fifteen countries in Group 1 (former British colonies controlled by indigenous governments or colonies being prepared for this condition); one out of three countries in Group 3 (Arab countries in North Africa), and this would have become three out of five if this paper had covered the UAR and Tunisia as well;

[2] See chap. 48 in this volume.

two out of twenty countries in Group 2 (former French, Belgian, Italian, and Spanish colonies); none out of two in Group 4 (countries that have not been colonies); and none out of eight in Group 6 (colonies still controlled by Portugal, France, or Spain). This is no accident resulting in a bias in survey. It is precisely what had been expected from earlier research findings and also from the experience of the United Nations Secretary General when undertaking an inquiry of a somewhat similar type.[3] Most of Africa that was or is controlled by France or Portugal failed to reply because their administrations have never concerned themselves with population policy and because their citizens have never had the choice between using modern family planning methods and not doing so.

In terms of family planning there are two leading sectors in Africa: the Arab north and those parts of Africa which are or have been British possessions. These are where most progress has taken place up to the present, where most is likely to occur in the immediate future, where the existing social structure and experience to date means that investment in family planning schemes is most likely to bring the first results in falling birth rates, and from where family planning institutions are likely to flow to the rest of Africa. The latter groups, those parts of Africa which are or have been British possessions, contain almost half the population of Africa. Fourteen out of seventeen countries in the group provided some kind of information for the surveys, and nine out of seventeen have family planning clinics. All have laws permitting the import and sale of contraceptives, and all have experience of a British ruling class containing many families practicing family planning. All permit abortion and sterilization under certain circumstances and have laws which could be interpreted more broadly in these matters should the need ever arise. A survey in Ghana showed that neither practice was so fundamentally opposed to indigenous mores as to merit ruling it out as a possibility at some future time.[4] On the other hand, in most of former French Africa the import, sale, or advertisement of contraceptives and the performing of operations inducing abortion or sterility are illegal.

In Commonwealth countries of Africa the chief brake on the family planning movement now is insufficient finance. As many associations will probably be increasingly looking overseas for funds, and as such an action could conceivably conflict with governmental policies, the survey of governmental policy asked a series of questions of each

---

[3] United Nations Economic and Social Council, *Inquiry among Governments on Problems Resulting from the Interaction of Economic Development and Population Changes: Report of the Secretary-General* (New York, 1964).

[4] See chap. 48 in this volume.

country about the official attitude on this matter. In most British or former British countries which replied, there would be no opposition to the receipt of such funds from international bodies, foreign governments, or private foreign sources for private family planning clinics or for government-backed schemes, should the latter be decided upon. Basutoland would prefer such assistance from an international body and for a government scheme. Malawi reported that the question has not yet arisen, and Tanzania replied that the government does not consider family planning necessary. In the Arab north, Morocco described private assistance to a private scheme as a "desirable procedure" and stated that it would welcome assistance from an international body in studying the implications of a family planning program. The only type of assistance it opposed was that from foreign governments. The replies from former French tropical Africa were different, but even here they were not rigidly opposed to assistance. For instance, Upper Volta replied to the question about assistance to a government scheme that the government did not intend to introduce one but failed to answer the question about assistance to a private scheme if established. Madagascar, which was firmly opposed to most forms of assistance, modified its reply on the matter of assistance to a government scheme from an international body to the effect that it was "opposed at present."

The major needs of the present family planning schemes are, apart from money, to convince their governments of the economic and social benefits accruing from a drop in birth rates, to establish courses in family planning, especially in the use of the IUD and oral contraceptives, to train African medical students in Africa and overseas, and to obtain help in producing publicity such as locally made films and in evaluating achievements.

The pressure upon societies and governments to interest themselves in family planning will undoubtedly increase. Most of the British or former British countries in Africa already have rates of population growth above 2.5% per annum. Birth rates in West Africa are so high that continued mortality decline there could eventually produce rates of natural increase in excess of 4% a year unless fertility declines. The Ghana survey showed that the demand for family planning is positively associated with educational levels attained, urban background, and change from the traditional way of life. In every country in Africa each of these characteristics is on the increase.

One can indicate some of the directions in which the family planning movement is likely to spread. The Ghana survey showed that there is already a market among the economically better-off groups in the towns. There is a case for establishing new clinics first in such areas, although political and social motives might dictate a primary interest in the plight of the urban and rural poor. Once an urban upper- and middle-class custom of family planning is established, it may spread surprisingly rapidly to other sections of society. African society is in many ways more mobile than that of Asia or Europe. Townspeople are constantly traveling back to visit relatives in the villages. Social and political revolution has been so recent that most wealthier or more educated people have close relatives who are poor and illiterate. In Ghana there would already be a demand in the richer, cash-crop rural areas. The spread will bring problems. The Ghana survey showed that about half the urban elite who desired family planning services would be prepared to accept complicated contraception, such as the taking of an oral contraceptive each day. The other half would not, and doubtless a much bigger proportion of their poorer and less educated fellow countrymen would not. The IUD might be the answer at least during a transitional period. Foam tablets (or patent products to be taken by mouth) are acceptable and are at present widely used, but the rate of failure is apparently very high. Traditional European methods, such as coitus interruptus or continence, are used by very few Africans.[5]

Family planning may well be supported in the not very distant future by nearly all the Commonwealth governments in Africa. They, like most African leaders, have a strong belief in modernization, and European innovation can often find acceptance much more readily in Africa than in many parts of Asia. As demographic analyses of the African position mount in number, along with United Nations and other surveys of the world situation, most governments will probably take an interest in population planning. They may well find that some aspects of local society do something to ease the spread of family planning. It is agreed in modern Africa that the extension of health services will be mainly carried out through a system of government clinics, and if these also incorporated family planning it would be readily accepted. In addition, it may well be that the Sierra Leonean experiment in using the midwives who are found throughout the country offers an economic way of extending the network of information and even services in many African countries.

[5] See chap. 48 in this volume.

15

WESTERN EUROPE

D. V. GLASS
The London School of Economics and Political Science

In the sense in which the term "program" applies to current policies in such countries as India and Pakistan, Western Europe has no family planning programs. Few countries in the region have a conscious, integrated population policy. Those that do—France, Belgium, and Sweden—are explicitly pro-family in attitude, though the assumptions and measures adopted differ markedly among them. In the remaining countries in the region, as in all other developed societies, pro-family measures of one kind or another are also the rule. They are not organized with a populationist objective in mind but reflect the now general concern with poverty and sickness and with the alleviation of certain types of inequalities.

During the past ten years, a change in the attitude to population growth has become visible in some European countries. The fears of the 1930's, based upon the expectation of declining numbers, have largely disappeared. Moreover, relatively high fertility, coupled with increased immigration, has provoked reverse views. So far, however, these have been private views and governmental policy has not been affected. No government in Western Europe has proposed a program for restricting the natural increase of its population. Yet almost every country has an organized birth control movement. The nature and status of the movement in a given country, and its contribution to the spread of birth control advice and practice, depend upon many factors which can best be illustrated by considering some aspects of the historical background.[1]

[1] In addition to the sources specifically mentioned in subsequent references, the material in this paper is also derived from the data used in two earlier publications by me, to which I shall not otherwise refer: "Family Limitation in Europe: A Survey of Recent

MALTHUSIAN BACKGROUND

All birth control movements in Western Europe stem directly or indirectly from the pioneer work of the Malthusian League in Britain in the 1870's. After the purely technical victory of Annie Besant and Charles Bradlaugh in their fight to republish Knowlton's *The Fruits of Philosophy*, C. R. Drysdale and his colleagues established an organization which campaigned on the basis of Malthus' theory and Francis Place's precepts of conduct. It was with this neo-Malthusian ideology that the movement spread to the Netherlands and to France and it was this type of attitude that Knut Wicksell tried to promote in Sweden. The spread was by no means wholly spontaneous. The early collaboration with the Netherlands may be seen from the fact that the very term "neo-Malthusian" was a Dutch invention, suggested to Drysdale as more appropriately describing the aims of his League. In France, the initiation of the movement may be dated from 1879 when, on the invitation of Paul Robin, Drysdale addressed a working-class conference in Marseilles, though the first French organization, the Ligue de la Régénération Humaine, was not set up until 1896.[2]

During their early phases, the various birth control movements were concerned primarily with propaganda via meetings and pamphlets. For actual birth control advice they depended mainly upon commercial publications or upon the collaboration of the few individuals of the medical profession who had accepted the unorthodox view that fertility control was no less legitimate than control of mortality. Among them was that rare person, Aletta Jacobs, who started prescribing the use of the Mensinga pessary in Amsterdam in 1882. The medical profession as a whole remained hostile until well into the present century,[3] as did the churches, whether Protestant or Catholic.

In Britain, when the Church of England was at last compelled, in 1908, to take cognizance of a subject formerly regarded as not fit to be discussed by Christians, its committee recommended "the prohibition of so-called Neo-Malthusian appliances" and "the prosecution of all who publicly and professionally assist preventive methods."[4] At

Studies," in C. V. Kiser (ed.), *Research in Family Planning* (Princeton, N.J., 1962); and *Population Policies and Movements in Europe* (Oxford, 1940).

[2] In 1879 Drysdale and Allbutt also delivered papers at the Amsterdam meeting of the International Medical Association. The first International Neo-Malthusian Conference was held in Paris in 1900, and there were further conferences in 1905, 1910, and 1911.

[3] On the attitudes of the medical profession in Britain, see J. Peel, "Contraception and the Medical Profession," *Population Studies*, November, 1964.

[4] Society for the Propagation of Christian Knowledge, *Conference of Bishops of the Anglican Communion . . . 1908* (Brighton, 1908), p. 147.

almost the same time, in 1907, the synod of the Netherlands Reformed Church referred to birth control as "the great sin against the Creator's commandment."[5] The influence of the Church of England in Britain was, however, relatively limited. Its authority with the middle class had been eroded by the Darwinian controversy and its appeal to the urban working class had long been declining. Non-conformist denominations were somewhat more flexible in their attitude and acted in some degree as a counterpoise.[6] Hence though Anglicans continued to show official hostility—or, at best, indifference—to birth control for a considerable time, their views did not prompt restrictive legislation.

In the Netherlands, on the other hand, the existence of a far larger proportion of Catholics helped to produce in both Catholic and Protestant groups what Van Heek has depicted as a kind of "front mentality" in respect of reproductive behavior.[7] Partly in consequence, in 1911, Article 451 of the penal code was secured, sharply restricting the possibility of disseminating birth control advice or of selling contraceptives, and conditioning the form subsequently taken by the Dutch birth control organization. Religious hostility continued to be evident between the wars, and it was not until the 1950's that the synod of the Reformed Church began to change its attitude.[8] By that time, Protestant churches elsewhere were moving in similar fashion—the view of the Church of England was officially revised in 1958—and the Roman Catholic Church had begun to reconsider its position.[9] Events had overtaken organized religions, now compelled to recognize the fact that birth prevention had permeated the societies in which they were trying to maintain or recapture their authority.

The antagonism of the churches was a "given" in respect of which the early birth control movement could do little directly. But there

[5] Nederlandse Vereniging Sexuele Hervorming, *With NVSH in Search of Proper Sex Relations* (The Hague, 1960) (unpaginated).

[6] Catholics were in a small minority and their "image" was somewhat tarnished by their identification with the Irish immigrants, against whom there had been much hostility.

[7] F. van Heek, "Roman-Catholicism and Fertility in the Netherlands," *Population Studies*, November, 1956.

[8] C. van Emde Boas, "The Churches and Ourselves," IPPF, *Proceedings of the Third Conference of the Region for Europe . . . , 1962* (Amsterdam, 1963), Addendum, and letter dated May 29, 1960. Article 240 of the penal code, revised in 1936, penalizes, among other actions, any attempt to give birth control information to persons under 18 years of age. The Dutch movement is based upon individual membership, for legally it is only within an association that birth control advice and appliances can be offered to members (NVSH, *op. cit.*). (Unless otherwise specified, references to IPPF conferences are to those of the region for Europe, Near East and Africa.)

[9] See F. Campbell, "Birth Control and the Christian Churches," *Population Studies*, November, 1960.

was one element for which the movement was responsible and which influenced the acceptability of the propaganda, namely, the attachment to Malthusian theory. For whatever the intellectual validity of the argument, its emotional appeal to the mass of the population was unlikely to be effective. Moreover, the very success of the spread of family limitation automatically helped to reduce the apparent relevance of Malthusianism. Even in Britain, once the birth rate had begun to fall, the devil of Malthus was raised again only during the period of unemployment shortly after World War I and, associated with the depression of the 1930's, was interpreted in quite different terms. By the 1890's Cannan was speculating upon a possible future fall in population in this country, rather than a continued rise, and by 1913 a self-appointed National Commission was looking into the causes of declining fertility.

In France, the Malthusian theme appeared still less appropriate. Fertility had been declining throughout the nineteenth century and the cry of *dénatalité* began to be heard soon after the Franco-Prussian war. Robin's Malthusian Ligue, founded in 1896, was immediately counterattacked by the Alliance Nationale, founded in the same year by Bertillon and soon supported by clerical and military circles. Its strength grew on the manpower losses of World War I. Concern with those losses largely accounts for the hasty passage of the 1920 Act prohibiting the spread of birth control information and the sale of contraceptives (other than the condom, defined not as a contraceptive but as a protection against venereal disease) and for the modification in 1923 of paragraph 317 of the penal code, aimed at increasing the effectiveness of the fight against abortion. The mounting threat of Italy and Germany between the wars gave further support to the Alliance Nationale and its affiliates.

The birth control movement, on the other hand, still emphasizing the Malthusian theme and associating population growth with the danger of war, appealed only to pacifist and fringe left-wing groups. The main working-class political parties were concerned with very different problems and their initial hostility to French pro-natalist policy was at least partly reduced when family allowances were generalized and made compulsory and was largely eliminated by the combination in 1939 of the Nazi threat and the passing of the comprehensive Code de la Famille. Eugène Humber, publisher of *La Grande Réforme*, the main remaining journal of the old-style birth control movement, died in prison in an air raid during the war—and with him what little was left of the earlier movement collapsed, a victim of its own fossilization, as well as of French pro-natalist repression.[10]

[10] The pro-natalist organizations adapted themselves far more than the birth control movement. Though the drive against abortion and contraception continued (and espe-

In other countries, however, the movement gradually adapted itself to changes in circumstances and needs. The Dutch Neo-Malthusian League was among the first to change. By 1894, its focus had shifted from Malthusianism as such to a less doctrinaire concern with population questions generally. Later, the emphasis was placed on "over-population" within the family, though this did not prevent the establishment, in 1899, of a counterorganization to attack neo-Malthusian propaganda, or the development of a "popular front," supported by religious organizations sufficiently powerful to persuade the Minister of Justice to refuse to renew the League's charter. But by 1931, when it established its first medically staffed birth control clinic, the League had lost its Malthusian vestiges, and this was finally and formally recognized by its absorption in the newly christened Netherlands Society for Sexual Reform in 1946.[11]

A corresponding change occurred in the British movement, though in a rather different way. For there the old Malthusian view continued to be expressed by the League in *New Generation,* the periodical which replaced *The Malthusian* in 1921. But the influence of this view diminished rapidly, while the newly emerging birth control organization proper was imbued with a different ideology, first proclaimed by Standring in 1919 in his journal, *Birth Control,* and taken up by Marie Stopes, who in 1921 established the first birth control clinic in Britain—namely, that birth control was "good" in its own right, regardless of any population theory.

TWENTIETH-CENTURY WELFARE VIEW

It is this welfare view which has generally obtained in the Family Planning Association, now covering the largest number of birth control clinics in any European country. In Sweden, too, the present birth control organizations derive from welfare motives rather than from nineteenth-century economic theory. There was, in fact, little action in Sweden springing from that source and the situation was

---

cially against abortion), there was an increasing pressure for realistic, positive measures for assisting families. And the propaganda tone also changed slightly, as witness the alteration in the name of the central organization from Alliance nationale pour l'accroissement de la population française to Alliance nationale contre la dépopulation. For a detailed account of the development of pro-family organizations in France—by one who clearly favors their views while critical of some of their activities—see R. Talmy, *Histoire du mouvement familial en France, 1896–1939* (2 vols.; Paris, 1962).

11 Boas, *op. cit.* As in a number of other countries, advice on, and the provision of, contraceptives are now only part of the activities of the NVSH. Other activities include sex education, marriage counseling, and the treatment of infertility.

made more difficult by the existence of legislation, passed in 1910, prohibiting the public sale of contraceptives. The birth control movement in Sweden today results from the initiative of Madame Elise Ottesen-Jensen in 1932, which produced the founding in 1934 of the National Association for Sex Education.[12]

The Association provided advice on birth control, helped to organize the wider sale of contraceptives, and promoted the diffusion of sex education proper. Its efforts were greatly assisted by the fact that when Sweden came to adopt a positive population policy, following the recommendations of the two Royal Commissions of 1935 and 1941, the basic premise of the policy was "voluntary parenthood," and this entailed the abolition of legal bars to the sale of contraceptives, the requirement (as from 1946) that all pharmacies must stock contraceptives, the liberalization (in 1938 and 1946) of the grounds on which abortion could legally be obtained, and the introduction of sex education into the school system.[13]

Elsewhere in Western Europe the birth control movements showed widely different rates of development. In Eire, at one end of the scale, the country moved from the Victorian silence of the nineteenth century to the rigorously Catholic-influenced prohibitions of early independence. There is still no movement and, in theory at least, no access to mechanical or chemical contraceptives. At the other end, in Germany, where the influence of the Malthusian League was already visible in the 1880's, there was almost an excessive efflorescence of organizations, some (in the period shortly after Warld War I) commercial, others established by voluntary organizations, and some deriving from sickness benefit funds which provided birth control advice. By 1932, there were fifteen main birth control organizations. Then, under the Nazis, the organizations were suppressed and the law modified to prohibit any further activity.

Other countries showed varying degrees of involvement. In Belgium, concern with *dénatalité* was similar to that in France and equally led in 1923 to legal action to restrict propaganda and the sale of contraceptives—though the law had (and still has) more loopholes than in France. In Denmark, in spite of the relatively favorable atti-

[12] Typescript by Madame Ottesen-Jensen, giving an account of the foundation and growth of the Riksförbundet för Sexuell Upplysning.

[13] Contrasting France and Sweden, it might almost be argued that the Code de la Famille had a demographic objective which entailed substantial social provisions, whereas the Swedish Royal Commissions had primarily social objectives, with demographic overtones. Of the various measures adopted in Sweden, that relating to sex education appears to have been least successful—largely because the average teacher does not feel competent to give the instruction required (see T. Sjövall, "Sweden," in IPPF, *Proceedings of the Third Conference*, p. 74).

tude of the medical profession—at least as expressed in a survey in 1932—there was only one birth control clinic before World War II, that established by the World League for Sexual Reform, while, according to the penal code, birth control propaganda was a punishable offense. By contrast, Norway had twelve clinics, independently run but springing from the initiative of Madame Anker Møller in 1924, and receiving grants from central and local authorities. Iceland had no clinics, but under the 1935 Act physicians were obliged to advise women who consulted them on birth control matters.

So much for the background. Though a matter of "history," it has been given in some detail for several reasons. First, to show that the groups which operated to promote birth control changed their character and motivation over time. They might have had more significant results if they had done so earlier; but that is a judgment based upon hindsight and it is by no means certain that, without a Malthusian drive, the initiators would have been sufficiently dogmatic or messianic to withstand the persistent antagonism of authority.[14] Second, to make it clear that, on the eve of World War II, the birth control movement in Western Europe still showed many characteristics derived from its original and no longer appropriate impetus.[15] Third, to emphasize the still relatively undeveloped state of organized birth control in most of the countries in the region. Even in those countries with the longest tradition—Britain and the Netherlands—birth control clinics as such began only after World War I and did not exist in substantial numbers until after World War II.[16] The direct contribution of the birth con-

[14] With the passing of the Neo-Malthusian motif from the European family planning movement, it is unfortunate that the term "Neo-Malthusian" continues to be used by French writers to describe policies to which it is not applicable. This is so, for example, in articles in *Population*, discussing family planning programs in Denmark and Sweden. And it is strange to find in such articles, under the same general heading, reference to legal castration—a practice which forms part of the administration of criminal law and has nothing whatever to do with family planning provisions.

[15] I include here the continued preference by birth control clinics for the diaphragm or cap as contraceptives—probably deriving from a period in which, for various reasons, it no doubt seemed most appropriate for women to be responsible for birth control practice. But the familial situation is now very different and, so far as the practicing public is concerned, the diaphragm by no means appears to be the preferred method. Reluctance to consider abortion is also a characteristic of many birth control organizations—in part because of the initial need (regarded both legally and "morally") to distinguish sharply between contraception and abortion, and in part because in some countries (especially in France) one of the main "selling points" of the birth control movements has been the claim that, without full access to contraception proper, massive recourse to illegal abortion would be inevitable. (Equally, in many East European countries, the recent drive to promote contraception is based upon a desire to reduce the known massive use of legal abortion.)

[16] In Britain in 1939, there were 66 clinics affiliated to the Family Planning Association and 5 affiliated to the Society for Constructive Birth Control. There were also

trol associations to the practice of family planning could scarcely have
been very significar.t.

POST–WORLD WAR II DEVELOPMENTS

Since World War II, however, there have been new and substantial
developments. One important factor has been the increasing recognition that birth prevention *is* widespread—much more widespread than
could be accounted for by activities of family planning organizations
—and that in general the practice is far from sophisticated. This conclusion, reached in advance of any serious field investigations, has been
confirmed by them.[17] Influenced both by the need for the adjustment
of doctrine to reality in Western society and by the concern of the
West with rising population growth in less developed societies, another relevant fact is the legitimation of family planning—initially by
governmental committees (especially by the Swedish and United
Kingdom Royal Commissions) and subsequently by the Protestant
churches.[18] At the operational level, the establishment of the IPPF in
1952 also helped, for it provided additional stimulus, experience, and
occasionally funds to countries wishing to embark upon more ambitious activities. Save for Eire, there are now birth control organizations

municipal clinics offering, as part of their work, birth control advice. The total number
of new patients attending the various clinics was probably not much above 20,000 (the
number had been 19,000 in 1937). It was after 1949—following the main report of the
Royal Commission on Population—that a sharp increase in provision took place, and by
1964 there were 455 clinics covered by the FPA, with almost 115,000 new patients (FPA,
Draft Annual Report 1964–65, p. 2). In addition, there were local authority clinics (118
in 1961; [F. Lafitte], *Family Planning in the Sixties: Report of the Family Planning
Association Working Party* [London, 1963], chap. 3) and some hospital clinics offering
advice to women requiring it on medical grounds. Yet, as the subsequent discussion
shows, the total direct impact was still relatively small.

[17] In his 1965 presidential address to the Population Association of America, Ronald
Freedman stressed the paucity of direct evidence regarding the role of birth prevention
in bringing about a decline in fertility in Britain and France and noted that the only
direct inquiry was that of Lewis-Fanning, based upon a sample of women hospital
patients. That is technically correct (and from that point of view it is a pity that
United States field studies, restricting themselves to current behavior, have made little
effort to see what can be learned by asking retrospective questions). But as an assessment
of the contribution of indirect approaches to the interpretation of fertility trends in
Western Europe during the past 150 years, the comment is hardly appropriate.

[18] Mrs. M. A. Pyke, chairman of the British FPA, wrote in 1956: "1949 was the great
year. The Royal Commission on Population published its Report in June and we saw
at once that we could not have written it better ourselves. . . . From then onwards, the
only real problem has been to prevent the Association from outgrowing its strength"
(quoted by F. Lafitte, *op. cit.,* Foreword, p. 1).

throughout Western Europe,[19] but the region still exhibits great variations in activity and effectiveness.[20]

BELGIUM AND FRANCE

Some of the more notable developments are those in Belgium and
France. Although far from among the most significant in terms of quantitative impact, they are of interest for their occurrence in countries
with laws designed to prohibit what is now being done. In Belgium,
where the law is less ironclad, the contradiction is not so sharp. Nevertheless it was not until after 1949—initially as a subdivision of the Dutch
movement—that a realistic organization developed in Belgium, taking
advantage of the fact that, as a non-profit-making body, it could escape
the penalties of paragraph 383 of the penal code. During the first ten
years there were crises and changes in personnel, but there is now
(since 1963), a national federation, uniting family planning groups in
the Flemish and French-speaking areas, and there are birth control
clinics in Ghent, Antwerp, Brussels and Liège, providing both advice
and contraceptives.[21]

The postwar movement in France has not been able to go so far.
It was founded, on an individual and family welfare basis, in 1956 by
Dr. M. A. Weill Hallé, with the title Maternité Heureuse. As in the
Netherlands its support is by individual membership, numbering
45,000 by the end of 1964. Proposals to change the existing law were
put before Parliament in 1956,[22] but the attempts failed and the group

[19] In reply to United Nations inquiries, the Irish government acknowledged the
desirability of "research into and dissemination of information on non-artificial methods
of family planning" but did not refer to artificial methods (U.N., *Inquiry among Governments on Problems Resulting from the Reciprocal Action of Economic Development
and Population Changes: Report of the Secretary-General*, E/3895, May 18, 1964, p. 75).
The National Maternity Hospital, Dublin, has a clinic providing advice on the rhythm
method of birth control.

[20] In what follows, the information given has been drawn not only from the sources
cited but also from unpublished and informal accounts provided by Mrs. Joan Rettie,
of the IPPF, to whom I am very greatly indebted, and I wish most warmly to thank her
for her help.

[21] R. de Belder, "Belgium," in IPPF, *Proceedings of the Second Conference of the
Region for Europe . . . 1960*, p. 137; E. Klein-Vercautere, "Belgium," IPPF, *Proc. of
Third Conference . . . 1962*, p. 49. It is worth noting that there is now a more professional interest in demography in Belgium, shown in the creation by the government
of the Centre d'étude de la population et de la famille, with a journal which has recently
published the results of an inquiry into "desired family size" (Gh. Julemont and
J. Morsa, "Le nombre d'enfants désirés: un essai," *Population et famille*, No. 4).

[22] There were two proposals to modify the law relating to birth control (expressed
as proposals "to prevent, by means of contraceptive prophylaxis, the increase in the

turned instead to the establishment of advice centers, of which there are now 68. The centers cannot supply contraceptives, but giving advice to a member of a closed group who asks for it cannot be designated as propaganda within the terms of the law. Also, the 500 doctors co-operating with the movement are covered by the professional secrecy which applies to all medical advice given by a doctor to a patient. The women themselves are then informed by the advice centers of ways of implementing the recommendations and of buying contraceptives and there are several means of doing so. Thus for the first time assistance—at least in terms of specific and practical information —is being given on a scale relatively large compared with what was given by organizations in France in the past, though small in relation to the number of potential consumers. Nevertheless, the impact of the new movement has been disproportionately powerful. It has given rise to, and has been aided by, wide discussion in the press, even when the reports have been hostile.[23]

---

number of criminal abortions") and one (put forward by the Communist group) to allow therapeutic abortion on certain specified grounds, including the type of medico-social grounds permitted in Sweden. See Assemblée Nationale, Session, 1955–1956, *Proposition de loi,* Nos. 715, 1252, and 1945. A useful discussion of the existing law and of its uncertainties is given in P. Douriez, "La contraception et la loi," *Le concours medical,* May 19, 1962, pp. 3143–49. In reality there has been no ban on the publication of books or articles explaining the rhythm method and there are on sale materials which, though not labeled "contraceptives," can be used as such. In addition, it appears that the law, presumably unintentionally, does not specifically prohibit the manufacture (as distinct from the sale) of contraceptives, and contraceptive jelly has recently been produced in France.

[23] C. Valabrègue, "France," in IPPF, *Proc. of Third Conference,* p. 57; H. Fabre, "Contraception versus abortion," *Proc. of Fourth Conference of the Region for Europe . . . 1964* (mimeographed); "Planned Parenthood in France: Report of Activities," *Proc. of Fourth Conference;* C. Valabrègue, *Contrôle des naissances et planning familial* (Paris, 1960), chaps. 9 and 10. Discussion was especially stimulated by the publication in *France-soir* in March, 1961, of a series of articles by Madeleine Franck, under the title "Contrôle des naissances: oui ou non." At the more specialized level, a powerful article by the French demographer Paul Vincent stressed the difference between pro-family policy (which he supported) and anti–birth control measures (which he attacked). He advocated the repeal of Articles 3 and 4 of the 1920 law, stating that such a repeal would eliminate one of the "grandes hypocrisies" of French population policy (P. Vincent, "La liberté de la conception: opinion d'un démographe," *Les Temps modernes,* April, 1957, pp. 1547–60). The interest of the French medical profession has also increased greatly during recent years. Thus almost a thousand individuals registered for a seminar in 1963 on contraception, the seminar being held at the faculty of medicine, Paris, organized under the auspices of the National Society for the Study of Sterility and Fertility, by Dr. R. Palmer, president of the French Society of Gynecologists. In addition to the services provided by the family planning organization (the Mouvement Francais pour le Planning Familial, as it is now called), quite explicit birth control advice is now given by the Mutuelle Générale de l'Education Nationale, an association which represents around a million members (the advice is available only to members) and which initiated clinic sessions in 1963. (See J. Rettie, "Developments in France,"

Academic studies must also have played a part—including articles in *Population* dealing with "desired family size" and with attitudes to birth control. A recent field inquiry into contraceptive practice based upon a random sample of 1,200 maternity cases in the Grenoble public hospital in 1961–62 showed a high incidence of birth control. Of the whole group, 69% reported its use prior to the current pregnancy, while the reported incidence was 82% among women aged 33–37 years. Their methods were crude: two-thirds of the birth controllers used coitus interruptus solely or in combination with some other method, and this appeared to be especially prevalent among practicing Catholics.[24] These findings confirm the voluminous, indirect evidence which has long been available. Legislators who support the present law can scarcely be comforted by the results of the inquiry.

There is in any case a growing uneasiness in respect of the basic illiberality of the law, and of the linking together of contraception and abortion as if they were equally unacceptable. Increasingly it is recognized that the present pressure for free access to contraception is not Malthusian but springs from woman's need to be able to decide whether and when she wishes to have a child. The official Commission de la Famille has gone so far as to acknowledge that the law in its present form is untenable and has recommended the establishment of a special commission to consider what modifications should be introduced. Action still lies in the future, but the possibility of change is now greater than at any other time during the past twenty years.[25]

GERMANY AND AUSTRIA

The problem in Germany and Austria has also been partly legal— in that the Himmler police ordinance remained in force after the war.

Family Planning, April, 1964, p. 28; and R. Boutet de Mouvel, "A French Experiment in Education," *Family Planning*, October, 1963, pp. 71–72.)

24 S. Siebert and J. Sutter, "Attitudes devant la maternité: une enquête à Grenoble," *Population*, October–December, 1963. The authors report evidence of high failure rates and suggest that 414 out of the 1,200 current pregnancies would have been avoided or delayed if an "ideal contraceptive" had been available. It is interesting that the condom—the one freely available contraceptive—appears to be so little used, accounting for only 4% of the methods reported. Perhaps this is because in France the condom appears to be particularly linked to "immorality," prostitution, and venereal disease.

25 The Commission de la Famille was established by a decree of April 8, 1960. Its general report on family policy was published in *C.A.F. Bulletin Mensuel*, March, 1962. There is also a series of special reports, so far available only in mimeographed form. Report No. X (3) (undated), entitled *Le contrôle des naissances*, concludes, *inter alia*, that the law of 1920 can no longer be maintained in its present form and recommends that the government end the confusion resulting from the assimilation, in the public health code, of the penalties for incitement to abortion with those for birth control propaganda.

In Austria this was repealed in 1952 and contraceptives were brought under the same kind of control as general medical preparations. Access to birth control is thus theoretically free and advice is in fact given in Vienna and in some hospitals in other places. But there is little in the way of an organization for promoting the spread of modern contraception.

In West Germany, repeal took longer; the situation was not finally clear until 1961. It was not easy to re-create a movement which had been so nearly suppressed by the Nazis, traces being left of only one organization, the Association for Public Health and Voluntary Parenthood, a remnant of which had continued to meet throughout the Nazi period. A new organization—Pro Familia—was founded in 1952, despite the uncertainty of the legal position. With some financial help from the IPPF, activities were expanded after 1957 and the new group was joined in 1958 by the older one. Even so, there was by no means any sizable support in the early years from the community—especially not from the churches—and little open discussion in the press or elsewhere.

The situation was improved somewhat by the publication of two series of articles in 1963 and 1964 in a widely read woman's magazine, *Constanze*. Drawing attention to what was being done in some other European countries—especially in Britain and Sweden—the authors, in their first series of articles, described the position in West Germany as thirty years behind the rest of Europe; and, in their second series, as being still one more year behind. They stressed the role of illegal abortion in Germany (and, of course, if doctors are heavily involved in it, this may help to account for their lack of interest in contraception).[26] They also cited the 1963 inquiry of the Institut für Demoskopie as showing that while two-thirds of the married couples in West Germany were in favor of birth control, half the couples used no form of control, about a fifth practiced the safe period and a similar proportion used birth control proper.[27]

[26] It has sometimes been argued that legalized abortion, with its heavy involvement of doctors, results in a lack of medical interest in contraception, and Japan has been cited as an illustration. But in Japan the practice of contraception has greatly increased during the past 20 years.

[27] The proportion of married couples in favor of birth control is considerably higher than that found by Baumert in his DIVO inquiry (see Glass in Kiser [ed.], *op. cit.*). The articles in *Constanze* were written by Elizabeth and Peter W. Rober, the first series (entitled "Aufklärung für Erwachsene") beginning September 3, 1963, and the second series ("Keine ungewollten Kinder mehr") August 18, 1964. In contrast to the reportedly low degree of birth control in practice by married couples, articles published in 1963 in *Stern* reported widespread premarital sexual relations. The information on birth control and on sexual relations derives from a repeat of the Institut für Demoskopie's earlier study, *Umfrage in die Intimsphäre*, the results being published in a series of articles

How far these articles influenced public opinion, it is difficult to gauge. They appear to have affected the authors themselves, in the sense that they established a birth control clinic. Now there are several other clinics; five in West Berlin, four of which are run by the General Health Insurance; one in Kassel and one in Frankfurt, the two latter being supported both by the city and the *Land*.[28] With the intensification of activity during the past year, it is hoped to open new clinics in Bavaria and the Rhineland.[29]

SWITZERLAND

Developments in Switzerland, like those in West Germany, have also been hampered until fairly recently by the unwillingness of the religious organizations to become involved. And cantonal independence has limited the possibilities of action on a national scale. The position is curious in that recourse to abortion tends to be easier than in many other countries, while sterilization is also used to limit family size.[30] Contraception proper is still largely a matter for private advice or for commercial distribution, but there have also been moves to

---

in *Stern*. Mr. Peter Rober was kind enough to send me copies of the material relating to birth control practice on the part of married couples. As regards husbands, 46% reported no birth control practice, 18% the safe period, 19% "preparations" (i.e., chemical and mechanical methods) and 17% "other precautions" (not defined but presumably mainly coitus interruptus). The corresponding proportions for wives were 41, 21, 8, and 14%, respectively. At the time of writing I have no information on the nature or size of the investigation.

28 I. Brandt, "Germany," *Proc. of Second Conference*, p. 151; I. Brandt, "Western Germany," *Proc. of Third Conference*, p. 62. According to the latter report, the Protestant churches had recently begun to show a positive attitude to birth control.

29 "Pro Familia—Annual Report for 1964" (typescript kindly sent to me by the executive director, Dr. Eva Hobbing, April 26, 1965). With the limited number of clinics and the relative lack of interest of the medical profession in birth control, "marriage hygiene" mail order businesses (*Versandhäuser*) play a very substantial part in the supply of contraceptives. This is discussed by E. and P. W. Rober in the book version of their articles, *Aufklärung für Erwachsene* (Hamburg, 1965), pp. 117–21, and the authors have kindly given me additional information on the subject (information from P. W. Rober, Aug. 31, 1965). Apparently, these mail order houses in general have around 3 million customers. One of the largest of the houses analyzed its activities and indicated that in 1961 some 26% of its sales (by value) were of contraceptive materials.

30 In Basel alone, according to Dr. Reimann-Hunziker, 600 cases per year. It is claimed that the use of sterilization hinders the development of birth control practice. See R. Reimann-Hunziker, "Induced Abortion in Switzerland," *Proc. of Third Conference*, p. 228. There have been no direct inquiries in Switzerland into the incidence of various types of birth prevention. Recent studies of "desired" and "expected" numbers of births in Zürich unfortunately contained no questions on birth control (see A. Miller, "Die gewünschte Kinderzahl und die ideale Familiengrösse," *Zürcher statistischen Nachrichten*, 1963, p. 3).

provide more in the way of a public service. Thus clinics attached to hospitals exist in Geneva (with stress on the safe period) and in Lausanne. More interesting—and perhaps most significant as an indication of future provisions—is the position of the Canton de Vaud, the health service of which joined the IPPF in 1957. In 1965, the parliament of the canton decided that family planning facilities should henceforth be part of the cantonal health service—an arrangement which so far has been achieved in few Western countries.[31]

FENNO-SCANDIAN COUNTRIES

The Fenno-Scandian countries continue to show considerable variation in organizations. In Iceland there has been little change. Private medical practice is still supposedly the primary source of advice, though there is a family planning clinic in Reykjavik, opened in 1964 by the Social Institute of Iceland and now (in 1965) attached to the National Church of Iceland, which, under the law, has the responsibility of giving general marriage guidance in connection with divorce petitions.[32] Norway, too, remains more or less as it was in 1960—with the emphasis mainly on providing advice through the public maternal health clinics, though there is some doubt whether such advice is always available. So far, efforts to set up a family planning association have not been successful.

In Finland, on the other hand, access to advice and to contraceptives is secured through a private organization, the Finnish Population and Family Welfare League. This was established in 1941, has very considerably influenced governmental social policy, and now has semi-official status. It has been heavily involved in the whole field of marriage guidance and it helped to draft the 1950 Act on abortion. Under this Act, the League was empowered to set up a series of social guidance clinics for dealing with applications for abortion, this work being financed by a state grant.

It is especially as a result of the campaign to substitute contraception for abortion, that the marriage guidance clinics have increasingly come to supply birth control advice, while women applying to the social guidance clinics also receive such advice.[33] In addition, all gyne-

[31] Information from Mrs. Joan Rettie, IPPF, July 9, 1965.

[32] Information from Hannes Jónsson, director of the Social Institute, Mar. 1, 1965. (The Institute has published books on marriage and the family and on birth control.) According to this information, medical practitioners were not very helpful in giving advice (at least until the advent of the pill), for they had had no training. The clinic gives advice and also sells contraceptives.

[33] The information on the number of clinics is not completely clear, but there appear to be five clinics, covering both marriage guidance and social guidance. The League

cologists and some municipal medical officers give birth control advice, and all contraceptives are fully available commercially. Nevertheless the League is doubtful whether the position is wholly satisfactory, especially as there is public pressure for a further widening of the grounds on which abortion can legally be procured. Hence efforts are being made to include instruction on birth control in the curriculum of all medical students, and to give midwives training, while the antenatal clinics (attended by over 90% of all pregnant women) are being asked to distribute a birth control handbook (published by the League) to all women bearing children in 1965 and 1966.[34]

By contrast with Finland, Danish efforts appear to consist as much in governmental and other discussions as in positive action. Here, too, the need arose partly out of the revisions of the law relating to abortion, particularly after the 1956 Act, and from a desire to persuade women to switch over from an "abortion mentality."[35] It was in this context that the Danish Family Planning Association, founded in 1956, began a campaign to disseminate information on birth control and provide pharmacies with contraceptive supplies. The Danish Medical Association published information for general practitioners on the various types of contraceptives. In theory, the 1956 Act authorized various public and private bodies to offer birth control advice, but little in the way of practical results followed, though there are clinics run by the FPA and by the state "Maternity Aid" Institute.[36] Since 1961 too, "human reproduction" has been a compulsory subject in

---

produces birth control handbooks and also a quarterly periodical sent to all doctors in Finland. See K. Turpeinen, "Finland," *Proc. of Second Conference,* p. 132, and *Proc. of Third Conference,* p. 54. See also *Väestöliitto: The Finnish Population and Family Welfare League* (1960), pp. 20–22. It should be remembered that Finland, like Sweden, has a strong pro-family policy involving allowances for children and household loans for newly married couples.

[34] In addition to the sources already cited, information was also kindly supplied by the chairman of the League, Professor V. J. Sukselainen, Mar. 25, 1965. It is clear from the discussion that there is no opposition from the churches (predominantly Lutheran). On the contrary, the marriage guidance centers of the Lutheran church refer their clients to the League clinics for birth control advice. Unlike most other comparable bodies, the League has its own Population Policy Research Institute. So far, however, no field study of birth control practice has been carried out—a projected study was postponed for financial reasons.

[35] Though the 1956 Act included socio-medical grounds for legal abortion, the decision on whether to allow an abortion—which formerly had been made by two doctors—was henceforth put into the hands of specially appointed councils. See M.-R. Mangin, "La politique néo-malthusienne au Danemark," *Population,* January–March, 1962.

[36] In general, birth control advice is given irrespective of the marital status of the person requesting it. This is so among all family planning associations in Europe, with the exception of Britain, where the extension to the unmarried is still not fully accepted.

school courses on biology. How far instruction goes depends upon the agreement of parents, as well as upon the willingness of teachers. The Danish FPA believes that abortion frequency has fallen since 1956, a decline it associates in part with its campaign.[37] Nevertheless the Association prefers that general practitioners give birth control advice and it helped draft a bill to provide that such advice be given to every woman six weeks after delivery.[38]

The build-up of birth control organizations in Sweden, aided by governmental action, was outlined earlier in this paper. Since World War II, the various activities have been amplified. The National Association for Sex Education still provides the most important underpinning, with six clinics, a substantial number of consultant doctors distributed in different parts of the country, and a postal advisory service. The Association also has twenty-five shops selling contraceptives and a number of authorized retailers, and a substantial volume of postal sales. As the major distributor and manufacturer of contraceptives, it has been an important influence both in improving standards of quality and in increasing access to modern techniques.[39] But the Association is now only one of several agencies offering birth control advice. The other main types are the maternity and child health centers, usually attached to district hospitals, and the centers which deal

[37] Legal abortions have fallen since 1955 (the peak year) but it is extremely difficult to be sure that this is also the case with illegal abortions. Dr. A. Braestrup, chairman of the FPA, believes this is so (see her article, "Fertilitet," *Ugeskr. Laeger*, Vol. 126, No. 51, 1964) and states that the number of applications for legal abortion has also declined. Some light may be thrown on this by an investigation, sponsored by the Commission on Sex Education, conducted in one county, into birth control, pregnancy, and abortion in that area. No national field studies of contraceptive practice have so far been undertaken. A proposal for such a study was prepared by H. Gille for the Danish National Institute for Social Research, but because of lack of funds only a pilot survey has so far been completed. This, which covered 200 interviews in 1963, asked *inter alia* about birth control practice during the previous month, and reported discordant replies by husbands and wives, similar to the findings of the PIC study in Britain (see subsequent discussion). Only 16% of the husbands but 35% of the wives reported no use of birth control, the main basis of the discrepancy being in respect of the reported use of coitus interruptus. (Information from E. Jørgensen, Danish National Institute, Apr. 13, 1965; and H. Gille, Apr. 22, 1965.)

[38] Information from Dr. A. Braestrup, Mar. 3, 1965. Also, FPA, "National Report of Denmark," *IPPF Fourth Conference . . . 1964* (mimeographed); and A. Braestrup, "Family Planning," reprint from *Denmark* (Ministry of Foreign Affairs) (Copenhagen, 1961).

[39] Chemical contraceptives are manufactured in Sweden; condoms and (since 1959) pessaries are imported. Imports were at about 207,000 gross of condoms in 1963 and 103,000 pessaries. The 1964 figures were 222,000 and 71,000, respectively. Oral contraceptives have been permitted in Sweden only since May, 1964, and IUD's are at present allowed only for research purposes. (Information from Dr. T. Sjövall, Apr. 4 and 12, 1965.)

primarily with applications for legal abortion. There are in addition hospital gynecologists and private medical practitioners, though their proportionate contribution is not known. Information via books and pamphlets is also important, especially now that the open sale of contraceptives is assured.[40]

As in Denmark, the number of applications for legal abortions has been falling in Sweden, since 1951.[41] It is likely that this fall is associated with the spread of birth control, for a survey conducted in spring 1963 suggests very wide practice. The inquiry was based upon a two-stage, random sample covering 872 married women, aged up to 45 years, with responses from 93% (810). Of the total, 91.6% acknowledged using some method to plan the number of their births, the proportion ranging from 96.3% for the top social group to 87.5% for farmers.[42] On the other hand, in spite of access to modern contraceptives, coitus interruptus was still a major technique, even among those women with the longest education, being second only to the condom; the former accounted for 24% of practice (by itself or as the chief means in a combination) and the latter for over 54%.[43] How this compares with the ways in which the knowledge of birth control was obtained, it is not at present possible to tell.[44]

[40] Under the Act of 1959, all shops (other than pharmacies or specialist shops for medical apparatus) selling contraceptives must obtain a license from the police. Contraceptives are also sold in automatic machines installed in barracks, factories, and the washrooms of cafés and restaurants (see J. Sutter, "Bilan de la politique néo-malthusienne en Suède [1939–57]," *Population*, August–September, 1960).

[41] In 1950, there were 6,884 applications, of which 5,751 were approved. For 1960, the figures are approximately 4,000 and 2,500. (T. Sjövall, "Sweden," in *Proc. of Third Conference*, p. 74.)

[42] The lowest percentages are among the childless (75.0%) and those with four or more children (82.4%). For other family sizes, the proportions were from 92.9 to 93.6 and 96.7% (1, 2, and 3 children) (*Ökat stöd till barnfamiljer*, Stat. Off. Utredingar, 1964, 36 [Stockholm, 1964], Table 6, p. 58). The inquiry was directed by Professor G. Karlsson, Uppsala University. I am indebted to Mrs. Inge Westergaard, who translated the document, and to Dr. E. V. Hofsten, who sent me the report.

[43] *Ibid.*, Table 14, p. 63. Included in the 54% for the condom is 8.1% for that method in conjunction with coitus interruptus. The table also includes (in its 100% total) 2.4% of "no technique"—that is, primarily childless women who said they were planning their families but, with no children so far, were not actually using birth control. The pessary as a sole or main method accounted for 13.1%.

[44] The schedule used in the inquiry (*ibid.*, p. 145, question 99) asked respondents how they had obtained their knowledge of birth control, but the results are not given in the report. The over-all findings of the inquiry contrast sharply with the experience of women applying for legal abortions. Thus among the 1,160 applying to the Stockholm Mental Health Agency in 1964, 531 said that they had never used any method, 254 reported condom, and 150 coitus interruptus (information from Dr. T. Sjövall, Apr. 4, 1965). The fact that the women attending National Association clinics are predominantly prescribed the diaphragm, does not necessarily mean that knowledge of the condom is not also spread by the Association's activities.

NETHERLANDS

Swedish institutions offering advice are now working within a society in which there are no longer legal hindrances to birth control—where, on the contrary, a variety of motives has resulted in strong public pressure to improve the knowledge and practice of contraception. In the Netherlands, the situation is different. There has so far been only one major institution, the Netherlands Society for Sexual Reform, and it has had to work in circumstances of semilegality, so to speak—by increasing its number of individual members. It is these members who provide the financial basis—an annual membership fee of 6 florins per person—and to whom it has the first responsibility. By mid-1964, there were 200,000 members and their fees have helped to build a large and impressive structure, covering thirty-three birth control clinics and nine consultation centers, with a substantial staff of doctors, trained and paid by the organization, the payment being met by the fees charged for consultation at the birth control clinics.

The organization consists of two bodies controlled by a single board of directors. The Society proper, covering ninety-six local sections, consists of the whole membership and is largely run by a core of some 5,000 activists; it is the members who provide from among themselves individuals who act as local "stockists" for the supply of condoms and jellies. The other body is the Netherlands Stichting, which supervises the medical side of the Society's activities. Membership of the Society consists predominantly of employees and skilled workers, in the 20–40-year age groups, and very largely Protestant in adherence, though 10% are Roman Catholics (as compared with 39% in the country as a whole). This latter fact is noteworthy not only in respect of affiliation by individuals whose church is in general opposed to the Society's objectives, but no less so in that in the Netherlands even fully acceptable activities tend to be organized in duplicated but separate religious structures.[45] The Society manufactures pessaries and spermicidal pastes; and though it usually prescribes a diaphragm or cap, it also sells condoms—indeed, its sales account for some 30% of the condoms sold in the country.[46] In recent years, there appears to have been a considerable swing to the use of condoms, so that increased membership has not meant a corresponding increase in the number of members attending the clinics.

The Society covers much more than birth control proper: infertil-

45 There is, indeed, something of a deliberate, religious "ghetto" mentality, so that schools and social services are organized separately for the different main religious groups.

46 Sales of condoms in 1962 in the Netherlands are reported at 68,000 gross (information from Dr. J. Schuyff, Executive Secretary, NVSH., May 11, 1965).

ity, marriage guidance and sex education in general are also its concern. It is active in spreading information and promoting discussions, publishes three magazines (one of which is sent monthly to every member), and helps to produce educational films. Yet it would be the first to acknowledge that there are still sizable gaps in the Netherlands. It has not been very successful in reaching farm workers or unskilled urban workers, for whom the presently available birth control techniques are not sufficiently effective or easy to use.

Outside its own clinics, private medical practitioners are still badly informed about contraception: a survey undertaken for the Society in 1961 reported that 87% of Dutch family doctors were uninformed or ill-informed on the subject.[47] And a further survey in 1963, commissioned by the Society, revealed a low level of birth control practice among married women other than those who were members of the NVSH. To the question, "Do you use birth control?" only 47% of the non-members answered yes, the proportion being substantially higher only for women with no religious affiliation (61%) or those in the upper social stratum (60%).[48] By contrast, the over-all proportion of yes answers was 93% for women who were members of the NVSH—not surprisingly, since they had presumably joined the Society because they wanted to use birth control. Among the latter women who answered yes, the condom and the diaphragm were the methods most frequently mentioned; for those controllers who were not members of the Society, the safe period, coitus interruptus, and the condom were the most frequently mentioned, in descending order.[49]

The situation may improve in the near future, for another survey

[47] The survey was carried out by the Stichting Bevolkingsbeleid, Voorst (information from Dr. J. Schuyff, May 11 and June 24, 1965).

[48] There was also a sizable proportion of women who reported all birth control methods (presumably including safe period) as ethically unacceptable—12% in total, 12% for Roman Catholics, and 18% among those belonging to the Reformed Church. The survey is reported in Nederlandse Stichting voor Statistiek, *Orale anti-conceptie en het gebruik van andere methoden ter voorkoming van zwangerschap*, September, 1963, the figures cited being from Tables 9 and 11, pp. 14 and 16. The highest practice is among women in the urban communities (60%). It should be noted that the survey consisted of two inquiries: (1) 307 completed interviews out of a random sample of 410 married women aged 21–44 years, members of the NVSH; (2) a quota sample of married women in the same age group in the country at large. This latter sample originally consisted of 524 married women of whom 120 were found to be members of the NVSH (an excessive proportion, which suggests that co-operation in the quota sample inquiry was influenced by attitudes to birth control). These 120 were transferred to category (1). Thus the final analyses were based upon (1), 427 members of the Society, and (2) 404 women who were *not* members. The figures cited above relate to the latter group.

[49] (a) Society "controllers"—of the methods mentioned, the condom accounted for over 40%, the diaphragm for 20%, and coitus interruptus for under 10%. (b) Other "controllers"—the safe period accounted for almost two-fifths, coitus interruptus for almost a quarter, and the condom for around a fifth (*ibid.*, Table 11).

commissioned by the NVSH—an inquiry among young men and women aged 21–22—appeared to show a widespread awareness of contraception on the part of the younger generation.[50] And the churches, as was noted earlier, have been changing their attitude— especially the Dutch Reformed Church, since the Pastoral Letter of 1952. With the situation in the Netherlands this change is more likely to lead to the establishment of an additional series of centers for the separate religious groups—this is already being done by the Protestants —than to the transformation of the NVSH into a universal body catering to all religions. In any case, much will depend upon whether, and how far, the state decides to concern itself with the problem of family limitation.[51]

BRITAIN

Finally, there is the question of the position of organized birth control facilities in Britain. Here the circumstances are more easily described, both because there has recently been a full-scale attempt at self-evaluation and because special analyses of the survey carried out by the Population Investigation Committee (PIC) were provided to assist that evaluation. Since the results of these studies are widely available, the discussion will be restricted to a consideration of the contribution of the existing Family Planning Association to the spread of birth control and to organizational matters that affect the future functioning of the system.[52] In this connection it should be emphasized that

[50] Nederlandse Stichting voor Statistiek, and Dr. Y. N. van der Veen, *Sexuele voorlichting aan jongeren*, September, 1963. The inquiry covered 398 members of the NVSH (the criterion included membership by parents or fiancé) and 600 non-members. Among the former, 100% reported a knowledge of birth control—about half having obtained it from NVSH sources. But even among the latter, awareness was reported by 88%— knowledge being obtained mainly from books or friends.

[51] Additional sources of information: NVSH, *op. cit.*; B. S. Witte, "National Report of Holland," *Fourth Conference . . . 1964* (mimeographed). The new interest of the Roman Catholic Church in the subject may be seen reflected, to some extent, in the study conducted by Timmermans in 1960–61, among young Roman Catholic married couples who attended his courses (on marriage and the family) in the western mining district of Limburg. See L. A. G. J. Timmermans, *Huwelijksbeleving van Katholieke jonggehuwden* (Utrecht-Nijmegen, 1964) (with English summary). See also T. Blankenstijn-Biersma, "The Netherlands," *Proc. of Second Conference . . . 1960*, p. 129. The changed attitude of the government is suggested by the appointment by the Minister of Health of an "advisory discussion group" to consider the legal position and possibility of official support of family planning in the Netherlands (information from Dr. C. Van Emde Boas, Sept. 23, 1965).

[52] The main relevant publications are: [F. Lafitte], *Family Planning in the Sixties: Report of the Family Planning Association Working Party* (London, 1963); C. P. Blacker, *Family Planning in the Sixties: Some Comments* (London, 1964) (mimeographed 4-page comment); G. Rowntree and R. M. Pierce, "Birth Control in Britain," *Population Studies*, July and November, 1961.

the working party began its inquiries in 1960 and that much of its information does not go beyond that year. Since then, however, various changes have taken place, to some of which reference will be made later.

By the end of 1960, there were 334 FPA clinics in operation in Britain. It had not been the intention of the birth control movement—even in the 1920's—to establish a large series of clinics. The aim had been far more to ensure that adequate advice be given through the existing network of publicly run and financed maternal welfare centers. When, in the 1930's, it was evident that such a development would at best be very slow, clinics were established as a necessary but by no means preferred alternative. However, a link with the local authorities was established, and part of the support of the FPA and its clinics consists of a concealed subsidy in the form of a nominal rent for premises usually charged to the clinics by local authorities and hospitals. The rest of the support comes from the annual membership fees paid by members of the local branches; consultancy fees paid by patients; fees charged for the training of doctors and nurses in contraceptive practice; and the profit made by selling contraceptives. These are obtained on specially favorable terms from manufacturers and are sold below normal retail price; even so, the profit on sales contributes about half the reported net income of FPA branches.

The number of new patients seeking advice on birth control at FPA clinics was around 101,000—of whom some 86,000 were already married. This is a substantial number, but the working party estimated that it involved a coverage of only about 11% of newly married women during the first year of their marriage. This estimate is at a fairly high point on a rising curve of clinic creation and attendance. For women married over a longer period—1950–59—the PIC survey found that, even of those who reported the use of birth control, only some 8% had obtained advice from clinics, while 11% had obtained it from doctors. Whichever estimate is taken, the direct contribution of the clinics is small.

A similar picture is obtained from information on the types of contraception recommended by the clinics compared with those reported by married couples in the PIC survey. For a sample month—November, 1960—the working party found that 86% of the new clients at the clinics were advised to use a cap immediately, and a further 11.5% to adopt a cap after first using a sheath. By contrast, in the PIC survey, taking the last type of contraceptive used by couples married in 1950–59 and reporting birth control practice, all female methods (including the cap) accounted for only 27.5% of contraceptive practice; the predominant types of birth control used were the sheath (solely or together with minor methods), 49%; coitus interruptus (also solely or with other minor methods), 15%; and a combination of the two techniques, 5.5%. This probably understates the role of coitus interruptus and hence overstates the contribution of the cap and of the clinics to total contraceptive practice.

In an earlier report on the results of the PIC inquiry into birth control in Britain, I suggested that among the more recent marriage cohorts (1950–59) the proportion of couples ultimately practicing birth control would probably not amount to much more than 75%.[53] Subsequently, however, it was possible to examine the data for segments of married life and to consider the differential reporting of men and women in respect of the use of coitus interruptus. On the basis of these further analyses I have estimated that, more realistically, among the 1950–54 marriage cohort, around 87% of couples will ultimately have used birth control, given the circumstances visible in the nearest earlier cohorts.[54] Against this figure, the quantitative contribution of the clinics would appear small, both absolutely and in relation to the enthusiasm and energy invested in the running of clinics.

But paralleling, and partly consequent upon, the inquiries of the working party, changes have been taking place in the activities of the FPA. The number of clinics has increased considerably, to 453 in 1964, and the number of new patients in that year was over 114,000. More significantly, many clinics are now prescribing oral contraceptives and thus breaking away from the traditional prescription.[55] There is also a growing interest in working outside of, or from, the clinics, instead of solely within them. Some years ago, Dr. Mary Peberdy began this experimentally in one city; her approach was endorsed, at least in principle, by the FPA in its report for 1964, which stated that "instead of concentrating on bringing people to our services, we can now begin to think more about taking our services to the people who need them most."[56]

[53] In Kiser (ed.), *op. cit.*, pp. 259–60.

[54] See the Appendix to D. V. Glass, "Fertility and Birth Control in Developed Societies . . . ," *Proceedings of the Seventh International Conference of the IPPF, Singapore, 1963* (Amsterdam, 1964). In referring to the raw data of the PIC survey, published in *Population Studies,* Louis Henry suggested that the results of field studies of birth control practice be treated with caution. They should be especially wherever coitus interruptus remains a major technique. But for various obvious reasons, indirect studies are not a substitute for direct inquiries. We need to improve our methods of investigation, be aware of their limitations, and use the results jointly with those of indirect assessments. See L. Henry, "A propos d'une enquête sur la contraception en Grande-Bretagne," *Population,* January–March, 1962. See also the discussion in *Proc. Royal Soc.,* Ser. B., Dec. 10, 1963, pp. 89–92.

[55] FPA, *Draft Annual Report 1964–65,* p. 2.

[56] *Draft Annual Report,* p. 1. Dr. Peberdy's experiment in Newcastle was begun in 1958; see her article "Home Help: An Experimental Service for Domiciliary Birth

There is also concern with providing birth control advice to the unmarried and not just to the married, and the FPA has become much more aware of the importance of inquiring into and evaluating its own activities. The Royal Commission on Population recommended that the provision of birth control advice should be accepted as part of the duties of the National Health Service, and that "the initial duty to give advice should rest with the family doctor."[57] So far, this recommendation has not been adopted. But if it should be, there will clearly have to be a major reconsideration of the functions of the FPA.

RESPECTABILITY REQUIRES NEW GUIDE LINES

Existing organizations in other countries in Western Europe will face the same problem, should similar circumstances arise. These organizations only too often grew up in adversity, run by groups prepared to be regarded as deviants. As hostility diminished, and as societies came to realize that birth control *had* spread in spite of the obstacles of law and custom, organized activity could be both expanded and modified.[58] But it does not follow that adaptation by piecemeal adjustment has resulted in systems which best suit present needs. There may still be far too much of a residue of the original forms and approaches, left over from a period in which health services were less developed, when access to the "family doctor" was restricted to the middle classes, when there were few "safe" techniques of birth control, and when in any case birth control was not a "respectable" subject. In some countries, no doubt, that earlier context still obtains,

---

Control," *Family Planning*, April, 1960. The 1964 report of the FPA notes that there were then domiciliary services in six urban communities, in two cases with financial assistance from the local authority, and that similar schemes were being initiated elsewhere. See also J. Peel and F. Schenk, "Domiciliary Birth Control," *Eugenics Review*, June, 1965.

[57] Royal Commission on Population, *Report*, Cmd. 7695, London, 1949, p. 194. It is to be hoped that the newly appointed Royal Commission on Medical Education will take this recommendation into account in considering the curriculum for medical students.

[58] The IPPF itself has also been changing considerably in recent years and has become much more apprized of the relevance of research. This paper has been concerned with "Western Europe" in the strict sense. Eastern Europe (including the German Democratic Republic) is considered in another paper in this volume (chap. 16, by K.-H. Mehlan), but Southern Europe has not been made the subject of a specific contribution. Hence it may be of interest to add a few notes on that region. So far as Spain and Portugal are concerned there is very little to report. In neither country are birth control organizations permitted. Whatever is done must be clandestine or involve resort to "natural" methods, such as coitus interruptus or the safe period. In Italy, the penal code prohibitions regarding birth control propaganda still apply; nevertheless propaganda has been spread and advice given by the Italian Association for Demographic Education, set up in 1953. Recently, internal difficulties have seriously hampered the development of organized national activity, but there are signs that these difficulties may now

though there have been modifications of it since World War II. But even for these countries a substantial review of aims and activities may soon become appropriate and one of the most valuable contributions of the IPPF would be to supply the guiding lines for such a review.

---

be in process of resolution. In Greece, there is no family planning association at present, though it is possible that one may be established in the not too distant future. At the same time, the demographic data make it quite clear that birth prevention—in some form or other—is fairly widespread in all four countries. In Greece, in particular, a recent study by V. G. Valaoras et al. ("Control of Family Size in Greece," *Population Studies,* March, 1965, pp. 265-78) suggests that coitus interruptus, the condom, and induced abortion are used by very substantial proportions of married couples.

16

THE SOCIALIST COUNTRIES
OF EUROPE

K.-H. MEHLAN, M.D.
Director, Institute of Hygiene
Dean, Medical Faculty, University of Rostock, German Democratic Republic

In the socialist countries of Eastern Europe, all children are wanted children. Responsible parenthood is a basic ingredient of socialist health programs and of socialist population policy which is frequently misinterpreted by demographers from Western countries, who contend that Marxist demographers are opposed to both Malthus and to responsible parenthood. Lenin stated: "Freedom of medical information and protection of the elementary rights of the citizen are one thing. The doctrine of neo-Malthusianism is another."[1]

Since socialism is characterized by the integration of political, economic, demographic, and preventive health measures, Marxists are opposed to the use of family planning as an independent means of combatting the socioeconomic causes of poverty. Engel's statement that people create their own history applies to their reproductive behavior as well. The reproductive behavior of the family in a socialist society develops in complete harmony between the individual and society. Marxists fear neither overpopulation nor underpopulation.

In the socialist countries, women have achieved equal legal status with men in all fields, and family planning contributes to their emancipation by combining happy maternity and creative work. On the basis of this political attitude, and to prevent illegal abortions, laws permitting abortion were enacted in the Soviet Union in 1955, in Bulgaria, Poland, Hungary, and Romania in 1956, in Czechoslovakia in 1957, and in Yugoslavia in 1960.

Except in Czechoslovakia, abortion is performed on demand unless

[1] Lenin, *Collected Works*, 23: 253.

medically contraindicated. In Czechoslovakia, specific social indications must be present, such as advanced age of the woman, at least three children, disability of the husband, broken marriage, unfavorable economic circumstances, or illegitimacy. In the German Democratic Republic, where the law of 1950 provided for abortion on medical and eugenic grounds only, a recent reinterpretation extended *de facto* recognition to socio-medical and ethical indications, including age of woman (40 years and older), number of children (five or more), rapid succession of births, intra-uterine damage to the fetus, cases of rape, and pregnancies of girls under 16 years of age.

Contraindications to abortion are similar in all countries: a period of gestation in excess of twelve weeks, an induced abortion within the preceding six months, or acute or chronic pathology of the genital organs.

The operation must be performed by a gynecologist and, in general, in a hospital. In cases of abortion for eugenic reasons, it is recommended that the woman be sterilized at the same time. Each case must be registered and reported to the public health authorities. Except in Poland and the German Democratic Republic, a fee is charged for voluntary abortion, while abortion on medical grounds is free in all countries.

In Czechoslovakia, the German Democratic Republic, and Yugoslavia, abortions are authorized by medical commissions, with the proviso that adverse decisions may be appealed to a higher medical body. In Romania and the USSR, women may go directly to the outpatient clinic; in Bulgaria and Hungary, to the hospital; and in Poland, to the family doctor. In these countries, the ultimate decision rests with the surgeon performing the operation. In some countries, instruction in contraception accompanies the authorization of induced abortion, and in Poland, Yugoslavia, and the USSR this procedure is compulsory.

The main objective in simplifying the administrative procedures is to minimize the time lag between the request for the operation and its performance. Experience shows that in some countries, administrative formalities extend beyond the period of gestation prescribed by the abortion laws of the socialist countries. Such delay may result in psychological tensions and cause some women to resort to criminal abortion.

New Techniques of Abortion

In the past, the usual procedure for inducing abortion has been dilation and curettage. A new procedure has recently been developed utilizing special instruments to evacuate the uterus. First, an electric instrument, resembling the traditional Hegar's dilator, is used to expand the cervix, a procedure which takes one to two minutes. In cases of pregnancy of less than twelve weeks duration, a vacuum-type apparatus, providing a negative pressure of 1–1.5 atmospheres and connected by a plastic or rubber tube to a hollow Hegar's dilator with a lateral hole, is inserted into the uterus to evacuate its contents. In the opinion of experienced gynecologists, this method reduces blood loss, infection, and lesions of the uterus.

TABLE 1

TOTAL AND LEGAL ABORTIONS, 1955–64

(In Thousands)

Country	1955	1956	1957	1958	1959	1960	1961	1962	1963	1964ᵃ
	Total Registered Abortions									
Bulgaria.........	19.1	40.0	46.2	55.5	63.8	74.1	88.7	97.8	103.8	......
Czechoslovakia...	35.1	34.1	37.5	89.1	105.5	114.6	120.3	115.9	99.9	99.0
Hungary.........	78.5	123.6	168.8	183.0	187.7	196.0	203.7	197.6	207.9	218.7
Poland.	101.6	104.3	121.8	126.4	161.5	223.8	216.6	210.7	260.3	246.8
Yugoslavia......	......	......	......	......	111.8	133.3	164.5	......	......	......
Romania.........	......	......	......	129.5	235.8	......	......	......	......	......
	Legal Abortions									
Bulgaria.........	......	......	30.9	37.5	45.6	54.8	68.8	76.7	83.3	......
Czechoslovakia...	2.1	3.1	7.3	61.4	79.1	88.3	94.3	89.8	70.5	70.7
Hungary.........	35.4	82.5	123.3	145.6	152.4	162.6	170.0	163.7	173.8	184.4
Poland..........	1.4	18.9	36.4	44.2	79.0	150.4	143.8	140.4	146.5	143.6
Yugoslavia......	......	......	......	......	54.5	76.7	104.7	......	......	......
Romania.........	......	......	......	112.1	219.1	......	......	......	......	......

ᵃ Provisional figures.

Some tests with antimetabolites as abortifacients have recently been initiated on a small scale. The antimetabolites used were azaurdine and peltatine, combined with estrogen. Given orally to pregnant women, these agents cause the death of the fetus but do not usually result in its expulsion from the uterine cavity.

EFFECT OF LEGISLATION

The immediate effect of the new legislation on abortion in the socialist countries has been to increase legal abortions, the rate of increase varying from country to country (see Table 1 and Fig. 1). While in some countries peak rates may not have been reached, a small decline has occurred in Czechoslovakia and Poland since 1962. In Hungary, the number of legal abortions exceeded the number of live births in each year beginning with 1959 (see Table 2). In Romania, the decline in the birth rate from 20.2 in 1959 to 15.7 in 1963 followed a sharp increase in the abortion rate in 1959, the last year for which data on abortions are available. Official estimates for Yugoslavia for 1964 amount to over 200,000 hospital abortions, of which 70% are legal and the remaining 30% are incomplete, either spontaneous or illegally induced. Data for the Soviet Union are not available.

That the liberalization of the laws on abortion has succeeded in reducing the number of criminal abortions may be deduced from the decline in deaths from such operations. In Poland, the number decreased from 76 in 1956 to 26 in 1959; in Czechoslovakia, from 53 in 1956 to 11 in 1962; and in Hungary, from 83 in 1956 to 24 in 1964. It is probable that other sequelae of criminal abortion, such as acute and chronic damage to health, including sterility, have also been reduced.

COMPLICATIONS AFTER LEGAL ABORTION

Acute complications and death after legal abortion are rare. In the years 1963 and 1964, there were no deaths among 140,000 cases of legal abortion in Czechoslovakia, and none among 67,000 operations in Bulgaria. In Hungary in 1963 and 1964, there were two deaths among 358,200 legal abortions; and in Yugoslavia in 1961, five among 104,700 operations.

It is difficult to give a precise account of the morbidity associated with legal abortion. In general, an insignificant number of cases of damage to health is reported, and even this number is declining as physicians become more experienced. In Czechoslovakia, early sequelae represented 5.2% of the cases in 1958 and 2.3% in 1963, and late sequelae 12% of the cases in 1958 and 4.9% in 1963. The figures for Slovenia for 1962 are 2.8% for early sequelae and 1.9% for late sequelae. Czernoch[2] reported the following data in cases of abortion in a large hospital in Prague: injuries, less than 0.1%; infections, less than 0.5%; and hemorrhage, 0.3%. The number of complications, particularly infections, appears to increase with duration of gestation, especially after the twelfth week. Special problems also exist in interrupting the first pregnancy in girls under 17 years of age. A stay in the hospital of less than three days following the operation also appears to increase the incidence of late sequelae.

[2] Ant. Czernoch, "Experiences in Czechoslovakia with the Effects and Consequences of Legalized Artificial Termination of Pregnancy," World Population Conference (WPC), Belgrade, 1965, Paper No. 337 (in English).

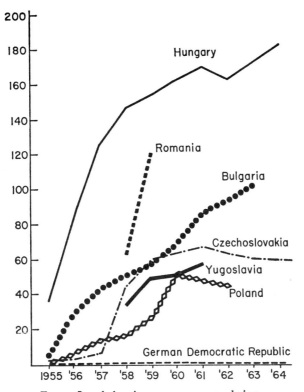

FIG. 1.—Legal abortions per 10,000 population

TABLE 2

LEGAL ABORTIONS PER 1,000 WOMEN 15–49 YEARS OF AGE
AND PER 100 LIVE BIRTHS, 1955–64

Country	1955	1956	1957	1958	1959	1960	1961	1962	1963	1964[a]
	Legal Abortions per 1,000 Women									
Bulgaria.......	.....	.....	16	19	23	27	34	38	41	.....
Czechoslovakia...	1	1	2	19	25	28	29	28	22	22
Hungary........	14	33	49	58	61	65	69	66	70	79
Poland..........	.....	3	5	6	11	21	20	20	24	20
Yugoslavia......	.....	.....	.....	.....	11	16	22	.....	.....	.....
Romania........	.....	.....	.....	26	51	.....	.....	.....	.....	.....
	Legal Abortions per 100 Live Births									
Bulgaria.......	.....	.....	22	27	33	39	50	57	63	.....
Czechoslovakia...	1	1	3	26	36	41	43	41	30	29
Hungary........	17	43	74	92	101	111	121	126	131	140
Poland..........	0	2	5	6	11	23	23	23	25	26
Yugoslavia......	.....	.....	.....	.....	13	18	25	.....	.....	.....
Romania........	.....	.....	.....	29	60	.....	.....	.....	.....	.....

[a] Provisional figures.

An increase in late sequelae has recently been reported from Czechoslovakia and Hungary. Slunsky[3] stated that the risk of spontaneous abortion, premature birth, stillbirth, and various birth complications is doubled by repeated abortions. Czernoch found that one-half of the women with cervical insufficiency among his hospital patients had previously undergone legal abortion. On the other hand, physicians in Czechoslovakia, Hungary, and Yugoslavia report a significant improvement in the ability to reach orgasm and in the sexual life of their patients following the legalization of abortion.

EFFECT ON FERTILITY RATES

In Bulgaria, Czechoslovakia, and Hungary, where fertility was relatively low before the enactment of the abortion law, the number of births decreased immediately and sharply. In the USSR, Poland, and Yugoslavia, on the other hand, where fertility was relatively high, the decline began later and, except in Poland, was relatively slow. The lowest live-birth rates are recorded in those countries in which the ratio of abortions to births is highest. In Czechoslovakia, the increase in births since 1963 has been associated with the decline in the number of abortions since 1962.

UNION OF SOVIET SOCIALIST REPUBLICS (USSR)

Abortion as a method of family planning was legalized in the USSR after intensive discussions because: (1) no highly effective contraceptives, acceptable to all classes of the population, were available; (2) there was a humanistic desire to wage an intensive campaign against illegal abortion; and (3) it seemed desirable to bring all pregnant women under medical supervision. Nevertheless, discussions at medical conferences in the USSR have led to the conclusion that induced abortion is not without some danger to the woman and must be replaced by effective contraception. The legalization of abortion is considered a temporary, emergency measure.

Simultaneously with the legalization of abortion, special provisions were made for the care of pregnant women and mothers. Vacations for pregnant women were fixed at 18 weeks with full pay, and medical care and hospitalization during delivery are free. Families with more than two children receive birth subsidies and children's allowances, and, after 1970, 75% of the expense for the maintenance and education of children will be paid by the state. Taxes on childless couples have been increased.

[3] *Ibid.*, quoting Slunsky.

A network of maternity centers, staffed with gynecologists, midwives, and lawyers, extends over the entire country. There is one gynecologist for every 3,000 women 15 years of age and over. Attached to each center is a special unit whose function is to reduce the number of legal abortions and of abortions performed outside of hospitals, and to encourage the use of contraception. The gynecologists and midwives are required to instruct the women in the use of contraception, and in many centers, there are stocks of informational material, as well as contraceptives for sale. The available contraceptives are condoms, diaphragms and cervical caps, Gramicidin paste, and vaginal tablets (Nicozeptin containing nicotinic acid, Lutenin with a vegetable agent, and Galazepnin). The tablets are reported to be 94% to 97% effective.

The gynecologist must discuss with each woman the reasons for her application for an abortion and must warn her of possible adverse sequelae. In cases of social difficulties, a lawyer is called in. However, if the woman insists, her application must be approved and she is sent to a hospital. The vacuum method of abortion is used and the patient must be hospitalized for at least three days. Although women are expected to go to the maternity center in their locality, they frequently travel to a larger town in order to conceal the fact that they are seeking an abortion. They are entitled to choose their own physician.

The maternity centers are required to give lectures on contraception, on the danger of abortion, and on marital problems. Since 1955, more intensive efforts have been made to reach the husband. Informational material to popularize contraception is produced by the Central Institute for Health Education in Moscow, and includes films, pamphlets, exhibitions, and posters. A film entitled "Wasted Youth" is specifically directed at young people.

Nearly 40% of the women who have had one or more abortions and have sexual intercourse regularly do not use any contraception. Many women become pregnant because of a failure of contraception and then refuse to continue its use. Furthermore, it is stated that in spite of the official promotion of contraception, people know little about it and the refusal rate remains high. Moreover, traditional attitudes, especially in the Asiatic republics, hinder extensive use of contraception.

EXTENT AND EFFECT OF LEGAL ABORTION

The pattern of abortion varies from republic to republic, with the largest differential between the European and Asiatic sectors of the USSR. In some large towns, the ratio of abortions to births is 1:1; in large industrial districts, it is 0.8:1; in many western districts, it is 0.5:1; and in the predominantly rural districts, 0.3:1.

In a study of 26,000 legal abortions in the period 1958–59, Sadvokasova[4] divided her urban and rural populations into four groups according to whether the reasons for the abortion justified its performance, i.e., whether the operation was avoidable (see Table 3). Sadvokasova also reported on incomplete abortions, most of which were illegally induced. Among these women, the proportion of primigravidae was 14%, compared with 10% for women having legal abortions, and the proportion of childless women was 20% compared

TABLE 3

DISTRIBUTION OF LEGAL ABORTIONS, 1958–59

(Per Cent)

Group	Urban	Rural
I. Absolutely avoidable (economic insecurity, unsatisfactory housing, no place for child)	35	26
II. Possibly avoidable (unmarried mother, marital conflicts, disease of partner)	17	18
III. Unavoidable (large family, newborn child in family)	10	10
IV. Unclear (mother or father does not wish child, other reasons)	38	46

with 10%, respectively. The ratio of working women to housewives among those having legal abortions was three to one. Among every 100 women having legal abortions, 10 were childless, 41 had one child, 16 had two children, and 33 had three or more children.

FACTORS AFFECTING FERTILITY

Crude birth rates in the USSR have declined from 27.7 in 1955 to 20.8 in 1964. The most important factors influencing fertility are:

1. *Increasing integration of women into communal activities.*— More than 83% of all women in the 15–59-year age group are working, and nearly one-half of all employees are women. Women account for 79% of the physicians, 70% of the teachers, 39% of the agronomers, 32% of the engineers, and 37% of all scientific workers. More than 800 women are members of the Academy of Sciences, or are professors. In 1958, compared with housewives in the same age groups, the fertility of working women in the 20–29-year age group was a fourth lower, and in the 30–39-year age group, one half lower. As

[4] Y. A. Sadvokasova, "Birth Control Measures and Their Influence on Reproduction," WPC, Belgrade, 1965, Paper No. 189 (in Russian).

early as 1929–33, Strumiliv[5] reported a birth rate of 87.7 per 1,000 working women compared with 169.1 per 1,000 housewives.

2. *Increasing urbanization and industrialization.*—During the past ten years, the birth rate in rural areas has been about one-fourth higher than in urban areas. In 1962, the birth rate for the rural population was 25.0 per 1,000 compared with 20.0 per 1,000 for the urban population. In the period 1950–62, the urban population has increased from 39% of the total to 52%.

3. *Rise in cultural and educational levels.*—While illiteracy was extensive in tsarist Russia, it has not existed in the Soviet Union for some time. In 1964, 32% of the population and 50% of the working population had at least a secondary school education.

TABLE 4

DISTRIBUTION OF FAMILIES BY NUMBER OF CHILDREN, 1962

(Per Cent)

Number of Children	Salaried Employees	Wage Earners	Collective Farmers
One child................	50	46	40
Two children.............	41	39	32
Three children............	8	12	19
Four children or more......	1	3	9

In a study of family size in the USSR in 1962, Ovsienko[6] reported the percentage distribution of families by number of children 16 years of age or younger and by working status of the head of the household (see Table 4). The figures show that the number of children in a family decreases with increasing education.

4. *Shift in age at marriage.*—The average age at marriage for women has increased from 23 years in 1910 to 27 years in 1960 (Urlanis).[7] In 1960, 25% of the brides were 20 years of age or younger, 66% were 25 years old or younger, 78% were 30 years or less, and 89% were 40 years old or less.

5. *Socio-psychological factors.*—Factors which favor an increase in family size are full employment, confidence in the future, increase in the number of institutions for child care, generous measures for protection of mothers and children, and increasing economic support for women with large families.

[5] *Ibid.*, quoting Strumiliv.

[6] V. E. Ovsienko, "Influence of Social and Economic Factors on Demographic Characteristics," WPC, Belgrade, 1965, Paper No. 230 (in Russian).

[7] B. T. S. Urlanis, "Trends and Factors of Natality in the USSR," WPC, Belgrade, 1965, Paper No. 2 (in Russian).

PEOPLE'S REPUBLIC OF HUNGARY

The legalization of abortion in Hungary was followed by a continuous increase in the number of legal abortions, which reached its maximum in 1964 with 75 abortions per 1,000 women of reproductive age. A total of 218,700 legal abortions was registered in that year compared with 132,000 births, or 165 abortions per 100 births. The number of other abortions treated in hospitals has remained unchanged. Miltényi[8] estimated that the number of induced abortions per married woman probably exceeded three by the end of her reproductive life. Changing attitudes toward family size, the ease of obtaining a legal abortion, and the limited use of contraception combined with its lack of effectiveness account for this unfavorable development.

According to Miltényi,[9] the main motivation for legal abortion

TABLE 5

LEGAL ABORTIONS BY NUMBER OF LIVING CHILDREN, 1962

(Per 1,000 Married Women)

Number of Children	Confinements	Legal Abortions	Ratio of Legal Abortions to Pregnancies[a]
None	236.9	48.5	17.0
One child	69.0	84.1	54.9
Two children	28.0	91.0	76.5
Three children or more	35.5	86.2	70.8

[a] Confinements plus legal abortions.

among married women is the number of living children, as shown in the figures for 1962 (see Table 5). While only one-sixth of the childless married women terminated their pregnancies by abortion (in most cases to postpone childbirth), the ratio of abortions to pregnancies for those having one child was more than one-half, and for those having two children, more than three-fourths. Of 100 women who had induced abortions in 1963, 56 had two or more children, 29 had one child, and 15 had no children.

The use of birth control is influenced by the number and sex of the children in the family; age seems less important than the availability of institutions for the care of infants. The level of induced

[8] K. Miltényi, "Demographic Significance of Induced Abortions," *Demográfia,* 3–4: 419–28 (1964) (in Hungarian); A. Klinger, "Demographic Effects of Abortion in Some Socialist Countries," WPC, Belgrade, 1965, Paper No. 88.

[9] K. Miltényi, "Social and Psychological Factors Affecting Fertility in a Legalized Abortion System," WPC, Belgrade, 1965, Paper No. 334 (in English).

abortion is influenced by the professional activity and occupation of the woman. The fertility of housewives is 86% higher that that of working women, although a small decline in the differential has been observed recently.

Families where the nature of the work of the husband and wife is fundamentally different are more inclined to resort to legal abortion, especially if the woman is in an occupational category considered to be of a lower status. The low birth rates in urban areas, especially in Budapest, may be attributed to a higher rate of induced abortion, although birth control is also undoubtedly more extensively used than in rural areas. Fertility is about twice as high among home owners as it is among families who rent or share their homes.

In 1964, 95% of the women applying for abortion gave personal reasons, and 5%, medical indications. About equal numbers of women stated that they already had a sufficient number of children; claimed such difficulties as short birth intervals, fear of delivery or illness, and advanced age; or reported unfavorable financial and living conditions.

Forty per cent of the women who had had an abortion stated that they intended to have a child within a short time after the operation, while 60% regarded their families as complete. Miltényi[10] concluded that a large proportion of legal abortions was due to a desire to postpone childbirth. However, on the basis of subsequent histories of these women, future births should not be expected.

To reduce the number of abortions, the government of Hungary has extended the duration of maternity leave from 12 to 20 weeks and permitted the mother to take unpaid leave up to the child's third birthday without any loss of her social security rights. In addition, family allowances are to be increased and education of the public in contraception is to be undertaken by the Ministry of Public Health.

Miltényi estimated that from 20% to 30% of all couples used contraception regularly and that this figure has remained constant for several years. Out of 100 women, 24 do not control the number of their births, 18 use legal abortion only, 18 use contraception only, and 37 use legal abortion or contraception. (The other 3 are unaccounted for.)

In a study of problems of family planning, Acsadi and Klinger[11] noted that, in 1964, 54% of the women had legal abortions because of contraceptive failures, and 46% did not use contraception systematically. Coitus interruptus was the most popular method of birth

[10] *Ibid.*

[11] György Acsadi and A. Klinger, "Some Problems of Fertility, Family Planning and Birth Control," *Demográfia*, 2–3: 176–219 (1959) (in Hungarian).

control, accounting for 52% of the practice, and the condom was second with 22%, the vaginal douche accounted for 8%, the rhythm method for 7%, chemical methods for 5%, diaphragms for 4%, and other methods for 2%. An increase in the use of diaphragms and jellies has been observed in recent years. While coitus interruptus was used among all social groups, it was most popular in rural areas, while diaphragms and jellies were preferred by women in the intellectual stratum.

Condoms, foam tablets, jelly (Timidon), and diaphragms (Palma) are manufactured locally. An ovulation inhibitor, similar to Lyndiol, is to be produced in the near future.

Hungary does not have a separate family planning program. Free consultations on contraception are given by gynecologists, and information may also be obtained from the abortion committees. Informational material, such as books and pamphlets, is available, and some educational services are provided by women's organizations. An independent family planning organization is being considered. Plans for a large-scale informational campaign have been deferred because of limited supplies and the poor quality of available contraceptive materials. However, medical students will in the future be instructed in contraceptive techniques. Various conferences of physicians have been held on legal abortions and an international symposium on family planning has been organized for September, 1965. Many physicians would like to see more active efforts leading to the development of effective contraceptive methods and for publicizing their use.

SOCIALIST FEDERAL REPUBLIC OF YUGOSLAVIA

According to the law of 1960, legal abortions may be performed for social reasons when it seems likely that the woman will be placed in difficult personal, familial, and economic circumstances as a result of her pregnancy. However, nearly 10% of all applications for abortion are denied by special commissions, made up of two physicians and one social worker, whose duty it is to review the applications. In Slovenia, 20% of the applications are denied. It is also the duty of the commissions to inform the applicants of possible adverse effects of abortion, to point out the advantages of contraception, and to refer them to a contraceptive clinic.

Health workers must conform more and more to their ethical code, which states: "A health worker should regard abortion as biologically, medically, psychologically, and sociologically harmful. Corresponding to the principle of socialist humanism and medical knowledge, human life must be respected from its beginning. Therefore, the health worker should conscientiously endeavor to see that the true humanistic privilege of maternity be valued above the privilege of abortion."[12]

Data on abortions for Yugoslavia as a whole are not available for any year after 1961. In Slovenia, however, in 1964 there were 9,392 legal and 5,993 other hospital abortions, and 29,221 births. The number of abortions in Slovenia has remained constant since 1961. Nearly 95% of the legal abortions were performed on social indications, the disparity between family size and the desire for a higher standard of living playing an important role. In a number of cases, abortion was permitted on neuro-psychological indications. Of the women having legal abortions, 78% were married, 16% unmarried, and 6% widowed or divorced. The modal age groups were 20–24 years and 25–29 years, with one-fourth of the abortions in each of these two groups.

Childless women made up about 11% of those having abortions; women with one or two children, 55%; with three or four children, 27%; and with five or more children, 7%. The ratio of abortions to births was 2.5:1.5 for female wage earners, 2.4:1.2 for female salaried employees, and 2.8:2.7 for housewives.

The government has undertaken an all-out program to solve the problems of family planning. Besides the ideological work of the commissions on legal abortion, much attention is given to the promotion of contraception. In 1964, a Co-ordinating Committee for Family Planning was established, which consists of representatives of the Federation of Women's Associations, the Young People's Friends Association, The Red Cross, the Ministry of Health, the social insurance system, and medical associations.[13]

During the past few years, instructions in family planning, sex, and human relations have been introduced into the curriculums of primary and secondary schools, teachers' training courses, colleges, and technical schools. "Schools for living," which provide premarital education, became popular in 1958, and "schools for parents" have also been founded. Slovenia alone has 255 such schools, with an attendance of over 10,000 in 1963.

Two family planning centers have been established in Slovenia, one under the guidance of Dr. L. Andolšek, and the other, under Dr. B. Tekavčić. The clinics are staffed with gynecologists, psychologists, mental hygienists, and social workers. The centers give contraceptive

[12] Herak-Szabo and Mojic, "Legal Abortion in Yugoslavia," Regional Conference IPPF, London, 1964, Paper No. 7.

[13] Mojic, Personal information and questionnaire on family planning situation in Yugoslavia, July, 1965.

advice, treat sub-fertility in both sexes, and provide consultative services on sexual disorders. A study on intra-uterine contraceptive devices is under way in Ljubljana.

Advice on contraception is available at all gynecological outpatient departments, at prenatal clinics, in the outpatient clinics of factories, and from general practitioners. Instruction in its use is given by gynecologists, general practitioners, midwives, and visiting nurses. Furthermore, social workers who are members of abortion committees are obliged to inform the woman, or the couple, about contraception before the application for abortion can be granted. The practice of paying a "control visit" to women who have been granted abortions is too new to judge its effectiveness in increasing the demand for contraceptives.

Contraceptives can be obtained from chemists' shops, condoms from drugstores, and some contraceptives, especially Emko foam, from some outpatient departments. They are available without charge (paid for by the social insurance system) except for diaphragms and condoms, and in some of the constituent republics, diaphragms are also free. The available products are: jellies (Contrafer Patentex Genosan), creams (Genotan), suppositories (Nona Gel), foam tablets (Contrafer), foam (Emko), and oral pills (Anovlar and Lyndiol). All contraceptives, except Emko, are manufactured in Yugoslavia.

A study of the use of contraceptive methods made by Andolšek[14] in 1963 showed that 44.2% of the population used coitus interruptus, 21.7% used diaphragms, 4.5% used condoms, 2.6% relied on chemical methods, 0.7% on rhythm, and 6.9% used combined methods. No contraception was used by 19.4% of the respondents.

Andolšek also reported that in spite of intensive efforts to encourage the use of contraception, 30% of all women indicated that legal abortion was the only method of birth control acceptable to them. In general, men refuse to use contraception, perhaps because the educational programs are directed toward women only. Although there is no prejudice against contraception on religious or traditional grounds, scattered opposition to contraception, but not to legal abortion, has been reported.

Future plans include the introduction of contraceptive services into every general health institution, registration of abortions, documentation of the distribution of contraceptives, courses on contraceptive techniques for the general practitioner, and a sufficient supply of good contraceptives. A separate organization for family planning is not

[14] L. Andolšek, Letter with personal information on family planning situation in Slovenia.

planned at the present time as this service is considered a part of maternal and child health programs.

CZECHOSLOVAKIA (CSSR)

The abolition of the fee for legal abortion and the liberalization of residence requirements in 1960 were followed by an increase in legal abortions and a decline in births in 1961. In December, 1962, new criteria for the interruption of pregnancy were established, especially concerning first pregnancies; fees and residence restrictions were reintroduced; and the commissions passing on abortion were reduced to one gynecologist and two laymen. In the following year, the number of live births increased by 24,000 and legal abortions declined by 20,000, while other hospital abortions increased by 3,000, and the number of deaths from abortion also increased. Although indications for legal abortion in the CSSR are more restrictive than in the Soviet Union, Hungary, or Romania, in the opinion of experts legal abortion will continue to be the most widely used method of birth control.

The proportion of married women among those having legal abortions declined from 86% in 1958 to 82% in 1962, and the proportion of housewives also fell, while the proportion of unmarried women rose and the proportion of working women increased from 50.6% in 1958 to 65.5% in 1962. Apparently, a shortage of institutions for the care of children contributes to the desire for smaller families.

The average age of women having legal abortions has remained at 30 years for the past six years. The reasons given in 1962 for requesting the operation included: more than three children (44%), poor health (15%), unmarried (14%), lack of housing (9%), and breakup of the marriage (7%).

According to a study by Srb and Kutschera,[15] 95% of all couples had definite ideas as to the number of children they wanted. Of the interviewed couples, 63% planned to have two children and 18% planned three children. The average for all couples was 2.3 children. About one-half of the couples (47%) stated that they knew about contraception before their marriage. Coitus interruptus only was used by 42.9% of the couples, condoms by 17.3%, the rhythm method by 5.6%, and diaphragms by 0.5%. Most of the remaining 33.7% used coitus interruptus, condoms, and other methods in combination.

Diaphragms, a contraceptive cream (Spofa), and condoms may be purchased in drugstores and in consultation centers. An ovulation inhibitor (Antigest) will be on the market by the end of 1965.

[15] V. Srb and M. Kutschera, "Marriage—Contraception—Abortion," *Demographie Revue* (CSSR), 1961, pp. 45–56, 139–56, 209–22, 311–30 (in Czech).

Consultation on contraception is a public health service available in all gynecological outpatient departments from physicians and midwives. Gynecologists must give free advice on contraception on request. The total number of consultation centers dealing with all aspects of fertility runs to nearly 2,000. Women who seek abortion are not required to have a consultation on contraception before the operation and, in general, do not have one until after the operation.

Several programs dealing with contraception have been broadcast over the radio recently, but on the whole there is little effort to publicize birth control. Contraception is not included in school curriculums, even in medical schools.

As in Hungary, contraception has not succeeded in reducing the number of abortions, and the number of pregnancies has increased steadily during the past few years. Nevertheless, a majority of couples try to use contraception before they resort to abortion to control the number of their children. The attitude of men toward contraception has been conditioned by intensive propaganda during their military service.

No independent family planning organization is in existence. A population commission has been set up in the Ministry of Public Health to deal with the problem of family planning.

PEOPLE'S REPUBLIC OF ROMANIA

In Romania, the ideal of responsible maternity is almost entirely implemented by legal abortion. Contraception plays an unimportant role. Stations equipped to handle abortions exist all over the country. There are no commissions to review applications, or to grant or deny requests. Women may go directly to the abortion ward of a hospital or to the outpatient clinic of a factory. If there are no medical contraindications and the pregnancy is not more than 12 weeks old, the operation is performed on the same day, and the patient may go home in two hours. The physicians, who work in shifts, are not allowed to perform more than ten abortions in one day. A fee of 30 lei or $2.50 is charged.

In the two years for which data are available since the passage of a liberalized abortion law, the number of abortions increased sharply— from 112,000 in 1958 to 229,000 in 1959. Data from hospitals in urban areas, available for the period 1957–62, reveal a three- or fourfold increase in abortions since 1958. The ratio of abortions to births in 1958 was 3.2:1 in the town of Arad and 3.5:1 at Filantropia Hospital, Bucharest. In 1961, the comparable ratios were 7.4:1 and 13:1, respectively. That the incidence of legal abortions in Romania is higher than in Hungary may be concluded from, among other things, the rapid decline in the number of births.

According to Zárnescu,[16] married women represented 94% of those having abortions, and housewives, between 40% and 60%; 10% were less than 20 years old; and nearly 70% were in the 20–29-year age group. Women who applied for an abortion in Bucharest in 1961 already had an average of 3.9 legal abortions. Personal reasons were given by 99% of the women and medical indications by only 1%.

The one-child family is considered ideal in Romania. Zárnescu computed a mean average of 1.3 children per family for Bucharest, and 0.7 children for educated mothers. The desire for children seemed to decrease and the number of legal abortions to increase with rising educational levels. Families with three or more children were rare at all educational levels.

According to Zárnescu, 96% of the women did not know about and did not use contraception. Even the most primitive types of traditional methods were almost unknown. Contraception was used by only one-third of the educated women. Recently, the stations for abortion have begun to inform women on the use of contraception. Besides the condom, a contraceptive cream has been available since 1964.

PEOPLE'S REPUBLIC OF POLAND

An independent Association for Responsible Motherhood[17] was founded in 1958, one year after the legalization of abortion. It collaborates with the Ministry of Public Health and its president is the Vice-Minister of Public Health. To achieve its goal of a "happy family," the Association promotes family planning and instruction in sex hygiene and education, discourages abortions, and provides premarital and marriage counseling services and consultations on sterility problems. The central office is in Warsaw and other offices are in Krakow and in each of the 18 districts, with branch offices in 310 counties and 150 villages. The offices are staffed with gynecologists, psychologists, lawyers, pedagogues, and sociologists.

Contraceptive consultations are given by gynecologists and midwives in all gynecological hospitals and outpatient departments to women seeking abortion, to mothers of large families, and to young couples. There are about 2,900 consultation centers in the country. The quality of this service varies considerably because many physi-

16 Quoted in K.-H. Mehlan, "Legal Abortions in Roumania," *Journal of Sex Research*, Vol. 1 (1965).

17 Letter and questionnaire from the Polish Association for Responsible Motherhood.

cians are not interested in contraception and prefer to perform abortions.

The activities of the Association for Responsible Motherhood are directed toward the female population. Men learn about family planning during their military service, and military medical officers are trained in contraception in courses given by the Association.

The following contraceptives are produced locally: condoms, foam tablets, suppositories, creams, diaphragms, and cervical caps. There is little demand for diaphragms and cervical caps because physicians are neither interested nor trained in fitting them. In general, only tablets and condoms are distributed through drugstores and through the offices of the Association for Responsible Motherhood. The social insurance system bears about 70% of the cost of contraceptive materials.

From about 48% to 60% of all women are given information on birth control methods in the various districts. During recent years, the number of pregnancies has declined and the number of legal and other hospital abortions (spontaneous and illegal) has remained constant.

Resistance to family planning on religious grounds from the largely Catholic population appears to be diminishing steadily. However, it is difficult to reach the lowest economic strata of the population through educational services, even though the Association's activities in this field are extensive. Reports on its work are made regularly over radio and television and appear in the newsreels, twelve movie shorts on family planning have been produced, and informational pamphlets and books are distributed. Physicians who are members of the Association lecture on contraception in the towns and larger villages. However, birth control has not been accepted as a part of the course on sex education in schools, and medical students are not trained in this field.

GERMAN DEMOCRATIC REPUBLIC

To reduce illegal abortions, the abortion law was extended in 1947 to include socio-medical, ethical, and eugenic indications, and, in practice, social indications were also accepted.[18] The immediate effect was an increase in the number of legal abortions to 26,000, or 15 per 10,000 population. The avowed goal, reduction of illegal abortions, was only partially achieved, along with a reduction in mortality from abortions. In 1950, because of a rise in the level of living and the extension of

[18] K.-H. Mehlan, *International Abortion Situation and Contraception* (Leipzig: Georg Thieme, 1961).

protective measures for the care of mothers and children, it was felt that indications for abortion could be restricted to medical and eugenic reasons only. The number of legal abortions declined subsequently to between 700 and 800 a year. In March, 1965, the law was reinterpreted to include socio-medical and ethical indications.

Although the number of women of reproductive age has declined by one-fourth, the number of births has remained constant. The general fertility rate increased from 66.0 in 1957–58 to 90.1 in 1963, and the crude birth rate from 10.4 in 1946 to 17.2 in 1964. The estimated total number of abortions, including legal, spontaneous, and illegal abortions, declined from 150,000 in 1950 to about 70,000–90,000 in 1962. In 1962 there was one abortion for every 3.7–5.0 births. During the past few years, abortions have increased faster than births in the age groups up to 21 years, among the unmarried, among women with one child or none, and in the larger towns.[19]

Since the incorporation of family planning into the public health system in 1963, all women can obtain free advice on birth control from public health service physicians and public health institutions, as well as from gynecologists. The following contraceptives may be purchased in drugstores: condoms, cream (Tutus), suppositories (Nona Gel), diaphragms (Primeros), and oral contraceptives (Ovosiston).

The program of the Association for Marriage and the Family, founded in 1963, includes: consultation on contraception and on sterility problems, premarital and marriage counseling, and sex education. The Association is supported by the Ministry of Public Health. There are six centers staffed with gynecologists, psychologists, and lawyers. Consultation in contraception and related fields is available in fifty outpatient clinics. The German Democratic Federation of Women has demanded the establishment of more birth control clinics and advisory centers to promote the health of women and family happiness.

A research institute for family planning in Rostock, under the author's guidance, conducts training courses for physicians and midwives. The medical faculty of the University of Rostock has for several years given lectures on family planning to its students, and a series of lectures on sex and on contraception, open to all students, was begun in the spring of 1964.[20] In general, however, training of physicians in contraceptive techniques is inadequate.

An intensive educational campaign has been carried on by the Association for Marriage and the Family since its inception in 1963. Dis-

[19] K.-H. Mehlan, "Reducing the Abortion Rate in the German Democratic Republic," WPC, Belgrade, 1965, Paper No. 279 (in English).

[20] K.-H. Mehlan, "Legalization of Abortion in Eastern Europe," Seventh Conference IPPF, Singapore, 1963 (*Excerpta Medica*, International Congress Series No. 72).

cussions dealing with marriage and family, including contraception, appear regularly on television and radio programs, and articles and readers' letters are published in newspapers, magazines. and women's journals. Several recent books and pamphlets on marriage, the family, and sex education also deal with contraception. The wide publicity given to contraception has stimulated visits to family planning clinics,

Future tasks are: (1) support of industry in the production of contraceptives, (2) postgraduate training for physicians in contraception and family problems, (3) lectures on contraception for all students, (4) incorporation of birth control into the programs of obstetrical departments and prenatal and infant care centers, and (5) premarital education. The intensive work already underway has succeeded in bringing about the recognition of family planning as an integral part of preventive health measures.

17

PUERTO RICO

JOSÉ NINE CURT, M.D.
Assistant Dean and Head
Department of Preventive Medicine and Public Health
School of Medicine, University of Puerto Rico

INTRODUCTION

Long before the modern world suddenly awakened to the so-called population explosion, many Puerto Ricans were aware of their country's population problem. Mortality rates were undergoing a remarkably rapid decline but because of the much slower decline in natality, the rate of population increase became a source of serious concern. The problem has attracted many brilliant minds, with approaches as varied as the interests and backgrounds they represent. As a health worker, I have viewed the population problem as a community health problem that arises out of our family care unit.

From this point of view, motivation looms as a most important element in a population control program. As Bernard Berelson of the Population Council said in March, 1965, at the seminar on demography at the School of Public Health of Puerto Rico, "People of high motivation can make any method work successfully." Nevertheless, it must be recognized that motivations are based on the cultural and religious convictions of the people involved, so that in establishing programs it is necessary to motivate through the institutions of the community.

At the same time, recognition by national leaders of the impact of population growth on the socioeconomic development of the nation, is a basic step toward solution of the population problem. The impetus for solution must come from national leaders, not from outside sources, and must be based on the prevailing culture, religion, resources, and psychology of the nation. The role of international agencies is to guide in the assessment of the problem and its proposed solutions, and when the time is ripe and propitious, to help with funds, equipment, and technical advice. Administratively, a population control or family planning program should be an integral part of the health program of a nation, specifically an activity of a maternal and child health program. Design of the program should be consistent with the elements of human rights and dignity; and procedures should ensure for all individuals the access to and free selection of alternative methods for family limitation and spacing.

The Setting

Only two decades ago Puerto Rico was among the most undeveloped countries of the world. Not only was it a land of hunger, indolence, and misery but, in the minds of many, a hopeless land. The scarcity of natural resources combined with an enormous population density was thought to be an irremediable malady. Several fortunate events, however, saved the island from disaster. We list the following as most important:

1. The New Deal Era, which affected favorably both the socioeconomic and the political aspects.
2. Improved education for all people.
3. Changes in the political structure, resulting from the above, which culminated in an honest and able public administration machinery.
4. Industrialization and economic development.
5. Health improvements.
6. Mass emigration of Puerto Ricans to the United States.

Thus, from a seemingly hopeless situation, a new Puerto Rico emerged. The socioeconomic progress has been amazing, not only for the achievements per se, but for the speed with which they occurred. During the last twenty years, per capita income and gross national product have increased more than 400%. Wages and salaries rose from $125 million in 1940 to $867 million in 1960. Industrialization received considerable impetus between 1940 and 1960; employment in manufacturing increased from 26,000 to 93,000; and income derived from this source increased almost 1,000%. Investment in Puerto Rico, which was $29 million in 1939–40, was $392 million in 1959–60 (a 1,252% increase).

Education, too, received unusual attention. The number of employed teachers rose from 6,000 in 1949 to 14,000 in 1958. School enrollment increased from 304,000 pupils to 679,000 during the same period. The relative increment has been greater at college level. Enrollment at the University of Puerto Rico, for example, increased

236% during this twenty-year period. As a result of these developments illiteracy declined from 32% in 1940 to 17% in 1960.

In the realm of public health, the utilization of modern health practices, including insecticides and antibiotics, together with economic improvement and other factors, has produced in the island one of the lowest mortality rates in the world. Malaria was completely eradicated in 1955, and tuberculosis, although still high compared with the United States, has been reduced by 90% since 1940. Similar declines have been observed in other infectious diseases, for example, in pneumonia, diarrhea, and enteritis. Infant and maternal mortality rates have been reduced by more than 60% during the past decades. Mortality among children 1–4 years of age in 1960 was only one-tenth of the figure recorded in 1940. Life expectancy at birth, which increased from 30 to 46 years during the first forty years of the present century, was almost 70 years in 1960.

Meanwhile, the crude birth rate declined from 40 in 1950 to 32 in 1960, which represents a marked deviation from the slowly declining trend observed during the first half of the century. The rate of population growth recorded during the decade 1950–60 was only 0.6% per year, as compared with almost 2% observed during the two preceding decades. The 0.6% population increase observed during the last decade constitutes a record (the lowest) for all the censal history of Puerto Rico (1765–1960) and was one of the lowest among all the countries of the world.

This succinctly describes Puerto Rico, an island whose only natural resources are its climate and a population with a true desire of improving their life conditions.[1]

HISTORICAL BACKGROUND OF FAMILY PLANNING

The problem of population growth was brought into the open in 1925 when Dr. Lanauze, a physician, organized the Birth Control League in Ponce. This institution soon disappeared as a result of the controversy aroused and nothing else was heard concerning the problem until 1932, when another birth control league appeared in San Juan. After a couple of years the clinic under its sponsorship ceased to exist because of the scarcity of its clientele. Zalduondo states, "The pressure of the church and the apathy of the people put a quick ending to the efforts of the league."[2]

[1] José Nine Curt, *Health in Puerto Rico* (3d ed., 1964); Antonio Samuel Medina, *Maternal and Child Health Care in Puerto Rico* (1964).

[2] Celestina Zalduondo, Presentation, Second Seminar on Family Planning at New York, 1963.

The great economic depression in the United States in the mid-thirties gave rise to several relief programs. In 1934–35 the Puerto Rico Emergency Relief Administration (PRERA), one of the federal relief agencies, decided to establish a series of maternal health clinics as part of a program of medical services. These were extended throughout the island after a successful trial with a pilot clinic at the hospital of the School of Tropical Medicine. Social workers referred individuals to the clinics from among the hundreds of thousands of individuals who applied to the relief stations, and community workers scouted people in their areas who might be interested in the services.

In 1963 these programs were discontinued in the United States on the grounds of a boost in the American economy. However, since our economy remained practically at the same low level, the United States Congress passed special legislation establishing an agency to care for the island's rehabilitation (Puerto Rico Reconstruction Administration). Efforts by this new agency to re-establish the clinics of its predecessor did not materialize, but in this same year (1936) the maternal health clinics under the direction of Dr. Belaval were reactivated under private sponsorship.

In 1937 Puerto Rico passed a law legalizing sterilization for socioeconomic as well as medical reasons and directed the Health Department to offer family planning services. At that time available methods were not generally acceptable; so sterilization was preferred. "It was widely used among the high-parity women, which had very little effect on the birth rate—but it was also abused extensively among very young women waiting in the outpatient dispensaries. Especially in the young women of low parity this resulted in much frustration and the development of guilt complexes with frequent psychosomatic disorders."[3] The Health Department continued to offer family planning services at the maternal health clinics but no major effort was made to launch an educational campaign. As a consequence the clientele of these health clinics dropped considerably.

In 1946 the Association of Population Studies was started as a voluntary agency. It evolved from a study and research unit into "an agency which offered direct contraceptive services to the families," changing its name to the Family Planning Association of Puerto Rico in the late fifties. Its main activities were (1) education about family planning and population growth; (2) direct services to families, including distribution of contraceptives, aid for sterilization (financial), and fertility services; and (3) research. The Association received initial

[3] Adaline P. Satterthwaite, "The Role of Ante-partum and Post-partum Education in Maternal Health," 1964.

financial support from the Planned Parenthood Association of America, because funds could not be obtained in the island. Since then, support has been through private sources in the United States.

In 1959 the voluntary Family Planning Association of Puerto Rico (formerly the Association of Population Studies) started a unique campaign utilizing lay voluntary leaders to distribute a vaginal contraceptive cream on an island-wide basis. Because of lack of financial support the agency was recently forced to reduce their services. In 1962, Mrs. Zalduondo, the executive director of the Family Planning Unit, gave the following as some of the greatest handicaps to their program: (1) indifferent attitude of the government; (2) hostile attitude of the church; (3) the Catholic indoctrination of physicians and other personnel against contraceptive services; (4) indifferent attitude of the press; (5) hypocrisy of civic leaders who themselves use contraceptive services but deny them to the poor; (6) ignorance of the public; and (7) lack of financial support.[4]

THE PRESENT APPROACH

The general framework of the family planning program rests on the proposition that in a pluralistic democracy with different groups of different beliefs and religious convictions, it is up to individuals to decide what they want for themselves and their families. Therefore all methods and procedures are to be offered and health workers must not impose their personal bias. We place strong emphasis on human dignity and individual rights in dealing with people.[5]

We see four major components in our approach to the problem. The first component is professional education within the program. We expect to teach Puerto Ricans and others the nature of the population problem, going into some detail about demography and population theories, and the social and economic factors affecting population dynamics. This formal education may vary from short one-day or one-week seminars to short courses of approximately one month to detailed formal instruction involving one or two semesters. Classroom teaching of a medical nature is provided by various departments within the medical school. Public health implications are discussed in the course on maternal and child health at the School of Public Health.

The second component of this program is the clinical service. These services are provided by the Department of Health supported by regular funds from the Maternal and Child Health Program. In the Northeast Region these clinics are an integral part of the regular post-partum

---

[4] *Ibid.*   [5] Nine Curt, *op. cit.*

clinic. Cases are drawn from existing prenatal and postnatal clinics. We offer a "full selection service" including the rhythm method, chemicals, the IUD or coil, and other available contraceptive agents. Conscientious efforts are being made to provide adequate instruction in the use of the rhythm method if the patient desires to use it. Each patient is given a list of methods for her own free choice. In this way we avoid meddling in religious convictions.

The third component of this program concerns education of the public, a responsibility we feel is a proper function of the different society groups. For example, the Family Planning Association should dedicate its effort to educate and orient people to request services, according to our social and cultural patterns. Education should proceed at the same pace as the development of clinical services, lest we fall into an imbalance between services and demand. Also, we have to consider the contribution of the Catholic church. We feel that in the confessional and in the pulpit as well as in informal conversations, the priest can offer information pertaining to responsible parenthood and improvement of health and can orient people to avail themselves of services and select methods according to their conscience.

The fourth component concerns research and evaluation. Research activities are varied and include effectiveness of the different methods. Another area of interest is the relationship between program activities and the stillbirth rate. We believe that the research and evaluation aspects of the program require a high level of competence and should be handled by professional personnel. It is the impression of many of my colleagues that much of the work that was done previously was well intentioned but lacked scientific validity. Our program requires constant evaluation so that it can be directed accordingly.

Furthermore, we may want to measure the effectiveness of services on the basis of the clinical trial model; for example, two similar villages having different programs of services or utilizing different educational techniques can be compared in relation to the impact of these variables on their fertility pattern.

PRESENT PROGRAM ACTIVITIES

Our program, operated by the School of Public Health, School of Medicine, and the Northeast Region of the Department of Health, covers the Northeast Region of Puerto Rico, an area of over 900,000 persons. Almost all the communities in this area have service activities. We do not give contraceptive information as such, but the Family Planning Association, a voluntary group, offers materials and services outside our program.

To integrate all four aspects of the program we have a co-ordinator who is directly responsible to the director of the School of Public Health. At the present time, we are utilizing physicians and nurses who are trained in our School of Medicine (at the University Hospital and the Nursemidwifery School). At the Nursemidwifery School, the problems and alternate solutions are an integral part of the program. The post-partum clinics are the main target of the program. As far as the rhythm clinics are concerned, these are being developed by Catholic physicians who are well versed in the method. We are also utilizing lay couples trained to use the method, who move from town to town forming groups for the exchange of information and follow-up. The services are free and are offered to all interested persons regardless of creed, race, or socioeconomic status. As already mentioned, we expect that the information will be disseminated through the community by different voluntary agencies or church groups. At the present time we are not using any mass media method to expand our program.

This paper has presented our efforts in Puerto Rico to develop a program to cope with the population problem. We recognize that each nation must decide for itself whether it has such a problem; we also respect the right of the individual to use or not use the services offered, and to have the freedom to choose that method which she finds appropriate.

18

CHILE

HERNÁN ROMERO, M.D., M. of Sc. in P.H.
Professor and Chairman of the Department of Social and Preventive Medicine
University of Chile
Adviser to the National Association of Family Protection of Chile

Chile may make two significant contributions to the world cause of family planning. To arrive at an effective solution, the problem of abortions has been studied for the past fifteen years under such favorable conditions that they would be difficult to duplicate elsewhere. A National Association of Family Protection (NAFP) has been organized (Asociación Chileno de Protección de la Familia). This is a voluntary group of doctors, other professional people, and the representatives from different activities in the community, and is officially backed by the National Health Service (Servicio Nacional de Salud). As the only institution of its kind in the country, it is succeeding in (1) combining and integrating the efforts of those individuals who are working or wish to work with similar purposes in different parts of the territory; (2) actually helping those efforts and initiating the formation of other groups which may embark on a similar kind of work, giving priority to those offering better possibilities of effective action, or serving sectors of the population whose needs are more urgent; and (3) centralizing and distributing resources of both national and foreign origin.

Through the appointment of subcommittees, various phases of the general program are tackled. The subcommittee on studies and research has prepared forms for recording observations, questionnaires that produce statistics of national validity. For the first phase, it appears obviously advisable to experiment with all birth control methods in order to determine which are (a) the most effective at the present moment, (b) the most accepted, and (c) the most economical. The Association does not merely authorize but actually encourages heads

235

of clinics and other health services to use different methods or combinations of methods. These plans must follow, however, the same general lines so that their acceptance, benefits, or shortcomings can be compared once again. For this purpose one of the research projects consists of the follow-up of a number of women (200 in each of six clinics) to determine the constancy and failures in the use of contraceptive devices, as well as how the latter are defined and evaluated.

The first educational film will be ready shortly. A considerable number of copies will be prepared to be exhibited simultaneously in Santiago and in the provinces and eventually in any other Spanish-speaking countries which may consider the film appropriate. A competition for the best script was held and a prize offered, and production is now in the hands of the department of experimental cinematography of the University of Chile. The subcommittee on education[1] also sponsors teaching programs in maternal and child welfare centers, in prenatal and mothers' clubs, the PTA, and in those groups of population which are mainly at the proletarian level. As a result of this system, leaders are selected who attempt to enlighten the community, obtain information of induced abortions, and serve as supply holders. The subcommittee on information has already issued the first number of a monthly publication.

Up to now, mass education has been dispensed with on the grounds that it would be unwise. On the one hand, much has been accomplished in overcoming resistance to the idea of birth control by people who oppose it or express worthwhile reservations on the subject, and it was felt that a frontal attack might induce undesirable reactions. On the other hand, experience has proved that social demand for birth control is so enormous that it cannot be satisfied with the organization and means at our disposal. To stimulate it might be premature. Many of us are controlling our impatience because we would like to test the degree and strength of the opposition and, naturally, defeat it with well-founded arguments and legitimate resources.

Antagonism does not noticeably interfere with our work. We know of a Catholic priest who carried out an intensive campaign against the IUD in a marginal population of some 35,000 inhabitants, basing his arguments on fear of infection and cancer, not on moral or religious ground. Applicants decreased temporarily. This is the most conspicuous but not the only example. On the other hand, the author's booklet entitled *Control de la natalidad: Prejuicios y controversias* ("Birth Control: Prejudices and Controversies"), published by the University of Chile Press, received favorable reviews in the papers, became a

[1] The Association has been in charge of the personnel of the department of preventive and social medicine under the leadership of Dr. Mariano Requena.

best-seller, and orders were received for it from several foreign countries. Numerous lectures and round-table and panel discussions, open to the public, have taken place in scientific societies, with tremendous success. None of the actions described above has produced adverse repercussions.

Unquestionably a complete airing of this matter would substantially facilitate the achievement of our main and final goal. We have reiterated that we aim to put contraceptive methods within easy reach of those wishing to use them and to inform others who may benefit from them. Undoubtedly many people are kept in the dark by the deliberate and even obstinate efforts of persons who accept only those methods they consider natural or who condemn the whole lot indiscriminately.

The NAFP was founded in 1962. During the first visit of Dr. Ofelia Mendoza of the staff of the International Planned Parenthood Federation, several persons met—all seriously concerned with the dreadful consequences which high fertility produces on individual and collective health, on the welfare and stability of the family, and on the national economy. Nothing exasperates this group more than the ever increasing disaster of illegal abortions in Chile. There were several doctors and services working quietly and resolutely on the application of anti-fertility methods. Under the direction of Dr. Amalia Ernst, a contraceptive clinic, annexed to the fertility service of the department of gynecology of the University of Chile, has been functioning since 1938. The need to intensify, combine, and extend the various efforts then appeared evident to all of us.

The Association, which was legalized in January, 1964, is composed, among others, of the following: the professors of obstetrics and gynecology and of preventive and social medicine of the University of Chile and Catholic University; the professor of maternal and child health in the School of Public Health; the presidents of the Collegio Medico and the Society of Obstetrics and Gynecology, as well as all the heads of these services in the Santiago hospitals. This represents an outstanding group of the medical profession. The Association has been permanently presided over by Dr. Luisa Pfau, whose prestige and devotion have contributed substantially to its success. Its headquarters were originally in the department of health promotion of the National Health Service, but now it has its own premises, equipment, and personnel, and holds sessions every month and oftener if necessary.

The NAFP is subsidized by the IPPF (Western Hemisphere)—$50,000 in 1964; $86,000 in 1965. Other foundations (Ford, Rockefeller, Pathfinder, and the Population Council) have provided a quantity of contraceptive devices and audiovisual material for health education and are also sponsoring various projects. We recently obtained official patronage of the Chilean government for the next World Congress which the IPPF will hold here early in 1967.

We are now endeavoring to centralize overseas help, to distribute it evenly and so ensure its adequate use. The Health Service contributes several material elements and personnel: doctors, midwives, social workers, nurses, and auxiliaries. With money from abroad, the Association has equipped several clinics and supplemented the budgets of some of them, while others still receive grants directly. Through the Association, fellowships have been obtained, numerous members have attended international congresses, and foreign professionals have come either as visitors or as fellows. Demography and birth control have been taught for years in the departments of preventive and social medicine and in the School of Public Health. Recently these subjects have been included in the university lectures of other professors who belong to the Association, as well as in the schools of nursing, obstetrics (midwives), and social service. Some members also form part of the Committee on Studies in Population Dynamics, which was created on the initiative of the dean of the faculty of medicine of the University of Chile.

A training program has been developed for the control of voluntary abortions and the use of contraceptives. Headed by Drs. Faúndes and M. Luisa García, it consists of a series of continuous courses, each of one-week duration, for a total of sixteen Latin American fellows who come two or three at a time. They spend the mornings in clinical work in various services; the afternoons of one week they spend, respectively: (1) in the Latin American Center of Demography (CELADE); (2) with Dr. Armijo's department to become acquainted with the problem of abortions and methods of investigating epidemiology; (3) with Dr. Requena to be trained in the study of attitudes and of the way to conduct fertility control campaigns among various segments of the population; (4) studying the physiology of conception and contraception with Drs. Zipper, Faúndes, and Zanartu. None of the professionals who organize and give the courses receives any remuneration. Funds are provided by the Public Welfare Foundation. A small sum has been reserved to pay the expenses of Chilean experts who will, upon request, advise their colleagues in other countries, and help finance contraceptive work which former students may initiate on their return.

SOME CONTROL PROGRAMS

Some of the programs are rather complex and none is more so than the so-called investigation and training in the biology of reproduction and in family studies. Under the direction of Drs. Puga and Zanartu of the university department of obstetrics, this program has the backing of the Ford Foundation and the Population Council. Apart from clinicians, the staff includes pathologists, cytologists, statisticians, biochemists, and experts on electronics, as well as several assistants (nurses, social workers, midwives, laboratory technicians, librarians, and others). It provides services to the half-million inhabitants of the northern area of Santiago and carries out research on new contraceptive methods and methods for application; fertility and the physiology of pregnancy and parturition; early diagnosis of cancer; lactation and the influence on lactation of anti-natal agents and their possible action on the development of the newborn.

The program proposes to reach 5,000 cases a year and is studying some 900 highly fertile women who use control devices (in groups of from 50 to 100) over a total of 10,000 menstrual periods. These women are submitted to cytological studies of the vagina, cervix, and endometrium, and even of the Fallopian tubes and ovary on the occasion of a laparotomy. The project also includes sociological studies on the structure of the family, the husband and wife relationship, sexual behavior, attitudes toward contraception, and so on. To ascertain rates of birth and abortion, life records are kept. With the advice of the department of preventive and social medicine of the university, demographic matters are explored, especially the effects of the rapid increase of population, which has doubled in the northern area in the last twenty years. The program also includes help to families in financial distress and provides teaching for medical students, doctors, paramedical personnel, sociologists, economists, priests, and community leaders. At the present time, it is working in conjunction with the University of Utah, the Worcester Foundation, and other foreign institutions and is sending members of the staff to the United States for advanced studies and specialized training. Several reports have been submitted to scientific congresses and numerous articles have appeared. Elaborate equipment and a good technical library are being assembled.

The program carried out by Dr. Ernst and his co-workers (in the department of gynecology, headed by Professor J. Wood) is particularly significant from a scientific and a practical viewpoint. Up to 1961 only those patients for whom pregnancy was absolutely forbidden because of health reasons were accepted and the work was performed unobtrusively. Diaphragms (Rameses) were used almost exclusively and still are considered the best method. Starting at that time, advice and various contraceptive devices have been provided free of charge to anyone requesting them. Over 3,500 cases are handled a year. The acceptance of progestagens and of the Zipper ring is just about equal. Every case receives complete gynecological examinations, cytodiagnosis for cancer, and treatment of gynecological pathology. Two very important investigations are underway. Seventy-five women from 21 to 40 years old who were receiving oral pills and had gone, at a certain moment, through 589 cycles, showed reversible changes of the endometrium which consisted of a lack of synchronization with the menstrual period, owing to early maturation of the lining's cells. Moreover, they suffered from headaches (11%), nausea (7%), vomiting (2%), and intolerance, so that the medication had to be discontinued in 7% of the cases. No alteration of the mammary glands or pregnancies were registered during the period under study.

In another group of 107 women who have worn the IUD for periods varying from 8 to 30 months, the condition of the endometrium, as well as tube permeability, has been verified (by hysterosalpingography and uterotubal insufflation). Both tubes were obstructed in 24% of the cases. Possible alterations in the cervico-vaginal segment which might interfere with the migration of the sperm have also been investigated. Among changes attributable to the device, hypermenorrhea, metrorrhagia, and pelvic aches have been found in 22 cases; functional disturbances consisting of anovarian cycles and discordance between the day of the cycle and the degree of mucosa maturation in 32 cases. Signs of endometritis were discovered in 20% of the samples submitted to histopathological investigation. All in all, the endometrium was disturbed in 44% of the cases. These findings, which substantially differ from those of other authors, make Dr. Ernst's team somewhat skeptical of the procedure. They use it extensively, however, because these damages are insignificant in comparison with the consequences of the induced abortions they are seeking to prevent.

Dr. Onofre Avendaño, vice-president of the NAFP, directs a multipurpose combination of services in the southern area that has succeeded in providing adequate protection for 8%—principally by means of the IUD—of the 120,000 women of reproductive age. In his group is Dr. Jaime Zipper, who originated the "Chilean" or "Dr. Zipper's ring," which is handmade of a thread of nylon about 2 meters in length and 0.35 mm. in diameter. The thread forms 20 interlaced turnings, with a final diameter of 25 mm. About 200 mm. of the ending is left free; in some cases the tail remains in the uterine cavity and removal requires an intra-uterine hook. An aluminum wire of 3 mm. in diameter with a groove in its end is used as an inserter. It does not require dilation of the cervical canal. The application is preceded by hysterometry.

Dr. Zipper has already used it on more than 7,000 women and analyzed the results of the first 3,000. The rate of spontaneous expulsion reached 17.2% for the first and 4.6% for the second. Removal for medical reasons was mainly due to metrorrhagia, the most common and troublesome difficulty. These have now been reduced to 5.7% by means of estrogens. Infections are comparatively rare, are easily eliminated through antibiotics, and do not usually require hospital care. In over 100 woman-years of exposure to risk, the device failed in 3.75 (pregnancies); in 1.69 of these cases, the ring was clearly in place. All in all, over 70% of the women have retained the ring for over a year and a half, a total of some 50,000 months. As Dr. Zipper is also an assistant at the University Institute of Physiology, he is investigating contraceptive mechanisms in experimental animals in the laboratory and has already obtained interesting results.

In collaboration with the School of Public Health of Harvard University, Dr. Requena is embarked on a program of abortion control in the 450,000 population—mostly workers and low middle class—of the western area of Santiago, where the birth rate is 40 per 1,000. After the completion of a pilot project (1962–63), he succeeded in 1964 in providing 10% of the women of reproductive age (6,525) with contraceptives, using IUD's in 93.1% of the cases, and, of them, the Lippes loop in 71%. Since he had already established that people were highly motivated but lacked knowledge and resources to control their fertility, he carried out an intensive educational campaign (214 lectures that covered some 4,000 persons, among other activities) and made contraceptives easily accessible in health centers. He aims to investigate several sides of the problem: attitudes, motivation, communication, evaluation, as well as social and psychological effects of long-term insertions, incidence of infections, and so on.

Today fertility control services exist in almost all Santiago public hospitals and in numerous maternal and child health centers located in different parts of the city. These provide contraceptive methods for 40,000–50,000 women a year and the numbers are increasing. The National Medical Service (Servicio Medico Nacional de Empleados) is supplying them regularly in the mother and child section, to the public service employees, and to employees in private enterprises, as well as to members of the Merchant Marine. The Catholic University Hospital carries out very conscientious work with oral pills and the rhythm method. In October, 1964, the NAFP sent a circular letter to sixty-five heads of obstetrical and gynecological services in provincial hospitals. The response was very enthusiastic and work has commenced in several of them.

On the whole, these specialists make the insertions as well as the first diaphragm application and the recommendation of other systems when necessary. Midwives[2] are in charge of the periodic control, and nursing assistants prepare the material. Both groups are playing a role of increasing importance. This can be readily understood as Chilean women traditionally call on the midwife for the care of their pregnancies and deliveries. Chilean midwives are professional women who have had three or four years of university study and abundant practical experience. Obstetricians use them as assistants not only in maternity cases but also in their private practice. There is no national program of education and training. As has already been said, university syllabi in medicine, nursing, obstetrics (midwives), and social work at present include material on birth control. In general, the best qualified specialists have been trained abroad, mainly in the United States, and they give in-service training to their staff.

Overseas visitors have been surprised at the number of women who come to the obstetrical and gynecological polyclinics and other services offering contraceptive methods. This influx is a clear sign of social demand, inasmuch as those seeking advice come of their own accord. A minor part can be attributed to the small degree of publicity which has already been mentioned, as well as to the advice given by doctors, nurses, and social workers to abortion cases, to multiparous women, and to other qualified cases in prenatal and postnatal care centers. Although it is obviously urgent to expand and increase these services, progress is slow because of limitations, especially of personnel and funds, and because of the desire to advance cautiously, providing, only and above all, efficient medical care.

Another barrier is the discovery of abundant gynecological pathology during the examination which precedes the insertion of the IUD or the initial application of the diaphragm or another agent of local action. As a result, two of the most valuable side products of the birth control program have been the extensive treatment of the above-mentioned pathology and the early diagnosis of cervical cancer, which is also systematically included. Most centers now perform the Schiller test and the cell frotis (Papanicolaou) as a routine. It is thus that the great disproportion (from four and more to one) exists between the number of consultations and insertions. In the absence of that pathology and of a possible pregnancy, the ring or the loop is applied in the first consultation and checked after one to three months, and then twice a year. These routines are subject to certain variations in order to determine which is the best. Some gynecologists simultaneously inject a slow action sulfonamide.

As far as choice is concerned, there are two relevant observations to

[2] Present laws (Health Code) forbid midwives to do anything but attend to pregnancies and deliveries; for the time being they cannot make insertions.

make. Almost nobody wants the rhythm method, and preference for
the IUD may be as much as 10:1 in relation to other systems. The
most popular IUD is the Zipper ring, but Lippes loops and Margulies
spirals (gifts of overseas foundations) are employed extensively. They
are all well accepted and do not produce serious complications. Lasting expulsions do not generally exceed 3%. In an experience covering
100 woman-years, only three births were recorded. Doctors assert
almost unanimously that objections, principally religious or moral, are
exceptional. On the contrary, a majority of women (around 75%)
and their consorts feel that birth control should be made universal
and that the church has no right to interfere in these matters. A small
percentage is in favor of legal abortion.

THE ABORTION PROBLEM

Around 1950, and as a part of a very extensive research study of
human reproduction, our department investigated for the first time in
Chile the problem of abortions.[3] We discovered the enormous frequency of involuntary miscarriages, a fact which seems typical of
underdeveloped countries and has interrelationships with stillbirths
and infant mortality. In a sample of 3,038 women, we found that out
of 10,612 pregnancies, 72.5% gave rise to live births, 1% to stillbirths, and 26.5% were voluntarily terminated. We analyzed the
distribution of abortions in relation to the age of the women (it increases up to 35 years and decreases later on, but sometimes covers
the entire reproductive period), the social class, civil status, and other
aspects. Complicated or incomplete abortions that required hospital
care were then 64,500 a year. Of the others we had no further information at that time.

In 1959 Tabah and Samuel[4] took a probability sample of some
2,000 women, between 20 and 50 years of age, in order to ascertain
fertility rates and attitudes concerning family formation. They concluded that the rate is only 50% in the upper cultural and economic
levels, that restriction is deliberate and has perceptibly increased in
the recent five-year period and that the majority of women consider
23 the ideal age for marrying to have four children born at two-
and-a-half-year intervals. Less than 20% opposed birth control on
principle; but even in this group some practice it. The proportion of

[3] H. Romero and Jerjes Vildosola, "Economia de vidas. II. Introducción al problema
de los abortos." *Rev. Chil. de Hig. y Med. Prev.*, 14 (4): 197-211 (1952).

[4] L. Tabah and R. Samuel, "Preliminary Findings of a Survey on Fertility and Attitudes toward Family Formation in Santiago, Chile," in *Research in Family Planning*,
ed. C. V. Kiser (Princeton: Princeton University Press, 1962), pp. 263-304.

abortions was one to three live births among married women and one to slightly over two for estranged or common-law wives.

In recent years, Drs. Rolando Armijo and Tegualda Monreal and Dr. Requena have engaged in long-range investigations of paramount interest and with the best techniques. Taking representative samples in Santiago in 1961, and in Concepción (a mining and industrial city of the south) and Antofagasta (a mining city of the north) in 1963–64, the first team has surveyed 3,776 women between 20 and 44 years of age. Of these, 46% declared that they had had abortions, and 23% that they had provoked them; 75% experienced three abortions; 8%, seven or more; and 15 women had a total of 187. Frequency is twice as high in married women as in spinsters. Although a majority resort to an interruption between the fourth and sixth pregnancies, the peak is reached between 25 and 29 years of age. Abortions, as well as infant mortality, have a marked inverse correlation with family income. In nine out of ten cases, the male approved the decision, and in one out of every eight it was carried out by the patient herself, usually through the introduction of a Nelaton catheter. As a rule these are the same women who attempt to control their fertility, often by absurd methods. Abortion is therefore the last resort when all else has failed. Along the same lines is the surprising fact that 13% of the middle-class women interviewed had been sterilized.

In a non-stratified and representative sample of people of reproductive age in a population of some 13,000 inhabitants who are under the care of the Comprehensive Medical Care Demonstration Center, Dr. Requena interviewed 580 women who had gone through 2,617 pregnancies. Of these, 34.7% of the pregnancies were interrupted, 11.3% spontaneously and 23.4% induced. Among the latter, it made no difference if the person was married or not; if she had received secondary education (university education was very rare); if she was a professional, employee, or housewife; or if she declared herself to be Catholic or non-religious. Curiously enough, frequency is greater among the most fervent believers (who go to church once or twice a week and to confession more often than other people) and considerably less among Evangelists; as was to be expected, the number is also greater among unskilled workers. As in the study of Armijo and Monreal, the peak is located among those who practice or believe in the practice of birth control. This group constitutes 18% of the sample, and, of them, only one-fourth employ effective methods; the rest resort to such unusual systems as warm wine, lemon, mustard, purgatives, post-coitum micturition, and the like. When offered a rational method, only 14.5% rejected it; nearly 50% preferred the

IUD; nearly 40%, pills; the rest chose diaphragms; and none accepted the rhythm method.

By now we know that one out of two or three pregnancies is interrupted and that two-thirds of abortions are induced. Furthermore, in one out of five pregnancies which come to term, interruption was contemplated. We also know that cases of complicated and incomplete abortion which come to the hospital for treatment make up 8.1% of all admissions and add up to 67 for every 100 deliveries. They comprise 35% of all operations performed in maternity cases and require 17% of the transfusions and 26.7% of the volume of blood used by emergency services. Those admissions increased from 12,963 in 1937 to 57,368 in 1960 (they multiplied 4.4 times as against 1.8 for deliveries). In that year, they represented 184,000 bed-days and produced, by this single fact alone, an expenditure exceeding $1 million. Each survivor of *Clostridium perfringens septicemia* costs over $3,000. In 1963 abortions were responsible for 39% of maternal mortality. Despite its magnitude, this calamity represents only the visible part of the iceberg. The hidden part is being explored in the different ways described above and also by other means.

Chile may not be typical with regard to induced abortion, but it does offer singularly favorable opportunities for investigation. The lessons to be learned may apply to other countries of similar economic and cultural conditions. The country is endowed with reliable statistics, public health and medical organizations with national programs, a group of professionals who are highly competent and genuinely interested in the problem, as well as accumulated information of undeniable value. Because public medicine is well developed, people are accustomed to dealing with doctors and their co-workers and trust them. Furthermore, the Chilean is not naturally inhibited and work has shown that it is not difficult to obtain data concerning even the most intimate aspects of individual lives.

HIGH FERTILITY AND ITS CONSEQUENCES

It will be of little use to provide numerical information on the work performed in the field of birth control. Partial programs have been carried out for some twenty-seven years and, because of their secretive nature, few traces have been left of the first phase. Others have begun in recent weeks or are in preparation and will soon start, and they differ in the procedures and the systems of work employed. In pharmacies, condoms are sold freely but do not receive as much acceptance as would be desirable. Diaphragms, imported from the

United States, are still less popular. Because of foreign exchange restrictions, pills of different makes come in limited quantities and the supply is rapidly exhausted. Rings are so profusely employed in private practice that the stock of nylon, with which they are made, runs out. For the time being it is impossible to assess the volume of these different commercial transactions. The NAFP proposes to make a complete evaluation of the achievements and problems of birth control toward the end of 1965, when several projects will close to change their orientations.

In view of the foregoing, it appears appropriate that the NAFP concentrate its efforts on investigating the size and characteristics of the problem of induced abortion, the causes and the way to combat them. Since abortion is now the most popular method of fertility control for people who are ignorant of other methods or who have no other means at their disposal or whose motivations are weak, the Association considers its duty to be to put the modern methods within easy reach of all and to popularize them. Experience has already shown that education should be continuous, especially when mass methods are not yet employed. Several doctors have noticed that, though demand for contraceptives is very substantial, it drops appreciably and immediately when teaching is discontinued. Experience has also shown that demand is greater when the work of teaching is merged with that dealing with mother and child and gynecology. This is partly because the mother often feels shame or timidity attending a service which is devoted exclusively to birth control, and in MCH or gynecology clinics a climate of mutual confidence is usually established.

Chile may benefit from a greater population that will increase its consumption power and the diversification of its economic activities. It is undoubtedly true, in any case, that a growth of 2.5% which adds over 200,000 individuals yearly to a population of some 8 million, makes for unfavorable age distribution (around 38% are below 15 years of age) and seriously interferes with economic development. According to the United Nations Economic Commission for Latin America, change in per capita income was 1.7% between 1950 and 1954, 0% in 1955, and —4% in 1956. In later years, it has had several negative values in spite of the determined efforts Chileans have made, for more than twenty years, to plan and promote the country's development.

It is the family, however, which suffers most from excessive fertility. The size of the family is unquestionably in inverse relationship to material welfare, even though family allowances in Chile are the most generous in Latin America. It appears suggestive that housewives who devote the biggest part of their income to food are precisely those most inclined to practice birth control. The greatest stumbling block to reducing infant mortality to below 110 per thousand is the precarious nutritional state of our poorer children. Because of these conditions, infections are easily acquired and take a more rapid and often deadly course. The mother does not realize the severity of the disease—in an infant always emaciated—and no matter how prompt the medical care, the child is already doomed. As has been stated before, induced abortions are responsible for nearly two-fifths of maternal mortality in Chile today.

19

LATIN AMERICA

RAMIRO DELGADO GARCÍA, M.D.
President, Interdisciplinary Committee, Division of Population Studies
Colombian Association of Medical Schools
Vice-President, Colombian Association for the Scientific Study of Population
Executive Secretary, University Committee for Population Research
Universidad del Valle, Colombia

CHARACTERISTICS OF FAMILY PLANNING PROGRAMS

There is no common denominator for family planning programs throughout Latin America. Each country is trying to adapt to its own particular circumstances, organizing private clinics or research units placed in specific cities and not yet attempting to cover the entire country. No government is directly sponsoring these programs which are, in general, led by the medical profession. Several countries still have legal restrictions limiting the sale or distribution of contraceptives. The Catholic church favors the idea of family planning in Latin America, provided the methods used are "natural," and the aim is the regulation of family size within the general context of responsible parenthood. However, because the average educational level of the Latin American population is low, and its motivation for small families is not well established, the conclusion is that the organization of Latin American national programs is still a matter for the future.

GOVERNMENT ATTITUDES TOWARD POPULATION STUDIES

Five ministries of health in as many countries have adopted a favorable attitude toward population studies and programs: The National Health Service of Chile is supporting the National Association of Fam-

This paper represents the personal opinions of the author, and has not been officially endorsed by the institutions of which he is a member.

ily Protection programs.[1] The Family Welfare Society of Guatemala has been officially recognized and is providing contraceptive services through the American Hospital in the city of Guatemala.[2] The Demographic Association of El Salvador, the Center for Population and Development Studies of Peru, and the Population Division of the Ministry of Health and Social Assistance of Venezuela are working in close collaboration with their respective governments in a careful study of socioeconomic and demographic problems of these countries, in order to determine by means of specific data (census analysis) and special surveys (abortions, sexual attitudes) the actual seriousness of the population situation.

There are demographic sections in the national planning offices of Ecuador, El Salvador, Nicaragua, Paraguay, Peru, Venezuela, and Chile. Moreover, statistical centers and demography departments exist in most of the Latin American countries.

The Latin American Demographic Center (CELADE) was created in 1957 under the auspices of the United Nations. It has promoted ambitious research and training programs in demography for Latin America.

In 1964, the Secretary General of the United Nations delivered among the governments of member nations the results of a survey conducted by the Economic and Social Council "concerning the particular problems to be faced as a result of the reciprocal action of economic development and population changes."[3] Eight countries from the Americas responded to the request expressing some concern as to the feasibility of attaining satisfactory progress in both economic and social development in the near future if the present high rate of population increase continues.

Thus, there is some hope that in the future traditional Latin American indifference toward population problems will be replaced by a positive policy that favors direct action and allows private institutions to provide service and advice in family planning.

Scope of Existing Family Planning Organizations

In Argentina, Brazil, Chile, Colombia, Costa Rica, Ecuador, El Salvador, Guatemala, Haiti, Honduras, Mexico, Peru, Uruguay, and

[1] See Romero paper in this volume (chap. 18).

[2] Ofelia Mendoza, "Population Growth: Its Impact on the Health, Nutrition, and Economic, Social, and Cultural Development of Latin America," Ninth Congress of the Pan-American Medical Women's Association, Los Angeles, Nov. 16, 1964.

[3] Report of the Secretary General to the General Assembly of the United Nations, E/3895, May 18, 1964, and E/3895/Add. 1, June 30, 1964.

Venezuela there are well-organized associations giving contraceptive services, mostly to the urban communities. But only in Chile and Colombia are these organizations well co-ordinated and attempting to cover the entire country.

The Chilean experience is fully described by Dr. Hernán Romero elsewhere in this volume (chap. 18).

THE COLOMBIAN APPROACH TO POPULATION RESEARCH AND SERVICE

During the past decade, several isolated individuals and institutions have been working on population studies. Last year it became apparent that an adequate co-ordination of these efforts would avoid duplications and permit better utilization of available human resources. The first assembly for the study of Colombian demographic problems was held in Bogotá, in May, 1964, under the auspices of the Colombian Association of Medical Schools and the Ford Foundation. This was a most successful meeting, in which leading universities from throughout the country, the Ministry of Health, the National Planning Office, the National Department of Statistics, as well as several private institutions of higher education and research were represented. Two organizations were created at this assembly: the Division of Population Studies of the Colombian Association of Medical Schools—deriving its membership from the associated institutions—which deals with research and operational aspects of population problems, and the Colombian Association for the Scientific Study of Population, which purports to educate and stimulate awareness of population problems among the diverse social levels: government, church, industry, education, community leaders, and so on; its members are private citizens.

The Division of Population Studies sponsors and co-ordinates eight population committees, located in the six principal cities of the country. These committees are also of an interdisciplinary nature and belong either to a medical school or a university. The activities of such committees are locally supervised and directed by an executive secretary, usually working full time in this endeavor. For the time being, priorities for research activities through these centers have been fixed as follows: (*a*) fertility, (*b*) family planning, (*c*) abortion surveys, and (*d*) socio-demographic studies.

In these areas, fourteen research programs have been launched in 1965. About one hundred persons from different professions, including physicians, economists, bio-statisticians, lawyers, social workers, nurses, and others are working full time in these programs. A minimum of 20% of the cost of the projects is being covered by the respective university or institution, with the rest provided by national and international agencies and private citizens. The total cost for the initial three-year program amounts to more than $500,000.

Moreover, the Division of Population Studies is encouraging adequate training for affiliated personnel. In 1965, the following fellowships for studies in foreign countries were awarded by the Division for Special Training in demography, family planning, communications, physiology of reproduction, and other fields: 16 to medical doctors; 5 to economists; 3 to sociologists; 2 to social workers; and 1 to a priest. The duration of the studies varies from two months to three years. Twice a year the Division organizes an intensive seminar on demography with the participation of national and foreign experts and the collaboration of the personnel directly involved in the research projects. Some of the institutions collaborating with technical and financial aid are Ford Foundation, Rockefeller Foundation, Milbank Memorial Fund, AID, Population Council, International Planned Parenthood Federation, University of Chicago, Cornell University, University of California, University of Michigan, CELADE, Columbia University, Universidad de Chile, and others.

The Colombian Association for the Scientific Study of Population distributes important documents dealing with population problems, family planning, and moral aspects of birth control. It also organizes round-table meetings, seminars, and conferences regarding population problems of both Colombia and the world. One of the main objectives of the Association is to facilitate communication and stimulate discussions among government officials, the church, scholars, and community leaders. Such a task is of the utmost importance because lack of understanding and knowledge among individuals from various social groups has been one of the most significant barriers impeding the adoption of population policies throughout the world. We hope to avoid such barriers in Colombia.

The great interest shown by the Colombian universities in community studies has favored the development of population programs. Special credit should be given to the Universidad del Valle, in Cali, for its continuous interest in matters related to the study of regional problems and for the establishment of a powerful and dynamic department of preventive medicine within its Medical School. This department is directing several pilot health centers in both urban and rural areas. In Candelaria, a rural zone near Cali, high birth rates were causing serious difficulties that affected the general health of the people. A careful survey showed that these birth rates reached the incredible figure of 60.3 per 1,000 population per year. Mothers were anxiously requesting information and advice on family planning, and they have been quite responsive to the programs being offered by the university's Pilot Health Center.

The Candelaria program has been followed by similar programs in other areas of the state and in many community centers. The specific importance of the Candelaria Family Planning Program is that it is organized in a well-controlled community of low socioeconomic conditions and is using the methods accepted by the moral precepts of the Catholic church, so that it will not provoke opposition and can be easily followed in other centers. One additional advantage of this program is the possibility of evaluating it accurately both at the family level and on a community-wide basis. Evidence thus derived, after some three years of experience, will help us to decide whether large-scale campaigns based on these methods are justifiable.

Of equal importance are two other studies which are organized by the Committee for Population Research of the Universidad del Valle: the analysis of census data of Valle State and a survey on the prevalence of abortion.

The general climate for population studies is rather good in Colombia. Public opinion has been made aware of the problem through the different mass media (press, radio, television) and is very receptive to discussion of population matters.

During August 11–14, 1965, the First Pan-American Assembly on Population was held in Cali, sponsored by the Universidad del Valle and the Colombian Association of Medical Schools, with the co-operation of the American Assembly of Columbia University and the Population Council of New York. Eighty outstanding hemispheric leaders in the fields of education, public affairs, mass communication, and the professions met for three days to discuss population problems in the Americas. At the end of the assembly a statement was approved by the participants (see Appendix). This report summarizes very well the present feeling throughout Latin America regarding the population problem.

APPENDIX

FINAL REPORT

of the
First Pan-American Assembly on Population
(Cali, Colombia, August, 1965)

At the close of their discussions the participants in the First Pan-American Assembly on Population reviewed as a group the following statement. The statement represents general agreement;

however no one was asked to sign it, and it should not be assumed that every participant necessarily subscribes to every recommendation.

INTRODUCTION

The extraordinary rates of population growth in many of the American countries in recent decades have aggravated and will continue to aggravate problems in almost every sphere of life, from the diet of the peasant to the investment necessary to accelerate economic and social development. There is considerable variation among the American nations in their demographic situation—size, density, population distribution and velocity of growth. While not faced with severe demographic problems at this time, Northern America is undergoing rates of population growth which may cause serious problems in the future. Most Latin American nations, on the other hand, have rates of population growth which are high, both in terms of their growth of national product, and in comparison with the demographic growth of nations in other areas or eras. As a result of rapid and continuing declines in death rates, along with continued high natality, the population of the region will double in about 25 years, but the number and severity of the problems will increase by an even higher factor.

Distribution

Although over-all population density in Latin America is low, the distribution of population is uneven. Since urban areas are growing much more rapidly than rural, the problem of mal-distribution is steadily growing more severe. The "bands of misery" around many Latin American cities grow thicker as rural inhabitants leave the farms, as a result of rural population growth and other social and economic changes.

Economic Development

Among the factors which impair economic development, excessively high rates of population growth may be cited, because they require higher proportions of national income to be saved and invested merely to maintain current levels of per-capita income. Further, because of the large proportion of young people in high fertility nations, capital is diverted from production to consumption. There is increasing difficulty in making per-capita improvements in community services when new population tends to absorb the new homes, classrooms and hospitals.

Family Welfare

High population growth rates also affect the family. The family with many children can save and invest very little and must spend a higher proportion of its income on consumption than the family with few children. Problems of the degree and kind of education are also aggravated. Equally important are aspects of health and morality. Scientific surveys indicate that the average Latin American woman (at least in cities) wants fewer children than she has, but as a result of reductions in infant mortality family size in Latin America has been increasing. Latin American women have not been unresponsive to this discrepancy, and high rates of induced abortion prevail in the countries studied thus far, creating a broad range of legal, moral and medical problems.

The above reasoning does not imply that Latin America is currently "over-populated," only that the present rates of growth are impeding social and economic development. Nor does it imply that Latin American nations should stop growing, or have some fixed population, but that a slower rate of population growth has many advantages. Most important of all, it does not imply that attention should be shifted from the great and imperative needs for basic social and economic reforms.

For the kind of problems we have been discussing, there are demographic and other than demographic solutions. The latter refer to the usual ingredients of economic and social development—investment, industrial and agricultural development, higher educational levels, a more balanced distribution of income, social security measures, etc. We have seen that these are difficult to achieve in the face of high rates of population growth, but even low rates, without growth in the factors cited above would result in intolerably slow social and economic improvements. While the present recommendations concentrate on population, it should be understood that a judicious combination of demographic and other solutions is essential.

In all instances, whether or not the approach be demographic, the ultimate ends of improvement in the cultural, economic, and physical well-being of the individual human being must be kept in view. Our recommendations are intended as means to these ends, as ways of further liberating man in his pursuit of higher goals.

RECOMMENDATIONS

1. Every nation, according to its special cultural, economic, religious and demographic circumstances, should develop a population policy embodying broad national objectives with respect to population distribution, velocity of population growth and levels of mortality, fertility and migration, as an integral part of its policy of economic development. The creation of such a policy should be preceded by adequate public discussion and thorough analysis of demographic, economic and social data.

2. American governments should assign high priority to the improvement of collection, processing and analysis of demographic and related data. Further, the appropriate ministries and planning boards dealing with such problems as health, education, housing and manpower, should include demographers as part of their personnel.

3. Governments should aim toward the enlightenment of the community with respect to family and sexual problems, with the end of encouraging responsible paternity. This means efforts to reduce illegitimacy and to encourage couples to have the number of children consistent with

their own ideals and compatible with the possibilities available to them for the education and care to which they are entitled.

4. Private national organizations have important roles to play in dealing with population problems. Until governments adopt policies, such agencies should serve to awaken public opinion, encourage government participation and serve as a continuing stimulus for programs in research, communication and service. By means of pilot programs they can demonstrate demand, feasibility and range of alternative population and sex education programs. Even after governments adopt a program, the private agency should remain a continuing stimulus for new ideas, pioneering new avenues of approach to family planning and sex education, and adopting experimental programs.

It is highly important that such organizations be composed of representatives from a broad spectrum of the professional community—such as physicians, sociologists, economists, businessmen, educators and clerics—as well as representatives of labor and farm organizations.

5. In realization of the educational aims of the governments enunciated previously, and, in recognition of the high incidence of criminal abortion, and, in recognition of the manifest desire of many couples to properly space their children's births, the governments, through their appropriate ministries, should make family planning services accessible to the people who desire them, and educate the people to their availability. These services should provide a sufficient variety of medically approved methods so that they can be chosen in accordance with the dictates of the individual conscience.

6. Considering the fact that most nations have excessively high rates of urban growth, special attention is needed to problems associated with internal migration and population density. With respect to external migration, governments should encourage personnel essential to economic and social development to remain in the region.

7. Recognition of the dangers of population growth and formulation of the policies which may be applied to population problems should not divert attention from the necessity for basic social and economic reforms.

8. Intergovernmental institutions should provide financial and technical assistance for the establishment of national population programs, providing information and consultative services with respect to administrative and technical alternatives in population programming.

9. Bilateral arrangements with foreign organizations of public and private character should be considered by governments and private institutions, for technical and financial assistance in the study, execution and evaluation of population programs.

10. Universities and other institutions of higher learning should:

> Seek ways of introducing the scientific study of population to all relevant university curricula in such fields as law, theology, education, economics, sociology, medicine, public health, biology and planning.

Cooperate with government and private agencies, and with each other, and take the lead in pure and applied research on population problems.

Promote the preparation and training of personnel and assist in the determination of the appropriate methods of education in sexual and family matters.

Be focal points for high level public discussion and diffusion of ideas on the population question.

Participate actively in programs related to population problems and coordinate by means of centers or work groups the interdisciplinary study, research and discussion indispensable to integrated planning for the solution of demographic problems.

11. Religious leaders should be continually provided with the best available scientific information on biological, social and economic aspects of population problems. This information should be made available to all levels of the church hierarchy. In turn, religious leaders of all faiths should intensify communication with scientists in order that the public may fully comprehend the continual development of church thought.

20

THE UNITED STATES

LESLIE CORSA, Jr., M.D.
Director, Center for Population Planning, University of Michigan

ORIGINS AND OPERATIONS

Organized social action in the United States to affect fertility rates of the American people through individual family control of the timing and number of offspring stems from many causes and covers a broad range of private and public activities. All possible social actions that have been taken to affect fertility[1] are beyond the scope of this paper but it should be emphasized from the start that actions unintentionally influencing birth rates and family size far outnumber actions intended to have influence. Here the focus is on organized efforts to make various methods of birth control known and used effectively by families. Principal efforts of this kind are carried out in the American culture and economy largely by private enterprise with significant contributions from private family planning agencies and, more recently, by government.

HISTORICAL DEVELOPMENT

Historically, these organized efforts represent a late stage of the North Atlantic demographic transition of the past few hundred years and can be said to have developed from the changes in industrialization, urbanization, mortality, and fertility between the American Revolution and the twentieth century. The historical development of contraceptive knowledge and technology in the United States has been well documented by Himes.[2]

[1] See Ronald Freedman, "The Sociology of Human Fertility," *Current Sociology*, 10–11:35 (1961–62).

[2] N. E. Himes, *Medical History of Contraception* (New York: Gamut Press, 1963).

Private family planning agencies in the United States owe much to Mrs. Margaret Sanger, the feminist rebel who so effectively promoted emancipation of women from unwanted pregnancies through contraception. She is credited with coining the phrase "birth control." The National (later American) Birth Control League (later Planned Parenthood Federation of America) was established in 1917 with Mrs. Sanger as president. Its Clinical Research Bureau (later Margaret Sanger Research Bureau) opened in 1923 and expanded under the direction of Dr. Hannah Stone (1925–41) and then of her husband, Dr. Abraham Stone (1941–58). In 1962, the Planned Parenthood Federation of America merged with the World Population Emergency Campaign to form the present Planned Parenthood–World Population as a single national organization for unified action on the population crisis under the presidency of Dr. Alan F. Guttmacher, a distinguished leader in American obstetrics.

Meanwhile, in 1952, the Population Council, a private foundation, was formed "to stimulate, encourage, promote, conduct and support significant activities in the broad field of population." Under the chairmanship of John D. Rockefeller 3rd and the presidency of Frank W. Notestein, it has provided key professional leadership in developing population research, training, and technical consultation in the social and medical sciences. Other foundations, notably Ford, Rockefeller, and Milbank, have provided essential research and training support in population in recent decades.

Because of religious and political controversy, local, state, and federal governments in the United States have excluded tax-supported family planning services until recent years, and many states still have some restrictive legislation. Only as late as June 7, 1965, did the United States Supreme Court declare unconstitutional the one remaining state law making contraceptive *use* illegal. This has meant that families of lowest incomes who rely upon tax funds for medical care have been deprived of birth control knowledge and services available to the average American through private resources. As public concerns about social, economic, and racial inequality, about rising illegitimacy, and about the higher fertility rates and tax costs of unwanted children among low-income families have heightened, civic and medical leaders have begun to incorporate birth control into existing tax-supported health services.

In 1959 the American Public Health Association, under the presidency of Dr. Leona Baumgartner, declared population problems a major public health concern and specified public health responsibilities for action.[3] This was followed in the next few years by similar statements from other national and state organizations and from some state health agencies. The 1963 American Assembly dealt with the population dilemma and called for "assumption of responsibility by the federal, state and local governments for making available information concerning the regulation of fertility and providing services to needy mothers compatible with the religious and ethical beliefs of the individual recipient. . . ."[4] The National Academy of Sciences issued a 1963 report on the growth of the world population[5] and a 1965 report on the growth of the United States population[6] recommending government action. Dr. John Rock, a prominent Catholic physician, supported government action in his 1963 book, *The Time Has Come*.[7] President Johnson, in his 1965 State of the Union message, promised to "seek new ways to use our knowledge to help deal with the explosion in world population and the growing scarcity of world resources." During this period, the number of states with local health departments providing family planning services rose from 7 in 1960 to 27 in 1965.

OBJECTIVES

The objectives of family planning programs in the United States are to enable individual families to have the number of children they want at the time they want them. No local or national goals exist in terms of fertility rates or of population growth or density although recognition of the multiple effects of these factors upon American life is growing. The cohorts of the sustained postwar baby boom starting in 1946 have produced social problems as they grew, none more acute than their current and increasing need for jobs and college education. Even affluent America is having trouble keeping up with the demands for housing, schools, hospitals, roads, and recreation space, to say nothing of such basic essentials as clean water and clean air for its highly

[3] American Public Health Association, "Policy Statement on the Population Problem," *American Journal of Public Health*, 49:1703 (1959); see also additional later policy statement, *ibid.*, 54:2102 (1964).

[4] American Assembly, Columbia University, *The Population Dilemma* (Englewood Cliffs, N.J.: Prentice-Hall, Inc., 1963).

[5] National Academy of Sciences, *The Growth of World Population*, Publication No. 1091 (Washington, D.C., 1963).

[6] National Academy of Sciences, *The Growth of U.S. Population*, Publication No. 1279 (Washington, D.C., 1965).

[7] John Rock, *The Time Has Come* (New York: Alfred Knopf, 1963).

urbanized, industrialized population of 195 million. Serious efforts to define optimum relations between population growth and density and the many facets of living are just beginning. Meanwhile, such objectives remain obscure beyond increasing public recognition that America's metropolitan and wilderness areas are becoming overcrowded. We are concerned here with present organized action to provide knowledge and methods of fertility control for those of our 35 million American families of reproductive age who want them.

PRIVATE ENTERPRISE

The large majority of Americans obtain their knowledge of human reproduction and fertility control as best they can. Their family planning services and supplies come from private physicians, pharmacists, and other consumer outlets for all kinds of contraceptives produced in sufficient quantities by American rubber, plastic, and pharmaceutical industries and distributed under the eye of the federal Food and Drug Administration. With the advent of new and better contraceptive methods requiring a physician's services, the interest of industry and physicians is growing rapidly. While limited data are available periodically about the quantities of contraceptives produced and distributed in the United States, the most useful information about the use of contraceptives comes from national household sample surveys, which will be discussed later.

Even more limited data are available on what family planning services physicians actually provide[8] and on what American medical schools teach of family planning.[9] Those available indicate that inadequate attention is given to family planning in most medical schools and that "the extent and kind of family planning information a doctor provides depends on what a patient requests and on what each doctor believes appropriate rather than on any definition by the profession of what the doctor should do."[10]

The American Medical Association, which during 1935–38 had taken positions on several aspects of contraception, made clear its present position in December, 1964, by stating that "the medical profession should accept a major responsibility in matters related to human reproduction as they affect the total population and the individual

[8] M. J. Cornish, F. A. Ruderman, and S. S. Spivack, *Doctors and Family Planning*, National Committee on Maternal Health, Inc., Publication No. 19 (New York, 1963).

[9] American Public Health Association, Maternal and Child Health Section, Committee on Family and Population Planning, "Preliminary Report on National Survey of Medical Education in Family Planning, 1964."

[10] Cornish *et al., op. cit.*

family." It also said that "in discharging this responsibility physicians must be prepared to provide counsel and guidance when the needs of their patients require it or refer the patients to appropriate persons" and specified American Medical Association responsibility to disseminate information to physicians on all phases of human reproduction and to help improve teaching in this field in medical schools.[11] The pharmaceutical industry, too, has recently provided impetus to postgraduate education of physicians on population matters. Physicians in the United States can be expected to be more active and more knowledgeable in family planning in the years ahead.

PRIVATE FAMILY PLANNING AGENCIES

Almost all private family planning agencies in the United States are affiliated with the Planned Parenthood Federation of America, which in December, 1964, included 138 local organizations in 35 states and the District of Columbia (see Fig. 1). Fifteen per cent were newly organized in 1964, another index of increased civic interest in family planning. These local planned parenthood organizations served 281,-960 patients during 1964, an increase of 21% over 1963, and of 127% over 1960, but still less than 6% of Planned Parenthood's national estimate of 5,000,000 medically indigent families needing family planning services. Nearly half of new patients came on recommendation of a "satisfied customer" and over 40% of all patients selected oral pills (intra-uterine devices were not generally available).[12] Planned Parenthood–World Population also conducts national and local informational and educational activities and conducts and supports investigations in medical and social sciences.

GOVERNMENT PROGRAMS

The firm trend in the United States to deny birth control no longer to families receiving their medical care primarily from government facilities or funds has already been mentioned. About 20–25% of American families, largely of lowest income, are in this category and receive their medical care from a variety of city, county, state, and federal hospitals or health services, or from private physicians and hospitals paid from tax funds. No national data are available on tax-supported hospital or welfare services in family planning or on tax-fi-

[11] American Medical Association, "Policies on Human Reproduction and Birth Control, Adopted December, 1964."

[12] Planned Parenthood–World Population, *Annual Report on 1964* (New York).

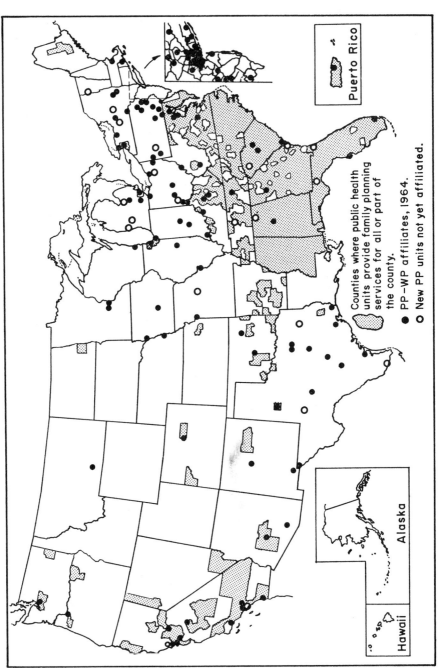

FIG. 1.—Family planning services in health departments, by county, 1965, and Planned Parenthood affiliates, by city

Counties where public health units provide family planning services for all or part of the county.

● PP–WP affiliates, 1964.

○ New PP units not yet affiliated.

Puerto Rico

Alaska

Hawaii

nanced private services but the change is well documented for state and local public health departments.[13]

Before the American Public Health Association's 1959 policy statement, only seven states (Alabama, Florida, Georgia, Mississippi, North Carolina, South Carolina, and Virginia) included family planning as a regular part of their public health services. California in 1961, Maryland in 1962, and Colorado and Kansas by mid-1963 had initiated some family planning clinical services but in a total of only eighteen local health departments. In three of those same states and four others (Delaware, Illinois, Nebraska, and Texas) health departments also reported providing space and other assistance for private agency clinics by 1963. Certain referral and educational activities occurred in a few other states. Just one year later in summer, 1964, the District of Columbia and eight additional states (Arkansas, Indiana, Kentucky, Michigan, North Dakota, Oklahoma, Oregon, and Tennessee) reported that they, too, provided some clinical services and the number of local health departments providing services in the earlier states had increased substantially. By mid-1965 Arizona, Maine, Missouri, Nevada, New Jersey, New Mexico, New York, Texas, Washington, and West Virginia were also providing direct services (see Fig. 1).

No national data are yet available on the number of families receiving family planning services through tax-supported programs, but if families of military personnel are excluded, it is certainly less than the number served by private agencies, although growing rapidly.

Despite the variety of government programs in the United States, they tend to have in common the following features:

1. They are administered as part of the regular maternal health services.
2. They are available primarily to low-income families.
3. They make available a variety of contraceptive methods so that families can choose one compatible with their beliefs and needs.
4. Professional services are provided largely by qualified physicians and nurses.
5. They make little effort to provide information to families not seeking service.
6. They are financed from various federal, state, and local tax sources and so incorporated in related maternal health services that accurate estimates of costs for family planning are not possible.

The following brief descriptions of program development and content in a few states are indicative of the present status of program operations in the United States.

[13] Johan W. Eliot, "The Development of Family Planning Services by State and Local Health Departments in the United States," *American Journal of Public Health* (in press).

North Carolina.[14]—Contraceptive services were first made available in North Carolina in 1937 through the initiative of several physicians, the approval of the State Board of Health and the State Medical Society, and financial support from the Pathfinder Fund. Service is provided through clinics run by autonomous county health departments covering all 100 counties. Originally the family planning clinics were set up as a separate service apart from the maternity services but gradually merged to become an essential part of maternal health care. The State Board of Health has provided consultation, literature, and financial support. By 1954, although approximately half of the women seen in prenatal clinics were receiving some degree of contraceptive services (diaphragms, suppositories, jellies, foams), the proportion continuing service was extremely meager, because of inadequacies in service and in contraceptive techniques available. With the advent of oral pills and intra-uterine devices there has been marked reactivation of programs but no specific evaluation has yet been done. The State Board of Health has been an active participant in a clinical field trial of intra-uterine devices since September, 1963.

Mecklenburg County Health Department in Charlotte provides a good example of a local program active since 1937.[15] The population includes 5,700 indigent women between 15 and 40 years old who have already borne more than one child. Currently about 800 women are receiving service from the single clinic in Charlotte and the number of new admissions per year is rising from recent levels of over 300. Oral pills have been increasingly popular since their addition in 1960, 66% of initial pill users continuing use for at least 24 months. Intra-uterine devices were added in 1964 and are rapidly gaining in popularity.

California.[16]—The first significant step in California was unanimous adoption by the Conference of Local Health Officers on October 26, 1961, of a state policy on family planning which specified health department responsibility for services. Several local health departments proceeded at once to implement this policy, one with federal funds made available by the State Department of Public Health. Strong supporting action came from state and local medical associations on the basis that an adequate maternal health program should include family planning. Strong support came also from many citizen groups, aided by Planned Parenthood–World Population, whose first regional field

14 Personal communication from Dr. James F. Donnelly, Director, Personal Health Division, North Carolina State Board of Public Health, May 24, 1965.

15 Elizabeth C. Corkey, "A Family Planning Program for the Low-Income Family," *Journal of Marriage and the Family*, 26:478 (1964).

16 Leslie Corsa, "Family Planning in California" (in preparation).

worker was based in San Francisco in 1963. By mid-1965, twenty-three local health departments serving 88% of the state's population operated family planning clinical services in forty-four locations and 43% of local departments receiving new state health financial allotments elected to use them for family planning. No statewide data are yet available on the numbers of families served but they are known to be increasing rapidly, and to represent only a small proportion of low-income families so far. The State Department of Public Health also provides technical consultation and training and has sponsored a co-operative clinical field trial of intra-uterine devices since early 1964.

Alameda and Contra Costa counties (population 1.6 million) east of San Francisco Bay provide an example of good services. The Contra Costa County Health Department was one of the first in the state to provide family planning services, starting in January, 1962, on the initiative of the health officer. Seventeen clinics per month are now held, one-third of them in the evening, in six different locations throughout the county, serving about 3,000 cases, including 610 new families during 1964. Oral contraceptives are most popular so far, although since addition of intra-uterine devices in July, 1964, an increasing number are selecting them.[17]

Alameda County Health Department's clinic service began in July, 1964, having developed earlier as part of a Ford Foundation–financed effort to combat urban decay and social disorganization in an area of Oakland.[18] Tax-supported family planning was made a public issue by the 1963 county grand jury, culminating in official authorization of health, welfare, and hospital family planning services by the predominantly Catholic Board of Supervisors in March, 1964. The Health Department, with assistance from a closely allied Public Health Research Association, operates twenty clinics per month in three different locations, serving about 1,500 families, all new in the past year. Approximately half are using oral pills and half intra-uterine devices. Since May 1, 1965, these clinics have been financed by a grant from the federal Office of Economic Opportunity. In addition, all 100 public health nurses have had special training and have been issued special field kits to facilitate family planning education during home visits. Services to unmarried mothers are not yet included. Efforts are now being extended to develop a strong education program in the public schools on family life.

Berkeley City Health Department, also in Alameda County, began

[17] Personal communications from H. Blum and Y. Togasaki, Contra Costa County Health Department, May, 1965.

[18] J. C. Malcolm, S. B. Gross, W. Johnson, L. Anderson, and P. Merisuo, "Family Planning Program of the Alameda County Health Department" (in preparation).

early in 1965 to operate two clinics as part of the maternity outpatient services of two local hospitals. Meanwhile, the private Planned Parenthood Association, which had operated a clinic in Oakland since 1929, opened two new suburban clinics. Both it and a new citizens' Council for Responsible Parenthood in Contra Costa County actively supported the development of tax-supported services as did the Alameda–Contra Costa Medical Association. As a result, the 60,000 medically indigent families in this area relying in 1960 on two clinics, both private, now have available fourteen, mostly tax-supported. But only a small proportion of the 60,000 are yet served.

Maryland.[19]—In Maryland the key initial action was adoption on October 28, 1962, by the State Board of Public Welfare of a policy in favor of family planning for married welfare clients, followed immediately by a recommendation to local health officers by the State Department of Health to co-operate by making family planning services available. In the succeeding two and a half years, twenty of the twenty-four local health departments have developed family planning services in fifty-four locations and served over 3,000 families during 1964. About 90% selected oral pills (intra-uterine devices were not generally available). In March, 1965, the State Board of Public Welfare amended its 1962 policy to allow referral of unmarried welfare clients.

Michigan.[20]—Michigan is a good example of a state that is just beginning to develop tax-supported services. The State Department of Health issued a policy statement supporting family planning in December, 1964, almost simultaneously with a similar declaration by the Detroit City Board of Health. So far the only active local health department program is that in Detroit financed by federal maternity and infant care project funds, with expansion contemplated as part of the poverty program, plus special research and training components in co-operation with the University of Michigan. Family planning services for low-income groups remain primarily available through private agencies in Ann Arbor, Detroit, Flint, and Grand Rapids, although a number of Michigan county departments of social welfare now pay for family planning medications prescribed by private physicians for welfare recipients. However, the new state legislation (effective July, 1965) authorizing health and welfare department family planning services and special appropriations for this purpose should enable more local services to develop soon.

[19] Personal communication from Dr. Edward Davens, Deputy Commissioner of Health, Maryland, June 2, 1965.

[20] Personal communication from Dr. Goldie B. Corneliuson, Director, Division of Maternal and Child Health, Michigan Department of Public Health, May 20, 1965.

United States government.—The federal government remained remarkably quiet during this period of nationwide ferment despite considerable internal recognition of the problems and desire to act. John F. Kennedy, the first President of the United States to be a Roman Catholic, made clear during his election campaign that national welfare would override his personal beliefs in such matters and did encourage research in human reproduction and dissemination of knowledge. But the turning point in national policy came with President Johnson's 1965 State of the Union message, followed promptly by specific policy statements by Surgeon General Luther B. Terry of the Public Health Service[21] and Administrator David Bell of the Agency for International Development[22] making both domestic and international family planning assistance, technical and financial, proper government business. The Children's Bureau has stated that its grants to the states may be used for family planning services, as may its newer special project funds for maternity and infant care projects. The Office of Economic Opportunity is also financing family planning service elements of community action plans, although currently under some restrictive special conditions. Federal welfare policy is less certain but should be influenced by the recent policy statement of the American Public Welfare Association[23] that public welfare agencies make available family planning resources consistent with client's beliefs. Senator Ernest Gruening of Alaska is conducting hearings on a bill intended to clarify United States congressional policy in this field.

District of Columbia.—The special status of the federal capital warrants special mention. The District is governed by a Board of Commissioners responsible to the United States Congress which determines the budget. Federal legislative action was, therefore, necessary to initiate the birth control program of the District, which became effective April 1, 1964, under an appropriation of $25,000. The program is administered by the Department of Public Health as part of maternal and child health services with Department of Public Welfare participation through information and referral, and with assistance from Planned Parenthood of Metropolitan Washington. The policy and procedures manual developed for this program is exemplary.[24]

[21] Luther B. Terry (Public Health Service, Department of Health, Education, and Welfare), "Memorandum on Population Field—Extramural Program Guide, January 6, 1965."

[22] U.S. Department of State, Agency for International Development, "A.I.D. Memorandum on Population, February 1965."

[23] American Public Welfare Association, "Policy Statement on Family Planning, Adopted November 23, 1964."

[24] District of Columbia Government, Department of Public Health, *Birth Control Program Policies and Procedures Manual* (Washington, D.C., 1964).

PUBLIC INFORMATION AND EDUCATION

One of the weakest spots in American family planning is the extent to which sex education is not taught in public schools and to which birth control information is not made readily available to the general public. The mass media have in recent years increased their coverage of population matters including some information on newer birth control methods, but emphasis has been on newsworthiness rather than on public information. More books on birth control are being published inexpensively for public consumption. National opinion surveys show a steady rise to the current 81% of Americans who think birth control information should be available to anyone who wants it and the current 69% who approve of schools giving courses in sex education.[25] Much remains to be done, not least the amendment of restrictive state laws, to ensure that basic knowledge of human reproduction and fertility control is readily and accurately available to all American children as they grow up.

RESEARCH AND TRAINING

Organized efforts to develop and disseminate new knowledge relevant to the solution of population problems represent areas of responsibility for which the United States has provided leadership. Development of demography, largely from bases in sociology and economics, has been outstanding, with strong support from the Population Council and from Ford, Milbank, Rockefeller, and other foundations, to major university demographic centers at Berkeley, Chicago, Cornell, Duke, Georgetown, Miami, Michigan, Pennsylvania, Princeton, Washington, and Wisconsin, and with increased activity in the Bureau of the Census.

Research and training in the biology of reproduction related to population control has moved more slowly because, being controversial, it has suffered in the national competition for funds and minds. Even without the massive biologic research effort urged by many,[26] American investigators and private organizations have pioneered many of the latest developments in contraceptive methods such as oral pills and intra-uterine devices. Recent increases in federal appropriations for such research to the National Institute of Child Health and Human Development will help, but a major push commensurate with need is not in sight.

[25] Gallup Poll, Princeton, N.J., 1965.

[26] See nn. 3, 4, 5, and 7 above.

Research and training in the public health aspects of population have come last with at least five major universities—Harvard, Johns Hopkins, Michigan, North Carolina, and Pittsburgh—initiating special programs in the past year.

INTERNATIONAL ASSISTANCE

Although the focus here is on family planning for the American people, no discussion of United States responsibility should omit reference to organized efforts in technical assistance to peoples and governments of other countries who request it. These range from the contributions of the Planned Parenthood Federation of America in the development of the International Planned Parenthood Federation to the leadership of the Population Council and the Ford Foundation in filling much of the initial world vacuum created by requests from foreign governments for technical assistance in family planning. The present willingness of the United States government to provide such technical assistance opens a new era.[27]

EVALUATION OF RESULTS

Determination of the worth of the above organized efforts in the absence of clearly specified objectives and of appropriate measurements becomes an exercise in arbitrary definition and estimation.

Although the ultimate objective of family planning programs is a better life for people, the critical program goal can be expressed in some fertility rate. In the absence of such a national goal for the United States we are left with the summation of millions of individual family goals: that the rate of *unwanted* babies be zero. This is much easier to say than to determine, because it is difficult to know whether or not a given birth is wanted, in the sense of not exceeding the number of children desired by the family or of being within reasonable time expectations. However, it would be operationally possible to determine for any specified population in the reproductive period those who do not want any offspring in a specified time period and by home, telephone, or birth registration follow up the actual number of births that do occur in that group in that time. The socially unwanted babies of unmarried parents are a special class that can be more simply determined from birth registrations.

Even without specific national goals, changes in fertility rates of the American people are of great importance for family planning programs, as is knowledge of changes in contraceptive usage and in other

[27] See n. 22 above.

influential factors, such as age of marriage, family size desires and expectations, and birth intervals. No attempt will be made to review here the many analyses of American fertility but the interested reader should be aware of the latest official analysis of United States natality statistics[28] and the latest official estimated projections of the United States population.[29] Fertility rates for the total population are slowly falling with the decreasing changes in such effects as earlier marriage and childbirths, births postponed by war, and more births of high parity following World War II, but one index of unwanted births, the illegitimacy ratio, continues to rise and sizable differentials in fertility rates by color and race persist.

CONTRACEPTIVE USAGE

The latest data on the use of contraception in the United States come from the second (1960) phase of the "Growth of American Families" study.[30] They are based upon home interviews of 2,414 married white women 18–39 years of age (representative of 18 million similar persons) and 270 non-white married women of the same ages (representative of 2 million similar persons). Of the white population about one-tenth are definitely sterile, largely because of surgical sterilizations, half of which were performed primarily for treatment of a pathological condition. Eighty-one per cent had used contraception by 1960 and an additional 6% expected to begin use later. The latter were mostly those who had married recently and planned to have one or more children before beginning use. Only 2% did not have or expect some form of limitation of their fertility. The less-educated are less likely to begin contraception before they have had several pregnancies and are more likely to discover impaired fecundity which makes it unnecessary to begin. Catholics, too, are more likely to delay use, and never begin, than are Protestants.

Full understanding of contraceptive usage data requires recognition of the various ways in which couples use contraception to control the number and spacing of their children. Almost two-thirds of newly-weds do not use contraception before the first conception. Couples

28 A. S. Linde, M. Okada, and H. M. Rosenberg, *Natality Statistics Analysis*, Public Health Service Publication No. 1000, Ser. 21, No. 1 (Washington, D.C.: National Center for Health Statistics, Government Printing Office, 1964).

29 J. S. Siegel, M. Zitter, and D. S. Akers, *Projections of the Population of the United States, by Age and Sex: 1964 to 1985*, Bureau of the Census, Current Population Reports Ser. P-25, No. 286 (Washington, D.C.: Government Printing Office, 1964).

30 P. K. Whelpton, A. A. Campbell, and J. E. Patterson, *Fertility and Family Planning in the United States* (Princeton: Princeton University Press, 1965).

using contraception to space wanted children tend to use it ineffectively. Most couples are able to prevent having more children than they want, although 17% had one or more excess births, presumably from ineffectiveness of contraceptive use.

Important differences exist between whites and non-whites. Although non-white wives want about the same number of children as white wives, they have had and expect more children, and use less contraception (in terms of delay and current and expected use). Present data suggest that as the influence of southeastern rural culture decreases, fertility differences between whites and non-whites will decrease. By 1960 non-white wives with some college education had had and expected fewer births than comparable whites.

Rapid change is occurring in the extent to which American families use different methods of contraception as new, more effective methods become available, but accurate current data are lacking. In 1955, married, white families reported using condoms (29%), diaphragm (26%), rhythm (24%), douche (11%), withdrawal (6%), jelly alone (4%), all other (7%).[31] In 1965 these methods continue to be important but a sizable population is now using oral pills, and a small but rapidly growing number is using intra-uterine devices. With the development of new methods has also come a surge of interest and concern for properly designed and executed field studies of effectiveness and safety of contraceptives, which have been badly needed. Illegal abortion continues to be a major means of preventing births and is increasing in importance as a cause of maternal death in the United States. Its frequency is unknown but is estimated to be between 200,000 and 1,200,000 per year.[32]

TERTIARY OBJECTIVES

Beyond the primary objective of changing fertility and the secondary objective of changing contraceptive usage are a host of tertiary objectives or program activities, most of which have already been mentioned. Evaluation of most of these has been in terms of some measure of activity, such as number of patients served, number of service locations and visits, amount and quality of public education and of professional training, or the number of dollars spent. Experimental studies to compare the effects or costs of different ways of

[31] R. Freedman, P. K. Whelpton, and A. A. Campbell, *Family Planning, Sterility and Population Growth* (New York: McGraw-Hill, 1959).

[32] M. S. Calderone (ed.), *Abortion in the United States* (New York: Hoeber-Harper, 1958).

changing the use, knowledge, and attitudes of people regarding reproduction and birth control are being developed and expanded.

MAJOR ACHIEVEMENTS

Now is not the time to emphasize past accomplishments in a field in ferment about foreseeable future problems. Recognition of these problems by the public and by many leaders in the United States has in itself been an important step. American contributions to the discovery and development of better contraceptive methods deserve credit as does American leadership, in turning new methods of survey research toward better understanding the many ways in which man controls his fertility. The churches in the United States are recognizing the important changes in man's knowledge and circumstances regarding fertility control. The medical profession is beginning to assume its rightful responsibilities. The universities are indicating that they will give proper priority to the needs for new knowledge and for its dissemination. The federal, state, and local governments are gradually losing their reluctance to face fertility issues and are now providing family planning services for low-income Americans and technical assistance in family planning for other nations who request it. The stage is set for significant achievements in the next decade.

MAJOR UNSOLVED PROBLEMS

So many individuals, committees, and conferences have spoken on what needs to be done regarding population problems and responsibilities of the United States that it would be redundant here to attempt more than a brief listing of the most important.

1. Definition of long-range American population and fertility goals. Greatly intensified scientific research on the causes and effects of population growth and density are an immediate prerequisite. Employment, education, housing, transportation, health, air and water pollution, natural resources, outdoor recreational space, urban living, economic development, social (particularly governmental) organization, and human genetics are among those factors which should receive prime attention.
2. Massive laboratory and field research on the biology of human reproduction to enable better understanding and control of human fertility.
3. Inclusion of all aspects of human reproduction as essential elements of public education for American children.
4. Greater information and availability of all methods of fertility control (including therapeutic abortion) for all people, with an immediate end to remaining outmoded legal barriers and to remaining deterrents to

services for the poor, not the least being segregation of medical care by economic status.

5. Expansion of university training in all fields relating to population, particularly demography, bio-medical sciences, behavioral sciences, economics, public health, public administration, genetics, and education.
6. Resolution of residual differences in religious beliefs about fertility.
7. Accelerated research and evaluation of present and new ways of informing and motivating the American people about population change and fertility control. Mass communication and economic incentives need early exploration.
8. Technical assistance in population for countries overseas requesting it, and support of efforts to make more assistance available from the United Nations (especially the World Health Organization and the United Nations Children's Fund).
9. Non-discriminatory immigration policies.

Most of these needs are being actively met by the varied resources of the United States but not one in the magnitude warranted by the tremendous effects of population growth in America, and in the world, on almost every facet of life. The present surge of interest in the United States and in so many other countries means with certainty that exciting changes affecting fertility and the welfare of all mankind will occur in the next decade in many parts of the globe. We welcome this and anticipate, too, that with the need to share discoveries and to compare experiences, population planning will continue as an ever growing force for international understanding.

21

FAMILY PLANNING AROUND THE WORLD

LEONA BAUMGARTNER, M.D.

Assistant Administrator for
Technical Cooperation and Research
Agency for International Development
Department of State, U.S.A.

In the past fifteen years, in almost every country of the world, there have been vast changes in many aspects of life, and these changes have come with amazing rapidity. In no area of discussion or activity has change been as marked, perhaps, as in the approach to the so-called problems of population. There have been changes in understanding the nature of the problems involved. There have been changes in the attitudes of people in all walks of life. There have been rapid changes in the actions of governments, churches, social institutions, and people themselves.

A very significant change is the recognition that rapid rates of population growth influence almost every aspect of economic and social development. It is only within the past fifteen years that many governments have realized that rapid population growth impedes their economic development. There is no simple problem—rather, there are many population problems—those related to employment, education, providing health services, transport, migration, housing, industrialization, agricultural productivity, and above all, in the developing countries, that of increasing per capita income.

Small wonder that today the governments of half the people in the developing regions are actively concerned with family planning. It must be emphasized, however, that this is not a sole solution to population problems. It is, of course, a base for solutions, and the topic we are brought together to discuss. But let it be remembered that as the interrelationships of the many problems associated with rapid population growth become better understood, there will be sounder bases for action on many other fronts. Continuing dialogues of those in the many fields affected by rapid population increase and continuing action-oriented research are alike important if the complicated nature of the problems involved is to be understood and balanced programs are to be developed. The goal is increasing movement toward a dynamic balance between the resources, the advancing abilities of people to use resources productively, and the changing numbers of people who must be sustained by the resources as used. The goal is not reducing, increasing, or stabilizing the numbers of people. It is helping make more possible a richer, fuller life—jobs; homes; resources; freedom from hunger, disease, ignorance; time for development of innate capacities—in short, enriching the quality of life for an increasing proportion of the world's people.

A WORLD VIEW

The problems of population are found everywhere but there are differences as well as similarities among the countries. Let us briefly sketch characteristic pictures in different parts of the world. Latin America is a continent rich in natural resources with many sparsely settled and underdeveloped areas. Most of its people are desperately poor; technology and education are limited in type and in diffusion. Until recently, there had been little change in most countries from the social and economic institutions laid down over many years. Today there is rapid change in most countries. The changes are hopeful for development in the long run, but in the short run they often threaten social and political stability. There is ferment for action—demands for schools, for transport, for housing, for better health services, better ways of life. Many migrate to cities seeking the new life. The rising numbers of illegal abortions disturb the clergy, the doctors, the elite, and leaders of government. Everywhere the demand for modernization is threatened by the high rate of population increase, which in Latin America is around 3%, the highest of any major region on the globe.

Africa, on the other hand, is still somewhat the continent of the unknown when it comes to population. Even semi-accurate figures of numbers are lacking in sub-Saharan Africa. The continent cannot be treated as a whole. Attitudes toward population control vary widely. The tide of rising expectations is dangerously high in many areas. The awareness of the relationship of population growth to economic development is scattered and scanty. In South Africa and in Tunisia and Egypt there are active family planning programs with strong government support. They are beginning in British Africa, where privately supported clinics, often attached to health demonstrations and to universities, are found. There is little sign of activity in the areas formerly attached to France and still held by Portugal. In Ethiopia and Morocco there are flickerings of interest. There is no apparent reason to believe that the high rate of population growth which can be anticipated with modernization in Africa will have an effect different from that elsewhere in the world. It must always be remembered that high rates of growth in the poorer countries are not likely to be compatible with the increasing standards of living which people demand. The problems of unstable governments, or lack of information, of nationalistic and tribal rivalries, all make imprudent any predictions of how the newly emerging African countries will handle their already increasing rates of population growth. The pressures for more schools and general education may well emerge as the most important pressure and lead to a demand for family planning sooner than now seems possible. The mobility of people between urban and rural areas is another important factor in the African scene, particularly in tropical Africa.

Mainland China has changed its verbal policies several times in the past two decades. Today its expanding family planning program may be related to an acceptance of the fact that its population growth rate of about 2.0%–2.5% or more will impede its economic development, though official justification for the programs is phrased in terms of social and family well-being. With the traditional family structure in China, the difficulties might seem to be large, but declining birth rates in Chinese populations outside China suggest that cultural barriers may not be insurmountable.

Japan, of course, has solved its problem of rapid population increase and, indeed, may need to add to its population in the years to come. Birth rates are declining in some areas of the western Pacific. In the rest of Asia, problems vary somewhat from country to country, but there is an over-all picture of a race between the numbers of people and development. As has been frequently pointed out, the people in these areas, by running fast like Alice in Wonderland, may be able to stay in the same miserable state. Things may not get much worse and famine may be averted, but certainly the better life, which all seek and which is now accepted as an essential right of human beings, is threatened by recent rapid increases in population.

Western Europe and North America have their own special problems. In the affluent, the industrialized, world there are pockets of poverty. There are too many with too little skill to fit into the automated society that is rapidly developing. Metropolitan areas with traffic congestion, air and water pollution, overcrowded schools, a greater.

demand for health services, a greater distance and difficulty in getting to recreational facilities, have a complicated series of problems associated with increasing population. In these countries, people commonly do regulate the size of their families and there are the trained health personnel to help them do so, but there is need to re-evaluate the future here, too.

It may be useful to reach slightly further back in history and take a quick look at Europe and the United States. This is useful largely because of a common misunderstanding on the part of some as to what happened there and a tendency to translate that experience into the 1960's. In these countries, death rates fell slowly and populations grew slowly. Life expectancy rose slowly. The scientific knowledge and social and economic change which affected birth and death rates came slowly. There were vast open spaces to which the people of Western Europe could and did migrate. This took off some of the pressure. As the immigrants arrived on the shores of North America, they had a vast continent to explore and develop. People themselves began to limit the size of their families. Thus, these countries were able to keep the balance of population and resources without widely organized or government-supported programs of population control. The situation was quite different in Western Europe and North America than it is today in the developing countries, where the conditions just described do not prevail. Under the conditions in some of the latter countries now, where substantially larger and larger proportions of children survive through their reproductive years, the increase of population becomes staggering. As someone has recently written, "the girl baby spared from death in early childhood contributes not only her own life to the world's people but the lives of the children she produces as she moves through her reproductive years, followed in turn by the lives of the children's children, and so on."

So much for an overview of the world situation which is the backdrop for this conference. What specifically is there to learn from the reports prepared for this conference? I should like to discuss them chiefly in terms of three questions. First, What are the common characteristics of family planning programs in the developing countries? Second, What are the common barriers to progress? And third, What next? The last becomes more or less obvious as one discusses the first two.

In reviewing these reports, we must remember that the authors were asked to describe what was going on currently in family planning programs in their own countries. The interrelationships with other facets of the population problem, some of which I have mentioned briefly above, were not to be discussed. I am sure that the authors will agree with me that this does not mean that these interrelationships are not important.

COMMON CHARACTERISTICS

If we look at the common characteristics of the family planning programs, I believe the strongest first impression is of the dynamic nature, the rapidly changing nature, of the situation in most of the countries. There have been enormous changes within a few years in the attitudes of government leaders and leaders of industry, labor, and social groups of all kinds. There have been changes in the attitudes of the people themselves. I was much interested this past winter (1964–65) to return to rural India to study this problem even as I had done a decade ago. The change as one talks today with a village midwife and village women, for example, is impressive. Women know now that there *is* something that can be done about not having so many children. They know that fewer children die in infancy. They are familiar with surrounding market areas and villages. In an increasing number of areas women travel on buses to get to towns. They are now, to a surprising extent, masters of their own destiny, and willing to explore what the world outside the village has to offer them. True, this change may not be deep, and it is not prudent to generalize, but let us rejoice that change is evident.

If one discusses the problem with top government officials, as I have in some seven countries in Africa, the Middle East, and Asia in the past six months, one finds a rapidly changing point of view. The same is true in the Western Hemisphere. In many countries the economic planners have begun to realize the enormous impact of the rapid growth of population on the economic development of their countries. So have political leaders in an increasing number of countries.

A second characteristic is the rapid supplementation of private efforts by governmental action—or the initiation of a major officially operated program. This trend is true in the United States today as well. Governments are increasingly realizing that population growth is, indeed, a matter of public concern, and that efforts to control excesses must be supported directly or indirectly by governments. The question of whether a national policy or a specific legislative act on population is essential to effective operations is open to question. Turkey has emphasized the importance of its legislation which revoked restrictive legislation and names the several ministries to be involved. Taiwan has a going program and no official policy or legislation specifically directed to family planning. It seems obvious that the historical background, political organization, and social realities of the national scene are the decisive factors in judging the necessity for and extent of governmental action.

A third characteristic is the quickening of interest in population problems of all kinds, including human reproduction, as a subject for research among persons trained in the biological and medical sciences, economists, those expert in the communications field, and, particularly, among the behavioral scientists.

A fourth characteristic, not as widely apparent, is a growing sense of urgency about these problems in many countries. This is particularly true in India, Pakistan, Korea, Taiwan, the UAR, Tunisia, Turkey, and Chile and some of the other Latin American countries. It is becoming true in the more affluent societies.

A fifth characteristic is a growing awareness of the interrelationship of population growth with other problems of development. This has accelerated the development of programs in many countries. In others it may spark interest, as, for example, it has in Kenya. Here it was the conclusions of studies indicating the great new demands for schools and teachers that led Mboya to consider assuming governmental responsibility for family planning and to request the Population Council to make recommendations about action on family planning.

A sixth trend is the eagerness with which new developments in technology are apparently being accepted and others demanded. For example, in the United States, where the oral pill has been available now for only a few years, its use, though not accurately documented, has obviously grown tremendously. Similarly, the IUD, with a much shorter history, is being widely accepted in both the affluent and the developing societies. New scientific developments will be eagerly sought after—sometimes even before their value has been established. A point not stressed enough, however, is that the use of simpler methods not dependent on doctors seems to open the way for the use of more sophisticated methods—the converse may also be true.

In many countries the great bottleneck is the lack of doctors and other health personnel. As long as the family planning technology used requires the attention of such persons on a patient-practitioner basis, large numbers of people cannot quickly be reached. It is thus possible that a wider use of non-medical methods—coitus interruptus, condoms, rhythm, foaming tablets, aerosols, and liquid and sponge—should be more actively pursued and their usefulness in opening the way for other methods more adequately investigated. It is clear, of course, that unless the materials themselves are effective and have no unpleasant side effects, they will not be accepted. Their use, however, may do some good so long as the people concerned are not led to believe that they are 100% perfect. Many products in common use in some areas do not meet acceptable criteria relating to effectiveness and side effects.

A seventh characteristic of current family planning efforts is an increasing interest on the part of doctors and other health personnel in programs of family planning. Just as in the Western world, this question has often been largely ignored by doctors in the developing countries. It was usually groups of dedicated women caught up in the "birth control" movement who opened the door. They have often found apathy and resistance in ministries of health and in the physicians, nurses, and midwives of their countries. Today this is becoming less and less true.

It is also clear that most countries which now have operating programs have chosen to relate their family planning programs to their other health programs, particularly those in maternal and child health. The value of this decision seems obvious.

The eighth characteristic is the greater knowledge about attitudes, motivation, and effective methods of communication that has been acquired by social science and research experts. In general, this suggests that resistance to change in family size may have been overestimated. The need to find better ways to overcome apathy remains. It seems important for the family to realize that under present conditions more of its children can live to maturity. In many a remote village where infant mortality rates are coming down, the native intelligence of the people has already discovered this fact. Dr. Carl Taylor tells a delightful story of talking with a group of village men in a Turkish village. He went around asking the simple question of how many brothers and sisters each man had and how many had lived to maturity. Then he asked about the individual's own family. After only three or four men had replied, one of them spoke up and said, "Don't bother any more, Doctor, we already know that today one doesn't have to have as many children as one had in the past in order to have sons and daughters in the fields and in the house." Stories like this contribute to the hope of success which many workers need—but, in fact, a constant search for the roots of apathy and resistance must be maintained. The early successes in Taiwan, India, Korea, and Thailand may merely be "skimming off the cream," reaching the already convinced.

A ninth most important point is that in many countries institutions and effective institutional leadership seem to lag behind public opinion in the acceptance of family planning. Though some may be involved, others essential to success of the country's efforts may be indifferent or overcautious. Health ministries and leaders may be too cautious or indifferent, education ministries or the armed forces may not co-operate, and so on.

Finally, it is increasingly clear that new "modern" values and ideas are spreading more rapidly—from country to country and from urban areas to villages and rural populations—than has commonly been believed.

COMMON BARRIERS

And now to the second question, that of the nature of the barriers impeding progress. Most of them can be divided into two groups. The first are those associated with doctrine or dogma, the commonly heard ideas that are used as reasons why nothing can be done. The second and more important are organizational, operational barriers.

DOGMA AND DOCTRINE

Several seem common in the first group. The first is the concept that more people make a stronger country. It is argued that more men mean greater military strength necessary to protect the country. This concept played an important role in Turkey for many years, for example, and is still heard there despite recent legislative action to remove the ban on contraceptives. It has been important in several Western European countries and is heard in most of tropical Africa. The concept has been, of course, closely related to shortages of men following wars. It was also related to age structures in countries where birth rates had been low, such as France. Related concepts of the "strong country" are also found summarized in the belief of business leaders that they need more people as consumers or of farmers that more children are essential to increasing their incomes. Careful analyses of the facts of the specific relationships between population and economic growth under differing conditions are essential to test the validity of these and related arguments.

Then there is the argument that a large family is necessary for survival or to prove virility, common in agricultural societies. There is abundant evidence that these beliefs can be and are being changed. People, after all, no matter how illiterate, are not stupid and do change under the influence of new ideas. Change becomes easier as they move away from a subsistence living where there is too little margin to gamble on a new idea. Families must see a possibility of economic improvement. To be sure, the ideal family size they advocate may not coincide with their practice. What is important is that the concept of ideal family size can and does change. Dr. Irene Taeuber suggests that in mainland China this change may come very rapidly, as it has in Chinese and Chinese-related cultures around mainland China's peripheries. Certainly, the cultures which perpetuated large families, the extended family, and ancestor worship are experiencing changes which favor smaller families.

Religion

The second barrier is religious opposition. This is often blamed for more resistance than it is responsible for. The ready acceptance of the particular family planning method approved by a specific religious group in the country, such as the rhythm method in the Roman Catholic church, is important. The recent interest which the Vatican has shown in re-examining its position is in line with its age-old practice of looking anew at the interpretation of its essential dogma. Certainly in pluralist and democratic societies there should be freedom of choice of methods, so that persons of all faiths are given equal opportunity to exercise their choice without offense to their consciences. Religious opposition, sometimes at least, seems to dissipate after family planning programs are operating. Singapore is a good example. Moslem, Buddhist, and Coptic faiths have no doctrines directly opposed to family planning—though, as in other groups, individual representatives of the church hierarchies interpret the doctrines of their respective churches differently.

Need for Well-developed Health Services

A third barrier is that commonly heard argument that nothing much can be done until the country has a network of well-developed health services. This is expressed in a variety of ways. Sometimes it is said that people won't accept family planning until cholera, malaria, small-pox, etc., are wiped out; or it is believed that women will not travel out of their villages for health services, or that a complete complement of rural maternal and child health services will need to be developed before one can inaugurate a family planning program. There are many variations on this theme. All seem not to be as important as previously thought. Obviously where health facilities and services are well developed, as in Ceylon and Taiwan, bringing family planning to the people is easier. A concomitant development of rural health services and family planning is important. But the readiness of thousands of people for family planning is often overlooked. What is needed is a sense of balance. It is quite possible that an active and effective family planning program will make possible a more vigorous rural health service. A critical question is whether an IUD program can go faster than the development of the rural health service or what minimum service is essential for the initiation of the IUD program. Administrative decisions need to be made, such as:

1. Who will insert the IUD?
2. What technique for cleanliness will be used?
3. How much after-care is necessary? Spontaneous abortions may increase but have not rural women always dealt with such abortions without expert medical care?
4. Can such a program be supported from the logistic point of view—personnel, supplies?
5. Where is there greater readiness to start? Where are the chances for success greater?

Certainly family planning services can be built into existing health services, or even help initiate or support them. It will be interesting to see, for example, if offering IUD insertions in post-partum clinics will make post-partum care itself more popular. Certainly the post-partum period is an ideal time to insert the IUD.

Another group of arguments also does not directly oppose family planning but relates to reasons why action should be delayed. "There isn't anything that can really be done anyway," "People aren't well enough motivated," "Technology isn't good enough—a better method is the first step." "Only female doctors can be used to put in IUD," and so on. Opinion polls, the advances in technology, and the experience in many countries have proved that these and similar ideas, though valid in part, are not reasons to delay action further.

Another argument used to postpone action or give it a low priority is the attitude that the problem can be solved by other means: increasing agricultural productivity, industrialization, improving the educational status of people. That activity is needed on all these fronts is perfectly clear. All take time and effort. Further efforts should not be wasted in bickering among the proponents of each approach. It is high time, for example, that agriculturists follow the example of the director of the Food and Agricultural Organization, Dr. Sen, and India's dynamic Minister of Agriculture, Dr. Subramanian, in supporting family planning vigorously while still working at their own jobs of increasing food production. Similarly, health experts should recognize, as many do, that family planning is not the sole solution to population problems.

It is further said that developing countries cannot afford family planning programs. Recent studies indicating that the economic returns of investing in family planning programs may far exceed those from investment in economic development should go a long way to remove this barrier in countries which have not already reached this conclusion. Economists may argue over relative figures, but the differences seem greater than had been realized. This whole area of the economics of family planning warrants further study.

Certainly the cost of contraceptives themselves should be no barrier. The IUD is cheap. In India and Hong Kong it is estimated that local manufacture will bring the cost of one IUD down to $0.02. Condoms, too, can be made inexpensively, though the countries with small demands will probably not find local manufacture profitable, as the initial cost is large and modern machines produce a very large volume. Such countries may find import cheaper. The cost of the physiological drugs at present seems high for the poor countries. That is, however, not their chief drawback. Anything which requires that a woman take a specific medication regularly and that a physician be available for possible continuing complications is not well adapted to the countries with poorly educated, not very highly motivated women and a shortage of doctors.

Money for staff may be a problem until government officials recognize the high returns realized from investing in family planning. Foreign exchange to finance vehicles to carry health personnel to rural areas and to purchase communication media may be a problem in some places. If one looks honestly at the gains made from family planning programs, however, it is quickly seen that money is not a real barrier. This has already been recognized by the planning commissions in India and Turkey, for example, which have said that they will make the necessary funds available.

Managerial and Operational Barriers

It is increasingly clear that the most serious immediate barriers to effective programs today are organizational, operational, and managerial. The technology is now sufficiently well advanced. There are effective, safe, cheap, and acceptable methods. There are millions of people saying that they wish to have smaller families. The major problems seem to be ones of logistics, tactics, administration. I include in these the necessary action, research, and evaluation essential to good administration in a modern sense. Money, with a few possible exceptions, is available. Trained people are often in short supply, but what needs to be taught can be readily taught, particularly if the professional leaders concerned can become flexible enough to adapt their sometimes rigid ideas of who should do what and if the use of existing personnel is maximized. More attention needs to be paid, incidentally, to the training of nurses and nurse-midwives. Basic, of course, to good administration is the will, the dedication, of those who work. Other points of importance will be discussed later.

WHAT NEXT?

Let me now focus more sharply on what next? Many points which favor success in family planning programs have already been touched on: vocal leadership; the readiness and practice of at least some segments of the population to limit family size; a lowering childhood mortality rate and a realization by parents that fewer children die; enough of a network of social exchange and communication that information moves from one area and group to another; enthusiastic and vocal support from political, business, and other leaders; enough social and economic change that there is a rising expectation of a better life; an effective organization.

EFFECTIVE MANAGEMENT AND SKILLFUL USE OF SCIENTIFICALLY SOUND TECHNOLOGY

I suggest that the current situation in family planning is not unlike that of the eradication of malaria from Brazil in the 1930's, or in the later conquests of yellow fever. Experts knew what needed to be done. The technology was good enough. Opposition to action was tolerable. The problems were largely logistic and administrative. The government and the Rockefeller Foundation joined skills and money to act. One paragraph from an administrative report of the time bears reviewing:

The methods here described should not be considered final but only as a stage of development reached—after an exceptional opportunity to work —throughout an enormous area in which conditions varied greatly from region to region, with adequate funds, personnel and authority on the most fascinating problem of pitting human intelligence and perspiration against the instinct and persistence of the mosquito. The victory has not been always on the side of intelligence and perspiration, and defeat has been due to limitations of one and the other.

The secret of success was the continuing discovery and correction of things that went wrong—the continuing desire to complete the task.

There are those who say that there are no analogies between malaria and family planning. "Malaria is different," they say. Of course it is, but both are programs that have to reach into every home and involve the active co-operation of millions of people. Those who sprayed homes with DDT had to win people's confidence too. They had to win it over again when DDT killed the gecko lizards which had destroyed the bugs that bit, and when DDT no longer worked on flies. They were welcomed one year and shut out the next.

I suggest the essential lesson for those in the population field to learn from the story of malaria and yellow fever control is that success came with sound administration, skillful use of a scientifically sound technology, appropriate training of workers, detailed supervision, continuing evaluation of results, and search for better methods.

The pragmatic approach involved is not a characteristic of most traditional societies. It is possibly one of the most helpful contributions which modern science and technology can make—even though highly organized government-sponsored family planning programs have not been the means by which low population growth rates have been achieved in countries where science and technology are well developed. But the managerial, administrative, applied scientific approach used in these countries is essential in family planning efforts everywhere. The approach has already paid dividends. Examples are found in many papers prepared for this conference. Taiwan attributes its success to this approach, characterized as "a series of pilot undertakings, studies and surveys." All led to changes in action, such as in the numbers of home visits, the type of mail and publicity campaigns, or the methods of spreading activities geographically.

REALISTIC TRAINING

Another facet of better organization that deserves attention is more realistic training goals. Training is often begun too late and is directly related to what the trainee is to do. Health man-power surveys document the potential numbers of personnel available in many countries. Capable administrators probably knew them already, within reasonable limits. The concepts found useful are simple. Figure out who is to do what and where. Teach only what is essential and relevant. Seek to "upgrade" auxiliary workers. Season heavily with inspiration to overcome that major barrier of apathy. Invest heavily in bringing people back for short training courses as indicated. Pre-test materials. Adapt to new conditions.

In view of the almost universally reported shortages of professional personnel and the necessity of carrying programs to rural areas, the wider use of auxiliary personnel is certainly indicated. Several conditions militate, however, against their use. Money for expanded training programs is seldom concentrated on them. Professional salaries are budgeted first and auxiliaries get what is left over. The Korean experiment testing the use of midwives to insert loops instead of physicians (but under their supervision), and the Turkish plan of using newly graduated physicians, should be watched carefully and repeated elsewhere. A wide variety of possibilities of using all kinds of workers in family planning programs should be tried.

MONETARY INCENTIVES

The experience of several countries using monetary incentives should also be carefully watched. If these induce doctors or other workers to spend more time on family planning or bring in more patients, the incentive is worth the money spent. Care, of course, must be taken not to cheapen the service in the eyes of patients or to encourage corruption.

BETTER SUPERVISION

Better supervision demands a very high priority. Human nature being what it is, up to 25% of the labor budget spent on checking work is not unreasonable. But the supervision must be of a creative type—not merely checking records in an office and filing reports with another supervisor higher up, but finding out in the field what works, what does not work, and why, and helping to develop those one supervises. Getting rid of excessive, detailed reports never used to determine or check on action is essential.

CONTINUING EVALUATION

All of this discussion implies the need for continuing evaluation. But evaluation of a program does not just happen; it must be carefully planned for. It must be closely related to—but also reasonably independent of—daily operations. Many countries have recognized the need for administrative evaluation—as distinct from day-to-day supervision. Some have set up special institutes designed to take care of this part of administration. The problem is to keep such institutes close enough to the field and to be clear for what purpose one is measuring, evaluating. The key to success is that evaluation of this type must be an integral part of administration. Results should lead to administrative change when indicated. Taiwan had most fruitful experiences in this type of endeavor. There is too little time and personnel to waste on studies that verify over and over again what is already known, as some demographic and attitudinal studies have done. Research workers, particularly in the social sciences, are needed to evaluate action—to explore unanswered questions.

In India, for example, a pending list of practical questions to which there are inadequate answers includes:

What is the increase in numbers of IUD's inserted if dais (i.e., indigenous midwives) are paid?

How much is the efficiency of a program increased if transport for staff is readily available?

What is the difference in acceptance of male and female doctors?

How effective is the malaria worker in getting data on births? Persuading people to use traditional contraceptives? sterilization? IUD?

What women reject the IUD?

What is the effectiveness of a loop program or condoms with and without a background of mass propaganda?

Studies of this type should be a part of administration in all countries. In those which have not accepted the IUD, does one need to retest its use in order to determine the scientific effect on the human reproduction system or in order to determine acceptance by patients and doctors and logistic problems involved in its use under local conditions? The purpose of the tests will change the type of study undertaken.

Another pertinent question is the value of semi-independent evaluations. Health officials have welcomed the periodic evaluations of their malaria programs by joint-country WHO teams. I suggest that similar joint evaluations of family planning programs by WHO or other international groups would be very useful. They would assist in sharing experiences with other countries and providing a periodic opportunity to view problems and progress anew. However, effective evaluation of family planning programs still awaits the development of the satisfactory measuring rods which many other public health programs have. Various regional and international groups can make substantial contributions to evaluation, as well as training. Let us call a five-year moratorium on international conferences that serve only to repeat what is already neatly printed in books. Let us concentrate on the work to be done at home and on working sessions like this conference.

RELATIONS OF GOVERNMENTAL AND NON-GOVERNMENTAL ACTIVITIES

Still other administrative problems brought up in conference papers concern the relations between governmental and non-governmental activities. There is general agreement on the value of professional or scientific advisory committees with persons from both groups. Involving leading practitioners of medicine and universities seems helpful. The contribution of lawyers in Tunisia seems to be unique. The potential contributions of the private business sector seem to have been overlooked. The continuing relationships of voluntary family planning groups with their government have sometimes proved difficult. The contrast between Hong Kong and Puerto Rico is striking. Egypt talks of the problem of bringing together the several privately sponsored groups that have grown up there. There is another puzzling problem. How will the many pioneering private agencies, to whom goes the credit for initiating so many programs, adjust to nationwide programs run largely by government? Can they live with the growing success of their efforts? There is more than enough for everyone to do—but who will do what?

The problems of communication are so widely discussed that I shall mention but a few aspects. The first is the general agreement that the appeal to families is not through discussion of the population explosion or the country's policy, but through discussion of their own problems. Families are not interested, according to experience in several countries, in how one gets pregnant or why they should practice family planning, but in methods and where they can get service. The converse of this is that political, business, and economic leaders need to know more of the interrelations of rapid population growth with other aspects of economic and social development. In Africa the great demand for schools and education emerges as a potent motivator for the new African leader. In Latin America the importance of using family planning as a means of combatting the rising number of illegal abortions is clear.

Experience has shown that knowing what attitudes and beliefs the particular target group in the population holds and tailoring the message to meet the group's interest is important. But action may also be delayed much longer than necessary by overrefinement of studies to determine attitudes of a large number of groups. In view of the apparent rapidity with which attitudes on population problems are changing, it is important to look carefully at the need for, as well as the kind of, studies that should be undertaken—lest the results be of academic interest only.

The relative roles of mass communication and person-to-person communication are of special interest. Certainly in Japan, with its industrialized, literate population, where the people, not the government, were prime movers in reducing the birth rate, mass media, including women's magazines, were of great importance. This is true in other industrialized countries. In Pakistan, the mass media approach as operated there was not deemed a success. The results of the recent Calcutta trials will be interesting to study. In Taiwan, Korea, and elsewhere the person-to-person route has played a leading role. The satisfied customer seems particularly effective in inducing other women to try the IUD. Effective diffusion begins when one has a large enough "critical mass," to borrow a phrase from nuclear physics. The diffusion of a negative effect must also be remembered.

A great deal more study appears necessary to know how and when to use mass media. Certainly pre-tests should be made of materials and methods of presentation. There seems to be no reason to believe, however, that condoms, for example, cannot be "sold" as easily as soap—but trials to test the theory seem warranted before this or other nation-wide advertising campaigns for any methods are undertaken.

It is axiomatic that supplies must be readily and continuously available when such mass campaigns are undertaken. The problem of maintaining supply lines, with or without large publicity campaigns, is crucial.

The value of mobile education vans is yet to be proved. Group techniques, in some hands, work. The "camp" technique for sterilizations was thought successful in India. The widespread change in attitudes so successfully achieved in India in the past ten years cannot apparently be attributed to any mode of communication. Both India and Pakistan have concluded that waiting for patients to come to their existing clinics did not work. Was the problem the kind of clinic? Why did women not use the services?

The Place of Research—Better Methods

The continuing need for research in many fields is evident. Science can never be content with present methods. Greater knowledge of the reproductive cycle should produce more accurate knowledge of the time of ovulation. Investigation of immunological methods is only beginning. A new method of interrupting early pregnancy as reported here from East Germany merits study. On and on go the possibilities.

So, too, in the economic, political, sociological, and communications fields the possibilities in research are great, and the needs urgent. A clear-cut responsibility rests on the more scientifically advanced countries to pursue with much greater vigor answers to these questions and those in the field of human reproduction both at home and abroad. Provision must be made for the training of research workers and for a continuing exchange of working experience as well as for international conferences. The new positions of the WHO and other United Nations groups should facilitate such exchanges.

CONCLUSION

What does all of this add up to? Can one summarize? Let me try. The rapidly rising rates of population growth in many parts of the world, a new awareness of the interrelatedness of population growth rates with many phases of economic and social development (employment, social unrest, urbanization, adequacies of food, education, transport, per capita income), the greater demands of people for a better standard of living, and improved methods by which pregnancies can be regulated have resulted in rapidly changing attitudes toward the importance of finding appropriate and acceptable ways of lowering birth rates. Political, social, and spiritual leaders, and the people themselves in many areas, are recognizing the need for specific action, instead of relying on other developments to solve their population problems. Governments in an increasing number of countries are, directly or indirectly, supporting family planning programs. The goal is not just fewer people. It is to give a greater opportunity to all for a fuller life—a chance for freedom from hunger, disease, ignorance, and poverty, for development of their own innate capacities, and for helping their children. Many people want smaller families in order to achieve these goals. Effective methods are available. Their widespread application comes next.

What lies immediately ahead is the hard and often dull job of planning and administering effective, efficient family planning programs; training thousands of workers; removing bureaucratic barriers; moving from pilot to mass operations; supporting the studies needed to improve administration. At the same time, the search for new methods of regulating pregnancy and a clearer understanding of human behavior and of the interrelations of population growth with the many aspects of life in the world's rapidly changing society must not be neglected. But the knowledge of how to administer effective family planning programs is largely available and the ways of finding answers to residual problems seem clear.

Further ahead lies a harder problem, one we have not discussed here but which we can, because of progress already made, now face. It is to assure the good life for which the world's people yearn. To find better ways to assure that kind of life is the next task. We are part of it. Our challenge is to administer and develop our present programs so that they will contribute to the evolution of that better living for those who will be born.

PART TWO

Organization and Administration of Programs

22

PROBLEMS IN STARTING A PROGRAM

NUSRET H. FIŞEK, M.D., Ph.D.

Undersecretary of State
Ministry of Health and Social Assistance, Turkey

INTRODUCTION

Population dynamics is so complex that to cover all problems involved would require someone well trained in demography, geography, economics, anthropology, education, obstetrics, public health administration, and several other subjects as well. Since I qualify in only one of the above-mentioned subjects, i.e., public health administration, I shall review the subject in the capacity of an administrator having five years' experience in starting a population control program in a country where birth control has been illegal for many decades.

The first problem in starting a program is to name and define it. Birth control, family planning, campaign against criminal abortion, human reproduction, and population control are terms used in different places and at different times in order to express more or less the same thing; but actually they are not synonymous. Birth control is the simplest among them. It is a physiological term and has no social implications such as family planning or population control; but certainly we control the size of the family and the population, if we control the births. If we launch a campaign against criminal abortion we may also achieve population control. If criminal abortion becomes a social problem in a country, it means that the motivation for using contraceptives and limiting family size is very high. To my mind, the preferable term is "population control" because it reflects the aim much better than the others. Surely a great problem of mankind in our time is to raise the standard of living in the developing countries, partly in order to achieve and maintain peace. Population control is one of the most effective means of attaining this goal, along with the increase of agricultural and industrial production. Some people feel that the term "population control" stirs up controversy unnecessarily, and they advocate talking about family planning. But I prefer to use a term that continually reminds us of the dangers of an unbalanced increase in population and stimulates our efforts to increase the number of accepters of birth control methods.

The elements of importance in starting a population control program may be classified as behavioral and social factors on the one hand and administrative problems on the other.

BEHAVIORAL AND SOCIAL FACTORS

We can discuss behavioral and social factors that may have an adverse effect on population control programs under three major headings: (1) attitude of the general public, (2) attitude of intellectuals, and (3) attitude of professionals.

Public attitudes.—The close co-operation of the public in limiting family size is essential for the successful implementation of a population control program. Accordingly, reliable information about the attitude of the public and related factors is required in preparing a program. In many places, the available "information" is based either on guesswork or on occasional contacts with the people. Hence, systematic attitude surveys are very useful for the administrators. They produce invaluable information about the interest of the public, family size, the place of women in the society, and other relevant factors.

Some of the common problems in developing countries where population control programs have been started are as follows:

1. The interest of the public is closely connected with educational level. The results of the Turkish attitude survey demonstrate the importance of education. For example, 5% of the illiterate men in Turkey practice family planning as compared with 28% of those having at least a junior high school education; 27% of the illiterate think that the population of Turkey is increasing too rapidly and that the rate should be decreased, as against 67% of those with at least a junior high school education. Education helps people learn more about sex physiology and the prevention of pregnancy, as well as the social aspects, and encourages more sense of responsibility for the care and training of children.

One point which requires careful attention is the difference between wishing and acting. Attitude surveys usually give us information about what the people think and want. Not until the program has begun can we truly gauge their determination to do something about the matter.

2. The desire for a big family is a serious problem because it usually is deeply rooted in social and economic considerations—the need for inexpensive labor; substantial gifts received by the father of a girl who is about to get married; support in vendettas; a kind of social insurance for parents who lose their working abilities; religious beliefs; tribal traditions; and the desire of minorities in a country to increase in number and hence strength.

3. In families where men and women have equal status and are together in social life, both husband and wife are usually very enthusiastic about family planning. Population control will not be an important problem in countries where a large majority of the families are of this type. Women, however, are helpless in controlling the number of children if they are considered responsible simply for housekeeping, bringing up the children, and satisfying the sexual pleasures of their husbands, and if they have separate lives with the other women. But such problems, evolving from women's inequality, are more easily overcome from the standpoint of practicing birth control than those stemming from the desire for big families. Still, the struggle for women's rights and education should be considered a significant part of any population control program.

The attitudes of the intellectuals.—By intellectuals I mean everyone from a member of Parliament to a minor government official, from a university professor to a young student. The intellectuals are a most influential group in the formation of public opinion and government policy. Their support can be instrumental in starting a population control program. The reactions of Turkish intellectuals to the change in Turkey's traditional population policy during the past year may be cited as an example.

The traditional Turkish population policy was, "More population, in the shortest time possible." Accordingly, the sale and use of contraceptives and propaganda in favor of birth control were forbidden by law. During the past four decades the Turkish nation has been indoctrinated with the absolute necessity of a large and increasing population. The demand has been influenced greatly by historical factors. Turkey was a large and very powerful empire in the sixteenth and seventeenth centuries. She lost her territories gradually and only in Asia Minor retained the boundaries she had at the time of World War I. The country was largely devastated by three wars between 1911 and 1922. The population of 10 million was scourged by contagious diseases such as malaria and typhus. Man power was the most important factor in the strength of the army and was also essential for agricultural development in those days. In these circumstances it was quite natural to expect and to demand an increase in population.

In spite of all efforts, the average annual rate of increase in the 1927–45 period remained around 17 per thousand population, so that population increase did not become a problem for Turkey during this period.

After 1945, the balance between the birth and death rates was disturbed because of improvements in health conditions, and the growth rate of the population increased steadily to nearly 30 per thousand in 1960. Such a rate has become a heavy burden on the Turkish economy. Moreover, criminal abortions increased as a result of the economic pressures on the family budget. The first move to legalize contraception came from obstetricians and the Ministry of Health. In 1960, economists in the State Planning Organization also recommended that the government change its population policy. These two groups succeeded in securing the support of the large majority of intellectuals, and Parliament accepted a new population control policy in 1962.

Although a majority of the intellectuals support the population control program, those opposing it are still strong and active. Turkish economists, without exception, support the program. Medical doctors generally agree that a birth control program is necessary in order to improve maternal and child health. To most Turkish lawyers, having or not having children is a matter of human freedom, and restrictions upon this freedom are unconstitutional. Yet there are doctors and lawyers who oppose population control. Some medical doctors believe that population control will diminish the military and political power of Turkey, or that it will shift the ratio of intellectuals to illiterates unfavorably. A lawyer who is a member of Parliament, in objecting to the proposed change in population policy, maintained that the optimum population for Turkey should be estimated before taking any step toward population control. A pharmacist, also a member of Parliament, compared the population density of Turkey and Belgium and concluded that there is enough space in Turkey for a larger population, not only today but also in the future. A veterinarian wrote dozens of articles in the newspapers condemning the population control measures and suggesting that this money could be more effectively spent on animal husbandry and the fishing industry. A teacher opposed the program on the ground that the availability of contraceptives would encourage unmarried girls to misbehave. Some politicians feared that such a program would be regarded as evidence of the inadequacy or the failure of the agricultural and industrial policy of the government. Some other intellectuals opposed the change by citing alleged harmful effects of contraceptives and insisting that the health of the people should not be endangered by permitting the sale of contraceptives.

Why are so many people against population control? The main reason, I believe, is their lack of knowledge of the relevant social and economic facts. I have talked with no opponent of population control who was not laboring under the misapprehension that he knew as much or more about population dynamics as demographers, social scientists, and economists. Factors influencing the attitudes of the intellectuals, such as nationalism, pride in numbers, hopes for the beneficial effects of population pressure, anticolonialism, usually result from ignorance on the part of intellectuals in subjects and fields not covered by their professional training. I believe that this may be said not only for Turkish intellectuals but for those of other countries as well.

Attitudes of professionals.—The attitudes of professionals such as obstetricians and midwives are of importance in starting and executing a program. Since their incomes are directly related to the number of births and abortions, they might be expected to oppose population control programs on that ground. Usually, this is not so. Throughout the world many obstetricians and gynecologists are the pioneers and leaders of population control programs. Since obstetricians and midwives are key figures in population programs, their enthusiastic participation should always be sought. The Turkish attitude survey demonstrates their important role—for example, 43% of the people who opposed birth control stated they might well change their point of view if a doctor told them that birth control was worthwhile, and 73% of the women stated that they wished to get information about birth control from midwives.

ADMINISTRATIVE PROBLEMS

Administrative problems are numerous and it is especially difficult to find solutions for them in large countries. Starting a program is somewhat easier in countries having a population of fewer than 30 million. The method of contraception to be used is of particular importance, since the whole administrative pattern is affected by the method chosen.

I shall discuss six main problems of administration, i.e., education of the public, meeting the requests for service, manpower requirements, supervision, finance, and evaluation.

Education of the public.—Education should be undertaken as a nationwide program and all available resources should be put to use to motivate the public—to teach people contraceptive methods and guide them to birth control facilities. Usually a new organization is not required, since other organizations to educate the public already exist, such as basic education units, agricultural extension services, and health education centers. A center for the preparation of educational materials and a field organization to support and improve field work may be needed if a satisfactory network of health education is lacking. In Turkey, the Ministry of Health co-operates with the armed forces, the Ministry of Education, the Ministry of Rural Affairs and Communal Development, voluntary organizations, and religious leaders in order to educate the public. For example, the Ministry of Rural Affairs organizes courses in rural areas to improve agriculture and teach home crafts, with home economists and community development workers who visit villages and houses regularly. No difficulty has been encountered here.

Meeting requests for services.—This is not a major problem in the cities. Maternity hospitals, maternal and child health centers, other health units, and private doctors are readily available to the public. The difficult thing is to work in rural areas, especially in countries where there is an insufficient health infrastructure. Unfortunately, this is true in the rural areas of almost every developing country, where increasing population is also an acute problem. There are alternative solutions to the problem. We can either set up a special organization for population control or strengthen or reorganize the existing rural health services and extend their responsibility to cover population control. Independent organizations for special problems, such as malaria eradication, have been tried in many countries. This is not advisable for population control.

There are three main reasons in support of an integrated service. First, population control is a continuous operation and requires confidence and close relations between the public and the workers in order to get satisfactory results. Second, women, especially in conservative countries, are shy and do not like to be seen taking an interest in birth control as such. It is much easier for them to apply to a multipurpose clinic or worker for advice on birth control. Third, since the type of personnel and equipment necessary to run a population control program would duplicate those of a maternal and child health clinic, an independent organization for population control would be an unnecessary and wasteful use of resources.

How are the health authorities likely to react to this additional responsibility? I am convinced that they will undertake it willingly because of the high priority it will be given by the Ministry of Health and because they will appreciate that population control is a most effective, yet unfortunately neglected, measure for the improvement of maternal and child health.

Man power.—Population control requires large numbers of trained administrators, health personnel, educators, and field workers able to operate and administer the programs. It is difficult to give a general guideline on how to solve manpower problems because conditions and problems vary from one country to another. It is the responsibility of the top administrative group and planners to study available man power, methods of contraception and education, needs and requests, and local conditions in order to devise a custom-made program for the country concerned.

However, I do wish to point out a common weakness of medical doctors and midwives in public health projects. Since they are accustomed to having patients or pregnant women come to them, they usually do not appreciate the necessity of working in the community and encouraging and motivating the people to seek help—which is essential for any public health project, especially population control. Therefore, administrators should do everything they can to instruct and lead health personnel in community work.

Supervision.—Administrators and planners know that the success of any program depends largely on the mechanism of supervision that they set up. Special emphasis should be placed on supervisory activities in a population control program because this is a new project and the staff will be inexperienced. Supervisors should always regard themselves as trouble-shooters and teachers of the staff.

Finance.—An estimated additional expenditure for a population control program is around 5 cents (U.S.) per capita per year. This is a negligible amount when compared to the cost of rural health services, which cost at least US$4.00 per capita annually. In small countries, neither additional expenditures for population programs nor the running expenditures for health services are prohibitively high. But the problem of finance may become a major problem for large countries. But even there, the potential economic benefits from a population control program are far greater than the probable costs (see chaps. 28, 57, and 58 in this volume).

Evaluation.—Any administrator must have information about the results of his work. Demographic data are essential in both starting and following up the program. Normally they are derived from a routine vital registration system. Unfortunately, such a system is lacking in many of the developing countries, and so a sampling survey technique must be used in order to obtain information. Demographic surveys are now being carried out in Pakistan and Thailand as well as in Turkey. By 1968, the Turkish survey will include 1.3 million persons annually—an estimated 4% of the total population. The major purpose of this survey is to provide reliable annual natality and mortality statistics on a regional basis.

CONCLUSION

Since the time of Malthus, almost nothing has been done to control population throughout the world except for spontaneous decreases in the birth rate of developed countries. After World War II, the advances in medicine and public health practice and the improvement of health services in the newly independent countries aggravated the population problem. Now, the average man realizes its importance, and the soundness of a population control policy is beyond any doubt. The big problem of starting a population control program is therefore solved.

The second point of importance is the recent advances in contraceptives. This reminds me of the point of view of public health scientists on the control of tuberculosis before the discovery of tuberculostatic drugs and the mass application of the B.C.G. vaccine. In those days, it was considered that the control of tuberculosis was related to the prosperity of the country and that nothing substantial could be done if the standards of living were not improved. A similar situation exists today for population control programs. Many people have maintained that population control will not take hold because it requires a certain level of education in a nation, and there have been several failures to support this viewpoint. But the new contraceptives have changed the outlook and opened horizons for a better future.

Our policy is sound and we have the means to achieve our goal. Anyone who is on the right track will reach his goal sooner or later if he is patient and not disappointed by occasional failures. What we must do is "keep working." To quote a Turkish proverb: "The determined dervish will get his wish."

23

PLANNING THE PROGRAM

JAE MO YANG, M.D., M.P.H., D.M.Sc.

Professor of Preventive Medicine, Yonsei University College of Medicine
Chairman, Board of Trustees, The Planned Parenthood Federation of Korea

INTRODUCTION

Each country will vary the strategy of its family planning program according to its government policies, educational level, available resources, religion, and cultural patterns. This report is based on five years' experience in Korea and includes some ideas which come less from scientific evidence than from my experiences, plans, and future hopes. Many of my statements are in agreement with those given by the vice-president of the Population Council, Dr. Bernard Berelson, in his "National Family Planning Programs: A Guide," published in *Studies in Family Planning*, December, 1964.

In planning the program it is important to keep the following facts in mind.

1. Because this program is a very novel one in most of the developing countries, it is common for their leaders to feel that further research and study is needed within each country to provide guidelines before any national program can be undertaken. I believe that at the present time enough experience has been accumulated to support the statement that there are only very minor differences in the major principles of organization and of administration of the family planning programs in different countries. These differences are not important in the over-all direction or success of the program. The most important factor in a successful program is strong leadership. I would not say that no research or study is needed in setting up a program, but I would urge any country to feel confident in launching a family planning program nationally if it will follow the basic principles which have already been found to be successful in other countries.

2. People as individuals have generally been ahead of their leaders in wanting and approving family planning, much more so than any of the government leaders had expected. Our surveys among a group of Roman Catholics revealed that their attitude and behavior were little different from that of non-Catholics, despite the very vocal stand of the Catholic hierarchy. If we are to stay in step with the times, we must make haste to provide the information and services so greatly needed without being overcautious and hesitant.

3. A program, once launched, will usually develop very rapidly if it is successful. Any program must be flexible enough to adjust to differences in the local situation, and to newly developing techniques. I would urge any administrator of a program to have the courage to introduce any new method or technique which he feels should be put to the test, and to revise his program as he feels necessary. To make this possible, it is essential that the administrator have as much autonomy as is practical.

4. Family planning is a critical and urgent need in most of the developing countries, though very few leaders or countries appreciate this crisis. We cannot afford the time required by the usual procedure of training public health workers. Rather than take several years to establish facilities, train teachers, and recruit and educate trainees, we must carry on these efforts simultaneously.

5. Few programs are more complex and delicate and also few programs are related to so many fields of work. Hence any family planning program must have the combined support of many groups—the ministries in the government, the social agencies, and others. If we are to avoid a situation in which everyone's concern becomes nobody's concern, care must be taken to devise a program which crystallizes vague ideas of co-operation into definite working relationships.

6. In order for family planning programs to become permanently established it is important that the government or association publicize a purpose which is more comprehensive than just family planning for economic reasons. The additional goals of respect for human life, prevention of induced abortions, protection of maternal health, improvement of family life and welfare, and promotion of responsible parenthood should all be emphasized. A word of caution must be given in the translation of "family planning" or "planned parenthood" into the local language of the community. We have found that in Korea, Japan, and China the term "birth limitation" was the widely used translation of the original "birth control." Sometimes "family planning" has been misinterpreted as meaning "induced abortion."

The terms "family planning," "family welfare," "pre-pregnancy health," and "planned birth and child raising" are widely used in

Asia. The words must convey the idea of a voluntary family planning program. Special education is usually necessary at first to ensure correct understanding of the meaning of the words used.

GOVERNMENT POLICY

In most of the developing countries, and particularly in Asia, strong government support is essential for any successful program of family planning, though the successful programs in Taiwan and Hong Kong prove it is not indispensable. Therefore, the first step in national development has been to make the family planning program a government program. We found that to government leaders and the general population, maternal health was not so persuasive an argument for family planning as were the economic and political reasons for such a program. Therefore, with government leaders the economic impact of the family planning program must be stressed.

In 1961 I was able to work closely with the Ministry of Health in setting up a family planning program following the advice given to the Supreme Council for National Reconstruction in preparing its first five-year plan (1962–66). The following seven points were proposed by the Ministry of Health to the Supreme Council.

1. Abolition of the law prohibiting importation of contraceptives.
2. Approval and encouragement of domestic production of contraceptives.
3. Contraceptives to be provided under the direction of doctors, midwives, and public health nurses.
4. Contraceptives to be provided by the government, free of charge, to the needy and to those approved by the Ministry of Health.
5. Establishment of family planning clinics by health centers and other facilities for medical care.
6. Campaigns for education of the people about the family planning program to be carried out by government and voluntary agencies.
7. Organization by the Minister of Health and Social Affairs of a Family Planning Advisory Committee to be consulted by the government in planning, organizing, setting-up, managing, and conducting research for a national family planning program.

The first proposed budget was the equivalent of US$2 million but the Ministry of Health reduced the annual budget to US$0.5 million in order to make the proposed budget more acceptable to the authorities and to emphasize the improved economics. The statistic showing a $2 billion economic gain by 1971 from a successful family planning program was very attractive to the members of the Supreme Council, which gave unanimous approval. The military government was eager to follow any program which would improve the national economy. I would, however, strongly recommend full contact with the responsible authorities concerned before any proposal regarding the program is submitted for a governmental decision.

Korea was fortunate that the public announcement made by the chairman of the Supreme Council in early December, 1961, not only supported the family planning program as a part of national policy but immediately silenced many fears by stating that the program would be a voluntary one carried out through education.

Since then, there has been considerable support of the program by annual messages from the head of the government. A New Year visit by the President to the Ministry of Health has publicized and greatly strengthened the program, as did the instructions to support the program of family planning sent in September, 1963, from the Prime Minister to all related ministries, such as the Ministries of Health and Welfare, Education, Defense, Justice, Economic Planning, Public Information, and to the Office of Cabinet Administration. The instructions clearly outlined each ministry's specific responsibility and function in supporting the efforts of the government to lower the exploding rate of population increase.

The actual work, however, was carried out by the Planned Parenthood Federation of Korea (PPFK) until 1963 when the government had a trained staff and was able to carry on the program. The resulting hiatus between enactment and execution allowed time for relief of the tension caused by those who opposed any program proposed by the military government. Because of government bureaucracy there is always a lag of a few years from the time a decision is made until the policy can be put into effect. This points up the value of having a strong voluntary organization which can react with flexibility and speed to changing situations.

GOAL

A nation's goal in its family planning program is usually expressed in terms of the reduction in the birth rate, or in the annual growth rate for the population. To be attractive to any government leader the goal must be ambitious, but it is wise not to be too ambitious. Once leaders in charge of a nation's economic improvement become convinced of the need for a family planning program, they often quickly become impatient with the speed of the program and overlook the human factors present. For example, even though the budget for the family planning program was available only from July, 1962, we were asked early in 1963 about the amount of reduction in the birth rate.

Because of the lack of any really reliable vital statistics in most of the developing countries, it is very difficult, if not impossible, to set any clear demographic goals or even truly to evaluate the program's achievements. The number (2.88%) which has been officially quoted as the annual population growth rate in Korea is simply a figure derived from the differences in census data in 1955 and 1960. If one considers the declining death rate, now found in most of the developing countries, the actual annual growth rate in 1960 and 1961 could easily be 3% or higher. This, with the improvement in reporting of birth statistics, would very likely cancel out any real achievements due to the program.

However, it is not unrealistic to anticipate a reduction in annual growth rate in five years from 3% to 2.5%; in ten years from 3% to 2%. Also, one could anticipate a reduction in the birth rate of from 40 to 25 in about ten years.

ORGANIZATION

From the first, the main responsibility for the national program was placed with the Ministry of Health and Social Affairs. In June, 1963, responsibility for the family planning program was given to the maternal and child health section of the ministry, which is directed by a medical doctor with a staff of eight assistants. This is in contrast to the advice given by the Population Council's advisory mission on family planning that there be at least a bureau of family planning with three sections: family planning, maternal and child health, and health education. If one considers the importance of the program, the work load of the staff, and the high proportion of the total health budget involved (23%), a section level is not high enough or strong enough in the organization of the program in the ministry. This relatively low status in the central government is reflected in the establishment of subsections for family planning at the level of the provincial governments.

Because of this, the PPFK was required to carry on most of the government programs during the first few years and has since been called upon to supplement the government in its program of training, production of educational materials, program evaluation, and international co-operation. The PPFK is fortunate to have as members many specialists from a wide variety of fields not on the staff of the Ministry of Health. Because it has a flexible program, the PPFK has been able to circumvent the delays and complex red tape of government bureaucracy. It has also been fortunate in having dedicated and enthusiastic leaders who were willing to undertake the risks of developing pilot projects for the program. Because of frequent meetings and active interest the advisory committee has provided valuable help to the program. And the Population Council has been providing invaluable assistance financially and through the advice of resident representatives or visiting staff.

TRAINING

From the beginning, the responsibility for training personnel has been delegated to the PPFK because there were many experts among its membership who could be mobilized as instructors. But, neither the PPFK nor the government had the budget and the time to provide the

TABLE 1

STAFF TRAINING IN KOREA

Category	Lecture and Seminar	Field Demonstration
Family planning workers:		
Pre-service............................	8 days	
In-service.............................	2 weeks	
Assistants to the family planning workers:		
Pre-service............................	4 days	1 week
In-service.............................	3 weeks	
Physician:		
Vasectomy............................	1 day	1 day
IUD..................................	1 day	1 day

facilities for training personnel. Therefore, any available space was utilized for the four-day training courses. They were given at nine different centers—medical or nursing school classrooms, even a meeting hall in the government capitol. Later, a three-week course was given in five centers for local training.

The trainees received a per diem to cover the costs of their lodging in homes near the training center. Because of the prompt receipt of a supplementary grant from the Population Council in New York, we were able to train 1,500 workers completely within a fourteen-month period. For an outline of the types of training, see Table 1. The teachers were prepared in three- to four-day seminars given by the PPFK, which prepared and provided the materials.

In order to keep all family planning workers and physicians up to date, monthly newsletters are prepared giving the progress of the program and new information as it becomes available. Also, an annual in-service refresher training period of two to three days is recommended.

Each year there is about a 10% attrition rate among the trained personnel, so that the basic training course needs to be continued to provide replacements.

Since the two-day training in IUD insertion or vasectomy for general practitioners has been found inadequate, additional training is planned by stationing a doctor with a mobile team in each province. Using a remodeled army ambulance, the local practitioner and specialist can go together to each village where the former will make the insertion under the supervision of the specialist. In this way we secure the co-operation of the local physician and help maintain his prestige and income. It is felt that about thirty IUD insertions are needed to provide sufficient experience for each of the trainees. With the support of the IPPF and others, we were able to establish a demonstration clinic where trainees could be taught. Moreover, several of the universities have set up demonstration clinics in their outpatient departments.

WAYS AND MEANS OF PROVIDING INFORMATION AND SERVICES

At first the main issues were whether the services of the family planning clinics should be free or paid for and whether the clinics should be located in the public health centers or in private physicians' offices.

Soon it was decided to place a family planning clinic in each of the 189 health centers scattered throughout the country. Each center is surrounded by about 150,000 people. Since these centers cover the entire population of the country, they are logical places to provide this service in their maternal and child health programs. Of course this does not preclude the establishment of the program in private or voluntary clinics.

Because of limitations of government supplies and budget, the decision was that the health center clinics would be used to provide services to the indigent. This decision has produced three problems. (1) The knowledge that free services are available has led the majority of women in the rural areas to claim indigency. (2) To qualify for free services women must have identification from the local township office, a procedure which is troublesome and may be expensive. (3) The health centers are not equipped to accept pay patients; so those who could pay are excluded from the services.

To solve the second problem, authorization was given to the family planning worker to screen the patients who were unable to pay for the services. In order to protect the worker, each recipient signed a receipt at the time she was treated. This made careful audits possible.

However, this arrangement places a heavy burden on the family planning worker; it is difficult for her to deliver the monthly supplies to her neighbors when she has to be out on home visits. A solution might be to have a leader among the village women delegated to take care of the distribution of supplies.

During the first two years when there were only two family planning workers in each center, the main activities were confined to educating the people through large and small group meetings of the villagers. Flip charts and slide projectors were provided for the workers. In only one or two villages were we able to provide for home visits, and intensive guidance was given to about 150 couples per worker. At the beginning of the project a great deal of assistance came from National Reconstruction workers. Later when assistants were trained they were added at a ratio of one to each township (about 12,000 people). Then it was possible to increase the number of group meetings and home visits until finally all villages could be covered. To fill the need for a bridge between the family planning workers and the village women, mother's classes are now organized under the leadership of about 29,000 volunteers.

In April, 1964, the PPFK conducted a survey to probe nationwide opinion about family planning. At that time we found that only 9% of the eligible women were currently practicing family planning, while 45% of the eligible couples wanted it. Hence we feel it is best to provide the necessary information and services to those who want them and are ready to practice family planning, rather than to spend much time and effort on changing the attitudes of those who are not interested. Instructions were given to the field workers to concentrate their efforts on the age group of 25–39 and on those who have had at least three children, particularly if they have had two sons, and also on women in the post-partum period. The workers emphasized the regular use of the traditional methods of contraception instead of spending much time and effort on increasing the number of users of the methods.

Our experience has shown that it is more difficult to get acceptance from the urban dweller than from those in rural areas, a fact which had not been anticipated. This is usually due to the "know it all" attitude and snobbishness among the higher classes of the city dwellers, who also are hard to reach. Because both the husband and wife among the lower classes are out working from early morning until late evening it is hard to reach them too. In April, 1964, only 5.9% of the eligible rural couples were practicing family planning, as compared with 19.2% of the urban couples. One year later the rural rate had risen to 14.1%, the urban rate to 21.0%. Thus, in spite of the heavy concentration of facilities and higher educational level in the cities, there was almost no increase in the urban percentage in contrast to an increase of 2.5 times in the rural percentage. The city people must not be neglected in family planning but must be reached through other channels, e.g., television, radio, magazines, newspapers, and other media of information. Also the services need to be provided through private practitioners, hospital clinics, and voluntary organizations.

Of great importance to a family planning program is the active participation of the private practitioner who needs to be oriented and encouraged so that adverse or harmful criticism may be avoided. Contraceptives provided at cost or even given without charge, and some monetary incentive, are helpful in securing the doctors' co-operation.

TABLE 2

INCIDENCE OF COMPLICATIONS, 1964

(Per Cent)

Degree	After Vasectomy	After IUD
Minimal...............	3	15
Moderate...............	....	3
Severe.................	0.5	0.5
Very severe...........	0.3	0.4
Moderately severe......	0.15	0.075
Minimally severe.......	0.05	0.025

At first the subsidy for a vasectomy was $4.00, but it has been reduced to $2.00. The subsidy for IUD insertion is the equivalent of $1.20. No other financial subsidy is given to either the workers or the patients. The government has recommended an increase in the subsidy and also a monetary incentive to the workers who bring in cases. Initially, the government subsidy was given only to urologists, surgeons, and obstetricians who did the vasectomy and IUD insertion. Later the subsidy was extended to any doctor who was recommended by the director of the health center after receiving the PPFK training.

During the time of the rapid expansion of the IUD insertion and vasectomy services in 1964, some problems developed. The incidence of complications is shown in Table 2. Although the number of serious problems was very small, there was a danger of unfavorable publicity which could jeopardize the program by damaging its reputation. It became necessary to seek out preventive measures and ways of minimizing the complications and handling them immediately.

After consultation with the Ministry of Health and the adviser from the Population Council, the medical advisory committee planned a national consultative clinic system at three levels: central, provincial, and county. A management committee was made responsible for selection of the consultative or referral clinics, for the training and guidance of those working in the family planning program, for the standardization of the follow-up care, and for the financial decisions on subsidies.

In order to minimize or prevent complications, additional field training will be given to the local doctors by a mobile team. Also, the basic drugs needed, such as antibiotics, sulfa drugs, oxytocis, and hemostatic agents, will be provided.

To expedite the use of the available funds from the government and the Population Council grants, which were pooled for the referral system, the PPFK was asked to be responsible for their administration.

A mobile team has been found to be very effective for IUD service in Korea. The PPFK bus staff averaged an insertion rate of more than thirty per day in the villages. It has been found that a small Jeep type of car is more suitable for transportation in the rural areas.

Koyang Gun has been used as a special study area. There we brought the crew and a folding examination table to the village in a Land Rover and set up a temporary clinic in one of the village offices.

Because of the monotony of the procedure it is very difficult to recruit a qualified physician even though the salary is relatively good. Paramedical personnel were trained by observing ten insertions following which they did thirty insertions under the close supervision of a well-qualified physician. Such paramedical personnel were known as nurses, not M.D.'s; yet there was little difference in their acceptance by village women or in the complications following insertion. The IUD was inserted at any time during the menstrual cycle in this trial.

To plan for a mobile family planning service for IUD insertion in a model rural community one should select a community of 150,000 population, including about eleven townships of about 12,000 people each and one central township of about 30,000 people. In this center the services would be provided through the health center or through the private practitioner. Each village is estimated to have about 1,000 people, making about twelve villages per township.

To make the most economic use of supplies and personnel, three villages are grouped together to form one unit for the IUD services. This means that each mobile service would be responsible for forty units. If each mobile car spent four days per week on the field, at the rate of one unit per day, sixteen units could be covered per month. These sixteen units would need to be revisited monthly for three months with subsequent follow-up visits every three months. In this way, over a nine-month period one mobile team could complete the entire ten townships for their first three months' consecutive follow-up. Thereafter the trimonthly visits to each unit would be scheduled. Villagers must be informed in advance about the date of visit of the team to their village.

Among a population of 120,000 about 13%–15% or 17,000 couples are under the age of 44. In this group, 30%–40% or 6,000 are potential users of contraception, about 5% of the entire population. According to our recent experience, in one small rural community 30% of the eligible couples had received an IUD insertion during the six months in which services were offered. This was an unusually successful experience.

In the model community of 120,000 people, however, let us assume that about 50%–70% of the 6,000 potential users, 3,000–4,000, have IUD insertions during the first year. The mobile staff can do about 15–20 insertions per visit day or about 240–320 insertions per month, a reasonable estimate. Even at $1.20 per insertion, the income of $288–$384 is enough to pay the salaries of the staff, and the monthly car maintenance costs ($100).

If it is not possible to secure full-time services of a well-qualified doctor to travel with the mobile team, it might be possible to use a well-trained nurse or midwife to do the screening of the patients and the insertion of the IUD under the supervision of the local practitioner in each area.

PERSONNEL

In the family planning program the key personnel are the workers at the clinics and in the field. Since 1962 there has been a gradual increase in the number of workers, so that in 1965 there is one family planning worker for each 50,000 population and one assistant family planning worker for each 12,000 population in rural areas, and one family planning worker for each 30,000 population in the city areas. Therefore one trained person is responsible for about 1,600 eligible couples or about 600 potential users of contraceptives. At the rate of thirty home visits per week she can cover about one-fifth of the eligible couples per month, a proportion which is felt to be a reasonable one at the present time. The worker's efficiency can be increased by use of a bicycle, although in hilly areas a motor-scooter might be more helpful.

If it becomes possible to expand the program and to obtain additional MCH workers, with the further responsibility of collecting vital statistics and other data, it would be well to plan to double the number of family planning workers to one for each 6,000 population.

In recruiting personnel, priority is given in the following order: to nurses or midwives, to college graduates, to high school graduates, to women between the ages of 22 and 49 (later revised to 20–44 to include the young graduate nurse), preferably married. Non-married young workers have been as well accepted as married and older people, and generally have been more active in the program. Men have been found to be less efficient and more likely to be given their employment on the basis of patronage.

The government provides only one nurse–family planning supervisor to each province which varies in population from 1.5 to 4 million. Even with the help of vehicles provided by the Population Council, this number of nurses is completely inadequate, since one alone must now try to cover from nine to thirty-four health centers. It would be wise to plan for two supervisors per province with an additional supervisor added for each ten centers over twenty.

Looking to the future, it would be wise to plan some increase of personnel in the main family planning office of the Ministry of Health, where at present there is a staff of nine.

METHODS OF CONTRACEPTION

According to the principle that "no single method will satisfy everyone," we taught and offered condoms, foam tablets, diaphragms, jelly, rhythm, and withdrawal as methods to be used in the early stages of development of the program. Clinical experience quickly showed that the diaphragm and withdrawal were not acceptable in Korea. Since the rhythm method has not been successful, it is no longer taught. After foam tablets became available in 1962, the government offered this locally produced product as well as condoms and jelly. As the demand for condoms increased they began to be produced locally. There was some complaint that the foam tablets deteriorated during storage.

In 1963 a clinical trial of the IUD was followed by a high degree of acceptance. Because of its many advantages, it was offered nationally after July, 1964. The present goal by 1967 is 1 million IUD's, 200,000 vasectomies, and 300,000 regular users of the conventional methods.

In the IUD supply, the proportion of sizes of the loop is 1:2:1 for 25 mm., 27.5 mm., and 30 mm.; and one inserter for every twenty loops. We do not know as yet whether the latter ratio holds when tincture of iodine is used to sterilize the inserter and loops.

For those who can afford them, the use of oral contraceptives is encouraged. The women who use these, however, do not get any subsidy. The government allows the importation of oral contraceptives after they had been tested by the PPFK over 2,400 woman-months of exposure.

After 1964, the advisory council set the proportion of the supplies of usual contraceptives at about 80% condoms, 15% foam tablets, 5% jelly. The council also set the standard month's supplies as 9 condoms, 16 foam tablets (one vial) and 30 grams of jelly, though field workers are allowed to make necessary adjustments.

It is important for each clinic to have a three-month supply of materials on hand and supplies should be planned by the year. It is also important, however, that supplies do not deteriorate during storage, and so each clinic should adjust its requests to its needs.

When the program was first begun in 1962 we were very conservative in offering sterilization. However, from 1963 it was actively promoted among those who had had three or more children. Government subsidy is limited to male sterilization.

At present the request for import tax exemption for all contraceptives is under negotiation with the Ministry of Finance. It has been recommended that the government provide a production subsidy so that contraceptives can be sold cheaply on the open market. It is also desirable for medical practitioners to have a free or at-cost supply of various contraceptives readily available.

PROGRAM EVALUATION AND RESEARCH

Most of the developing countries do not as yet have accurate and adequate vital statistics. Any scientific research on fertility control must be made on the basis of accurate and complete data, not only on attitudes and behavior related to family planning, but also on basic facts concerning fertility, births, deaths, and population migration. Most governments and family planning associations are unable to support such research and are reluctant to initiate any such program.

Korea was fortunate in 1961 when the visit of Dr. M. C. Balfour of the Population Council brought the happy information that the Council was interested in bringing us technical and financial assistance in this field. A two-year pilot study in Koyang Gun was promptly proposed, to be carried on by Yonsei University. The main purpose of this study was to clarify and demonstrate whether or not an intensive family planning program could really have an effect on the birth rate. In 1964, with the support of the Council, a large-scale urban research project was begun in Sungdong Ku, Seoul, under the direction of Seoul National University. This project was developed as a pilot study seeking the most efficient methods of education and information in family planning.

In 1963 the Medical Advisory Committee of the PPFK, with the support of the Council, started a large-scale study on the use of the IUD at twenty-four clinics; mostly university, missionary, and provincial hospitals participated in this study. The Koyang study was later enlarged to include investigation of the most efficient methods of organization of the IUD service, as well as how to improve the securing of vital statistics and how to improve and efficiently record and report the work of the service.

In April, 1964, a nationwide sample survey was initiated on attitudes toward family planning and its acceptance and use. At present, the PPFK and Yonsei University are evaluating the use of a mobile van and the clinical use of an oral contraceptive.

Most of the above studies aim at prompt answers to practical problems arising out of the family planning programs. In 1965, under the joint auspices of the Ministry of Health, the PPFK, and the Population Council, an evaluation team was organized to give an objective and neutral evaluation of the work of the family planning program.

The staff of a university is well qualified to carry on this type of research, and their active support and participation in the program brings considerable favorable publicity.

BUDGET

The budget request should be modest and realistic at the inception of the program and expand gradually as confidence and capability increase. However, it must not be so modest that the program will suffer. In general, a budget ranging from $0.05 to $0.10 per capita seems to be the desirable one in developing countries. The current year's budget in Korea is about $0.036 per capita, and the proposal for next year will be about $0.075 per capita.

Usually about one-third of the budget is allotted to salary and allowances. Another one-third covers subsidies to physicians for IUD insertions and vasectomy operations, including the cost for the care of complications. The rest covers the contraceptive supplies, information and education, maintenance of transportation, and administrative expenses.

Currently the salary and traveling allowances for the workers in Korea are $240 per worker per year, which is inadequate. The government is planning to increase the salaries of government employees by 30% in 1966.

The ideal and reasonable salaries and allowances would be:

$300 × 1,500 asst. FP workers. $450,000
$360 × 500 FP workers. $180,000
$400 × 200 head workers and supervisors. . . .$ 80,000

$710,000 ($0.025 per capita)

An ideal budget for physician subsidies would be:

$2 × 300,000 . . . . $600,000
$5 ×   20,000 . . . . $100,000
_____
                          $700,000 ($0.025 per capita)

Taking account of 64,000 unwanted pregnancies prevented in a year by 300,000 IUD's and 20,000 vasectomies, the cost per prevented birth might be approximately $15 in the current year, and $30 in 1966. The equipment to set up one unit of an IUD clinic costs about $400, and the expendables cost about $20 per month.

The above-mentioned budgets and costs do not include the expenses necessary for research, evaluation, and technical assistance, which would be the equivalent of 20% of the current year's government budget.

Summary of Main Points

1. Do not hesitate to launch a national program. People are ready to accept, and there is a fair amount of basic knowledge and experience to guide you.

2. Keep the program flexible, and tackle the problem with emergency measures.

3. Any successful program must have strong leadership and the co-operation of all concerned.

4. Be careful in the semantics of "family planning." The terms must be comprehensible and clear, and must stress the voluntary and contraceptive character of the action.

5. Government support is essential in most of the developing countries, but it usually takes two or three years to establish it.

6. Therefore, the organization of a strong voluntary association capable of flexible and rapid action is essential, particularly in the early stage of a government program.

7. The goal must be ambitious, but not unrealistic.

8. Set the organization as high as possible in the administrative hierarchy. But ideal organization alone is not all. Again a voluntary organization could have a supplementary role.

9. Sufficient pre-service training, though desirable, is often impossible. Solve this problem by supplementary in-service training. Do not make training wait until you have your own teaching staff and facilities fully established.

10. Aim to provide information and service to motivated couples, and leave the others until later. Concentrate on younger couples with high parity.

11. Start in the areas where you can find a team of strong local leaders. The city people are not always easy to approach; therefore, home visiting may have less effect in cities. Use mass media.

12. Visit one out of every three or four families, in consideration of the diffusion effect and operational costs.

13. The IUD is the best method at present in most developing countries. Aim at 70%–80% with the IUD, the rest with sterilization and condom.

14. Mobile teams seem to be highly effective, not only for the IUD service, but also for the field training of local practitioners.

15. Insertion of the IUD at any time by well-trained paramedical personnel might solve the problem of remote rural or island areas.

16. For the IUD and vasectomy, some arrangement for the care of complications is needed in most developing countries.

17. Roughly 5% of the entire population or 35% of the eligible couples will be the potential number of current users of contraceptives if your program is successful. Aim to cover at least half of that during the first year of the program.

18. One family planning worker for every 12,000 population seems to be a modest ratio, and one for every 6,000 is ideal. The majority should be female workers, particularly for the IUD.

19. Keep the supplies as plentiful and cheap as possible, not only for the clinics, but also for practitioners and for commercial channels.

20. Evaluation and research are necessary to solve any practical problems arising from the on-going program and to improve the program promptly.

21. A modest but sufficient budget would be about $0.05–$0.10 per capita, about 30%–50% of that to cover salaries and personnel allowances.

24

ORGANIZATIONAL STRUCTURE IN FAMILY PLANNING PROGRAMS

MOYE W. FREYMANN, M.D., Dr.P.H.

Chief Consultant in Health and Family Planning, Ford Foundation India Office
Director, University of North Carolina Population Center

One increasingly hears the question, "What is the optimal organizational structure of an official family planning program?" A review of the many family planning efforts now emerging in the world provides no simple answer. Obviously, such programs must be pragmatically fitted to particular local resources and conditions.

Are there no general guidelines, then, for the administrator working on a new family planning program, or wishing to improve an existing one? Where can he find some valid principles, some underlying ideas, some way of organizing the experience gained in such programs?

In seeking them, I have found useful the following two basic concepts: (1) The objectives of a family planning program can be dissected into a kind of hierarchy. The ultimate objectives of the program can be specified; to reach them the achievement of certain intermediate objectives is assumed to be necessary; achieving each of them, in turn, will depend on certain performance objectives, or program activities. Among all the possible program activities, those categories of activities which appear to be especially salient to achievement of the ultimate goals of a family planning program can be termed the basic organizational functions of such a program. (2) Given such a set of basic functions, consideration of the "total organizational structure" of a family planning program in any particular situation will require considering *all* the organizational mechanisms (of various types, wherever they are located) which serve to carry out these basic functions in that situation.

Application of the first concept to family planning programs in

321

various countries reveals many common functional features. It is possible from these to construct a broad, functional matrix which can be used in approaching any new family planning program situation. According to local circumstances, efficient fulfillment of each of the basic functions may entail different types of activities, carried out through diverse organizational means. In a given situation, some functions may already be fulfilled; some may be handled by various existing organizational entities; and some may require establishing new structural units. A common functional body thus may manifest itself in a variety of organizational forms.

For the family planning administrator, a more explicit appreciation of the general functional framework which underlies organizational structure may help him make better plans and decisions. It may also

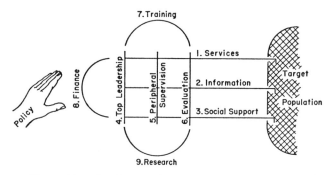

FIG. 1.—Functional matrix for a family planning program

facilitate the cumulation of a body of valid experience from family planning programs in different areas. An attempt is made below, therefore, first to sketch a broad functional schema for family planning programs, and second to comment on organizational implications of each of the functional elements.

A FUNCTIONAL MATRIX

Let us look at the diagram at Figure 1. On the right side is represented the general "target" population. This target population has its own internal structure, with distinct channels of influence and communication. The task of the external family planning program structure is to engage with this internal structure in such ways as to catalyze and mobilize those forces within the population which favor the spread of family planning practices.

The family planning program structure in Figure 1 looks like a key; this is appropriate, since such a program is meant to be a key to a human social problem. The force behind the key is the hand of public policy. The key itself contains nine lines, each line representing a basic functional element. These elements fall into three groups: instrumental functions, control functions, and supporting functions.

The instrumental functions are those which directly lock into and activate the forces within the target population group. (1) *Provision of services* of an acceptable type with maximum convenience is of primary import. In most populations, at least some people are immediately ready to limit births if acceptable contraceptive supplies and services are truly made conveniently available. Satisfying this group, especially, is essential for the spread of such practices to others. (2) *Provision of information* about the advantages of family planning and about contraceptive methods, their safety, and their availability will facilitate both the use of services and the process of group endorsement. (3) *Generating social support for small family size* is a distinct function that deserves special emphasis. If social pressure favoring smaller family size comes from within their own group, people themselves will seek out information and contraceptive methods. Without such social support, they may ignore information and available services.

The control functions of a family planning program serve to build, direct, and co-ordinate the instrumental functions. (4) *Top leadership* is needed to give strong direction to a program which is of an unprecedented, critical, and complex nature. (5) *Peripheral supervision* is needed to represent this new program at lower administrative levels, to elicit the participation of other staff and of local leaders, and to help identify and solve problems of implementation. (6) *Program evaluation* activities must provide the "feedback" information that program administrators need to monitor and improve the program.

The supporting functions feed into and sustain the control functions. (7) *Training* of new and old staff is needed to equip them for new functions and relationships. (8) *Financial support* must be provided in sufficient magnitude and duration, with special arrangements for flexibility and for some unusual types of subsidy needs. (9) *Research support* is needed to provide new knowledge and to clarify problems arising as the program advances.

Let us now consider some of the organizational aspects of each of these major functional needs. Illustrations will be drawn primarily from Asia; the principal documentation is provided by the papers prepared for the Geneva conference.

INSTRUMENTAL FUNCTIONS

PROVISION OF SERVICES

Intra-uterine contraceptive devices.—Use of the organizational structure of maternal and child health services and of maternity hospitals for providing IUD services has shown its effectiveness in many countries. Private practitioners as a group must also be involved, as demonstrated in Taiwan and Korea. Where doctors are scarce, they can work on an itinerant basis, providing scheduled services at different locations. In India, another useful organizational device is the "camp"; after careful preparation in a rural area, large numbers of women gather at a given point to be served by a team of doctors and nurses.

An important organizational lesson learned from experience with IUD's is that their effective use requires a strong infrastructure of permanent, auxiliary health personnel. Nursing and midwifery staff are especially needed to educate and inform the women, to involve indigenous midwives, to organize clinic sessions, to provide continuing reassurance, and to detect and handle possible later complaints. In India, male workers also have played a key role in the organizational and group-education support for this service.

In the initial enthusiasm for the IUD, some observers suggested that simply providing for IUD insertion services alone might meet the family planning needs of high fertility areas. Surely the IUD gives a tremendous boost to the process of family planning program development. However, where data have been collected on the use of IUD's in a known population group over a period of time, in India, Pakistan, Thailand, and Taiwan, the familiar S-shaped curve seems to emerge, with a leveling-off well below what is needed for adequate fertility moderation. To suggest that any other organizational inputs should be withheld at this time would seem quite shortsighted.

Sterilization.—The primary principle in organizing services for voluntary sterilization is truly convenient availability, with a minimum of physical, psychological, and financial obstacles. Expectations that voluntary sterilization will not be popular in a given area will be self-confirming, when the service is not made conveniently available. In India, even with availability of the IUD, male vasectomy services through clinics and camps have continued to be utilized. In parts of the United States also, this method has demonstrated its potential popularity. For female sterilization, the problem of availability is complicated by hospital-bed shortages. In general, sterilization services seem to require more effort for group educational support and somewhat less effort for follow-up work, than is required for the IUD services.

Condoms.—The traditional type of family planning clinic has proved inadequate for distribution of condoms, as for provision of other mass services in high fertility areas. In India, several states have developed systems of "depot-holders," whereby condoms are supplied to rural health workers, shopkeepers, or local leaders for free distribution. When supported with supervisory and educational services, this system has produced a leap in the consumption of condoms in the area served.

The most favorable organizational structure for condom distribution appears to be the commercial distribution network, which carries daily commodities to the common people with remarkable efficiency even in remote areas. A group of marketing specialists in India has proposed a simple method for government subsidy of the price of condoms, to be distributed on a massive and continuing basis through commercial channels. with support of a vigorous advertising campaign. This promises to be much more effective and less expensive than any other distribution system; it desperately needs some large-scale demonstrations.

Oral contraceptives.—The orals have proved their popularity in economically favored areas. But the present products still have severe limitations. For rural high fertility areas they appear to require an organizational supporting structure much more elaborate than can be expected in most such areas in the near future.

Induced abortion.—Abortion must be mentioned as a service to be made available in conjunction with family planning programs; it is not advocated as a desirable, routine "family planning method." But any new family planning program is bound to involve contraceptive failures. Women who find themselves with an unwanted pregnancy, the world over, are likely to resort to induced abortion under unsanitary conditions. This is a common cause of maternal morbidity and death. It is only humane to try to minimize the illness and death of mothers by not excluding them from the use of available medical facilities for this purpose when they seek it. Certain controls and conditions can indeed be imposed. The kinds of organizational arrangements for providing such service along medically and ethically appropriate lines are now illustrated in Scandinavian and Eastern European countries.

PROVISION OF INFORMATION

Publicity departments.—The government ministry dealing with public information and mass media services must feel a real responsibility for support of the family planning efforts. This may require development of a special family planning unit in this ministry. In many countries, commercial advertising organizations also provide a considerable reservoir of talent useful to the program. Enlisting the participation of such organizations deserves special effort.

Postal system.—Experiences in India and the United States have shown that printed materials sent with little cost through the postal system to local leaders or individuals may have surprisingly good effects in providing information and stimulating discussion.

Governmental and industrial groups.—Governmental organizations having close contact with the people must equip their personnel to answer questions and provide information about family planning. In addition to the maternal and child health services, other health services and agricultural extension services offer important information channels. Industrial and labor union leaders can also help to spread information within their own organizations.

Indigenous communications systems.—Some of the Indian states have employed traditional minstrels and drama troupes to spread the message of family planning. In the United States, Boy Scouts have been used to help distribute information on the program. A special type of information network arose when Madras State in India offered a small financial reward to "canvassers" for each new vasectomy case they introduced. The reward in some cases was shared with intermediate informers, to produce an information system reaching as far as 400 miles away.

GENERATING SOCIAL SUPPORT

Obviously, public statements of national and local leaders have an important, general legitimizing function. Certain types of social legislation also may have a pervasive general effect. In addition, there are some specific organizational means available for fulfilling this function.

Political organizations.—Political parties are likely to be highly sensitive and effective in the matter of helping to legitimize new ideas. In Tunisia, the political support to the family planning program has appeared to be extremely useful. In Maharashtra State in India, the grass-roots organization of the Congress party is said to have given most valuable, behind-the-scenes support. The possible danger that a program might become a political issue would have to be weighed in any situation.

Religious hierarchies.—In many countries the religious organizational structure has powerful capacities for social endorsement. Obviously, the active enlistment of this structure (or at least its supportive neutrality) can have crucial importance.

Formal education structure.—The formal educational system has a powerful normative influence, and it reaches a large segment of the population about to move into the reproductive age. Too often, discussion of ways for educationists to participate in family planning programs has been diverted by Western preoccupations with sex education and social adjustment for adolescents. In high fertility areas the most valuable contribution may be some simple steps at the primary school level to establish an image of the small family as normal, proper, and advantageous. For example, reading materials should provide illustrations of happy, smaller families. In addition, geography and mathematics teaching can instill an appreciation of the balance between population and resources. More specific family planning information can be left to sources outside the educational system.

Community-level and group-level education.—Within smaller social units, a critical step in the adoption of a new practice is the achievement of a group consensus that the practice is proper for that particular group. Skilled community educators can help to catalyze the process of discussion which leads to consensus. They can also help to strengthen the quality of leadership for this purpose within the group. In many family planning programs, full-time community educational personnel are therefore being located at key positions in the organizational structure. In India these workers include the district family planning extension educator and the block family planning extension educator. Similar staff members are in position in Taiwan and other countries.

CONTROL FUNCTIONS

Top Leadership

Status and location.—The newness and the urgency of this type of program call for leadership having high status, visibility, and nearness to the seat of governmental power. Its complexity also calls for coordination of the activities of different governmental ministries and institutions. These considerations would suggest that the program director and his executive organization may best be located at ministerial level; or perhaps at the next lower level, responsible to an interministerial council.

In most countries, however, the executive leadership has been placed within the health ministry. This does have advantages: the legitimization provided by association with health and welfare activities, the direct access to medical resources, and the fact that the general network of health services may be one of the few governmental structures which reaches out into close contact with the general population. Disadvantages may be a lower status and priority and the resistance of some health officials to accepting leadership for the many diverse aspects, medical as well as non-medical, of a total family planning program.

As a general rule, the importance of giving the central program leadership an autonomous, interministerial status could be considered as directly proportional to the urgency of the program and inversely proportional to the stage of development of effective local health services in the nation. If local health services are intensively organized throughout the country, then they indeed can provide an effective vehicle for many aspects of the program. If not, then there will be much greater need to mobilize and build other organizational channels.

The situations in Ceylon and Pakistan may be contrasted. Though they share a similar tradition of health administration, Ceylon has been fortunate in achieving a much more concentrated network of health staff. In Ceylon, family planning services seem likely to progress well within the existing health framework. Pakistan, however, has had to look beyond this and to build special mechanisms to handle certain aspects of the program.

Man and mandate.—Obviously, the men selected for national and provincial leadership of such programs should be very forceful, imaginative, and effective administrators. Of equal importance, however, is the mandate they receive: they must have strong powers of administrative decision and financial action. Traditional governmental bureaucracies tend to withhold such powers and may subvert the effectiveness of even the strongest administrator. Indeed, it may be harder to find the mandate than the man.

However, unsophisticated observers may focus only on the more tangible, personal element in this equation, missing the fundamental administrative element. Conservative administrators within a governmental system may also welcome overemphasis on charisma and avoidance of the need for administrative innovation. Strength of one of the elements may to some extent strengthen the other. But the program needs the best of both.

Federal systems.—The functions of central leadership in a federal governmental system are quite different from those at state level, or from those in a non-federal system. The federal leader is not responsible for direct execution but for maximizing the conditions needed for effective program execution within the states. His office must be particularly organized to develop general policy aspects, to handle problems of financial support to state governments, to arrange for basic supplies and materials, to engage the participation of various relevant ministries, institutions, or other organizational units, and to provide technical and moral support to state administrators.

PERIPHERAL SUPERVISION

Full-time staff at every administrative level.—For a new and multi-faceted program of this nature, full-time personnel are required at each major level of development administration, down to the periphery. At one level there may be several specialists, on medical, educational, statistical, and supply aspects of the program. Although they may have direct operational responsibilities, this does not mean that they will do all the work. They must represent the total program at each level and elicit the maximum contribution to it from other official and non-official resources, help co-ordinate the various aspects of the program, and report on the progress of its implementation at that level.

A strong vertical line of technical supervision of the full-time family planning personnel, between administrative levels, is also essential. Even though such staff may be administratively attached to the general unit of the health department at each level, specialized technical supervision from above is required to help them solve field problems and grow professionally and to protect them from diversion of their energies to other programs.

Attachment to the general health structure.—Full-time family planning personnel are usually attached to the general health program structure, as in Taiwan, Korea, India, and other countries. From this association they derive administrative support, the benefit of identification with the health and welfare efforts, and important access to other health services staff. The extent of such advantages will depend much on the stage of development of the basic health structure. In some situations, a voluntary organization may provide a sufficiently extensive base for support of family planning staff. In India, where a rural health unit is not present, they may be attached to the community development organization. Pakistan will depend more on the basic local government structure.

Use of multipurpose field staff.—At the point of actual delivery of health services to the public, these are almost inevitably combined in a generalist type of worker such as the nurse-midwife or sanitarian. Presence of some such multipurpose field workers seems almost essential for the solid development of certain features of a total family planning program, as noted for example in the previous comments on IUD services. In countries where the health service infrastructure is well developed, the importance of the roles played by such workers may go unnoticed or may simply be taken for granted. But in countries where the basic structure is not yet widely established, striking differences can be observed between areas where such staff are or are not yet posted. It is fully justifiable for the family planning budget to be used to accelerate the fuller development of this infrastructure, as an investment toward an effective long-range program. Such direct financial support may indeed give greater leverage to insist that the peripheral staff should now give top priority to family planning services.

EVALUATION

Stimulus to better planning.—Not the least of the benefits of building a good program evaluation system is that it forces more precise thinking about the ultimate objectives, intermediate objectives, and performance objectives of the program, and how they are expected to tie together. It helps to clarify thinking about how various organizational mechanisms should serve the objectives and helps to identify inconsistencies, overlaps, and unreal expectations.

Three levels of evaluation.—Measuring the extent of achievement of program objectives involves at least three different types of measurement problems and the use of correspondingly different organizational bases. At the level of ultimate objectives, the task of measuring change in fertility trends will require the mobilization of the vital statistics registration system and of special demographic resources. Measuring the achievement of the intermediate levels of objectives, such as changes in knowledge and attitudes and use of contraceptive methods, may be approached through special social surveys and through simple data collected by service facilities (e.g., IUD insertions). Measuring the achievement of administrative performance objectives will involve information on staff deployment, utilization, and costs. These data can be obtained from the various types of organizational entities involved in the total program: clinical service facilities, information and educational agencies, contraceptive distribution systems, etc.

External vs. internal evaluations.—In the early stages of a program, external sources can be called on for general evaluations and recommendations. However, program evaluation should be viewed primarily as a "feedback" device for the administrator. As systems of observation and measurement are refined, they should become routine and integral parts of the program organization. External participation in evaluation activities can then fit into a well-defined framework, to provide occasional independent checks and additional stimulation as may be desired for specific aspects of the program.

SUPPORTING FUNCTIONS

TRAINING

Training centers.—Development of effective training courses for family planning field staff requires rather special administrative conditions. The training center faculty must work very closely with the field service organization in adjacent areas, to work out demonstrations of improved program practices. Curriculum content must be built on such "live" experience; and trainees must be able to see convincingly effective field programs. The faculty must also be encouraged to experiment freely with the use of teaching staff. In order to obtain the high degree of flexibility required for these purposes, use of some type of semiautonomous body as the agent for training services is very advantageous. In India, the Central Family Planning Institute has been established to help ensure such special conditions. In Korea, the government subsidizes the voluntary family planning association for this purpose.

Supervisors as trainers.—A common tendency is to consider staff "trained" after passing a short course. The most important training, ultimately, will be the experience which workers gain as they encounter problems in the field and solve them with the support and guidance of their supervisors. As a general principle, the more junior the worker and the more general his functions, the higher must be the ratio of supervisor to worker for effective learning and performance. A related principle is the "distal-peripheral" order of staffing in a new program. In the haste to launch massive programs, administrators may be pressed to fill the more easily recruited junior positions at the periphery, before the intermediate supervisory positions; this can produce chaos. The ideal would be for senior and intermediate staff to be in position and have ample time to become acquainted with the people and problems in their area before taking on the extra burden of orienting and supervising junior staff.

Basic professional courses.—The basic education of health personnel and other development workers must help them recognize that family planning responsibilities are an essential part of their professional roles. Adding effective family planning content to traditional curriculums is not easy, and certainly cannot be done by fiat alone. The family planning organization must include specialized training staff who can work directly with the faculties of basic courses for health personnel to develop the family planning content of such courses.

FINANCES

Special boards.—In order to increase fiscal flexibility, to preserve fiscal responsibility, and to help involve various official departments and private groups in the program, special paragovernmental boards, committees, or agencies may be created with powers to supervise the expenditure of family planning budget funds. This extremely useful device is found in many forms, from the boards set up in Pakistan at national, provincial, and local levels to guide the whole program to the specialized use of an agency in Taiwan to pay fees to doctors for IUD insertions.

Institutional grants and contractual services.—The wide spectrum of specialized services required by a family planning program, as well as the needs for flexibility, calls for liberal use of grants and contractual arrangements with specialized institutions and agencies.

Long-term financial support.—One of the problems arising from the "staff-rich" and long-term nature of the program is that it obviously may entail a heavy continuing financial obligation. Financial authorities may balk at approving the necessary magnitude of staffing needed to achieve a "critical mass," or may resist giving assurance for long-term support. Both can seriously blunt the efficiency of implementation. A recent evaluation of the India program indicated that the lack of long-term financial assurances was the most serious single factor inhibiting the growth of state family planning programs. Financial authorities need help in appreciating the relative annual costs of uncontrolled population growth versus the program costs. Useful also is the assurance that staff employed for family planning work can be applied, in due course, to building up the general health services.

Incentive schemes.—Special types of incentives can give valuable impetus to the program in the early stage. These should ideally be for countable, discrete units of accomplishment by service personnel. In the India and Taiwan experience, for example, small payments are made available to those who refer cases for IUD or sterilization, and for medical and auxiliary personnel providing such services. In India, also, a small payment is made to sterilization cases to compensate for time lost from work. Providing supplementary pay for full-time family planning personnel may also help greatly to increase the attraction of the field, but is no substitute for the incentives for specific job performance.

RESEARCH

Relationships to program.—Research concerned with reproductive biology, clinical contraception, population statistics, and the behavioral aspects of the population field can enrich the program in at least three ways: (1) fundamental new knowledge produced in the country can strengthen the program content; (2) new developments discovered elsewhere can be confirmed and further refined for local application; and (3) new problems which arise in the course of the program can be referred quickly to competent scientists for clarification. Thus, research facilities can be considered a basic part of the over-all family planning program organizational system.

Use of independent institutions.—Research activities are best developed in existing independent institutions, which can be financially assisted to augment their research strengths. Also, to fill certain gaps special research institutions can be established, as the Central Family Planning Institute and the Demographic Research Centers in India and the National Research Institute for Family Planning in Pakistan.

Co-ordination.—In a large family planning program, special provision must be made for a central co-ordinating mechanism that can (1) maintain contact with research facilities and inform them of questions considered most crucial to the program, (2) help to increase research productiveness by facilitating scientific interchange between institutions, and (3) help to administer financial aid to them. In India, these purposes have been partially served by scientific advisory groups in the fields of reproduction research, demographic research, and communications and action research. These services are now more specifically delegated to the Central Family Planning Institute.

SUMMARY

Beneath the superficial differences in family planning program structures is a basic framework of general family planning program functions. These may be conceived of as instrumental functions (provision of services and supplies, provision of information, and generating social support); control functions (top leadership, peripheral supervision, and evaluation); and supporting functions (training, financial support, and research).

The administrator concerned with over-all development of a family planning program system, in a given situation, must include in his purview all those organizational mechanisms which may serve potentially to carry out the functional needs of such a system. He must be ready to mobilize many different kinds of existing organizational structures, as well as to devise appropriate new structures for this purpose. This paper attempts to identify the types and characteristics of organizational means that may be used to fulfill basic family planning functions.

Although family planning programs now carry extreme urgency, it is obvious that every aspect of a program cannot be developed at once. But the important dimension of timing and priorities is beyond the scope of the present paper. Berelson and others have usefully discussed this aspect, and it still deserves more detailed study. Here we can simply note that program implementation obviously must be phased according to considerations of ideal strategy, along with sensitive consideration of the specific interests, capacities, and resources existing in a given situation.

The point of this paper, however, is that the administrator does now have some guidelines to what is involved ultimately in order to do the whole job and to do it well.

The analytic scheme presented above, and the observations hung thereon, are still at a crude level. With time, they can be refined. Let us get on with the job of developing the conceptual tools needed to organize our experiences and observations in this field, to make them additive, and to make them available to others for use and further testing. Perhaps the Bhagavad-Gita refers not only to karma but to family planning administrators, in saying, "They who understand the particular and not the general will stumble on, through many births."

25

PERSONNEL PROBLEMS IN FAMILY PLANNING PROGRAMS

S. C. HSU, M.D., M.P.H.
Chief, Rural Health Division
Sino-American Joint Commission on Rural Reconstruction
Taiwan, China

The problems of personnel in organizing and administering family planning programs vary with the stages of development of the countries concerned. They also vary with the nature of the programs, which may be either pilot projects sponsored by voluntary agencies or nationwide programs with governmental blessings. Based on the experience gained in Taiwan, this paper deals with the personnel problems generally encountered in developing countries where controlled population growth is a prerequisite for accelerated socioeconomic development and where financial resources for family planning are available.

Types of Personnel Needed

In the main, there are four kinds of personnel needed for such programs: (1) administrative personnel in charge of the family planning program at various political levels—central, provincial, county and city, and township; (2) professional and technical, including obstetrical and gynecological doctors, general practitioners, nurses, midwives, health educators, demographers, artists, and others; (3) subprofessional, including assistant family planning workers or prepregnancy health (PPH) workers; (4) non-professional, including a great variety of individuals whose potentiality and numerical strength to promote the family planning program may be great indeed. Persons who can be motivated and organized to assist the educational phase of family planning are primary school teachers, home economists and other extension workers of farmers' associations, community development workers, population registration clerks and village clerks of township offices, members of women's associations, village chiefs and neighborhood elders and their spouses, and other local leaders.

The functions of personnel engaged in the family planning program may be divided into administrative, medical, motivational, and supportive aspects.

Administrative personnel.—At the central level it is important to develop a nucleus of personnel whose functions are:

1. To establish policy guidelines adapted to various political conditions.
2. To draw up annual budgets and obtain financial support from governmental and non-governmental resources.
3. To formulate achievement goals—long-range and annual.
4. To evaluate the achievements and operation of the program.
5. To work out ways and means to reach the projected goal within a shorter period of time; to promote the effectiveness and efficiency of various types of workers; to co-ordinate family planning with and integrate it into the general health program; to make it possible for government at all levels to finance the program, and for workers in the government and voluntary organizations to participate actively in the family planning and health program; and to convince the medical profession of the effectiveness and safety of IUD contraception and to obtain their support for it.
6. To arrange with and assist voluntary agencies such as the family planning associations, the Maternal and Child Health Association, the Farmers' Association, and the Red Cross to undertake that part of the program which the government cannot do well or is not ready to handle, such as conducting training courses, providing contraceptive materials, publicity, and payment of doctors' fees.

At the provincial and county or city levels, administrative personnel organize and operate the family planning program in their respective jurisdictions according to the policy, goals, and plans formulated at the central level. Their duties also include supervising and evaluating the performance of subordinate units and workers; enlisting the support of competent government organizations and voluntary agencies in matters relating to finance, personnel, and morale; conducting various training courses; and recruiting workers upon request from planners at the central level.

At the local township level, wherever local self-government is highly developed, the township organizations can be the most important sources of financial support and working personnel. To promote the intensive village community-health development program, of which family planning is a phase, the health officer of every township health station should be the *ex officio* administrator to supervise the grassroots family planning workers and should allow his entire staff, particularly the nurses and midwives, to participate in the family planning education program.

Professional and technical personnel.—The main functions of professional and technical personnel in the family planning program are motivational and medical activities and the training and organization of personnel available at the township level.

The motivational objective is to educate the public on the desirability of family planning, to provide the necessary information about various contraceptive methods, and to motivate the eligibles to adopt them. Activities concerned with education and motivation include preparing and disseminating educational materials and information, holding group meetings, making home visits, and accompanying selected cases to the doctor's office for contraceptive treatment.

The medical objective is to let the trained medical doctors in both private and public clinics and hospitals handle the reversible, non-reversible, and oral contraceptive methods and to let the trained nursing-midwifery personnel handle the traditional types of contraception.

The aim in the organization and training of local personnel is to help the local governments organize and train the available personnel from relevant local organizations and make the intensive village health improvement and family planning program an integral part of township government's activities.

Sub-professional workers.—In places where auxiliary medical personnel are not available when a sizable family planning program is launched, family planning or PPH workers may be trained to motivate people, mainly eligible women, by means of group meetings and home visits.

Non-professional workers.—After proper organization and health training, non-professional workers are divided into teams to visit selected villages in order to organize and train small groups of village people in personal hygiene; in home sanitation, with emphasis on cleanliness, orderliness, beautification, pest control; and in family planning. All families in the villages take part in the work of home improvement and family planning through their own efforts and with their own resources.

PROBLEMS OF RECRUITMENT

Administrative personnel.—Probably the most important and also the most difficult recruitment problem is that of finding capable administrative personnel at all levels. More often than not, the personnel are already there and no room is left for selection. Therefore, competent administrators may have to be developed rather than recruited. To develop the potentialities of administrative personnel, reasonable remuneration, advance training, and a congenial working environment are essential. In addition to the keen competition by United Nations organizations and other agencies for competent personnel, there is the problem of keeping our own men content and willing to remain on their challenging jobs at home once they become experienced and attractive offers for their services come from abroad.

Professional and technical personnel.—Health organizations in rural areas in developing countries are constantly faced with the difficulty of getting and keeping qualified medical and health personnel. This is due to the scarcity of trained indigenous personnel in rural areas where life is monotonous, facilities are meager, and chances for satisfying personal needs are few. These conditions together with unattractive salaries and amenities tend to keep qualified individuals away from rural areas.

Owing to the uneven distribution of medical doctors, it is often difficult to obtain the services of competent persons to do contraceptive work in remote areas.

Sub-professional workers.—Owing to uneven development there may even be difficulty in recruiting indigenous sub-professional workers in some remote townships. Since available jobs are few and under-employment is increasing in the rural areas of many developing countries, local political pressure may be brought to bear on officers responsible for recruitment. In this connection, the experience in Taiwan of recruiting sub-professional workers may be of some interest. We have found that married women between the ages of 30 and 44 are preferable because they can motivate more women to accept IUD's than those of other age groups. Unmarried girls above 23 years old are comparatively more effective in pushing the family planning program than the younger age groups. The longer they stay on their jobs, the higher is their efficiency. For example, the average number of IUD cases recruited in April, 1965, by each PPH worker who had served less than two months was 13.7. It was 14.8 for those who had served from two to six months, 21.5 for those from six to twelve months, 18.6 for those from 12 to 24 months, and up to 28 for those with 24–36 months of service. These results show the value of the self-confidence and skill of experienced workers and point up the harmfulness to the program of a high rate of turnover in personnel. In Taiwan we make it a point to recruit local workers who have no housing problem and to offer them relatively attractive pay. Consequently, the annual resignation rate of PPH workers has been quite low.

Non-professional workers.—Initially, our most serious problem in Taiwan was the scarcity of organizers capable of persuading local governments and interested organizations to let their staff members participate in the intensive village health improvement and family planning programs. But successful demonstrations finally induced the local governments to include such programs among their responsibilities.

Problems of Training

Once the situation becomes favorable for its development, a family planning program usually expands so fast that it outgrows the existing facilities. To meet the urgent needs, the training of personnel should be short in duration and concentrate on enabling workers to perform a single duty and attain one common goal. However, the subject matter of training for each category of workers should vary with their functions.

Administrative personnel.—It is a good investment to give advanced training to a few medico-health personnel who have shown their potentiality and competence and to afford opportunities to leaders to visit other countries which have started vigorous socioeconomic development and family planning programs.

The responsible administrative personnel at the provincial level should be gathered together at the central level, and administrative personnel at the county-municipal level should be gathered together at the provincial level for orientation and discussion on matters concerning policy, mobilization and recruiting of personnel, budgeting, organization, and implementation of the family planning program. Sessions should last only a few days but should be held at least once a year at the central level and twice a year at the provincial level.

Professional and technical personnel.—On IUD contraception, one half-day of orientation and demonstration is found adequate for obstetricians and gynecologists in private practice, while at least three half-days of orientation and practice are needed for general practitioners so that each of them, under supervision, can perform about half a dozen insertions. Since the doctors must continue to supervise their own clinics, it is preferable to divide the training into half-day sessions conducted in the county-municipal health bureau or other conveniently located hospital. In places where there are transportation problems or training facilities are lacking, one-day training for obstetricians and gynecologists and three-day training for general practitioners in small groups at specially designated training centers are desirable. Work in non-reversible contraception and Papanicolaou examination requires longer training periods in accordance with the specific recommendations of experts.

Sub-professional workers.—The initial training for assistant family planning workers in Korea is four days at one of the four training centers and one week at the local health bureaus before they are sent to work at the township level. Later they are given three-week refresher courses at the training center.

The initial period of training for pre-pregnancy health workers in Taiwan and in Hong Kong is two weeks. The number of trainees in each class varies from 22 to 36. The contents of the training curriculum are as follows:

Knowledge about population: (1) The world population and population policies in other countries. (2) Modern family planning movements. (3) The population in Taiwan and common terms used in the study of population. (4) Family planning program—development, objective, and achievement.

Knowledge about medical aspects of the program: (1) Anatomy and physiology of the female reproductive organs. (2) Physiology of pregnancy. (3) Common illnesses of women. (4) Maternal and child health problems. (5) Induced abortion. (6) Sterility. (7) Nutritional problems of mothers and children.

Family planning methods and practices: (1) Historical review of the IUD, the Ota ring in particular. (2) New IUD study and movie entitled "The Margulies Coil." (3) Traditional methods (condom, diaphragm, jelly, foam tablet, safety period, basic body temperature, and others): four hours of presentation and four sessions of group practice. (4) Oral contraceptives. (5) Current status of fertility control. (6) Sterilization.

Health education: (1) Principles of working with people. (2) Family planning concept and discussions. (3) Intensive village health education movement. (4) Home visit techniques: three hours of demonstration and two days of field practice. (5) How to organize neighborhood meetings: two hours of demonstration, three evenings of field practice. (6) Presentation and demonstration of teaching materials—film strip, flip books, etc.; three hours of presentation and five sessions of group practice. (7) Guidelines for loop education. (8) Public speaking: four hours of practice.

Evaluation: (1) Effectiveness of various contraceptive methods. (2) How to increase the number of loop users. (3) Evaluation procedures for field workers. (4) Evaluation of training courses. (5) Evaluation of the trainees after training. (6) Working procedures and discussion. (7) General discussion with the local health authorities on functions and working relations. (8) Fertility survey—attitudes, knowledge, and practice.

Others: (1) Village health work among military dependents. (2) Regulations concerning government employees. (3) Health services and security problem. (4) The China Maternal and Child Health Association—general description of its functions, services, and work procedures. (5) Distribution of materials. (6) Salaries and per diem rates.

Non-professional workers.—At the initial stage, much effort is required to convince the heads of local organizations in townships selected for demonstration to take part in an intensive village improvement committee and to designate its members to form a working group. On an average the working group of a township consists of about thirty members. A nursing team of two to three persons is sent to help the township committee train the group members on how to mobilize and teach village people to undertake a campaign on personal hygiene, home sanitation, and family planning. The group members form teams; each member must be fully prepared for the task before starting village work. It will take two to three days to train the township working group. According to the size of the village, the time required for the training of village people, who are divided into groups of around ten families each for the purpose, and for actually carrying out home improvements through their own efforts and resources, will vary from two to four weeks.

The organization and training of township officials and the village people are simple, if approached in the right way. They can be counted on to carry on family planning as an integral part of the community development—village health improvement program when special resources for implementing the family planning program as a separate and independent undertaking are no longer needed or justified.

VALUE OF VARIOUS INCENTIVES FOR FIELD WORKERS

Incentives are especially important to family planning programs at the promotional stage. The important ones and their value are summarized as follows:

Subsidies to key personnel.—Subsidies ranging from US$10 to US$30 a month per person to one or two key personnel at the county-municipal level and from US$20 to US$50 per person per month to a few important persons at the provincial and central levels will certainly ensure their full co-operation and wholehearted support in the still sensitive field of family planning.

Reasonable salaries.—Salaries relatively higher than the prevailing scale will attract and keep the better workers.

Special favors.—Special favors, such as granting of extra vacations or leaves of absence with pay after completion of a difficult task or when ill, or simple entertainment by superiors to express their appreciation, will boost the morale of the workers and their confidence in their superiors.

Provision of uniforms, badges, raincoats.—The provision of attractive uniforms and badges will increase the workers' prestige and will be generally welcomed by them, while provision of raincoats, bicycles, and so on will increase their efficiency.

Furnished accommodations and household servant.—Provision of furnished accommodations at headquarters and employment of a servant to keep house for field workers are important measures to keep up the morale and efficiency of personnel.

Promotion and advanced study.—To promote competent field workers to be supervisors and offer them opportunities for advanced studies or a study tour abroad will improve the quality of their services and attract more qualified workers to join the program.

PROCEDURES FOR PROPER SUPERVISION

When the family planning program gets underway and develops rapidly, the key personnel may, unless someone keeps a close watch over them, become so enmeshed in the enormous task of recruiting, training, and assigning workers, preparing reports, undertaking surveys and researches, looking after visitors, and so forth as to overlook supervision altogether. The following are suggested procedures for proper supervision:

Designation of administrative personnel.—Chief supervisory personnel at central, provincial, county-municipal, and township levels should be assigned administrative functions and deal mainly with spot checking of workers at lower levels.

Appointment of supervisors at the county-municipal level.—In addition to the designation of the chief nurses of county and municipal health bureaus to serve as supervisors of field workers assigned to work in their areas, the central and provincial headquarters should send regional supervisors, preferably not less than one for every two counties and one for each municipality. That is to say, each regional supervisor will on the average look after fifteen PPH workers or assistant family planning workers instead of eighteen, as it is in Taiwan at present. The county health bureau supervisors have other functions besides family planning, but the regional supervisors are concerned only with the family planning program. The regional supervisors are expected to go out to live and work with field workers, particularly those whose abilities and performance are below par. The regional supervisors may be selected from among the field workers or be specially recruited.

Establishing targets.—Publication of monthly targets and actual accomplishments, particularly loop insertions for each area and each field worker, will serve as a guide for the regional supervisors to select their field workers in an effort to achieve better performance.

Preparation of supervisors.—It is found that a one- or two-day discussion session is adequate for county-municipal health bureau supervisors on general supervision problems, including checking of coupons from and forwarding payments to private practitioners. For proper preparation of regional supervisors a two-week workshop is needed to familiarize them with the contents and methods of supervising their field workers and preparing reports.

Expert supervision over private practitioners.—In addition to the general supervision rendered by county-municipal health bureaus, there is also need of expert supervision over the medical work of private practitioners. Unfortunately, this aspect is often neglected or inadequately carried out owing to the lack of highly trained obstetricians and gynecologists in government medico-health organizations.

CONCLUSION

In developing countries where the existing health facilities and available professional personnel are inadequate to cope with the sudden development of a nationwide family planning program, there is need and justification to employ and train sub-professional workers to carry the major load of motivational activities among the people and to restrict the performance of certain contraceptive treatments to recognized obstetrical and gynecological doctors. However, adequate provision should be made so that when the family planning program has passed the promotional stage and become a regular routine activity, it may be effortlessly integrated into the general health program as a normal function of local health organizations. According to the views of the obstetricians, gynecologists, and health authorities, IUD insertions may be gradually assigned to selected general practitioners, health bureau and health station doctors, and even trained nursing-midwifery personnel in places where doctors are not available.

26

INFORMATIONAL AND EDUCATIONAL PROGRAMS

PAUL HARTMAN
The Population Council Representative, Korea

In Korea at present, among the total population of approximately 28 million, it is estimated that there are some 3.6 million married couples in the 20–44 year age group. This is the target group we are trying to reach as soon as possible, because we are reasonably certain that some 1.6 million of these couples have had all the children they want and are looking for a contraceptive method that they can use successfully. In addition, we believe that many of the other 2 million couples want this information now in order to space their children.

So our job in the area of public information is to help the workers reach this group; and a sample survey last April indicated that we had approached about 84% of them. Furthermore, the survey showed that 64% of the eligibles knew a method and some 16% were using it. Among this practicing group, some 23% had selected the IUD as their method; and among this group 20% were in the 25–29 age group and are assumed to be using it for spacing purposes.

This appears to us to be a reasonable degree of progress in reaching the target group since initiation of the family planning program in 1962, particularly in view of the limitations of staff, facilities, and budget for planning and carrying out public information programs in family planning. The capabilities of the Ministry of Health and Social Affairs are basically limited to the workers in the program; a small planning, supervisory, and administrative staff at headquarters; and limited funds for the purchase of equipment, supplies, and the contract production of printed materials and audiovisual aids. In brief, to carry out public information activities on the scale required and to procure the additional program materials and aids necessary, the ministry or, more specifically, the maternal and child health and family planning section, depends upon the co-operation and assistance of other official agencies, voluntary organizations, and professional and business groups in Korea, and whatever other assistance it can secure from outside sources.

In Korea, the family planning program is a priority project of the government. All groups are co-operative in our informational efforts, particularly the Ministries of Public Information, Agriculture, Education, and Transportation. Among the voluntary organizations is the Planned Parenthood Federation of Korea (PPFK), which has been assigned all training responsibilities of physicians and workers by the ministry and, in addition, is most active in helping to plan and carry out the public information program.

And finally, as external assistance, the ministry has had direct technical, logistical, and supplementary budget support from the Population Council, as well as indirect guideline assistance from the research-and-action study projects the Council has sponsored in Korea aimed at the development and evaluation of new methods and materials which might prove helpful in reaching eligible couples and improving their ability to practice family planning successfully.

The Target Group

Fortunately, in Korea the attitude toward the use of contraceptives is permissive. In fact, results of a national survey taken in April, 1965, among some 3,000 couples under age 44 indicated that about 91% in the urban areas and about 87% in the rural areas approved the use of contraceptives. Furthermore, in the cities, about 6% had no opinion and even more (about 8%) in the country indicated they had an open mind on the subject. The majority of city couples indicated they would like to have two sons and one daughter, whereas the rural couples wanted two sons and perhaps two daughters before completing their family. However, the problem is that most people do not know how to do anything about it. In fact, this is still the major problem in Korea, since even after three and a half years of effort, 34% among the urban couples and almost 38% among the rural still do not know a contraceptive method. This points out the vital role of the family planning workers and the limitation of public information channels as a teaching medium.

On the positive side, however, once they are reached, most of the wives want to know a method and how to use it. They are not interested in learning about the reproductive process. Their motivation is further indicated by the fact that many of them will practice induced abortion if they do not know how to practice family planning effectively. In fact, sample surveys indicate that about 25% have been resorting to the practice of induced abortion in the cities and about 4% in the rural areas.

CHANNELS OF COMMUNICATION

The mass media.—In Korea, communication channels via the mass media are good, and we receive a lot of free time and space. There are two national broadcasting systems in Korea (one government-controlled) and four limited-range stations serving the two major cities of Seoul and Pusan. About 36% of all the homeowners either have a radio or a speaker connected to a centrally located receiver and amplifier. At present there are some 60,000 television receivers in the major cities of Seoul and Pusan whose viewers have a choice of two channels. The Ministry of Public Information licenses and regulates all mass communication channels: radio, television, newspapers, theaters, and public bulletin boards. Also, the ministry has staff and facilities to produce 16 mm. and 35 mm. films, and its personnel film, process, and distribute a newsreel each week to the nation's 538 theaterrs. It has, so far, made two family planning movies and one short trailer, which is often attached to newsreels. The high degree of co-operation we have received from the ministry and from commercial broadcasting companies is reflected in the results of the April survey—almost 46% of the eligibles stated that they had heard about the program over the radio.

The April survey also revealed the co-operation of publishers and the effectiveness of the 32 newspapers, with a nationwide daily circulation of some 1,350,000 copies, since about 25% said they had read about the program in the papers. Likewise, almost 16% said they had read about it in magazines, of which there are presently 130 (9 for women) published in Korea.

Public meetings.—Through the channel of public meetings, which includes the showing of movies and slides and distribution of family planning literature (of which we have produced over 3 million copies), much assistance is received from the local staff members of the agricultural extension offices located in each of the nation's 139 counties. The members of this group are well informed on the subject through close contact with our field workers and through lectures and materials they have received from PPFK headquarters and provincial representatives. In addition, the local staff members of the 104 Ministry of Public Information offices who hold numerous meetings, give talks over local radio amplifiers, show movies, and service bulletin boards in their areas are always willing to include material on family planning in their activities. Most helpful, too, have been the 28 audio-visual mobile units operated by the Ministry of Agriculture and the three operated by the preventive medicine section of the Ministry of Health. While the specific degree of impact this channel has made in spreading the word about family planning is difficult to measure, it is certainly involved in the 21% who stated they had heard about the program through local "lectures."

Special events.—Also difficult to measure is the effectiveness of the "special events" channel, which includes all the other channels but has been isolated in this paper for the purpose of illustrating the importance of establishing a specific period during the year for highlighting or calling the public's attention *en masse* to the problem of population control and what is being and should be done about it. This public enlightenment period in Korea is the month of May, which coincides with both "Mother's Day" and "Children's Day." In Korea last May, for example, a nationwide publicity campaign was carried out, a commemorative postage stamp issued, the "Family Planning Song" heard frequently over the radio, huge street "arches" and "towers" constructed in the major cities, posters distributed, exhibits placed in store windows, citations awarded at municipal auditoriums, windshield stickers placed on public conveyances, and hand fans, counter cards, slogan banners, and leaflets distributed.

The workers.—All family planning field workers "wear two hats," as teachers and public information officers, since specific personnel to carry out the latter task as a full-time job are not employed in the Korean national program. As a result, the workers need adequate practical training in this area, if they are to carry it out with any degree of self-confidence and get any results. For example, if the worker is expected to seek the co-operation of local news agencies, radio station officials, voluntary, business, professional, and fraternal groups and to provide them with news items and reference materials and to offer to serve as a guest speaker, she must know what to prepare, how to prepare it, and be adequately equipped and supplied. Also, and most important, she must have practice in *doing* it in a simulated situation among a friendly group. In brief, students learn by doing, learn best from each other, and use their knowledge most effectively if they are comfortable and confident of their ability.

This same type of practical training, using the equipment and supplies provided each worker (home visiting flip chart, small group meeting flannel board with illustrations, and demonstration pelvic model showing a loop in place and vasectomy "operation"), is also given to help them when they don their "teaching hats." The effectiveness of this training and their ability to secure local co-operation are shown by the 51% of the eligibles who stated they had heard about the program from the workers and the 35% who had heard about it from their village chiefs.

Word-of-mouth.—Among the channels of communication in Korea found most effective in spreading the word about family planning are, first, the eligibles themselves. In the survey last April, over 64% stated they had heard about the program from a neighbor or friend and about 34% from a relative. Even more important from the standpoint of saving the workers' time, trouble, and expense in reaching eligibles is the accumulating evidence resulting from an action-research project presently being carried out in one area of the city of Seoul. This project is aimed at determining the specific effectiveness of the influence of mass media, letter campaigns, home visits, and group meetings in stimulating eligibles to visit a family planning center for further information or services. For example, in this study, which includes some 45,000 eligible women, 45% of the total who have visited one of the four family planning centers in the area stated they had been influenced to do so by a neighbor, friend, or relative. Moreover, results of this survey clearly indicate that the use of paid "commercials" over mass media channels alone can stimulate motivated couples to action, as 12% of the center visitors stated they had come as a result of an invitation heard over the radio, 5% through a newspaper advertisement, and 1% by television.

IMPORTANCE OF SERVICE

So, in our analysis of the most effective family planning communication channels, we have concluded that the best promoters of the program in Korea are the eligibles and participants themselves. Moreover, the future of the program no doubt will depend on how successful we are in making certain that their reaction to the service is positive—that is, that contact with the service was satisfactory. In this respect, it is unfortunate that the IUD, the most acceptable and effective method we have to offer, is also capable of producing disappointed or dissatisfied participants. For example, even under the most desirable conditions we know, there will be a certain number of eager applicants with contraindications and many who will experience difficulties following insertion. All such cases are potential sources for disseminating information harmful to the steady growth of the program if they are not handled carefully, offered an acceptable substitute, and properly treated. So in shifting family planning to the doctor's office, we have shifted the responsibility for success directly to the doctors and indirectly to the personnel charged with helping them render a quality service. Never before have I been so aware of the significance of the "good doctor-patient relationship" or realized the full meaning and importance of the follow-up. In the most practical sense, service is our most important product.

"Ask about the loop" is what we have been saying through every available channel of communication since this device was introduced a year ago. Our aim is to make the loop a respected household word and its shape familiar to married couples through exhibiting the real article at every opportunity and by imprinting its image on about everything we distribute to our target group. The terms "simple," "reliable," "effective," and "economical" will, we hope, become synonymous with its shape as they have become its ever present public companions. In brief, the loop is the focal point of all of our promotional activities. Wherever possible, this copy is supported by illustrations intended to be interesting and stimulating. The message is always *positive* in approach: "Practice Family Planning"; *personalized:* "For Better Education (opportunity, health, improved living standards, etc.) for Your Children (or family)"; *directive:* "Visit Your Doctor (health center or township worker)"; and *specific:* "Ask about the Loop, the new modern way of practicing family planning that's so simple. . . ." The April survey indicated that less than a year after its introduction as a method, almost 71% of the eligibles knew about it; so the message is getting through to people.

However, getting the message to the target group in as many forms and as often as possible is a problem wherever staff, facilities, and funds are limited and success is primarily dependent on the co-operation of other agencies and groups. Even under permissive circumstances in Korea, considerable effort is required to bring our information to the eligibles via the co-operation route. Meetings are held frequently with key agencies and groups to keep them informed, provide them with the latest data, exchange ideas, make suggestions, and so on. Reference materials are distributed to all newspaper and magazine publishers and radio and television directors, and news conferences are held regularly to report latest developments and progress. In addition, lectures are given and the "take-home" materials provided at national and provincial in-service training courses for government officials and at the various military reserve officers training centers. Furthermore, those directly concerned with the program do all they can to "spread the word" by serving as guest speakers, arranging for and giving radio and television programs, and being interviewed over such media. Also, those of us behind the scenes are busy preparing posters, leaflets, exhibits, and other materials to support the total effort, to distribute through our workers in health centers and township offices, and to display on bulletin boards throughout the nation.

PROGRAM LEADERSHIP AND GUIDANCE

Development of the public information program in Korea and all materials to support its various activities are under the leadership and guidance of an information and education committee, composed of representatives from the Ministry of Health and Social Affairs and the Planned Parenthood Federation. To assist this committee, technical advisers from all professions serve regularly as consultants. Actual preparation of materials, production, distribution, and, in many instances, utilization is carried out by the professional and administrative staff members of the ministry and the PPFK, with technical and supplementary budget support from the Population Council. Many of our ideas for new materials and practically all the evaluation of those produced come straight from our field workers. From their comments plus those of local officials and the data collected from surveys it seems clear that carrying out public information activities has helped to expedite nationwide introduction of the service, to stimulate motivated eligibles to visit family planning centers on ther own, to initiate and generate word-of-mouth communication about the service, to prepare eligibles and thus make the field workers' job more efficient, and, finally, to maintain public interest and support of the program.

27

FAMILY PLANNING AND THE
SCHOOL CURRICULUM

SLOAN R. WAYLAND
Teachers College, Columbia University

The great faith which people in developing countries have in formal education is well known. For the individual, the education system is seen as a means of social mobility; and for the nation, education is looked to as the means of developing common communication skills, transmitting basic cultural values and furthering the specialized skills which the nation needs for its social and economic development. Is there a place for family planning in such an education system?

In certain aspects of the school curriculum (such as mathematics) the content is essentially international, with such variations as may be deemed necessary for the teaching-learning process. In other aspects, the same course subjects may appear in different countries, but the detailed content is local in character, such as reading and writing in the local language. In still other areas, the content may be similar in many ways, but special attention or emphasis may be given to the local aspects of the general content. Examples of the latter may be seen in courses in geography and history. In some instances, content which is essentially local in character is a part of the curriculum, and in this category may come those programs designed to develop attitudes and understandings appropriate for the achievement of public policy in such countries. This may be as general as the country's national plan, or as specific as the promotion of a national savings scheme.

Within this context of both universal and local goals, education is organized along lines which have remarkable similarity in country after country. Education systems are probably the most universal formal human institution that man has created. Children, beginning at the age of 6 or 7, are assembled daily at a local site under the supervision of an adult who has been through the system himself and has received some amount of specialized training. The teachers, utilizing an officially approved program of study embodied in a textbook, work with the students over the years until the students either drop out or are excluded from the system because they have not attained a minimum level of performance on an essentially standardized testing scale. Various forms of formal and informal control are established, including control of the training and placement of teachers, approval of course syllabi and textbooks, an inspectoral system, and standardized examinations. Some of the variations which appear in detail from country to country represent alternative means of achieving similar ends, or are variations forced by local circumstances which will be modified as soon as these circumstances no longer obtain.

One other aspect of the role of formal education needs to be examined. This aspect may be posed as a question: To what extent, or under what circumstances, may an education system serve as a means of social change? As a public institution, working largely with dependent members of the society and staffed by persons under public supervision, can the education system be expected to work deliberately for changing the institutions of the society? It is evident that education for an individual does change his life chances. Certain latent consequences have been frequently observed, such as the movement to the city of the more educated and the intentional control of size of family by those with more education. Changes in the levels of skills within a population as products of an education system provide a basis for new levels of economic activity.

Social science research to date has not provided us with a sharp picture of the role of the education system in social change. The following facts seem to be fairly well established.

1. Education systems are most effective in transmitting information and developing specific skills.

2. Teaching of attitudes which are in harmony with the general community values is easier than teaching those which represent changes from family and community values.

3. The transmission of information and the development of skills involve attitude formation as a latent consequence, but some changes may be achieved when deliberately planned.

With this general analysis as a background, let us now turn to the specific area of family planning. In the section below, attention will be given to the following aspects of the problem.

1. What are feasible goals for the education system which will support in some measure the objectives of family planning?

2. What is the present status of curriculum in countries with explicit family planning policies?

3. What courses of action seem to be the most promising?

FEASIBLE GOALS FOR EDUCATION SYSTEMS

The current characteristics of education systems constitute a framework within which realistic goals have to be formulated. One of the major features serving as a limitation on the goals is the pattern of school enrollment and student survival. Several specific points may be noted here: (1) School systems in developing countries are reaching only a limited proportion of the total school-age population, and the high drop-out rate is particularly marked in those segments of the population where the birth rate is the highest. (2) Typically, the enrollment in such settings tends to be higher for males than females. (3) The preparation of teachers and the availability of instructional materials are likely to be at the lowest level in schools for those segments of the population where the birth rate is the highest.

Another factor which has to be taken into account is the level of maturity of the population being served. The specific actions involved in family planning are, of course, faced by individuals past puberty and in effect after the student has left the education system. In certain areas of the school curriculum, opportunities for action, even by the relatively young, are present. For example, many areas of health or agriculture or basic technical skills may be taught in elementary schools with opportunities for action in everyday life. Although there is a gap in many aspects of the school curriculum between the time when the teaching occurs and action is involved, the field of family planning is, by its nature, one in which any learning that takes place is in anticipation of future rules. This is true in most developing countries—even for the secondary and university students—since they typically do not enter into marriage until after they have gone as high as they can in the education system. In addition, social controls exercised on young people are such that free sex play is usually much more limited than in many Western countries.

One additional feature of the school system needs to be underlined. The curriculum of the schools suffers almost invariably from an effort to include more than time and energy will allow. To introduce a new substantive area forces some hard choices as to what aspects of the current curriculum will be modified in order to include the new. Another consequence is that the sense of urgency and priority which leads to the inclusion of the new becomes diluted when the new finds its place in the middle of an already overcrowded program.

The prevailing image of the appropriate content of an education system also has to be taken into account. This problem may be highlighted by polarizing the alternatives. In the first instance, and by far the prevailing pattern, the education system is seen as an arrangement for transmitting systematic bodies of knowledge and developing basic academic skills. Schools select those who demonstrate competence in the acquisition of the knowledge and skills. The personal needs and life circumstances of the individual students are, in a sense, irrelevant, and the current problems of the society are not seen as a basis for the development of the details of a curriculum.

The alternative view is a strategy which holds that education is a process which can be of value to students as persons as well as to society. By building the content of the curriculum around the immediate experiences of life, the motivation of students to learn is increased, and the content of that learning has relevance for personal and social problems at each age level. It is the significance of the problem which establishes its eligibility for inclusion rather than the logic of an historical academic discipline.

Although no curriculum is a pure type of either of these alternatives, education systems do differ in their traditions in the degree to which they are more like one or the other. In school systems in which the first of these two orientations is dominant, family planning content of any type will need to be put in its most appropriate place within the disciplines which are the basic elements in the curriculum. In the other type of system, the population problem may be treated explicitly in its own right, or as a part of some other problem with which it is integrally related.

A final problem may be noted which acts to limit the goals which will be viewed as feasible. The educational structure and content of the systems in developing countries have as their models their counterparts in the more developed societies. None of these societies has adopted family planning as an explicit public policy, and the school systems in these countries have not developed patterns which might serve as models for the developing societies. Experience in family life education, in sex education, and in population studies in Europe and the United States may be of some value, but these programs do not provide a body of knowledge which has the same degree of relevance as many other aspects of the education system. The absence of such an experience is enough for some educators in the developing societies to raise a question as to the legitimacy of such an effort.

Given these characteristics of education systems, as well as others not noted, what may be considered feasible goals for a school system? In the light of the comments made above, it is clear that these goals will have to be worked out in each country by collaborative effort between the family planning leaders and leading educators.

Several general types of goals may be expected. In the first place, it should be emphasized as strongly as possible that teaching *about* the technical or clinical means of birth control is not necessarily a part of the task of the education system. For understandable reasons, the major focus of attention of many in the family planning field has been on the means of control, and the assumption is frequently made that the content of a school program should have the same focus. This is an erroneous assumption. Many important contributions of a fundamental nature may be made without specific attention to the means for effecting family planning. This question will be re-examined after looking at the range of possible objectives.

The following list of possible contributions of the formal education system is based on the assumption that the population problem is a long-range one and that basic understandings and attitudes by the new generation are of basic importance. Furthermore, it is assumed that the nature of the problem and the consequences of actions taken to meet it are such that a narrow clinical-medical approach is not enough.

POSSIBLE GOALS OF AN EDUCATION SYSTEM

This list is intended to be suggestive and not comprehensive. Furthermore, no effort has been made to differentiate between the goals for different levels of students or for different subgroups such as boys or girls.

1. For the individual's own personal behavior patterns and attitudes
   a) Acceptance of the small family as a proper and desirable norm
   b) Understanding that uncontrolled reproduction is not necessary to ensure a desirable family size
   c) Understanding that the size of family can be controlled by deliberate planning
   d) Acceptance of marriage at a mature age as a desirable pattern
   e) Appreciation of the advantages of planning, including health and economic gains from spacing and limitation in total number of children, and of the health, education, and other opportunities for children that may be more adequately provided for in the small family
   f) Knowledge about the process by which human life begins
   g) Appreciation of an acceptance of community resources, such as family planning clinics, as legitimate agencies for use by married couples

2. For the individual's role as citizen and community member
    a) Understanding of the dynamics of population growth and of the current and projected characteristics of the population of his own country and of other regions
    b) Knowledge of the policy of his country and of others, and appreciation of the factors which have led to it
    c) Recognition that reduction in the rate of population growth is possible if the established agencies in the community are given support by community leaders and responsible citizens
    d) Understanding of the ways in which uncontrolled growth makes difficult the achievement of the economic, education, and health aspirations of the nation
    e) Understanding of the importance of accurate and complete vital statistics for planning in the nation
    f) Appreciation of the possible courses of action open to an individual in the community who understands the social significance of family planning

To this list may be added specific information about means of control where the cultural setting makes such an approach acceptable.

Present Status of Curriculum Related to Family Planning

During the period from March to August, 1965, educators in some ten countries were interviewed, and the curriculums of those countries examined. These countries include five in which family planning on an officially sponsored basis is underway in some degree and five in which there is no official program. Of course, the officially sponsored programs are relatively recent developments.

In an examination of the current syllabi, the basically international character of curriculum structure noted earlier became evident. It is clear that the public actions which have been taken in instituting public family planning programs have not come about as a consequence of an effective education program in the schools. There is essentially no difference in the attention given to population in countries with or without family planning programs at this date.

In most countries, including the United States, biology courses skirt the subject of the process of human reproduction. The "new biology" does include this area specifically, but most countries have not made serious revisions in this area. Syllabi for courses in personal hygiene sometimes include references to human reproduction, but this area is very frequently skipped by instructors who do not feel comfortable in dealing with it.

On the other hand, geography courses usually include some attention to such topics as size, distribution, and growth of population. The depth here is usually limited, and the significance of the growth of population is not emphasized. In courses dealing with recent history or national development, certain basic demographic materials are included, but, again, they are treated superficially.

In other substantive areas where support to family planning objectives might be developed, such as in home economics or school health programs, the potential is not realized.

From the interviews held with educators in the countries with public family planning programs, it is clear that educators are concerned about the population problem in their own countries and are ready to give serious thought to the appropriate action within the education system. In the recently established program in Turkey, the role of the Ministry of Education is specifically recognized in the implementing code.

In summary, the curriculums of schools have not yet given the attention to population problems and family planning which the situation warrants. The structure of the curriculum in most countries is such that additional attention can be given without providing special courses. Educators seem to be becoming aware of the potential contribution which the education system can make.

POTENTIAL COURSES OF ACTION

The modification of the content of the school curriculum in any society is a complicated process which can, in the most favorable of circumstances, become fully effected only after a substantial period of time. The proposed changes in the content have to be reviewed by a number of interested parties, and differences worked out. Competition for scarce time in the school year is such that a change in one phase of the curriculum cannot be made without disturbing established patterns. After approval of changes has been made, special attention must be given to preparing teachers to handle the new materials: this means revisions in the curriculums of teacher-training programs for the pre-service teacher. For the main body of teachers in the field, in-service education may be necessary, or at least provision of special materials which will aid them in handling the changes. Appropriate changes in textbooks for students and teachers must also be made. Since the external examination structure is a very important element in the operation of the education system—particularly at the secondary level—attention to this area is also important. Lack of effective implementation at any one of these points may prevent the innovation from becoming an institutionalized part of the curriculum.

The details of the process of curriculum innovation, of course, vary from country to country. In a country such as India where the field of education is a state subject, the central government is limited in what it can do, and the process noted above may need to be carried out in each of the several states. In view of all these factors, it seems desirable that a professional educator who is thoroughly familiar with the process of curriculum change become a staff member of family planning agencies.

Since curriculum change is a complicated process, there is a great advantage to be gained if desired changes relevant to family planning objectives can be included in general programs of curriculum revision. In many of the countries visited, special groups are at work on various aspects of the curriculum. One of the functions of the educator referred to above would be to keep in touch with such developments and try to gain acceptance of appropriate materials.

The second course of action which is believed to be of high priority is the determination in each country of the objectives which the education system may be expected to meet in the family planning area. The special traditions of each education system, and the cultural values of the society in which the education system operates, constitute a framework within which feasible objectives may be set. Some of the special factors which may condition these objectives were noted earlier in this paper. Direct discussion between family planning personnel and educators will be fruitful in setting these objectives and will also set up a pattern of communication which may continue through other phases of the program. If the first suggestion has been followed, namely, the appointment of an educator to the staff of family planning agencies, the specification of educational objectives may be easier.

The third major suggestion is that priority be given to the teacher-training institutions, and particularly the institutions training elementary school teachers. The control of elementary teacher-training institutions is typically in the Ministry of Education and results may be easier to obtain than in the universities where secondary teachers are usually trained. In addition, the elementary school teacher may be an important source of influence in the rural community, above and beyond his work in the school.

Special programs and special materials aimed at the teacher-in-training, at both the elementary and secondary levels, may be of great importance, regardless of the formal changes in the curriculum. Short courses or conferences of teachers held at strategic points in the country is another means of reaching teachers who are already in the field.

The fourth suggestion is concerned with sections of the curriculum where relevant content may be most easily added, or existing content modified. These subjects are biology, geography, recent national history, and home economics.

General social studies of the type which may be found in most schools in the United States are seldom provided in other countries. The courses in geography and those history courses dealing with the recent past tend to be courses which are taken by all students in the early secondary level, and, in some instances, by all at the latter part of the secondary level. These courses provide a framework in which population problems in their world, as well as local, dimensions may be considered. In countries in which a national policy has been established, the factors which led to this decision may be examined here. In other countries, including those in which an official family planning program is not likely to be established, the manner in which rapid growth of population is affecting various aspects of life may be considered here. In such situations, the basis of the approach is that, regardless of whether family planning is practiced or not, population growth and its consequences ought to be understood by all citizens in the society. What they choose to do about it will then be done in the light of an understanding of the problem.

There is no body of evidence to prove that an understanding of the process of reproduction will change attitudes toward family planning. However, as noted above, this is too important an area of human knowledge to be left outside the curriculum. In many countries, systematic biology is a part of the science and mathematics track in the secondary schools, and thus reaches only a portion of the students. It may be desirable to explore possibilities of inclusion of this area in other related courses which do reach a wider range of students.

The field of home economics seems to be potentially an important area, particularly in view of the significance of the IUD. Home economics is a new field in many countries and is in the process of major reformulation in many other countries. The content of home economics as it is being currently developed gives considerable attention to family life in its social aspects. Child-rearing, health of the mother and of children, and other aspects are considered. Within the content of this program, the processes of reproduction and the problems of family living which result from lack of spacing of children and from large families may be readily included. Attention may well be given to the curriculums of the training schools for home economists before curriculum modifications are planned for the secondary and lower levels.

CONCLUSION

Although education systems have not been leaders in the process of creating public understanding about population dynamics, there is good evidence to indicate that many new steps will be taken in the next few years. Since this is a new field and no well-established models are available, the experience of one country will be of special interest to educators in other countries. Up to this time, the family planning personnel, operating out of ministries of health, have had limited contacts with ministries of education. In view of potential contributions which education systems can make over the long period of time during which nations will be facing population problems, active collaboration is needed. With over 40% of the population in many developing countries under the age of 15, an effective school program reaching whatever portion of the group that goes to school for any extended period should be viewed as an important complement to those activities focused on the childbearing population.

28

BUDGET AND TIMETABLE

S. M. KEENY
Resident Representative for East Asia
The Population Council

BUDGET

The broad estimate.—To begin with, the family planning sections of the so-called budgets of five-year plans should not be taken literally. Even their makers did not expect that the money would be spent evenly over the period; it takes time to "tool up" for any big operation. What is important is that these big plans commit the government, beginning with the planning board, to a wholly new level of activity, put Finance on notice that the money may be required, and start the long process of bringing the idea out of the clouds and down to earth.

Then the annual budget.—To a smaller extent, the problem of lack of precision persists even in the annual budgets. In a world governed by reason, annual budgets should be exercises in foresight by experts. But the rule of reason is not yet universal, especially in governmental procedures. Moreover, in the first years, there is little experience to be used as a guide. Also, however compelling the case for family planning, its budgets must run all the usual gantlets. Even if the top directive is firm, there will be delays, mostly routine but a few intentional—and all costly to the program. The main thing in the early budgets is to get enough money so that there will be no shortage even if the sanctions come through as requested and faster than expected.

They come in all sizes.—How big is a family planning budget? That of course depends largely on the population but also on the elaborateness of the plan. Four samples are given in Table 1 (all sums in this paper are given in United States dollars unless otherwise specified). The figures for India and Pakistan are estimates for the future. The actual figures may be lower, especially if there are delays in getting the

363

plan underway. The figures for Korea and Taiwan are approximate actuals for 1965. Even the higher figures are modest by Western standards. So much can be accomplished for so little only because salaries are so low.

The per capita ratio between Pakistan, the highest, and Taiwan, the lowest, is almost 5:1. Taiwan, however, gets a relatively higher amount of foreign aid for research and program support; also the Taiwan money will probably not be enough to do the job when more women have to be recruited for spacing children. But, after these adjustments, the ratio will still be at least 3:1.

What is the explanation? It does not lie in wide differences in salaries. The higher officials in Pakistan are better paid than in Taiwan, but they are relatively few. The bulk of the staff—the field workers

TABLE 1

FAMILY PLANNING BUDGETS

(Per Year)

Country	Total Cost	Per Capita
India	$40 million[a]	0.083
Pakistan	12 million[a]	0.12
Korea	1 million	0.033
Taiwan	0.3 million	0.025

[a] Average for the proposed next five-year plans.

who meet the people—in all the countries work for from $20 to $25 a month.

The main differences are: (1) India and Pakistan have a far higher percentage of illiteracy and have assumed that much more education on family planning is necessary than is provided in Korea and Taiwan. This is probably true in general; it has not been demonstrated that it is necessary for the loop program. (2) In India and Pakistan there are a variety of incentive payments that are not found in Korea and Taiwan. (3) All of the countries except Taiwan pay for all contraceptives distributed. In Korea, this is 22.6% of the whole national family planning budget. (4) All the four countries except Taiwan pay all costs of inserting loops. In Taiwan, all except the indigent (limited to 10%) pay half. This means a saving of 30% of the budget. Thus, the country with the highest per capita income—at least double that of the other three—can operate the program at the lowest cost.

What is the money spent for?—In Korea, 33.8% of the national budget goes for operating expenses (including only half the salaries of field workers, the other half coming from local governments); 32.8%, for the cost and insertion of intra-uterine devices; 22.6% for traditional contraceptives; 5.3% for sterilization; and 5.5% for education, evaluation, and other expenses.

How are budgets built?—If there is a five-year plan and a government policy, as in India or Pakistan, the usual method is to allow one worker for so many population (usually one per 10,000–30,000) and then build the budget on the time-hallowed pattern, with all costs on the usual scale, sometimes regardless of whether the resulting machine can do the work or not. Taiwan allows one worker for about 30,000 population; Korea, one for each 15,000.

In the relatively small demonstration countries of Korea and Taiwan, the procedure has been relatively simple. It was assumed that the major method was to be the loop, and the budget was built around this idea. The target was to reduce the natural increase per year roughly from 3% to 2%, mostly by actions taken in the first five years of the action program. In Taiwan, this came to 600,000 loops in five years for a population of 12 million. This was 5% of the total population but more than one-third of all the married women between 20 and 39. In Korea the target of 1 million loops was set lower (3.3% of the population) because of the relative popularity of vasectomy; but it is being found that, as loops become acceptable, the percentage of vasectomies declines.

Don't forget the objective.—The main purpose, of course, is to reduce the birth rate. It was assumed that five loops inserted, of which three at least would remain in until the end of the five-year period, would prevent one birth a year. In Taiwan, with about 420,000 births a year, the effect by 1969 would be a reduction of 120,000 births annually. The other 20,000 would have to come from the use of traditional methods.

A loop for $2.50.—The Taiwan budget came to only NT$60 million ($1.5 million) for the five years, or the equivalent of $300,000 a year. This works out at the low figure of $2.50 per loop inserted. (The Taiwanese woman pays 75 cents herself in addition.) Even at the most conservative estimate of how long the loops will remain in, the cost per baby prevented is under $5.00. (The cost for feeding a child for fifteen years at 10 cents a day is $547.50; its education for six years in Taiwan costs the government about $135.)

Some points to watch.—(1) The budget is often too inflexible, so that it is hard to make changes within the year as necessary. (2) Too little money is allowed for training doctors and field workers. (3) The amount for travel and per diem, especially for supervisors, is always too small. (This job cannot be done from a desk.) (4) Reporting and analysis are much too slow.

In Taiwan, it is known before the end of February what happened in January, down to the achievement of the last worker in the field. This cannot be done on big programs; but speed is of the essence.

How to get the money.—This was rather a special problem in Taiwan. Since the island has no official policy on family planning, the money could not come from the regular annual budget. Fortunately, however, there was available accumulated interest from United States counterpart funds. The problem was to convince the Economic Planning Board that family planning had a bearing on the economic future of the island. A projection of the cost of educating the rapidly increasing number of children, including the additional three years of compulsory schooling planned, provided the clinching argument. The money for five years was approved.

In Korea there was a strong national policy; but there was also little money in the Treasury. Here the usual battle of the budget had to be fought. At one stage a proposed horizontal cut would have left the program with 2,000 workers in the field and no money for nearly half the insertions in the plan. Reason (and pressure) prevailed.

In summary, with the knowledge we now have, it seems possible to reduce the annual increase of population by one-third within ten years at a cost less than that of a national campaign against malaria.

TIMETABLE

First, get the money.—The timetable for the long process of budget review must be determined and followed precisely. Those who come later or are careless in their follow-up will eat crumbs. Also, at each stage of budget scrutiny, it is imperative to have an influential spokesman who is both informed and convincing.

In India and Pakistan the problem now is less how to get the necessary funds approved than to get the funds actually released. The administrative wheels grind slowly, especially when new people have to be hired, new posts created, new buildings built, and foreign exchange released. Taiwan and Korea are mostly spared these horrors.

Keep it simple.—If the loop is used as the main method of family planning, the organization can and should be simple. Since the best advertisement for the program is the satisfied wearer, the object should be to get as many loops as possible inserted satisfactorily and quickly in women in the maximum number of communities. Essentially, all that is needed is a willing woman, a doctor trained and equipped, and a field worker to bring the two together. Other aspects of an over-all campaign may take more time, but the loop program should not wait for them.

A target for everybody.—If five-year plans are to be achieved, there must be a target for each year. Against the goal of 1 million loops, Korea inserted about 110,000 in 1964, with the action program starting in the second quarter. The target for 1965 is 200,000, with the program running ahead of schedule. The peak will be 300,000 in 1966. Thereafter the number may decline a bit as the percentage of loops for spacing rises.

These targets and timetables must be in the minds not only of the leaders but also of every worker, who needs also to know what her share of the job is. Exceeding the target month after month builds confidence as nothing else can.

Needed—a flow chart.—The heart of the matter in working out a timetable is to start first on the things that will take longest or are the first in a series of steps. Not all the items in a schedule need be started at the same time. But the central staff must be strong enough to make a number of moves at the same time. A common fault is to get so involved with one item as to forget half a dozen others of equal or greater importance and urgency.

A year to get a car.—An example of the first step is transport. In Taiwan and Korea this problem has been simplified. There is no special transport for family planning workers except for a few top supervisors. But in India and Pakistan several thousand vehicles will be required. Even if they are made in the country, as in India, one must get in the queue early. If they must be imported, as in Pakistan, one must get the foreign exchange sanctioned and an import license—and must then wait another six months for the vehicles. One year from the decision to receipt of the vehicle is the least one should plan on. How many to order will depend on how many full-time doctors will be available. If they must be women, it is even harder to estimate the number. It is better, however, to have too many vehicles than too few: in a country starving for transport any surplus can usually be transferred to another project. The absence of transport, moreover, need not hold up a vigorous start in a loop program. Even in India, one-third of the population is in cities, towns, and rural areas close to health centers and can be reached by transport already available.

Training comes early.—High on the list is the selection and preparation of the top training staff, of both doctors and field workers. The former should be specialists, preferably selected from those who have participated in testing the loop as a method. They should be thoroughly familiar with the side effects that are to be expected and should be skilled in advising how to meet the situation without removing the loop. Above all, they should be competent, patient teachers, able to put themselves in the position of the general practitioners who will be most of their pupils.

The trainers of field workers should be selected from experienced teachers or supervisors who know the possibilities and limitations of the persons they are going to train. They need to know how to select the essentials for a course that may be only two or three weeks long.

All of these top staff members should be willing and able to travel—and given enough money to do so. It is much cheaper to train the workers in places close to their work than to bring them all to where the teachers happen to be living.

Everything ready on time.—The preparation of teaching materials, though apparently simple, usually turns out to be more complicated than expected. All the materials to be used, such as flip charts and flannel boards, must be pretested and ready in advance for demonstration and for immediate distribution. Summaries of the content of lectures should be mimeographed in advance, together with copies of all report sheets, etc. If fliers are to be used (as they should be wherever the women can read), they should be ready too—several thousand for each worker. In short, the worker should be fully equipped to get busy the day after she returns from training. A year of preparation is not too long: six months for preparing the material, three for having it made or printed, and three for getting it distributed, with a margin for safety.

In the same way, the loops, inserters, and surgical instruments required should be ready at each point where doctors are being trained. Each doctor should get his first stock of loops and the surgical items he does not have.

In the training of doctors, practice in making insertions is essential. If the training is done in maternity hospitals, arrangements can be made (with a small incentive payment if necessary) to have enough cases ready. After the doctor's work has been approved, he should be ready to insert loops the day after he returns home.

Where to get the loops.—It is usually best to import the first lot until arrangements for local manufacture can be made. Loops are usually packaged in 100's, which means that, if two sizes are used, each doctor needs 200 to start with. The first order, then, will be at least 200 times the number of doctors to be trained in the first six months. In general, the loops ordered should be at least twice and preferably three times the number expected to be inserted in the first year. There must be reserves at all levels.

Inserters at the rate of one for each twenty loops should also be ordered. The supply line for them is as important as that for loops. They can be made locally; but, if a Teflon core is wanted, this material must usually be imported.

If you want to make your own.—At least the larger countries will want to make their own loops to save money and to be sure to have

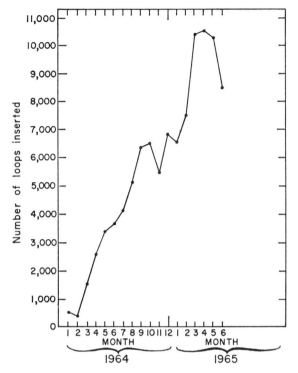

Fig. 1.—Taiwan IUD Program, 1964–65. The drop in June, 1965, was due to harvest and in-service training. Cumulative totals were: June, 1964–12,123; December, 1964–46,449; and June, 1965–53,727. Target for 1965: 100,000.

TABLE 2

PERSONNEL RESPONSIBLE FOR IUD INSER-
TIONS, TAIWAN, 1964–65

Date	Doctors[a]	Field Workers[b]
June, 1964.............	253	122
December, 1964........	369	136
March, 1965...........	405	247
June, 1965.............	473	265

[a] Nearly all private.
[b] Full-time or equivalent.

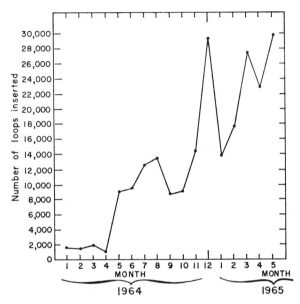

FIG. 2.—Korea IUD Program, 1964–65. Number of workers: doctors—about 1,000 in late 1964; about 1,400 in mid-1965; field workers—about 2,000 from May, 1964. Target for 1965: 200,000 insertions. (Data from Ministry of Health.)

TABLE 3

KOREA IUD PROGRAM ACHIEVEMENT, 1962–65

Date	Clinical Research	Free Service	Paid Service	Total
1962–63..........	1,493	....	....	1,493
1964..............	15,000	91,461	4,370	110,831
1965ᵃ.............	2,470	56,148	562	59,180
Total..........	18,963	147,609	4,932	171,504

ᵃ By end of March, 1965. Excludes 23,720 for April and 29,675 for May.

stocks always available. This is simple enough if the work can be done in a going plastics factory, but more complicated if the work must be done in the "public sector," which sometimes has no such factory. It is best to order the molds from the maker in the United States who specializes in this kind of precision work. Four cavities (dies used in IUD manufacture, costing about $500 each) are more than enough for Korea. India expects to meet her requirements for the next couple of years with eight cavities (four each of two sizes) by running two or even three shifts if necessary.

Before the mold can be made, one must know on what kind of injection machine it is to be used. If a machine made in the country is not available, the time required to get one from abroad may be at least nine months, so that local manufacture may be delayed a year or more. If a local machine can be bought from stock, the time may be cut to as little as three months.

There must always be available enough plastic (Alathon 20), pure barium sulphate, and string that meets specifications.

Keep them fresh.—Supplies of foam tablets usually present fewer problems. It is essential that at least six months' supply be in the line— but not much more, to prevent deterioration. The quality must be high—not only effective for spermicidal effect, but free from ingredients that cause excessive burning or that do not dissolve completely.

Condom-making is not easy.—The biggest problem of all in the timetable is the local manufacture of condoms. Few, if any, countries in Asia except Japan are producing really good condoms. The essentials are good latex and small amounts of a few chemicals, adequate machinery, a high degree of skill in working latex, and electronic testing. Korea makes its own condoms but has had trouble with its electronic tester. India has a good but expensive plan for setting up a condom factory in the public sector.

The timetable for getting local production may vary from one year for the relatively simple Japanese equipment to three or more for an elaborate modern American plant.

How to cut costs on imports.—In the meantime condoms must be imported. If purchases are made through local agents, the "wholesale" price is very high. India has been paying from $2.50 to more than $5.00 a gross. This price can be greatly reduced by central buying. The Japanese price for satisfactory condoms is about $1.00 a gross in the usual drugstore pack. This can be cut to 60 cents a gross in polyethylene bags of one gross each for orders of a million or more per month plus import tax, which in some countries, such as Taiwan, is more than the cost of the condoms *ex* factory.

Timetable: four to six months from the time the order is placed (with letter of credit) to delivery where needed.

Fix the responsibility.—Responsibility for all the actions listed should be assigned to specific persons competent to get the job done, with deadlines and a schedule for reporting progress.

Begin by beginning.—Some of these waiting times seem long but they are based on hard experience. The start of a program need not wait on these more elaborate arrangements. To begin with, in a loop program, only a few items are necessary. The basic principle is to start *now*, wherever there is an opening. The results may come much faster than expected. (See Fig. 1 and Table 2; Fig. 2 and Table 3.)

PART THREE

Contraceptive Methods: Programmatic Implications

29

CONTRACEPTIVE METHODS: USE, SAFETY, AND EFFECTIVENESS

ANNA L. SOUTHAM, M.D.
Associate Professor of Obstetrics and Gynecology
Columbia University, College of Physicians and Surgeons
Medical Consultant, The Population Council

Instructions for decreasing or increasing fertility are included in ancient medical literature. These as well as folklore and the practices of preliterate peoples of modern times have sometimes a mystical and sometimes a scientifically sound mode of action but their existence reflects a desire, universal both in time and place.[1] All modern methods of birth control are based on utilization of known physiologic processes or their modification, but many are only refinements of methods originating in antiquity.

METHODS OF CONTRACEPTION

Intra-uterine contraception is unique in that it requires only initial motivation to provide years of effective, reversible contraception. The insertion of a foreign body into the uterine cavity to prevent conception has been practiced for centuries, and this method has been subjected to intermittent scientific investigation for decades. Several papers on intra-uterine contraception presented at the Fifth International Conference on Planned Parenthood in Tokyo in 1955 stimulated little interest.[2] Since 1962, however, carefully controlled studies through-

---

[1] N. E. Himes, *Medical History of Contraception* (New York: Gamut Press, 1963); B. E. Finch and H. Green, *Contraception through the Ages* (London: Peter Owen, 1963).

[2] "Overpopulation and Family Planning," Report of the Proceedings of the Fifth International Conference on Planned Parenthood, 1955 (London: International Planned Parenthood Federation, 1955).

out the world have been directed toward determining the safety, effectiveness, and acceptibility of intra-uterine contraception.[3] The presence of a foreign body in the uterus produces changes in uterine and tubal motility. Studies utilizing monkeys with devices suggest that ova which normally remain in the Fallopian tube for three days pass rapidly from the area where fertilization could occur. The devices do not interfere with sperm migration. Suggestions that they act by producing abortion or uterine infection have been disproved. Intra-uterine contraception prevents tubal, as well as intra-uterine, pregnancy, again suggesting rapid transport of ova through the tubes.

Several different intra-uterine devices are currently being evaluated throughout the world. Polyethylene, stainless steel, nylon, silkworm gut, and other materials have been utilized. The polyethylene devices are flexible and can be threaded into a catheter or cervical cannula similar in size and design to those generally used by gynecologists for diagnostic procedures. The cannula is then inserted through the cervical canal and the intra-uterine device is pushed into the cavity with a small probe. Other devices may require a slight amount of dilatation which can be done without anesthesia and without appreciable discomfort to the woman. They are inserted in the uterine cavity in a partially collapsed state with either a notched uterine sound or a modified uterine dressing forceps. Some of the devices have an attached cervical extension, a marker which extends through the external os. Visibility of this marker gives assurance that the device is in place and also makes its removal simple. Completely intra-uterine devices are removed by inserting a slender hooked instrument into the uterus. Pregnancy occurs at the expected rate following removal of contraceptive devices.

Steroid contraception is the answer to the search for an oral preparation to prevent pregnancy, a search which preceded its scientific achievement by centuries. Norman Himes, in his review of the medical history of contraception published in 1936, states that oral preparations used by preliterate and ancient people were "undoubtedly ineffective since no drug taken by mouth is known to Western science that will prevent conception or abort." However, the concept that a substance in the corpus luteum inhibits ovulation belongs to the nineteenth century.[4] Haberlandt in 1928 temporarily inhibited fertility

[3] C. Tietze and S. Lewit (eds.), *Proceedings of the Conference on Intra-uterine Contraceptive Devices, 1962*, Excerpta Medica, International Congress Ser. 54 (Amsterdam, 1962); S. J. Segal, A. L. Southam, and K. D. Shafer (eds.), *Proceedings of the Second International Conference on Intra-uterine Contraception, 1964*, Excerpta Medica, International Congress Ser. 86 (Amsterdam, 1964).

[4] J. Beard, *The Span of Gestation and the Course of Birth* (Jena, 1897).

by implanting ovaries from pregnant into non-pregnant animals.[5] In 1930 he reported preliminary studies in humans using an oral ovarian preparation called Infecundin. Konikow reports this work and states, "no doubt the idea of preventing conception by the swallowing of a few tablets is very tempting since it would mean that we had attained our desired goal of simplicity. However, it seems to me that we must proceed very cautiously and await the result of most extensive experiments—first on animals and later on women—before accepting this method."[6] Twenty-five years later the first scientific clinical data were presented which indicated the validity of this approach.[7]

A number of synthetic steroid compounds share the ovulation-inhibiting properties of naturally occurring ovarian and placental hormones. When taken during the appropriate time in the menstrual cycle (usually day 5 to day 25), these compounds prevent the orderly release of pituitary gonadotrophins leading to ovulation. On cessation of drug therapy, the endometrium, which has been stimulated by the synthetic compounds, is shed and withdrawal bleeding resembling normal menstruation occurs. The lack of ovulation in women using this method of birth control has been documented by studies which show inactive ovaries with absence of corpora lutea during drug therapy and a rapid return to normal activity and ovulation after discontinuing medication. Other mechanisms have been suggested and challenged.[8] Since progestins in adequate doses change cervical mucus in such a way that sperm migration is decreased, a physiological sperm barrier may be produced. However, the effect of synthetic progestins is variable and modified by the estrogen content of the tablets and this mechanism is not thought to be a significant factor in effectiveness. The endometrial response to synthetic progestins differs from that seen in normal cycles and implantation may be prevented. However, implantation occurs normally if only a few tablets are missed or if medication is started too late in the cycle to prevent ovulation. A direct effect on the ovary has been invoked to explain the effectiveness

[5] L. Haberlandt, "Über hormonale Sterilisierung des weiblichen Tierkörpers," *München medizinische Wochenschrift*, 68: 1577 (1921).

[6] A. F. Konikow, *Physicians' Manual of Birth Control* (New York: Bucholz Publishing Co., 1931).

[7] G. Pincus, "Some Effects of Progesterone and Related Compounds upon Reproduction and Early Development in Mammals," *Overpopulation and Family Planning* (London: The Fifth International Conference on Planned Parenthood, 1955), pp. 175–84.

[8] J. Rock, "Let's Be Honest about the Pill!" *Journal of the Medical Association*, 192: 141–42 (May 3, 1965).

of the compounds. This is unlikely, since progestins do not prevent the ovarian response to exogenous gonadotrophins in women.[9]

The list of compounds available for oral contraception is growing rapidly.[10] They consist in general of orally active estrogens and progestins taken either in sequence or in combination. The estrogen in most instances is either mestranol or ethynylestradiol; the estrogen component is important for endometrial development as well as for its gonadotrophin inhibiting properties. The progestin component may be one of several 17-hydroxyprogesterone derivatives or may be one of many 19-norsteroid compounds possessing the progesterone-like activity necessary to produce predictable withdrawal bleeding. The progestins alone, in adequate doses, may inhibit ovulation but in the currently available tablets this is either completely or chiefly the function of the estrogen component. The entire literature on steroid contraception has been summarized by Pincus.[11]

Long-acting injectable steroids are being investigated and show promise.[12] The use of these would require less motivation than daily tablet-taking. However, a preparation, once injected, cannot be quickly withdrawn, and side effects thus become a more important consideration.

The rhythm method depends on periodic continence so timed that competent spermatozoa and fertilizable ova are not in the Fallopian tube at the same time. Forty years have elapsed since this method was first accurately described.[13] More precise information concerning the effective life span of spermatozoa in the human female genital tract and a method for predicting the somewhat variable time of ovulation could give the rhythm method a theoretical effectiveness second to no other. Hartman has extensively reviewed the scientific knowledge which

---

[9] E. Johannisson, K. G. Tillinger, and E. Diczfalusy, "Effect of Oral Contraceptives on the Ovarian Reaction to Human Gonadotrophins in Amenorrheic Women," *Fertility and Sterility*, 16: 292–304 (May–June, 1965); M. L. Taymor and T. Rizkallah, "Effect of Norethindrone Acetate upon Gonadotrophin-induced Ovarian Function," *Journal of Clinical Endocrinology and Metabolism*, 25: 843 (June, 1965).

[10] M. C. N. Jackson, "Oral Contraception in Practice," *Journal of Reproduction and Fertility*, 6: 153–73 (1963); J. W. Goldzieher, "Newer Drugs in Oral Contraception," *Medicina clinica*, 48: 529–45 (March, 1964); G. Pincus, *The Control of Fertility* (New York: Academic Press, 1965).

[11] Pincus, *Control of Fertility*.

[12] M. T. Felton, H. W. Hoelscher, and D. P. Swartz, "An Injectable Progestin-Estrogen Contraceptive Program" (in press).

[13] K. Ogino, "Ovulationstermin," *Nippon Fruzinka Gakkei Zasshi*, 1919: 1924; H. Knaus, *Periodic Fertility and Sterility in Woman—a Natural Method of Birth Control* (Vienna: Wilhelm Maudrich, 1934).

forms the basis for determining the fertile time.[14] In most experimental animals, the functional survival time of spermatozoa does not exceed forty-eight hours, and the ovum must be promptly fertilized if it is to develop normally. By four to eight hours after ovulation, fertilization, if it occurs, results in a high percentage of abnormal embryos which are incapable of surviving. If the same situation pertains in humans, conception is possible for not more than three days during each menstrual cycle. However, there is some evidence that sperm retain their fertilizing capacity for five or six days in the Fallopian tubes of the mare and conceptions have been reported with controlled insemination in humans done five or six days before the estimated time of ovulation. Much indirect evidence has accumulated suggesting that the most fertile time in women is about fifteen days before the next expected menstrual period, or within the forty-eight hours before the basal body temperature chart reflects the thermogenic effects of progesterone. There is a widespread erroneous belief that the temperature rise marks the most fertile time of a woman's cycle. Many couples, with apparent infertility, have been incorrectly advised to abstain from intercourse before the temperature rise in order to "save" sperm for the supposed moment of ovulation. These infertile couples are actually practicing effective rhythm contraception and conceive promptly when coitus occurs a day or two earlier. Infertility has also been observed when religious continence delays sexual intercourse to the post-ovulatory temperature rise, or to a time that is less than fourteen days before the next menstrual period. The length of time from ovulation to menstruation is relatively constant. Variations in the length of the menstrual cycle are due to variations in the pre-ovulatory phase—the time required for a follicle to grow to maturity and release an ovum following onset of the preceding menstrual period. Few women have absolutely regular cycles and ovulation cannot yet be predicted far enough in advance of the event to define the onset of the fertile time. The information that ovulation has occurred can be obtained from numerous tests and signs. The simplest and least expensive so far is observation of the basal body temperature pattern. Restricting coitus to the post-ovulatory phase should result in no failures. The length of necessary pre-ovulatory continence is uncertain.

Lactational amenorrhea is associated with sub-fertility and breast-feeding and is sometimes deliberately prolonged in an attempt to extend this protection. Malkani and Mirchandani have reviewed the literature on lactation and found in their own series that the mean

[14] C. G. Hartman, *Science and the Safe Period* (Baltimore: Williams and Wilkins Co., 1962).

duration of lactational amenorrhea was only 5.25 months.[15] The duration of post-partum amenorrhea is definitely longer in women who breast-feed their infants than in those who do not. Lactation may be one of the factors responsible for the longer time required for conception after the first pregnancy but its ineffectiveness as a birth control measure is evident from the high birth rate in countries where post-partum lactation is characteristically long. The mechanism by which lactation inhibits ovulation in the human is not completely clear; gonadotrophin release tends to be decreased. Non-puerperal galactorrhea may be associated with amenorrhea and sterility, and certain tranquilizers produce a similar clinical picture in nulliparous women. Methods of reinforcing the post-partum ovarian quiescence during lactation could have important contraceptive implications.

Condoms, coitus interruptus, and continence prevent deposition of spermatozoa into the female genital tract. Linen sheaths and penile coverings made of animal intestines were used for the prevention of disease at least as early as the Middle Ages. According to one legend the condom acquired its name from a court physician of Charles II who invented it to prevent pregnancy. Dr. Condom was knighted for his contribution.[16] The use of a condom does not require medical supervision and the simple technique is understood by all. Reliability of the method depends on careful control of manufacturing processes, since defects in the material or breakage during use have been causes of failure. The world-wide use of condoms indicates the high acceptability of the method.[17] References to coitus interruptus or ejaculation outside of the female genital tract are frequent in ancient as well as in recent literature. In some countries this is the most widely used of all contraceptive methods,[18] and high demographic effectiveness has been established if this method indeed was responsible for the decline in birth rates more than a century ago in Western Europe.

Abstinence, by definition, is a completely effective method for preventing conception. It is part of the cultural pattern in some societies to place a taboo on sexual contact for periods of time following childbirth.[19] Mauldin's summary would indicate that this method has been used at least part of the time by a significant number of couples throughout the world.[20]

[15] P. K. Malkani and J. J. Mirchandani, "Menstruation during Lactation: A Clinical Study," *Journal of Obstetrics and Gynaecology of India*, 11: 1 (September, 1960).

[16] Himes, *op. cit.*

[17] W. P. Mauldin, "Fertility Studies: Knowledge, Attitude, and Practice," *Studies in Family Planning* (Population Council), No. 7, June, 1965.

[18] *Ibid.*   [19] Himes, *op. cit.*   [20] Mauldin, *op. cit.*

Vaginal methods utilize suppositories, tablets, creams, and foams to make an environment completely unfavorable for sperm survival, and to occlude the cervical os. Diaphragms, cervical caps, sponges, and various types of tampons provide additional barriers to sperm migration into the cervix. The ancient Egyptians prepared suppositories for contraception by fermenting acacia tips and honey to produce lactic acid, an effective spermicidal agent. The practice of placing leaves or other occlusive materials in the vagina prior to coitus is very old and is still used in primitive cultures today. Half a lemon from which the pulp had been removed has been used as a cervical cap, and Soranus recommended insertion of cotton lint into the cervical canal to prevent pregnancy. A number of highly spermicidal chemicals are utilized in the manufacture of vaginal preparations. These have been tested for safety and effectiveness.[21] The aerosol creams are packaged with compressed freon which produces a foam when released into the vagina. Foam tablets combine the active agent with sodium bicarbonate and tartaric acid to produce carbon dioxide. Gelatin, glycerine, and other substances are used as vehicles in jellies, creams, and pastes. The chemical spermicides must be placed in the vagina just before intercourse or their effectiveness diminishes.

A number of different types of diaphragms are available[22] and the correct size and type must be selected by a physician. The woman must be taught to insert it and check its proper placement. This method, properly taught, requires more physician-time than any other. The diaphragm is always used in conjunction with a spermicidal agent. Cervical caps are made of rubber, plastic, or metal and fit the cervix snugly.[23] They are designed to be left in place and removed only during menstruation. The advisability of retaining cervical secretions for this period of time might be questioned. Spermicidal chemicals are also required with this method.

The post-coital douche attempts to remove semen from the vagina before sperm can reach the upper genital tract. This method has been delicately recommended in nineteenth-century literature for "feminine hygiene." The post-coital douche is obsolete and ineffective.

THE SAFETY OF CONTRACEPTIVE METHODS

In pilot projects, women using steroid and intra-uterine contraception have benefited from medical vigilance available to few. Side

[21] R. L. Kleinman (ed.), *International Planned Parenthood Federation Medical Handbook, Part 1, Contraception* (London: International Planned Parenthood Federation, 1964); M. S. Calderone (ed.), *Manual of Contraceptive Practice* (Baltimore: Williams and Wilkins Co., 1964).

[22] Kleinman, *op. cit.*; Calderone, *op. cit.*   [23] Kleinman, *op. cit.*

effects have been carefully documented and evaluated and contraindications have been defined.[24]

The Cooperative Statistical Program for the Evaluation of Intra-uterine Contraceptive Devices under the direction of NCMH (The National Committee on Maternal Health, Inc.) resulted in the rapid accumulation of data. Two international conferences sponsored by the Population Council have made the world-wide experience available to all. These studies form the basis for the side effects and contraindications to intra-uterine contraception listed in Tables 1 and 2. The frequency of side effects is rather similar in various studies. Those compiled in the NCMH study will be quoted, since they are based on the results of thirty-eight different investigators.[25] Nearly 14% of women experience expulsion of the device, but this varies with design. About 11% of the devices were removed within one year for medical reasons (not all related to the method), and two-thirds of these were for pain and bleeding. Pelvic inflammatory disease occurred in 171 of 16,734 women in the study or in slightly more than 1%. Approximately one-third of these infections were classified as severe. The device was removed in only 71 cases; the remaining 85 were successfully treated with the device in place. The relationship of the method to this reported side effect is uncertain, since more than half the cases had a previous history of pelvic inflammation. However, the insertion of the device may have been responsible for reactivation and the presence of infection is a contraindication to use of this method. Rare complications[26] include perforation of the uterus, and these were noted more frequently with the bow-shaped device. With other designs, there has been approximately one perforation for each 2,500 insertions. Removal has occasionally been difficult, more often with the tailless devices, and retraction of the cervical appendage into the uterus has been noted.

Many of the side effects associated with the use of steroid contraceptives are similar to symptoms of early pregnancy (see Table 1). Symptoms decrease with continued use because of increased tolerance and because women with continued symptoms change to other methods. It is impossible to compare the relative frequency of side effects encountered with various preparations, but fewer side effects are apparently encountered as the progestin content of the compounds is

[24] Tietze and Lewit, *op. cit.*; Segal, Southam, and Shafer, *op. cit.*; Pincus, *Control of Fertility.*

[25] Segal, Southam, and Shafer, *op. cit.*

[26] C. Tietze, "Cooperative Statistical Program for the Evaluation of Intra-uterine Contraceptive Devices," Fifth Progress Report, February 28, 1965, National Committee on Maternal Health, Inc., 1965.

TABLE 1

Side Effects Associated with Contraception

Side Effects	Method				
	IUD	Steroid	Condom	Vaginal	Dia-phragm Cap
Metabolic changes		×			
Allergic reactions		×	×	×	×
Skin changes		×			
Visual disturbances		×			
Dizziness		×			
Depression		×			
Nausea		×			
Menstrual changes	×	×			
Vaginitis		×			
Cervical erosion		×			
Pain or irritation	×		×	×	×
Infection	×				×
Uterine perforation	×				
Expulsion or displacement	×		×		×

TABLE 2

Contraindications to Contraceptive Methods

Condition	Method			
	IUD	Steroid	Rhythm	Dia-phragm
Thrombophlebitis		×		
Thromboembolism		×		
Cardiovascular accident		×		
Cardiac disease		×		
Renal disease		×		
Liver disease		×		
Impaired vision		×		
Exophthalmus		×		
Abnormal bleeding	×	×		
Irregular cycles			×	
Breast cancer		×		
Genital cancer	×	×		
Uterine fibroids	?	?		
Pelvic infection	×			
Nulliparity	×			
Repeated expulsion	×			
Defective pelvic supports				×

revised downward.[27] The metabolic changes are also similar to those seen in early pregnancy. Alterations in thyroid and adrenal function tests have been noted. Glucose tolerance decreases and the insulin requirements for diabetics may increase. Some of the factors concerned with blood-clotting mechanisms change. Abnormal liver function tests have been encountered, but their significance is as yet undetermined. Large amounts of an oral contraceptive compound have been given to patients with rheumatoid arthritis and the metabolic changes noted were consistent with a glucocorticoid effect.[28] The contraindications to steroid contraception listed by the various pharmaceutical companies vary considerably (see Table 2). They are often conditions in which pregnancy itself is urgently contraindicated and in which a highly effective contraceptive method is mandatory.

Concern exists regarding possible carcinogenic effects of various contraceptive methods. The problem is complicated by lack of information on the expected incidence of pre-malignant and malignant changes in the female genital tract in various populations. The carefully controlled family planning projects in Puerto Rico and Haiti have provided useful information. A comparative study in patients using a variety of methods has been reported by Pincus.[29] Eight hundred and seventy-three women on oral methods are included; 185 were biopsied because of suspicious cervical lesions or smears, and 8 revealed cancer. Only 1 had a negative smear at entry into the study. Fifteen of 651 women using intra-uterine contraceptive devices required cervical biopsy, and only 1 had cancer. Forty-one patients using vaginal methods required cervical biopsy and 4 had cancer. Seven of 101 women not using contraceptive techniques were found to have cancer on cervical biopsy. A decrease in the number of suspicious smears in long-term users of steroid contraception was found. The large number of biopsies done in the Puerto Rican study could explain this, since a well-done cervical biopsy is often adequate treatment for eliminating

[27] Pincus, *Control of Fertility.*

[28] *Ibid.*; C. S. Hollander, A. M. Garcia, S. N. Sturgis, and H. A. Selenkow, "Effect of an Ovulatory Suppressant on the Serum Protein-bound Iodine and the Red-Cell Uptake of Radioactive Triiodothyronine," *New England Journal of Medicine,* 269: 501–4 (1963); M. G. Metcalf and D. W. Beaven, "Plasma-corticosteroid Levels in Women Receiving Oral Contraceptive Tablets," *Lancet,* 1095 (Nov. 23, 1963); H. Gershberg, Z. Javier, and M. Hulse, "Glucose Tolerance in Women Receiving an Ovulatory Suppressant," *Diabetes,* 13: 378–82 (July–August, 1964); R. R. Margulis, J. L. Ambrus, I. B. Mink, and J. C. Stryker, "Progestational Agents and Blood Coagulation," *American Journal of Obstetrics and Gynecology,* Vol. 93 (1965); N. E. Borglin, "Oral Contraceptives and Liver Damage," *British Medical Journal,* 1: 1289–90 (May 15, 1965); H. Waine, E. H. Frieden, H. I. Caplan, and T. Cole, "Metabolic Effects of Enovid in Rheumatoid Patients," *Arthritis and Rheumatism,* 6: 796 (1963).

[29] Pincus, *Control of Fertility.*

areas of cervical dysplasia. A similar decrease in suspicious smears was found as the duration of intra-uterine contraception increased.[30] Three per cent of 1,201 women developed suspicious smears after nine months of use; half of these reverted to negative in the ensuing few months. The higher number of positive smears found in women using vaginal methods may reflect the decreased frequency of cervical biopsy and not a harmful effect of spermicidal agents.[31] Many long-term cytological studies are in progress as part of steroid and intra-uterine contraception projects. Reports from investigators all over the world indicate that neither method increases the risk of genital tract cancer.

EFFECTIVENESS OF CONTRACEPTIVES

Effectiveness of contraception is measured by failure rates and expressed as unintended pregnancies per hundred woman-years of use. Table 3 shows failure rates compiled from several sources.[32] Failure rates reflect the use effectiveness of a method, since no distinction is made between method failure and patient failure. Theoretical effectiveness measures the potential protection provided by a method which is consistently and properly used. Since very high and very low failure rates have been reported for older methods of contraception, it is apparent that use effectiveness depends on motivation and acceptability. Parents who have the desired number of children experience lower failure rates than those who are simply delaying another pregnancy.[33] Older studies show a positive correlation between successful use of contraception and education. In pilot studies where motivation is constantly reinforced or when only initial motivation is needed, the difference between use effectiveness and theoretical effectiveness largely disappears. The length of time that the necessary motivation can be maintained, however, is related to the acceptability of the method, and continued use becomes more important than low pregnancy rates for a short period of time. The only actual comparison between the two newer methods in the same population group is that from Humacoa,

[30] G. Pincus, C. R. Garcia, and H. Rocamora, "Vaginal and Cervical Histology of Women Using Plastic Intra-uterine Devices," *Intra-uterine Contraception*, ed. S. J. Segal, A. L. Southam, and K. D. Shafer, Excerpta Medica, International Congress Ser. 86 (Amsterdam, 1964), p. 235.

[31] Pincus, *Control of Fertility*.

[32] *Ibid.*; Kleinman, *op. cit.*; Calderone, *op. cit.*; Tietze, *op. cit.*; C. G. Hartman, "Annotated List of Published Reports on Clinical Trials with Contraceptives," *Fertility and Sterility*, 10: 177–89 (1959).

[33] P. C. Sagi, R. G. Potter, and C. F. Westoff, "Contraceptive Effectiveness as a Function of Desired Family Size," *Population Studies*, 15: 291 (1962).

Puerto Rico.[34] Patients were offered their choice; half chose oral and half chose intra-uterine contraception. By the end of two years 70% of women were continuing intra-uterine contraception and 40% were still using tablets. With the better intra-uterine device 83% continued its use.

TABLE 3

REPORTED FAILURE RATES FOR
CONTRACEPTIVE METHODS

METHOD	PREGNANCY RATES PER 100 YEARS OF USE	
	High	Low
Aerosol foam....................	....	29
Foam tablets..................	43	12
Suppositories................	42	4
Jelly or cream	38	4
Douche.....................	41	21
Diaphragm and jelly..........	35	4
Sponge and foam powder......	35	28
Condom.....................	28	7
Coitus interruptus...........	38	10
Abstinence..................	....	0
Rhythm....................	38	0
Lactation...................	26	24
Steroid contraception........	2.7	0
	Average	
Intra-uterine contraception, Lippes loop (large)........ 0–12 months............. 12–24 months.............	2.4 1.4	

The frequency with which individuals choose any one method and the rate with which they change from one to another vary widely. In addition, side effects, contraindications, and availability of trained personnel limit the choice. There is, as yet, no universal method and each of those available may have unique indications.

[34] A. P. Satterthwaite, E. Arandes, and M. E. Negron, "Experience with Intra-uterine Devices in Puerto Rico," *Intra-uterine Contraception*, ed. Segal *et al.*, pp. 76–83.

30

CURRENT LABORATORY STUDIES ON FERTILITY REGULATION: EVALUATION OF THEIR POSSIBILITIES

KENNETH A. LAURENCE
Assistant Director, Bio-Medical Division, The Population Council

It is only within recent years that it has been possible to apply the technological advances made by the basic research laboratories to improve contraceptive methods for humans. There is no doubt that continuing basic studies in the physiology and biochemistry of reproduction will bring even greater changes in our concepts concerning the regulation of fertility in the not too distant future.

There are a number of promising laboratory procedures now available which can effectively confer a state of temporary infertility in experimental animals. Most of these techniques have not yet reached the stage of perfection which would permit extensive human studies. There are, however, other procedures which are being tested in humans but in small pilot projects. It is thought that many of these studies will be sufficiently advanced for extensive human studies in the very near future.

Some of these more important leads are in the following areas: immuno-reproduction, reversible vasectomy procedures, antizygotic agents, and injectable steroids for ovulation suppression.

RECENT ADVANCES IN IMMUNO-REPRODUCTION

Interest in the specialized area of immuno-reproduction is almost as old as the general field of immunology itself. During the early developmental stages of this scientific discipline, researchers whose names were later to appear on the honor roll of outstanding biologists began investigations on the antigenicity of the reproductive organs. As early as 1899–1900, reports by Landsteiner, Metchnikoff, and Metalnikoff describing the immunologic response of animals to injection of sperm or testicular extracts made their appearance in the scientific literature.[1] Since these reports, well over 150 reports involving more than 225 different experiments have reached the literature.

These reports from 1899 through 1961 are discussed in an excellent review article by Tyler.[2] The appearance of this article stimulated the organization of a Conference on Immuno-Reproduction which was held in the fall of 1962.[3] This conference served three purposes. First, it acquainted the immunologists with work already accomplished in the area of immuno-reproduction. Second, it enabled the conference organizers to probe the opinions of the group with the aim of finding the most promising direction to take in future studies. Third, the conference stimulated the participants to undertake studies in immuno-reproduction in their own laboratories.

As a result of the Conference on Immuno-Reproduction, and the pressing need for additional acceptable methods for physiological control of fertility, a great many studies have been initiated to find an inoculation that could effectively confer a state of temporary sterility in humans. In addition, basic immunologic studies, relating the antigenicity of the reproductive organs to the entire process of reproduction have been initiated.

There are perhaps five major areas under intensive study, in which immunologic techniques are being employed to affect the reproductive process.

1. Active immunization of the male with sperm or testes extracts to stop spermatogenesis.
2. Active immunization of the female with sperm to "protect" the female from pregnancy.
3. Active immunization of the female with extracts of tissues specific to pregnancy (placenta, umbilical cord, fetal membranes).
4. Active immunization of either male or female to neutralize gonadotrophin activity or other reproductive hormone function.
5. Immunologic analysis to predict ovulation time.

[1] K. Landsteiner, "Zur Kenntnis der spezifisch auf Blutkörperchen wirkenden Sera," *Zentralblatt für Bakteriologie*, 25: 546 (1899); E. Metchnikoff, "Recherches sur la spermatoxine et l'antispermatoxine," *Annales Institut Pasteur*, 14: 1 (1900); S. Metalnikoff, "Etudes sur la spermatoxine," *Ann. Inst. Pasteur*, 14: 577 (1900).

[2] A. Tyler, "Approaches to the Control of Fertility Based on Immunological Phenomena," *Journal of Reproduction and Fertility*, 2: 473 (1961).

[3] A. Tyler (ed.), *Proceedings of a Conference on Immuno-Reproduction*, issued by the Population Council, 1962; K. A. Laurence, "Report on a Conference on Immuno-Reproduction," *Eugenics Quarterly*, 10: 79 (1963).

Each of these five areas has been studied to some extent. Major emphasis, however, has been placed on the first two categories: (1) active immunization of the male, (2) active immunization of the female with sperm antigens. These two specific areas seem to hold the most promise for a direct immunologic control of fertility in the near future.

ACTIVE IMMUNIZATION OF THE MALE

In 1953 Freund made the observation that immunization of male laboratory animals with homologous testicular tissue in adjuvants generally results in impairment of their spermatogenic cycle.[4] Within a two-month period, complete exfoliation of immature germinal elements can occur.[5] In addition, manifestations of generalized immediate hypersensitivity as well as delayed cutaneous sensitivity to testicular extracts become apparent. The auto-immunized animals also have been shown to possess circulating antibodies capable of immobilizing sperm in the presence of complement,[6] of passive transfer of cutaneous anaphylaxis,[7] or of passive sensitization of tissue *in vitro*.[8] In attempts to identify the immunologic mechanism involved in the development of allergic aspermatogenesis, Laurence *et al.*[9] demonstrated that there is no direct correlation between humoral antibody titer and testicular lesions and that this system is apparently associated with delayed hypersensitivity and tissue-fixed antibody. Peritoneal exudative leukocytes obtained from testes-sensitized donor animals have the capacity to transfer the aspermatogenic lesions to normal secondary recipients

[4] J. Freund, M. M. Lipton, and G. E. Thompson, "Aspermatogenesis in the Guinea Pig Induced by Testicular Tissue and Adjuvants," *Journal of Experimental Medicine*, 97: 711 (1953), and "Impairment of Spermatogenesis in the Rat after Cutaneous Injection of Testicular Suspension and Adjuvant," *Proceedings of the Society for Experimental Biology and Medicine*, 1954.

[5] S. Katsh and D. W. Bishop, "Effects of Homologous Testicular and Brain and Heterologous Testicular Homogenates Combined with Adjuvant upon the Testes of Guinea Pig," *Journal of Embryology and Experimental Morphology*, 6: 94–104 (1958).

[6] J. Freund, G. E. Thompson, and M. M. Lipton, "Aspermatogenesis, Anaphylaxis and Cutaneous Sensitivity Induced in the Guinea Pig by Homologous Testicular Extracts," *J. Exper. Med.*, 101: 591 (1955).

[7] D. W. Bishop, R. Norbaitz, and M. Lessof, "Induced Aspermatogenesis in Adult Guinea Pigs Injected with Testicular Antigen and Adjuvant in Neonatal Stages," *Developmental Biology*, 3: 444 (1961).

[8] J. Baum, B. Boughton, J. L. Morgan, and H. O. Shild, "Autosensitization by Sperm in Guinea Pigs," *Immunology*, 4: 95 (1961).

[9] K. A. Laurence, O. Carpuk, and M. Perlbachs, "Transfer of Testicular Lesions by Leukocytes from Testes-immunized Rats," *International Journal of Fertility*, 10: 13 (1965).

while "classical antibody" cannot accomplish this feat in transfer studies.[10]

If such a vaccine is to be used to regulate fertility in the human male, what must also be determined is the effectiveness of the vaccine, the duration of the effect, and, most important, whether there is complete reversibility of the infertile condition. The only human study of induced allergic aspermatogenesis has revealed that this phenomenon can occur in the human male. Mancini reported that the testicular reaction simulated exactly what has been observed in the male guinea pig.[11] Laurence et al. recently reported that this actively induced aspermatogenesis which occurs in over 90% of the guinea pigs within six to seven weeks after injection is only a temporary condition and that the animals recover normal spermatogenic activity spontaneously on the average of five and a half months after being azoospermic.[12] Animals which have demonstrated complete spermatogenic recovery also have demonstrated complete recovery of fertility as well. Guinea pigs fathered by recovered male guinea pigs appear normal in all respects.

This potential method, however, has a serious side effect which makes its use for humans unlikely for the time being. A granulomatous lesion occurs at the site of injection as a result of the vehicle employed (paraffin oil adjuvant). The search for an adjuvant which simulates the immune response of the paraffin oil adjuvant without causing the cutaneous lesion is now underway. Preliminary results employing polyvinyl pyrollidone (K-30) as a substitute for Freund's adjuvant indicate that this substance acts as a slow releasing factor for the testes antigen and has given encouraging results by inducing testicular lesions without the severe cutaneous reaction. Only a passing erythematous reaction at the injection site is observed. The ability of the vehicle with testes antigens to induce allergic aspermatogenesis is somewhat less than that obtained by the Freund adjuvant technique, but it is sufficiently potent to warrant further study.

ACTIVE IMMUNIZATION OF THE FEMALE

Sperm immunization.—Impairment of fertility in the female guinea pig also occurs after immunization with sperm, or testes extract com-

[10] K. A. Laurence and M. Perlbachs, "Studies on the Relationship of Delayed Hypersensitivity to Experimental Aspermatogenesis in Rats," *Bacteriology Proceedings,* 1962: 88 (1962).

[11] R. E. Mancini et al., "Immunological and Testicular Response in Man . . . ," *Journal of Clinical Endocrinology and Metabolism,* 25: 859–75 (July, 1965).

[12] K. A. Laurence, O. Carpuk, A. Lefevre, and D. Mauldin, "Allergic Aspermatogenesis in the Guinea Pig: Induction and Recovery Studies," *Int. J. Fertil.* (1965).

bined with adjuvant. The period of infertility is variable, and the time of recovery is often difficult to determine. Isojima, Behrman, and Katsh have all reported successful impairment of pregnancy.[13] Behrman's studies are of particular interest, since the inoculation process is by a transvaginal method, and as such can resemble a naturally occurring infertility which often becomes apparent in females. A small percentage of infertility in the human female, with no other known cause of infertility, demonstrates sperm agglutinating antibodies in their circulating fluids.[14] Whether these naturally occurring antibodies are the responsible agents for adversely affecting fertilization has not yet been adequately studied. It has been indicated that there is a direct correlation between the antibody titer and infertile condition.[15]

The experimental studies on the female, however, suffer from the same side effects that occur in the male—that is, the use of Freund's adjuvant and the development of the granulomatous lesions.

Antigens specific to pregnancy.—The use of tissues specifically related to pregnancy has received some attention recently. Studies in our laboratory employing antigens derived from full-term placental tissue reveal that pregnancy can be prevented in some animals. However, since the capacity to form antibodies in each individual is variable in terms of quantity as well as quality, abortion can also occur as a result of the immunization process. In addition, some of the normal, placental immunized animals are unaffected by this immunologic procedure.

Serious side effects may also occur in association with the placental injection and development of antibodies. The similarity of the placental antigens to kidney antigens can elicit a nephrotoxic condition. This is a serious matter, but is only a question of purification and isolation of specific placental antigens to eliminate the production of non-specific formation of anti-kidney antibodies.

Immunization with gonadotrophins.—Recent studies in our laboratory have indicated that antibodies specifically developed in rabbits against bovine luteinizing hormone (LH) can neutralize the endog-

[13] S. Isojima, R. M. Graham, and J. B. Graham, "Sterility in Female Guinea Pigs Induced by Injection with Testes," *Science*, 129: 44 (1959); S. J. Behrman and Y. Otani, "Trans-vaginal Immunization of the Guinea Pig with Homologous Testes and Epididymal Sperm," *Int. J. Fertil.*, 8: 829 (1963); S. Katsh, "Infertility in Female Guinea Pigs Induced by Injection of Homologous Sperm," *American Journal of Obstetrics and Gynecology*, 78: 276 (1959).

[14] N. T. Nakabayashi, E. T. Tyler, and A. Tyler, "Immunologic Aspects of Infertility," *Fertility and Sterility*, 12: 544 (1961); S. Segal, E. T. Tyler, S. Rao, Ph. Rumke, and N. T. Nakabayashi, "Immunologic Factors in Infertility," chap. 23 in *Sterility: Office Management of the Infertile Couple*, ed. E. T. Tyler (New York: McGraw-Hill Book Co., 1961).

[15] R. R. Franklin and C. D. Dukes, "Antispermatazool Antibody and Unexplained Infertility," *Amer. J. Obstet. Gynec.*, 89: 6 (1964).

enous secretion of leuteinizing hormones in rats by passive transfer experiments.[16] The passive neutralization of rat LH results in an extended period of diestrus. This study has revealed the close similarity in antigenic structure between the bovine LH and the rat LH antigens.

Active immunization of female rats with bovine LH in Freund's adjuvant, on a schedule of three weekly injections of 0.5 mg. LH, results in an extended and persistent diestrus by the end of the third week of observation. The persistence of this phase has lasted as long as three weeks or more in many animals.

The recent development of more refined chemical and physical procedures for purification and isolation of pituitary gonadotrophins has opened up this new approach to fertility regulation in addition to the development of immunologic procedures for prediction of ovulation time and determination of pregnancy. With further studies it may be possible to immunize either males or females with FSH and LH, respectively, to inhibit sperm production without affecting libido or to prevent ovulation and implantation in the female.

Immunologic detection of ovulation.—The development of immunoassay procedures for detection of pituitary hormones is steadily progressing. It is now possible to follow a complete cycle and measure quantitatively the amount of LH being excreted daily by the human female.[17] It is hoped that in the near future it may be possible to develop the test more specifically to determine the exact time of ovulation in the human.

Conclusions.—There is little doubt that an inoculation that could effectively confer a state of temporary sterility in humans would be a welcomed and highly acceptable method of birth control. Confidence in immunologic techniques has been established over the years as a result of the effectiveness of vaccines in controlling many of the diseases which formerly ravaged the world's population. It has been felt that, by applying procedures which have prevented widespread dissemination of the bacterial and viral diseases, perhaps the regulation of fertility processes can be accomplished and population growth can also be controlled.

This area of investigation is by no means a new approach to the problem. For many years specialists in the area have studied the potentialities of developing a vaccine for fertility regulation in animal experimentation. Some early reports of success have been matched later

16 K. A. Laurence, O. Carpuk, and O. Wahby, "Neutralization of Endogenous LH in Rats by Antibodies," *Excerpta Medica*, International Congress Series, No. 99 (October, 1965).

17 C. Gemzell, "Purified Protein Hormones in Human Endocrinology," *Techniques in Endocrine Research*, ed. P. Eckstein and F. Knowles (New York: Academic Press, 1963), p. 213.

by some even more convincing denials. It is thus apparent that the application of vaccines has been and still remains only a potential birth control method.

With development of new ideas and techniques a greater knowledge of reproductive physiology has occurred. As a result, it is now reasonable to anticipate development of several techniques which could inhibit fertility by stimulating antibody formation against one or another reproductive process.

The same technical procedures may also be applicable to regularize ovulation cycles or to determine more accurately the timing of ovulation in the human. Further studies in immuno-reproduction seem warranted.

VASECTOMY PROCEDURES

Vasectomy is one of the various methods recommended and often used for birth control purposes. The surgical procedure has been receiving an increased amount of attention the last few years. There are several national programs which include vasectomy as one of their family planning techniques. The governments of Korea and India for example provide free services to enable individuals who desire it to have the sterilization process performed. From 1962 to 1964, over 66,000 men were vasectomized in Korea.[18] In India over 450,000 vasectomies were performed from 1956 through 1964. The popularity of the method would undoubtedly increase if the prospective patient could be reassured that the sterility condition was only temporary and could be reversed when desired.

At the moment, reversibility of the operation depends upon a tedious, and often difficult procedure for reanastomosis of the severed vas deferens. Since the early reports by Martini in 1902 of a successful operation to rejoin the vas,[19] several later reports indicate that, with newly developed surgical procedure, the restoration of fertility is at least a possibility.[20] Lee's studies indicate that it is possible to use a splint to permit re-epithelialization of the anastomatic point.[21] As a

[18] H. Y. Lee, *Sterilization in the Male* (Seoul, Korea: Haimoonsa, 1963).

[19] J. L. Waller and T. A. Turner, "Anastomosis of the Vas after Vasectomy," *Journal of Urology*, 88: 409 (1962).

[20] S. S. Schmidt, "Anastomosis of the Vas Deferens: An Experimental Study. 4. The Use of Fine Polyethylene Tubing as a Splint," *J. Urol.*, 85: 838 (1961); S. I. Roland, "Splinted and Nonsplinted Vasotomy," *Fertility and Sterility*, 12: 191 (1961).

[21] H. Y. Lee, "Studies on Vasectomy. II. Comparative Studies of Splinting Materials on the Vas Anastomosis of Animals and a Report of Consecutive Successful Anastomosis of the Human," *Korean Journal of Urology*, 5: 43 (1964).

result, recanalization occurs and sperm can be found in the post-operative semen samples.

In another series of experiments, Lee injected Biowax, a substance used for plastic operations, into the lumen of the vas and successfully occluded the passageway.[22] This material has remained *in situ* as long as sixty days with little or no tissue reaction. However, long-term effects have not yet been determined.

Work along similar lines has been done in our own laboratories. In our experiments, Silastic, a silicone rubber, was used instead of the Biowax. This material is a thick liquid, which on the addition of a catalyst turns to a soft rubber material. The Silastic material, injected into the lumen of the vas deferens immediately after the addition of the catalyst was observed to block sperm passage completely in rabbits. Within three to four weeks after this procedure, the animals became azoospermic and remained in this condition for several months, at which time the animals were sacrificed. No tissue reactions were observed at this time. Long-term studies are now underway to determine whether continuing contact of the Silastic creates any serious tissue reactions. The occlusion of the vas with Silastic need be only a temporary condition. The Silastic can be removed from the tube by operative procedures, and the small incision in the vas repaired. This procedure will thus offer an individual an opportunity to regain fertility after extended periods of azoospermia with only a minor surgical manipulation of the vas deferens.

Antizygotic Agents

In laboratory studies, a series of non-steroidal compounds which display both estrogenic and mild anti-estrogenic characteristics, have proved to have remarkable anti-fertility activity in rats. At low dosage, these compounds (ethamoxytriphetol, clomiphene, and derivatives of 2,3-diphenylindene) demonstrate 100% effectiveness if administered to female rats after mating but before the implantation process. This effective period is during the four to five days the zygotes are in tubal transport and free in the uterine lumen.

The biological action of these compounds may be associated with both a rapid journey through the Fallopian tube passage and an accompanying effect on the endometrial tissue to prevent decidualization.

If the potent anti-fertility effect in animals would carry over to humans, this would offer an excellent fertility control method. Until now, however, clinical trials have been disappointing. Trials with

22 H. Y. Lee, "Studies on Vasectomy. I. Experimental Studies on Nonoperative Blockage of Vas Deferens and Permanent Introduction of Nonreactive Foreign Body in Vas," *New Medical Journal,* 7: 117 (1964).

clomiphene pointed out that this compound had ovulation-inducing properties. The expected antizygotic activity, however, was not tested, and this phase of the program has been obscured by the ovulation-induction studies. Other compounds of the same family are now being studied with the expectation that there will develop a compound which can effectively interfere with the implantation process specifically. This indeed will be an important and acceptable fertility control measure in some cultures.[23]

INJECTABLE OVULATION INHIBITORS

Studies on the development of ovulation suppressants which possess long-lasting activity have recently been initiated. The objective of these studies has been to find a combination of a long-lasting progestational drug with a long-acting estrogen which could be employed instead of the short-acting oral preparations which are now in favor. Recent reports by Swartz as well as Taymor indicate that an injectable preparation, a combination of dihydroxy progesterone acetophenid with estradiol ananthate, can simulate the natural menstrual cycle without the ovulation process. Taymor reports a mean cycle time of 27.4 days with an injection of this compound on day 8 of the normal cycle.[24] A variation of two days from the pretreatment mean occurred in 16% of the cases. This study is still small, involving only 31 women and 143 cycles, but the results are encouraging. The acceptability by the patient of a monthly injection process, however, is a rather serious consideration. Only further studies will reveal the acceptability of such a method for fertility regulation.

CONCLUSIONS

This paper has discussed only a few of the many promising leads in fertility control now being explored in basic research laboratories. It is safe to assume that many more potential birth control measures will be developed as a result of the broad study programs in the physiology of reproduction now being undertaken in academic institutions throughout the world. It is apparent from this report that the researchers are not concentrating on searching for a "perfect" contraceptive method but are exploring the possibilities of finding several procedures which may be found acceptable for the diverse needs of the world's population.

[23] S. J. Segal, "Fertility Control: Charted and Uncharted Horizons," *Advances in Planned Parenthood*, ed. A. J. Sobrero and S. Lewit (Cambridge, Mass.: Schenkman Publishing Co., 1965).

[24] M. Taymor, personal communication, 1965.

31

THE RHYTHM METHOD

ANIBAL RODRIGUEZ, M.D.
Universidad Católica de Chile

GENERAL CONSIDERATIONS

Chile has an area of 750,000 square kilometers and approximately 8 million inhabitants, with a population density of about 10.6 inhabitants per square kilometer. Despite the fact that the population is classified as 90% Roman Catholic, there are 96,000 induced abortions recorded each year. This means that one known induced abortion is performed for every three live births. Presently 40% of the obstetrical mortality—28 per 10,000 live births—is due to induced abortion and its complications.

Because of its relevance to our population, we studied the rhythm method from different angles. Two years ago we investigated this practice among 104 women in the post-partum period. In this study 396 menstrual cycles were followed to correlate the findings of Ogino-Knaus with the records of the basal body temperature. The number of cycles per mother was: minimum, 1; maximum, 12; mean, 3.8. Two hundred and sixty-six menstrual cycles were found to be ovulatory and 130 were anovulatory; 52 of the anovulatory cycles were recorded while the women were under the influence of oral progestagens.

In Figure 1, the occurrence of ovulation is represented according to the day of the menstrual cycle. The rise in the basal body temperature, which is generally accepted as an indirect but accurate criterion for ovulation, appeared most frequently on day 15. This "ovulation day," however, varied from day 8 to day 32.

In 1923 Ogino reported on a study of ovaries at laparotomy. He found that rupture of the follicles occurred between the twelfth and the sixteenth days of the menstrual cycle. Knaus, on the other hand,

397

maintained that ovulation always took place on the fifteenth day preceding the next menstrual period. Figure 2 shows our series of cases in which approximately 50% of the "ovulation days" fell outside the range of those stated by Ogino and Knaus. Therefore, according to this study, to estimate the ovulation date on the basis of the Ogino-Knaus reports is rather inaccurate and unreliable. Estimation should be substantiated by recording the daily basal body temperature for each individual.

Studies of endometrial biopsies taken during the first post-partum menses showed a marked difference in the endometria of mothers who breast-fed their babies and those who did not. In most cases the endometrial biopsies of the former reflected an anovulatory menstrual

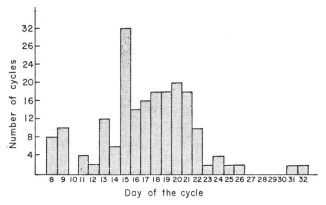

FIG. 1.—Day of ovulation in 196 cycles of non-lactating mothers. (Courtesy of Departamento Maternidad, Universidad Católica de Chile.)

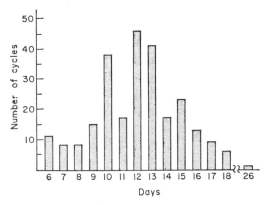

FIG. 2.—Duration of the progestative phase in 256 ovulatory cycles according to the basal temperature curve. (Courtesy of Departamento Maternidad, Universidad Católica de Chile.)

bleeding, whereas the endometria of non-nursing mothers showed secretory phase (Fig. 3).

In another study biopsies were performed during the first spontaneous menstrual bleeding on thirty-four post-partum women and two post-abortion cases. The duration of the post-partum amenorrhea averaged 75 days, with a range of 30 to 190 days. The endometrium was found to be in the proliferative phase in twenty-three cases and showed progestational effects in eleven cases. In two cases it was indeterminate. The morphology of these endometria varied somewhat from the histology of the specimens obtained after a normal menstrual cycle. The most striking variation was found in the glands. The most significant finding in this small series of cases, however, was that in seven biopsies (19.5%) the diagnosis of concomitant endometritis was

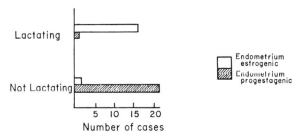

FIG. 3.—Biopsies of endometrium and lactation. (Courtesy of Departamento Maternidad, Universidad Católica de Chile.)

made and that in another seven cases placental tissue was retained in an incomplete abortion. In other words, in 39% of the cases some clinically unsuspected pathology was found histologically. These findings may be of importance in evaluating endometrial biopsies obtained from women using other types of contraceptive methods, such as the intra-uterine devices.

MATERIAL AND METHOD

From three outpatient gynecological services in Santiago plus a few private patients we studied 2,657 women of middle-class status. Their daily basal body temperatures were recorded from 12 to 50 months with an average of 24 months. The data included basal body temperature records for a period of 6 menstrual cycles in 200 women and for a period of 12 cycles in 150 women for a total of 3,000 menstrual cycles. The temperature record was biphasic and easy to interpret in 80% of the cycles, biphasic but difficult to interpret in 19%, monophasic or indicative of anovulatory cycles in 0.5%. The difference in temperature between the two phases of the biphasic cycles was 0.3°–0.5° C. in 75% of the cases, and greater than 0.5° C. in the remaining 25%. A pre-ovulatory dip in temperature was observed in 22% of the cases. The rise in temperature was rapid in 60% of the records studied and was gradual in 35%.

The change in the level of the temperature occurred between the twelfth and the sixteenth days of the cycle in 89% of the biphasic records and from the seventh to the twenty-second days in the remaining 11%. All these patients practiced the "rigid rhythm method" as proposed by Ferin. Sexual intercourse was performed only after two days of a clear and sustained rise of the body temperature taken on awakening.

In this series of 2,657 women who were studied for a total of 127,536 menstrual cycles, 244 unwanted pregnancies occurred. These pregnancies occurred on an average of eight months following the initiation of the method. The failure, or pregnancy, rate calculated according to Tietze, excluding 3,904 cycles during which the women were not exposed to pregnancy, was 2.36 per hundred years of exposure:

$$R = \frac{244 \times 1,200}{123,632} = 2.36.$$

DISCUSSION

The first requisite for a birth control method is to be innocuous. From this point of view, for those couples duly motivated and psychologically prepared, the rhythm method is harmless. Acceptability is the second important criterion with regard to which I quote Tietze to the effect that "the use-effectiveness of a method becomes to a considerable extent a function of its acceptance." In practice the rhythm method is a very restrictive and difficult method to follow. Only a small proportion of the general population may use and benefit from it, but we must know well how to advise the practice in terms of its possibilities and its drawbacks.

As for effectiveness, the third criterion, it must be recognized that the ovulation inhibitors are unquestionably the best protection available against unwanted pregnancy. Nevertheless, we must also remember, with Raoul Palmer, that a method which has a failure rate of two to four per hundred years of exposure is quite satisfactory. On this basis the rhythm method, properly taught and rigidly followed, offers satisfactory protection to those couples willing and able to follow it. The word "couple" rather than "woman" is used advisedly because, more so than with other methods, the rhythm method requires the participation of both spouses, with mandatory co-operation and responsibility of the husband. The motivation of the couple must also be sustained by the advising physician. The difficulty of the method results from the natural pressures and strains that produce violation of the abstinence schedule to prevent conception.

In choosing a method of family planning, the woman, or preferably the couple, should have the prerogative of a free choice among the different medically approved methods. For the choice to be meaningful, the couple must have sufficient understanding of the nature and technique of the various methods for proper evaluation in terms of their religious scruples, psychological orientation, income level, and other relevant factors. Implicit in this is the duty of the doctor not to impose his own beliefs or disbeliefs upon the choice of method. In presenting the rhythm method, we discuss its advantages freely and extensively, but we also point out the responsibilities and hardships to which both spouses will be subjected in its practice and the need to collaborate to make their family planning experience a success.

32

THE PLACE OF CONVENTIONAL METHODS IN FAMILY PLANNING PROGRAMS

JOHN F. KANTNER
Executive Associate, Demographic Division, The Population Council

There is a tendency with respect to almost any technological innovation to discount the further utility of old methods and devices in the flush of enthusiasm over new departures. The super novae of the day are the IUD's and oral contraceptives. This is indeed a new and exciting era but we would be misadvised to break completely with the past. Books are still read since the advent of television, airplanes are still made with propellers, and decisions are reached without benefit of computers. For the reason that the new almost never completely replaces the old, and may even lead to a rediscovery of forgotten virtues, we need to consider the place of conventional methods of contraception in a modern contraceptive program.

CONTRACEPTIVE SYSTEMS

A much neglected point of view in family planning strategy is the idea of a contraceptive system. To call to mind the analogy of military weapons systems may indicate the mode of thought that is required. Such an approach seeks to identify all objectives in an operation, to select the appropriate weaponry for each, and, most importantly, to consider the interrelations of component pieces of equipment. Regarded in these terms many family planning programs are pre-Napoleonic. Particularly with respect to conventional methods our thinking tends to be highly residual and, in my view, overlooks their importance in the total system. In part this is so because we have given too little attention to what can be achieved outside of the official or non-voluntary sphere, in part also because we have perhaps assigned too large a sector to the IUD. Let us look at both of these points, taking the latter first.

A fairly usual statement these days goes something like this: "There are some 20% of women for whom the IUD is not suited. For them and for couples who may prefer some other method, orals and conventional contraceptives should be made available." Accordingly about 80% of couples would use IUD's, the rest having recourse to other methods. This is of course a quite unsubstantial statistic which derives from the sorting of cases by choice of method that has gone on in IUD clinics. It is invalid as an indication of *average* IUD demand, since it overlooks the attrition among IUD wearers. As a first

TABLE 1

RETENTION RATES AMONG IUD WEARERS BY
QUARTERLY TIME INTERVALS

Quarter	Retained Devices per 1,000 Initial Insertions	Quarter	Retained Devices per 1,000 Initial Insertions
1st...........	852	7th..........	610
2d............	785	8th..........	594
3d............	734	9th..........	570
4th...........	694	10th.........	546
5th...........	655	11th.........	523
6th...........	624	12th.........	500

SOURCE: C. Tietze, Cooperative Statistical Program for the Evaluation of Intra-uterine Contraceptive Devices, Fifth Progress Report, Feb. 25, 1965 (New York: National Committee on Maternal Health), computed from Table A/4.

approximation to a more realistic figure we might look at the attrition rates computed from the data provided in the Cooperative Statistical Program for the Evaluation of Intra-uterine Contraceptive Devices.[1] This is the most comprehensive series of data available and perhaps reflects better than average follow-up. From data on expulsion rates, including pregnancies with device undetermined, the retention rates shown in Table 1 have been computed. It will be noted that at the end of twelve quarters or three years, only half of the devices are *in situ*. This figure may be somewhat low as a representation of average attrition because reinsertions are not counted. It may also underestimate what can be achieved eventually with improved devices and technique. Nevertheless, the results as we now have them underscore perhaps more fully than has generally been realized, the important role of alternative methods in a complete contraceptive system. If

[1] Christopher Tietze, Cooperative Statistical Program for the Evaluation of Intra-uterine Contraceptive Devices, Fifth Progress Report, Feb. 25, 1965 (New York: National Committee on Maternal Health).

further allowance is made for women who cannot accept the IUD and for nulliparous and other low-parity women who may prefer a more casual method, it seems reasonable to conclude that for at least half the couples using contraception, alternative methods will be required. Among the alternatives, the conventional methods have certain unique advantages which should ensure their place within contraceptive systems for a good long while. Some of the programmatic aspects relating to the use of conventional techniques will be discussed shortly. First, a brief discussion of the methods to be considered.

METHODS

A discussion of "programmatic implications" of conventional contraceptive methods will vary in length and substance depending on the methods to be discussed. The most tried method of them all, coitus interruptus, would seem to make no demands on a program beyond some elementary presentation of the facts of life. On the other hand, methods involving the supply and distribution of devices of one sort or another plus education in their use pose a wide range of problems. In practice several "conventional" methods have performed very poorly, so poorly in fact that their place in a contraceptive system designed for relatively poor, uneducated, uncertainly motivated populations can be seriously questioned. I refer here to foam tablets, aerosol foams, and vaginal douches, which, as shown in Dr. Southam's review of failure rates, are associated with pregnancy rates ranging from 12 to 43 per 100 years of use—of less dependability on the average than coitus interruptus, rhythm, or lactation. Such methods whose marginal efficiency is no greater than those requiring instruction only are hardly worth including in a contraceptive system.

Three female methods—suppositories, jelly or cream alone, and diaphragm and jelly—have, at least under some conditions, yielded pregnancy rates as low as 4 per 100 years of use. They have also been disastrous under other conditions. One is reluctant to exclude them from the system, however, since they represent the only reasonable alternative female method for women who will not or cannot use either the IUD or orals. In view of the demands made on scarce professional man power in the fitting of diaphragms, however, it can be argued that mass programs could well offer only jelly or cream as a topical female contraceptive.

Among conventional methods, the most important by far is the condom. In effectiveness it compares favorably with the best vaginal method and has frequently proved more acceptable, a shift from vaginal preparations to condoms being fairly common as family planning programs progress. Moreover, being a male method and the only one at present other than coitus interruptus, it gains in importance by the fact that obtaining contraceptive supplies is frequently the man's responsibility. The full potentiality of the condom in a contraceptive system is frequently underestimated. It has succeeded well in some programs, only moderately well in others. The fault is not always with the method as such but may reflect programmatic weaknesses ranging all the way from inferior packaging to unimaginative distribution and promotion.

PROGRAMMATIC ASPECTS

Family planning programs, especially the mass, government-backed programs that are being established in a number of countries are cumbersome creatures. They require tables of organization, budgets, personnel transfers, conferences, reports, files, and memorandums—and above all *time*. As in other government planning efforts there is sometimes a tendency to overlook what can be accomplished with existing organizations and personnel, not only as the official program is getting underway but also as a supplement to it. One can only welcome the appearance of national programs run through the agencies of government, but it is well to recognize that creating new agencies to deal with unfamiliar problems is difficult and by itself may not be able to do the entire job. Official programs can amplify their impact by taking advantage of and reinforcing efforts outside the sphere of government operations. In this realm of activity conventional methods are especially important, for their use can be stimulated without an elaborate build-up of administrative structures or the training of professional personnel.

The proposed marketing plan for condoms prepared by the Institute of Management in Calcutta is a pertinent illustration. This is an imaginative plan for making contraceptives available quickly and on a large scale by making use of commercial channels for the distribution of consumable commodities.[2] The plan calls for the full operation of 400,000 retail outlets for the sale of condoms thirty months after preliminary approval of the scheme. It is based on the subsidized sale of condoms at a level that puts purchase within the means of low-income users and yet provides a profit to the seller. It utilizes the existing network of wholesalers, distributors, and retailers and enlists the profit incentive in the cause of family planning promotion. The notion of a contraceptive system is well illustrated by this proposal,

[2] "Proposals for Family Planning Promotion: A Marketing Plan," *Studies in Family Planning*, No. 6, March, 1965.

since widespread adoption of the condom is seen not only as a goal in itself but as a step toward the adoption of more sophisticated methods. In addition the plan includes a large-scale government-supported promotional campaign aimed at increasing interest in and knowledge about all methods of contraception. "Only about 10% of the total (advertising) bill would specifically support the sale of condoms through retail outlets. Perhaps another 5% might be viewed as directly promoting the condom method. . . . In other words we view the main task of advertising in the program as the stimulation of the practice of family planning." This is an attempt, then, to mobilize the private sector with essential support from public funds. Such a scheme has still to be tested on a suitable scale. Results to date from efforts to promote commercial distribution on a more limited scale are presented in chapter 40 in this volume.

In general the charge that opportunities for private sector promotion and distribution of conventional contraceptives have been overlooked appears justified. One outstanding exception to this, however, is Japan, where programs have been undertaken by industry groups. In this case the dynamism was again, in part, profit incentive. It differed from the Indian marketing plan in that the realization of economic advantage was indirect rather than direct. From Muramatsu's account (see chap. 1) one might conclude that the relative success of these programs as compared to government programs was related to the greater administrative flexibility of the industrial establishment in the handling of budgets, to freedom in hiring and disposition of personnel, and to the fact that "selling" and promotion were familiar activities. This is not to argue that the promotion and distribution of conventional contraceptives should be put in private rather than government hands. It is rather that government programs should note the unique advantages of certain non-government channels and seek ways to exploit them.

While private distribution appears to hold great possibilities, there are other promising prospects for the promotion of conventional methods. One of these is through special programs, organized within the national program, designed to reach special publics such as military groups, post-partum cases, and other temporarily institutionalized populations. Conventional methods have a place in all such special programs, in particular those aimed at men. Given the opportunity, men are apt to be fully as interested in contraception as women.

Distribution through the mails, another scheme suited to conventional methods, has not received wide attention, perhaps because in many countries the mails would add an additional hazard to regularity of use. The rather meager results available at this writing do not offer much cause for optimism, but further testing is needed.

Family planning field workers are obviously important for the promotion of all methods and can be of special use with respect to conventional methods. An important question in this regard is, What makes a good field worker? From the experience of many different programs operating under widely different conditions one might infer that field workers can be effective when their roles are seen as valid, when there is some degree of organization of their activities, and when they have an incentive for doing the job. Field workers will not be effective merely because someone thinks that logically they ought to be. Thus experience with "community leaders or influentials" has sometimes been disappointing because family planning is not an area in which leaders lead or exert their influence. Midwives "ought" to be interested, but often when they realize how much work is involved and with what little tangible reward, they are not. From Pakistan, Gardezi[3] reports that many midwives have taken up their occupation in response to economic hardship rather than as a semi-professional calling. Muramatsu notes that midwives were interested in having the official title of "family planning instructor" but "they soon realized ... that family planning teaching was time-consuming and painstaking but not necessarily economically gainful. In consequence, family planning clinics held at health centers were not active, nor were home visits to be carried out by the instructors."

The unpaid volunteer worker is another type of field worker who has been tried in different places. Some have been very useful but, as a group, such workers are subject to high rates of turnover and require intensively organized supervision. In an interesting study in East Pakistan, volunteers organized and supervised by a trained field worker obtained roughly twice the number of acceptors for condoms and foam tablets as did a group of unassisted volunteers working in a similar area but organized on their own initiative into committees. Parenthetically, the interpretation of this particular experience is made more interesting yet more perplexing by the fact that the more successful group of organized volunteers consisted only of male workers. They recruited very few women directly but secured a larger total number of couples.

Paying a field worker is of course one way to give him a sense of responsibility toward his job. Evidence on this point is not as firm as

[3] Hasan Nawaz Gardezi, "Midwife as a Local Functionary and Her Role in Family Planning: Some Research Findings," paper prepared for the United Nations World Population Conference, Belgrade, 1965.

we would like and consists essentially of the fact that in some places paid workers have performed well. In Japan, for example, paid field workers made a significant difference, obtaining nearly twice as many users as were obtained from areas of similar size where they did not operate.[4] Payment is only one way, however, to make a job seem worth doing and meaningful to the worker himself. An illustration of this comes from Tunisia where local organizations and government workers were mobilized for promotional work as part of their official and political obligations. In the two areas where they operated, business at the local clinics picked up noticeably (see chap. 13). At Comilla in East Pakistan, a village organizer approach using local residents with backstopping from the local Academy for Rural Development seems to have succeeded in creating an accepted and sustained role for family planning workers. Gratifyingly high rates of acceptance and continued use appear to have been achieved. It is still more of a hypothesis than a conclusion but it would appear that, given proper support and incentive, personnel having relatively little formal training can perform effectively as field recruiters. They can also readily master the facts regarding the use of conventional contraception, and the importance of these methods should be emphasized in the instruction that they receive.

In sum, this paper has pointed out the important role that conventional contraception still plays in a modern contraceptive system. It has called attention to certain possibilities for expanding the scope of operations of national programs through collaboration between the public and private sectors, a collaboration that is especially feasible with respect to the distribution of conventional methods of contraception. The point was made also that conventional contraception fits well into programs aimed at special publics and that this is especially true with regard to programs aimed at reaching men. Finally, the promotion of conventional contraception is one of the tasks of the family planning field workers even though their job will include recruitment for other methods as well. Experience suggests that this job can be done effectively when there are adequate incentive and organization. Given these, the family planning worker can be a valuable element in the operation of a contraceptive system.

[4] Yoshio Koya, *Pioneering in Family Planning* (Tokyo: Japan Medical Publishers, Inc., 1963), p. 124.

33

ORAL CONTRACEPTIVES

ADALINE P. SATTERTHWAITE, M.D.
Research Associate, Department of Obstetrics and Gynecology
University of Puerto Rico School of Medicine
Technical Assistance Division, The Population Council

The hormonal control of fertility through the physiological inhibition of ovulation by synthetically produced, orally effective progestational agents has revolutionized the whole approach to family planning. Woman is now in a position to control procreation precisely and scientifically with the daily ingestion of a tablet at a time unrelated to the sexual act. Numerous clinical studies of these progestational steroids have demonstrated their safeness for the periods of usage under study, their effectiveness—both theoretical and practical, their acceptability, and the reversibility of their action.[1]

The oral contraceptives contain a balance of an estrogen, either ethynyl estradiol or its 3-methyl ether (mestranol), which in itself inhibits ovulation, and one of the 19 nor-steroids or 17 hydroxyprogesterone derivatives which also inhibit ovulation but in addition have an

[1] H. H. Cook, C. J. Gamble, and A. P. Satterthwaite, "Oral Contraception by Norethynodrel," *American Journal of Obstetrics and Gynecology*, 82: 437 (1961); J. W. Goldzieher, "Newer Drugs in Oral Contraception," *The Medical Clinics of North America*, 48: 529–45 (March, 1964); C. R. Garcia, A. P. Satterthwaite, and G. Pincus, "Contraception Using Oral Progestin-Estrogen Medication," International Congress Ser. 72, Excerpta Medica Foundation 3-7 (1963); E. Mears, "The Mode of Action of Oral Contraceptives," *Eugenics Review*, 65: 195–201 (January, 1965); E. Rice-Wray, A. Cervantes, J. Gutierrez, A. Aranda Rosell, and J. W. Goldzieher, "The Acceptability of Oral Progestins in Fertility Control," *Metabolism*, 14: 451–56 (March, 1965); A. P. Satterthwaite, "A Comparative Study of Low Dosage Oral Contraceptives," *Applied Therapeutics*, 6: 410–18 (May, 1964); A. P. Satterthwaite, and C. J. Gamble, "Conception Control with Norethynodrel," *Journal of the American Medical Women's Association*, 17: 797 (1962); J. Rock, "Let's Be Honest about the Pill," *Journal of the American Medical Association*, 192: 401–2 (May, 3, 1965); J. Rock, C. R. Garcia, and G. Pincus, "Use of Some Progestational 19 Nor-steroids in Gynecology," *American Journal of Obstetrics*, 79: 758 (1960).

effect on the spermatozoidal permeability of cervical mucus and so alter the endometrium as possibly to promote a hostile environment for implantation, should escape ovulation occur. The progestin-estrogen combination promotes better cycle control. The progestins can be divided into four main groups: those which have predominantly estrogenic effect; those with a progesterone-like action; those which are neutral or "hermaphrodite"; and one which is a testosterone derivative (see Table 1).[2]

The fact that there are so many different products on the market and that so many pharmaceutical houses have been investing vast sums of money in the development of newer agents with fewer side effects and with greater potency which reduces the size and cost of doses is evidence of the expanding market in the richer countries of the world. Further evidence is found in the action of one Wall Street investment firm which hired a biochemist to produce a technological service report on investment guidelines in oral contraceptives.[3] The declining birth rate in the United States has been ascribed to the wide use of the "pills." Assuming that the "pill" is almost 100% effective, if we could greatly reduce the cost of production, is not this the answer to the problem of population growth in the developing countries of the world? We would like to point out some of the practical difficulties which we have encountered in our experience with oral contraceptives.

Some of the earliest large-scale clinical trials of the oral progestagens were started in Puerto Rico nine years ago. Since 1959 there has been so much controversy in the press, television, and radio that there are few corners of the island where the "pill" is not known and accepted or condemned with equally violent emotion. This degree of sophistication was responsible for the difficulties encountered in trying to carry out a study of genital cancer using randomized selection of patients on oral and vaginal methods. The women who came to the family planning clinics were already prejudiced in favor of one method or another.

Our own studies with the oral contraceptives began in 1957 at the Ryder Memorial Hospital in Humacao, Puerto Rico. In the course of seven years we have admitted 1,771 women to six different studies

[2] Mears, op. cit.; Celso-Ramon Garcia and Gregory Pincus, "Clinical Considerations of Oral Hormonal Control of Fertility," Clinical Obstetrics and Gynecology, 7: 844 (September, 1964); J. W. Goldzieher and E. Rice-Wray, "Steroidal Anti-fertility Agents," Ergebnisse der Physiologie, biologischen Chemie und experimentellen Pharmakologie, 1965.

[3] J. Balog, Technological Service Report, Nos. 3 and 4, Steroid Hormones, September, 1963, and April, 1964 (Auerback, Pollak and Richardson, Institutional Research Department).

covering progestin-estrogen combinations, a pure progestin, and sequential therapy with an experience of more than 40,000 treatment cycles. Chloasma and weight changes are objective signs of systemic progestational medication which we have observed most frequently. We have fortunately not observed the more serious sequelae reported by some investigators. In presenting our experience we wish to emphasize cumulative rates of termination and post-termination conception

TABLE 1

ORAL PROGESTINS AVAILABLE AS CONTRACEPTIVES

PROGESTIN	MG.	ESTROGEN MCGM.		TRADE NAME
		EE3ME	EE	
I. 19 nor-steroids:				
A. Estrogen-like norethynodrel	10	150	....	Enovid,[a] Enavids (Searle)
	5	75	....	Enovid[a]
	2.5	100	....	Enovid E,[a] Conovid
3-Desoxynorethindrone	5	....	....	Lynestrenol (Organon)
	5	150	....	Lyndiol (Organon)
	2.5	75	....	Lyndiol (Organon)
B. Progesterone-like norethindrone	5	....	....	Norlutin (Parke-Davis)[a]
	10	60	....	Orthonovum (Ortho)[a]
	5	150	....	Orthonovum (Ortho)[a]
	2	100	....	Orthonovum,[a] Norinyl (Syntex)[a]
Norethindrone acetate	5	....	....	Norlutate (Parke-Davis)[a]
	4	....	50	Anovlar (Schering)
	2.5	....	50	Norlestrin (Parke-Davis),[a] Gestest (Squibb)
Ethynodiol diacetate	2	100	....	Metrulen (Searle)
	1	100	....	Ovulen (Searle)
	0.5	100	....	Ovulen (Searle)
II. 17 hydroxyprogesterone derivatives:				
Neutral or "hermaphrodite" medroxyprogesterone acetate	2.5	....	....	Provera (Upjohn)[a]
	10	....	....	Provera (Upjohn)[a]
	10	....	50	Provest (Upjohn)[a]
	5	....	50	Farlutal (Farmitalia)
	2	....	20	Protex (Leo Pharm.)
Megestrol acetate	4	....	50	Volidan (B.D.H.) Noracyclin (Ciba)
Chlormadinone	2	80 sequential	....	Lutoral (Lilly), C-quens (Lilly),[a] 15 tab. Mestranol and 5 tab. combined
III. Testosterone derivatives: Dimethisterone	25	....	100	Sequential Oracon (Mead-Johnson)[a] 16 tab. EE & 5 days combined

[a] Approved by the U.S. Food and Drug Administration.

rates as a measure of practical use-effectiveness. Table 2 summarizes the various studies in progress.

In the original study with norethynodrel 10 mg. and later 5 mg. we made house-to-house visits in the slum area of the town to solicit acceptors. Later we included women from the post-partum clinics of the hospital.[4] In the course of four years, 838 women were admitted to the

TABLE 2

EXPERIENCE WITH ORAL CONTRACEPTION IN HUMACAO, PUERTO RICO, APRIL, 1957, TO MARCH, 1965

Compound Tested	Women Admitted	Treatment Cycles	Total Active Users	Continuous Users
April, 1957, to October, 1961: Norethynodrel, 10 mg. Mestranol, 0.15 mg. Norethynodrel, 5 mg. Mestranol, 0.075 mg.	838	24,882	151	102 (51–110 cycles)
Comparative study: November, 1961, to November, 1962 Norethynodrel, 2.5 mg. Mestranol, 0.1 mg. Norethindrone 2 mg. Mestranol 0.1 mg. Ethynodiol diacetate 1.0 mg. Mestranol 0.1 mg.	562	12,095	175	127 (32–53 cycles)
December, 1962, to April, 1963 ORF 1658, 5 mg.	60	....	16	....
August, 1963, to December, 1963 ORF 1658, 1 mg.	74	....	17	....
December, 1963, to March, 1964 Ethynodiol diacetate, 0.5 mg. Mestranol, 0.1 mg.	103	....	62	58 (13–25 cycles)
Sequential therapy: ORF 1658-E, 2 mg. (6) Mestranol, 0.1 mg. (14)	194	....	124	....
Total admissions.	1,831	....	545	(30%)

study. Of these, 102 women or 12% of total users have been continuously using norethynodrel 5 mg. from 51 to 110 treatment cycles (four to eight years). Another 49 women are again actively using the medication after discontinuing therapy for one of a number of reasons. Of the women who have discontinued medication and remained at risk of pregnancy, 343 have been pregnant 449 times.

In 1961 a study was begun of three low-dosage progestational agents, norethindrone 2 mg., norethynodrel 2.5 mg., and ethynodiol diacetate 1.0 mg. all with the same estrogen (mestranol 0.1 mg.).[5] Six

[4] Cook, Gamble, and Satterthwaite, *op. cit.*

[5] Satterthwaite, "A Comparative Study ..." (see n. 1).

hundred women were admitted to the study but only 562 actually started medication. When this trial was reported last year, 317 women or 56% of total users, had already discontinued medication for the reasons shown in Tables 3 and 4. This group of patients was followed until June, 1965, twenty months after the last admission to the series. There are now 127 continuous users, while 435 (77.4%) have discontinued; 77 women restarted after termination for various reasons, and,

TABLE 3

REASONS FOR TERMINATION

Reason	Number Terminated	Total Users (per cent)
Total...................	317	56
Side effects.............	97	17
Personal reasons.........	106	18
Non-relevant reasons....	124	21

TABLE 4

SIDE EFFECTS MENTIONED AS REASONS
FOR TERMINATION

Side Effects	Number Terminated	Total Users (per cent)
Total........................	97	17
Nausea, vomiting, epigastric discomfort....................	39	7.1
Headache, dizziness, nervousness	31	5.3
Weight change................	10	1.7
Chloasma....................	10	1.7
Breast engorgement...........	2	0.4
Breakthrough bleeding.........	2	0.4
Loss of libido................	1	0.2
Vaginal discomfort............	1	0.2
Possible thrombophlebitis.......	1	0.2

of these, 48 are still active users. However, in order to look at the present results in a form comparable to that suggested by the National Committee on Maternal Health for the intra-uterine devices we will study the cumulative rates of discontinuing medication in terms of treatment cycles for each 100 first admissions.[6]

Table 5 shows the reasons for discontinuance of medication following the first admission only, by number of women and treatment cycles. Column A gives the periods of use expressed in treatment

[6] C. Tietze, *Cooperative Statistical Program for the Evaluation of Intra-uterine Contraceptive Devices,* Fifth Progress Report, Feb. 28, 1965.

cycles. Column B represents the aggregate experience in treatment cycles for each period of use. Column C includes those pregnancies which occurred from missing tablets or failure to return for medication in time. In one case this has happened on two occasions, each time after 12 cycles of treatment. Column D includes those discontinued because of all physical complaints whether considered by the investigator to be related to the medication or not, and discontinuance of the treatment for intercurrent conditions or on the recommendation of a private physician. Column E includes discontinuance for nonmedical reasons—fear of cancer or of thromboembolic disease, husband's objection, religious scruples, and so on—or abandoning contra-

TABLE 5

REASONS FOR DISCONTINUANCE OF MEDICATION FOLLOWING FIRST ADMISSION ONLY, BY NUMBER OF WOMEN AND TREATMENT CYCLE

Period of Use (Treatment Cycle) (A)	Aggregate Treatment Cycles (B)	Accidental Pregnancies (C)	Medical Reasons (D)	Personal Reasons (E)	Non-relevant Reasons (F)	Lost to Follow-up (G)	Total Discontinued (H)
1.........	562	....	10	9	18	3	40
2.........	522	....	9	2	7	3	21
3.........	501	....	9	7	5	1	22
4–6.......	1,366	....	19	23	22	8	72
7–9.......	1,170	....	20	6	17	5	48
10–12......	1,041	....	13	12	12	3	40
13–18......	1,788	1	20	6	28	3	58
19–24......	1,437	1	15	4	30	3	52
25–30......	1,151	1	8	3	21	5	38
31–36......	956	....	6	7	12	3	28
37–42......	823	1	1	2	7	1	12
43–48......	778	....	1	1	1	1	4
Total......	12,095	4	131	82	180	39	435

ceptive practice. Patients in this category often failed to return to the clinic to get supplies in time, returning only when pregnant. Column F includes termination for a desired pregnancy, separation from spouse, menopause, sterilization, or moving from the study locale. Column G gives the women whom we were unable to locate on the initial and all subsequent visits. Column H represents the total number of women discontinued in each period.

Table 6 shows the cumulative rates of discontinuance of medication per 100 first admissions for all types of termination and for terminations due to medical reasons only and for all relevant terminations. This figure is 57% as compared with 77% for all terminations and probably represents more accurately the degree of inacceptability of the method. Table 7 is illustrative of the method of calculation of cumulative rates.

Table 8 shows the follow-up of the first admission terminations. Of the 435 women who discontinued (terminated the first admission) 314 were revisited within the past year. Of the 209 who remained at risk of pregnancy, 196 had 228 pregnancies (see Table 9); 181 babies including one set of twin girls have been delivered. This table shows the outcome of the pregnancies in the women discontinuing medication by cycle. Four women suffered total losses, but in only two were congenital defects apparent (one cleft palate and one congenital heart disease). One woman (case no. 1069) had a history of repeated fetal loss.

The cumulative rate of conception of the women discontinuing oral contraception and remaining at risk of pregnancy is shown in Table 10.

TABLE 6

CUMULATIVE RATES OF TERMINATION OF MEDICATION PER 100 FIRST ADMISSIONS FOR ALL TYPES OF TERMINATION, FOR RELEVANT TERMINATIONS AND TERMINATIONS FOR MEDICAL REASONS ONLY

Period of Use (Treatment Cycles)	All Terminations	Relevant Terminations	Termination for Medical Reasons
3	14.8	9.8	5.0
6	26.7	19.5	8.9
12	41.8	31.1	16.8
24	61.7	43.2	27.2
36	73.8	54.3	33.9
48	77.2	56.9	38.3

TABLE 7

ILLUSTRATIVE COMPUTATION OF CUMULATIVE TERMINATION FOR MEDICAL REASONS

PERIOD OF USE (Treatment Cycles) (A)	AGGREGATE TREATMENT CYCLES (B)	NUMBER TERMINATED (C)	MONTHLY RATES		CUMULATIVE RATES		RATE PER 100 ADMISSIONS (per cent) (H)
			Terminated (D)	Continuing (E)	Continuing (F)	Terminated (G)	
1	562	10	0.0182	0.9818	0.9818	0.0182	....
2	522	9	0.0153	0.9847	0.9658	0.0342	....
3	501	9	0.0159	0.9841	0.9504	0.0496	5
4–6	1,366	19	0.0139	0.9587	0.9111	0.0889	8.9
7–9	1,170	20	0.0171	0.9496	0.8652	0.1348	....
10–12	1,041	13	0.0125	0.9629	0.8321	0.1679	16.8
13–18	1,788	20	0.0112	0.9314	0.7740	0.2260	....
19–24	1,437	15	0.0104	0.9408	0.7282	0.2718	27.2
25–30	1,151	8	0.0069	0.9563	0.6963	0.3137	....
31–36	956	6	0.0083	0.9493	0.6610	0.3389	33.9
37–42	823	1	0.0012	0.9409	0.6219	0.3780	....
43–48	778	1	0.0013	0.9922	0.6170	0.3830	38.3
Total	12,095	131	....	....	....	....	....

Without medication, 54% had conceived three months after termination of medication, 73% after six months, and 88% by the end of a year. Referring again to Table 8 it will be noted that 148 of the women whose pregnancies have terminated have subsequently sought some type of contraception, as follows: 34 (23%) were sterilized, 50 (34%) had intra-uterine devices inserted, and 64 (43%) restarted orals.

In the first four years, from 1959 to 1961, of the women in the original oral contraceptive series using norethynodrel, 53% discontinued; and in the second low-dose series, from 1961 to 1965, 78% discontinued. Unquestionably an important factor in the decreasing

TABLE 8

FOLLOW-UP OF FIRST ADMISSION TERMINATIONS

Number terminated..................... 435
Number revisited in past year........... 314
Number at risk of pregnancy........... 209
Women becoming pregnant............. 196
Subsequent status:
    Restarted orals...................... 64
    Inserted IUD....................... 50
    Sterilized.......................... 34

TABLE 9

PATIENTS DISCONTINUING MEDICATION: OUTCOME OF PREGNANCIES

Treatment Cycles	Women Using Medication at Start of Study Period	Women Discontinuing during Period	Delivered	Undelivered	Aborted	Total Loss or Defects
1...............	562	40	16	3	1	1[a]
2...............	522	21	9	0	0	0
3...............	501	22	9	2	2	0
4–6.............	479	72	38	2	6	1[b]
7–9.............	407	48	33	5	1	3[c]
10–12...........	359	40	27	2	2	0
13–18...........	319	58	22	4	1	0
19–24...........	261	52	18	1	0	1[d]
25–30...........	209	38	7	3	0	1[e]
31–36...........	171	28	22	8	0	0
37–42...........	143	12	0	2	1	0
43–48...........	131	4	0	1	0	0
49–54...........	127	0	....	....	....	....
Total.........	....	435	181	33	14	7

[a] Case No. 1002, Abruptio placenta—stillborn.
[b] No. 1363, Neonatal death.
[c] No. 1069, (1) Abortion; (2) stillborn, premature; (3) full-term, normally delivered male, died 43 days postnatally—congenital heart defect.
[d] No. 1956, Twin girls normal.
[e] No. 1223, Cleft palate; neonatal death.

acceptability was the introduction of the intra-uterine device in 1961. It had its effect upon all of the oral users—by 1965 (after eight years) we had only 12% of the original women still using norethynodrel after 51–110 cycles.

In the past four years 105 pill users have switched to intra-uterine devices while 57 IUD users who could not use the method have changed to pills.

In Table 11 one can see the comparison of women freely choosing between oral and intra-uterine contraception for the one-year period

TABLE 10

CUMULATIVE PREGNANCY RATE OF WOMEN DISCONTINUING ORAL
CONTRACEPTION AND REMAINING AT RISK OF PREGNANCY

Months after Termination	Number Did Not Conceive	Number Conceived	Total	Months Exposure	Conception	Cumulative Conception Rate (per cent)
0.........	....	29	29	214	....	....
1.........	2	22	24	185	....	....
2.........	1	35	36	161	....	....
3.........	1	27	28	125	0.5362	54
4.........	4	10	14	97	....	....
5.........	2	15	17	83	....	....
6.........	1	13	14	66	0.7248	73
7.........	....	6	6	52	....	....
8.........	1	9	10	46	....	....
9.........	2	3	5	36	0.8215	82
10.........	....	2	2	31	....	....
11.........	....	6	6	29	....	....
12.........	1	2	3	23	0.8783	88
Longer......	3	17	20	20	....	....
Total.....	18	196	214	1,168	....	....

TABLE 11

RYDER MEMORIAL HOSPITAL, HUMACAO: COMPARISON OF WOMEN
BY CONTRACEPTIVE METHOD CHOSEN FROM NOVEMBER,
1961, TO NOVEMBER, 1962, FOLLOWED TO MAY, 1965

	Oral Contraceptive	IUD
Number of women	600	608
Per cent over 30 years of age	12	24
Per cent with 4 or more children	25	40
Per cent active at end of two-year period	43	70
Per cent active at end of three and a half year period...............................	22	50
Per cent lost to follow-up..................	20	15
Subsequent pregnancies after termination....	228	130

from November, 1961, to November, 1962. It will be noted that the groups are almost equally divided, although the oral acceptors are somewhat younger and with fewer children, indicating that they were spacers rather than terminators. It is true that many of the IUD users had hoped for sterilization and accepted the IUD as a substitute. At the end of the two years 70% of the women who used the IUD were still active, while only 43% of the oral users were continuing. Of those revisited after three and a half years, 50% were still using the IUD and 22% were using pills. These results are obtained in research conditions where we have good follow-up.[7]

In Humacao, we have continued to offer all methods. Approximately 50% of the women coming to the clinic for family planning choose orals and the remainder the IUD. Since December, 1962, we have admitted another 430 women to oral contraceptive studies, of whom about 50% are still active. We are having approximately the same experience at the Bayamon Health Center, where we are also carrying out clinical trials. Of 279 women who started oral contraception a year ago, 47% are still active.

In studying the cumulative admissions to the family planning clinic in the health centers of the northeast health region[8] since January, 1965, where two-thirds of the women are from rural areas, we find that 60% accepted the IUD, 30% accepted the orals, and 10% the other methods. The only exception was in one small, largely Catholic town where the pills outnumber the IUD because the priest has given special dispensation for use of the pills in cycle regulation (see Fig. 1).

Studying the endometrial changes observed in combined therapy with norethindrone 2 mg. and mestranol 0.1 mg. on the twenty-day regimen from cycle day 5 through 24, one can understand the reasons for the reduction in menstrual flow observed. The early progesterone effect with the full-blown secretory changes are seen in the glands at the ninth to the eleventh day of the cycle. There is subsequent regression of the glands to a straight inactive phase although the stroma continues to progress to a rather extensive predecidual reaction. The glands and stroma are characteristically out of phase. The endometrium returns to normal by the second post-treatment cycle.[9]

[7] A. P. Satterthwaite, E. Arandes, and E. D. Negron, "Experience with Intra-uterine Devices in Puerto Rico," *Intra-uterine Contraception*, ed. S. J. Segal, A. L. Southam, and K. Shafer, 76–83 (Amsterdam: Excerpta Medica, International Congress Ser. 86, 1964).

[8] A. P. Satterthwaite, "The Role of Ante-partum and Post-partum Education in Maternal Health," *Journal of the American Medical Women's Association*, 20: 738–42 (August, 1965).

[9] *Ibid.*; M. Roland, M. J. Clyman, A. Decker, and W. B. Ober, "Classification of Endometrial Responses to Synthetic Progestagen-Estrogen Compounds," *Fertility and*

We have also studied wedge-biopsies of the ovaries of women on oral progestins. We find an inactive ovary with a pearly white thickened cortex and no follicle development. However, as early as twenty days following discontinuance of medication we have noted a corpus luteum at laparotomy.

The lower the dose of the progestin, the more frequently break-through bleeding occurs. This is especially true in the early cycles

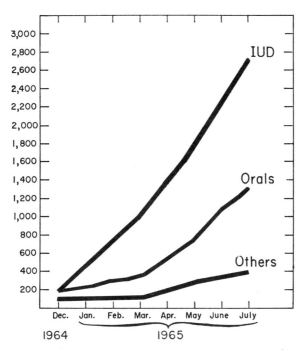

Fig. 1.—Cumulative admissions, family planning clinics, northeast health region, Puerto Rico.

when the women are apt to forget to take the pills regularly. This problem of irregular bleeding from irregular use or from low-dosage level causes much confusion. Many women discontinue treatment be-cause of this. Other causes of failure come because of the "silent men-struation" or amenorrhea. In spite of repeated admonitions to the women that they must not wait more than seven days without pills to

Sterility, 15(2): 143–63 (1964); G. M. Ryan, J. Craig, and D. Reid, "Histology of the Uterus and Ovaries after Long-Term Cyclic Norethynodrel Therapy," *Am. J. Obst. and Gynec.,* 90: 715–25 (Nov. 15, 1964); J. A. Board and D. S. Borland, "Endometrial Effects of Mestranol-Norethindrone Sequential Therapy for Oral Contraception," *Obst. and Gynec.,* 24: 655–58 (November, 1964).

see if they bleed, they often do not come back in time and are already pregnant when they do return to clinic.

The development of sequential therapy with the estrogen given from day 5 through day 20 and the combined estrogen-progestin combination in the last five or six days of the treatment cycle is designed to reduce the expense of the course of treatment and certainly does cause less alteration in the endometrial pattern with a more normal menstrual flow. The sequential therapy has been shown to be slightly less effective than the combined therapy. There are occasional escape ovulations. There is also more chance for error; for in spite of elaborate packaging some women take the combined pills first and this induces bleeding.[10]

IMPLICATIONS OF ORAL CONTRACEPTIVES IN THE FAMILY PLANNING PROGRAM

Both the oral contraceptives and the IUD's—the more sophisticated and more effective female methods of fertility control—require physician time. Indeed, the degree of acceptability and satisfaction in continued use is directly related to the confidence which the women have in the medical personnel with whom they come in contact. Time and patience are necessary to explain carefully the use of the orals. Illiterate women may be successfully managed as long as proper arrangements are made for the dispensing of supplies with each "menstrual period." For those who can read, printed instructions and calendars to mark are valuable adjuncts, and several months' supplies may be given at one time.

Nevertheless, in spite of low dosage and the introduction of sequential therapy, there is still a recurring monthly expense which is excessively high for many developing countries. Likewise there is need for sustained motivation to secure supplies and to continue to use them. It is so easy to forget pills or to fail to return for supplies in time. Especially is this a problem for those with the largest families who most need the protection.

It is true that we had better acceptance of the discipline of daily pill-taking before the IUD's were added to the program. It was the same effect we had noticed earlier when pills had been added to the aerosol foam (EMKO) program. Not only do patients flock to the latest fashion, but as soon as they gain confidence, they choose the method which offers better protection for least effort. Furthermore, there seems to be a psychological factor in preferring that a third party

---

[10] Goldzieher, *op. cit.*; Rock, Garcia, and Pincus, *op. cit.*

be responsible for producing the contraceptive effect at a time unrelated to sexual intercourse. What can be better than prolonged protection produced by a single action?

On the basis of the sales reported by pharmaceutical companies, it is estimated that more than 25% of the eligible women in the United States are using oral contraceptives, many with very little medical supervision after the first prescription. In Latin American countries, for example, there is a large over-the-counter sale, without medical prescription being necessary. Considering that self-medication is widely and effectively used, one wonders whether widespread programs using paramedical personnel for distribution might not be feasible. Again one returns to the chief problem of maintaining sufficient motivation to carry out a repeated action day after day. Further studies are necessary to elucidate the actual use-effectiveness and cost of operation of programs with various methods. In any event, effective public health family planning programs must offer several methods since no one method will meet the needs of every couple. Although the oral contraceptives offer the highest degree of effectiveness for the individual woman under the conditions of private practice, in the public health program their usefulness is limited.

1. A family planning program which offers only oral contraception will have a better record of acceptability and continuous use of the pills than a program which is combined with IUD's.

2. In spite of the high acceptability of the oral contraceptives, close supervision is necessary to maintain adequate motivation on the part of the women to continue the regimen faithfully from month to month.

3. The recurring monthly expense for supplies is high compared with other methods and may be prohibitive for mass programs in some developing countries.

4. For an effective large-scale program the availability of supplies at the local level is indispensable. However, even though the women have the supplies, there is no assurance that they will be used.

5. It is easier to discontinue pill-taking than to return to the clinic for removal of an IUD.

6. Possible inhibition of lactation and other metabolic changes (e.g., effect on liver function) may be of more importance in some developing countries with lower nutritional levels.

7. Suspension of medication results in rapid re-establishment of fertility.

8. The oral contraceptives offer an important adjunct in family planning programs because there are always couples who find this regimen particularly acceptable and who cannot tolerate other methods.

In summary, there is no ideal method for every couple. The oral contraceptives offer a useful and effective method of family planning in certain situations; but widespread application in public health programs seems to be of limited value. After forty-eight treatment cycles the cumulative rate of termination in our series ranged from 77% per 100 first admissions for all reasons to 57% per 100 first admissions for relevant reasons. The search for better methods of fertility inhibition must continue.

34

MASS USE OF INTRA-UTERINE CONTRACEPTIVE DEVICES IN KOREA

TAEK IL KIM, M.D.
Chief, Maternal and Child Health Section, Ministry of Health and Social Affairs

and

SYNG WOOK KIM, M.D.
Department of Obstetrics and Gynecology, School of Medicine
Seoul National University

INTRODUCTION

At both of the conferences on intra-uterine contraceptive devices, sponsored by the Population Council in April, 1962, and October, 1964, results obtained with several newly developed devices were presented. Discussion centered on their shapes, sizes, material composition, safety, effectiveness, acceptability, and the possibility of their widespread use as a method of regulating fertility. These evaluation conferences indicated that the IUD method of birth control is highly effective, reversible, and essentially safe, and if this method could be widely applied, it might well produce astounding reductions in population growth.

Reports from Taiwan, Hong Kong, and Korea, made at the IPPF Western Pacific Regional Conference held in Seoul, May, 1965, indicated that IUD's are already playing an important role in the family planning programs in these countries.

DEVELOPMENT OF NATIONAL PROGRAM

Following the introduction of the Lippes loop into Korea in September, 1962, a twenty-month period was devoted to clinical trials, recognition by the medical society, adoption by the government, participation of general practitioners, and introduction of the Lippes loop through the regular national family planning program.

An evaluation of the safety and effectiveness of the Lippes loop was first initiated by the Planned Parenthood Federation of Korea in 1962. Two medical school hospitals and a missionary mobile clinic participated during the first year of evaluation. Then in December, 1963, the evaluation was extended to IUD clinics in twenty-one medical school and provincial hospitals throughout the country with government support. Finally, in May, 1964, loop insertion became a regular part of the national family planning program.

During the twenty-month research evaluation period, a total of 7,364 women were fitted with the Lippes loop. Another 244,450 women were fitted with the loop during the fourteen months between May, 1964 (when the government included the IUD as a regular part of the national family planning program), and July, 1965.

TABLE 1

CHRONOLOGICAL INCREASE OF
PARTICIPATING CLINICS

End of 1963	3
January–April, 1964	24
May, 1964	144
June–September, 1964	445
October, 1964–May, 1965	719
June, 1965	1,088

IUD CLINICS

Insertion by an obstetrical-gynecological specialist is, of course, preferable, but since the majority of the specialists reside in cities, it has been necessary to designate general practitioners and their clinics as IUD referral centers in most of the rural areas. Both specialists and general practitioners were given a two-day orientation course on the IUD before designation of their clinics as referral centers—one day for lecture and discussion, and the next day for clinical observation and on-the-job training. However, because of limited budget, facilities, and time, we were obliged to have more than forty or fifty doctors, sometimes one hundred in each class. We found that the classes were far too large and the time far too short. Therefore, we are planning in the future, if more doctors are required, to give a week of intensive training to a limited number of trainees and also to give refresher courses for those previously trained to assure high quality service.

The number of participating clinics as shown in Table 1 has been increased to 1,088 as of June, 1965. Ninety per cent of the designated doctors are general practitioners and 10% are specialists in obstetrics and gynecology (OBG). Six per cent of the total are women doctors.

The IUD clinics are evenly distributed throughout the country.

There are 189 health centers in Korea and each center, covering an average of 150,000 people has several fixed clinics under its jurisdiction. The number of IUD clinics under the jurisdiction of a health center varies and their distribution is shown in Table 2.

Of the approximate 28 million population in Korea, it is estimated that 3.6 million are married and in the 20–44 age bracket. According to these figures, we now have one IUD doctor per 3,300 eligible couples.

If we assume that one insertion is made per day at each IUD clinic, it would be possible to fit IUD's in 326,400 women per year in 300 working days. As this is roughly 9% of the total number of eligible couples, it indicates it should not be necessary to increase the number of clinics if we set our annual target at service to 10% of the eligibles.

TABLE 2

DISTRIBUTION OF IUD CLINICS
BY HEALTH CENTER

Number of Clinics	Per Cent of Health Centers
1–3	23.3
4–6	46.0
7–9	22.2
10 or more	8.5

However, since a large number of married couples reside in remote areas and on Korea's many islands, there is need for a mobile service to supplement the 1,088 permanent clinics now in operation.

MOBILE SERVICE AND INSERTION BY PARAMEDICAL PERSONNEL

As the following review points out, the experience in Korea with the operation of a mobile IUD service and insertion by paramedical personnel has been limited.

Mobile service.—A missionary clinic located in Seoul has established nurse and health stations in several of the resettlement areas around the city. The nurses who manage these stations are aided by itinerant physicians who regularly make the rounds of the stations with a mobile van to provide medical care and insert IUD's. Sometimes, more than sixty insertions have been carried out in a day. The wearers were then followed up by the station nurse. Minor complications such as mild bleeding or cramps were treated by the nurses and severe cases were referred to the physician at the mission headquarters.

As this missionary clinic is also one of the twenty-four research clinics, careful records were kept; they show that more than 84% of the IUD acceptors had two or more follow-up examinations during the first year. Their records also indicate a 7% expulsion rate, an 18% removal rate, and a two per hundred woman-years pregnancy rate.

IPPF provided the Planned Parenthood Federation of Korea with a mobile van which is equipped with educational equipment and has facilities for surgical and gynecological service. This van was staffed with four full-time workers, i.e., an OBG specialist, a nurse, a social worker, and a driver. Insertions were performed in the van. Township family planning workers recruited clients according to the visiting schedule of the van to each town. During the seven-month period from September, 1964, through March, 1965, the mobile unit served 89 days (averaging 12–13 days per month) and fitted a total of 2,934 women (averaging 33 per day) with IUD's. The cost of providing this service averaged about $1.20 per insertion, which is almost the same as the amount paid by the government as subsidy per insertion. However, at present this mobile service is temporarily terminated owing to the resignation of the doctor, who was paid only $150 a month. The duty of following up the women who were fitted with IUD's by the mobile unit was left to the nearest local doctor. Therefore, we have no record of the clinical results from the mobile service carried out by the PPFK van.

Development of new IUD service methods.—Since April, 1965, the Population Council has sponsored field research to assess various methods in terms of acceptance rate and the control and care of side effects in order to provide guidelines for future IUD service in Korea. Subjects such as the efficiency of mobile teams in IUD insertions, insertions by paramedical personnel, and insertion at any time of the menstrual cycle are being investigated. Investigative methods are as follows:

1. Insertion of the IUD by physicians on limited days, with consideration for the ovulation period of each patient.
2. Insertion by a paramedical person on limited days in women screened by a visiting physician.
3. Insertion by a physician any time of the month without consideration of the ovulation period.
4. Insertion by a paramedical person at any time of the month in the women screened by a physician.
5. And, finally, both screening and insertion done by a paramedical person at any time of the month.

Also, in this study the acceptance rate and the control and care of side effects of each method will be evaluated. However, at present, data for evaluation are too limited for meaningful comparison of methods to side effects.

SCREENING, FOLLOW-UP, AND AFTER-CARE

Screening.—IUD insertions in the mass program are to be made soon after the cessation of a menstrual period and at least two months after a delivery or soon after the cessation of the first menstrual period following an abortion. A woman must be married and fertile as evidenced by having borne at least one child. Also, of course, she must not be pregnant and not have any disorders considered to contraindicate the use of the loop, such as presence of fibroids, acute and subacute pelvic inflammatory diseases, carcinoma or suspicious carcinoma, and a history of recent metrorrhagia or menorrhagia. Laboratory examination is not required for confirming the above-mentioned disorders because it is actually impossible in mass use of the device.

During twelve months—June, 1964, through May, 1965—13.3% of the total clients who applied for IUD's were rejected for various rea-

TABLE 3

FREQUENCY OF FOLLOW-UP VISITS

	Number	Per Cent
0		24.3
1		30.0
2		18.9
3		13.3
4		13.5

sons. This rejection rate dropped from 15.9% to 10.9% during the latter half of the above period as the ability of clients to judge their qualifications for IUD had been improved through the educational effort of field workers and mass media programs.

Follow-up.—All women fitted with the loop at the research clinics were required to return monthly for three months, then quarterly for three visits and semiannually thereafter. In the mass program, four visits for six months following insertion, i.e., monthly for three months and one more visit three months thereafter were required. But, since December, 1964, the schedule of just two follow-up checks by the physician, i.e., one month and six months after insertion, and one interim follow-up by family planning field workers three months after insertion is being followed.

The frequency and percentage of acceptors returning for a follow-up check are shown in Table 3. According to the clinical research and field trials, a schedule of one follow-up check one year after insertion, unless any problem arises, is planned tentatively for adoption in the future.

After-care.—How to minimize side effects and how to provide the best post-insertion care are the most important problems in Korea. At present the government is paying the physician $1.20 in subsidy for each insertion and six months' follow-up, but this is too low a fee in the event of a side effect which necessitates some medical care. In such cases, at present, the acceptor has to pay for the medical care; otherwise, the device has to be removed even for mild complications.

According to the records from IUD clinics, 12.7% of wearers needed some kind of medical care and 5.7% needed both removal and medical care.

Since the beginning of 1965 many discussions have been held by the medical committee on how to manage these patients with side effects. It has been decided to set up a referral service center staffed with an OBG specialist and provided with equipment for OBG service in several areas. In addition, the government will provide all the IUD clinics with basic drugs for minor complications.

Also, recognizing the fact that intensive refresher training of general practitioners who comprise 90% of all IUD doctors is desperately needed for minimizing side effects and providing the most effective control of the complications, twelve training teams will be organized and mobile units operated from September, 1965, with the assistance of foreign aid. The primary missions of these teams are the on-the-job training of general practitioners, and consultation for the management of side effects.

Medical Evaluation and Comparison: Research Clinics and Mass Use

A brief summary of the results of clinical research and mass use is shown in Table 4. As shown in the table, both expulsion and removal rates are lower among the mass use group than in the research group. Less complete record-keeping or poor description in the former group and a shorter period of observation are assumed as the reasons for the lower rate. Another reason is that many of the women seek medical care at another reliable clinic rather than the clinic where the devices were fitted; thus, records at the insertion clinic disclose no difficulties. The difference between the results of the two groups is not significant statistically. Therefore, we can assume that there is no significant hazard in the mass application of IUD's by general practitioners who have had little experience in gynecological examination, diagnosis, and treatment. But we still believe that severe complications were more frequent in the insertions at the IUD clinics by general practitioners rather than at the research clinics staffed by OBG specialists.

Work Load and Expected Effectiveness in Reducing Birth Rate with IUD

Korea has a goal of 1 million insertions by the end of 1971. To achieve this goal, 200,000 or 300,000 insertions are scheduled annually. If the expulsion and removal rate is assumed as 20% in the year of insertion and 10% from the next year annually, a total of 1.8 million insertions have to be carried out to reach the goal of 1 million wearers by the end of 1971. The number of eligible couples between 20 and 44 years of age at the end of 1971 was estimated as 4.2 million. Accordingly, if we achieve our goal, 24.5% of all eligible couples will be fitted with IUD's by the end of 1971. If we assume the birth rate in this age group to be 25% we can reduce the number of births annually by 250,000, if we can maintain 1 million continuous wearers of IUD's.

TABLE 4

COMPARISON BETWEEN THE RESULTS OF
CLINICAL RESEARCH AND MASS USE

Cases	Research Clinic	Mass Use
Total cases analyzed......	6,938	12,203
Total carrying to date....	3,718	7,771
Total discontinued.......	1,089	1,284
Not contacted...........	2,136 (30.8%)[a]	3,148 (25.8%)[b]

Analysis of Discontinued

Total discontinued........	1,089 (15.5%)	1,284 (10.6%)
Pregnancies...........	0.9%	0.2%
Expulsions...........	3.8%	2.5%
Removals............	10.8%	7.9%
Pain...............	3.7%	2.6%
Bleeding...........	3.9%	3.0%
Infection...........	0.4%	0.4%
Leukorrhea.........	0.4%	0.4%
Others.............	2.4%	1.5%

Major Side Effects with or without Removal

Pain.....................	16.7%	21.8%
Bleeding...............	23.4%	33.8%
Menorrhagia.............	20.7%	27.5%

[a] Failed to return for two or more scheduled follow-up visits.
[b] Failed to return after insertion.

COMMENTS

There is no significant difference between the results of IUD services provided by specialists at the research clinics on a small scale and those provided by general practitioners on a large, national scale. This indicates that it is quite possible to carry out an effective national IUD program.

In a mass program, administrative problems rather than those of a medical nature will require more attention to assure effectiveness, and it seems essential to secure the active participation and assistance of local practicing physicians.

Our experience indicates that several methods must be developed in order to provide clients residing in specific areas with an economical and convenient service. For example, employment of various methods, such as fixed clinic service, mobile service, and paying and free service, is required for operation of the most efficient, effective, and economical service.

In Korea where the distribution of local clinics is fairly even, designation of the pre-existing clinics as fixed IUD clinics seems to be the method of choice for mass application, and the other methods should be properly employed for the specific areas. If mobile service should be employed, it is more effective to provide IUD service in conjunction with the general public health service.

Even though no evidence of hazard can be elicited from the experimental insertions by paramedical personnel in Korea, we must also consider the legal aspect. At present, by law only physicians can do insertions.

As for the time of insertion, we are still holding to the standard of insertion soon after the cessation of menses. Since some clients falsified their menstrual period termination date to avoid rejection, we have been forced to revise the coupon which clients sign. Now the coupon includes the date they say their periods had ceased, so we are released from the responsibility of pregnancy before insertion.

As acceptability of the loop is steadily increasing, 1 million insertions —i.e., a quarter of all the eligible couples—during the next five years seems quite possible, if proper service can be provided.

35

A FAMILY PLANNING PROGRAM RELATED
TO MATERNITY SERVICE

HOWARD C. TAYLOR, Jr., M.D.

Chairman Emeritus, Department of Obstetrics and Gynecology
Columbia University College of Physicians and Surgeons
Medical Consultant, The Population Council

The advent of the progestins and the rediscovery of the intra-uterine device have inaugurated a new era in the drive to provide women with the means to plan their pregnancies and thus to place some restraint on population increase. For the first time, there are available methods which are highly effective and reasonably simple. The opportunities afforded by these new methods have brought with them a needed re-emphasis on means of contact, of education, and of motivation of people.

In a broad sense, this paper is concerned with the advantages of a system in which family planning would be treated as an integral part of the health and medical organization for maternity care. Such an approach is to be contrasted with a program stressing general, perhaps somewhat random, public education along with birth control clinics or other services for all who may, as a result of general propaganda, be inspired to attend. The two systems are, of course, not mutually exclusive, nor would they be competitive in practice. Undoubtedly elements of each must enter into every national or regional program and, indeed, in time one system might evolve into the other. However, the fact of limited funds and energies makes it essential to examine relative advantages in order to decide where the major effort should be placed to produce the greatest effect. My discussion of this subject will be divided into four sections:

1. The statistical advantages of the introduction of contraception in the post-partum period

2. The educational opportunities afforded during pregnancy and the puerperium
3. Essentials in a pregnancy–post-partum program
4. A view of some maternity services about the world with respect to their suitability for a post-partum family planning program

THE STATISTICAL ADVANTAGES OF THE INTRODUCTION OF
CONTRACEPTION IN THE POST-PARTUM PERIOD

Only a little consideration is needed to show that contraceptive advice given shortly after parturition will be more effective, in preventing conception, than advice offered at some later date.

TABLE 1

RELATIVE EFFECTIVENESS OF BEGINNING
CONTRACEPTION AT VARIOUS MONTHS
AFTER FIRST POST-PARTUM PERIOD

Months after First Post-partum Menstrual Period	Pregnant at End of Month (per cent)	Pregnancy Potential at Beginning of Month
0	4.8	0.321
1	18.7	.315
2	37.6	.292
3	53.0	.247
4	61.9	.190
5	67.5	.147
6	71.3	.117
7	74.2	.098
8	76.4	.086
9	78.3	.079
10	79.8	.073
11	81.2	.069
12	82.5	0.066

Working with principles described in several of his own previous publications,[1] Christopher Tietze has kindly prepared for me a table which shows the diminishing "pregnancy potential" (per cycle) as the months pass after the first post-partum menstrual period (Table 1).[2] This table assumes that contraception is not being used and, further, that there is a 5% incidence of infertility after any delivery. The table is constructed on the basis of months after the first menstrual period and not after date of delivery. Certain observations, however, permit

[1] "Differential Fecundity and Effectiveness of Contraception," *Eugenics Review*, 50: 231–37 (1959); "The Effect of Breast Feeding on the Rate of Conception" (Publication No. 21 of the National Committee on Maternal Health), *Proceedings of the International Population Conference, New York, 1961*, 2: 129–36.

[2] Christopher Tietze, personal communication.

approximate rules for recalculating the table's figures as months after delivery.[3] Thus it appears that in the absence of lactation, the median duration of post-partum amenorrhea is from six to eight weeks and when breast feeding is practiced, about three-fourths of the average period of lactation (Tietze).

The data show that, assuming no contraception, about half of the women will have conceived within three months of the first post-partum menstrual period and about four-fifths within one year. To state this somewhat differently, four-fifths of the pregnancy potential will be dissipated by the end of the first year.

In groups of women applying for contraceptive advice at some date remote from the first post-partum menstrual period, there is evidence that one is dealing with women of relatively low fertility or with some, perhaps many, who have been practicing some form of birth control with at least partial success. In these, the application of a birth control device or prescription will represent little net gain in conceptions prevented. One returns therefore to the original proposition of this section, namely, that contraception begun a year after a delivery is far less productive of results, statistically speaking, than that begun in the post-partum period before the time of the first ovulation.

THE EDUCATIONAL OPPORTUNITIES AFFORDED DURING PREGNANCY AND THE PUERPERIUM

The period of pregnancy and the puerperium offer unique opportunities to reach the women of any country in a systematic manner, at a time when contact with persons for whom the woman has respect is at its maximum and, furthermore, when the subject of family planning is clearly most relevant.

Universality.—In many countries, supervision of either the actual delivery or some part of the ante-partum period is nearly universal. In almost all others, the development of a program for general maternal care is fairly high on the list of health priorities. The pregnant woman, ideally and often in fact, is under the influence of this system for several months of her pregnancy and perhaps for several weeks thereafter. The latter period of contact may be prolonged if the mother returns with her infant for child health supervision.

The maternal health organization provides, therefore, a basis for a systematic and nearly universal organization for education in matters

[3] L. Mayer, "Häufigkeit der Menstruation während des Stillens," *Beiträge zur Geburtshilfe und Gynäkologie*, 2: 136–42 (1873): A. Sharman, "Menstruation after Childbirth," *Journal of Obstetrics and Gynecology of the British Empire*, 58: 440–45 (1951).

pertaining to reproduction. The women of the country should all come under the influence of this system, preferably in convenient annual "classes," with the regularity of children entering the first grade of the primary schools.

Instruction after the first child and regular repetition.—A particular advantage to this approach is that the woman will be introduced to the idea of family planning with emphasis on the principle of "child spacing," after her first delivery. Whether or not she heeds the advice at this time, the seed of the idea will have been planted, and after a second, third, or fourth child, with the regular repetition of the same advice, action will probably be taken.

Psychological advantages.—The obstetrical hospitals and maternity clinics appear, then, to offer an excellent organization, almost ready built, for the development of an educational system concerned with family planning. The susceptibility of the patient to advice given must also be thought of as reaching a peak during her pregnancy and puerperium. The physician, or his midwife or nurse associates, has already been accorded the role of guide and protector to assure a safe delivery and with the happy event accomplished, advice from the same source will surely have a special significance. Beyond this, the very fact of a recent birth must give rise to a consideration of the next one. The relevance and, indeed, the urgency of family planning to the recently delivered woman are quite clear. With a trusted authority at hand, the psychological setting could scarcely be improved upon.

Technical advantage.—A small point, perhaps, but one which should be mentioned, is that the intra-uterine device can be inserted particularly easily during the puerperium. Whether the device can be inserted, with a reasonable chance of its remaining in place, during the first post-partum hours or days, is a point still to be determined. It is clear, however, that for several weeks, the cervical canal remains readily dilatable so that passage of the inserter is particularly easy.

Discipline and evaluation.—The integration of a family planning program with pregnancy and delivery would provide an opportunity, and a special reason, for birth registration in countries where this is not yet universal. A system by which birth certificates contained a section to be checked by the attendant to show that birth control advice had been given would provide a needed discipline for the obstetrical attendants. (A similar system has been used successfully in the United States to popularize other routine procedures in pregnancy, such as the serological tests.) The advantages of such a plan for the eventual evaluation of the work on a demographic basis would be very great.

ESSENTIALS IN A PREGNANCY–POST-PARTUM PROGRAM

At this point it is proper to pause to consider briefly the essential elements in a family planning program integrated with a maternity service. In a general way, the needs may be summed up by stating that pregnancy should become *a period of education* and the post-partum weeks *a time of decision* on the part of the patient and prescription of the selected means of contraception by the medical attendant. A little imagination can supply many details by which the system could be elaborated.

The ante-partum weeks.—Good health practice requires that the expectant mother make regular visits to an ante-partum clinic for an initial health examination and for subsequent observations of weight, renal function, and blood pressure. These visits provide the time for the informal or formal introduction of the idea of family planning. In many maternity services there are already regularly organized "mothers' classes," in which reassuring information is given about health matters of importance during pregnancy and thereafter. Where such "mothers' classes" do not exist, they should be developed. Little change in the organization of the mothers' classes as they now exist would be required to add discussions of the physiology of conception and thus lead to the topic of family planning. The classes should be conducted by the nurse, midwife, or physician upon whom the woman can best bestow her confidence.

The lying-in period.—The days immediately after delivery, the "lying-in period," should be used to sharpen the woman's interest and to impart the idea that a decision about family planning must be made before a predictable first ovulation, this time depending to a degree on her intent with respect to lactation. The importance of a post-partum visit, within six weeks, should be stressed and a definite appointment given. All women, whether delivered in a hospital or at home, should have this bedside visit.

The post-partum clinic.—The post-partum clinic should be developed as an essential part of good maternity care. The importance of this visit, at about the sixth week, should be related to the health needs of the mother and her child, as well as to family planning.

Advice on family planning may, however, soon come to be the most important function of the post-partum clinic. Here again emphasis is best placed on the health advantage, to mother and child, of an appropriate interval between pregnancies. Finally, it is at this time that definite steps should be taken, by insertion or prescription, to provide the mother with the means to delay her next pregnancy.

Once again it should be emphasized that as fast as such a system could be instituted, there should be a cross check between recorded births and birth control advice given. This is needed both for over-all evaluation and as a sort of disciplinary check on the attendant's observation of the agreed-upon routines.

A VIEW OF SOME MATERNITY SERVICES ABOUT THE WORLD
WITH RESPECT TO THEIR SUITABILITY FOR A POST-PARTUM
PROGRAM OF FAMILY PLANNING

If it is indeed true, as has been suggested here, that pregnancy offers the unrivaled opportunity for education, and that the post-partum period is the critical one for decision and action, then the status of maternity services throughout the world becomes a crucial point for examination. It is necessary, in planning, that we should know the place where women are delivered and the capabilities of the attendant who is in charge. These points determine the accessibility of the woman to the sources of information and of prescription.

The auspices under which pregnancy is supervised and labor conducted may be arranged in a rough order of descending contact between the woman and the sources of information.

Hospital deliveries by physician or midwife.—Here the greatest opportunity is offered for education and instruction. The problems are those of medical enlightenment and development of an effective organization.

Home deliveries by physician or qualified midwife.—Here the opportunities are nearly as great as in the hospital deliveries, except that systematic organization is not as easy and responsibility for giving family planning information rests on the individual attendant.

Home deliveries by unqualified persons but with some ante-partum visits to an organized clinic.—At this point, the line of communication greatly weakens. There remain the brief moments when the expectant mother is being checked by the physician or health worker, when she may be told of the importance to her of child spacing and of the opportunity offered her if she will return for a post-partum visit.

Home deliveries without qualified supervision during pregnancy or at delivery.—This group, which is a sizable one in many developing countries, of course offers the greatest problem. The long-term effort should be toward the expansion of maternity services, so that no woman will have to accept the risk of a completely unsupervised pregnancy. For the immediate future, efforts should be made, by appropriate health or social workers, to detect in the cities and villages the women who are pregnant or nursing and to persuade these to go to a post-partum family planning clinic before another conception occurs. Although these women may be relatively inaccessible to the health and medical authorities, the whole problem will become somewhat easier if it is recognized that the women immediately and primarily at risk are the ones toward whom the greatest educational efforts should be directed.

To provide a quick view of the world situation, with respect to obstetrical service, an inquiry with six questions was mailed to various correspondents throughout the world. The results are shown in Tables 2 and 3. These figures should not in all cases be taken as precisely accu-

TABLE 2

PLACE AND SUPERVISION OF DELIVERY IN VARIOUS CITIES

City	Hospital or Nursing Home (per cent)	Supervised Domiciliary Delivery (per cent)	Unsupervised Home Delivery (per cent)
Osaka.............	86.7	13.2	0.05
Seoul.............	11.0	12.0	77.0
Taipei.............	28.2	70.8	1.0
Hong Kong.......	98.7	1.3	0.0
Manila...........	77.2	22.7ᵃ	....
Singapore.........	69.1	30.2	0.6
Madras City......	53.4	39.6	6.0
Delhi.............	35.2	47.3	17.5
Istanbul..........	86.6	13.4	0.0
Nairobi...........	50.0	10.0	40.0
London...........	53.7	46.3	0.0
Caracas...........	99.0	0.79	0.13
Buenos Aires (1948– 52 average)	76.9	23.1	0.0
Sydney...........	99.0	1.0	0.0

ᵃ Outside of hospitals; degree of supervision unspecified.

rate, but rather as representing the intelligent estimates of responsible persons. Furthermore, meanings of the terms used in the simple questionnaire may have been differently interpreted by different respondents, and some figures may, therefore, have been placed in the wrong columns. In spite of this, some general conclusions may be reached.

In the cities throughout the world, a surprisingly large percentage of women are delivered in hospitals or maternity nursing homes. When this figure is low, it is often balanced, as in Britain, by a high figure for supervised domiciliary delivery. A few exceptions exist but, in general, women living in cities throughout the world have access to educational and implementative programs carried out in relation to pregnancy and delivery.

When, on the other hand, one looks at statistics for countries as a whole, which include the large rural populations, one often finds that a half of all deliveries take place without trained attendants. These unsupervised deliveries are most frequent in the countries in which the population problem is most urgent. These are the women who are the most difficult to reach, and doubtless will be the last to be convinced of the importance and necessity of family planning.

GENERAL COMMENT

There is no intent to suggest that all other means of bringing birth control to the people be abandoned and that the exclusive effort be

TABLE 3

PLACE AND SUPERVISION OF DELIVERY IN VARIOUS
COUNTRIES OR STATES

Country or State	Hospital or Nursing Home (per cent)	Supervised Domiciliary Delivery (per cent)	No Trained Attendant (per cent)
Japan	66.2	32.5	1.3
Korea	3.0	3.0	94.0
Taiwan	14.1	51.8	34.1
Philippines	16.7	83.2[a]	....
Madras State	16.5	33.2	50.4
Turkey	15.3	8.1	76.6
Kenya	15.0	15.0	70.0
United Kingdom	49.1	48.8	2.1
Venezuela	88.4	8.3	33.3
Argentina	45.0	45.0	10.0
New South Wales	99.5	0.5	0.0

[a] Outside of hospitals; degree of supervision unspecified.

made through a program integrated with maternity services. My purpose has been to raise the question of whether *the chief formal effort* should not be made within this framework.

There are three ways by which birth control may become general practice.

First, it has been argued that through industrialization and improved standards of living and education, birth control will come almost spontaneously to be practiced. This, indeed, was the course followed in Europe, but the process apparently took many decades.

Second, through various types of general education and availability of clinics, it appears that the most educated and susceptible groups of a population may be quickly reached. From these it is supposed the knowledge and practice of family planning will gradually spread. To stress this approach is at least to attempt the easiest job first, but we do not know how rapidly the process of dissemination will take place, or when women of relatively low parity will begin to volunteer in significant numbers.

The third method is the one advocated in this paper; that there should be a concentration of effort on a single phase of our social organization, that concerned with maternal care. It has been pointed out that women who have just completed a pregnancy are the ones chiefly at risk and personally most concerned. To work primarily with them would be placing the emphasis where maximum results could be obtained with a minimum of effort.

Should the latter course be decided upon, family planning and maternity care would have similar objectives and would become important allies. In order to attain the necessary access to the women of the world, organizations concerned with family planning would work for the extension of maternity clinics, until all women were included. They would strive for the reduction in perinatal mortality to remove the sensed need of women to overproduce in order to be sure of sufficient surviving children. They would emphasize the importance, in spite of difficulties, of obtaining total birth registration, as a disciplinary technique to assure that all women receive birth control advice and in order that results may be quickly evaluated.

These proposals may seem utopian, but as a statement of a final objective may point to the immediate road to be taken. The question has at least been asked whether the improved organization of maternity care, and the integration with this of family planning programs, may not after all be the shortest route to the ultimate goal.

36

POST-PARTUM INSERTION OF A
STANDARD LIPPES LOOP

L. L. WILLIAMS, F.R.C.S.
Senior Medical Officer, Victoria Jubilee
Hospital, Kingston, Jamaica
West Indies

POPULATION TRENDS IN JAMAICA

The population of Jamaica at the end of 1963 was 1,706,318, and the population density 403 per square mile. Over the past 100 years, the population increased gradually up to 1930, more sharply over the next 30 years, and most steeply between 1960 and 1964. If the present trend continues and migration from Jamaica is restricted, the population will continue to rise precipitously to an estimated 2.5 million in 1971. Between 1938 and 1948 the birth rate in Jamaica actually declined, but it rose again in 1951 above the 1938 level. From 1952 on, it rose gradually to a peak of 42.1 in 1960, fell in 1962, but in 1963—the last year for which figures are available—it stood at 40.5. In that year the largest number of births for any one year was recorded: 69,266.

The present birth rate places Jamaica among the highly fertile areas in the world. Reduced to a language that the Jamaican man in the street can understand, a baby is born every nine minutes. At the same time, the death rate has decreased over the same period from 16.75 to 8.6—among the lowest in the world. The infant mortality rate in 1963 was 49.2 in contrast to the 1938 figure of 129.2.

Furthermore, migration to the United Kingdom, which for a time afforded an outlet to the expanding population and reached a peak of 40,000 in 1961, fell sharply during the next two years to 7,500 in 1963, as a result of the Commonwealth Immigration Act of 1962.

The population density is greatest in the capital city of Kingston:

443

14,868 per square mile. In 1964, 15,000 births or 21.6% of the island's total births occurred in the Victoria Jubilee Hospital. It has 164 beds and provides 70% of the public (non-private) beds for a population of 420,000 in the adjoining parishes of Kingston and St. Andrew.

ATTITUDES TOWARD CONTRACEPTION

Before April, 1964, facilities for advice on family planning were limited to two clinics, one in Kingston and the other in the rural parish of St. Ann. These clinics were operated by the Family Planning Association of Jamaica, and to this voluntary organization, founded in 1939, must be given the credit for establishing and pioneering the concept of family planning in Jamaica.

However, as late as the period 1960–64, contraception had reached only a small fraction of the 15–44 age group of the population in the areas where these clinics were located. There seem to be two possible reasons for this: either an uninformed and poorly motivated public, or rejection of traditional methods of contraception because of recurrent cost, inconvenience, or difficulties of application. Poor motivation seemed unlikely in view of the great demand made on us for sterilization procedures at the Victoria Jubilee Hospital—a demand which had become increasingly difficult to cope with in view of staff shortages and extreme pressure on beds.

An intra-uterine contraceptive device program seemed likely to be successful. A single sampling of thirty-four patients about to be discharged from the puerperal wards of the hospital showed that twenty patients were interested, and thus encouraged us to proceed further. Accordingly, in April, 1964, our program was launched with a grant provided by the Population Council. An indirect approach through printed invitations yielded only ninety patients in the first month and was abandoned in favor of a personal interview with the clinic nurse on her visit to the wards each morning, and a firm appointment for insertion was then made for each interested patient. The response was immediately overwhelming.

INSERTION CLINICS

Clinics are held twice a week and each clinic is limited to twenty-five new patients. The program was restricted to post-partum patients. Patients who recently had had an abortion were rejected because we were afraid that the success of the program, at least until it was well established, might be compromised by including these patients in whom there might be a residue of pelvic infection. No post-partum patient applying for insertion has, so far, been rejected. A Lippes No.

3 device was used in all insertions, which were made any time after the sixth post-partum week. We prefer to wait a minimum of eight weeks after Caesarean section.

We think it is an advantage for one physician to do all the physical examinations, the patients then passing to another physician for insertion. In this way, we believe that we can achieve better asepsis in our technique as well as speed up the flow of patients through the clinic. In our view, the disadvantage of an insertion being made by anyone other than the examiner is more theoretical than real. In any event, any deviation from the normal, e.g., a retroverted uterus, can be brought to the attention of the inserter who may then confirm the examiner's findings before insertion.

TABLE 1

AGE DISTRIBUTION

Age	Number	Per Cent
Less than 15.........	1	....
15–19..............	56	4.2
20–24..............	416	31.6
25–29..............	433	32.8
30–34..............	261	19.8
35.................	149	11.3
Total............	1,316	100

Among our patients, 55.4% had not yet begun to menstruate at the time of insertion. In the remaining 44.6% who had re-established menstruation, insertions were made at any time in the menstrual cycle. There is, of course, the risk of insertion in an early pregnant uterus if the insertion is done during the second half of the cycle. Against this must be weighed the inconvenience to the patient of another visit to the clinic and the difficulty of matching each patient's cycle to clinics that are held only twice a week. It is clear that the recommendation that insertions be made on certain days of the period, though desirable, is not practical in a large clinic.

A total of 1,316 patients had insertions between April 1, 1964 and March 31, 1965, representing 8,062 woman-months of experience. Papanicolaou smears were taken routinely. Follow-up visits were scheduled at intervals of three months, six months, and one year. Patients were, however, free to return at any time if they needed advice or treatment.

The social characteristics of our patients are given in Tables 1, 2, and 3. A total of 6,177 children had been born to these women, and 5,693 had survived.

SYMPTOMS—AN ANALYSIS

In our follow-up interviews, 280 patients (21.2%) complained of symptoms, the three main ones being pain, bleeding, and discharge (see Table 4). Of these patients, 214 had a single symptom and 66 had two or more symptoms. The breakdown is based on what, on analysis, appeared to have been the patient's leading symptom when two or more symptoms existed—hereafter referred to as a primary symptom. Where another symptom was present but was not the chief cause of complaint, it will be referred to as a secondary symptom.

TABLE 2

MARITAL STATUS

Status	Number	Per Cent
Single.............	612	46.5
Common law........	377	28.6
Married............	321	24.4
Divorced/separated...	5	0.4
Widowed...........	1	....
Total.............	1,316	100

TABLE 3

LIVING CHILDREN

Children	Number of Women	Per Cent
1.............	31	2.3
2.............	162	12.2
3.............	282	21.4
4.............	279	21.1
5.............	223	16.9
6.............	152	11.6
7.............	93	7.1
8.............	48	3.6
9.............	46	3.5
Total.......	1,316	100

Pain was the most common complaint. It was a primary symptom in eighty-eight patients and a secondary symptom in thirty-eight others. The incidence is greatest in the first three months after insertion. Four patients complained of dyspareunia. Twenty-one patients showed evidence of pelvic infection—nineteen mild and two severe. One patient was hospitalized, and all responded to antibiotics. Pain was the leading cause of removal of the device in this series (21 out of 75 removals), in fifteen cases at the request of the patient.

Metrorrhagia was a primary symptom in seventy-four patients and a secondary symptom in six others. By far the maximum incidence was during the first month; it was a negligible symptom after the third month.

Menorrhagia, while third in order of incidence, is to the patient the most alarming symptom. It was a primary symptom in sixty-four patients and a secondary symptom in two others. Of the four major symptoms, it is the only one of any significance beyond the third post-insertion month. It was a cause for removal in nine patients, in six at their request. These patients very often present themselves during an episode of bleeding. More than any other symptom it demands active treatment by the physician. Yet treatment was unsatisfactory

TABLE 4

SYMPTOMS FOLLOWING LOOP INSERTION

Symptom	Number	Per Cent
Pain..................	88	31.4
Metrorrhagia..........	74	26.1
Menorrhagia...........	64	22.8
Discharge.............	36	12.9
Dysmenorrhoea........	8	2.9
Polymenorrhoea........	4	1.5
Miscellaneous..........	6	2.1
Total..............	280	100

and was limited to the empiric administration of vitamin K, Ergometrine, iron, and antibiotics in cases where the bleeding was thought to be associated with low-grade pelvic infection.

Vaginal discharge was a leading symptom in thirty-six patients and a secondary symptom in thirty-four others. It is a negligible symptom beyond the third month. By itself, it was a cause for removal in three patients and, in combination with pain, a cause for removal in five others.

Dysmenorrhoea is excessively rare, occurring in eight patients as a primary symptom and in three as a secondary symptom. It was not a cause for removal in this series.

Expulsion occurred in 110 patients (8.2%), in 75% of the cases occurring in the first three months. Of the total, eighty-five patients expelled once, and fifty-five were reinserted and all retained the device; twenty-five patients expelled twice, and nine had insertions for the third time and so far have retained the device. In all, forty-six patients have discontinued the use of the device because of expulsion.

Removal occurred in the case of seventy-five patients (5.9%), for reasons given in Table 5.

Pregnancy.—There were twenty-four pregnancies in this series, giving a failure rate of 3.6 per 100 woman-years of exposure calculated on the Pearl formula. In the 55.4% of women who had not yet begun to menstruate at the time of insertion, no allowance has been made for the dual protection against pregnancy afforded by the amenorrhoea of lactation during which fertility is suspended. In retrospect four patients were probably pregnant at insertion. One patient had expelled on two occasions and had probably become pregnant at a time when she was not protected. One patient had removed the device herself immediately after a period because it "made her sick." This was her first period after her recent confinement, and it was to be her last before her next one.

Two pregnancies have ended in abortion. One is remarkable for the fact that the device was not expelled at the time of abortion, nor could it be recovered when the uterus was explored under anesthesia.

TABLE 5

REASONS FOR REMOVAL OF LOOPS

Reasons	Number	Per Cent
Pain	21	29.1
Emigration	12	16.7
Menorrhagia	9	12.5
Metrorrhagia	7	9.7
Pain and discharge	5	6.9
Discharge	3	4.2
Miscellaneous	15	20.8
Total	75	100

X-ray examination showed that it was outside the pelvis. On laparotomy it was found attached to the omentum in the abdominal cavity but examination of the uterus showed no evidence where perforation might have occurred, nor was there anything to suggest this in the patient's history from the time of insertion.

An unintended pregnancy when failure occurs is a catastrophe in the life of these patients. The diagnosis is received in stunned silence, very often followed by tears, on occasions by an angry outburst. As we are more and more impressed by the implicit faith our patients have placed in this method of contraception, we are increasingly convinced of the necessity of making our patients understand from the outset that the device, while offering a considerable degree of safety, does not guarantee total protection. It is our policy to offer sterilization to all our failures.

What of the future? It is now the declared policy of the government of Jamaica to provide advice on all methods of contraception, free of cost and without persuasion, for all who desire it. In a combined program with the Jamaica Family Planning Association, it is proposed that thirty insertion centers be established throughout the island roughly on the basis of one center to 60,000 population. Twenty-five centers have so far been formed but few are working to full capacity because of the shortage of medical personnel. The 4,800 insertions performed in the first year fall far short of the 20,000 insertions per year estimated necessary to stabilize the population at its present level. Nevertheless, a start has been made and over the past year we have come a long way, to the day when the Governor General of Jamaica, speaking at the recent opening of the new Kingston Clinic of the Jamaica Family Planning Association, had this to say:

Family planning has come to stay; it is not a passing shadow. The stark reality of its necessity is upon us and those who have not yet realized that they ought to take hold of the opportunity to disseminate useful knowledge and information to those who are devoid of it, are enemies of their own country and their own destiny.

37

THE TRAINING OF THE NURSE-MIDWIFE FOR A NATIONAL PROGRAM IN BARBADOS COMBINING THE IUD AND CERVICAL CYTOLOGY

G. T. M. CUMMINS, M.R.C.O.G.
Chief, Obstetrics and Gynaecology
Queen Elizabeth Hospital

and

HENRY W. VAILLANT, M.D.
Field Research Assistant, National Institute of Child
Health and Human Development, U.S.A.

In Barbados we have recently inaugurated an island-wide program with two objectives: (1) to introduce the Lippes loop as a mass contraceptive measure, utilizing nurse-midwives as inserters, and (2) to screen the population of childbearing women annually for cervical cancer by exfoliative cytology. We anticipate that out of a total population of 245,000, of which 57,000 are of childbearing age, about 40,000 women will have Papanicolaou smears annually, and about 10,000 active loop cases will be enrolled.

Before the program began, the volume of exfoliative cytology performed in the island was minimal, consisting of several hundred smears per year taken in private practice. Contraceptive advice and supplies had been available for about a decade from the Family Planning Association of Barbados, a voluntary organization partially supported by a small government grant. Since January, 1964, the Association had been using IUD's, first the Margulies spiral and later the Lippes loop. These had been inserted by a voluntary panel of eight doctors. At the end of sixteen months about 800 IUD's had been inserted.

In May, 1965, a Population Council grant permitted an expansion of the IUD program and the development of a cytology program. Three nurse-midwife teams, composed of a nurse-midwife and nurse-assistant, have been trained in the last three months to carry out the bulk of the double program. The reasons for training paramedical personnel were the following:

1. Barbados shares with the rest of the world a shortage of doctors, having only one per 3,000 people.
2. Barbados has well-trained nurse-midwives available.
3. Volunteer private physicians have only limited time to give to the Family Planning Association and had been doing only 50–100 insertions a month.
4. The actual techniques of insertion and smear-taking are not elaborate and seemed within the capabilities of nurse-midwives.
5. The nurse-midwife could be employed at reasonable cost to work full time, thus rapidly widening the scope of both the IUD and the cytology programs.

The problems that we anticipated in a project using nurse-midwives were: (1) Because of the intimate nature of contraception, patients might well prefer doctors to nurses. (2) The opportunity to recognize significant clinical conditions at the time of insertion might be lost. Contraindications to the use of the IUD might be overlooked. (3) Inept techniques might produce serious complications. (4) Legal problems might arise.

At the same time, we felt these disadvantages were countered by the following factors: (1) Intrinsic in the training of the nurse-midwife is the tradition of calling in the doctor for complications. (2) The nurse-midwife is legally accredited to carry out limited practice in this specialty of medicine. (3) The clinical knowledge required for IUD insertion is limited and could be taught in a short period. (4) Any errors made during the training period would be more than compensated for by the unwanted children and abortions prevented, and the cervical cancer that would ultimately be prevented by the program. (5) The nurse-midwife could be backed up by a medical consultant on call.

To expand the function of the nurse-midwife, she was provided with an assistant. This assistant helps her in much the same way as a skilled nurse helps a doctor, taking care of details and leaving the nurse-midwife free to concentrate on the job at hand. The assistants chosen have had some training in nursing without necessarily having received a diploma. Their salary is therefore less than that of a trained nurse.

Because the insertion itself is rather simple, some have advocated a short, intensive period of training for the IUD inserter. We do not share this concept. The nurse-midwife requires some gynecological experience inasmuch as most of her formal training has dealt only with obstetrics. She should not only be capable of doing almost all insertions herself, but should also be a competent observer of certain gynecological conditions. Gross gynecological abnormalities should be noted even if no diagnosis is made. Referral can then be made to a medical consultant. Early pregnancy must always be recognized. The ability to recognize complications of insertion is essential so that a consultant can be called promptly.

No particular training course can guarantee the fulfillment of these objectives. The training of each nurse-midwife and her assistant is a highly personal matter, analogous to the training of a physician. Our two-month training course has consisted of the following weekly programs:

1. Four half-days in apprenticeship to an obstetrician-gynecologist during surgery, antenatal examinations, gynecological clinics, and loop insertions.
2. Two half-days of apprenticeship to an internist with emphasis on IUD insertions and proper techniques of obtaining Papanicolaou smears.
3. Two half-days of rounds, didactic lectures, and reading.
4. Two half-days of unsupervised in-service experience doing Papanicolaou smears, operating a clinic independently, and performing simple insertions. A doctor is always on call during these sessions, but the lack of his immediate presence helps to build confidence in the trainee that she can practice on her own. The number of these independent sessions is then gradually increased commensurate with the individual skill of the team.

At present, three nurse-midwife teams have been trained and operate clinics independently all over the island. They continue to have about one day each week of review, lectures, and rounds so that their extensive activities do not dull their capacity for self-criticism.

The results at the end of the first three months (during which much of the trainees' time was spent in teaching sessions) are encouraging. There are now approximately 1,600 Lippes loops in place and 1,200 Papanicolaou smears have been taken. The volume of activities of the nurse-midwives increases each week as is shown in Table 1. The nurse-midwives have performed 688 Papanicolaou smears and 204 IUD insertions. Because of the brief observation period, only thirty-three of the patients have returned for a routine two-month follow-up visit. Nineteen have returned with specific complaints of bleeding or cramps, expulsions, and pelvic inflammatory disease. These cases necessitated two removals of the device. In addition, two significant complications related to loop insertion have been encountered, one uterine perforation which led to no subsequent illness and one insertion into a pregnant uterus which has so far not resulted in abortion. These cases are summarized in Table 2.

Certain factors which are less easy to tabulate are equally significant in such a program. The most important of these is the attitude of the island's physicians. In general, they have been politely skeptical, but they are gradually being convinced of the usefulness and skill of the nurse-midwives. The nurse-midwives of the island have also changed their attitude. Early in the program, many were unwilling to apply, fearing lawsuits and the disfavor of the medical profession.

TABLE 1

ACTIVITIES OF BARBADOS NURSE-MIDWIVES

Dates (1965)	Papanicolaou Smears	Loop Insertions
June 1–30	96	10
July 1–31	299	91
August 1–16	293	103
Total	688	204

TABLE 2

COMPLICATIONS OF IUD INSERTIONS BY
BARBADOS NURSE-MIDWIVES
JUNE 1–AUGUST 16, 1965

Bleeding or cramps	13
Expulsions	3
Pelvic inflammatory disease	3
Medically indicated removals	2
Insertion in pregnant uterus	1
Uterine perforation	1

Now that the program is well underway, however, there are continual new applications for project posts from the island's nurse-midwives. The patients' acceptance of the nurse-midwives has been virtually universal in public clinics.

The physician has not been entirely replaced, however. One remains on call for the clinics, handling problems by telephone. Another is usually on hand for follow-up visits, in which such complaints as bleeding, abdominal pain, or repeated expulsions can be managed. We do not feel that the nurse-midwife can be given the responsibility of prescribing analgesics, hemostatic drugs, or hormones.

Although no decisive conclusion can be drawn from our brief experience, the results of the project so far support the feasibility of training nurse-midwives to carry out such a program.

38

THE UNITED STATES MEDICAL PROFESSION
AND FAMILY PLANNING

ALAN F. GUTTMACHER, M.D.
President, Planned Parenthood—World Population
New York City

In the United States, until the last five or six years, the medical profession has been resistant to becoming involved in the whole area of preventing conception. It has preferred to remain in a neutral corner, neither condemning nor approving. Both socioeconomically and politically, American doctors are conservative; in such fields they do not lead, they follow unless their incomes are threatened.

In the twentieth century the American medical profession has been content to permit laymen to spearhead movements to liberalize restrictive laws and attitudes toward conception control which arose in the nineteenth century.

The sterilization movement was begun by eugenicists who forecast that America would eventually be taken over by mental and social incompetents by virtue of their outbreeding the competents. It is only in the last several years that any consideration has been given to sterilization as a means of relief for the excessively fertile couple from their uncontrollable fertility. In 1940 Eastman[1] and Yerushalmy[2] showed that both maternal and fetal risk rose gradually after a sixth birth and appreciably after an eighth. Therefore, after that time on the basis of medical risk alone—not socioeconomic relief—Eastman initiated voluntary puerperal sterilization for any woman with an eighth or greater birth. In 1952 at the Mt. Sinai Hospital in New York the Obstetrical and Gynecological Service instituted sterilization of any

[1] N. J. Eastman, "Hazards of Pregnancy and Labor in the Grande Multipara," *New York State Journal of Medicine*, 40:1708 (1940).

[2] J. Yerushalmy, C. E. Palmer, and M. Kramer, "Studies in Childbirth Mortality. II. Age and Purity as Factors in Puerperal Mortality," *Public Health Reports*, 55:1195 (1940).

mother who desired it with her sixth living child irrespective of age, with a fifth living child when she is 30–35 years old, and with a fourth living child when older. It was publicly stressed that such sterilizations were not done on the grounds of medical risk, as obstetrics had improved so markedly since the late thirties and high-parity births in 1952 were very infrequently attended by death. The true indication was spelled out, which I cannot help feeling also partly motivated Eastman's statement about women who had borne eight children—namely, relief from the socioeconomic burden of uncontrollable, excessive fertility. (The rule introduced at Mt. Sinai, using parity and age as sliding criteria for sterilization, has become known as the Law from Mt. Sinai.) Using the numbers of living children as an indication for puerperal sterilization in the absence of maternal disease is still considered semi-radical by much of the American medical profession. If a group of ordinary parents promulgated such rules instead of physicians, it is more likely that thoughtful supplication for the procedure by a mature couple with normal intelligence might be grounds for sterilization irrespective of family size.

The lay public has long been in clandestine rebellion against the highly restrictive abortion laws of the fifty states—laws no doubt suggested by doctors of medicine and divinity, written by lawyers, and framed into statutes by legislators. The medical profession has zealously avoided giving either leadership or counsel to the rebellion. This is in spite of the fact that it recognizes that the antiquated abortion laws, like the prohibition law of the twenties, can never work, for they are contrary to the desires and interests of the populace. The medical profession is cognizant of the fact that the abortion racket is the third largest in America, involving as racketeers, in many instances, members of their own profession. Physicians witness daily inequities in the applicaton of therapeutic abortion, leading to a five-to-one ratio in favor of the private over the clinic patient and a virtual absence of legal abortion in municipal hospitals. Medicine silently compels women impregnated through rape or incest to bear their bastards and refuses to apply modern genetics and teratology to fetal outcome in support of therapeutic abortion for eugenic reasons. Neither the American Medical Association nor the College of Obstetrics nor any other national group of medical leaders has taken any positive action about induced abortion;[3] they abdicate the leadership to

[3]Local medical groups have discussed the problem within the last three years. The California Obstetrical and Gynecological Society passed a resolution to reform the California statute and testified in favor of the Bielenson bill at a legislative hearing. In November, 1965, the chairman of the New York County Medical Society appointed a committee of doctors to review the New York State abortion statute and bring in recommendations. The American College of Obstetrics and Gynecology has scheduled a panel discussion of abortion statutes at its May, 1966, annual meeting.

such groups as the American Law Institute and the Los Angeles County Grand Jurors Association, both of which have made recommendations toward the liberalization of existing statutes.

MEDICAL CONSERVATISM ON BIRTH CONTROL

A third and far more widely applicable technique of conception control is the use of contraception. Historically it antedates sterilization, but anthropologists are unable to determine whether abortion or contraception is the older. Both were securely entrenched when the first extant written records of medicine—the early Egyptian medical papyri—were penned 4,000 years ago.

Why has the American medical profession been so conservative in its attitude toward contraception? I believe there are six reasons.

1. *Preserve life.*—A physician's training gives primacy to the preservation of life, no matter how distorted and wretched that life may be. Therefore to prevent the creation of life is often perceived as antithetic to his primary purpose.

2. *Non nocere* (do not harm).—This is the physician's credo. The Lying-in Hospital of Chicago during the tenure of its founder, one of America's great obstetricians, Dr. Joseph B. DeLee, had a tablet with the words *"non nocere"* in each delivery room on the wall facing the obstetrician as he sat upon his stool prepared to carry out the delivery. And the dictum is carried over into general medical philosophy. In medical practice a sin of omission is less likely to be regarded as seriously as a sin of commission—that is, it is less grievous to do harm to a patient by doing nothing when action is indicated than by doing something when the action harms the patient. Obviously, if the student or resident absorbs this philosophy, doing nothing when in doubt is preferable to taking a risk. I believe that the do-nothing attitude of the medical profession toward contraception stems in part from this.

3. *Popularity with colleagues.*—Medical practice is a strange hybrid; it is part business and part profession. When viewed in this light some actions by physicians are easier to interpret. A specialist in medicine has two sources of clients—those who come on their own initiative and those referred by physicians or previous patients. Therefore, with an eye to the practical, he counts the favor and good will of all. By remaining neutral he is unlikely to offend anyone. Therefore, why take on so controversial a socio-medical matter as contraception, when maintaining neutrality is better for business, especially referred business from colleagues?

4. *Staying in step with medical politics.*—The lowest rung on the

ladder of American medical politics is occupied by the local county or city medical society. In many respects they resemble ward units in general political structure. Each is likely to have a sprinkling of outstanding members, but they tend to be absorbed in the number and spirit of the majority. In occasional instances, when a local medical society has an outstanding physician as temporary leader, social progress may be made. Ordinarily, however, the main focus of interest for the city or county medical society is pocketbook security for the brotherhood. Politically, a practicing physician usually runs with the medical crowd, is numbered among them, and is entitled to all the rights and privileges appertaining to the majority. Until recently, local medical societies could not be persuaded to take a stand on contraception and therefore physician members felt it wiser and safer to take no stand individually. In the last decade, however, birth control has been increasingly removed from the unmentionable category and more and more local medical societies have endorsed the aims of family planning. In vigilant guardianship of the vested financial interests of the brotherhood, many local societies at the same time are likely to endorse a community birth control program only so long as an agreed minimum income is imposed as an eligibility rule for patients receiving contraceptive care at such clinics.

5. *"Won't play God" syndrome.*—When it comes to many of the social problems of medicine—less often in regard to contraception and more frequently in the areas of sterilization, therapeutic abortion, donor artificial insemination, and withholding resuscitative techniques to seriously malformed infants in the delivery room—doctors retreat behind the cliché that they "won't play God." This type of intellectual cowardice, this mental retreat, is irrational. It lacks logic completely, because through the nature of his work a doctor is constantly intruding himself into the work of the Deity. Does he wait for God to show his decision by making some outward manifestation before he undertakes a Caesarean section, orders a transfusion, or performs a risk-fraught open-heart operation? When it comes to donor insemination and sterilization, the "won't play God" group seems to feel that the Deity has a monopoly on the bestowal and withdrawal of fertility; yet the same men will not hesitate to perform a tuboplasty on the wife when the chance for surgical success is remote or to explode the anovulatory ovary.

6. *Catholic hospital staff privileges.*—Until the recent ecumenical spirit softened the Catholic anti–birth control position, most Catholic hospitals gave non-Catholic physicians the choice of staff privileges or working in planned parenthood centers. Several examples could be cited, such as Poughkeepsie and Albany, New York. In some in-

stances, the issue was taken to the courts and it was ruled that any hospital could establish its own criteria of staff membership, among them non-participation in planned parenthood centers. Obviously, this presented a practical problem to many non-Catholic doctors, especially in small communities where the Catholic institution might be the only or the best hospital. In addition, many physicians feared that public approval by them of family planning might also alienate the good will of Catholic colleagues and patients.

In my view, then, American physicians were, and are still to a lesser extent, reluctant to support the birth control movement because of these six factors—dedication to the preservation of life, innate conservatism of the profession, unwillingness to antagonize, a wish to be in agreement with local medical politics, unwillingness to take over God's prerogatives, and fear of Catholic reprisal.

PERSONAL EXPERIENCE IN THIS FIELD

To recall the history of my own involvement in the birth control movement almost forty years ago in Baltimore seems pertinent before making recommendations about how to secure greater involvement of the medical profession. Recommendations are necessarily deeply colored by one's own experiences, which therefore seem a useful, indeed fair, introduction.

In 1925, when I began an obstetrical residency at the Johns Hopkins Hospital, the institution was not only completely segregated along color lines but along social lines as well. There were three postpartum floors—B2 for colored patients, B3 for white ward patients, and B4 for private white patients. It did not take long to observe that colored patients came in each year for an annual model; white private patients delivered a first, second, or third child, rarely more; and the fertility of the white clinic patient was as intermediate as the hospital floor she occupied. At first I was puzzled, but a little reading in the departmental library and superficial interrogation of patients demonstrated that there are no ethnic or social differences in fecundity, simply differences in fertility due to the knowledge and use of contraception. As a young and perhaps idealistic physician, I was scandalized by such undemocratic stratification of socio-medical facilities and I became interested in contraception, not for itself, but in an attempt to equalize the distribution of medical care among all ethnic and social groups.

Dr. J. Whitridge Williams, the distinguished professor of obstetrics at the Hopkins, was a remarkable person. Fashioned from old Rhode Island and Virginia ancestors, he was a William Welch–trained pathologist and the author of America's leading obstetrical textbook. He lived and reacted as an aristocrat but rarely allowed his emotions to dominate his actions. He had a commanding personality, and this, combined with the stature of his position and his intelligence, made him a strong force in both Hopkins medical affairs and American medicine. Dr. Williams exhibited deep concern and understanding for the socio-medical problems of the clinic patients—a concern, to be sure, with strong paternalistic overtones. He believed in sterilization and practiced its performance liberally. He chafed under the restrictive Maryland abortion statute but applied it strictly.

At that time neither Baltimore nor the Hopkins had a birth control clinic, but a group of prominent citizens including four members of the medical faculty determined in 1927 to establish one. Contraception was still too controversial to allow the clinic within the confines of the Hopkins Hospital, so Dr. Donald Hooker, a professor of physiology with independent means, purchased a dwelling five blocks distant. In addition to Dr. Hooker, the other faculty members involved were Dr. Williams, Dr. Adolf Meyer, the distinguished professor of psychiatry, and Dr. Raymond Pearl, the eminent biometrician. The clinic flourished from the moment it opened. That does not mean it did not meet with opposition, but the armor of the Hopkins afforded the clinic the necessary protection, for in Baltimore Johns Hopkins can do no wrong.

I soon associated myself with the Baltimore birth control clinic, first as a physician-worker, then as a member and later chairman of its Medical Advisory Committee. About 1930 the Johns Hopkins began giving contraceptive advice to its own post-partum patients.

MEDICAL INVOLVEMENT

My many years of work in the field of contraception, particularly the past three years as president of Planned Parenthood has taught me some practical points in regard to the involvement of the medical profession.

1. If one wishes to start a Planned Parenthood affiliate in a new community, the movement must be broadly based, including correct medical leadership. Just any doctor is not enough; wrong medical sponsorship can wreck the effort. A list should be prepared of the most important non-Catholic physicians in the order of their community standing and the number one doctor should first be invited to become chairman of the local medical advisory committee. If he refuses, number two should be asked, and so on. The chairman then invites other physicians to join him. Since the chairman has stature

in the community, other doctors feel secure in aligning themselves with him and with the Planned Parenthood movement.

2. The medical chairman and the members of his committee, preferably including an officer of the local medical society, should inform the local medical society of their plans for a birth control center and arbitrate any differences which may exist in regard to fee schedule, means test for clinic eligibility, and so on. They should then ask for formal approval of the new organization by the society.

3. When possible, a nucleus of female physicians should be enrolled as clinicians. Married female physicians often find such part-time clinic work compatible with family duties. To be sure, male doctors can also be used as clinicians. Each physician should be paid approximately $20 for a two-hour session. In some communities it is difficult to enroll a sufficient medical staff, and senior residents from the obstetrical-gynecological service of a teaching hospital are used to supplement the practicing physicians. This has the disadvantage of annual rotation of personnel, but the advantage of indoctrinating medical leaders of the future in Planned Parenthood medicine.

4. The introduction of a contraceptive clinic into a voluntary hospital depends very largely on the interest and depth of conviction of the chief of obstetrics and gynecology. In some institutions the permission of both the lay and the medical boards of the institution may be required.

5. Introduction of a contraceptive clinic into a municipal hospital may be a complicated process, as the 1958 hospital battle in New York City and the current Cook County struggle in Chicago attest. In this situation there are two obstacles, medical and political.

In New York City, before 1958, no patient in the huge municipal hospital system could be advised about contraception, receive supplies, or even be referred from a city hospital to an outside agency for such service. When the situation was analyzed, it turned out that this ban was based not on written but on unwritten law. Dr. Louis Hellman, the chief of obstetrics and gynecology at Brooklyn's Kings County Hospital, attempted to breach the ban; he planned to fit a severe diabetic, recently delivered by Caesarean section, with a contraceptive diaphragm. On orders from the then commissioner of hospitals he was prevented from implementing the therapy he believed necessary. That same day the ruling by the commissioner reached the press, and the response of the non-Catholic community was so great that no political power could resist it. The daily press attacked the action in a unanimous stand, as did radio and television, and perhaps most important to the outcome, so did the influential Public Health Committee of the New York Academy of Medicine. Protestants and Jews closed ranks and in September, 1958, the Board of Hospitals, composed of ten distinguished, non-political, medical and lay citizens voted 8 to 2 to replace the unwritten ban with a written permissive ruling. By 1964 all sixteen of the municipal hospitals in New York City offered contraceptive services. The number of patients given contraceptive service in the city hospitals of New York rose from 0 in 1958 to 22,000 by 1964. Details of this dramatic happening have been recorded in a publication by the Planned Parenthood Federation, *The Anatomy of a Victory*.

6. For a doctor lacking in fortitude, it is extremely important to have the stamp of approval of his guild organizations upon an idea or an action. In seeking organizational approval for contraception, one must originate the action from within, perhaps not infrequently after judicious prodding from without. One highly motivated protagonist of contraception who is a member of the inner council of a medical organization can usually get the stamp of approval of the whole group. Most doctors are not opposed to contraception—as a matter of fact they approve it—but they lack the initiative and the selflessness to initiate action.

Among important medical leadership organizations that have recently endorsed contraception are the American Public Health Association, the American College of Obstetrics and Gynecology, the American Osteopathic Society, and the American Medical Association, as well as many individual city, county, and state medical societies.

7. Unquestionably the most effective way to arouse the interest of the next generation of American physicians in family planning is through the curriculums of the medical schools. Population dynamics and the control of conception cut across several disciplines—preventive medicine, obstetrics and gynecology, genetics, medicine, social medicine, physiology, therapeutics, and others. In the ideal, each department would introduce the topic at the point where it fits into its program. The medical student should be led to regard the control of conception as a natural component of complete medical care, just as he regards vaccination against poliomyelitis, eradication of malaria, or a balanced diet. Contraception should be divested of its moral overtones, like properly prescribed eyeglasses, vitamin supplements, or therapy for infertility.

Realistically, few if any American medical schools do justice in their curriculums to the importance of conception control. Cutting across so many disciplines, it is neglected by them all. In an attempt to fill this void in part, the Planned Parenthood Federation has made a forty-five-minute film for first- and second-year medical students, called "Fertility Control and the Physician." The project was financed by a grant from the Commonwealth Fund, and the script reviewed by a group of scientific consultants. The film demonstrates the existence of the global problem resulting from the excessive rate of population growth and calls the student's attention to the problem's cause in the world's high birth rate and the decreasing low death rate. It presents the common methods of conception control and the involvement of physicians in the work, in both private and clinical practice. The film also presents public health programs in birth control, here and abroad. In addition, it presents some aspects of current research in contraception.

Our task is to inform the student about the medical-social problems created by unwanted pregnancies and the means that science has today, and the better means it will have tomorrow, toward their solution. If progress is to be made, the coming medical generation must become deeply involved in birth control.

39

ABORTION PROGRAMS

ANDRAS KLINGER
Hungarian Central Office of Statistics

Among birth control methods, induced abortion is known to occupy a very important place in every country. Its role in family planning varies, however, and is measured with different degrees of
accuracy according to its legality in the country involved. This
summary deals with the legal aspects of abortion which permit broad
masses of women to adopt it as a means of influencing their family
size.

We are concerned with the legality of abortion which permits the
interruption of pregnancy, not only for health and biological reasons,
but also according to the will of the woman (family) on the basis of
socioeconomic or other family considerations. Our experience is derived mostly from the situation in Hungary but also includes the
situation in some other European socialist countries in which the
practice or legal rules are similar to those in Hungary.

In Hungary the legal rules permitting induced abortion came into
force in 1956. The Order of the Council of Ministers, issued in June,
1956, authorizes the woman (mother) to make a conscious determination of desired family size and permits her to interrupt an undesired
pregnancy by means of induced abortion.

Induced abortion was legalized on similar principles in the Soviet
Union, Bulgaria, Czechoslovakia, and Romania between 1955 and
1957, as well as in Yugoslavia in 1960.

To deal with the practical aspects of the law, most countries have
established committees to receive applications and grant the necessary
permission. In Hungary, these committees—which work partly in
co-operation with the specialized organs of the health service, with
the outpatient departments—consist of three members. The chairman

of the committee is always a doctor, one of its members is the head (or delegate) of the socio-political group of the local administrative organ, and the other member is a delegate of the local women's association. The committees hold their sessions twice a week and receive the applicant women. Before applying for permission the women undergo a gynecological examination in the course of which the duration of their pregnancy is determined.

The induced interruption of pregnancy is permitted, in general, on the basis of two types of circumstances. One is the rather universal consideration of health indications, the other involves circumstances of a social and family nature. Most countries make this distinction between the two groups of causes in their legislation. In Hungary the committee permits the interruption of pregnancy in the following cases: (1) if the interruption of pregnancy is necessary in order to save the life of the pregnant woman or to protect her from a grave illness or from the worsening of her illness or if the fetus to be born will presumably be exposed to a grave injury; (2) if the interruption of pregnancy is justified by personal or family circumstances deserving acknowledgment or if the applicant insists on the interruption of pregnancy.

Instead of these general statements, the legal rules of other countries specify more concrete causes for permission. Thus, besides health causes the legal rules in Czechoslovakia permit induced interruption of pregnancy in the following cases considered to deserve special attention: (1) advanced age of the woman, (2) (at least) three living children, (3) loss or disability of the husband, (4) disruption of family life, (5) endangering the living standard if the economic responsibility for the family or the child falls mostly on the woman, (6) an unmarried woman, and (7) circumstances under which the pregnancy was caused, e.g., by violence or crime.

In some countries, permission is formulated in more general terms. In Poland, induced interruption of pregnancy is permitted in instances of a "serious social position" of the woman and in Yugoslavia the law specifies "grave personal or material circumstances" of the woman.

According to the practice in Hungary, the proportion of induced abortions performed for illness is relatively very low: in 1964 less than 4%, with the other 96% permitted on the basis of other (social or family) causes. The ratio of abortions permitted because of illness did not exceed 5%–6% in any year.

Conclusions on the probable factors involved in induced abortions permitted for "other" causes can be drawn from the data of two sample surveys. In the course of two months (October, 1960, and

April, 1964) after their induced abortions, women were questioned on their birth control and family planning practices, as well as on their subjective motives for the induced abortion. On the basis of these investigations we found that about one-third of the surgically aborted women applied for the interruption of pregnancy because they did not want to have more children. Bad dwelling accounted for another sixth while unfavorable marital or family status was the reason for another 10% in the first survey and 15% in the second. As can be seen in Table 1, low income declined from 13% in the first survey to 9% in the second.

A similar survey of about 26,000 women in the Soviet Union in

TABLE 1

DISTRIBUTION BY SUBJECTIVE MOTIVE OF WOMEN UNDERGOING
INDUCED ABORTION FOR CAUSES OTHER THAN ILLNESS

(Per Cent)

Motives	October, 1960	April, 1964
Number of children is enough............	30.5	32.7
Youngest child is still small.............	9.7	8.0
Fear of confinement or illness...........	10.3	8.1
Advanced age.........................	4.1	3.9
Unfavorable marital or family status......	9.7	14.5
Bad dwelling circumstances.............	15.2	16.1
Low income...........................	13.4	9.2
Saving purposes.......................	1.8	3.0
Difficulty caused by a child in one's work..	3.8	3.2
Other and unknown....................	1.5	1.3
Total.............................	100.0	100.0
Total number of women..............	12,333	13,892

1958–59 found that about one-third of the women simply said they did not want to maintain their pregnancy. About 10% accounted for such factors as uncertain marital circumstances, the difficulty of caring for the child, or the problems of bringing up a small child already born.

Beside the subjective motive, duration of the pregnancy is also a factor in permission for induced abortion. This is unambiguously stipulated in the legal rules which prescribe that induced abortions can be carried out only during the first three months (12 weeks) of the pregnancy, and after this only if, after thorough considerations, the state of the woman's health makes it absolutely necessary. In Hungary, as an exception, induced interruption of pregnancy is permitted for girl-mothers between 16 and 20 years of age if the pregnancy has not exceeded 18 weeks. According to the sample survey of 1964, 38%

of the women applying for induced abortion were in the fourth to seventh week, 57% in the eighth to eleventh week, and only 5% in the twelfth to nineteenth week of the pregnancy.

The Hungarian legal rules permitting induced abortion prescribe that they be carried out in the gynecological wards of hospitals or in maternity homes. Induced abortions must not be performed in out-patient departments, a condition which safeguards the health of the mother. In general, hospitalization for three days after the operation is deemed necessary, but under proper circumstances the aborted woman is discharged on the second day because hospitals are over-crowded.

The fact that artificial interruption of pregnancy is permitted does not mean that our health policy regards induced abortion as the only or best means of birth control. Its only purpose is to make it possible for women who conceive through ignorance or unsatisfactory knowledge of prevention to terminate an undesirable pregnancy. The Hungarian legal rules, therefore, try to connect permission to interrupt pregnancy with information on contraception and the dangers of induced abortion. In some cases, in compliance with the law, the committee attempts to dissuade the woman from requesting permission when the grounds are other than health considerations.

The order of 1961, as a supplement to the basic legal rule, makes it the duty of the committees to speed the explanatory activity so as to have the time, where it seems advisable, to convince the applicant to maintain her pregnancy. To this end the committee deals with the requests of childless women or women with one child at a separate session, drawing their attention to the possible injury to health and emphasizing the necessity of using contraceptives. Decisions are not made at this first "informatory" session but the committee asks the woman to go home and think over what she has heard, to talk the question over with her husband, and to report at the next session of the committee.

In most committees this informatory work is rather formal and yields little practical result. Since the character of the committee is mainly consultative, its major authority being to reject the request only if the duration of pregnancy exceeds 12 weeks (or in some cases 18 weeks), most women (knowing this) return for permission to interrupt pregnancy, which the committee is obliged to grant. Thus the activity of the committee in this field is unfruitful and its sphere of authority to refuse permission can be regarded as rather limited.

Since the interruption of pregnancy for causes other than illness takes place at the will of the woman, the law provides that payment by the social insurance scheme apply only to those abortions performed for illness. For all other cases, expenses of the first three days of hospital treatment are borne by the applicant or her husband; or if the applicant is under age (under 18 years of age) and has no income, a responsible relative is obliged to pay. However, beginning with the fourth day of hospitalization, the applicant is entitled to all the services she normally would receive under the social insurance system. In practice, these provisions mean the payment of 360 forints (about $16.00) for induced abortion based on non-medical reasons. This amount (representing about one-fifth of the average monthly earnings of the employed) does not cause any difficulty to applicants and does not hinder them from applying for permission to interrupt unwanted pregnancies.

The subjective motives explain why the pregnancy is unwanted but what explains the lack of prevention of conception? According to sample surveys, in Hungary only 52% of the surgically aborted women employed regular prevention against conception in 1960; in 1964 the figure was 54%. Another sample survey (the so-called TCS study on fertility, family planning, and birth control carried out in 1958–60) showed that only 21% of Hungarian women practice birth control by contraception, 18% by interruption of pregnancy, and 37% by both methods. This means that 58% of the women employ contraception; most of them, however, are unsuccessful.

Of the aborted women who became pregnant despite regular contraceptive use, 63% in 1960 and 44% in 1964 attributed the pregnancy to occasional omission or negligence. Another 21% in 1960 and 27% in 1964 claimed the pregnancy was due to improper use of the method employed, while those who considered defective contraceptives responsible increased from 4% in 1960 to 13% in 1964. These data are given in Table 2.

The relatively great number of undesired conceptions which take place in spite of prevention can be explained by the fact that Hungarian women use relatively primitive and inefficient methods of contraception. Coitus interruptus, the oldest means of prevention, represents the greatest proportion. According to the TCS study, the majority of contraceptors, 52%, use this method. It will be noted, too, in Table 3, that of the aborted contraceptors (who had a child), 54% in 1960 and 44% in 1964 relied on coitus interruptus. While the trend is in the right direction, the decrease in the use of this method should be greater considering the availability of more effective methods. In this connection, however, the greater clinical effectiveness and greater adoption of the more modern methods is offset by irregularity in their use as well as by misuse. Thus, for example, one-third of the aborted women who used the diaphragm as a contraceptive became pregnant when they failed to use it, an additional third because they applied it incorrectly, and 13% because of a defect in the appliance.

Another frequently used means of prevention is the condom, which, according to the data of the TCS study, was used in 22% of the cases. Its use among childbearing and aborted women with children increased from 17% in 1960 to 25% in 1964. In one-third of the aborted cases among women relying on this method, conception was due to negligence in its use, and an additional one-third to a defect in the condom.

TABLE 2

DISTRIBUTION BY CAUSE OF PREGNANCY OF
SURGICALLY ABORTED WOMEN WHO
WERE REGULAR CONTRACEPTORS

(Per Cent)

Cause of Pregnancy	October, 1960	April, 1964
Negligence in prevention.........	62.8	43.3
Improper use of contraceptives.....	20.5	27.3
Defective contraceptive..........	4.1	13.3
Other.......................	2.3	3.2
Unknown ("She does not know")...	10.3	12.7
Total.......................	100.0[a]	100.0[a]
Total number of women.........	7,058	7,827

[a] The ratio of women applying prevention to all surgically aborted women was 51.6% in 1960 and 53.6% in 1964.

TABLE 3

DISTRIBUTION OF THREE GROUPS OF WOMEN BY MAJOR
METHOD OF BIRTH PREVENTION

(Per Cent)

METHOD OF PREVENTION	DATA OF THE TCS STUDY (women 15–49 yrs. old)	CHILDBEARING AND ABORTED	
		October, 1960, Survey	April, 1964, Survey
Coitus interruptus.........	52	54	44
Ogino-Knaus.............	7	2	2
Condom.................	22	17	25
Diaphragm..............	4	4	12
Timidon jelly............	1	6	7
Vaginal irrigation.........	8	8	6
Other and unknown........	6	9	4
Total.................	100	100	100
Total number of women..	3,821	8,908	10,678

The legal rules also contain provisions intended to protect health by restricting the number of permissions in a given time interval. Thus, the Czechoslovak, Bulgarian, and Soviet rules permit an induced abortion only if more than six months have elapsed since the previous induced abortion.

In spite of these stipulations, abortions occur at rather frequent intervals. In the Soviet Union for instance, according to the data of the investigation of 1958–59, 16% of the aborting women had more than one induced abortion within a year; in Hungary 22% of the women surgically aborted in April, 1964, had also had an induced abortion in 1963. The latter proportion was 41% among those who had had an

TABLE 4

SURGICALLY ABORTED WOMEN BY
ABORTION ORDER

(Per Cent)

Abortion Order	October, 1960	April, 1964
1............	47.1	40.0
2............	27.4	28.6
3............	13.6	15.5
4............	6.7	8.4
5 and more....	5.2	7.5
Total.......	100.0	100.0
Total number of women..	13,675	14,640

induced abortion even earlier (54% of the aborting women were among this group).

As shown in Table 4, in Hungary the aborting women experiencing their third or higher order abortion increased from 25.5% in 1960 to 31.4% in 1964. Although these data have not been standardized for age or duration of marriage, they suggest an increasing tendency among women who resort to this method of birth limitation in the first place to continue to rely on its use. Fifth and higher order abortions accounted for 7.5% of surgical induced abortions in 1964 compared with 5.2% in 1960. Moreover, among the women aborting for the fifth or more time in 1964, 52% had also had an induced abortion the year before.

Induced abortion rates in Hungary are highest among women with two children, but the data presented in Table 5 show a pronounced increase between 1960 and 1964 in resort to induced abortion by childless women and women with only one child. Among childless married women, 54 per 1,000 were found in 1964 to have experienced an induced abortion compared with 33 in 1960, an increase of 64%. Rates among women with only one child are now almost as high as among women with two children, 97 compared with 101, respectively, among 1,000 married women, while the differential between one- and two-child married women in 1960 was 85 to 101 per 1,000 such women. In general, after two children, the frequency of abortions tends to decrease. These findings are generally characteristic of the other countries, although in Bulgaria there are no great differences in the proportion of abortions among those with different numbers of children except that it is relatively higher among childless women.

TABLE 5

INDUCED ABORTION RATES OF WOMEN AGED 15–49
WITH SPECIFIED NUMBER OF CHILDREN

(Per 1,000)

NUMBER OF CHILDREN	ALL WOMEN		MARRIED WOMEN	
	1960	1964	1960	1964
0.............	23	35	33	54
1.............	80	94	85	97
2.............	95	98	101	101
3 and more.....	85	89	90	91
Total........	65	74	83	91
Total number of women...	162,160	184,367	142,260	160,101

In the Soviet Union among surgically aborted women the proportion of those who are pregnant for the first time accounts for 4%–6%; according to the number of children the greatest proportion of women with one child can be found in the towns, and the greatest proportion with two children in the villages; the proportion of the childless is 10% and 6%, respectively. (In Hungary, of surgically aborted women in 1964, the proportion of childless was 16%, of whom 58% were unmarried.)

Number of children is, of course, a link between age of woman and frequency of abortion. According to the Hungarian data, the relatively highest abortion rates are found among women 25–29 years old. By 1964 this age group had experienced 145 induced abortions per 1,000 total women and 156 per 1,000 married women. Rates are also high among the 20–24 and 30–34 age groups, as can be seen in Table 6. According to the Czechoslovak data of 1962, the highest frequency of abortions has been experienced among women aged

25–34. All these data indicate the insistence of women still in the prime reproductive years to limit their families to one or two children.

The increasing trend of induced abortions among young unmarried women is especially noteworthy. In 1964, when 32 per 1,000 women aged 15–19 experienced induced abortion, nearly 7,000 or 2% of the unmarried women under age 20 reported to the committees for permission to interrupt pregnancy. Among married women of similar age the proportion was 12%. From this, it is clear that lack of information and thus lack of knowledge of means of prevention cause a great number of pregnancies and therefore are responsible for a great number

TABLE 6

INDUCED ABORTION RATES BY AGE

(Per 1,000 Women in Specified Age Group)

AGE GROUP	ALL WOMEN		MARRIED WOMEN	
	1960	1964	1960	1964
15–19.........	22.5	31.6	89.2	120.1
20–24.........	102.3	121.1	130.8	151.4
25–29.........	126.9	144.8	137.7	156.0
30–34.........	101.7	116.7	109.8	123.7
35–39.........	63.5	65.7	64.9	71.1
40–49.........	12.0	14.0	14.7	15.9
15–49.........	65.2	74.3	82.9	91.2
Total number of women...	162,160	184,382	146,260	160,509

of induced abortions among young girls. (It should be noted that although women under 18 years of age are allowed to apply to the abortion committees, parental permission is indispensable for the performance of an induced abortion in a hospital.)

In permitting induced abortion, the laws not only protect the freedom of women but ensure that the operations are performed under proper medical and sanitary conditions. Before the legalization of induced abortion, the incidence of illegal abortions was very high, estimated at about 100,000 per year in Hungary and between 100,000 and 300,000 in Czechoslovakia in the early 1950's. Moreover, because of their clandestine and illicit nature, these induced abortions were often performed, not by doctors under antiseptic conditions, but by midwives and even laymen, as a result of which the mortality rate was unnecessarily high. In Hungary, for example, some 80 to 100 women died annually as a result of illegal abortion.

Although the legalization of induced abortion now ensures its performance under proper medical auspices, this still remains an undesirable method of birth limitation. Repeated induced abortion endangers the health of the woman and children born subsequently. There is a correlation, for example, between the frequency of induced abortion and the proportion of premature births (see Table 7). Defining as premature a newborn child weighing under 2,500 grams, we find the per cent of premature births increases with an increase in the mother's induced abortion history. According to birth data from April, 1964, the ratio of premature births among women who had no induced abortion was 10%; the same figure was 14% among those with one induced abortion, 16% after two induced abortions, and 21% after three or more induced abortions.

TABLE 7

PREMATURE LIVE BIRTHS (UNDER 2,500 gm.)
BY NUMBER OF INDUCED
ABORTIONS OF MOTHER

(Per Cent)

PREVIOUS INDUCED ABORTIONS	PREMATURE LIVE BIRTHS	
	October, 1960	April, 1964
0	8.0	10.1
1	11.1	14.4
2	12.2	16.0
3 and more	13.9	20.5
Total	8.3	11.0
Total number of women	766	1,163

Thus, the impact of premature birth on infant mortality and on the mental and physical development of the child is connected with the frequency of abortions. These relationships have not yet been studied in detail, but it is clear that induced abortion plays an important role in the development of a later child. It might be noted that in Budapest, where the frequency of induced abortion is highest, the frequency of premature births is very high.

Mortality resulting from induced abortion is now very low. In Hungary, 20–25 women die yearly of abortion, but most of these cases involve spontaneous abortion or abortion performed without permission. The number of deaths resulting from permitted abortions is only 2 or 3 annually. The complications of induced abortion are, however, more significant. According to the data of 1964, shown in

Table 8, 1.3 per 1,000 experienced perforation of the uterus; 8.5, feverish conditions; and 16.4, after-hemorrhage. The low mortality suggests that these complications are successfully treated, but the after-effects of these complications cannot be followed up. At any rate, their frequency indicates the dangers of induced abortion.

In the countries for which data are available, the number of registered abortions increased immediately under the impact of legalization and continued to rise. Rates, however, may have reached a plateau in Poland and since 1961 have been declining in Czechoslovakia. As shown in Table 9, Hungary has the highest rate, 91 induced abortions per 1,000 married women aged 15–49 in 1964, a level that exceeded live births by 40%. Among the other European socialist countries, induced abortions are still high in Bulgaria, 41 per 1,000

TABLE 8

COMPLICATIONS OF PERMITTED INDUCED ABORTIONS, 1964

Complication	Number of Cases	Number per 1,000 Induced Abortions
Perforation of the uterus.........	232	1.3
Feverish conditions (genital)......	691	3.7
After-hemorrhage................	1,141	6.2
Repeated hospital treatment within 4 weeks after abortion:		
Due to fever...................	872	4.7
Due to hemorrhage............	1,879	10.2

TABLE 9

LEGALIZED INDUCED ABORTION RATES IN SEVERAL COUNTRIES, 1954–63

YEAR	RATES PER 1,000 WOMEN AGED 15–49					RATES PER 100 LIVE BIRTHS				
	Bulgaria	Czechoslovakia	Hungary	Poland	Yugoslavia	Bulgaria	Czechoslovakia	Hungary	Poland	Yugoslavia
1954..........	1	1	6	......	......	1	1	7	......	......
1955..........	......	1	14	0	......	......	1	17	0	......
1956..........	......	1	33	3	......	......	1	43	2	......
1957..........	16	2	49	5	......	22	3	74	5	......
1958..........	19	19	58	6	......	27	26	92	6	......
1959..........	23	25	61	11	11	33	36	101	11	13
1960..........	27	28	65	21	16	39	41	111	23	18
1961..........	34	29	69	20	22	50	43	121	23	25
1962..........	38	28	66	20	......	57	41	126	23	......
1963..........	41	22	70	......	......	63	30	131	......	......
1964..........	......	17	74	......	......	......	29	140	......	......

women of childbearing ages, but are relatively lower (about 20) in Czechoslovakia, Poland, and Yugoslavia. (For birth rates, see Table 10.)

To sum up, one can state that the legalization of induced abortions influences considerably the number of live births and is thus an important means of family planning. Induced abortion, however, cannot be viewed as a proper and suitable means of birth control. It can be regarded only as an interim, auxiliary method pending the adoption

TABLE 10

LIVE BIRTH RATES PER 1,000 POPULATION IN EUROPEAN SOCIALIST COUNTRIES, 1954–64

Country	1954	1955	1956	1957	1958	1959	1960	1961	1962	1963	1964
Bulgaria	20.2	20.1	19.5	18.4	17.9	17.6	17.8	17.4	16.7	16.4	16.1
Czechoslovakia	20.6	20.3	19.8	18.9	17.4	16.0	15.9	15.8	15.7	16.9	17.1
German Democratic Republic	16.6	16.7	16.2	15.9	15.6	16.9	17.0	17.0	17.4	17.6	17.6
Hungary	23.0	21.4	19.5	17.0	16.0	15.2	14.7	14.0	12.9	13.1	13.0
Poland	29.1	29.1	28.0	27.6	26.3	24.7	22.6	20.9	19.6	19.0	18.1
Romania	24.8	25.6	24.2	22.9	21.6	20.2	19.1	17.5	16.2	15.7	15.2
USSR	26.6	25.7	25.2	25.4	25.3	25.0	24.9	23.8	22.4	21.2	19.7
Yugoslavia	28.5	26.8	25.9	23.7	24.0	23.3	23.5	22.7	21.9	21.4	20.8

by the population of proper means of birth prevention. Under present circumstances, inasmuch as contraceptive methods are still primitive in most European socialist countries, induced abortion is applied as one of the chief means of birth control. Its deleterious effect on health is sufficient reason to change the present-day situation. This, however, cannot be achieved by administrative measures prohibiting induced abortions but by disseminating knowledge of modern contraceptive methods, making supplies readily available, and teaching effective use. The health policy of the individual countries now takes cognizance of these needs so that women may prevent conception rather than interrupt unwanted pregnancies.

40

A COMMERCIAL SYSTEM FOR INTRODUCING
FAMILY PLANNING IN COMILLA, PAKISTAN

AKHTER HAMEED KHAN
Pakistan Academy for Rural Development, Comilla

and

HARVEY M. CHOLDIN
The Population Council

BACKGROUND

The government of Pakistan, since the Second Five-Year Plan in 1961, has been working to introduce family planning.[1] The Second Five-Year Plan, 1960–65, organized the promotion of family planning through clinics and other installations of the Health Department. Conventional contraceptives were to be distributed through the clinics, and clinical contraceptives were to be prescribed and supplied. On a pilot basis, fieldwork approaches were tested, including home visits, small group teaching, promotion by village women, and other methods.

The national scheme had its operational drawbacks in a shortage of medical and paramedical personnel and overtaxed clinical facilities. Some of the pilot projects suffered from a lack of large-scale reproducibility.

In this context, a new scheme was tested, at the Pakistan Academy for Rural Development, Comilla, East Pakistan, where one of the pilot projects had been in the field for two years. In early 1964 this new scheme started introducing family planning and distributing contraceptives through commercial channels. This paper presents the experience to date of this commercial project.

[1] Pakistan Planning Commission, *The Second Five-Year Plan (1960–1965)* (Karachi, 1960), p. 360.

477

EAST PAKISTAN AND THE COMILLA AREA

Before independence and partition in 1947, East Pakistan formed an agricultural hinterland to Calcutta, producing rice and jute. At that time the area had no modern manufacturing industries at all and was not urbanized. As recently as 1961 only 5.2% of the population lived in urban centers of 5,000 or more population.[2] The people of East Pakistan are mostly Moslems, though there is a sizable minority population of Hindus. The area has experienced more than eighty years of accelerating population growth, with the 1881 population doubled by 1961. The 1961 population, according to the census, was 50,850,000,[3] and the rate of natural increase is estimated by the Planning Commission at 2.6%.[4] The over-all population density, one of the highest among the world's rural areas, was 923 per square mile in 1961.[5]

Comilla District and Kotwali Thana, the areas of the pilot project, may be considered typical of the province as a whole, although they are among the most densely populated areas of the province, the district having a density of 1,639 per square mile.[6] The area is characterized by poverty, a low rate of literacy, a village way of life, and traditional agriculture. The evidence is that family planning with conventional contraceptives was all but unknown in 1961. There are no data on folk methods of family planning.

One special feature of the local culture bearing upon the introduction of family planning is the *purdah* system, meaning seclusion of women. In the villages the women are restricted to the areas near their own residences and are not to be seen by males other than certain relatives. Females, except the very poorest, do not work in the fields and do not leave the villages. Girls attend school for a year or so. Less than 10% of females in the province are literate.[7] All this makes it very difficult to contact women in teaching programs.

INTEGRATED CHANGE PROGRAM AT THE ACADEMY
FOR RURAL DEVELOPMENT

In Kotwali Thana, an administrative sub-area of Comilla District, various pilot projects to introduce change in the villages were started

[2]Sultan Hashmi, *Main Features of the Demographic Conditions in Pakistan* (Karachi: Central Statistical Office, 1963), p. 18.

[3]*Ibid.*, p. 5.

[4]Karol J. Krotki and Nazir Ahmed, "Vital Rates in East and West Pakistan from the P.G.E. Experiment," *Pakistan Development Review*, 4:751 (1964). Krotki and Ahmed estimate the growth rate to be as high as 3.7%.

[5]Pakistan, Census of Pakistan, Population, East Pakistan, Vol. 2 (1961), Karachi, p. II-2.

[6]*Ibid.*, p. II-11.   [7]*Ibid.*, p. IV-5.

in 1959 and 1960 and are still being developed. A network of village agricultural co-operative societies was built with a co-operate federation. A public works project was developed to give responsibility to local councils and to build local roads, drainage systems, and public buildings. Programs of women's education and school development are being tested.

These projects have been developed as working models of feasible rural-development schemes. Government departments may then evaluate them, duplicating those of merit. This expansion process has taken place with various projects or parts of them. The project staff observes the field work closely in the experimental area and revises the systems until they appear to be workable.

First Comilla Family Planning Project

Family planning was introduced as an adjunct to the attempts to improve the farmers' economic condition. The first scheme worked through the network of village agricultural co-operative societies, groups of village males with an average of forty-five members. The project continued to work closely with the co-operatives and the women's education project from 1961 through 1963. Now, however, its dependence upon the co-operative system is very slight. The headquarters of the project staff is at a thana development center which houses all the pilot projects.

At first, the method of promoting family planning was essentially that in each of the ten participating villages a housewife of the village was a paid family planning organizer. She was trained at the development center and returned there weekly for continued teaching and discussion. She visited the housewives of her village repeatedly to teach family planning and to sell supplies to the users. Thus the participating villages received a very intensive program.

The lessons learned from this experiment, which lasted more than two years, were (1) There was considerable acceptance of family planning in the villages—41% tried and 22% continued using family planning in the first two years, among the married women of child-bearing age with one child or more. (In an additional twelve villages a lower percentage accepted family planning but a higher percentage of those accepting continued use.) (2) The illiterate population was capable of using the contraceptives effectively. (Condoms and foam tablets were the contraceptives used in the project.) (3) A non-medical fieldwork approach was possible. (4) The illiterate segments of the population were as receptive as the literate. (5) No organized opposition was forthcoming.

However, it was observed that the methods of the first pilot project had features which limited replication. The record-keeping system necessitated literate organizers, who were hard to find among the village women. The use of women as organizers necessitated a backing-up effort, the women's education program. Also, it was felt that the villagers might resent the fact that they could get the contraceptives only from a single source, with records kept of their purchases. This problem of non-privacy was suspected to be a built-in retardant to the system. There was also the desirability of finding agents who could approach males.

CHANGE TO COMMERCIAL APPROACH

The lessons and drawbacks of the organizer method led to a decision to expand the family planning work and to revise the methods.

The aim was to create a program in which male as well as female agents were employed and in which there was a multiplicity of places where a man could buy contraceptives more or less secretly.

The scheme of the new system was to put contraceptives into regular shops and bazaars where the agents (shopkeepers and others) could sell them at a profit. The public was to be informed about family planning by publicity shows in the market. The agents were to be recruited and supplied and the publicity was to be arranged by the project staff. The project was mixed—government and commercial.

In contrast to family planning programs elsewhere, the project had these features: (1) It relied mainly on a local form of mass communications, rather than upon intensive teaching and "motivating" of individuals and small groups. (2) Therefore, it was aimed at the segment of the population most motivated or ready to adopt family planning. (3) It had an extensive non-clinical contraceptive distribution scheme.

OUTLINE OF THE PROGRAM

A four-point plan was prepared in the first weeks of the project, which in outline has been followed in the year and a half of field work.

1. A nucleus staff was created, consisting of a training officer, a male field worker, and a female field worker. This staff had a one-room office at the development center. The female worker was later moved to the offices of the women's education program.

The training officer was a young man, a college graduate with advanced work in health education. In duplicating this plan, a college graduate should be required for this post. The male assistant was a so-called village doctor and the female was a former community development field worker who had studied to matriculation level. The training officer had a Jeep at his disposal and the male assistant a bicycle. The female assistant made her field visits by bicycle-rickshaw.

During the course of the first year of field work the record-keeping and office activities expanded to such an extent that two more workers, assistants to the field workers, were appointed.

2. After appointment of the staff, field workers of the research section of the Academy made a listing of all the shops in the thana.

3. A large number of agents were recruited quickly in the rural areas of the thana. At first they were recruited through the local government councils and the co-operative federation: the councils offered names of shopkeepers in their areas, and the federation asked the heads of the village co-operatives to become family planning agents. Female agents were recruited from among the women participating in the women's education pilot project. The number of agents grew quickly and within three months there were 111 agents, 61 male and 50 female. The field workers later began to recruit shopkeepers without introduction through the local councils and the number of agents continued to rise. In May, 1965, there were 268 agents, 163 male and 105 female.

The Health Department supplied the contraceptives (condoms and foam tablets) to the project at no cost. The staff then distributed the contraceptives to the agents, the first consignment on credit, the following ones on cash or credit. The agents bought the supplies at a small price and were instructed to resell them at double the price they paid. The price to agents was 6 paisa per dozen, and the price indicated to the consumer on the printed literature was 12 paisa per dozen (12 paisa are worth 1.3 cents).

4. Publicity was to be generated throughout the area by indigenous publicity methods, printed materials, and meetings of local organizations. The main effort was put into the indigenous publicity methods. (Indigenous methods were chosen because of equipment-operating problems when family planning and other projects at Comilla used movies.) First a musical medicine hawker was hired to explain family planning at the bazaars. But after that attempt failed (because of staff difficulties in dealing with the hawker), a group of musicians and singers was hired.

The singing group was briefed on the essentials of family planning and of the project. Then they composed a series of songs in the local styles and began performances in the bazaars and later in villages.

Their shows bring together large audiences ranging from about 300 to 500 men in a three-hour show in a bazaar and one or two thousand in a five-hour show in a village. Their songs emphasize economics and welfare and the education of children, in relation to the need for family planning. They also answer questions from the audience.

The pace of the publicity program has been kept at a high level. After the first group of agents started work they almost unanimously requested publicity on family planning in their areas, stating that their customers did not know about it. An average of eight shows per month are now given in bazaars and nine in villages. Soon, portable tape recorders will be used to play the shows for village women, since they cannot attend the regular shows.

The main visual and printed devices used are small signboards, posters, and instruction sheets in simple Bengali. Each shop has a metal sign outside indicating that contraceptives are available. Inside are family planning posters and illustrated printed instruction sheets explaining the use of the contraceptives.

ACTIVITIES OF AGENTS

During the period the project has been in the field, the research staff has studied its progress through small informal surveys of the agents and through records on the quantities of supplies taken by the agents. Some of the observations have led to changes in the operating scheme. The following picture emerges from the surveys.

The typical shopkeeper hung the posters in his shop and nailed the metal signboard to the outside of his shop. Some kept a supply box in a prominent location. Some grocers tied the condoms in little packets and hung them from strings at the front of the shops, in the way they display little envelopes of tea.

The shopkeeper's degree of interest in family planning activities is not clear. As for the margin of profit at the suggested price, they say that it can be profitable to them if they sell large quantities. Some of the agents sell the supplies at prices higher than the regular price.

Unsuccessful agents sell one or two pieces to a few persons soon after receiving the first consignment and never get regular or repeated customers. Successful agents develop regular customers who buy contraceptives by the dozen or half-dozen.

Most of the male agents say they talk about family planning in their shops and that others also discuss it there. In a survey of sixty male agents, fifty said that people have talked about family planning in their shops and forty-seven said people have asked them questions about it. The most frequent question is how to use the contraceptives, reported by eighteen agents, and the second most frequent question refers to the religious aspect, reported by thirteen agents. Forty-nine agents said they did not feel uneasy in talking about family planning.

Most of the agents surveyed approved of family planning and understood the arguments for it. Forty-five said they thought villagers should practice family planning, four did not, and eleven did not know. The most frequently mentioned reason why villagers should plan families was economic—the difficulty of supporting a large family, mentioned by twenty-five agents. Presumably, those not approving of family planning became agents because they were afraid to refuse the field worker, whom they knew to be a government officer.

Most female agents are participants in the various women's education projects. All are village housewives or widows. Some are in

TABLE 1

NUMBER OF AGENTS AT END
OF SPECIFIED MONTHS

Month	Males	Females	Total
1964:			
March.........	50	39	89
June..........	115	71	186
September.....	143	105	248
December......	148	90	238
1965:			
March.........	151	96	247
May..........	163	105	268

midwifery training; some are village literacy teachers; some are teachers of other subjects, such as nutrition or sewing. All these women come weekly to the center for classes and meetings of the other programs, and the family planning staff sees them on the class days. Other female agents do not come to the center; the field staff visits them in their villages.

GROWTH OF THE PROGRAM

After the program was established and some initial experience had been registered, evaluation showed the need for two fundamental changes. Recruitment of agents had been substantial in the early months (Table 1), but some of them were not active. In May, 1964, the staff began to drop inactive agents. Officers of village cooperative societies were found to be inactive and most were dropped. Recruitment of new agents continued throughout the period. The distribution of supplies fluctuated without rising after most of the agents had received their first allotments by June, 1964. For four or five months after that there was no growth in supplies distributed.

Two Additions to the System

In December it was decided that the training officer needed to improve his information about the agents' performance and about his staff's field work. There were then over two hundred agents, and a system was needed to give up-to-date information on the field situation.

A card system for record-keeping was devised with a card for each

TABLE 2

Contraceptives Taken by Agents

(In Dozens)

Month	Condom	Foam Tablet	Total
1964:			
June............	803	851	1,654
July............	525	500	1,025
August..........	508	413	921
September.......	387	411	798
October.........	436	494	930
November.......	414	254	668
December........	765	533	1,298
1965:			
January.........	390	290	680
February........	482	469	951
March..........	1,237	737	1,974
April...........	1,556	912	2,468
May............	796	496	1,292

agent, indicating allotments of supplies and staff visits. Weekly and monthly summaries were made by sub-areas of the thana to give the officer an over-all picture of the situation.

To make better contact with the male agents, a system of chief agents was introduced two months later. The project area was divided into nine zones. Nine of the best agents were recruited to become chief agents. Their duties are to visit the male agents in their zones fortnightly for discussion and to replenish supplies. They meet weekly at the center to discuss progress in the field.

After the introduction of the new record system (December) and the chief-agent system (March), the distribution of supplies rose considerably. The large increases shown in Table 2 for March and April are due partly to overstocking by the agents, causing the drop in May. But in June the figure for the total line was approximately 1,880, and there was no doubt that a genuine advance had occurred.

After several months of field work a detailed manual, explaining how to set up and run such an operation, was prepared.

DIFFERENTIAL PERFORMANCE OF AGENTS

Male vs. female agents.—In an average month in 1965, 43% of all agents took resupplies. About the same proportion of female and male agents take resupplies, although females take smaller allotments. The likelihood of getting an active and interested agent is higher among females than among males in this setting, especially with the presence of the women's education project.

Males are more likely to sell condoms, females foam tablets, but males sell some tablets and females some condoms. Males sell more condoms in a ratio of 2:1, females more tablets in a ratio of 3:2.

DUPLICATION FOR ALL OF EAST PAKISTAN

The commercial system of distributing contraceptives (though perhaps not the indigenous publicity plan) is to be set up in all 411 thanas of East Pakistan in the next two years. This will be done under the non-medical portion of the East Pakistan family planning program, as part of the Third National Five-Year Plan (starting July, 1965). The administrators now have a model, already tested in the field, which is ready to be incorporated into the plan. Moreover, in the next five years the pilot project will have a close relationship to the expanded program in Comilla District. It will continue to study the situation in the field and look for new field-work methods for the larger program.

We contend that this kind of small-scale experimentation in the field has proven fruitful. Careful work and observation at this level allow development of the kind of details and procedures needed, without large-scale errors. In this case, the working model was ready within fifteen months.

Regarding the future, we have seen an upward trend in the monthly distribution of supplies, and it cannot be predicted how far up it will go. The specific research needed now is a sample survey of the target population to ascertain what proportion has adopted family planning and who the adopters are.

41

DISTRIBUTION OF CONTRACEPTIVE SUPPLIES THROUGH COMMERCIAL CHANNELS

HARRY L. LEVIN
Consultant for Distribution Channels
The Population Council

The effort to win widespread distribution and use of contraceptives by the people of the world has just begun. Much has happened, particularly in recent months, but much remains to be done. A comprehensive look at today's situation would indicate that there are more contraceptives and types of contraceptives available than ever before—new products such as pills, IUD's, and aerosol foams, and substantial production of traditional products such as condoms, foam tablets, and jellies. In all probability, there is more development still ahead. The big question is whether the contraceptive products available will be used soon enough and broadly enough to affect population growth.

The Present Distribution

This paper provides background information about the present distribution of contraceptive products in the "free" world. Unfortunately, data are not yet adequately available for the European, the African, and the South American markets; so the information in this report from those areas is limited, as is the information for the Communist world. It is hoped that subsequent reports will update the findings for those areas.

Let us begin with the question, How many oral contraceptive pill users are there in the world today? At the beginning of 1965, there appeared to be a total of about 5.5 to 6 million pill users, and the numbers of acceptors is increasing so rapidly that by the beginning of 1966 the users total about 8 to 8.5 million. Table 1 gives some idea of present consumption and the approximate distribution of pill users. As an approximation, in January, 1965, these figures ranged from a high of about 20% of the estimated number of married women in the reproductive ages in Australia, somewhat under 15% in the United States and under 10% in Canada, to about 4% in the United Kingdom, 1% in Latin America, and down to under 0.1% in the Far East, the Near East, and Africa.

Oral contraceptives are now being manufactured in at least the following countries: United States, United Kingdom, West Germany,

TABLE 1

NUMBER AND DISTRIBUTION OF PILL USERS[a]

COUNTRY	NUMBER OF USERS	
	January, 1965	January, 1966
United States.............	4,000,000	5,000,000
Latin America............	500,000	1,250,000
Australia.................	320,000	425,000
United Kingdom..........	275,000	400,000
Europe...................	250,000	375,000
Canada...................	250,000	400,000
Far East.................	150,000	300,000
Japan.................	50,000	90,000
Singapore..............	40,000	60,000
Hong Kong.............	20,000	30,000
South Korea............	6,000	10,000
Other Countries.........	34,000	110,000
Near East (and UAR)......	145,000	400,000
Africa...................	50,000	90,000

[a] Data provided by private market research organizations, pharmaceutical manufacturers, and government sources and combined into present form. Details are privileged and not available for publication.

Holland, Mexico, Japan, United Arab Republic, East Germany, and Italy. Mainland China is also reliably reported to be in this category.

According to sampling studies, many adopters of oral contraceptives had formerly used diaphragms, particularly in the highly developed countries. For example, there were estimated to be about 3 million diaphragm users in the United States in 1960 and about 50,000 in the United Kingdom. Sales of diaphragms have dropped sharply since that time, in favor of the pill, so that now there are estimated to be only about 2 million diaphragm users in the United States. Use of this method of contraception appears to be rather small in most other parts of the world, except probably in Japan and Western Europe, but hard data are almost impossible to gather.

The other newly developed contraceptive is the intra-uterine device. Since it is mainly under the control of national programs, at least in the developing countries and for the time being, the approximate figures on initial insertions, mainly of the Lippes loops as of mid-1965, are fairly reliable (see Table 2). In addition, the Ota ring is marketed to the extent of about 300,000 a year in Japan (including export), and about 10,000 devices are reported to have been inserted in Chile (including the nylon device known as the "Zipper ring"). The IUD figure for the United States is not known, since it is largely subject to commercial confidentiality, but an educated guess would place the figure at about 200,000. At present, the IUD is being made in the United States, Chile, Japan, India, Pakistan, South Korea, Taiwan, Hong Kong, and possibly mainland China.

Significant quantities of latex rubber condoms are being manufactured in Czechoslovakia, Yugoslavia, Germany, Hungary, India,

TABLE 2

NUMBER AND DISTRIBUTION OF
INITIAL IUD INSERTIONS

Country	Number of Users
South Korea	254,000
Taiwan	116,000
India (reported)	100,000
Hong Kong	31,000
Pakistan	20,000
Tunisia	10,000
Thailand	9,000
Puerto Rico	5,000

Japan, South Korea, mainland China, South Africa, Argentina, Uruguay, Brazil, Mexico, Italy, the United Kingdom, Canada, Australia, and the United States. Small numbers of cemented natural rubber and latex condoms are being manufactured in many other countries of the world.

To calculate users of condoms is quite difficult (mainly because individual frequencies are unknown), so the figures in Table 3 refer only to annual production. Thus there is an estimated production of at least 8 million gross outside the United States, and an estimated unused plant capacity of another 10 million gross annually.

Finally, there are a variety of contraceptives like aerosol foams, vaginal foam tablets, creams, and vaginal jellies. Again, it is difficult to reach sound data on users, owing to differing frequencies of use as well as the complication of transforming information on production, sale, or import into actual use. However, sampling estimates would indicate the rough picture of users shown in Table 4. Since many countries produce these items, no effort is made to enumerate them here.

Thus the total world market for contraceptives of all types appears to be relatively small at the present time, especially compared to the expressed interest. As a rough indication, it appears from the above survey that there are now of the order of 25–30 million users of contraceptives throughout the non-Communist world, out of an estimated total number of married couples with women in the child-bearing years of perhaps 500 million. If these figures are approximately

TABLE 3

ANNUAL PRODUCTION OF CONDOMS

Country	Gross
United States.............	5,000,000[a]
United Kingdom..........	2,500,000
Japan....................	2,500,000[b]
Germany.................	1,700,000
India....................	205,000
South Korea..............	100,000

[a] Ninety per cent for domestic market.
[b] For domestic use.

TABLE 4

ESTIMATED USERS OF CONTRACEPTIVES
OTHER THAN PILLS, IUD'S,
OR CONDOMS

Country	Number of Users
United States............	3,000,000[a]
United Kingdom and Europe (including USSR)..	1,000,000
Japan....................	500,000[b]
India....................	130,000[c]
Pakistan................	32,000[d]
Singapore...............	9,000[e]

[a] Of whom as many as 2 million may use these products in conjunction with condoms or diaphragms.
[b] 250,000 jelly, 250,000 foam tablets.
[c] 50,000 jelly, 80,000 foam tablets.
[d] 12,000 jelly, 20,000 foam tablets.
[e] 1,000 jelly, 8,000 foam tablets.

correct, about 5% of the total target population are practicing contraception, or about 8% of the "eligible" population (excluding those currently pregnant, lactating, or presumed sterile), or about 15% of the "currently eligible" (further excluding those actively wanting another child now). Naturally, most of that group is found in the developed world. In short, there is a long way to go before this market is satisfied.

Furthermore, again as a rough estimate of order of magnitude, it appears that in mid-1965 contraception promoted by public governmental programs was used by fewer than 1.5 million of the total

25–30 million users referred to above. The rest, of course, used private initiative and commercially obtained supplies. (These figures do not take into account methods such as coitus interruptus or rhythm for which no supplies are required.)

At the same time, there is no world shortage of production capacity for any of the items mentioned, and a survey of the present manufacturers shows that there is no "supply problem." The available facilities of world production can readily meet a substantial increased demand for products, and the capital requirements and technology required for further expansion to meet increased demands are readily available and eagerly waiting to be developed. Hence, supply will and can rise to almost any level the demand can set for it. If one thing can be predicted for certain, it is that in the next ten years new producers and new products will appear on the market, and competition will stimulate the creation of new markets as well as cause price reductions in old markets.

MARKETING NETWORK

Against this profile of use and supply, let us consider the present marketing and distribution network for the various products. At the present time, oral contraceptives and IUD's are generally distributed through the medical community, and product marketing by manufacturers is carried on in the "ethical drug" tradition. Advertising, when employed, is institutional, and, except in rare instances, direct efforts to promote these products at the consumer level is limited.

Condoms, aerosol foams, tablets, and jellies are generally distributed and marketed through regular drug channels. In many areas of the world, because of the residual cultural stigmas about sex and contraception, these products tend to be under-the-counter items; and even though in some areas of the world they are widely displayed, their marketing is often inhibited as a result of that characterization. Typically, these products are not actively promoted directly to consumers.

What are some of the deterrents to more widespread distribution of such products?

Pills and condoms, which at the moment account for the major share of the world's contraceptive use, are not easily manufactured by every country. As a result, many countries must import these items; and hard currency, involving balance-of-trade considerations, must be employed in their purchase. In general, very limited resources are available for this purpose.

The price of a year's supply of pills is high when measured against disposable income in the developing countries; and a year's supply of condoms, although much lower in comparison, is still high when compared to income levels. Import licenses, customs duties, taxes, freight, and the complex distribution pattern involving importers, agents, distributors, wholesalers, retailers, or dispensing physicians, all of whom must be recompensed for their performance in the marketing chain, compound the price structure.

Products that are not imported are free from the restraints of the import-export balance-of-trade requirements, but the same complicated distribution network prevails. Prices rise as the products passes through many channels before finally coming into the hands of the consumer. Advertising and product promotion is very limited, and so is market penetration.

What are some of the first things to do if wider distribution is to be achieved? (1) Hard currency should be made freely available for the import of necessary items. (2) Local manufacture should be encouraged where feasible. (3) Universal distribution through existing networks of marketing and distribution should be undertaken. Contraceptive products should be as widely and readily available as soap, kerosene, matches, rice, and other products. (4) Widespread advertising and promotion should be undertaken through all available media. (5) The distribution network should be simplified so as to eliminate the chain of middle-men and the attendant profits. (6) Cost reduction or subsidy should be considered to bring a year's contraceptive supply into the price range of all consumers. (7) Extra incentives should be built into the marketing network chain. This is true particularly for the last agent, who has a face-to-face opportunity to influence the consumer and whose motivation for making the sale can thus be increased.

SUGGESTIONS FOR IMPROVING DISTRIBUTION

To begin with, all contraceptive products, all advertising, all marketing, all packaging, and all individuals, organizations, vehicles, and facilities engaged in promoting family planning might be put under one identification umbrella in order to unify these diverse elements into one cohesive and recognizable effort—a product image, so to speak.

In other words, the field might consider the national or international adoption of an IID—an Instant Identification Device that could serve to bring easy recognition to the concept of family planning or population control. This IID should be a simple symbol that is readily reproducible in black and white. Any symbol that is easily recognizable, distinctive, and universally inoffensive would be acceptable. If this new symbol were to appear on every piece of literature relating to family planning, in every poster, on every piece of advertising matter, in every movie, in every store window where contraceptives were sold, on every building where family planning is offered; if every worker involved in family planning wore the symbol; and if all products useful for family planning bore this symbol on their package—then all these diverse activities would reinforce one another and a substantial impact might be produced. This symbol would then identify places, people, organizations, and products involved in family planning. A symbol could bridge the gap of illiteracy and the problem of cultural inhibitions, since any person recognizing the symbol could instantly identify and seek out products or help regardless of ability to read and with less possibility of exposure to embarrassing situations. The symbol would cost little or nothing, could be implemented immediately, and might produce a significant marketing impact.

Second, further consideration should be given to the employment of indigenous midwives as promotional agents and as sales outlets for family planning supplies. In most parts of the world, the traditional midwife or "granny" is the regular consultant on births and family planning matters and is reported to be present at over 90% of all rural births. Any birth control program that reduces births successfully will threaten the income of these trusted advisers and may well generate hostility and resentment from them. If these midwives are brought into programs by making them part of a network of sales agents selling traditional supplies and serving as distributors of coupons for IUD insertions, pills, and vasectomies, the negative effects can be blunted and the replacement of lost income from reduced births can be turned into a positive force in the form of profits or fees.

The network of midwives is easily identifiable; they are acknowledged consultants on birth and related items; they have the greatest chance to identify post-partum timing for contraception; and they are trusted members of their local communities rather than "strangers." Experience of this type of approach in Comilla, Pakistan, was sufficiently encouraging that the approach was incorporated into the new national Pakistan program. Results obtained by the Japanese Family Planning Association using a technique of marketing through midwife sales agents seem to indicate that such programs might succeed very well.

Third, since prices are such an important ingredient in the supply and distribution problem, a co-operative effort by several developing countries to combine their purchasing power might reduce prices on contraceptive materials. Manufacturers can and do offer identical products at different price levels depending upon such factors as packaging, size of the orders, spacing and placement of orders into slow or idle production time, and simplified billing, bookkeeping, and shipping procedures.

Thus the standardization of products, packaging, purchasing, billing, and shipping could result in many advantages. Moreover, the co-operative could establish standards, provide uniform testing, act as a clearinghouse for orders, and negotiate with manufacturers to the mutual benefit of all concerned. Politically, an international co-operative may be hard to organize, but if formed, it would be self-sustaining and could probably produce a marked reduction in prices for those products with which it concerned itself.

Finally, one important change should be sought in the distribution of family planning items at what marketing people call "the point of sale." In the world today, family planning workers and others are often more likely to extol the virtue of family planning in the abstract than to ask for specific action. But marketing people know that sales of products go up when salespeople remember to "ask for the order."

In Taiwan, the insertion of IUD's increased significantly when this notion was applied. Family planning workers were distributing coupons for insertion of IUD's by private doctors at a special rate. Then the workers, in addition to distributing coupons, actually scheduled an appointment at a specific place and time. The increases in insertions were encouraging. According to marketing men, efforts that not only explain but also ask for specific action and commitment are more likely to gain significant results than those that do not.

It is clear that the private sector is and has been making the major contribution in carrying the message of contraception, and the practice, to the peoples of the world. Based on combined numbers of users and acceptors resulting from both private and public efforts there appears to be much room for improvement. It seems desirable to involve the private sector of the world, with all its marketing and merchandising skills and "know how," to assist in marketing the innovation of contraception.

42

PROBLEMS OF IUD MANUFACTURE

PAUL H. BRONNENKANT
President, Hallmark Plastics, Inc.
Buffalo, New York

While the problems of IUD manufacture might very well apply in general to other similar devices, the IUD activity at Hallmark Plastics has been confined to the development and production of one type only, namely, the Lippes loop. Therefore, the contents of this paper stem from experience with that specific item.

It is quite normal to expect numerous problems in conjunction with any new development, and this little gem, in spite of its present deceptively simple appearance, was no exception. While the initial steps taken are now past history, a brief rundown from the beginning appears to be in order, to provide background for its present state of existence and to serve as a springboard for further research and development.

In retrospect, the first major hurdle was that of establishing effective mental communication between the doctor and the engineer. This entailed, among other things, the doctor's giving capsule courses of instruction on reproductive anatomy and the definition of the uterus in dimensionable terms. The doctor had the general shape and desired characteristics of the device in his mind. The manufacturer's function was to crystallize the doctor's ideas into tangible, three-dimensional reality.

After thorough analysis of the available information furnished by the doctor, involving lengthy discussions and numerous sketches, the first dozen samples were fabricated by hand from strips of polyethylene sheet stock. The doctor himself attached some suture to the lower end of each and provided himself with improvised means of insertion.

Comments on the clinical aspects, and resultant conclusions, are beyond the scope of this paper, but whatever the doctor did with

495

those first samples provided the impetus for an expanded research program requiring a greater number of devices than was practical to make by hand.

This program gave rise to more exacting requirements. The material, for example, had to have flexibility along with a degree of stiffness. It needed memory, or the ability to reassume its shape after having been deformed. Chemical inertness in the presence of body fluids, and X-ray opacity were also desired. Uniformity of size and shape became obviously important, as well as a smooth contour with complete absence of sharp projections.

Familiarity with specific characteristics of a wide range of plastics indicated that a suitable material was available within the elastomeric family of polyolefins. The injection molding process was chosen, particularly in view of the potential accuracy, surface finish, and consistency of production available by this method.

While it is within standard practice to make molds for free-form objects from models, it was decided to design the loop geometrically, in order to be able to define it entirely with fixed dimensions.

One of the finest mold-making firms available was engaged to prepare the first experimental mold, capable of producing one loop at a time. Cavity halves were cut into tool steel on a pantograph machine, working from a four times size master, which had been carefully cut from an accurately expanded layout of the final piece dimensions. Particular emphasis was placed upon identical matching of the two halves, in order to minimize the possibility of any deviation at the parting line which might result in a sharp projection on the molded part. In this area the mold-maker was grudgingly allowed a tolerance of 0.002 inch.

When the mold was finished and placed in a molding machine, material evaluation was begun. Samples from a wide range of low-, medium-, and high-density polyethylenes, as well as polypropylene, were molded and submitted for examination. Pertinent properties of these materials varied from 0.905 to 0.960 in density, and the melt flow index ranged from 1.0 to 28.0. Softening point temperatures were between 180° and 260° F., and yield strengths from 1,100 to 3,300 psi were represented. The material finally selected was DuPont's Alaton 20, a low density polyethylene having the following values for those properties named:

Melt index	1.9
Density	0.919
Vicat softening point	205° F
Yield strength	1,400 psi

Another interesting property was a flexural modulus of 26,000 psi, as compared to values in the 21,000 psi range for other materials having similar density and melt index.

In the meantime, attempts to persuade the material supplier, as well as reprocessors, to furnish small quantities of the material in an X-ray opaque state, were totally unsuccessful. In spite of the lack of specialized equipment for this purpose, a crude but effective means for incorporating barium sulphate into a homogeneous blend with polyethylene was developed, using existing machinery at the molding plant.

Pilot production was begun, with the doctor himself attaching the sutures after the molded loops were delivered. Several types of surgical suture were evaluated, resulting in the selection of a 10-mil-oriented linear polyethylene monofilament, because of its properties of tensile strength, chemical inertness, and resistance to absorption of liquids.

Initially, no special provision was made for suture attachment. It was literally sewn on, by perforating the end of the loop with a needle, drawing the suture through, and knotting it into place. Several alternate methods of attachment were tried and discarded before the present method, facilitated by a hole molded into the end of the loop, was established.

In conjunction with the then growing possibility of extended usage of loops beyond the confines of the local clinic, was the need for a safe, positive, and standardized means of insertion. The major requirements were:

1. Ease of insertion into the uterus without dilation
2. Free passage of the loop
3. Flexibility to permit coincidence with varied uterine structures
4. Provision for orienting the loop to a predictable plane
5. A guard to prevent penetration beyond a specified depth
6. Convenient means for manipulation

The doctor, in his earliest efforts, had selected Teflon tubing for its flexibility and inherent lubricity, and a small-diameter flexible plastic rod as a means of propulsion. In view of anticipated complications in the assembly of Teflon to other components, tubing from different materials including cellulose acetate, rigid PVC, low- and high-density polyethylenes, polypropylene, and even nylon were submitted as alternates but were all rejected by the doctor as being inferior to Teflon in providing ease of passage for the loops.

Teflon tubing, therefore, became the basis for evolution of the present inserter. The tubing was custom-extruded with an oval cross section to provide orientation and held to a wall thickness of only 0.015

inch. Fastening of a guard to such a thin wall by normal mechanical means was obviously impractical. Since there was no available substance for chemical adhesion to Teflon, a length of elastomeric vinyl tubing was expanded over the Teflon and allowed to shrink down tightly upon it. Molded vinyl ferrules were then cemented to the vinyl tube—one to serve as a penetration guard, and the other as a terminal finger grip, with both oriented to the major axis of the oval tubing. The plunger was molded with a button-like head on the handling end, and from the semi-rigid materials tried, polypropylene was ultimately selected.

With loop No. 1 in limited production, it was not long until a modified design was requested. Back on the drawing board, the doctor's new requirements, based upon his experience with the existing prototypes, were reflected in the form of loop No. 2. After design approval, another single cavity was made, installed, and run in the experimental mold base. Eventually, the same procedure was followed for loops Nos. 3 and 4.

Later, as more widespread usage developed, and with the advent of the Population Council's interest in the loop as an aid to its far-flung family planning activities, a four-cavity production mold, with extra interchangeable cavities of all sizes, was built to insure a supply of whatever sizes the demand might call for.

The current selection had been identified numerically in the order of development, and in the same order bore the nominal size designations of 25, 31, 30, and 27.5 mm., respectively. It was generally agreed that a more logical progression would be by size, and therefore re-identification was made alphabetically, with A as the smallest and D the largest, as shown in Figure 1.

Many new problems arise in getting loop manufacture started in other countries around the world. These follow no predictable pattern, as they are induced by variables ranging from systems of measurement to administrative policy. The initiation of a new factory for the sole purpose of loop manufacture, as opposed to the introduction of a loop mold into an existing plastics plant, can have serious implications. The availability of proper material can affect an entire program. Incidentals such as the conflict between American Standard, Metric, and British Whitworth screw threads can result in frustrating delays.

While there is no pat formula for starting loop molding activities in any country, the following general recommendations are offered:

1. Determine that quantity requirement is sufficient to warrant manufacture in the first place. Purchase of loops from an existing source may be more advantageous.
2. Consider manufacture by local plastic molders who may already have

FIG. 1.—The Lippes loop, graduated sizes from *A* (*smallest*) to *D* (largest), and, *below*, the inserter.

The following series of illustrations is intended to present a visual cross section of current loop-manufacturing activities in the United States, as well as in a number of other localities around the world.

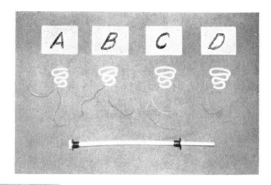

FIG. 2.—Typical injection mold. This one, in fact, is the experimental unit containing four cavity inserts for various sizes. The two objects on the left are a matched pair of cavity inserts from a production mold. These tools are very accurately made from high-grade tool steel, heat-treated to a Rockwell C hardness of 50–54, to withstand many thousands of clamping cycles.

FIG. 3.—A four-cavity mold in the open position in a molding machine, just prior to the removal of a shot of loops. This machine, with which most of the United States production has been made, is rated at 25 gm. or 9 oz. capacity, with a screw-fed preplasticizer. More to the point, it has a production capacity approaching 500 loops per hour. It is capable of fully automatic performance, but is constantly attended by an operator whose primary function is 100% inspection of the product.

FIG. 4.—A set of eight loops from an eight-cavity mold prepared to accommodate growing needs. The machine in the background is a larger counterpart of the machine in Figure 3, having a rated capacity of 100 gm. or 3.5 oz. Its production rate from this mold approaches 1,000 loops per hour.

FIG. 5.—The method of suture attachment—a double strand, passed through the molded-in hole, having the closed end interlocked around the body of the loop and tied on the opposite side of the hole to retain its position.

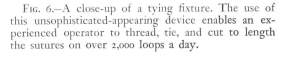

FIG. 6.—A close-up of a tying fixture. The use of this unsophisticated-appearing device enables an experienced operator to thread, tie, and cut to length the sutures on over 2,000 loops a day.

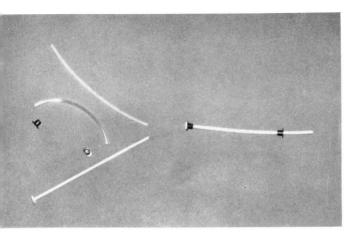

Fig. 7.—The component parts comprising the present inserter assembly. At the upper left is the oval sectioned Teflon extrusion, with the vinyl outer tube shown immediately below. Beneath that can be seen the two molded vinyl ferrules or guards, and the molded polypropylene plunger appears at bottom left. The object to the right is, obviously, the finished inserter.

Fig. 8.—Strands of material emerging from the head of an extruder in Korea, showing the means used to blend polyethylene with barium sulphate at the outset of loop manufacture in that country.

Fig. 9.—A historic moment as the first authentic loop production begins in Korea. Here is an American mold in an Italian machine, set up and run by a Korean technician, producing loops with a connotation of international status.

Fig. 10.—An electro-hydraulically powered but manually controlled molding machine made in India. Similar machines are also being used for limited loop production from small molds in Taiwan and Hong Kong. Since it lacks instrumentation for timing and accurate temperature control, the quality of its output is largely dependent upon the skill of the operator.

Fig. 11.—Three completely manual molding devices encountered in Pakistan. This type of equipment is also used to some extent in other parts of the world, including the United States. While it is possible to mold satisfactory parts with these, the process is cumbersome, and the product, even from an excellent mold, is entirely dependent upon the operator's dexterity. A production rate of even 60 satisfactory pieces an hour would be considered good.

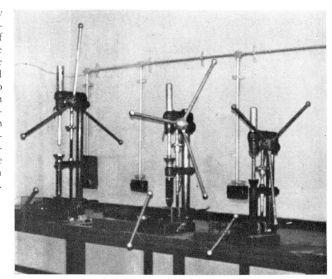

Fig. 12.—A fully automatic machine, made in India under British license. It is the type recently installed at the new IUD factory in Kanpur, India, to produce loops from an eight-cavity mold made in the United States. This combination of mold and machine has a realistic production potential of more than 20,000 pieces per day, which is in keeping with the mass production requirements of a family planning program as extensive as India's.

suitable machinery at their disposal. Many of these people are well qualified, and there is no substitute for experience.

3. Insist on the highest quality molds available, as the product will not be any better than the mold that forms it.

4. If, for political or other reasons, manufacture must be performed in the public sector, it is strongly urged that reputable molding specialists be recruited from private industry, with the authority to use their knowledge and experience in the program's best interests.

5. Consider quality first, and cost second. While cost or price comparisons are important, a product such as the loop performs too vital a function to have its quality jeopardized for the sake of apparent cost saving. It would be false economy indeed, if a family planning program, costing hundreds of thousands of dollars, was endangered in an effort to save hundreds of thousands of pennies.

The problems of IUD manufacture are basically the same as those encountered in any light manufacturing operation, with the emphasis on quality and dependability. The major issues occur during the development stages, and in the preparatory steps prior to production. At the production level there are the ever present potential problems of mold damage, machine failure, material contamination, faulty assembly, and so forth, but these can be controlled to a high degree by the use of orderly procedures and an eternally vigilant inspection department.

Achieving product standardization and attaining a substantial plateau of productive output does not mean, however, that the ultimate has been achieved. Nothing is so good that it cannot be made better, and efforts to improve both product and process should continue in order to remain effective in the constant presence of change.

PART FOUR

Research and Evaluation

43

A FAMILY LIFE STUDY IN EAST JAVA: PRELIMINARY FINDINGS

HALVOR GILLE

Office of Social Affairs, United Nations, Geneva

and

R. H. PARDOKO

Public Health Institute, Surabaya, Indonesia

INTRODUCTION

Java is one of the most densely populated areas in the world. It has about two-thirds of Indonesia's total population of 105 million (1965), but it covers only about 7% of the total land area of the country. The population density in Java is 477 inhabitants per square kilometer as compared with 65 per square kilometer for Indonesia as a whole. The rate of population growth of Java is estimated to be 2.2% per annum, which is about the same as for all Indonesia, estimated at 2.3% per annum.[1]

The rapid rate of population growth and the high population density are serious problems which have aggravated the social and economic conditions on the island. The government has sought various remedies such as transmigration of people from Java to the sparsely populated outer islands, improvement in agricultural productivity through application of modern methods of cultivation, industrialization, and better utilization of forest resources. So far limitation of population growth and fertility control have not been adopted as a governmental policy as they have been in some other countries in Asia.

Ideas about family planning are only beginning to spread among educated people in urban areas. The rural population traditionally favors large families. As soon as he reaches school age, every child

---

[1]Indonesia, *Statistical Pocket-Book of Indonesia* (Djakarta, 1962).

born into a farmer's family is put to work on the land during the peak periods of planting and harvesting, when all available labor is used. The desire for many children may lead to a relative disregard of the consequences to the health of the mother and child. In spite of efforts made toward improving sanitary and health conditions through health education and health centers, mortality and morbidity are still believed to be high.

Very limited information is available on population trends, levels and differentials of fertility, and attitudes, behavior, and knowledge of the population with regard to human reproduction. Sources of demographic information are mainly limited to the population census of 1961 (taken for the first time since 1930), the incomplete vital statistics registration, and a demographic survey introduced in 1962 to estimate periodically the rate of population growth. These sources provide little information on the economic, social, and other factors affecting demographic behavior and attitudes toward family building. The need for information of this kind is clearly indicated by the fact that steps have been taken recently to provide, on a small scale, advice and facilities for family planning through maternal and child welfare services in various urban areas in the country, a policy mainly aimed at protecting the health and the welfare of mothers and children. As a first attempt to provide some much needed data on family life and living conditions, required to plan possible measures to deal with population problems, the Public Health Institute in Surabaya initiated, with assistance from the Population Council, a family life study in East Java in 1961.

STUDY DESIGN AND FIELD WORK

The study was designed to obtain, in selected villages in East Java, information on living conditions, on behavior, attitudes, and knowledge related to family building, and the changes therein over a period of time. In the regency of Surabaya the two sub-districts of Tjermee and Duduk Sampejan were selected for the study. These two sub-districts are located 20–25 miles west of the city of Surabaya in a poor and, even for Java, very densely populated area.[2] It is a flat area which is flooded during the rainy season and very dry during most of the rest of the year. In the dry season even drinking water becomes very scarce. Lack of irrigation facilities generally limits the number of crops to one a year. The farmers all own the land they are cultivating

[2]The population density in the rural area of Surabaya is more than 50% above the average density in rural areas in Java as a whole (667 and 428 persons per square kilometer, respectively).

but the holdings are small, usually less than one acre. Almost all villagers in the two areas are Moslems but many of them (about half of the married women) do not claim to observe the Moslem religion or to obey its laws.

In the Tjermee sub-district seven villages were selected for inclusion in the study. They are in a fairly isolated location and some of them can be reached only by foot, being one or two miles off the nearest road. The main means of livelihood in the villages is agriculture, except in one village where weaving is widely practiced.

Three villages were selected in the Duduk Sampejan area (abbreviated to Duduk below). They are located on or near the main road running from Surabaya to central Java. The railroad from Surabaya to Samarang also runs through the area, providing an easy connection with the former city. The level of living is on the whole higher than in the Tjermee area, since fish cultivation in the saltwater ponds is a widespread practice in addition to farming.

From complete lists of more than 2,500 households in the ten villages in the two areas, 1,002 households were selected at random for the study, about 500 in each of the two sub-districts. In the 1,002 households there were 4,215 persons in all, 2,228 in Tjermee and 1,987 in Duduk.[3]

Through house-to-house interviewing, the data were collected by three teams, each consisting of one male and one female health worker. In the households selected, the male workers interviewed the married men and the female workers the married women. Husband and wife were, if possible, interviewed at the same time but separately in order to obtain independent replies.

It was deemed necessary to undertake the study in several stages, partly to acquaint the families with the project gradually and to approach questions about family planning cautiously, and partly to obtain information on changes in living conditions and attitudes over a period of years. For the first round of interviews, which took place in 1961, a household schedule and two individual schedules, one for men and one for women, were used. These schedules included questions on the living conditions of the household, the social, economic, and demographic characteristics of its members, the number of births and deaths which had occurred in the previous twelve months and some questions addressed to married persons about marriage and childbearing. For the second round, a supplementary schedule was used which included a few additional questions on attitudes toward birth spacing.

[3]The sample constituted 7.0% and 8.7%, respectively, of the total population in the two sub-districts.

In the third round, the same families were visited. Detailed questions on knowledge of the physiology of human reproduction and on family planning and willingness to use family planning were put to husband and wife in marriages where the wife was under forty years of age. At the same time some of the questions included in the two earlier rounds were repeated.

Following the third round, an action program was introduced in the areas by furnishing information on family planning to all couples in the villages. All those accepting family planning were offered contraceptives, and routine visits were made.

At the present time results are available only from the first two rounds of the study.[4] The third round is still in the process of tabulation.

GENERAL CHARACTERISTICS OF THE FAMILIES IN THE SAMPLE

Sex distribution.—About 54% of the sample are females and 46% males. The sex ratio is approximately the same in the two districts, although there is a slightly smaller proportion of men in Duduk than in Tjermee.

Age distribution.—Of the total sample, 40% are under 15 years of age and 55% are 15–59 years (Table 1). Those in the working ages constitute a considerably higher proportion in Tjermee than in Duduk, in particular for men, suggesting that a number of adults from Duduk had left the latter area for work, probably in the city of Surabaya. At the same time some under-reporting of girls seems indicated by the comparatively small proportion of females in the age group 0–14 years (38%).

Some underenumeration of infants and young children might be expected and seems to have occurred. At the same time the very small number in the age groups 10–14 and 15–19, as compared with the younger groups, may reflect to some extent an outmigration of young people from the area. This seems indicated by the fact that the ratio between the age groups 10–14 and 5–9 is substantially smaller in Duduk (42%), which is more likely to be influenced by migration in view of its location, than in Tjermee (71%). However, migration cannot fully explain the present age distribution, especially as other evidence from the survey does not seem to suggest generally a very high mobility of the population (nearly four-fifths of the adults had stayed all their life in the villages concerned), although adverse economic conditions in the area recently have undoubtedly increased outmigration in the younger adult groups. The small number of persons

[4]Unless otherwise stated the data described in the paper are from the first round.

in their teens and early twenties as compared with the larger younger age groups, is probably due considerably to the low level of fertility and high infant and early childhood mortality which undoubtedly prevailed in Java under the severe conditions during World War II and the subsequent war for independence.

Marital status.—Among persons 15 years of age and above, 70% of the men and 68% of the women were married (Table 2). Widowhood

TABLE 1

SAMPLE BY SEX AND AGE

| AGE GROUPS | NUMBER | | PERCENTAGE | | | | | | |
| | | | Tjermee | | Duduk | | Total Sample | | |
	Males	Females	Males	Females	Males	Females	Males	Females	Both Sexes
0–14	839	864	40.3	34.9	46.6	41.4	43.2	38.0	40.4
15–59	1,011	1,317	54.7	59.1	49.1	56.6	52.1	57.9	55.3
60 and over	91	93	5.0	6.0	4.3	2.0	4.7	4.1	4.3
Total	1,941	2,274	100.0	100.0	100.0	100.0	100.0	100.0	100.0

NOTE: According to a 1% sample tabulation of the 1961 national population census the age distribution in rural areas in Indonesia as a whole was (in per cent):

Age groups	Males	Females
0–14	43.6	41.4
15–59	52.0	54.3
60 and over	4.4	4.3
	100.0	100.0

A detailed breakdown for the child and youth population is as follows:

Under 1 year	121	0– 4 years	715
1 year	120	5– 9 years	635
2 years	135	10–14 years	353
3 years	173	15–19 years	294
4 years	166	20–24 years	374
		25–29 years	400

was reported by only 3% of the men but by 20% of the women, and divorce by 5% of the men and 7% of the women. About 22% of the married women had been married once before and 12% several times. Among married women under 40 years of age, 12% had been married once before and 9% several times. The smaller number of married men than married women is caused by the many husbands who were away from home, most of them because of work in another area, particularly in Surabaya city; for about 19% of the married women aged 15–39 years, the husband was not present.

Education and literacy.—Fifty-two per cent of males and 80% of females 10 years or older had not received any education. In the Tjermee area there were more persons without any education than in Duduk (among males 56% and 48%, respectively).

Only 33% of the ever-married men and 12% of the women were able to read and write (Latin characters); in the district of Duduk the literacy rates were higher, namely 43% for males and 16% for females. The spoken language was Javanese. Only 35% of the men and 13% of the women understood the national language, Bahasa, but more in the Duduk district than in Tjermee.[5]

TABLE 2

MARITAL STATUS OF PERSONS 15 YEARS AND OVER[a]

STATUS	NUMBER		PERCENTAGE						
			Tjermee		Duduk		Total		
	Males	Females	Males	Females	Males	Females	Males	Females	Both Sexes
Married......	776	959	64.8	63.6	77.6	73.5	70.4	68.0	69.1
Widowed.....	32	279	2.9	22.9	2.9	16.0	2.9	19.8	12.4
Divorced.....	50	102	6.5	7.7	2.1	6.6	4.6	7.2	6.0
Single........	244	70	25.8	5.8	17.4	3.9	22.1	5.0	12.5
Total.......	1,102	1,410	100.0	100.0	100.0	100.0	100.0	100.0	100.0

[a] Only 10 ever-married women were under age 15.

Occupation and employment.—For persons 15 years and over who were working and gave information, the occupational distribution is given in Table 3.

Around 46% of all married women were working. Among women with one or more children under age 5, 43% were working. In the group of women with older children and with none under age 5, 52% were working. The percentage of women who were working was much higher in Tjermee than in Duduk. For example, in Tjermee 53% of the women with small children were working, but in Duduk only 34% were.

The employed women were working on the average 6.5 hours a day; nearly one-third of them worked 8 hours or more. In the Duduk district nearly 10% of them worked even 10 hours or more, but in Tjermee only 4% worked that long. Women with small children

[5]Information on literacy was obtained in response to questions put to the respondents in the first round. Their ability to read and write was not tested in the course of the interview but was tested in the third round, from which the data are not yet available.

worked on the average about as long as other women. There were no major differences in the duration of work in the two main areas.

Household types.—A household was defined in the survey as a group of people cooking their main food in the same pan. Such a group of people normally living under one roof consisted of a nuclear family with or without relatives or other persons. On the average there were 4.6 persons per household. In Tjermee the household size was slightly higher than in Duduk (4.8 and 4.4, respectively). Two-thirds of all households had at least four members; 30% had six or more, and 2% ten or more. In three-fourths of all the households there was a married

TABLE 3

OCCUPATION OF PERSONS 15 YEARS AND OVER

OCCUPATION	NUMBER	PERCENTAGE				Total
		Tjermee		Duduk		
		Males	Females	Males	Females	
Farmer..............	863	63.1	39.1	57.4	59.7	55.0
Laborer..............	462	26.8	51.8	19.2	17.9	29.4
Merchant............	186	8.6	9.1	11.6	20.8	11.9
Government official......	56	1.5	....	11.3	1.6	3.6
Military..............	2	....	....	0.5	....	0.1
Total..............	1,569	100.0	100.0	100.0	100.0	100.0

NOTE: Information on occupation was not available from 943 respondents—702 of them women. Nearly all of them were not gainfully occupied.

woman in the reproductive age group, 15–39 years. More than one-third of such households had live-in relatives or other adults in addition to the married couple and their children. In about one-fifth of the households the husband was absent from home at the time of the survey, usually for work elsewhere. Households with the husband absent were found more frequently in Duduk than in Tjermee.

Housing conditions.—Each household occupied in most cases a dwelling of its own. Only 2% of the households were under the same roof with another household. Most of the houses are made of bamboo-matting walls covered with a tile roof. One-fifth of the houses included in the survey had walls made of wooden boards and only one house had brick walls.

The general design of the houses is very simple, usually consisting of one rectangular room with a small kitchen attached to it. The room is used not only as a living room but also as a bedroom for part of, or all of, the household and is sometimes also shared with the cattle.

There are generally no windows, and the floor is made of packed earth. The furniture is usually limited to a table, a few chairs, and one or two broad, benchlike pieces used as beds. Nearly all families own their dwellings, but a few cases of renting exist in Duduk district.

Sleeping quarters.—Nearly half of the households with a married woman aged 15–39 years had no separate bedroom, and all members, on the average 4.7 persons, slept together in the one single room of the house (Table 4). The overcrowding was generally worse in Duduk, where nearly 60% of the households had no bedroom. (In Tjermee only 31% of the households had no bedroom.) But at the same time the households without a bedroom were on the average smaller in Duduk than in Tjermee (4.6 and 5.1 persons, respectively). About 40% of all households had one bedroom, with an average household size of 4.8. Only 13% had two or more bedrooms, with an average of 5.9 persons per household.

The overcrowded housing conditions and the limited possibilities for privacy are especially apparent from information about bed facilities. In most households several persons shared a bed. In households with a married woman aged 15–39 years, about 32% had only one

TABLE 4

BEDROOMS IN HOUSEHOLDS WITH A MARRIED WOMAN AGED 15–39 YEARS

BEDROOMS	NUMBER OF HOUSEHOLDS	PERCENTAGE			AVERAGE NUMBER OF PERSONS PER HOUSEHOLD
		Tjermee	Duduk	Total	
None............	317	31.4	59.1	46.9	4.7
1................	269	49.2	32.4	39.8	4.8
2 or more........	90	19.4	8.5	13.3	5.9
Total..........	676	100.0	100.0	100.0	4.9

TABLE 5

BEDS IN HOUSEHOLDS WITH A MARRIED WOMAN AGED 15–39 YEARS

BEDS	NUMBER OF HOUSEHOLDS	PERCENTAGE			AVERAGE NUMBER OF PERSONS PER HOUSEHOLD
		Tjermee	Duduk	Total	
None............	89	3.7	20.7	13.2	4.4
1................	215	26.1	36.3	31.8	4.5
2................	263	46.8	32.6	38.9	5.0
3 or more........	109	23.4	10.4	16.1	5.9
Total..........	676	100.0	100.0	100.0	4.9

bed, although the average family size was 4.5 persons. Around 39% had two beds for an average number of 5 persons (Table 5). In 13% of the households, consisting of 4.4 persons on the average, there were no beds at all. The bed facilities were more limited in Duduk than in Tjermee, but at the same time the household size was substantially lower in the former area than in the latter (on the average 4.6 and 5.4 persons, respectively).

Sanitation.—The chalk layer in the ground makes it difficult to dig water wells in the area. Therefore rainwater stored in some open reservoirs and ponds located outside the villages provides the drinking water for the people and cattle. Less than one-third (30%) of the families in the Tjermee villages boiled the water before drinking, but in the Duduk district nearly half of them followed this procedure. Contrariwise, half the families in Duduk versus over one-third in Tjermee did not use any latrine. The majority of the families in Duduk who used a latrine used public latrines, but in Tjermee private latrines were generally used.

AGES AT FIRST MENSTRUATION AND MARRIAGE

Age at first menstruation.—Among ever-married women the ages reported for first menstruation were as follows: before 13 years of age, 109 (8.3%); before 15 years of age, 406 (30.9%); before 17 years of age, 1,178 (89.6%); and before 20 years of age, 1,296 (98.6%); age 20 years or later, 19 (1.4%). (Thirty-five women did not give any information.) The mean age at first menstruation was 15.3 years in Tjermee and 14.8 years in Duduk.

Women who menstruated at a comparatively early age often married earlier than other women. Thus 58% of women who menstruated for the first time before age 13 married also at that age. Such an early age at marriage was reported by 34% of the women who menstruated at age 13–14, by 13% of the women menstruating at age 15–16, and by only 11% of women menstruating at an older age.

Age at marriage.—Women marry at an early age, as in several other Asian countries, India in particular. The mean age at first marriage was 15.7 years. Of all persons ever-married at the time of the interview, more than two-thirds of the women had married before they were 17 years old. More than one-fifth of them married before age 13 (Table 6). Differences in age at marriage for literate and illiterate women were small and not statistically significant. The pattern of age at marriage was about the same in the two areas under study. The men married generally much later; only 5% of them married before age 17 and the majority married after they were 20 years old. At age

20–24 years 62% of the men were still bachelors but only 9% of the women were spinsters.

Marriage is almost universal in the population concerned. At age 35–39 years only 1% of the men and 0.6% of the women had not yet married. Among all men aged 40 and over, 1% were unmarried and among women, 0.3%. Polygamic marriages were not reported.

Attitude toward age at marriage.—There seems to be a prevailing opinion among many villagers that a low age at marriage for girls is

TABLE 6

AGE AT MARRIAGE BY COHORTS OF EVER-MARRIED MALES AND FEMALES

(Per Cent)

MARRIED UNDER (years of age)	YEARS OF BIRTH OF COHORT							
	1920 or Earlier		1921–30		1931–40		All (1940 or Earlier)	
	Males	Females	Males	Females	Males	Females	Males	Females
13.........	0.5	27.9	0.4	25.0	....	14.5	0.4	22.4
15.........	0.5	38.5	0.8	37.8	0.5	26.0	0.6	33.9
17.........	4.0	73.4	5.7	72.9	4.8	60.9	4.7	68.8
20.........	18.7	87.2	25.0	89.3	23.8	88.5	21.8	88.2
25.........	61.4	98.9	75.4	98.2	....	....	....	....
30.........	87.7	99.8	97.3	....	....	....	....	....
40.........	98.5[a]	100.0	....	....	....	....	....	....
Total.....	100.0	100.0	100.0	100.0	100.0	100.0	100.0	100.0
Number of ever-married.	396	462	264	328	189	435	849	1,225

NOTE: In addition, there were nine ever-married women who did not give information on age at marriage.

[a] 6 men were married at age 40 or over.

not desirable. The mean desired age as stated by ever-married persons was 17.3 years which is substantially above the actual age at marriage as reported above. About 30% of them stated that they would like their daughter, if any, to marry only at 19 or 20 years of age. Of the men, 71%, and, of the women, 59% favored 17 or above as the most appropriate age. Literate persons generally expressed preference for a higher age at marriage than did illiterate persons. An age at marriage of 17 years or above was favored by about 75% of the literate but by only about 60% of the illiterate persons.

A comparison between the desired age and the actual age at which the respondents themselves had married, showed that 60% of the ever-married women wanted their daughters to marry at a higher age than that at which they themselves had actually married. A substantially higher age at marriage was generally favored—in two-fifths of the cases, five years higher or more was suggested. About 20% of the women mentioned the same age at which they themselves had married and nearly as many proposed a lower age though generally only one or two years lower.

Matching of the answers given by husbands and wives to the question about the desirable age at marriage for their daughters (if any), showed identical replies for about 28% of the couples. In 30% of the cases the husband expressed a desire for a higher age at marriage than the wife; in 23%, a lower age. In the rest of the cases one or both of the spouses did not express any opinion about the desired age.

PREGNANCIES AND BIRTHS

Women married once and still married, who were 40 years old and over, reported they had had on the average 4.4 pregnancies and those aged 50 years and over, 5.3 pregnancies. They had on the average 4.4 pregnancies after 20–24 years of marriage and 4.7 pregnancies after 30 years or more of marriage (when most of them had completed their reproductive cycle). There was no significant difference between completed fertility in the two study areas.

Among married women of all ages the literate had higher fertility than the illiterate, but for women with completed fertility the material was insufficient to establish any significant difference. Little difference in fertility was found between women who were observing the Moslem religion and those who were not.

About 97% of all pregnancies had terminated in live birth, 1% in stillbirth, and nearly 2% in miscarriage or abortion. Deliveries were usually attended by indigenous midwives. Not even 4% of all deliveries in the area under study had been attended by a trained midwife or a doctor.

About 12% of all live-born children reported by married women died within the first year of life. The infant mortality rate was higher in Duduk (139 per 1,000 live births) than in Tjermee (102). About 18% of the children born alive died before the age of five. It is likely that the under-reporting of births mentioned above, particularly in Tjermee, was linked to a considerable extent with births where the child had died, supporting the notion that infant and early childhood mortality is also under-reported.

ACTUAL AND DESIRED BIRTH INTERVALS

An attempt was made to estimate the dates of births as accurately as possible by using a list of special events in the villages concerned to support the respondents' memory, by estimating the age of children present during the interview, and by checking the information obtained against the village records of vital events. Matching of the husband's and wife's answers concerning the length of intervals between live births showed a high degree of concurrence. Discrepancies of one month or more occurred in only 2%–3%, or fewer, of the cases for various birth intervals, but for the interval between marriage and first birth, disagreements occurred more frequently (discrepancies of one month or more in 17% of the cases).

The average pregnancy intervals for women married once and still married were around three years (35 months) and the birth intervals slightly longer (38 months). The intervals tended to decline with increasing pregnancy and birth order. Generally the longest interval was found between marriage and the first event (associated with the delay in cohabitation after early marriage). An inverse correlation seems also to exist between age at marriage and birth intervals. A preliminary examination of the data suggests higher average pregnancy intervals for illiterate than for literate women (36 months as compared with 32 months), but if a breakdown is made according to present age of the women this differential tends to disappear.

It is common practice for women throughout rural Java to breastfeed their infants for several years, if possible. In the study area 64% of the women aged 15–39 years, with children, reported that they had nursed their babies for 24 months or more. Most of the rest reported lactation periods between 12 and 23 months. The illiterate women tended to have nursed their babies longer than literate women. There was no significant difference in lactation practice between the two groups of villages.

The preferred birth interval seemed to be around three years as stated by about one-third of all married men and a similar proportion of married women under age 40. The next highest preference among women was four years, but among men only two years as stated by 18% and 19% respectively. A comparison of the replies given by husband and wife shows that the same answer was given in about half of all cases from whom information was obtained. In the remaining half, two-thirds of the husbands stated shorter birth intervals than the wife. A difference in the average birth interval of one year was most common.

DESIRED FAMILY SIZE

Information on desired family size was obtained by inquiring in the first round about the ideal number of children the respondents would have liked to have, assuming that they had just married, and by asking in the second round if they wanted to have a child in addition to the children they already had at the time of the interview.

The average family size desired as the ideal was 4.3 children. The men generally indicated a preference for more children than women; the means were 4.7 and 4.0, respectively. There is a correlation between ideal family size and the number of children the respondents actually had (Table 7). Married couples who had no children or only one or two considered around four children to be the most desirable number. Families with three or four children felt that at least one

TABLE 7

NUMBER OF CHILDREN STATED AS IDEAL

NUMBER OF CHILDREN LIVING	NUMBER OF RESPONDENTS	AVERAGE IDEAL NUMBER OF CHILDREN	RESPONDENTS STATING HIGHER IDEAL NUMBER THAN PRESENT FAMILY SIZE (per cent)	
			Males	Females
0..........	407	3.5	99	100
1..........	346	3.6	88	91
2..........	307	4.0	80	75
3..........	250	4.3	51	62
4..........	225	5.2	51	35
5 or more.....	212	4.8	42	24
Married persons aged 15 or over	1,747	4.3	75	71

more child, on the average, would be desirable. Only in families with five or more children was the average ideal below the actual family size. Even in the latter families more than two-fifths of the men and about one-quarter of the women had an ideal exceeding the number of children they already had.

For about one-fourth of the married men and women the ideal number of children coincided with the number they actually had. About 42% of the families with five children or more held this view. Only 3%-4% of all respondents stated an ideal below the number of children they had, but in families with seven or more children one-third of the respondents did so.

Sex preference.—A strong preference for boys, similar to that noted in many studies in other Asian countries, was not found in the study. The same number of boys and girls was wanted by 55% of the married women and by 45% of the men. A preference for more boys was expressed by 24% of the women but nearly as many (21%) wanted more girls than boys. Of the men, 32% wanted to have more boys, but 24% desired more girls.

Desire for another child.—The answers to the less hypothetical question about having another child give an impression rather similar to the above, although this information is limited to families where the wife is 15–39 years of age (Table 8). The proportion of respondents wanting another child declines with increasing family size. More than two-fifths (42%) of the married women, and over half

TABLE 8

MARRIED WOMEN AGED 15–39 YEARS AND THEIR HUSBANDS
WANTING ANOTHER CHILD, BY NUMBER
OF LIVING CHILDREN (SECOND ROUND)

NUMBER OF LIVING CHILDREN	NUMBER OF RESPONDENTS		PERCENTAGE WANTING ANOTHER CHILD	
	Males	Females	Males	Females
0.............	73	125	....	....
1.............	69	125	85.5	81.6
2.............	60	118	78.4	77.1
3.............	45	90	71.2	62.2
4.............	43	84	60.6	42.8
5 or more......	15	38	26.7	39.4
Total........	305	580	....	....

NOTE: No reply was given by 58 married women and 333 men, the majority of the latter were not reached for interviewing in the second round.

(52%) of the men with four children or more, wanted another child. The men more often wanted another child than the women, except among those who already had five children or more (but most of these husbands did not express any view or did not reply).

The desire for another child was generally more pronounced among literate than illiterate married men and women. The percentage of the literate wanting another child declined from 90% among married persons with one living child to 59% among those with four living children, but for illiterate persons it declined from 78% in one-child families to 44% in four-child families. In the families with five or more living children there was no significant difference between the attitudes of literate and illiterate married men and women.

Comparison of husband and wife replies.—Husband and wife replies in Table 7 were identical for 42% of the couples where both spouses replied (586 couples). In 38% of the cases the husband stated a larger ideal number of children, generally one or two children more than the wife. In the remaining cases the husband's ideal family size was below the wife's, generally by one or two children. The question about whether another child was wanted was answered identically by husband and wife in a large proportion (80%) of cases in which both spouses replied and expressed an opinion, but the room for deviating replies was also more limited with a yes-no question.

Reasons for wanting or not wanting more children.—Among married women (aged 15–39 years) and their husbands who replied to a question about the reasons for desiring more children (613 persons) most of them stated that they were young and had not yet obtained the family size they wanted. A fatalistic reply like "Will of God" was given by only about 7% of the respondents, most of them men. However, among couples with four children or more, about 14% mentioned "Will of God" as a reason (second round).

The majority of the comparatively few respondents who did not want more children (244 persons) merely stated that they did not like a family life with many children, without specifying further. About one-fourth considered themselves too old to have more children, although they were still in the reproductive ages. Hardly 10% mentioned adverse effects on the family's economic conditions.

Discussion on desired family size.—Discussions between husband and wife about desired family size seem not to be very common. Only 28% of the married persons (wife aged 15–49 years) mentioned that such a discussion had taken place. Among literate persons about 36% had discussed this subject with their spouse. Matching of the replies given by husband and wife shows that in more than four-fifths of all cases the same reply was given. A larger percentage of the literate respondents than the illiterate stated that they had had discussion, but the difference was not statistically significant (second round).

KNOWLEDGE OF AND WILLINGNESS TO USE METHODS OF
FAMILY PLANNING

Knowledge of family planning.—Very few of the villagers had any knowledge of family planning. Among all ever-married persons who were asked whether they had heard of and understood what methods of birth spacing were, only two persons replied that they had heard of birth spacing and knew something about methods, and four had heard of it but did not know how it was done (Table 9).

Willingness to use methods of family planning.—In the first round a question was put to the married persons about their willingness to use methods to regulate births "if such means were available to doctors." A large number answered in the affirmative. Among literate persons

84% and among illiterate persons 65% expressed willingness (Table 10).

More than four-fifths of all males expressed interest in family planning but hardly two-thirds of the women did so. However, these findings might be subject to serious doubts. There is no indication that married couples with many children (many of them having expressed interest in limiting the number of births) were more willing to use family planning than couples with only a few or no children. It is questionable whether the villagers understood what the question really was about, since their knowledge of family planning was almost totally

TABLE 9

KNOWLEDGE ABOUT FAMILY PLANNING AMONG
EVER-MARRIED PERSONS (SECOND ROUND)

DEGREE OF KNOWLEDGE	NUMBER	PERCENTAGE	
		Males	Females
Had heard of birth spacing but did not know how...	4	....	0.3
Had heard of birth spacing and knew how.........	2	0.1	0.1
Had never heard of birth spacing.................	140	6.2	6.5
Had never heard of birth spacing and understood the question only with some difficulty..............	999	29.1	57.4
Did not understand the question at all............	1,049	64.6	35.7
Total..	2,194	100.0	100.0

TABLE 10

WILLINGNESS TO USE FAMILY PLANNING
METHODS, IF AVAILABLE

(Married Women Aged 15–39 Years and Some of Their Husbands)

RESPONDENTS	NUMBER OF PERSONS	PERCENTAGE WILLING TO USE METHODS		
		Literate	Illiterate	Total
Males....................	425	88.6	77.2	83.8
Females.................	739	77.5	61.1	64.3
Total.................	1,164	84.5	64.9	71.4
Married persons with:				
0–1 child..............	550	85.1	69.4	75.8
2–3 children...........	424	84.6	60.8	67.7
4 children and over......	190	81.0	63.5	67.4
Total.................	1,164	84.5	65.0	71.5

absent (as indicated above) and no detailed explanations were made during the interview.

SEXUAL RELATIONS

Premarital experience.—None of the ever-married women indicated that they had had any premarital experience. Among men, however, 13% stated that they had had sexual relations before marriage. There was no correlation between age at marriage and the extent of premarital experience among the men, except that the percentage of those with such experience was somewhat higher among men who

TABLE 11

DISTRIBUTION BY AGE AT FIRST INTERCOURSE FOR
EVER-MARRIED PERSONS BY YEARS OF BIRTH

(Per Cent)

FIRST INTERCOURSE	YEARS OF BIRTH							
	1920 or Earlier		1921–30		1931–40		1941 or Later	
	Males	Females	Males	Females	Males	Females	Males	Females
Under age 13.........	....	4.1	....	2.1	....	0.7	....	4.3
13–14.................	....	9.0	....	8.8	....	9.3	....	15.5
15–16.................	3.0	41.3	4.6	40.3	3.7	41.0	(11.1)	42.2
17–19.................	10.1	27.2	15.9	30.3	16.9	30.3	(22.2)	18.2
20 years and over.....	82.9	16.5	78.4	16.8	70.4	15.5	....	....
Unknown............	4.0	1.9	1.1	1.8	9.0	3.2	(66.7)	19.8
Total..............	100.0	100.0	100.0	100.0	100.0	100.0	100.0	100.0
Number of ever-married..........	396	467	264	328	189	439	9	116

married very late (23% for men who married after age 30 as compared with 12%–13% in other age groups). There was no major difference in the frequency between the two areas of the study.

Age at first intercourse.—The various age levels at which ever-married persons had first intercourse are outlined in Table 11.

Only a small percentage of the men had had first intercourse before age 17 and around 20% or fewer before age 20. More than half of the women had had first intercourse before age 17. The pattern of age at first intercourse did not vary extensively for the different groups of birth cohorts (except for the youngest cohorts, where the number was rather small). There was no significant difference in the pattern between Tjermee and Duduk.

The very low ages at which women married were not reflected in similarly low ages at first intercourse. Whereas, for example, about 22% of the women married before age 13, and 34% before age 15, only 3% and 13%, respectively, had intercourse for the first time at that age. Many young married couples undoubtedly do not begin sexual intercourse immediately after marriage; young brides often remain with their parents for a period of time before joining their husbands.

The "correlation" between age at marriage and age at first intercourse for women is outlined in Table 12. Among women marrying under 13 years of age, 88% started cohabitation later, the majority of them only at age 15 or above. About two-thirds of women married at

TABLE 12

AGE AT MARRIAGE AND AT FIRST INTERCOURSE FOR EVER-MARRIED WOMEN

AGE AT MARRIAGE	AGE AT FIRST INTERCOURSE (number of females)						
	Under 13 Years	13–14 Years	15–16 Years	17–19 Years	20 Years and Over	Unknown	Total
Under 13 years....	34	77	122	41	14	7	295
13–14 years.......	....	52	72	26	2	6	158
15–16 years.......	....	1	357	98	15	15	486
17–19 years.......	....	....	2	215	32	9	258
20 years and over..	....	....	1	....	139	4	144
Unknown.........	....	....	....	....	....	9	9
Total...........	34	130	554	380	202	50	1,350

age 13–14 experienced their first intercourse after that age. Only one-fourth of the women married at 15 or 16 years of age had first intercourse at a later age. In a few cases (4) an age lower at first intercourse than at marriage was recorded. This seems inconsistent with the fact that none of the women admitted premarital experience. The discrepancy may be due to incorrect information on the latter or, more likely, misstatements of age.

Sexual experience outside marriage.—Such practice appears not very common in the population under study. Only 2% of the married men and 1% of the women admitted sexual relations outside marriage.

Interval between childbirth and subsequent intercourse.—The information obtained indicated fairly long intervals. More than one-fourth of the married women under age 40 stated an interval of 6 to 11 months and nearly half of them 12 to 23 months. Around 4% stated even 24 months or more.

Frequency of intercourse in marriage.—Married persons aged 15–49 living with spouse were asked about intercourse within the last month prior to the interview. About 57% mentioned a frequency of 1–3 times in the last month, 8% 4–7 times and nearly 2% 8 times or more. One-third of them stated that they had not had any intercourse or they did not reply (Table 13). The women stated on average slightly lower frequencies than the men. The reliability of answers on such a personal question may be doubtful although the fairly low frequency rates are not inconsistent with what has been found in studies in some other Asian countries. Matching of husband's and wife's replies shows that exactly the same answer was given by about half of the couples

TABLE 13

FREQUENCY OF INTERCOURSE IN MARRIAGE DURING
ONE MONTH PRECEDING INTERVIEW

(Married Persons Aged 15–49 Years, Spouse Cohabiting)

	NUMBER	TIMES OF INTERCOURSE (per cent)				
		None or No Reply	1–3	4–7	8 or More	Total
Married men[a]	427	24.6	64.9	9.8	0.7	100.0
Married women	819	37.7	53.5	7.0	1.8	100.0
All	1,246	33.2	57.4	7.9	1.5	100.0

[a] Numerous men were unavailable for interviewing because they were working.

(52%) and answers deviating by 1 or 2 times by about one-third (35%).

CONCLUSION

The present study is a first attempt in Indonesia to provide basic demographic and socioeconomic data required for the planning of an experimental action program in the field of population as well as the base-line data needed to measure the effects, if any, of such a program. The findings of the first two rounds presented in this paper are subject to further analysis and to supplementary information collected in the third round as well as in the pilot action program. In spite of the preliminary nature of the findings, they show clearly the poor living conditions of the villagers, low age at marriage, high birth rate, large family norms, and almost no knowledge and practice of family planning. A considerable number of respondents expressed willingness to use family planning but few of them indicated concern about the consequences of many childbirths. The extent of their real interest in family planning is doubtful and needs further investigation.

44

FAMILY GROWTH AND FAMILY PLANNING IN A RURAL DISTRICT OF THAILAND

AMOS H. HAWLEY

Demographic Adviser
The Population Council

and

VISID PRACHUABMOH

Faculty of Political Science
Chulalongkorn University

Although Thailand's rate of population growth, estimated to be about 3% per year, places it among the world's most rapidly growing nations, it is fortunate in having at the moment no serious pressure of numbers on resources or economic opportunities. Economic growth is 5% or more per year. Agricultural resources, though they are amenable to a more intensive cultivation than they now receive, yield a substantial surplus for export. Nevertheless, the short-run future is clouded by a very real prospect that the population, should the present growth rate continue, will increase from the 27 million of 1960 to 53 million in 1980. Thus, unless economic growth can be sharply accelerated, the increments of growth will be devoted mainly to feeding, clothing, housing, and servicing the expanding generations.

These circumstances and their consequences were discussed at considerable length in a National Population Seminar, held in Bangkok, in March, 1963. The consensus reached in those discussions was that Thailand was in the unique position of being able to foresee the effects of present trends and to take action before its problems became serious. It was further agreed that exploratory steps should be taken toward the development of a national population policy. One step which was recommended was the initiation of a family planning pilot project to gather information on the feasibility of family planning and the response of the people to such a service. Accordingly, at the request of the National Research Council, the Population Council, which had assisted in the organization of the seminar, provided funds and technical advisers for the pilot project. An area was selected—Photharam Amphur, Ratburi Changwad, situated some 85 kilometers west of Bangkok—and the project was launched in mid-1964 under the joint auspices of the National Research Council and the Ministry of Health. It began with a field study designed to provide baseline data for the later measurement of change. An action program began soon afterward. In this paper we are concerned only with the findings of the field survey of the Family Health Research Project.

To put forth any expectations concerning fertility patterns, trends, or attitudes prevailing in the study area in advance of the survey would be foolhardy. There is no precedent in Thailand, at least not in published form, for the kind of investigation we wish to pursue. This report, then, is necessarily descriptive and analytical.

The survey was carried out during the first two weeks of August, 1964. A simple, random sample of 25% of all households in the amphur was drawn from house registers made available by the district officer. (One section, having approximately 600 households, was excluded from the universe population because of its inaccessibility and the wide scatter of houses there.) The sampling process yielded 2,538 households. Each of the households in the sample was visited by a trained midwife interviewer and an interview was held with one married woman in each household who was 20 to 45 years of age and whose husband was living. In only 7 of the 2,538 houses could no one be found, after repeated visits, to inform the interviewer whether an eligible respondent lived there. Of the eligible respondents located none refused to be interviewed. Completed interviews number 1,207.

CHARACTERISTICS OF THE SAMPLE POPULATION

Photharam is primarily a rural district. Except for a market center, which contains about one-eighth of the total population, settlement is scattered over open country. Yet agricultural households comprise only 63% of all households. Photharam is similar in that respect to the changwad in which it is located. But that proportion is well below the 78% for the kingdom as a whole, exclusive of the Bangkok metropolitan area. Of the remaining households in the study area, 14% of the heads are engaged in white-collar occupations and 21% are craftsmen and service workers of various kinds. Less than 2% of all household heads are unemployed.

The district has not, in recent years, had to rely to any appreciable extent on migration to maintain its population. Most of the residents are native to the locality; 87% of the wives and 82% of the husbands were born in Photharam. Two-thirds of the remainder of both wives and husbands were born either in other amphurs of Ratburi Changwad or in adjacent changwads. Only 6 wives and 31 husbands are foreign-born.

It appears from the age composition of wives in the sample that the district has had and may continue to have a net outmigration of its young adults (Table 1). Women in the youngest age group are but half as numerous as they are in the changwad and in the kingdom, while older women are much more numerous in Photharam. Furthermore, inflation of the sample produces a total population 10,000 fewer

TABLE 1

DISTRIBUTION OF MARRIED WOMEN,
20–44 YEARS OF AGE

(Per Cent)

Age	Photharam (survey)	Ratburi (census)	Kingdom (census)
All ages.........	100	100	100
20–24..........	10	18	20
25–29..........	23	24	25
30–34..........	26	24	23
35–39..........	22	18	18
40–44..........	19	16	14

than the 73,000 reported in the census of 1960. (That census' migration data for Ratburi Changwad show a net loss of population between 1955 and 1960 of 5,360 people. There is reason to believe that this figure is an understatement of the actual net loss.) In this connection it is interesting that only seventy-four of the women stated that they and their husbands had plans to move and of those nineteen definitely intended to leave the changwad. But these small numbers are no indication of probable migration, for very likely in Thailand as elsewhere migration draws most heavily from young unmarried people.

The evidence of population loss through migration, together with the rather large proportion of husbands in service and other non-agricultural occupations, suggests that economic opportunities in Photharam are more than fully manned. Further evidence of population pressure on oportunities appears in the fact that almost one-third (30.1%) of the farm women asserted that their farms are inadequate to feed their families. The farms of husbands of women who made that statement have an average size of 10.5 rai (one rai equals two-fifths of an acre) and support an average size household of 7.4 persons.

Women who declared the lands their husbands cultivated to be adequate live on farms of 19.7 rai on the average. The average size of their households is 6.8 persons. Farm and non-farm households are equal in size—7 persons per household.

The nuclear family, comprising husband, wife, and children, is the model type in the district. Fifty-three per cent of all households are of this type. Usually, however, a young couple begins married life in the household of one of the parental families, frequently that of the wife. As the couple grows older it withdraws from mixed households to constitute with its children a separate household (Table 2). Per-

TABLE 2

DISTRIBUTION OF COUPLES BY AGE OF WIFE AND TYPE OF HOUSEHOLD

(Per Cent)

Age of Wife	Man, Wife Only	Man, Wife, Children	Man, Wife, Children, Parent(s)	Man, Wife, Children, Other Relatives	Man, Wife, Children, Relatives, Parent(s)	Other	Total
All ages.......	1	53	18	6	18	4	100
20–24.........	1	17	21	5	36	20	100
25–29.........	1	35	22	7	33	2	100
30–34.........	1	55	20	6	16	2	100
35–39.........	1	61	17	7	12	2	100
40–44.........	2	76	13	6	2	1	100

haps the withdrawal is aided by the deaths of parents and the later marriages of brothers and sisters.

Over 80% of husbands as well as of wives have had four years or less of formal education. But three times as many men (11%) as women (3%) continue in school beyond the fourth grade. Illiteracy among women amounts to 19%; but another 33% say that they read only with difficulty. It is not surprising, therefore, to find that the printed word is not often consulted. A mere 1% depend on the newspaper for general information. That might be due as much to the unavailability of newspapers in the locality as to reading difficulty. A larger proportion (7.8%) rely on the radio. For the most part, news and general information enter the area and circulate by word of mouth. The village head man is regarded as the most important carrier of information. The village head man is a locally elected official who, without salary or civil service status, acts as a liaison between the district officer and the people. The district officer, a career agent of the Ministry of Interior, has broad administrative responsibilities.

Women in the sample are in general 3.5 years younger than their husbands. The mean age of women at marriage is 21 years, a rather low marriage age for women in an agrarian and largely self-sufficient economy. Moreover, the data in Table 3 indicate that the mean age at marriage has been declining. Each younger group of women has married at an earlier age. The reason for this trend—the only clear indication of changing behavior to emerge from our data—is obscure. It is possible, of course, that there is a systematic error in reporting the date of marriage; the older the woman, the greater may be the tendency to understate the duration of marriage.[1]

TABLE 3

MEAN AGE AT MARRIAGE OF WOMEN WHO MARRY AT DIFFERENT
LIFE STAGES, BY CURRENT AGE

AGE	MARRIED BEFORE AGE					TOTAL
	25	30	35	40	45	
All ages..........	19.9	21.1	21.5	22.0	22.7	21.0[a]
20–24.............	18.7	....	....	....	....	18.7
25–29	19.5	19.9	....	....	....	19.9
30–34.............	20.1	21.0	21.2	....	....	21.2
35–39.............	20.2	21.2	21.5	21.6	....	21.6
40–44.............	20.6	21.8	22.0	22.6	22.7	22.7

[a] SD = 3.92.

REPRODUCTIVE EXPERIENCE

The pregnancy and reproductive history of women in the sample is briefly summarized in Table 4. The average number of pregnancies per woman rises from 1.5 in the youngest age group to almost 7 in the oldest group. Pregnancy wastage—stillbirths and miscarriages, apparent in the differences between pregnancies and live births—varies around 6%. Given the rather questionable assumption that the reporting of such events is reasonably complete, that figure is relatively low for a population with little education and very inadequate medical services.[2]

Reproductive history is more fully described in Table 5. The data in this table permit comparisons of the rates at which women at dif-

[1]Age and dates reported by the respondents are approximate as often as not. Rural people in Thailand have no pressing reason for giving close attention to time. The extent of error is minimized, of course, by the aggregate treatment of the data. All dates were reported in terms of lunar months and the twelve-year Chinese cycle. They were converted to the Western calendar in the coding process.

[2]Infant mortality rates for children born to women in the sample, for five recent years, are 1962—95.2; 1961—111.8; 1960—118.8; 1959—76.7; 1958—72.8. The five-year average is 95.1. The very low rates in 1958 and 1959 suggest that women might have forgotten live-born children who lived but a few days or weeks.

ferent ages had live births when they were at corresponding periods in their reproductive life spans. Thus it is possible to follow the reproductive careers of different age cohorts as they move through the years of marriage. The striking fact in Table 5 is that no consistent pattern of variation in fertility rates appears within duration of marriage classes. In other words, there is no evidence of a trend of change despite the apparent downward movement of average age at time of marriage observed in Table 2. The variations which are present may result from small numbers, but more than likely they are due to inaccurate reporting of dates of birth by mothers. The annual fertility rate remains fairly constant through the first ten years of married life. After a decade of marriage has passed, the annual rate declines slowly

TABLE 4

PREGNANCIES, LIVE BIRTHS, AND LIVING
CHILDREN PER MARRIED
WOMAN, BY AGE

Age	Pregnancies	Live Births	Living Children
All ages.........	4.6	4.4	3.8
20–24...........	1.5	1.4	1.2
25–29...........	3.1	2.9	2.6
30–34...........	4.5	4.3	3.6
35–39...........	5.7	5.4	4.7
40–44...........	6.6	6.2	5.2

to about 24 per 100 women for those married 20–25 years. The cumulative effects of these age-nuptial specific fertility rates are shown in Table 6. There it will be seen that women who have nearly completed their reproductive periods—40–44 years of age—and who have been married 30 years or more, have had approximately 8 live births per woman.

Whether there has been any decline of fertility can be investigated further. To do so we shall employ the dual hypothesis that fertility decline will follow upon the adoption of urban technology, as happened earlier in the Western world, and that the decline will occur first in groups that have moved furthest in that direction and latest in groups that have changed the least. In other words, an inverse association of fertility with extent of involvement in urban culture or with measures of socioeconomic status is symptomatic of a change having occurred in the level of fertility.

As a first step, a modernization scale was developed. The scale rests on ownership or non-ownership of fourteen different items, to each of which is arbitrarily assigned a weight more or less representa-

TABLE 5

Live Births per 100 Women, by Age and Duration of Marriage Cohorts

Age	Number of Women	Number of Births	Births per 100 Women	
			5-Year Average	Annual Average
First 5 Years of Marriage				
All ages.........	1,171	2,356[a]	201	40
20–24...........	123	230[a]	187	37
25–29...........	222	478[a]	215	43
30–34...........	309	670[a]	217	43
35–39...........	282	548[a]	194	39
40–44...........	235	430[a]	183	37
Second 5 Years of Marriage				
All ages.........	1,021	1,887	185	37
20–24...........	33	70[a]	212	41
25–29...........	179	337	188	38
30–34...........	294	578	197	39
35–39...........	281	517	184	37
40–44...........	234	385	164	33
Third 5 Years of Marriage				
All ages.........	783	1,230	157	31
20–24...........	....	....	....	....
25–29...........	55	93[a]	169	33
30–34...........	232	358	154	31
35–39...........	266	402	151	30
40–44...........	230	377	164	33
Fourth 5 Years of Marriage				
All ages.........	451	640	142	28
20–24...........	....	....	....	....
25–29...........	....	....	....	....
30–34...........	51	78[a]	152	30
35–39...........	175	262	150	30
40–44...........	225	308	137	27
Fifth 5 Years of Marriage				
All ages.........	204	250	122	24
20–24...........	....	....	....	....
25–29...........	....	....	....	....
30–34...........	....	....	....	....
35–39...........	55	79[a]	143	29
40–44...........	154	145	111	22

[a] Adjusted to a full five-year period.

tive of its cost or importance.[3] Births per woman in each scale position are shown in Table 7. The fertility rates presented there are more or less constant over the several modernization scale intervals within each age group. There appears to be one exception, however: relatively low rates occur among women with the highest modernization scores

TABLE 6

LIVE BIRTHS PER 100 MARRIED WOMEN, BY DATE OF MARRIAGE AND AGE

Age	1960–64	1955–59	1950–54	1945–49	1940–44	1935–39	Total
All ages.......	249[a]	290	433	565	671	773	438
20–24.........	231[a]	224	b				232
25–29.........	265[a]	294	427	b			291
30–34.........	b	321	456	581	b		429
35–39.........	b	273	412	608	696	b	542
40–44.........	b	b	485	596	674	781	643

[a] Adjusted to a full five years.
[b] Number is less than 25.

TABLE 7

LIVE BIRTHS PER WOMAN, BY AGE AND SELECTED
SOCIOECONOMIC CHARACTERISTICS

Socioeconomic Characteristic	All Ages	20–24	25–29	30–34	35–39	40–44
All women..............	4.4	1.5	2.9	4.3	5.4	6.2
Modernization scale:						
Under 5..............	4.5	1.4	3.5	4.1	5.4	6.4
5–9.................	4.5	1.4	2.9	4.4	5.7	6.0
10–14..............	4.4	1.5	3.1	4.4	5.4	6.4
15–19..............	4.8	1.4	2.4	4.6	5.8	8.2
20 and over..........	3.8	1.4	2.7	3.4	4.9	5.2
Occupation of husbands:						
Non-farm............	4.2	1.4	3.0	4.3	5.2	6.0
White collar........	4.5	1.7	2.9	4.4	5.3	5.9
Blue collar.........	3.9	1.3	3.0	4.3	5.1	6.1
Farm................	4.5	1.5	2.9	4.2	5.4	6.4
Size of farm:						
Under 10 rai..........	4.5	1.4	3.2	4.6	5.3	6.1
10–19 rai............	4.6	1.7	3.0	4.2	5.2	6.8
20 rai and over........	4.3	1.2	2.7	3.8	5.7	6.0
Education of wife:						
None................	5.5	1.8	3.2	4.2	5.5	6.8
1–4 years............	4.3	1.4	3.0	4.3	5.4	6.1
5 years and over.......	3.7	1.3	2.6	4.2	5.0	4.9

in most age classes. It is possible that a reduction of fertility has begun. But no supporting evidence is found when rates are calculated for broad occupation classes, also shown in Table 7. Nor is there any clear

[3] The items and their weights are: automobile, 15; motorcycle, 8; television, 7; well, electric pump, 6; electric fan, 6; electric iron, 6; sewing machine, 6; radio, 5; bicycle, 5; newspaper subscription, 4; well, no pump, 3; sanitary latrine, 3; clock or watch, 2; thermos bottle, 1.

tendency for a consistent inverse pattern of rates to appear among farmers' wives classified by size of farm cultivated. Still, in two age groups—the 25–29 and the 30–34—an inverse association of size of farm with fertility rate is apparent. That could be either a chance occurrence or another indication of the beginnings of fertility change.

The possibility that some of the intimations of fertility decline might be more than an illusion finds some support in the bottom panel of Table 7. There an inverse relationship between education and fertility rate, similar to that which long prevailed in Western populations, stands out unequivocally. As later paragraphs will confirm, that set of differences cannot have resulted from differences in contraceptive practice. It might be that persons with higher levels of education are more inclined to practice abstention from sexual intercourse. One form of abstention is shown in Table 8. i.e., later age at marriage. Yet

TABLE 8

MEAN AGE AT MARRIAGE, BY AGE AND EDUCATION OF WIFE

AGE	EDUCATION			
	None	1–4 Years	5 Years and Over	Total
All ages......	20.9	20.5	21.3	21.0
20–24........	17.7	19.0	18.8	18.7
25–29........	19.4	19.8	21.1	19.9
30–34........	21.2	21.4	21.2	21.2
35–39........	21.3	19.6	22.6	21.6
40–44........	21.4	22.0	22.8	22.7

the differences in mean age at marriage are not alone enough to account for all of the observed fertility differences. A complementary factor, however, is that the more highly educated women terminate reproductive activity at an earlier age.[4] In other words, it seems that the more highly educated set lower numbers of children as their goals and begin abstention after those numbers are attained.

Not only is the incidence of still births and miscarriages relatively low, as we noted earlier, but also the lack of fecundity is infrequent. Twenty-six women, or slightly more than 2% of the total, are childless after three or more years of marriage. And of the women who have borne children the number who feel uncertain about their ability to have more children, exclusive of those who have been sterilized, is very small. Even so, the average of 26.6 months between live births (22 months between pregnancies) indicates a rather restrained exer-

[4]The intervals from marriage to first birth and the interbirth intervals do not vary systematically with education.

cise of fecundity.[5] How that is accomplished is unknown. It does not appear to be due to husbands living apart from their wives. Eighty-five women reported that their husbands do not live with them regularly.[6] But the average number of months since their last pregnancies is 25, while the corresponding average for all other women is 29 months. Women whose husbands are living apart have lower fertility rates (3.5 live births per woman) than do women whose husbands live regularly with them (4.4 live births per woman). That difference stems mainly from the fact that women in the former group are two years younger than are other women. In any case, the number of women whose husbands do not live with them regularly is too small to exert any important effect on measures of behavior in the entire sample.

TABLE 9

NUMBER AND PROPORTION OF WOMEN WHO WANT AND DO NOT WANT
MORE CHILDREN, BY NUMBER THEY HAVE AT PRESENT

NUMBER OF CHILDREN AT PRESENT	NUMBER			PER CENT		
	Want More Children	Do Not Want More Children	Total	Want More Children	Do Not Want More Children	Total
All women.........	340	865	1,205[a]	28	72	100
0.................	43	6	49	88	12	100
1.................	96	41	137	70	30	100
2.................	95	88	183	52	48	100
3.................	58	140	198	29	71	100
4.................	29	171	200	15	85	100
5.................	11	158	169	6	94	100
6 or more........	8	261	269	3	97	100

[a] No answer given by two respondents.

THE PROSPECT FOR FUTURE REPRODUCTION

The presence of rather high fertility rates among the women of Photharam should not be construed as reflecting a desire for large numbers of children. In fact, 72% of the women declared that they want no more children, including half of the 183 women (15%) who were pregnant at the time of the survey. The desire for more children is concentrated among women below 30 years of age and, too, among those who have the fewest children. Table 9 shows a steep decline in the proportions of women who want more children as the number

[5] This also assumes complete reporting of pregnancies and births in the interviews.

[6] Some of these women are minor wives. The husbands of others are absent either for reasons of military service or employment elsewhere.

they have is increased. Of the women who want more, 95% have four children or fewer now; 56% have three or fewer.

The desire to stop having children begins earlier in Photharam than in other areas of Asia for which comparable data are available (Table 10). Japan is the one exception.

The interest in having more children appears to have different objectives in different stages of the reproductive span. The youngest women are most concerned with acquiring a family and they seem willing to accept whatever comes to them. Women 25–35 years of age, having already had a few children, turn their hopes toward achieving a balanced distribution of sexes among their progeny. After age 35 the few who still want more children have all or nearly all of one sex

TABLE 10

WOMEN IN SELECTED AREAS OF ASIA WHO DO NOT WANT
MORE CHILDREN, BY NUMBER THEY HAVE[a]

(Per Cent)

AREA	NUMBER THEY HAVE				ALL
	2	3	4	5 or More	
Photharam..........	48	71	86	96	72
Ceylon..............	29	57	69	88	44
Japan..............	76	95	98	99	72
India...............	27	42	75	85	37
Pakistan (West).......	29	45	66	75	46
Taiwan..............	24	54	76	88	....

[a] Comparative information supplied by W. Parker Mauldin of the Population Council.

and would like at least one or one more of the opposite sex. Unlike most Asian peoples, women in Photharam express no strong preference for one sex or the other; female children are wanted as frequently as are male children. When aspirations are added to the children women already have, the results are as shown in Table 11.

What would be the effect of the number of additional children wanted on the completed fertility of women? This question can be answered by adding children wanted to the children women already have, as is done in Table 12. That total, it will be observed, shows a number of children per woman, for those who want more children, less than the number for women who do not want more children. In the two youngest age groups the have-plus-want total for women who want more exceeds the number for women who want no more. But in the older age groups the combined total drops below that for women who want no more. For the entire group the have-plus-want number is 20% lower than the number for women who have all the children they want.

Another approach to the matter of desirable family size was attempted with the question: "If you were starting over again and could have just the number of children you wanted, how many would that be?" The answers to that question reveal that the "ideal" number of children, expressed as an average per woman, is exactly the same as the actual average, that is, 3.8 children (Table 13). The similarity of the two figures is, of course, a coincidence; they result from different weightings in the several age groups. For young women the "ideal" is greater than the actual, but after age 30 the "ideal" number falls below the actual number.

TABLE 11

SEX OF CHILDREN WANTED ADDED TO SEX OF EXISTING CHILDREN, BY AGE OF WOMEN WHO WANT MORE CHILDREN

(Per Cent)

Age	Sexes Equal	Sexes Unequal by One	Sexes Unequal by Two or More	All of One Sex	Sex Unspecified	Total
All ages.....	40	39	14	4	3	100
20–24.......	44	33	6	9	8	100
25–29.......	40	41	16	1	2	100
30–34.......	42	41	15	2	....	100
35–39.......	29	32	31	8	....	100
40–44.......	28	32	36	4	....	100

TABLE 12

NUMBER OF CHILDREN PER WOMAN: WOMEN WHO DO AND DO NOT WANT MORE CHILDREN, BY AGE

AGE	NUMBER HAVE		WOMEN WHO WANT MORE CHILDREN	
	Women Who Want No More	Women Who Want More	Additional Number Wanted	Number Wanted Added to Number They Have
All ages..........	4.5	2.0	1.8	3.8
20–24..........	1.8	1.1	1.9	3.0
25–29..........	3.3	1.9	1.8	3.7
30–34..........	4.2	2.3	1.6	3.9
35–39..........	5.0	2.9	1.6	4.5
40–44..........	5.5	3.3	1.8	5.1

If we consider the difference between the actual and "ideal" numbers of children for women of near-completed fertility, those 40–44 years of age, and assume the "ideal" to be a potentially determining principle of action, it would appear that women in Photharam would have, were it within their power to control reproduction, one child less than they have, a reduction of 20% in their fertility. Or, if the "ideal" number expressed by women 20–24 years of age were to become an effective determinant, the lifetime fertility of Photharam women would be reduced by almost 50%.

As a matter of fact, however, the age of a woman has less to do with the "ideal" number than does the number of children she already has. That is apparent in Table 14. It is also to be noted that women adjust

TABLE 13

COMPARISON OF ACTUAL AND "IDEAL"
NUMBER OF CHILDREN PER
WOMAN, BY AGE

Age	Actual Number of Children	"Ideal" Number of Children
All ages..........	3.8	3.8
20–24............	1.3	2.8
25–29............	2.6	3.4
30–34............	3.7	3.6
35–39............	4.6	4.1
40–44............	5.2	4.2

TABLE 14

"IDEAL" NUMBER OF CHILDREN PER WOMAN, BY AGE AND
BY NUMBER OF EXISTING CHILDREN

NUMBER EXISTING	AGE OF WOMEN					
	20–24	25–29	30–34	35–39	40–44	All
0..........	2.4	3.1[a]	2.5[a]	3.0[a]	[b]	2.7
1..........	2.8	2.6	2.6	2.2[a]	2.3	2.6
2..........	2.8	2.9	2.9	2.6	2.7	2.8
3..........	3.9[a]	3.7	3.4	3.4	3.9	3.6
4..........	[b]	4.0	4.0	4.2	4.3	4.4
5..........	....	4.0[a]	4.3	4.6	4.3	4.4
6..........	....	[b]	5.0	4.7	4.6	4.6
7..........	....	[b]	6.0[a]	4.9	4.8	4.9
8..........	....	....	5.2[a]	4.9	4.7	4.8
9 or more....	....	....	....	[b]	4.5[a]	4.3[a]

[a] Number less than 15.
[b] Number less than 10.

the "ideal" number upward with each additional child they have until they have had four children. After that size of family has been attained, the "ideal" lags behind the number of children they have, though it continues to rise as size of family increases. There is a tendency to report the number of existing children as the "ideal."

Some cross-cultural comparisons of "ideal" numbers of children are presented in Table 15. Photharam stands well above Ceylon and Japan, roughly on a par with Taiwan, but below other Asian coun-

TABLE 15

WOMEN WHOSE "IDEAL" NUMBER OF CHILDREN IS
4 OR 5 OR MORE: SAMPLE STUDIES
IN SELECTED AREAS[a]

(Per Cent)

Area	Year	4 Children or More	5 Children or More
Asia:			
Photharam	1964	54	26
Ceylon	1963	23	12
Indonesia	1961–62	66	36
Japan	1961	22	8
Korea	1962	80	45
Pakistan-West . . .	1960	64	25
Taiwan	1962	57	18
Europe:			
Austria	1960	4	. . . .
France	1960	17	. . . .
Great Britain	1960	23	. . . .
Hungary	1958–60	13	6
Italy	1960	18	. . . .
Netherlands	1960	39	. . . .
Norway	1960	25	. . . .
W. Germany	1960	4	. . . .
United States	1960	40	15

[a] Comparative information supplied by W. Parker Mauldin of the Population Council.

tries in the list. Among Western nations none have "ideal" numbers similar to those in Photharam. The United States and the Netherlands are not far below Photharam, however, in the percentage for whom the "ideal" is four or more children.

Interestingly enough, the "ideal" number of children has no relationship to size of farm when the influence of age is controlled (Table 16). Nor is there an important difference between farm and nonfarm "ideals." It seems inconsistent, however, that women who declare their farms to be inadequate to feed their families mention a larger "ideal" number than do women who feel their farms are adequate. But that anomaly stems from the facts that inadequacy of farm is characteristic of the least educated and that the "ideal" number of children varies inversely with education, as may be seen in Table 17.

ATTITUDES TOWARD FAMILY LIMITATION

In view of the large number of women who do not want more children and of the rather modest size of family deemed desirable, it seems that many women might wish to practice some form of family limitation. To discover to what extent this might be true, three questions, widely spaced in the interview, were asked of each woman: (1) "If you knew of a simple, harmless method of keeping from get-

TABLE 16

"IDEAL" NUMBER OF CHILDREN PER WOMAN, BY SIZE OF FARM CULTIVATED, AGE, AND ADEQUACY OF FARM FOR FEEDING FAMILY

AGE AND ADEQUACY OF FARM	NUMBER OF RAI CULTIVATED BY FARM FAMILIES						NON-FARM
	Under 10	10–19	20–29	30–39	40 and Over	All Farms	
All ages........	3.7	3.9	3.6	3.6	3.9	3.8	3.9
Adequate.....	3.5	3.8	3.5	3.5	3.9	3.6	....
Inadequate....	3.9	4.2	3.8	3.8	3.8	4.0	....
20–24.........	2.8	2.8	2.8	2.0	2.8	2.7	3.1
Adequate.....	2.9	2.6	2.9	2.0	2.3	2.6	....
Inadequate....	2.6	3.3	2.0	2.0	4.0	2.8	....
25–29.........	3.2	4.0	3.1	3.1	3.8	3.4	3.6
Adequate.....	2.6	4.3	3.0	3.0	3.8	3.4	....
Inadequate....	3.5	3.3	4.3	4.0	....	3.5	....
30–34.........	3.8	3.5	3.5	3.6	4.7	3.6	3.8
Adequate.....	3.6	3.4	3.5	3.7	4.7	3.6	....
Inadequate....	4.1	3.9	3.8	3.0	....	3.9	....
35–39.........	4.1	4.0	4.2	3.9	4.1	4.1	4.3
Adequate.....	3.9	4.0	4.2	3.8	4.2	4.0	....
Inadequate....	4.2	4.1	3.7	4.2	3.5	4.1	....
40–44.........	4.3	4.4	4.0	4.0	4.0	4.2	4.2
Adequate.....	4.0	4.1	3.8	4.0	3.9	4.0	....
Inadequate....	4.5	5.2	5.0	4.0	4.0	4.8	....

TABLE 17

"IDEAL" NUMBER OF CHILDREN OF FARM WOMEN, BY EDUCATION

Education	Per Cent with Inadequate Farms	"Ideal" Number of Children per Woman
None.............	48	4.0
1–4 years..........	28	3.7
5 or more years....	18	3.4

ting pregnant too often and of having too many children (more than you want), would you approve or disapprove of its use?" (2) "Would you like to do something to keep from getting pregnant in the future?" and (3) "Are you interested in learning more about how to keep from getting pregnant too often or having too many children (more than you want)?" To the first question 53% of the women indicated approval and another 13% stated a qualified approval. In answer to the second question 59% said they would like to do something to limit childbearing. And two-thirds of all women expressed a desire for information about methods of family limitation.

The three questions permit us to construct a rough scale of motivation toward or readiness for family planning. Women who answered all three questions affirmatively may be described as highly motivated. Those who gave a qualified approval of contraception in general but

TABLE 18

MOTIVATION OF WOMEN TOWARD FAMILY PLANNING

Category	Per Cent	Cumulative Per Cent
Highly motivated.........	39.7	39.7
Moderately motivated......	6.2	45.9
Qualifiedly motivated.......	9.8	55.7
Potentially motivated.......	12.7	68.4
Not motivated.............	24.2	92.6
Inconsistent..............	7.4	100.0

who answered the remaining questions positively are regarded as moderately motivated. Some women indicated disapproval of contraceptive practice, which evidently meant disapproval in principle but not in practice, for they stated that they wish to do something to regulate the number of children they have and they want to learn how to do that. Those women are described as having a qualified motivation. Another group of women do not wish to do anything to limit conception but they wish to learn how to do so; we refer to those women as potentially motivated. Women who answered the three questions negatively are regarded as not motivated. There remains a small group who gave inconsistent answers to the three questions. The percentage falling into these several motivation categories are shown in Table 18.

More than two-thirds of the women indicated some degree of motivation, while less than one-quarter lack any inclination to engage in family planning. For the most part, the highly motivated are young women. The proportion with lesser degrees of motivation increases with age. Absence of motivation is found mainly among older women.

Motivation or the lack of it is not a function of the desire for more children. As may be seen in Table 19, women who want more children are evenly divided with reference to readiness and non-readiness to practice family planning. On the other hand, over one-third of those who do not want more children have no desire to do anything to control reproduction. Those who want more children and who also want to practice family limitation have on the average 1.2 children. They would like to have another 1.9 children apiece before beginning

TABLE 19

WOMEN INTERESTED IN BIRTH CONTROL, AND REASONS
FOR NOT WANTING TO DO ANYTHING

INTEREST AND REASONS	NUMBER		PER CENT	
	Want More Children	Do Not Want More Children	Want More Children	Do Not Want More Children
All women........................	340	865	100	100
Want to do something..............	169	533	50	62
No answer.......................	5	30	1	3
Do not want to do anything.........	171	332	50	38
Reason:				
Fear cannot have more children...	126	121	38	15
Dangerous to health............	13	60	4	7
Sinful........................	8	33	2	4
Nature will decide..............	7	17	2	2
No knowledge..................	1	17	....	2
Too old.......................	....	20	....	2
Other.........................	8	27	2	3
No answer....................	3	1	1	....

the practice. Women who want more children but do not wish to do anything to control reproduction have somewhat larger families—an average of 1.9 children. Among the women who do not want more children those who wish to engage in family planning have the largest families—4.7 children—whereas women who want no more children but do not wish to use contraception have 4.1 children.

Readiness to engage in family planning is also unaffected by such considerations as how the woman feels while pregnant or the length of time it takes to recover from a pregnancy. The overriding reason given for approval of contraceptive practice is the desire to adapt the number of children to the household's ability to rear and prepare progeny for adult life.

The reasons given for unwillingness to do something to control births are given in Table 19. The ignorance they display needs no comment. The "it is sinful" reason is of interest, however, for it rests on a confusion of contraception with abortion. But for most women there is no such confusion. Nor does approval of the one practice imply approval of the second. Over 90% of all women disapprove of abortion; a mere 5% condone the practice (Table 20).

Our inquiry into attitudes toward family planning was extended into the thoughts of the respondents concerning the social and institutional context in which such a practice should be pursued. Of the several questions in this vein one of the more interesting is: "Do you think the government in Bangkok should have a program to inform people how to keep from getting pregnant too often or having too many children?" The replies, set forth in Table 21, are strongly in favor of a government program; a mere 10% are definitely negative. The proportion in favor of a program sponsored by the national government rises with education of the respondents and the proportion undecided on the issue declines correspondingly. There seems to be little room for doubt that the people want help from their government

TABLE 20

ATTITUDE TOWARD ABORTION, BY READINESS
TO DO SOMETHING TO LIMIT BIRTHS

READINESS TO DO SOMETHING	DISAPPROVE		APPROVE ABORTION	No ANSWER	TOTAL
	Strongly or Very Strongly	Not So Strongly			
Total..............	90	3	5	2	100
Would like to.........	89	3	7	1	100
Would not like to......	92	2	5	1	100
Undecided...........	80	....	....	20	100

TABLE 21

DISTRIBUTION OF ATTITUDES TOWARD A GOVERNMENT
PROGRAM OF FAMILY PLANNING EDUCATION,
BY EDUCATION OF RESPONDENT

(Per Cent)

Education	Yes	No	Undecided	Total
All...............	57	10	33	100
No education.......	48	10	42	100
1–4 years..........	58	10	32	100
5 years and over.....	62	11	27	100

in controlling family growth. A related question was also asked, namely, "If you were thinking of doing something about keeping from getting pregnant too often or having too many children, would you feel better about it if it was approved by the government, the governor of your changwad, the district officer, the head man of your village, a medical person, or whom?" Two-thirds of the replies favored endorsement by one or another arm of the government, particularly by the district officer.[7] It is also noteworthy that a large majority (76%) think that the population of their district should grow slowly rather than grow rapidly or not at all. They are aware, too, that the decline in mortality and the consequently greater probability of survival of offspring has reduced the need for as many births as occurred in former times.

KNOWLEDGE OF FAMILY LIMITATION METHODS

Despite the rather widespread interest in limiting the size of the family, knowledge of how to accomplish that objective is very meager. Two-thirds of the married women interviewed have no knowledge whatsoever of contraceptive methods. The 432 women who claim some knowledge provided 793 replies to questions about eleven different methods. Eighty per cent of those replies pertain to sterilization—both ligation and vasectomy. Among the few answers which dealt with less drastic methods, the oral pill, the condom, and the foam tablet occurred most frequently. The term "knowledge" must be used advisedly here, however, for all but a few women had only heard about the methods they mentioned. Contraceptive knowledge, such as it is, is more general in the market place of the amphur than in the outlying sections; it also varies directly with education and with age up to 30–39 years.

Apart from the forty-two couples of whom one or the other member has been sterilized, contraceptive practice is confined currently to eight couples, three of whom are relying on herbs. Not more than nineteen couples have ever practiced contraception.

The very scant knowledge about family limitation methods reflects a general lack of sophistication in matters of maternal health and the physiology of reproduction. This is evident in their attachment to the granny midwife, an unlearned, folk practitioner. As shown in Table 22, three-fourths of the women prefer to have their babies delivered by the granny midwife. The proportion is higher in the older than in

[7]The fact that village head men are the most important carriers of news does not seem to confer upon them any of the prestige of authority. Authority at the local level resides, in the eyes of the people and correctly so, primarily with the district officer.

the younger ages. The latter are somewhat more disposed to prefer trained attendants at delivery. But only twenty-six women in the entire sample stated a preference for a doctor.

Both the quality of medical service to which the women have had access and the education they have been able to obtain have denied them simple knowledge of reproductive processes. A mere 1% know which days in the monthly cycle conception is most probable (Table 23). The proportion who say they do not know the answer to that question declines with education, but the proportion who give wrong answers increases in the higher educational levels. Likewise, not more than 3% know the number of days that conception is possible (Table 24). Again educational experience seems to have been of no help in providing that kind of knowledge. In view of the rather primitive

TABLE 22

DISTRIBUTION OF PREFERRED PLACE AND TYPE OF
ATTENDANT AT DELIVERY OF BIRTH, BY AGE

(Per Cent)

AGE	PREFERRED PLACE OF DELIVERY						NO ANSWER	TOTAL
	At Home				Hospital			
	Granny Midwife	Government Midwife	Public Health Nurse	Self, Husband, Other	Public Health Nurse	Doctor		
All ages......	75	10	6	4	2	2	1	100
20–24........	68	14	7	3	3	3	2	100
25–29........	75	13	4	3	2	2	1	100
30–34........	77	8	7	3	2	2	1	100
35–39........	76	11	5	3	1	3	1	100
40–44........	80	8	5	4	1	1	1	100

TABLE 23

DAYS OF MONTH DURING WHICH WOMEN THINK CONCEPTION
IS MOST PROBABLE, BY EDUCATION

(Per Cent)

Education	Just before Menstruation	Just after Menstruation	Between Menstruation	Don't Know	Total
All women............	3	12	1	84	100
No education.........	4	7	2	87	100
1–4 years............	2	12	1	85	100
5 years and over.......	4	16	3	77	100

level of knowledge about elementary physiological processes, it is not surprising that there should be very little awareness of methods of family limitation. The appreciation of feminine hygiene must be equally undeveloped.

CONCLUSION

Population in the district we have studied seems to be in a very early stage of demographic transition. While the death rate, now around 17 per thousand, has decreased by 50% or more in recent years, the fertility rate remains at its pre-urban or pre-industrial level, though traces of the beginnings of decline may be faintly discernible.

TABLE 24

NUMBER OF DAYS IN MONTH DURING WHICH WOMEN
THINK CONCEPTION IS POSSIBLE

(Per Cent)

Education	Every Day	Several Days	10 Days	20 Days	Don't Know	Total
All women...............	....	2	4	3	91	100
No education...........	1	2	2	1	94	100
1–4 years..............		2	4	3	91	100
5 years and over........	....	....	9	2	89	100

Situated as it is within the outer reaches of metropolitan influence, Photharam seems to be drawing toward the threshold of significant changes in its mode of life.

Industrial technology in the form of consumer goods has invaded the area perhaps to the limit of the purchasing power of the people. Sanitary technology has also been put to work in the district, but one wonders how much of the knowledge is actually imparted to the people. Nevertheless, procreative life is still conducted in ways dictated by traditional lore. The granny midwife holds a strong appeal for all but a few. As a consequence, no doubt, women are almost totally ignorant of the elementary workings of their reproductive systems. Nor has more than a small minority had any introduction to modern means of fertility control.

Apparently, however, rumors, vague and inchoate for most people, that there are simple, harmless ways of controlling the number of births have spread through the area. For there is considerable unrest among women over their inability to adapt the sizes of their families to the resources of their households. Seven of every ten women want no more children than they have. That attitude becomes almost universal by the time the fifth child is born. It rests in part on a general awareness that mortality decline has greatly improved the probability of survival of existing children. Hence there is a keen interest in learning more about family planning methods. Two-thirds of the women wish either to learn about the methods or to begin practice. They feel, too, that their government should have a program to assist them in reaching that objective. Endorsement by the government of family planning practice takes precedence over endorsement from any other source.

For these reasons we conclude that the people of Photharam are ready to move quickly into the second phase of the demographic transition, that of fertility decline. They await only the opportunity.

45

RECENT TRENDS IN FAMILY PLANNING RESEARCH IN INDIA

C. CHANDRASEKARAN
Director, Demographic Training and Research Centre
Chembur, Bombay, India

INTRODUCTION

Family planning research began to attract the attention of social scientists in India about fifteen years ago when the First Five-Year Plan was being formulated. Earlier, studies had been undertaken to compare fertility and family planning practices in certain cross sections of the population and even to investigate such difficult topics as sex habits and coital patterns.[1] But it was only toward the year 1950 that really serious consideration was given to fertility and family planning studies, owing partly to the need for checking the rate of population growth.

Initially, attempts were largely restricted to exploratory investigations. Before 1960 no less than twenty-six studies were undertaken in different parts of the country to assess in a general way the attitudes of the people toward family planning, and to obtain data on the extent of knowledge and use of contraceptive methods in various sections of the community.[2] At the same time, a small number of well-directed community studies were undertaken to find out the effectiveness of specific programs aimed at popularizing one or more methods of family planning. Such studies (especially the ones undertaken in Ramanagaram and Lodi Colony, in Ludhiana, and in Singur) also

[1]C. Chandrasekaran *et al.*, "The Reproductive Pattern of Bengalee Women," All India Institute of Hygiene and Public Health, Calcutta (unpublished); G. S. Ghurye, "Sex Habits of a Sample of Middle Class People of Bombay," in *Indian Population Problems*, ed. G. S. Ghurye (Bombay: Karnatak Publishing House, n.d.), pp. SA 52–SA 63.

[2]S. N. Agarwala, *Attitude towards Family Planning in India*, Institute of Economic Growth, Occasional Paper No. 5 (Delhi, 1962).

obtained data on attitudes, knowledge, and practice regarding family planning as a preliminary to setting up programs.[3]

The body of data obtained from such exploratory investigations and community studies encouraged extending family planning throughout the country. At the same time, the need for evaluating the program periodically and modifying it in order to increase its effectiveness also became apparent. The Indian program, in its initial stages, relied heavily on the use of clinics for the dissemination of information on family planning and for the distribution of contraceptives. When sterilization was also accepted as a method of family planning, surgical facilities to conduct operations on a large scale had to be provided. Recently the program has been redesigned to make the "extension" approach its main pivot.[4]

These changes in the family planning program have affected the nature of research that is being undertaken. The earlier *ad hoc* surveys to assess attitudes or behavior have given way to studies in action-research settings. Eight studies, promoted by the Family Planning Communication Action-Research Committee of the government of India, are now in progress and three workshops have been held to discuss specific problems related to this research.[5] These studies are complex in character. They seem to call for new concepts and methods in experimental designs, if the changes arising from several interrelated elements in the programs are to be assessed.[6]

As emphasis has shifted away from studies in cross-sectional settings, toward changes resulting from specific action, the need has

[3]Government of India, Ministry of Health, "Final Report of Pilot Studies on Rhythm Method of Family Planning," Director General of Health Services, New Delhi (mimeographed); J. B. Wyon and J. E. Gordon, "A Long-Term Prospective-Type Field Study of Population Dynamics in the Punjab, India," in *Research in Family Planning*, ed. C. V. Kiser (Princeton: Princeton University Press, 1962), pp. 17–32; K. K. Mathen, "Preliminary Lessons Learned from the Rural Population Control Study of Singur," *ibid.*, pp. 33–49.

[4]B. L. Raina, *Family Planning Programme, Report for 1962–63*, Directorate General of Health Services, Ministry of Health, New Delhi (1964).

[5]The eight family planning communication action-research projects are undertaken at (*i*) All India Institute of Hygiene and Public Health, Calcutta, (*ii*) Central Family Planning Institute, New Delhi, (*iii*) Demographic Training and Research Centre, Bombay, (*iv*) Indian Statistical Institute, Calcutta, (*v*) Institute of Rural Health and Family Planning, Gandhigram, (*vi*) Lady Hardinge Medical College, New Delhi, (*vii*) Planning Research and Action Institute, Lucknow, and (*viii*) University of Kerala, Trivandrum.

[6]C. Chandrasekaran and M. W. Freymann, "Evaluating the Effects of Community Efforts To Modify Family Size," Symposium: Research Issues in Public Health and Population Change, University of Pittsburgh, June, 1964; C. Chandrasekaran, "Problems of Research Design and Methods in Studies of Effectiveness of Policy Measures Aimed at Influencing Fertility," paper submitted to the World Population Conference, Belgrade, August 30–September 10, 1965.

grown for clearly defining objectives and for developing sensitive indices for measuring changes in attitudinal and behavioral character- istics. This need is being met by attempts to devise fresh procedures for assessing knowledge, attitudes and behavior with respect to family planning.

In this paper, some of the recent researches pertaining to the as- sessment of knowledge, attitude and practice relating to family plan- ning will be described. This will be followed by a discussion of some of the problems of research design and evaluation procedures that arise in action-research settings.

ASSESSMENT OF KNOWLEDGE, ATTITUDE, AND PRACTICE

ASSESSMENT OF KNOWLEDGE

Knowledge that family planning is possible and that methods exist for controlling the number of children to be born is so fundamental to the spread of a family planning program that most exploratory sur- veys conducted in this field have attempted to elicit information on these topics. There have been difficulties in framing the questions and in obtaining accurate responses. While, on the one hand, expressions for "family planning" have not been in common use in most Indian languages, the avoidance or delay of pregnancy through abstinence is strongly ingrained in the Indian culture. Exclusion of abstinence, in reckoning the extent of knowledge of methods in the community, has been a feature of many Indian surveys. The Mysore Population Study adopted this procedure and so did the National Sample Survey in its survey on family planning in the urban areas of India from July, 1960, to June, 1961.[7] According to this National Sample Survey, in which men with wives under 45 years of age were interviewed, 70% were aware of family planning, of whom about 40% knew of at least one family planning method other than abstinence. The accuracy of such estimates is open to criticism both because of "response errors" and "interviewer bias." With respect to ascertaining knowledge of meth- ods, a direct question on all the methods known, without the use of probes explaining the methods, might result in an underestimate. The use of such probes, on the other hand, might give overestimates, since, as pointed out elsewhere, the explanation involves the risk of imparting so much knowledge that the respondent would on that

[7]United Nations, *The Mysore Population Study*, ST/SOA/Ser. A/34, Department of Economic and Social Affairs, (New York, 1961); National Sample Survey, "Report No. 116/1, Tables with Notes on Family Planning, Sixteenth Round," Indian Statistical Institute, Calcutta (1963) (draft).

account feel familiar with the method even though he had not known about it earlier.[8]

There is also the basic question of what "knowledge" of a method actually connotes. Some surveys have used a liberal definition. In one survey, a person who had never seen a condom but knew that certain types of covering can be used by the man for the purpose of preventing pregnancy was recorded as having knowledge of the method.[9] Recently the Survey of Family Planning Clinics in Greater Bombay attempted to gauge the extent of correct use of those methods that had been recommended to women attending clinics in Greater Bombay. As an illustration, the following were the questions asked of women who had been advised to use diaphragm and jelly.[10]

1. Could you tell me how you used (the method)?
2. (a) When do you put it in? (b) How long is it after you put it in that you have relations? (c) If you have relations later than two hours after you put it in, is there something you do before relations?
3. Do you know what the jelly is for?
4. Is there anything you do to your private parts after you have relations?
5. When do you take it out?
6. How long is it after you have relations that you take it out?
7. What do you do with it after you take it out?

These data have been utilized by Patankar to estimate the extent of knowledge about use of diaphragm and jelly, the underlying assumption in the analysis being that practice is determined by the extent of knowledge. The analysis was carried out using six main headings and a scoring system, and the results obtained are shown in Table 1.[11] Women scored poorly on "effect of jelly" and "action to be taken soon after intercourse." Incidentally, the figures shown in Table 1 also bring out the greater difficulty of imparting knowledge on scientific aspects of the method as against practical instructions for its use.

A retrospective survey of a random sample of women in the action-research area of the Demographic Training and Research Centre, Chembur, Bombay, attempted to evaluate the extent of knowledge imparted through a program of group meetings or home visits which

[8]United Nations, *Mysore Population Study.*

[9]*Ibid.*

[10]C. Chandrasekaran and K. Kuder, *Family Planning through Clinics: Report of a Survey of Family Planning Clinics in Greater Bombay* (Bombay: Allied Publishers Private Ltd., 1965).

[11]T. Patankar, "Communication of Instructions for the Use of Diaphragm and Jelly Method between the Clinic Staff and the Clientele of Greater Bombay," paper submitted to the Demographic Training and Research Centre, Bombay, as part of the training program, 1964–65 (1965) (mimeographed).

had been in operation for about four months.[12] For this purpose a scoring system was used to grade knowledge with respect to each method known to a woman. Her total score was obtained by totaling the scores for all the methods known to her. The distribution of the total scores for the 164 women interviewed is given in Table 2.

Studies with respect to knowledge of the existence of family planning clinics and of their activities were particularly important before the recent reorganization of the program with its emphasis on extension education. The need for using probes to increase the accuracy of information obtained in a single interview was highlighted in the baseline survey in the action-research area in Chembur.[13] The leading

TABLE 1

DISTRIBUTION ACCORDING TO LEVEL OF KNOWLEDGE
ABOUT DIAPHRAGM AND JELLY METHOD[a]

(Per Cent)

KNOWLEDGE	LEVEL OF KNOWLEDGE			
	High	Medium	Low	All Women
1. Way of putting in the diaphragm.......	92.3	4.8	2.9	100.0
2. Time for putting in the diaphragm......	23.3	69.5	7.2	100.0
3. Effect of jelly........................	3.8	63.3	32.9	100.0
4. Period of keeping the diaphragm in after intercourse.........................	80.5	8.6	10.9	100.0
5. Action to be taken after intercourse.....	39.0	32.4	28.6	100.0
6. Maintenance of the diaphragm.........	67.6	28.1	4.3	100.0

[a] Represents 210 women who had attended the Greater Bombay family planning clinics and had, at least once, used the diaphragm and jelly method prescribed by the clinic.

question, "Have you ever heard or known of a family planning clinic?" was followed by the question, "Have you ever heard or known of any place where the wife or husband can go and get some advice in family planning?" for those who answered no to the first question. At a later stage in the interview, those who answered no to the second question also were asked, "Have you heard or known of a place where a couple can get advice on how to keep the cradle away (to prevent pregnancy)?" In putting the leading question, expressions such as *pariwar niyojan kendra*, which have recently gained currency, were used for "family planning clinic." In the second question the

[12]Demographic Training and Research Centre, Bombay, "Report of the Evaluation Survey," Family Planning Communication Action-Research Project, Chembur, 1964 (unpublished).

[13]Demographic Training and Research Centre, Bombay, "Report of the Base-line Survey on Knowledge, Attitude and Practice of Family Planning," Family Planning Communication Action-Research Project, Chembur, 1963 (unpublished).

formal word *kendra* was substituted by a simpler expression. In the third question even the expression "family planning" was paraphrased. Two hundred and twenty-six women were interviewed. Analysis of the data showed that, of the 47% of the women interviewed who knew of a family planning clinic, 38% were identified through the first question, 6% through the second question, and 3% through the third question.[14] It is probable that had the same survey been conducted in rural areas, a larger percentage would have been identified through the second or third question. In the Survey of Family Planning Clinics in Greater Bombay, a question, "How did you first come to know that this clinic gives help in family planning?" was asked.

TABLE 2

DISTRIBUTION BY KNOWLEDGE OF ALL FAMILY
PLANNING METHODS[a]

(Per Cent)

Knowledge Score (Level of Knowledge)	Exposed to Program	Not Exposed to Program	Total
0 (no knowledge)................	19.7	48.9	35.4
1–3 (fair knowledge).............	14.5	12.5	13.4
4–6 (fairly good knowledge).......	19.7	27.3	23.8
7–9 (good knowledge)............	15.8	10.2	12.8
10 or more (very good knowledge)...	30.3	1.1	14.6
Total......................	100.0	100.0	100.0
Number of women in the sample.	76	88	164

[a] Total scores of women "exposed" and "not exposed" to the program in the Chembur area.

The most often cited source was "health visitor or social worker" and "relative or friend." It was only with the better-educated and well-to-do women that the signboard of the clinic was the source of knowledge.[15]

In the baseline survey in Chembur, the perception of a family planning clinic was obtained by responses of the women to such questions as, "Can you tell me something about what goes on in a family planning clinic?" or, "What help do you think people can get from the family planning clinic?" Of the 107 women who knew of the family planning clinic, 34 did not know exactly what went on there. The responses of the other 73 women showed that they had no misconceptions about the services rendered at a family planning clinic.[16]

[14]*Ibid.*

[15]Chandrasekaran and Kuder, *op. cit.*

[16]See n. 13 above.

ASSESSMENT OF ATTITUDE

Considerable attention has been given in past surveys to the opinions of people on adoption of family planning and related topics, such as size of family, spacing between children, and desire for additional children. These exploratory studies were primarily intended to find out whether there would be any resistance to family planning programs in India and also to study the socioeconomic differences, if any, between people holding different attitudes.

Interest at present lies not only in measuring the prevalence of opinions and attitudes but also in assessing the changes resulting from action programs. For the purpose of such evaluation, the need has been felt to develop such sensitive tools for measuring attitudes as standardized attitude scales and projective devices.

Measurement of group norms for family size.—Group support for the idea of small family size is a precursor to large-scale acceptance of family planning, and research is now underway in different action-research projects in India to develop suitable tools for measurement of attitudes toward small family size. The basic assumption which underlies such attempts is that social attitudes held in common reflect to a large extent the social norm prevailing in a given population group.

In the family planning action-research project of the Institute of Rural Health and Family Planning, Gandhigram, Madras State, a modified Thurstone's scale has been developed for measuring changes in attitudes favoring small family size.[17] A 5-point scale rather than a 7-, 9-, or 11-point scale has been adopted to suit the rural population. A box consisting of five compartments, each compartment having a distinct color and representing one scale position in the continuum, from the "least favorable" to the "most favorable," has been designed and is used for the judges to discriminate easily the position of the statement on the five-point scale. Out of one hundred statements collected expressing attitudes regarding a small family, twenty-eight were retained after screening and were given to seventy-five judges for assigning the scale value of each statement. Ultimately, an analysis of score distribution of each statement and the test of internal consistency led to the selection of ten statements to form the scale.

The Chembur family planning action-research program has recently been attempting to develop an attitude inventory to measure favor-

[17]A. Govindachari, "Modified Thurstone Scale of Attitude Measurement," paper presented at the Third Family Planning Communication Action-Research Workshop, Demographic Training and Research Centre, Bombay, April, 1965.

ableness to small family size by Likert's summated rating technique.[18] As a first step, the responses obtained from sixty interviews to each question in the six following areas have been assigned predetermined score values: (*a*) ideals of reproduction, (*b*) attitude toward small family size, (*c*) desire for more children, (*d*) value attached to children, (*e*) perceptions about the current infant mortality situation, and (*f*) attitude toward family planning. Item selection was done with the help of internal consistency checks. A set of fourteen questions has been selected to form the inventory.

Apart from attempts to develop attitude scales, other devices such as projective techniques are being used to assess attitudes toward small size of family. For example, the family planning action-research program undertaken by the Planning Research and Action Institute, Lucknow, Uttar Pradesh, is doing this. A visual stimulus in the shape of two pictures, one depicting a large and the other a small family, together with a verbal stimulus on the basis of an interview guide containing six questions, was provided to the subjects. These elicited responses on both general and particular aspects of the problem.[19] In addition, the typical expressions in the local dialect were recorded verbatim, and content analysis was done to gauge the true basis of the beliefs expressed. Detailed interviews gave insight into subjects' values and beliefs and into the way they conceptualized their problems.

Though many studies indicate that people do not favor very large families, it is also true that a strong distaste exists for childlessness and one-child families. This suggests that the perceived differences between families of two sizes may vary according to the sizes being compared. An exploratory study to measure perceived differences between different family sizes is in progress at the family planning action-research program undertaken by the University of Kerala, using the procedure developed by C. H. Coombs.[20]

As sophisticated techniques like attitude scales and projective techniques are yet to be generally standardized, the interview method is still in common use.

[18]S. P. Mohanty, "Measurement of Favourableness to a Small Family Size by a Summated Rating Scale Technique," paper presented at the Third Family Planning Communication Action-Research Workshop, Demographic Training and Research Centre, Bombay, April, 1965.

[19]Sunil Misra, "Use of Projective Techniques in the Study of Attitudes," paper presented at the Third Family Planning Communication Action-Research Workshop, Demographic Training and Research Centre, Bombay, April, 1965.

[20]Demographic Section, Department of Statistics, University of Kerala, "An Exploratory Study To Measure the Perceived Difference between Different Family Sizes," paper presented at the Third Family Planning Communication Action-Research Workshop, Demographic Training and Research Centre, Bombay, April, 1965; C. H. Coombs, *Theory of Data* (New York: John Wiley & Sons, 1964).

The National Sample Survey (sixteenth round) on family planning, conducted in urban areas, obtained information on ideal family size and on desire for additional children.[21] The average number of children considered ideal for a family was found to be 3.2. Among husbands who had three living children, about 9% expressed a desire for more children, 70% did not desire more, and about 10% were indifferent. For the remaining 11%, the information was not recorded. The most significant reason for desiring more children was found to be "the need to insure family survival." Financial difficulties were mentioned as reasons by the majority of husbands not desiring more children.

In a survey conducted in four villages near Delhi, information was obtained on attitude toward family size and spacing between children.[22] Although the questionnaire was structured, efforts were made to reach depth by probing. The most common reply for the ideal number of children was 4, consisting of either 3 males and 1 female or 2 males and 2 females. The ideal average spacing between births was 3.8 years. An intensive survey of a village in Kerala showed that there was not much difference among income groups with regard to opinion about spacing between births.[23]

Attitude toward clinic services.—The Survey of Family Planning Clinics in Greater Bombay made an attempt to ascertain the impressions women had at their first visit to the clinic, with respect to such aspects as distance between clinic and home, suitability of clinic hours, length of waiting time in the clinic, being seen by other women in the clinic, vaginal examination, and questions put by the clinic staff.[24] The clinic was rarely considered far from the home, as women were generally visiting neighborhood clinics. It was only the educated and well-to-do women who attended a clinic situated far away from home. The women showed a preference for clinics to be open during the afternoons rather than in the forenoons. Nearly 65% of the women reported that they did not have to wait long in the clinic, while two-fifths felt shy at being seen by other women at the clinic. Those who were afraid of the vaginal examination constituted only a third of the women interviewed, and a still smaller proportion stated that they were afraid of the questions the clinic staff asked.

[21]National Sample Survey report (n. 7 above).

[22]S. N. Agarwala, "A Family Planning Survey in Four Delhi Villages," *Population Studies*, 15 (2): 110–20 (November, 1961).

[23]Demographic Research Centre, Government of Kerala, "Report on the Intensive Village Survey in Sreekariyam," Paper No. 24, Bureau of Economics and Statistics, Trivandrum, 1963 (mimeographed).

[24]Chandrasekaran and Kuder, *op. cit.*

The women were also asked to indicate whether they were satisfied with the clinic services. Most of the women (95%) expressed satisfaction with the services and the staff at the clinic. This favorable attitude was also supported by the fact that, on an average, every woman who took advice from the clinic had advised two other women to go to the clinic.

Attitudes of service givers.—With the mobilization of all possible resources to augment family planning services, there has been a growing need to assess the attitudes of persons engaged in providing services toward family planning and toward their own roles.

A study undertaken by the family planning action-research project at the Lady Hardinge Medical College, New Delhi, is attempting to assess the attitudes of medical students toward family planning in their roles as potential service givers.[25] With the Guttman's Cornell technique, a set of statements has been developed for constructing an attitude scale. Out of a total of fifty-five statements only two were rejected. This set of fifty-three statements, put in the form of a questionnaire, was further pretested and a set of twenty-two statements formed the scale. The statements were administered to the target population, and a set of ten statements having coefficient of reproducibility of 0.89 and marginal reproducibility of 0.86 has been retained to form a scale.

The family planning action-research program at Chembur studied the attitude of voluntary family planning workers toward their role.[26] All nineteen participants of the first orientation training program were included in the study. The method used for collecting data was the case study technique in which unstructured depth interviews were conducted. The data were collected three months after the completion of the training and were subjected to content analysis. Some of the main findings of the study were that participation in the program gave the voluntary workers a sense of fulfillment, they were in a position to analyze the positive and the negative aspects of the methods of approach they used for motivation, and they had a favorable opinion about the community they lived in and saw prospects of effective contribution to the program.

[25]S. Fareed Ahmed, "Study of Attitude of Medical Students towards Family Planning as Potential Service Givers," paper presented at the Third Family Planning Communication Action-Research Workshop, Demographic Training and Research Centre, Bombay, April, 1965.

[26]Karkal Malini, "Attitude of Voluntary Workers Giving Family Planning Services, towards Their Role," paper presented at the Third Family Planning Communication Action-Research Workshop, Demographic Training and Research Centre, Bombay, April, 1965.

ASSESSMENT OF PRACTICE

Many cross-sectional studies have been conducted in India to assess the extent of contraceptive practice. In rural areas the extent of practice has been generally so low that the use of a detailed schedule has hardly proved worthwhile. In the Mysore Population Study, for instance, for every interval between successive pregnancies, information was sought on all the contraceptive methods used, whether they were used until the next pregnancy occurred, whether the methods were used "always," "usually," or "sometimes," and reasons for stopping the method (where applicable).[27] In the rural areas only 3.4% of the women reported practice of any method, and this method was invariably abstinence. Even in Bangalore City only 4% of the couples reported use of methods other than abstinence. In large cities like Calcutta or Bombay where the practice of contraception is higher, obtaining a detailed history of contraception use by individual couples has been found to be of value.[28] In many recent surveys contraceptive usage has been obtained in terms of "ever-used" or "currently used." The time when contraception was first begun has been obtained in terms of the number of pregnancies completed before its use.

The practice of contraception is still at a low level. The National Sample Survey has estimated that 5% of the husbands in urban areas (places with 5,000 or more in population), with wives below 45 years of age, had ever practiced a method other than abstinence.[29] The baseline survey conducted in the action-research area in Chembur showed, according to the wives' responses, that 30% had ever used contraception. Of these, 3% had begun using contraceptives even before the first pregnancy, 32% after the first pregnancy, 24% after the second pregnancy, 22% after the third pregnancy, and the remaining 19% after the fourth or subsequent pregnancies.[30] In the Bombay Birth Study, conducted from August, 1961, to February, 1962 (concerned primarily with the evaluation of the accuracy of the data on parity as given in the birth registration forms), a random sample of women for whom births had occurred in Bombay during a twelve-month period prior to the starting of the investigation was interviewed. Information on the practice of contraception was also obtained at the interview.

[27]United Nations, *Mysore Population Study.*

[28]S. J. Poti *et al.,* "Reliability of Data Relating to Contraceptive Practices," in *Research in Family Planning,* ed. Kiser, pp. 51–65; D. L. Sills, "On the Art of Asking 'Why Not?'" *Fourth All India Conference on Family Planning,* Report of the Proceedings, Family Planning Association of India, Bombay (Hyderabad, 1961), pp. 26–36.

[29]National Sample Survey report (n. 7 above).   [30]See n. 13 above.

According to this survey 51% had knowledge of one or more methods of family planning and 15% were currently using a family planning method.[31] The difficulty in obtaining data with respect to use of contraceptives is well realized. In the pilot study of the rhythm method of family planning at Lodi Colony, information on past use of a method of birth control was available from two sources—the preliminary attitude survey of women, conducted in their homes by women interviewers; and the interview of the women in the clinic by a lady doctor.[32] For 319 women for whom information was available from both sources, the home interviews showed 53% as having used

TABLE 3

NUMBER OF "EVER-USERS" AND "CURRENT USERS" OF
SPECIFIED FAMILY PLANNING METHODS[a]

METHOD	EVER-USERS REPORTED BY			CURRENT USERS REPORTED BY		
	Husband	Wife	Both Husband and Wife	Husband	Wife	Both Husband and Wife
Condom..........	46	30	20	26	15	10
Abstinence........	8	3	0	5	1	0
Rhythm..........	24	10	5	15	7	4
Withdrawal.......	8	25	7	5	14	4

[a] Represents 198 couples surveyed in the baseline survey of the Chembur experiment.

a method, 19% as not having used a method, and 28% with indefinite answers, while the interview in the clinic showed 83% as having used a method, 13% as not having used a method, and 4% with indefinite answers. The Calcutta survey has reported in detail the differences in the responses of wives and husbands with respect to contraceptive use.[33] It was found that wives, especially those in the lower social class, were too shy to disclose use of appliance methods, but their reports were better in the case of rhythm method and coitus interruptus.

The baseline survey conducted in the action-research area in Chembur has shown large differences in the use of specific methods as obtained from interviews with the wife and the husband.[34] As seen from Table 3, both with respect to "ever-used" and "currently used," wives reported less frequently the use of condom and rhythm method,

[31]Sills, op. cit.

[32]Government of India, Ministry of Health, "Final Report . . ." (n. 3 above).

[33]Poti et al., op. cit.

[34]M. B. Jahina, "Discrepancies in the Responses of Husbands and Wives Regarding the Couple's Practice of Family Planning," Family Planning Communication Action-Research Project, Demographic Training and Research Centre, Bombay (unpublished).

and more frequently the use of withdrawal. This survey showed that with respect to "sterilization," it is only rarely that a discrepancy arises between the responses of the wife and husband.

An attempt to classify "ever-users" of a method of family planning into different categories according to the extent of use of the method was made in the study *Family Planning through Clinics*.[35] Although this classification was aimed primarily at studying the acceptability of the method advised at the clinic, the procedure used might have wider applications in the measurement of practice of the method. On the basis of the information obtained during the interview, women were classified into the following five categories:

a) Women who received a method but did not make any use of it
b) Women who used the method once or twice and gave it up
c) Women who used the method three or more times, and then gave it up
d) Women who used the method three or more times, stopped its use because protection was not required at the time, and were not using it at the time of the survey
e) Women who were using the method at the time of the survey

Women belonging to both group *c* and group *d* had used the method recommended at the clinic three or more times but were not using it at the time of the survey. During the survey, a question was asked about the intention to use the method in the future, but responses to this question were not considered adequate to be taken into account in classifying women into groups *c* and *d*. Instead, this classification was made on the basis of the reasons stated for stopping the use of the method. Those who gave the impression that they had discontinued using the method were classified under group *c*. Those who indicated that the use had been suspended temporarily for reasons such as pregnancy, divorce, or ill health were included in group *d*. In their attitude toward continuance of the method, women in group *d* can be considered as intermediate between those in groups *c* and *e*.

The above classification can also be looked at in another way. Women in group *a* could be considered as having given up the method in the "evaluation" stage, and those in the other four groups as having passed on to the "trial" stage. Women classified in group *b* could be considered as having given up the method in the "trial" stage. All the women classified in groups *c*, *d*, and *e* had passed through the "acceptance" stage but those in group *c* could be considered as not having gone on to the "adoption" stage, while those belonging to *d* and *e* had done so.

Women for whom the diaphragm and jelly method was prescribed

[35]Chandrasekaran and Kuder, *op. cit.*

at the family planning clinics in Greater Bombay were classified into the above five groups as shown in Table 4.

In the action-research study undertaken by the Lucknow project, a novel way was tried for obtaining information on the acceptability and the regularity of use of the method supplied by the action-research unit.[36] The interviewers did not use any forms, nor did they make any notes in the presence of the respondents. They acted as if their main interest was in informing the couples about the proper use of the methods, and during the informal discussions that ensued they tried to obtain information on date of supply, quantity supplied, quantity left unused, supply channel, frequency of use, and so on. The significant points were noted down afterward.

TABLE 4

DISTRIBUTION OF WOMEN FOR WHOM THE DIAPHRAGM AND JELLY
METHOD WAS PRESCRIBED AT THE CLINIC, ACCORDING
TO THE EXTENT TO WHICH IT WAS USED

Extent of Use	Number of Women	Per Cent
a) Did not give trial........................	48	18.1
b) Gave trial, but did not accept.............	20	7.5
c) Accepted, but did not adopt..............	54	20.4
d) Adopted, not using at the time of survey...	41	15.5
e) Adopted, using at the time of survey.......	102	38.5
All women........................	265	100.0

RESEARCH DESIGN AND EVALUATION PROCEDURES IN ACTION-RESEARCH STUDIES

Action-research is quite different from ordinary surveys of knowledge, attitudes, and practice. Its principles have been discussed by Freymann and Lionberger and others.[37] Branching out from an "ultimate impact objective" are subsidiary objectives, all of which together constitute the program. Careful analysis of this type will not

[36]Planning Research and Action Institute, Lucknow, "Project Report," presented at the Third Family Planning Communication Action-Research Workshop, Demographic Training and Research Centre, Bombay, April, 1965.

[37]M. W. Freymann and H. F. Lionberger, "A Model for Family Planning Action-Research," in *Research in Family Planning*, ed. Kiser, pp. 443–61; Chandrasekaran and Freymann, *op. cit.*; Chandrasekaran, *op. cit.* (n. 6 above) (the three workshops held for research workers in family planning communication-action-research also dealt with these problems, with special reference to India); and Demographic Training and Research Centre, Bombay, "Project Report," presented at the Third Family Planning Communication Action-Research Workshop, Demographic Training and Research Centre, Bombay, April, 1965.

only make programing more rational, it will also guide the necessary evaluative research. Some observations follow which apply to the emerging specialty of action-research in family planning.

1. Most of the projects do not use external "controls" as understood in classical designs, partly because it is hard to keep a control group in the "no treatment" condition.[38]

2. Replication is difficult, but one of its purposes, to insure that the "treatment effect" is really due to the treatment, can be approached through internal evidence on whether concomitant changes occur in relevant attitudes and behavior.

3. Determination of precisely what causes the observed effects cannot be made with high precision. But often the main action-research aims do not require this.[39]

4. It is important in action-research to detect program effects promptly and accurately. The Household Fertility Survey[40] in the project areas illustrates this for changes in fertility indices, including the new "live-birth pregnancy rate."[41]

5. Baseline surveys can give benchmarks for measurement of change, but they can also inform action. They are, of course, common for obtaining data on knowledge, attitudes, and practice. In some areas they are done on existing family planning services, and even on the attitudes of medical practitioners and on marketing facilities.[42]

6. The retrospective "after only" survey has possibilities for assessing program impact. Its use in Chembur only four months after action began elicited reports of rises in contraceptive awareness, knowledge, and use during the action period. Reasons for these changes were investigated and questions asked about the agency responsible for any new knowledge reported. (Table 2 gives partial data.)

[38]Demographic Section, Department of Statistics, University of Kerala, "Project Report," presented at the Third Family Planning Communication Action-Research Workshop, Demographic Training and Research Centre, Bombay, April, 1965.

[39]Chandrasekaran, "Problems of Research Design . . ." (n. 6 above).

[40]Central Family Planning Institute (Statistical Division), "Standard Fertility Study Manual," compiled on behalf of the collaborating projects, New Delhi, 1965.

[41]Chandrasekaran and Freymann, *op. cit.*; R. S. S. Sarma, "Use of Birth Registration Records To Estimate the Trend in the Number of Births in Action Areas for Family Planning Research, Located within Greater Bombay," Family Planning Communication Action-Research Project, Demographic Training and Research Centre, Bombay (unpublished).

[42]Karkal Malini and M. B. Jahina, "Family Planning in Private Medical Practice," Family Planning Communication Action-Research Project, Demographic Training and Research Centre, Bombay (unpublished); Karkal Malini *et al.*, "Availability of Contraceptives on Sale in Chembur," Family Planning Communication Action-Research Project, Demographic Training and Research Centre, Bombay (unpublished).

46

FACTORS AFFECTING MOSLEM NATALITY

DUDLEY KIRK
Director, Demographic Division
The Population Council

This paper differs in scope and approach from others presented for this session of the Conference.[1] The author has not conducted an attitude survey in Moslem countries, but rather a study of common factors affecting the present and future level of natality in Islam as a whole. This is supplemented by a summary of the empirical studies done in specific Moslem countries, which are or will be more fully reported in separate publications by those who supervised the investigations.

Religion is often mentioned as a factor potentially affecting natality, but studies of this subject are most frequently focused on Roman Catholics because of the church's well-known doctrines concerning family planning and birth control. Most writers on the demography of the developing countries have stressed the absence of specific prohibitions on contraception in other major religions. They have often relegated the influence of religion on natality to rather vague effects, attributed to some religions, in engendering a fatalistic view of life unfavorable to the initiative and motivations required to adopt family planning.

In my judgment this restricted view is in error, at least as concerns the Moslem world. Empirically Islam has been a more effective barrier to the diffusion of family planning than Catholicism. The monolithic character of Islam in this regard is overlooked because of its enormous territory, its linguistic diversity, its political atomization, and the absence of a central religious hierarchy. What follows is a study of (1) the distinctive aspects of Moslem natality, (2) their

[1]Session on Research and Evaluation, International Conference on Family Planning Programs, Geneva, August 23–27, 1965.

possible explanation, and (3) evidences of prospective and potentially very rapid changes, including those from field studies of knowledge, attitudes, and practices relating to family planning.

Islam, or the community of Moslem peoples, includes some 500 million adherents. Its heartland is a solid bloc of Moslem settlement and nomadic occupation, extending from the Straits of Gibraltar and Dakar in the west some 5,000 miles into Chinese Sinkiang and to the borders of India in the east. In a rough way this enormous area of contiguous Moslem settlement is coterminous with the great continuous arid region of Northern Africa, Asia Minor, and Central Asia. Separated by a thousand miles of Indian territory are some forty-five million Moslems in the enclave of East Pakistan, and as many more are scattered through India itself. In Southeast Asia, and even farther separated from the Moslem heartland, is a bloc of close to 100 million Moslems in Indonesia, Malaysia, and the southern Philippines. Mohammedanism is the dominant religion in at least twenty-two countries and important in many more. The chief areas of Moslem settlement cover an area roughly equivalent to that of the North American continent, with about twice the population.

Moslem Natality

Few Moslem countries have official vital statistics complete enough to provide reliable measures of natality. But progress in measurement is being made by national and international agencies even in the absence of reliable vital statistics. Estimates of birth rates are variously derived from sample surveys in the countries concerned or indirectly from the census age distributions, usually computed by the "reverse-survival" method. Use of population models and stable age distribution theory where data are otherwise unavailable has provided another approach,[2] but this has not been used in the present study, which relies chiefly on the compilations of the United Nations. These are presented in Table 1. None of the individual figures should be regarded as highly accurate, but collectively they are thought to represent a reasonably accurate picture.

Insofar as data are available, Moslem countries range from annual birth rates in the low 40's (per thousand population) to very high rates, up to 60, estimated for certain Moslem countries of West Africa. Aside from the sub-Saharan area, Moslem natality seems to be concentrated within a rather narrow range. Among the five Arab coun-

[2]This approach has been used in the African Demography Project of the Office of Population Research, Princeton University. Cf. Lorimer, Brass, and van de Walle, "Demography," in *The African World*, ed. Robert A. Lystad (New York: Praeger, 1965).

TABLE 1

POPULATION, CRUDE BIRTH RATES, AND GROSS REPRODUCTION RATES
IN MOSLEM COUNTRIES[a] FROM UNITED NATIONS SOURCES[b]

MOSLEM COUNTRIES	ESTIMATED POPULATION 1963 (millions)	NATALITY DATA			
		Basis[c]	Year	Estimated Crude Birth Rate[d]	Estimated Gross Reproduction Rate[e]
North Africa:					
Algeria	11.6	C (2)	1944–49	45	3.0
(Moslems)		B	1959–60	47–50	
Libya	1.5	C (2)	1944–49	43	3.0
Morocco	12.7	C (2)	1955–60	47	2.9
(Moslems)		B	1962	46	
Tunisia	4.5	A	1960–63	43	3.1[f]
U.A.R.	28.0	C (1)	1950–55	45	2.8
		A	1960–63	43	
Middle East:					
Afghanistan	14.9		Not available		
Iran	22.2	C (2)	1946–51	48	3.1
		B	1959	44	
		B	1963	45–48	
Iraq	6.9	C (2)	1947–52	48	3.3
Jordan	1.8	C (1)	1951–56	45	3.4
		A	1960–63	46	
Saudi Arabia	6.6		Not available		
Syria	5.3		Not available		
Turkey	30.0	C (2)	1950–55	43	2.9
Yemen	5.0		Not available		
South Asia:					
Indonesia	100.8	C (2)	1951–56	52	2.8
		B and C (2)	1962	43	
Pakistan	98.6	C (2)	1946–61	48	3.3
		B	1962	43–46[g]	
Europe:					
Albania	1.8	A	1960–62	41	3.4[f]
Subsaharan Africa:					
Mali	4.4	B	1960–61	56	3.4
Mauritania	1.0	E	1962	49	
Niger	3.1	B	1959–60	61	3.5
Senegal	3.4	B	1957	45	
		B	1960–61	43	
		B	1963	48–54[h]	
Somalia	2.3		Not available		
Sudan	12.8	B	1955–56	52 (45–54)	3.0–3.5

[a] Including only countries having large Moslem majorities and with a total population of one million or more. Other countries with probable Moslem majorities or strong Moslem pluralities include Guinée, Nigeria, Lebanon, and Malaysia. The first two apparently have very high birth rates as determined from survey and census data; the reported national birth rate in Lebanon in 1961 was 42, the Moslem rate undoubtedly being higher than the Christian; the reported birth rate of Malays (i.e., Moslems) in Malaya averaged 41 in 1960–63 with a gross reproduction rate of 2.9 in 1960.

[b] All data, unless otherwise indicated, are from *United Nations Demographic Yearbook*, 1963 and *United Nations Population Bulletin No. 7*, 1965.

[c] Bases for rates: A—official birth registration statistics; B—sample survey data; C—"reverse-survival" estimates: (1) based on relatively satisfactory census data on population by age groups; (2) based on age data of relatively poor or uncertain reliability.

[d] Annual birth rates per 1,000 population.

[e] As defined in sources given in note [b] above.

[f] 1960.

[g] From early results of *Population Growth Estimation Study*. More recent results are presented in a paper based on this study by Karol J. Krotki, "The Problem of Estimating Vital Rates in Pakistan," United Nations World Population Conference (Belgrade), August 30–September 10, 1965. They give substantially higher figures on the assumption that the sample registration alone was (perhaps 10%) incomplete. The latter give birth rates of approximately 45 for West Pakistan and 55 for East Pakistan in 1962–63.

[h] Two surveys reported by Pierre Cantrelle, "Observation démographique répétée en milieu rural au Sénégal," United Nations World Population Conference (Belgrade) August 30–September 10, 1965.

tries of North Africa the birth rates obtained from a variety of sources are clustered from 43–50 and the computed gross reproduction rates range from 2.8 to 3.1. The Middle Eastern countries display a similar homogeneity in natality. Again the computed gross reproduction rates vary only from 2.9 in Turkey to 3.4 in Jordan. There are almost no data for the original homeland of Islam in the Arabian peninsula except for Aden and Kuwait, where the reported birth rates of 47–48 (1962) are consistent with the figures for other Arab countries.

West Pakistan appears to have a birth rate comparable to her Moslem neighbors to the west.[3] However, there is strong suggestion from field studies of continuous registration that the birth rate in East Pakistan is significantly higher, perhaps over 50.[4] A very high birth rate of 52 was determined for Indonesia from its census of 1961 but a relatively low gross reproduction rate of 2.8 was computed from the same data. The discrepancy is ascribed to distortions of the population age structure due to war and civil war that resulted in birth deficits in the 1940's and relatively small numbers of older children in 1961. A United Nations expert, posted in Indonesia, using the same data but making corrections for systematic biases in age reporting and using post-censal checks, estimated a birth rate of 43 (42 in Java and 45 in the outer islands).[5] Natality in Indonesia is clearly high but how high remains a matter for speculation. The birth rate for Moslem Malays in Malaysia is, however, believed to be accurately recorded (43.3 in 1960).

Moslem areas in Europe and the Soviet Union report somewhat lower birth rates but in all of these there are substantial non-Moslem populations that may affect the birth rates recorded for the total populations. Albania and the neighboring Moslem areas of Yugoslavia (Kosovo and Metokija) report birth rates of about 40, by contrast with 18 for Greece and an average of 22 for Yugoslavia as a whole. The five Soviet republics in which nationalities of Moslem background were a majority reported birth rates (1962) from 34 to 40 as compared with 20 for the RSFSR.[6]

[3]A number of studies listed in chapter 4, "Levels and Trends of Fertility in Asia," *United Nations Population Bulletin No. 7*, 1965, have found birth rates in the range of 41–50 in West Pakistan, including field surveys and analyses of both the 1951 and 1961 census data.

[4]See footnote g to Table 1.

[5]Vaino Kannisto, "Population Increase in Indonesia," 1963, quoted in *United Nations Population Bulletin No. 7*, 1965. Computed rates in this general range (i.e., 40–43 for Java, 1954–58) are also given in Hilde Wander, *Die Beziehung Bevölkerungs und Wirtschaftsentwicklung dargestellt am Beispeil Indonesiens* (Institut für Weltwirtschaft an der Universität Kiel No. 70, 1965), pp. 87 ff.

[6]USSR, *Vestnik statistiki*, No. 8, 1963, p. 92. The official birth rates in 1962 are as follows: Azerbaidzhan SSR (40), Tadzhik SSR (34), Turkman SSR (40), and Uzbek

There is greater variability in the natality of Moslems south of the Sahara, where the Moslem religion and way of life fuse with tropical African cultures and religions. In Zanzibar natality of Afro-Arab women is estimated by Blacker to be barely at the level of replacement, a condition which he finds only partly explained by the high incidence of sterility and venereal disease.[7] Other Moslem groups of comparatively low natality have been identified in East Africa, in the Camerouns, and elsewhere, again at least partly determined by a high incidence of sterility. On the other hand some of the highest birth rates ever recorded have been reported for Moslem (and other populations) of West Africa. The latter rates are, however, of especially dubious validity. They are obtained from sample surveys designed to record births during the preceding twelve-month period. It is believed that such surveys in Africa tend to exaggerate the crude birth rate because of inclusion of births which actually occurred prior to the reference period.[8] Nevertheless, in the absence of other evidence the presumption is that natality is variable and in some places very high among some Moslem populations of this region, though perhaps not so high as recorded in the surveys.[9]

Despite serious limitations of the data the evidence points to a rather narrow range of variability in Moslem natality, with birth rates generally in the 40's and gross reproduction rates in the range of 2.8–3.4 for the continuous bloc of Moslems living in the vast region from North Africa to Central Asia and West Pakistan. It appears likely that there is greater variability among the Moslems south of the Sahara, and that the Moslems of the Indo-Pakistan subcontinent, particularly in East Pakistan, have a different pattern.

SSR (40). The Soviet Union has conducted a vigorous campaign against the practice of Mohammedanism (as against other religions) and therefore does not recognize religious classifications—only nationalities. In each of these four republics about three-fourths of the population were reported to be of traditional Moslem nationalities in the census of 1959. The birth rate in the Kirgiz SSR (about three-fifths Moslem) was 34, and in Kazak SSR (less than half Moslem) it was 33. In the RSFR much the highest birth rate (41 in 1959) was reported in Daghestan, which is predominantly Moslem. The author is indebted to Mr. Allen Hetmanek of the U.S. Library of Congress and Mr. James Brackett of the U.S. Census Bureau for making these data available.

[7]J. G. C. Blacker, "Population Growth and Differential Fertility in Zanzibar Protectorate," *Population Studies*, 15 (3): 258–66 (March, 1962).

[8]*United Nations Population Bulletin No. 7*, 1965, chap. 3, "Levels and Trends of Fertility in Africa."

[9]It may well be that Moslem and earlier tropical African values on fertility reinforce each other. In a representative sample study of attitudes concerning "the best number of children in completed families" the modal size of family recommended by the male respondents was in the range of 5–9 in coastal and central Ghana (50% of respondents in each case) but 10–14 (28%) in northern Ghana, which has strong Moslem influence. J. C. Caldwell, "Fertility Attitudes in Three Economically Contrasting Research Regions of Ghana," to be published in *Population Studies*, 1966.

For the few Moslem countries for which there is a continuous record, there is little evidence of fundamental trends in natality either up or down. Aside from temporary reductions in the birth rate attributable to wars the birth rate in Egypt has apparently remained stable since the beginning of the century.[10] Though some Moslem populations such as the Algerian have been in close contact with the West for a long time, there is little evidence of the declines in the birth rate that have swept through Western populations[11] and more recently have appeared among East Asian populations.

As a consequence Moslem populations generally show higher natality than their non-Moslem neighbors. As noted above, Moslems in Europe and the Soviet Union have very much higher natality than Christian and other non-Moslem groups. Albania and the related Moslem districts in Yugoslavia are the only high natality areas remaining on the European continent. In the Soviet Union the Moslem republics stand out as the remaining areas of high natality in that country. In the Near East the sharp discontinuity is suggested by the birth rate in Turkey, estimated at 43, as compared with 18 for Greece. All available data show that the Moslems in North Africa had far higher natality than the dominant European minorities before the countries in this region achieved independence. The Arabs have a much higher birth rate than Jews in Israel. Moslems have higher natality than indigenous Christians in Lebanon and the United Arab Republic.[12]

While conditions are very different in South and Southeast Asia, there is evidence that again Moslems show higher natality than their Hindu and Buddhist neighbors, for example, in India and in Malaysia. Historically Moslems had consistently higher rates of natural increase in pre-partition India than Hindus, strongly suggesting higher natality, since there seems to be little reason for supposing lower mortality among Moslems. This hypothesis is borne out by other measures (e.g., ratios of children to women from the censuses). More recently some survey data show higher natality for the Moslems remaining in India where other conditions, for example, residence and economic class, are

[10]M. A. El Badry, "Trends in the Components of Population Growth in the Arab Countries of the Middle East," Conference on Demographic and Economic Trends, New York, October 10–12, 1963.

[11]Cf. Jacques Breil, La population en Algérie (Paris: Imprimerie nationale, 1957), p. 110. Had we more complete information we might see the beginnings of decline in the birth rate on the Western pattern in the secular states of Turkey and Albania. In Turkey census data show lower than average ratios of children to women in the more urbanized and developed regions of European Turkey and Western Anatolia.

[12]El Badry, op. cit.

held constant.[13] Others do not show such differentiation,[14] and so it would be rash to generalize about the remaining Moslem minority which lives under very diverse conditions in the different regions of the country. But there seems little doubt that natality in present-day Pakistan is higher than in India and that in the subcontinent as a whole Moslems have higher natality. Finally, in Malaysia, where Moslems are a plurality living beside an almost equally large population of Chinese origin, birth rates and reproduction rates are higher for the Moslem Malays. It should be pointed out, however, that this is a recent development; until quite recently the Chinese, largely of immigrant background, showed higher birth rates than the indigenous Malay population, partly because the Chinese had an age distribution more favorable to high birth rates. In the past few years Chinese birth rates have shown a steady downward trend, associated with a rising age at marriage and probably with the beginnings of contraceptive practice on the Western model.[15]

The above observations are demonstrable only in relation to populations adhering to one or another of the major world religions. Where Moslems live beside, or are fused with, tribal groups (e.g., in tropical Africa and in Indonesia) such consistent differentials are not observed.

Conclusions.—Within the important limitations of the data it may be said that Moslem natality (1) is almost universally high, (2) shows no evidence of important trends over time, and (3) is generally higher than that of neighboring peoples of other major religions.

Such observations do not apply to any other major world religion. Roman Catholic populations range in reported birth rates (1963) from 17 in Belgium to just under 50 in Costa Rica, and from gross reproduction rates of slightly above 1.0 in several European countries to 3.6 in Costa Rica. Among populations of Eastern Orthodox tradition

[13]Cf. United Nations, Department of Economic and Social Affairs, *The Mysore Population Study*, U.N. Population Studies, No. 34 (New York, 1961); J. N. Sinha, "Differential Fertility and Family Limitation in an Urban Community of Uttar Pradesh," *Population Studies*, 11:157–69 (November, 1957); J. R. Rele, "Fertility Differentials in India: Evidence from a Rural Background," *Milbank Memorial Fund Quarterly*, 41(2): 183–200 (April, 1963).

[14]Cf. V. M. Dandekar and K. Dandekar, *Survey of Fertility and Mortality in Poona District* (Poona: Gokhale Institute of Politics and Economics, Publication No. 27, 1953), pp. 63, 101.

[15]Another possible exception exists in the Philippines, where lower ratios of children to women have been reported in the censuses for Moslem than for Christian women. These data are suspect and are being re-examined for possible greater underenumeration of Moslem children and special biases in age reporting for Moslems (e.g., overstatement of age of children) that might affect such measures. Private communications from Drs. Mercedes Concepción and Frank Lorimer of the Population Center, University of the Philippines.

(now largely Communist) birth rates are almost universally low, from 16.2 (1962) in Romania to 20.2 in the RSFSR and 22.2 in White Russia. Protestant and Jewish populations also have birth rates in this general range. In the spheres of Buddhist and Confucian influence birth rates range from 17 in Japan to over 40 in Thailand and several other Buddhist Southeast Asian countries (though only in the middle 30's in Ceylon); gross reproduction rates range from about 1 in Japan to well over 2 in Thailand. The birth rate is low in Japan and falling in Taiwan, Hong Kong, Singapore, and probably Korea (present trends in Communist China are unknown). The religious group most comparable to the Moslems in natality is the Hindus, among whom natality is generally high, though not quite so high as among the Moslems of the Indo-Pakistan subcontinent.

It would seem that Moslem institutions, more than those of other world religions, favor a generally high natality. Religion and high natality are more closely correlated for Moslems than for any other major religious group. The next sections will explore possible reasons why Islam displays this uniformity.

The factors favoring high birth rates may be conveniently discussed at three levels: (1) general cultural and religious factors, (2) specific characteristics of Moslem belief and practice related to the family, and (3) mechanisms by which these determine natality.

GENERAL FACTORS FAVORING HIGH BIRTH RATES IN MOSLEM COUNTRIES

Moslem countries are all in the category of developing nations, and all have low indices of material development. These are usually lower than those of non-Moslem neighbors. High levels of education, industrialization, and other aspects of modernization associated with declines in the birth rate have not made strong headway as yet in Moslem countries. In fact, class differentials in natality in the UAR, for example, suggest that a general rise in the level of living might at first tend to *raise* the birth rate, because of better nutrition, health, and other factors.

Islam partakes of the pro-natalist social forces that exist generally in peasant and pastoral societies. High mortality, especially of infants and children, have in the past called for unrestricted reproduction. Sons are valued for many purposes: for continuity of family line and landownership; for contribution to agricultural labor; to strengthen family numbers in village rivalry and strife; for support in old age; for religious intervention at and after death. As in other developing societies, particularly in Asia, the joint family system in Islam buffers the direct burdens of childbearing on the parents.

Moslem influence is strongly conservative. In many ways *all* religions are conservative, but it is often noted that this is especially true of Islam, in which religion and way of life are so intertwined as to be inseparable. Mohammedanism shares with other religions injunctions to marry and multiply. Children are among the richest blessing that Allah bestows—He will provide for the souls He permits to come into the world. Moslems share with other religions important fatalistic themes that might well dispose them against conscious efforts to control family size or on occasion to adopt health measures that would reduce illness and postpone death. But these ideas are characteristic of many traditional societies; the difference is the tenacity with which old beliefs and practices are maintained by Moslems and influence life today. The contribution of this general conservatism to the maintenance of pre-modern natality is diffuse, difficult to measure, but probably very important.

The persistent resistance of Moslems to change has both historical and religious origins. The last of the world religions to appear, it has a strong tradition of military conquest and cultural domination. It has had over a millennium of conflict with Christianity and therefore has a conscious resistance to modern (often identified as Christian) influences which threaten the integrity of Islam. A large part of Islam, much the greater part, has within a generation been under the domination of European countries, and many Moslems have found solace and effective resistance in the continuing practice of their faith. The religions of the Orient, for example, do not have this deep-seated historical sense of conflict with the Western (i.e., Christian and Jewish) influences. Moslem sensitivities have understandably led to a cultural wall against diffusion from Europe despite proximity, political connections, and long-standing trade and communication.

The nature of the Moslem religion also is relevant to conservative influences. Mohammedanism is often described as a religion of practice rather than doctrine. True Believers are united by their faith in simple doctrine, with nothing comparable, for example, to the Christian concept of the Trinity. Essentially, all that is required is affirmation of belief in One God, who is Allah, and in Mohammed, as the Messenger of God. More important than doctrine in Islam is conformity to religious and social practices which are so closely interwoven in Moslem life.[16] Several of these that seem most pertinent will be discussed in the next section.

[16]These views of Islam are presented in standard works, including Louis Gardet, *La Cité musulmane: vie sociale et politique* (Paris: Librairie Philosophique J. Vrin, 1954);

SPECIAL MOSLEM CHARACTERISTICS THAT MIGHT
BE EXPECTED TO FAVOR HIGH BIRTH RATES

Three of these characteristics will be discussed briefly below: (1) marriage institutions, (2) emphasis on sexuality, and (3) subordination of women.[17]

The traditional Moslem family is strongly patrilinear and patrilocal with male dominance and responsibility specifically prescribed by the Koran. The Moslem family derives from the agnate family of Mohammed's day. Polygamy was customary and Moslem doctrine prescribes that in the event of plural marriage the husband must treat his wives equally; there has been much dispute over whether this also means that he should distribute his favors equally among them. Divorce is theoretically easy but is in fact restrained by the fact that the husband must return the dowry with the wife, sacrifice the wedding bond, or in other ways pay a substantial penalty. Religious precepts are favorable to early remarriage of the widowed and the divorced; the scriptures require only a sufficient interval (3–4 months) to determine whether or not the woman was pregnant at the time of separation and thereby establish legitimate male responsibility for offspring.

Moslem doctrine holds that pleasures of the flesh, and specifically sexual intercourse, are a God-given virtue to be enjoyed and conjugal obligation to be fulfilled. The great medieval theologian Al-Ghazzali held that Mohammed was superior to Christ in that the latter never successfully integrated family life and sexual pleasure into Christian belief. While Mohammedanism imposed dietary restrictions and restraints relating to art and music, there is a striking absence of the value that is placed on sexual asceticism in Christianity, in Buddhism, and in Hinduism.[18] A celibate clergy or celibate religious orders are foreign to Islam. In traditional Moslem belief the permanent state

---

G. E. von Grunebaum, *Islam* (London: Routledge & Kegan Paul, 1961) and *Medieval Islam* (Chicago: University of Chicago Press, 1946); and, with more sociological orientation, Morroe Berger, *The Arab World Today* (New York: Doubleday, 1962), and Clifford Geertz, *The Religion of Java* (Glencoe, Ill.: Free Press, 1960).

[17]These subjects are discussed, with extensive citations to other sources, in Mahmoud Seklani, "La fecondité dans les pays arabes," *Population* (Paris), 15(5): 831–56 (October–December, 1960); Special issue of *Confluent* on "Problèmes démographiques au Maghreb," particularly articles by J.G., "L'Islam face à la prévention des naissances," and Hédi Madani, "Le control des naissances et l'Islam," No. 50, April–June, 1965; and William J. Goode, *World Revolution and Family Patterns* (New York: Free Press–Macmillan, 1963), esp. chap. 3.

[18]Perhaps more evident in Christianity and Buddhism than in Hinduism, where fertility has been glorified in the construction of temples, etc. Nevertheless, there is a strong theme of the value of sexual asceticism in Hinduism (e.g., in teachings of Gandhi).

of celibacy is abnormal for men and unthinkable for able-bodied women.

The place of women in traditional Moslem society was an unusually subordinate one. In Moslem practice women were and still are commonly not permitted to enter the mosque proper or to participate directly in its religious ceremonies. They were supposed to wear the veil, and on the Indian subcontinent to observe the often unhealthful seclusion of purdah. These restrictions were not always practical or enforceable, especially among the poor, but they have had prestige and were applied most rigorously among the upper and middle classes that otherwise would have been most receptive to modern influences. While the position of women is changing rapidly in the more progressive Moslem states, earlier attitudes are reflected, for example, in the low level of education of Moslem women. Less than 10% of the women over age 15 are literate in Morocco, Iran, Iraq, Pakistan, and doubtless most of the Moslem countries for which there are no data. In each case the number of male literates is three to four times greater. Only in the Soviet Moslem republics, in Albania, and in Indonesia are more than a fourth of the women reported as literate. Male dominance within marriage is thus strengthened by the greater education of males and by the differences in age at marriage—women are characteristically married young to more mature men, usually in their twenties.[19]

MECHANISMS BY WHICH MOSLEM PRACTICES MAY DETERMINE NATALITY

These traditional family institutions and the traditional role of women affect natality through (1) proportion of the reproductive life that is spent in marital or other sexual unions and (2) within such unions the practices determining exposure to pregnancy. Statistical information is available on the first but not generally on the second. In the ten Moslem countries for which comparable data are available 70%–86% of all females aged 15–44 are married. This is a higher proportion than exists in the Far East and Southeast Asia and in almost all Western countries, which range from a low of 47% in Ireland to a high of 71% in the United States. It is apparent that Moslem women spend a larger part of their reproductive life in marriage than do their sisters in these other major regions. This is the result of the following several (in some cases contradictory) influences:

  1. In accordance with Moslem practice marriage of women is wellnigh universal. In those countries for which data are available 3% or

[19]Data in this and the succeeding paragraphs were computed from compilations in the United Nations, *Demographic Yearbook*, recent issues.

less (more often only 1%) are not married by the end of the reproductive period.

2. Age at marriage is low for women in all Moslem countries. In the ten countries for which reasonably comparable information was available from recent censuses, the proportion of females married among all females aged 15–19 ranges from 31% in the UAR to 73% in Pakistan.[20] In the latter, age at marriage approximates the early Moslem rule of marriage at puberty. The percentages were in the range 31–40 for Middle Eastern countries (Iran, Iraq, Turkey, Tunisia and the UAR) and 49% in Morocco. A figure of 57% for Kuwait confirms fragmentary evidence that age at marriage in the Arabian peninsula is lower, as it is also in West Africa (60% in Guinea). The figure for Moslem Malays is 40% and this is thought to be comparable for their ethnic cousins in Indonesia.[21] Differential age at marriage may well be a factor in the somewhat higher birth rates in Pakistan than in other Moslem countries, and in the very high birth rates apparently prevailing in West Africa. It is certainly an important element in the generally higher natality of Moslems.

3. Widowhood during the reproductive years is more common than in the West owing to higher mortality, which of course varies from country to country. This tends to reduce natality. Widowhood is generally declining with reductions in mortality.

4. As might be expected, divorce is more common in Islam than elsewhere. The reported figures, which probably understate the fact, show higher divorce rates than in the West and in the non-Moslem countries of Asia. The reported rates are not so high as to seriously jeopardize reproduction (e.g., annual rates of less than 1.5 per thousand population in Turkey, Albania, and Iraq and 2–3 in Morocco and the UAR).[22]

5. The effects of widowhood and divorce on natality are tempered in Moslem countries by institutions favoring the early remarriage of widows and divorcees. The proportions of marriages involving a widow or a divorced person are much higher than in the West (except in Albania and Turkey, which more closely follow the European pattern). Furthermore, in the United Arab Republic, for example, 8% of all Moslem grooms were (in 1955) reported as marrying an addi-

[20]These may be compared with 1% women married in this age group in Ireland and in Japan, 3% in France, 8% in Korea, 12–13% in the Philippines and Thailand, 16% in the United States, and 70% in India.

[21]To be contrasted with the figures for the Christian Philippines and Buddhist Thailand above. T. E. Smith, "Population Characteristics of South and South-East Asia," in *Women in the New Asia*, ed. Barbara Ward (Paris: UNESCO, 1963), p. 507.

[22]These may be compared with estimated United States rates of 2.12 to 2.35 for the years 1954–60, which are the highest for Western countries.

tional wife, suggesting that at least here polygamy was an appreciable factor in increasing the possibilities for women of marriage and remarriage.

6. Nevertheless polygamy is probably more a spectacular feature of Moslem institutions than a decisive factor in Moslem natality. There is inadequate evidence on its prevalence but available information suggests that some nine-tenths of Arab farmers, for example, are monogamous, and polygamy is most commonly adopted when the first wife fails to produce a child. Polygamy is more common among the Arab Bedouins and the Moslems south of the Sahara, where Moslem customs in this matter converge with earlier tribal practices. But among the more advanced Moslem countries polygamy is in disrepute and in some instances (e.g., Tunisia) has been made illegal and is presumably declining.

There is an extensive and inconclusive literature about the effects of polygamy on the total birth rate of the communities concerned.[23] One thing is clear—in Moslem societies it does promote opportunities for marriage of all females, single, widowed, and divorced. It may be recalled that the Prophet's nine wives were mostly widows. Plural marriage can be important to natality in societies where mortality is high, as it has been in Moslem countries, and where the difference in age at marriage between bride and groom (e.g., five years) is greater than in Western societies. Polygamy is certainly a pro-natalist factor in promoting marriage opportunities for women.[24]

There is only the most fragmentary evidence on the relation of Moslem institutions to practices determining the risk of pregnancy within marriage. Ritual abstinence is apparently less common among Moslems than, for instance, among Hindus, though abstinence is required during the daylight hours of Ramadan, the month of fasting. Moslem customs do not require prolonged abstinence following childbirth, and Moslem women do not so frequently return to their parents' home for confinement as, for example, do Hindus; so postpartum separation is likely to be shorter. Such factors may explain the somewhat higher birth rates of Moslems than Hindus in the Indian subcontinent despite similar patterns of early marriage, high rates of

[23]Cf. United Nations, *Population Bulletin No. 7*, 1965, esp. chap. 3, "Levels and Trends of Fertility in Africa."

[24]The opposite argument rests on comparisons that show higher average numbers of children born to women in monogamous than in polygamous unions, presumably because of differences in frequency of intercourse and the greater age of polygamous men (in most cultures polygamy is a luxury, usually requiring the accumulation of capital). But such comparisons are biased by the fact that barrenness of the first wife is the most common reason for marrying another—hence polygamous unions have a disproportionate number of sterile women.

widow remarriage, and high proportions of reproductive life spent by women in marriage.[25]

In a society which emphasizes the value, even the religious merit, of sexual exuberance within marriage it might be hypothesized that the frequency of intercourse might be higher than in societies more restrained on this subject. This might be expected to contribute to a higher birth rate. There is almost no direct evidence. Very fragmentary and inconclusive data show higher frequencies of intercourse for Moslems in special studies in Lebanon and Bengal, but the populations included were small and the data are verbal responses that might reflect cultural biases as well as real differences.[26] Similar problems arise in evaluating the possible effects of polygamy (referred to above) and of the joint or extended family, which is an ideal over much of the Moslem world. In the Bengal field study reported by Nag, women living in simple or nuclear families were found to have both higher coital frequency and higher natality than women in joint families. This is ascribed to the lack of privacy and greater adherence to traditional periods of abstinence in joint households.[27] There is too little evidence on the true prevalence of the extended family, quite aside from other problems, to make any generalizations on this subject.

Aside from the above, physiological factors in Islam would generally work against the attainment of maximum fertility. Problems of epidemic disease and malnutrition, still common in the Moslem world, probably reduce the capacity to conceive and certainly the capacity to carry pregnancy full term, but this influence is not now measurable. Further, Moslem women do indulge in prolonged lactation after childbirth; this practice presumably reduces natality somewhat. These several physiological influences are not specifically Moslem; they reduce natality below physiological potentialities in most traditional societies.

In sum, the traditional Islamic way of life is culturally favorable to high natality in the absence of voluntary restriction of births within marriage. The maximum potential fertility is reduced by high mortality and widowhood and probably by adverse physiological factors such as malnutrition and disease and by certain practices such as prolonged lactation. The general effect of modernization should be to

[25]Census data for India and Pakistan suggest little difference in the proportion of widows remarrying despite the Brahmin prohibition against this practice.

[26]David Yaukey, *Fertility Differentials in a Modernizing Country* (Princeton: Princeton University Press, 1961), p. 201; and Moni Nag, *Factors Affecting Human Fertility in Nonindustrial Societies: A Cross-Cultural Study*, Yale University Publications in Anthropology, 1962, pp. 72–73.

[27]Moni Nag, "Family Type and Fertility," World Population Conference, Belgrade, August 30–September 10, 1965.

ameliorate the adverse factors and hence raise the birth rate in the absence of voluntary control of family size.

Mohammedan doctrine does not prohibit the voluntary restriction of births, though as a militant religion Islam historically put pressure on men to produce numerous children and especially sons. Nevertheless there are clear authoritative statements, for example by the highly respected medieval theologian Al-Ghazzali, that would permit the practice of birth control (i.e., coitus interruptus) under certain conditions.[28] Also important are the *fatwas* made by religious authorities in the light of modern conditions. Because Islam does not have the hierarchical structure of the Roman Catholic Church, these pronouncements do not have the authority of a papal encyclical, but they have significant influence. One of the clearest and most authoritative of these, by the Mufti of Egypt, came to the conclusion that "it is permissible for either husband or wife, by mutual consent, to take any measures to prevent semen entering the uterus, in order to prevent conception."[29] While this conclusion has not gone unchallenged, the preponderance of religious authority has not been unfavorable to birth control. On the other hand, abortion after the "quickening" of the embryo is absolutely forbidden. The existing pronouncements on family limitation did not contemplate and hence do not pass judgment on the use of radically new methods such as the oral contraceptives and intra-uterine devices.

The above describes the traditional factors affecting natality in Islam. They explain why Moslems have not adopted family planning on the European pattern despite geographical proximity and long association with Europe. This is the cultural background within which rapid changes may now be occurring in the more advanced Moslem countries, though not yet general enough to be reflected in measurable declines in the birth rate. The next section deals with empirical studies of what Moslems *today* know, think, and do about family planning.

THE MOSLEM WORLD TODAY: FIELD STUDIES OF KNOWLEDGE,
    ATTITUDES, AND PRACTICES RELATING TO
    FAMILY LIMITATION

There is now a rapidly growing number of such studies of general populations in Moslem countries. The most ambitious of these is a

[28]Akhter Hameed Khan, *Islamic Opinions on Contraception*, (Comilla, East Pakistan: Pakistan Academy for Village Development, 1961). Includes translations of extracts from Al-Ghazzali and Ibn Kaiyim.

[29]"A Mohammedan 'Fatwa' on Contraception," *Human Fertility*, 10 (2): 45–46 (June, 1945). Includes translation of Arabic original published in the *Journal of the Egyptian Medical Association*, 20 (7): 54–56 (July, 1937).

survey of a national sample in Turkey, taken preparatory to the adoption of a government program to promote family planning in that country. There are several studies in Pakistan, which has had a government family planning program for several years. Two studies were conducted on a comparable basis in the UAR and in Lebanon. Studies are being conducted in Tunisia and in Indonesia, the first results of which were presented to this conference (as reported in chapters 43 and 47 in this volume). While these various studies were conducted under different auspices and are in some respects not comparable, they lead to certain consistent results. These are summarized below, though so brief a statement cannot hope to do justice to the individual studies involved.[30]

Such studies are feasible.—They can provide valuable and reliable information for general populations, as opposed to clinic or other unrepresentative groups. This is true despite initial skepticism encountered in every country concerning the feasibility of obtaining responses on such delicate subjects in a household survey.

Knowledge.—Men and women in Moslem countries, as elsewhere, display ignorance about the physiology of reproduction, as, for example, the time of ovulation and the fertile period in the menstrual cycle. Knowledge of modern methods of birth control (i.e., other than abstinence or abortion) is largely confined to the small educated minority in the cities. In Turkey, perhaps the most advanced Moslem country, only 43% of the national sample said they knew of *any* method of contraception. In rural Lebanon and rural Egypt, very few respondents reported such knowledge.

Desired family size.—All the studies show that a substantial proportion of couples in both urban and rural areas is concerned about the size of their families and do not want more children. In each of the studies where the appropriate questions were asked, a large proportion of the respondents gave as an ideal family size a smaller number of children than the actual number in completed families in their own

[30]Results of the studies are available in the following publications: "Turkey: National Survey on Population," *Studies in Family Planning*, No. 5, December, 1964 (Population Council, New York); Social Sciences Research Centre, University of the Panjab, *Knowledge of and Attitudes towards Family Planning*, Family Planning Association of Pakistan, Lahore, Pakistan; A. Majeed Khan, *Rural Pilot Family Planning Action Programme: First Annual Report, March, 1961–May, 1962*, Pakistan Academy for Rural Development, Comilla, East Pakistan; Beryl J. Roberts, David Yaukey, William Griffiths, Elizabeth W. Clark, A. B. M. Shafiullah, and Raisunnessa Huq, "Family Planning Survey in Dacca, East Pakistan," *Demography*, Vol. 2, 1965; Hanna Rizk, "Social and Psychological Factors Affecting Fertility in the United Arab Republic," *Marriage and Family Living*, 25 (1): 69–73 (February, 1963); David Yaukey, *Fertility Differences in a Modernizing Country: A Survey of Lebanese Couples* (Princeton: Princeton University Press, 1961).

society.[31] Women in Moslem countries apparently want fewer children than their husbands, though the difference is not large. Families with one or more sons are more interested in limiting family size than those having only daughters. Among Moslem countries, only in Turkey has the small family norm gained general acceptance, though even here only in principle, not in fact. The modal number of children desired by both men and women is 3, the average (mean) being 3.7 for men and 3.2 for women. In actual fact Turkish women completing the childbearing period report an average of 6.3 pregnancies, 5.8 live births, and 4.1 living children. Only about one-fourth of the Turkish couples in their thirties, married 10–14 years, and already having three children want more children. This position is not now representative of more than the most progressive Moslem populations but probably indicates the direction in which the more advanced Moslem countries are going. A very different atmosphere of opinion exists in the more rural populations: in the UAR study, for example, one-third of the women in the younger reproductive ages thought questions on desired size of family meaningless "because God alone determines the number of children a wife might have."[32]

Practice of family planning.—Despite widespread favorable attitudes toward the restriction of family size, the actual practice of birth control by Moslems is very limited. As stated by the author of the UAR study, "It is evident from this analysis that while more than half the wives in this study consider their families too large, yet they could not or would not limit them to the desired size."[33] Among the rural Moslem populations studied, the existing practice of contraception was negligible except in Turkey, where there was definite progression from 6% practicing in rural areas, 18% in the town, 21% in the cities, and 29% in the metropolitan areas. In the Dacca sample (an educated and urban group) the proportion ever having practiced contraception was 36% or 21% depending on whether one relies on the reports of the husbands or of the wives, and in Lahore the comparable figures are 18% and 8% for a somewhat broader urban sample. The highest figures reported for any Moslem population are those reported by Yaukey for Beirut, which is a cosmopolitan and Westernized city:

---

[31]A compilation of responses on "desired family size" and on persons stating they do not want more children for many studies including several in Moslem countries are presented in W. Parker Mauldin, "Fertility Studies: Knowledge, Attitude, and Practice," *Studies in Family Planning*, No. 7, pp. 1–10 (June, 1965). As the author points out, however, specific comparisons are treacherous because the responses are often to different questions, put in different ways, to different types of samples. This is particularly true of the studies made in Moslem areas; so no attempt has been made here to make numerical comparisons.

[32]Rizk, *op. cit.*, p. 72.   [33]*Ibid.*

for women married ten years or more, 60% of the uneducated and 83% of the educated reported some attempts at control of contraception.[34]

Reduction of the birth rate owing to family planning.—Where such information was obtained, the studies show smaller family size among the better educated urban couples included in the samples. In Moslem countries, as everywhere, education is highly correlated with knowledge of contraceptive methods, with favorable attitudes toward their use, and with the actual practice of family planning. As in most Western countries the educated were the first to adopt family limitation. But as yet these groups are too small to have any measurable impact on the birth rate of Moslem populations as a whole. It is possible that among the Moslem populations most exposed to European influence (in Albania, in Western Turkey, and among the Soviet Moslem Republics) the birth rate has begun to decline on the Western model and that this may soon become evident in statistical data.

Now a new factor has entered—*the intervention of governments.* The high birth rates and accelerating rates of population growth in relation to economic growth have caused concern in Moslem countries. Several of the above studies were undertaken as result of government concern about population growth and of government interest in introducing family planning programs. Moslem countries have been among the first to adopt such programs: four of these are described in papers in this volume, on national programs in Pakistan, Turkey, the UAR and Tunisia (chaps. 10, 11, 12, 13). None of these has yet been on a scale sufficient to affect the national birth rates of the countries concerned. But the results of the above studies suggest that in each of these countries, at least, there is a major reservoir of couples already motivated to adopt family planning if given the relevant information and services suited to their needs. The latter offer a major opportunity for government family planning programs if the necessary administrative services can be established. Nevertheless government programs may have to give more attention to stimulating motivation for family planning, especially among men, than would be true in other major religious groups.

GENERAL CONCLUSIONS

Conclusions relevant to family planning programs may be summarized as follows:

1. Islamic countries uniformly have high birth rates.

[34]David Yaukey, "Some Immediate Determinants of Fertility Differences in Lebanon," *Marriage and Family Living,* 25 (1): 27–34 (February, 1963). Other data in this paragraph from sources given in note 30.

2. These are supported by distinctive Islamic attitudes and practices in family life rather than by political or religious doctrine.

3. The "normal" diffusion of birth control to and within Moslem countries on the European pattern has been inhibited by the cultural discontinuity between Moslem peoples and their neighbors.

4. The continuing high birth rates in Moslem countries, matched with encouraging progress in reducing deaths, now lead to rapid population growth and its especially high visibility as a handicap to economic and social progress.

5. As a result several Moslem countries have adopted measures to introduce birth control.

6. KAP and other studies show: (*a*) that a substantial number of couples in all Moslem societies studied have favorable attitudes toward family limitation and would like to practice it given suitable methods—where the question was asked (Turkey) the respondents said they favored a government birth control program; (*b*) that the actual practice of birth control is still limited to a small urban and educated minority; (*c*) that efforts to introduce birth control on a large scale encounter much more salient lack of motivation, than, for example, in Buddhist and Far Eastern countries.[35]

7. Despite these difficulties the present attitudes and programs of governments, and the availability of more suitable contraceptive methods, augur much more rapid adoption of family planning in Moslem countries than could have been expected even a few years ago.

[35]Cf. action research experiments in Pakistan: "Pakistan: The Medical Research Project at Lulliani," and "Pakistan: The Public Health Education Research Project in Dacca," *Studies in Family Planning*, No. 4, pp. 5–9 (August, 1964) and No. 5, pp. 6–12 (December, 1964); in Indonesia, in paper by Gille and Pardoko, and in Tunisia, in paper by Morsa, chapters 43 and 47 in this volume. These may be compared with other experiments, e.g., those described in "India: The Singur Study"; "Korea: The Koyang Study"; "Ceylon: The Swedish-Ceylon Family Planning Project"; "Taiwan: The Taichung Program of Pre-Pregnancy Health," *Studies in Family Planning*, No. 1, pp. 1–4 (July, 1963); No. 2, pp. 7–9 and 9–12 (December, 1963); No. 4, p. 12 (August, 1964).

47

THE TUNISIA SURVEY: A PRELIMINARY ANALYSIS

JEAN MORSA
University of Brussels

Like most Moslem countries, Tunisia displays very high fertility. The current estimated birth rate is above 45 per 1,000 population. From this fact, we can safely conclude that differences in family size among different population groups are small. For the most part, they will not result from a deliberate or conscious effort, but from differences in demographic characteristics of the groups compared: differences in age composition, marriage duration, health condition, and so on. The practice of family planning is not to be expected except in very small groups, located in the upper strata, and among highly educated and Westernized people.

This paper reports findings from the before-survey of a family planning experiment now in progress. Such a survey is quite novel in Tunisia. It should give us a better understanding of the factors associated with high fertility and of the conditions making for a change. It should permit us to obtain data pointing to an interest in family planning and to measure the proportion of couples who have already taken action (however inefficient it may be). It also gives us an opportunity to examine the channels by which family limitation spreads in a society and to ascertain which groups are more prepared for such a radical departure from their traditional way of life.

The experimental design calls for an action program in twelve centers. In each of these centers, a survey was organized, in the spring of 1964, based on an area sample.[1] To aid in evaluating the action program, data for each center are analyzed separately. But here I

[1]There is no other valid basis. Usually, a map was drawn from an aerial photograph. There are differences in sampling fractions. Unless otherwise stated, the results presented here are weighted to account for these differences.

shall make groupings. I shall first present data for all areas together; then, taking into account differentiations within the country, I shall consider a first group (Group A), composed mainly of the coastal centers (Bizerte, Beja, Sfax, Monastir, Nabeul, Ariana), and a second (Group B), composed of centers situated in the interior (Maktar, Tozeur, El Djem, Tunis-Bellevue).[2] As will be seen, we shall have to consider Bellevue and Maktar separately.

In these ten centers, 2,175 valid questionnaires were completed. The interviewers were *sages-femmes, aides soignantes,* and *animatrices* (midwives and paramedical and social personnel) working under the supervision of a Belgian assistant.[3] They were told to interview all married women under 40 years of age, living with their husbands, in the assigned blocks.

MARITAL FERTILITY

As expected, marital fertility is very high. In the age group 30–39, 7.1 pregnancies are reported, 5.9 live births, and 4.7 living children. This high fertility is partly a consequence of the high infant and child mortality. The ratio of the mean number of living children to the mean number of children born alive (women aged 30–39) gives an index of this mortality. Its value is impressive: less than 0.8. The data gathered for each center show a marked dispersion: from 0.84 (Beja) and 0.83 (Sfax) to 0.74 (El Djem) and 0.68 (Tozeur).

Now, if we turn to the mean number of additional children the wives want, we find it inversely correlated to the survival ratio: where infant mortality is lower, people appear to be less anxious to have an additional child[4] and the proportion of women who want no more

[2]Data for Sousse are left out of the present analysis, because the survey there started later. The before-survey was not conducted in the city of Tunis, although the action program was implemented there, because of unresolved sampling problems. Actually, the groupings are not entirely satisfactory. They will be revised as soon as other data come in. I think Bizerte and Sfax (and perhaps Sousse) could form a single group. But, at present, similarities in educational level, employment structure, and so on lead us to join the others cited, even if attitudes toward family size and family planning are different, especially at Monastir, where the population appears to be more conservative. It might come as a surprise to see Tunis-Bellevue considered as a center from the interior. It is a suburb of Tunis which is not representative of the town itself: it is an extremely poor area, inhabited for the most part by people coming from small places in the interior (Kef, Kasserine). In fact, it is there that the illiteracy rate is highest, that one finds a high proportion of unemployed, and so forth.

[3]Miss Julemont, who also helped me in the calculations. I thank her for her help and her dedication to her work.

[4]Kendall's rank order coefficient: 0.46. It increases to 0.61 if Monastir is excluded. Monastir raises particular problems: with 4.3 living children, wives want 1.2 additional children. Only 43% said they want no more (age group 30–39).

children increases. In the same age group (30–39)[5] positive correlations are found between number of children born alive, or number of living children, and socioeconomic factors such as occupation of husband, school attendance, or total monthly income (non-monetary income included). At the same time, if one adds to the number of living children, the number of additional ones still wanted, it is clear that the ultimate differentials in completed family size would be very

TABLE 1

MARITAL FERTILITY AND DESIRED FAMILY SIZE

	WIFE'S AGE	
	Up to 30 Years	30–39 Years
Median age..........................	25	34.5
Number of pregnancies (mean)........	3.5	7.1
Number of live births (mean).........	2.7	5.9
Number of living children (mean).....	2.3	4.7
Survival coefficient[a]................	0.84	0.79
Wives who want no more children (per cent).............................	34	72
Number of additional children wife wants (mean).....................	1.5	0.6
Number of additional children husband wants (wife's report) (mean)........	1.7	0.8
Desired family size.................	3.6	4.0
Ideal number of children............	4.1	4.3
Wives desiring 5 or more children (per cent).............................	16	28
Ideal: 5 or more....................	17	26

[a] Number of living children divided by number of live births.

small (Table 2, cols. 5 and 9). These data are rough, but if such correlations are confirmed, and if they persist, family size might exhibit little tendency to decrease in the near future, in the absence of special action programs.

DESIRED FAMILY SIZE

It has to be said at once that our questions on desired family size did not seem to be meaningless to the interviewed women. Only 4.5% could not give a precise answer to the question on ideal family size; and only 5% could not answer the more hypothetical, abstract question on desired family size.

Ideal family size, as expressed by the interviewees, is smaller than

[5]We shall here concentrate on this age group. For the younger group, more detailed data are needed, especially by marriage duration.

the family they have at present, 4.3 against 4.7.[6] If the additional children the wife still wants to have are added to the present number of living children, offspring would amount to 5.3 (ignoring future mortality).

Wives think their husbands want slightly more children than they themselves want. This probably is related to cultural traits. High

TABLE 2

ADDITIONAL CHILDREN WANTED, BY AGE OF WIFE, NUMBER OF CHILDREN BORN ALIVE, LIVING CHILDREN, AND SELECTED SOCIOECONOMIC CHARACTERISTICS

SOCIOECONOMIC CHARACTERISTIC	UP TO 30 YEARS				30–39 YEARS			
	Born Alive	Liv-ing	Additional Children Wanted	Children Wanted plus Number Living	Born Alive	Liv-ing	Additional Children Wanted	Children Wanted plus Number Living
(1)	(2)	(3)	(4)	(5)	(6)	(7)	(8)	(9)
Occupation of husband:								
Clerical.............	2.6	2.3	1.3	3.6	6.3	5.3	0.2	5.5
Shopkeeper.........	....	....	....	....	....	....	....	....
Handicraft.........	3.1	2.4	1.4	3.8	5.9	4.7	0.6	5.3
Manual worker......	2.7	2.3	1.6	3.9	5.8	4.9	0.5	5.4
Unemployed........	3.0	2.4	1.5	3.9	5.3	3.9	0.8	4.7
Farmer............	2.7	2.2	1.6	3.8	5.8	4.2	0.6	4.8
Agricultural worker..	1.9	1.7	1.5	3.2	5.3	3.9	0.8	4.7
School attendance of husband:								
None..............	3.0	2.4	1.6	4.0	5.9	4.6	0.6	5.2
Traditional........	2.9	2.4	1.4	3.8	5.9	4.7	0.5	5.2
Primary............	2.4	2.1	1.4	3.5	6.1	4.8	0.5	5.3
Higher.............	2.2	2.1	1.3	3.4	5.6	4.9	0.4	5.3
Total income (monthly)								
Less than 10 dinars..	2.6	2.0	1.7	3.7	5.6	3.9	0.9	4.8
10–19 dinars.......	2.7	2.2	1.7	3.9	5.7	4.5	0.7	5.2
20–29 dinars.......	2.7	2.3	1.5	3.8	6.0	4.7	0.4	5.1
30 or more dinars...	2.8	2.6	1.3	3.9	6.8	5.7	0.3	6.0

fertility is praised; it is necessary to have the first child as soon as possible after marriage. This general emphasis, eventually associated with penalties,[7] leads the wife to understand that her main role is to produce offspring, and possibly to think that "others" want her to produce more children than she herself would wish. Nevertheless, 72% of the wives (aged 30–39) want no more children; 64% think their husbands feel the same.

[6] The Tunisian government, in some respects, implicitly supports a norm of 4 children. For instance, for workers who are entitled to receive family allowances, payments are made only for the first 4 children.

[7] Repudiation was to follow if too long a delay appeared between marriage and the first pregnancy. The Tunisian government has made it more difficult to obtain a divorce.

TABLE 3

WIVES WANTING OR NOT WANTING ADDITIONAL CHILDREN,
BY NUMBER OF LIVING CHILDREN AND AGE OF WIFE
(UNWEIGHTED SUM FOR NINE CENTERS)

NUMBER OF LIVING CHILDREN	AGE OF WIFE				TOTAL
	Up to 25	25–29	30–34	35–39	
Per Cent Wanting Additional Children[a]					
0.............	93	97	96	95	94
1.............	88	90	93	75	88
2.............	72	67	80	68	71
3.............	60	53	44	61	53
4.............	28	29	23	31	27
5.............	11	31	19	10	19
6 or more......	0	13	6	5	6
Total........	76	54	33	24	48
Per Cent Not Wanting Additional Children[a]					
0.............	1	0	4	0	1
1.............	10	3	7	20	9
2.............	23	32	20	32	26
3.............	38	44	53	36	44
4.............	69	63	75	63	68
5.............	89	67	79	86	79
6 or more......	100	88	91	95	92
Total........	20	43	65	73	49
Number of Cases Involved					
0.............	121	62	25	19	227
1.............	188	62	28	20	298
2.............	127	89	40	25	282
3.............	79	122	80	31	312
4.............	39	89	107	59	294
5.............	9	64	102	71	246
6 or more......	2	56	140	199	397
Total........	565	544	522	424	2,056

[a] The proportion of women not answering the question or who answered "don't know" is not shown but may be computed by subtracting percentages wanting and not wanting more children from 100.

It is interesting to examine the distribution, by number of living children, of the percentage of wives who want additional children (Table 3). Clearly, increased family size leads steadily to diminished interest in further childbearing. This distribution was established for nine centers (Ariana excepted). When data are properly weighted, only 13% of wives aged 30–39, with 4 or more living children, want additional children.

KNOWLEDGE AND PRACTICE OF FAMILY LIMITATION

The over-all percentage of wives who reported knowledge and practice (at any time) of any method of family limitation is 15.4%.[8] It is higher at Beja (24%), Sfax (23%), Bizerte (17%), and Monastir (16%); it is lower at Nabeul (11%), Tunis-Bellevue (8%), and Maktar (7%). The number of cases reported at Tozeur and El Djem is negligible. If these last two centers are excluded, 18% of the wives reported practice. Those who report knowledge, report practice at the same time.

Size of town alone does not explain the variation in these percentages; other factors are also at work. First, it is notable that the population at Tozeur and El Djem is older: the proportion of wives in the age group 30–39 is higher than that in the lower group. This situation is not found elsewhere. Probably this is the result of a net emigration. Moreover, in each age group, the proportion of husbands employed in agriculture is around 55%. Elsewhere, it is 5% or 6%.

It is in our second group (Group B: Tunis-Bellevue, Maktar, El Djem, Tozeur) that unemployment (including *chantiers de chomage*) is highest: 13% (7% in our Group A). At Tunis-Bellevue and Maktar, the proportion of manual workers is higher than elsewhere.

To summarize:

Group A: Prevalence of clerical workers (14%) and people working in trade (30%), as against 9% and 18% in Group B.
Group B: Prevalence of agriculture (El Djem–Tozeur) or of manual workers (53% at Tunis-Bellevue–Maktar, as against 41% in Group A) and unemployment.

At the same time, the level of income is lower in Group B, especially at Tozeur and El Djem (60% earn a monthly income of less than 10 dinars). The proportion of husbands who did not go to school is higher; so is the proportion of illiterate wives.

But everywhere, the situation in the younger groups is better: the improvement is continuous as far as men are concerned; it is more

[8]Before the new family planning program was started, the Tunisian government had made some contraceptives available to the population.

sudden for women. The situation is far from bright, but we have here a factor of importance, if a change in fertility is to be expected. Table 4 summarizes the pertinent data.

That young wives are beginning to receive some education is a testimony that there is some change in their social position.[9] I suspect that other signs point in the same direction. It seems to me (but I do not yet have on hand the data needed to prove or disprove this) that, in the younger generation, the difference in age between husband and wife is smaller. Slowly, the proportion of wives who are less subordinate seems to increase. But, of course, if there is a change, it is still slight,[10] and the traditional mores are widely prevalent.

For instance, the proportion of wives who stress the importance of having sons,[11] remains very high, in the younger groups as well. Only 11% state that they have no sex preference, and there is no variation from one age group to another.

All these factors have an immediate bearing on the practice of contraception. This is shown by Table 5, in which the reported practice of family limitation is classified by age of wife, group of centers (Tozeur and El Djem, where no cases were reported, are excluded), and several socioeconomic factors. Slight variations occur with age of wife. The over-all percentage is 18%; it is 14% for wives less than 25 years old, 19% for wives 25–29 years old; 20% for wives 30–35 years old, and 17% for the older group.[12]

As expected, the attempts to practice any method of family limitation are, as a rule, more numerous in the six "coastal" centers. In the centers of Group A, 31% of the clerical workers report use, and the highest proportion is in the lower age group (38%). For people engaged in trade and handicraft, we found 22%, and 16% for manual workers. Most unemployed did not try to limit their family size: only 8% report use of any method.

The amount of practice varies with income: it increases from 9% for the most disadvantaged, to 27% for people with a relatively high

[9]In some respects the Moslem woman always remains a minor: when a girl, she depends on her father, afterward on her husband, and later in life on her elder son.

[10]However, it is quite clear from our data that Tunisia is engaged in a most valuable effort in the educational field.

[11]The importance of having sons was ascertained by several questions, an approximate translation of which would read as follows: "Do you think you shall go and live with your elder son when you are older?" "Suppose you had only daughters. Would you have one more child hoping it is a son?" "Do you think it is more important to have sons than to have daughters?" As an index, we counted the number of answers: 18% gave three positive answers; 12%, none.

[12]If Tozeur and El Djem were included, the percentages would be respectively: 15% and 12; 17; 17; 14.

TABLE 4

SELECTED SOCIOECONOMIC CHARACTERISTICS: DISTRIBUTION (PER CENT) IN EACH AGE GROUP

SOCIOECONOMIC CHARACTERISTIC	AGE OF WIFE															
	Ten Centers				Coastal Centers				Interior				Bellevue–Maktar			
	Up to 25	25–29	30–34	35–39	Up to 25	25–29	30–34	35–39	Up to 25	25–29	30–34	35–39	Up to 25	25–29	30–34	35–39
Income (monthly):																
Less than 10 dinars...	21	18	26	29	13	10	19	20	38	33	39	43	28	24	19	28
10–19 dinars......	38	42	33	29	40	49	34	37	34	29	31	18	38	29	38	19
20–29 dinars......	21	20	19	19	21	19	20	18	19	21	16	22	22	28	25	27
30 or more dinars....	20	20	22	23	26	22	27	27	9	16	14	17	12	19	18	26
Education of husband:																
No school........	42	46	52	56	35	37	43	50	59	70	68	68	63	72	72	68
Traditional.......	15	17	17	14	14	19	18	11	17	14	15	20	15	15	13	17
Primary..........	36	32	28	26	42	39	35	34	20	14	14	11	19	10	12	13
Higher...........	7	5	3	4	9	5	4	5	(4)[a]	(2)	(3)	(1)	(3)	(3)	(3)	(x)[b]
Education of wife:																
None............	76	87	90	93	72	85	87	91	86	93	96	96	91	91	95	97
Some school.......	24	13	10	7	28	15	13	9	14	7	4	4	9	9	5	3

[a] Percentages in parentheses: number of cases too small.

[b] x: negligible.

TABLE 5

WIVES REPORTING USE OF ANY METHOD OF CONTRACEPTION

(Per Cent)

SOCIOECONOMIC CHARACTERISTIC	AGE OF WIFE							
	Coastal Centers				Bellevue–Maktar			
	Up to 25	25–29	30–34	35–39	Up to 25	25–29	30–34	35–39
Occupation of husband:								
Clerical.	38	26	31	30	3	29	31	(1)[a]
Shopkeeper.	. . . . .	. . . . .	. . . . .	. . . . .	. . . . .	. . . . .	. . . . .	. . . . .
Handicraft.	16	27	25	29	5	6	7	(11)
Manual worker.	10	21	20	14	6	10	9	2
Farmer.	(41)	(32)	(. . . . .)	(23)	. . . . .	. . . . .	. . . . .	. . . . .
Agricultural worker. .	(0)	(10)	(16)	(10)	. . . . .	. . . . .	. . . . .	. . . . .
Unemployed.	7	6	10	8	x[b]	1	8	1
Monthly income:								
Less than 10 dinars. .	5	6	9	13	x	x	0	6
10–19 dinars.	9	18	23	13	3	3	9	0
20–29 dinars.	15	32	28	15	1	7	5	15
30 or more dinars. . .	18	29	29	36	11	32	40	6
Education of husband:								
None.	6	16	13	14	4	5	6	4
Traditional.	18	23	24	23	2	13	9	0
Primary.	16	22	32	24	10	10	34	(4)
High.	35	45	31	55	x	x	x	x
Education of wife:								
None.	11	18	20	19	4	7	9	4
Some.	22	43	38	35	(12)	(41)	(65)	(48)
Household equipment:[c]								
0.	0	0	7	19	9	x	6	10
1.	8	12	13	3	x	0	10	10
2.	11	14	15	14	x	0	x	8
3.	5	13	17	14	3	8	11	0
4.	19	18	29	17	x	24	9	0
5.	2	33	26	17	(0)	(11)	(17)	(21)
6 or more.	28	39	34	47	(19)	(45)	(35)	(2)
Exposure to mass media:[d]								
Husband:								
0.	7	8	15	11	3	x	3	4
1.	8	26	12	14	3	4	10	10
2.	11	21	34	23	(1)	24	9	0
3.	24	37	35	42	10	32	45	(2)
Wife:								
0.	11	7	19	10	4	2	5	3
1.	7	21	33	16	x	8	11	8
2.	16	30	27	39	16	37	22	(1)
3.	27	53	45	54	x	x	x	x
Organization of family:								
Nuclear.	15	35	20	19	5	10	13	4
Couple with former generation.	16	23	19	29	5	6	18	13
Other.	6	20	23	17	0	5	x	(0)
Importance of son:[e]								
3 yes.	9	6	15	14	5	3	4	0
2 or 1 yes.	11	23	21	18	2	11	12	7
0.	31	34	34	36	(23)	(27)	(33)	(14)

[a] Percentages in parentheses: number of cases too small.   [b] x: negligible.

[c] Number of modern objects owned or elements of comfort.

[d] Exposure to none, one, two, or three mass media (newspaper, radio, cinema).

[e] As ascertained by three questions. Positive answers stress the importance of the son.

income (30 dinars or more). (At Bellevue–Maktar, it increases to 22% in the group with a high income.) At the same time, it increases with literacy of husband: 12% report practice among those whose husbands did not attend school at all, but 36% among those whose husbands went to a secondary or superior school. (At Bellevue–Maktar, 28% for this last group.) Of the wives who did not go to school, 16% report practice, as against 32% of those who went to school. (At Bellevue–Maktar, 44% in the last group.)

Household equipment is a correlate of socioeconomic status.[13] Among couples who have none of the objects cited, few report attempts to practice any method. Typically 10%–15% of those having 1 to 3 of the listed items of equipment report practice of contraception. As the number of items of household equipment increases above 3, reported practice of contraception increases.

Wives were asked about exposure to mass media: if they had a radio; if they read (or heard) regularly a newspaper and went to the pictures. The same questions were asked the husband. Practice is more widespread among those exposed to these three media (but few wives have access to the three).

Diffusion of contraception is lowest among couples living in large families; 15% in Group A and practically negligible in Bellevue–Maktar. If the importance of having sons is an index of traditionalism, wives who stick to tradition are less prone to adopt family limitation: 11% in Group A, 3% at Bellevue–Maktar, as against 33% and 25%, respectively, if they play down the importance of sons.

ATTITUDES TOWARD FAMILY PLANNING

Despite this relatively low degree of practice, and its low effectiveness, a large proportion of respondents say they are interested in knowing about methods of family limitation and state they would make use of them. In Table 6 the proportions of interested respondents are noted, for every socioeconomic factor examined, and for two age groups of wives. In general, the centers of Group B show less interest, and, in this group, Tunis-Bellevue and Maktar still less (see, as an extreme example, the figures for "organization of family"). It will be remembered that the educational level is higher in Tozeur and El Djem.

Table 7 shows that interest in methods of family limitation increases with number of living children, especially when the wife wants no more children (bottom panel of table).

[13]Interviewees were asked if they owned radio, watch, bicycle (or other modern means of transportation), iron, icebox, and if their house had running water, electricity, and private toilet.

TABLE 6

WIVES WHO SAID THEY WOULD MAKE USE OF CONTRACEPTIVE MEANS
(Per Cent)

SOCIOECONOMIC CHARACTERISTIC	AGE OF WIFE					
	Coastal Centers		Interior		Bellevue–Maktar	
	Up to 30	30–39	Up to 30	30–39	Up to 30	30–39
Occupation of husband:						
Clerical.........	71	75	68	87	63	84
Shopkeeper, Handicraft....	67	75	56	69	56	64
Manual worker...	68	80	64	66	60	65
Farmer..........	....	....	57	92	....	....
Agricultural worker........	....	....	68	71	....	....
Unemployed.....	83	91	63	59	60	69
Monthly income:						
Less than 10 dinars........	76	71	58	70	52	55
10–19 dinars.....	71	74	59	65	57	63
20–29 dinars.....	69	85	72	68	75	63
30 or more dinars.	68	80	78	81	75	79
Education of husband:						
None...........	74	79	60	68	56	63
Traditional......	61	70	71	77	69	68
Primary.........	70	80	66	72	76	75
Higher..........	86	80	79	80	79	80
Education of wife:						
None...........	71	64	64	71	63	65
Some...........	74	81	59	89	60	81
Household equipment:						
0..............	67	76	49	58	42	45
1..............	75	78	67	75	66	65
2..............	69	69	71	86	74	82
3..............	68	75	73	69	75	62
4..............	74	86	65	71	60	72
5..............	74	80	45	79	56	72
6 or more.......	74	82	73	73	71	69
Exposure to mass media:						
Husband:						
0.............	66	82	59	70	55	60
1.............	73	75	69	73	70	76
2.............	71	75	68	83	65	79
3.............	68	82	64	73	64	65
Wife:						
0.............	69	80	60	69	57	60
1.............	76	75	68	73	63	71
2.............	72	84	63	74	60	55
3.............	66	76	69	84	70	94
Organization of family:						
Nuclear........	74	79	64	75	58	70
Couple with former generation..........	68	79	71	74	75	69
Other..........	73	77	35	47	27	48
Importance of son:						
3 yes...........	70	73	47	58	45	59
2 or 1 yes.......	71	79	65	74	61	68
0..............	81	85	79	70	75	69

TABLE 7

DISTRIBUTION OF RESPONDENTS BY WILLINGNESS TO USE FAMILY LIMITATION METHODS[a]

(Per Cent)

WILLINGNESS	NUMBER OF LIVING CHILDREN							
	0	1	2	3	4	5	6 or More	Total
Among Wives Wanting Additional Children								
Both husband and wife willing.	28	55	55	64	64	54	57	52
Wife only willing............	3	10	5	10	6	15	7	7
Neither willing.............	69	35	40	26	30	31	36	41
Total...................	100	100	100	100	100	100	100	100
Number of respondents.....	222	274	207	171	81	48	28	1,031
Among Wives Not Wanting Additional Children								
Both husband and wife willing..	50	71	76	81	85	86	83	83
Wife only willing.............	....	11	13	10	10	9	9	10
Neither willing.............	50	18	11	10	5	5	8	7
Total...................	100	100	100	100	100	100	100	100
Number of respondents.....	2	28	79	147	219	210	393	1,078

[a] Three per cent of the respondents (66) do not fall into either of the two categories shown. They either failed to answer the question on wanting additional children or else answered "don't know."

TABLE 8

COUPLES WITH BOTH HUSBAND AND WIFE WILLING TO USE FAMILY LIMITATION METHODS, BY NUMBER OF LIVING CHILDREN, AND WIVES WANTING ADDITIONAL CHILDREN AMONG SUCH COUPLES[a]

	NUMBER OF LIVING CHILDREN							
	0	1	2	3	4	5	6 or More	Total
Willing (per cent)............	29	57	60	72	80	80	81	68
Number of respondents.......	224	302	286	318	300	258	421	2,109
Wives wanting more children, among those willing (per cent)	99	90	65	50	22	12	5	37
Number of respondents.......	64	171	173	229	239	207	343	1,426

[a] The table omits the same 66 respondents (3% of total) omitted in Table 7.

The proportion willing to use methods of family limitation rises rapidly with number of living children, to 80% with four or more (Table 8). Among those who are willing, the proportion wanting more children decreases sharply with number of living children. Table 3, however, shows much the same decrease among all women.

To sum up, when data are properly weighted, *wives with four or more living children* represent 62% of the entire interviewed group. Among them, 70% have the number of children they want and both husband and wife are willing to make use of a family limitation method. Ten per cent want more children (but husband and wife would both approve family limitation). Nine per cent of the wives state they would make use of contraceptive means, if available, but that their husbands would object. In only 11% of the cases do both husband and wife reject these methods and refuse to make use of them. Thus wives with four or more living children seem to represent an important ready segment of the population.

This is only a first sketch. But from it emerges the fact that a substantial core of the Tunisian couples are concerned with the size of their families and that they offer good prospects for action in the experiment now underway.

48

FAMILY FORMATION AND LIMITATION IN GHANA: A STUDY OF THE RESIDENTS OF ECONOMICALLY SUPERIOR URBAN AREAS

JOHN C. CALDWELL
Demographic Department, The Australian National University

INTRODUCTION

Between 1962 and 1964 eight demographic field surveys were carried out as part of the Population Council Demography Program at the University of Ghana. Six of these formed an integrated effort to understand aspects of family formation and of possible change in that formation.[1] Conjugal biographies were constructed so that a knowledge could be achieved of unstable and polygamous marriage and conjugal partnerships with a view to applying to West African society analytic techniques developed elsewhere. A survey of rural population investigated attitudes toward family size. Two more specialized studies sought information on the relationships between family size and assistance for aged parents and the effect of extended family obligations in reducing economic gains to be achieved by limiting the size of the nuclear family. An inquiry was made into the quality of the birth registration data available from the special registration areas. At the same time a survey was made of family formation and family

[1]All these surveys plus two others on rural-urban and international migration were financed by the Population Council. The facilities of the University of Ghana and the Australian National University have been used for the work and its analysis. Many of the general findings, without technical detail, will shortly be published in the "population" volume of the *Social and Economic Survey of Ghana*, ed. W. E. Birmingham, I. Neustadt, and E. N. Omaboe (London: Allen & Unwin).

planning among the urban elite. The last is the principal subject of this report.

The analysis of the 1960 population census data in conjunction with survey findings[2] had shown that population pressures might well be making themselves felt both in the country as a whole and within individual families. The total fertility rate averages about 7.3, while the estimated crude birth and death rates of just over 50 and 20 per thousand, respectively, yield a natural increase of at least 3% per annum. In fact, if both the 1948 and 1960 censuses are taken to be accurate, the average annual rate of population growth during the intercensal period was 4.2%, and, subtracting the increase attributable directly or indirectly to immigration, the rate of natural increase was about 3.5%. When deficiencies in the 1948 enumeration are taken into account, the true figures are estimated to be just over 3.5% for population growth and slightly under 3% for natural increase.

Despite the very high birth rates in Ghana the surveys revealed that by the early 1960's economic and social development had wrought such fundamental changes in the traditional society that over two-fifths of the respondents in the rural areas of southern Ghana disagreed with the flat assertion that "it is a good thing for people to have a lot of children." Even in the more traditional north almost one-fifth fell into this category. Furthermore, the problems of the large family were seen mainly in terms of economic strain. Over two-thirds of the respondents in the south and one-half in the north claimed that numerous children made the parents poorer. This has not always been the case, and it still is not in most subsistence farming areas. The change has been partly a product of the penetration of the cash economy and has been accelerated very greatly by the attempt to introduce universal schooling. Thus, four-fifths of southern rural parents and two-thirds of northern ones said that children aged 10–14 attending day school could not earn their keep. For children who did not go to school the proportions were one-half and one-quarter, respectively. This helps to explain the fact that only 10% of the rural parents in the south averred that large families were a good economic proposition as compared with 40% in the north, where mass schooling is not yet really underway.

Thus, even among the three-quarters of Ghanaians who still live a rural way of life, some pressures arising from the raising of a large family are already being felt. Almost a quarter of the respondents in the south and not much less than a tenth in the north advised an ideal family size of less than five children. Most respondents had heard that

[2]Reference to such analysis here and elsewhere in the paper is to the author's contribution to the *Social and Economic Survey of Ghana*.

some women attempted to prevent conception or produce abortion. In the south over a fifth of the respondents were prepared to state their approval of such actions in certain circumstances, although the proportion fell almost to a fortieth in the north. On the other hand, everywhere only about half of all respondents were willing to assert unqualified disapproval of such actions.

Ghana is, therefore, a society in social transition. There seemed at first to be a case for organizing a nationwide investigation into family change and the demand for family limitation, carried out at much greater depth than had been the case in the rural survey. The time will soon come when such a study will be highly desirable. But investment of major effort in such a venture now would ignore what is known about social change in Ghana and many other parts of tropical Africa. In the past century economic and social modernization has flowed into the country through the coastal ports and towns and has first affected the most urbanized and educated groups within the country. It is reasonable to assume that family planning will not become established among the rural population until it is already practiced in the towns and will probably not be in much demand among the poor until the economically and educationally better endowed have accepted it. Subsequently, the practice will probably spread quite rapidly, for rural-urban and occupational mobility are astonishingly great in Ghana. There is continual movement from the countryside to the larger towns and back again, and consequently every village possesses its proportion of residents who are keen to exhibit aspects of town life.[3] Similarly, occupational advancement has often been so rapid in recent years, and socioeconomic class divisions so fluid, that most educated and wealthier people have close relatives among the urban and rural poor. In these circumstances it was decided that the most fruitful inquiry would be one confined to the higher socioeconomic groups in those parts of the country where a genuinely urban way of life had developed.

SURVEY OF POPULATION ATTITUDES IN ECONOMICALLY SUPERIOR URBAN AREAS

In terms of present-day size, a considerable history as a large center, and the development of town traditions, perhaps only four of Ghana's

[3]The rural-urban migration survey showed that of all persons in Ghana regarded as belonging to rural households (whether actually there or in the towns at the time of the survey) only half rarely or never visited a large town. Those living semipermanently in the towns numbered 9%; those temporarily in the towns, 2%; those temporarily back in the villages from the towns, 6%; and those temporarily back in the villages after living in the towns, 8%. Almost a quarter visited large towns fairly frequently.

towns can be regarded as generating a true urban way of life. They are Accra, Kumasi, Takoradi-Sekondi, and Cape Coast. In 1960 the combined population of these four towns was just over three-quarters of a million, or about one-ninth of the population of the country. During 1963 we determined by inspection a position on a socio-economic scale for each of the suburbs of these towns, based mainly on the quality of the residences and sample surveys of the occupations and education of the householders. In Ghana's towns there is a pro-nounced relationship between socioeconomic status and housing and also between the former and education. When detailed statistics became available from the 1960 census, it was found that all occupa-tional and educational indices that could be constructed from these data confirmed our selection of the suburbs of higher socioeconomic status. These suburbs housed 36% of the population of the four towns at the time of the 1960 census. Within many of them, individual small areas or even single blocks of substandard housing were eliminated by inspection, thus reducing the population of the areas to be examined by about one-third. The final surveyed area contained about 185,000 inhabitants at the time of the 1960 census, making up approximately one-quarter of the population of the four towns and about 2.75% of that of the whole country.

The whole population of this area did not make up the universe of the inquiry, for preliminary trial surveys had shown that large num-bers of poorer persons live in upper-class households and residential areas, some as servants and some residing with wealthier relatives. Upper-class houses sometimes contain sub-tenants of lower socio-economic position. Thus, it was decided that the only way of confin-ing the survey to the upper socioeconomic groups was to include as respondents only the householders (i.e., the owners, lessees, or renters) of the houses. We had estimated that there were between nine and ten thousand houses in the survey area, and hence a sampling ratio of one house in thirty would yield somewhat more than three hundred interviews. In the absence of a complete house list, a systematic sample was organized along selected interviewing routes which gave each house the same chance of selection. The respondents in the survey will sometimes be described in this paper as the "urban elite." Strictly speaking, all that is meant by this is that their living conditions, as measured by type and place, are the most superior in urban Ghana.

We wished to interview both wives and husbands, but at the same time full and intimate answers were desired. Preliminary testing showed that the formal organization needed to secure interviews with both spouses created a degree of suspicion that jeopardized the whole undertaking. The existence of polygamy and unstable marriage posed further problems. Rather reluctantly, we decided to undertake two separate unconnected surveys, one of females and the other of males. The areas surveyed were identical, although quite different systematic samples were constructed. The interviewing schedules differed only in a few small points. In the survey of females, only married women between 15 and 44 years of age were interviewed. If the householder's wife were not of this age, another house was substituted according to a formula. In fact surprisingly few substitutions were necessary. With the polygamous marriages where both wives lived under the same roof, it was found necessary, in order not to arouse ill feeling, to interview the first wife to present herself. In the survey of males, interviews were held only with males who had wives, or senior wives in the polygamous marriages, between 15 and 44 years of age. All respondents had to be Africans. The substitution scheme was also to be used in cases of refusal to be interviewed, but most interviewers did not have to use it, although several visits were sometimes necessary before a suitable interviewing time was found.

One advantage of the two surveys was that they served as a check on each other, and in fact there were no cases of significant differences between the two surveys with regard to information of the type which would be expected not to vary between the sexes. There was a difference in the number of interviews, a discrepancy arising largely out of two errors in interpreting the limits of the survey areas. Thus the female survey consisted of 331 interviews and the male one of 296 interviews.

One might well ask what the probable size of this elite group is in the whole country. Taking the female survey, it may be noted that 331 interviews with a sampling ratio of 1 in 30 suggests a universe of about 10,000. This number would be raised by polygamous marriages to somewhere between 10,000 and 11,000, depending on how many of the other wives lived under the same roof. This represents about three-quarters of 1% of females, aged 15–44, in the country, and about 1% of those currently married and living with their spouses.[4] But, of course, there are more females of a social type similar to the elite group who were not included in the survey universe. Some lived as sub-tenants within the houses of the survey area, some lived in poorer areas or in smaller towns or even as teachers or wives of administrators in rural areas. No sound estimate is possible of their numbers or of precisely who is qualified for inclusion among the group most affected by social change, for some have obviously lived in less wealthy surroundings and others in areas of less urban sophistication. It is instructive to note

[4]Estimates of proportions married by age are drawn from the research program's conjugal biographies project.

that the survey universe contained only one-half as many females who had been to a university as the 1960 census had enumerated in the whole country. Since 1960 the number of graduates in the country had grown markedly, but this may be offset by the considerable number of non-African female graduates in the country. Taking into account all these qualifications, it would still be safe to say that probably at least twice as many women in the country have thoughts and experiences similar to the women in the survey universe. Their total number would exceed 20,000 or 2% of those females between 15 and 44 who currently are married and living with their spouses.

The survey sought a wide variety of information about changing social relations with particular reference to the family. Questions about family planning formed only a small part of the whole study, and the answers to the family planning questions can be fully understood only in the larger context. Nevertheless, in this paper the focus will be restricted to matters pertinent to family planning and only the salient points will be summarized.

CHARACTERISTICS OF THE URBAN ELITE

The reactions of the urban elite to the possibilities of family planning will depend to a considerable extent upon who constitute this group. That its members do not represent a cross section of the Ghanaian community is perhaps shown best by its educational and religious composition. What might in more temperate climates be called "white collar" jobs are in Ghana found increasingly only in government employ and to a very large extent require educational qualifications. Thus, all but 1.3% of male respondents had been to school and over half had at least some secondary education or its equivalent. Educational standards among wives were also high, so disproving the persistent myth that highly educated Ghanaian males prefer simple, uneducated wives. One-sixth of the female respondents had either had no schooling or refused to answer the question, but over a third had some secondary education or its equivalent. This was in a country where at the time of the 1960 census fewer than a tenth of all females between 15 and 54 years of age had ever been to school and fewer than 1 in every 150 had any secondary education or its equivalent.

The religious breakdown of the respondents was even more revealing. Although in Ghana as a whole adherents of traditional religions and Islam make up half the population and Catholics constitute the largest single Christian denomination, no males and only one female in the survey gave their religion as traditional, two males and one female stated that they were Moslems, and only one in nine claimed to be Catholics. Over three-quarters returned themselves as Protestants and a further 7% as just Christian. The numbers failing to answer or stating that they adhered to no religion were very small. The overwhelmingly Christian nature of the urban elite can be explained simply enough. They hold positions which require the education which for long was provided either by mission schools or often by government schools which assumed that they were Christian but non-sectarian. Thus the urban elite in Ghana are in the main reasonably well-educated Protestants. The number with little education was usually so small that answers to questions in the schedule could hardly be meaningfully analyzed in terms of their replies. Indeed, often there were so few Catholics in various categories that it was difficult to seek for significant differences between their answers and those of the Protestants.

Other characteristics of the sample can be briefly summarized. The average age at first marriage had been 21 years for females and 26 years for males. The age difference between spouses was about 7 years, the apparent discrepancy here being explained by polygamous marriages and subsequent marriages. About three-quarters of the marriages were first marriages and about five-sixths of them were monogamous. Even in the case of polygamous marriages, most contained only two wives. The great majority of respondents resided permanently with their spouses. The mortality which had been experienced by the children of the respondents was not much above the average obtained in economically developed countries. Thus, in many ways the urban elite were far more "Westernized" than most of their fellow countrymen.

Almost three-quarters of the husbands' jobs were professional, technical, administrative, executive, or teaching. Among the wives, one-third were full-time housewives and almost another third were employed in teaching, clerical, or technical capacities. Less than one in six was engaged in small-scale retailing, by far the most important occupation of urban women. Fewer than a third of the respondents had been born in the four large centers being surveyed, which in fact had been very much smaller when they were born. About half came from villages and approximately two-fifths were born of farming parents. In contrast, probably well over nine-tenths of all Ghanaian population of this age came from farming stock.

THE FAMILY

The families surveyed were a relatively new phenomenon in Ghana and most were aware of the fact. Only a sixth of the respondents saw no difference between their families' ways of life and that traditionally experienced in the country. Those who did see differences described them mostly in terms of the increased importance of the nuclear family, citing the affection and attention given to its members or money spent on them. About half the families had no one else living with them but the nuclear family. Over a third of all wives were taken out socially by their husbands at least once a week, and over a quarter of the parents took their children out at least once a month. In fact, when a rather extreme description of a "Westernized family"—monogamous, stable, family- and even child-centered—was read to them, two-fifths of the respondents asserted that there were no shortcomings in such a system, while only one in twenty could find nothing to praise. A quarter of the respondents specifically remarked that one of the virtues of such a system was in its assistance to children's development. More change is expected. Over half the respondents felt that Ghanaian society would have to come to accept unmarried adult females as part of their society. Nevertheless, many aspects of older Ghanaian society remain, even if in a lower key. Only 28% of wives are fully supported economically by their husbands. The rest contribute something to their own support and that of their children.

Family Size and Pregnancy

There is evidence in Ghana of an urban-rural fertility differential, although, in view of the continued importance of rural-urban migration in building town population, some of this may spring from a tendency of the less fertile to move to the urban areas. Completed fertility in the whole country probably averages about 7.3 children per female,[5] but that of urban areas is about 8% below the national average or 10% below that obtaining in rural areas. In southern Ghana large towns exhibit fertility levels about one-eighth below that of the surrounding regions.

There was no evidence from the survey that female respondents experienced fertility below the average of all females within the four towns. However, it is possible that the respondents showed more than average care in reporting deceased children and that this covered a small differential. Even without this proviso, the urban elite under 30 years of age appear to be slightly less fertile, and this may be an indication of changes in process. The oldest female respondents averaged about 6.3 children. The male average was somewhat higher because of polygamy, and will be higher still when all the wives of polygamous

[5] For this analysis and that immediately following, see the author's contribution to the *Social and Economic Survey of Ghana*, cited in n. 1.

males have completed their reproductive span. Apart from age, the only characteristic of the respondents which showed significant differences in fertility was that of education. Among both female and male respondents, parents with secondary school or higher education exhibited fertility levels of only about 90% of those with less education. It will be seen later that they are much more likely to be practicing contraception. There were no fertility differentials by religion.

Family size is now considerably greater than desired family size. Even computed by adding the number of extra children still wanted to those already possessed by respondents, the average desired is only about five. The average number which would be recommended to a friend or a daughter or son just getting married is 4.5. Interestingly

TABLE 1

PREGNANCY CONDITIONS AND ATTITUDES[a]

(Per Cent)

	Female Survey	Male Survey
Now pregnant...................	17	21
Favorable to pregnancy.........	15	18
Not favorable................	1	3
Not now pregnant..............	78	72
Favorable to non-pregnancy.....	44	41
Not favorable................	28	26
Summary:		
Favoring pregnancy............	44	44
Not favoring pregnancy.........	45	44
No answer....................	11	12

[a] All percentages are of total respondents in each survey. Residual percentages are no-answers. Pregnancy figures in male survey refer to any wife pregnant in polygamous marriages.

enough, the males almost invariably assumed that the male friend or son would remain monogamously married. Even more interesting is the fact that there is no association between the present size of family and recommended family size. Two-thirds of Ghanaians of the type surveyed want four or five children, and those who have many more or fewer do so because they cannot control events.

Table 1 presents an analysis of the pregnancy condition and the desire for pregnancy of female respondents and of the wives of male respondents at the time of the survey. The difference in the pregnancy proportions between the two surveys is explained by polygamous marriages. At any given time, one might expect to find half the wives or husbands among the urban elite favoring pregnancy and half opposed. However, among those favoring pregnancy, over a third of the cases were ones where pregnancy had already occurred and was cheerfully accepted. Very few, as yet, fail to accept pregnancy with equanimity. Where pregnancy had not occurred, almost three-fifths hoped that it would not do so at least in the near future. This, then, is a measure of the potential demand for family planning. At any given time, about 45% of wives are not pregnant and do not desire to become so. In some cases they may just have borne a baby. But it would be safe to say that well over a third of the wives might at the time of the survey have accepted advice on how to postpone pregnancy, if they felt such advice to be acceptable morally, aesthetically, and physically.

TABLE 2

FAMILY PLANNING—COMMUNICATION AND KNOWLEDGE[a]

COMMUNICATION AND KNOWLEDGE	FEMALE SURVEY ($n=331$)		MALE SURVEY ($n=296$)	
	Number	Per Cent	Number	Per Cent
Respondents who have discussed with their spouses the best number of children to have....	219	66	213	72
Respondents who believe that some people can plan their families' size.....................	203	61	206	70
Respondents knowing method of preventing pregnancy...................................	172	52	163	55
Respondents with a knowledge of modern contraceptives.................................	159	48	128	43
Respondents who have discussed family planning with their spouses........................	138	42	127	43
All respondents who believe that they could discuss family planning with their spouses........	257	78	241	81
Respondents who know someone who obtains contraceptive materials from doctors or chemists..	162	49	121	41

[a] All percentages are of total respondents in each survey.

FAMILY PLANNING—COMMUNICATION AND KNOWLEDGE

Necessary in most successful family planning is the willingness and ability of married couples to discuss the subject. The initial step, and one that usually implies at least a hope that family size may be limited to some figure, is talking about the desired number of children. This can mark the main breakthrough from traditional attitudes. It can be seen from Table 2 that such discussions had taken place among two-thirds or more of the urban elite couples. Of those who have not spoken on the matter, very few respondents thought that it would be difficult to do so. The amount of education received by the respondents was postitively related to the holding of such discussions, as was the existence of monogamous marriage. As might be expected, polygamous males tend to be traditionalists. A somewhat larger proportion of Protestants than Catholics had held such discussions, but the margin was insufficient to be significant even at the 5% level. Among male respondents a somewhat greater proportion of respondents with large families than with small families had held such discussions, but again the difference was not significant.

The next step in the break with tradition is the realization that some people can in fact control the size of their families and that such size is not always determined merely by the Will of God or a chance of Fate, using fate in a much stronger sense than contemporary Western society usually does. Table 2 shows that three-fifths of female respondents and seven-tenths of males do think that such control can be achieved. There has, of course, long been a European community in the four major towns, which has ostensibly achieved such control, although the clarity of the demonstration has been somewhat obscured by the practice of educating children abroad.

In fact, over half of the respondents in each survey claimed to know of some way of preventing conception, and nearly half knew something of modern contraceptives. Foam tablets, jellies, and condoms have for long been sold in pharmacies or department stores in each of the four towns. Originally the chief market was the British expatriate population, and it is believed that the public display of contraceptives for sale has declined since independence. Only one respondent mentioned knowledge of diaphragms, and she had not used one. Only four female respondents and no male respondents claimed to use traditional contraceptive medicines, and most obviously did not take the contraceptive claims of such concoctions very seriously. The survey established that only chemical or mechanical contraceptives are likely to be of any importance in limiting Ghanaian families for other methods of doing so do not find much favor in the culture. Twelve female and nineteen male respondents described rhythm methods, but of the twenty-seven who claimed to use such methods only two were Catholics. Coitus interruptus was used by only four respondents and continence by only eleven. Sterilization was described by ten respondents, none of whom had employed the method within their family.

The knowledge of a method of avoiding pregnancy was positively associated with the amount of education received by respondents. Among female respondents only, it was also significantly related to religion, Catholics being less likely to claim knowledge of a method, and to age, in that fewer wives under 25 years of age knew of any methods. Among males there was a positive association between such knowledge and urban origin, but among females the relationship failed to be significant at the 5% level.

Over two-fifths of the respondents in each survey had actually discussed family planning methods with their spouses. Almost twice as many thought that they could do so. African society is open and frank and does not readily produce gulfs between the sexes or other groupings which cannot be easily bridged by discussion. Of those who had held such discussions, the spouses saw eye to eye in nine-tenths of all cases. Of the fifth of all respondents who did not agree readily that they could discuss family planning with their spouses, most gave such explanations as "We don't discuss such things," "It has not occurred to me," or that the spouse would be hurt or would not listen.

A final test of the effectiveness of communication among this group

TABLE 3

THE PRACTICE OF FAMILY PLANNING[a]

RESPONDENTS' STATEMENTS	FEMALE SURVEY ($n = 331$)		MALE SURVEY ($n = 296$)	
	Number	Per Cent	Number	Per Cent
They had used a method to prevent pregnancy...	109	33	97	33
Their method for preventing pregnancy always worked successfully....................	72	22	62	21
They had used the method to postpone deliberately at least one pregnancy for more than two years.............................	15	5	27	9
They expected to use a method already known to them for preventing pregnancy in the future...	122	37	119	40
They had obtained contraceptive materials from doctors or chemists.....................	91	27	81	27
They were still obtaining contraceptive materials at the time of the survey.................	88	27	81	27
They intended to obtain contraceptive materials in the future............................	93	28	88	30

[a] All percentages are of total respondents in each survey.

was provided by asking respondents, irrespective of whether they were aware of any contraceptive methods, whether they knew anyone who actually obtained contraceptive materials from doctors or chemists. Almost half of all female respondents and two-fifths of male respondents did.

THE PRACTICE OF FAMILY PLANNING

Table 3 shows that one-third of all respondents in each survey claim to have used a method for preventing pregnancy. Among male respondents there is a positive association with education, but among the females the figures are suggestive but not significant. The only other characteristic related to the use of such a method is religion, but the correlation is not strong. It is significant at the 5% level in the female survey only because disproportionately more Catholics than Protestants claim to know of no methods, and in the male survey only among the older respondents.

No more than two-thirds of those who had used such methods said that they always worked. Thus, a fifth of all respondents in each survey claimed to be able successfully to use methods for preventing pregnancy. Only 15 females and 27 males, forming 5% and 9% of the surveys, respectively, asserted that they had successfully used such methods to postpone pregnancies for over two years. Thus, one should not make too extravagant claims for the use of contraceptive techniques among Ghana's urban elite. The main reason for failure is probably the widespread reliance on foam tablets. Although only a third of the respondents had already used a method for preventing pregnancy, around two-fifths expected to do so in the future.

Over a quarter of the respondents in each survey claimed to have bought contraceptive materials at some stage, and practically all of this group were still doing so at the time of the survey. The characteristic of respondents most clearly and positively related to the use of modern contraceptives was education. Only 23% of females with educational attainments lower than secondary school have used contraceptives compared with 41% of those more highly educated. The comparable figures for male respondents were 21% and 38% respectively. There were significant negative relationships with unstable marriage and polygamy. Thus, contraceptive users are more likely to be found among those participating in the least traditional form of marital union, stable and monogamous marriage.

Other correlations were less striking. In the case of males the association with urban birthplace was significant at the 0.1% level but among female respondents it just failed to be significant at the 5% level. Similarly, males born to farming parents were clearly less likely to employ contraceptives than those from non-agricultural origins, but the position among the female respondents was not so simple. Protestant females were significantly more likely to use contraceptives than were Catholic females, but a similar relationship did not hold among males. The husband's occupation was of some importance, but in Ghana this is fairly closely related to education anyway. Among males, whose views on public and private matters seemed to be more logically related than those of the female respondents, there was a close relationship between the use of contraceptives and apprehension about the high rate of population increase in the country.

Two characteristics, which might be expected to show some association with the use of contraceptives, failed to do so. They were the ages of the respondents and the number of children already born. The explanation is probably much the same for the two cases. With increasing age the proportion of more traditionally inclined respondents rises, but this is offset by the increasing pressures of larger families. Large families may exert more pressure upon some parents to find methods of birth control, but this cannot be detected statistically, because these same families contain a disproportionate number of fathers with traditional outlooks, partly because they are more likely to have been fathered by polygamous males than are the smaller families.

Therefore, the most likely couples to be using contraceptives are well-educated Protestants, born in urban areas, and participating in a stable, monogamous marriage. The chances are probably increased by the husband's being employed in a professional or administrative capacity.

INTEREST IN FAMILY PLANNING SERVICES

The actual use of contraceptives has probably been limited more by lack of knowledge than by anything else. Only 28% and 30% of the female and male respondents, respectively, were either using contraceptives or expected to do so. But these respondents formed something like two-thirds of all who knew anything about modern contraceptives. In the next part of the survey we attempted to assess the potential demand for birth control if the necessary knowledge could be provided.

Respondents were first asked if they would use a method for preventing pregnancy, or, if already using a method, a more effective one, if a doctor told them how to do it. Table 4 shows that over three-fifths of all female respondents and almost three-quarters of male respondents agreed that they would. However, when they were asked if they would still use such a method if it were complicated and took a lot of trouble, those assenting fell to 25% and 35%, respectively. Perhaps we alarmed them by overstressing the possible complexities. But the implication remains that the proportion of the surveyed community using family planning methods could be doubled from a third to two-thirds providing only that the methods employed were regarded as being fairly simple. Perhaps the foam tablets already used are so regarded and perhaps IUD's would also be. It is more doubtful whether oral contraceptives would qualify.

The nature of family planning clinics was explained to respondents, and they were then asked whether they favored their establishment in Ghana. Almost three-quarters of the female respondents and a slightly smaller proportion of the males stated that they would. Such agreement was not related to education received, as were the more difficult matters of actually learning about or using contraceptives. In fact the only characteristic significantly related to the answers given to this question was religion, and that was significant at the 5% level in the female survey alone. The setting-up of clinics was favored by 76% of Protestant females and 62% of Catholic females, and by 70% of Protestant males and 59% of Catholic males.

Respondents were then asked if they or their spouses, depending on the type of contraception employed, would use family planning clinics if these were established. Numbers assenting fell slightly from those recorded for the previous question. There were various reasons.

TABLE 4

INTEREST IN FAMILY PLANNING SERVICES[a]

RESPONDENTS' STATEMENTS	FEMALE SURVEY (n = 331)		MALE SURVEY (n = 296)	
	Number	Per Cent	Number	Per Cent
They would use a way (or a better way) for preventing pregnancy, if told how by a doctor.....	204	62	214	72
They would use a way (or a better way) for preventing pregnancy, if told by a doctor, even if the method were complicated and took quite a lot of trouble...............................	83	25	105	35
They favored the establishment of family planning clinics in Ghana......................	241	73	201	68
They would use family planning clinics, if established.......................................	210	63	199	67

[a] All percentages are of total respondents in each survey.

Some women were approaching the end of the reproductive span and did not expect to become pregnant again. Others were young and did not wish to prevent pregnancies in the foreseeable future. Still others were willing to agree to the establishment of institutions which they were not themselves prepared to use. Nevertheless, around two-thirds of all respondents would wish to use family planning clinics if they were established.

The willingness to use clinics was found in both surveys to be positively associated with the participation in discussions with spouses on the desirable number of children, the belief that family size can be controlled, the current use of contraceptives, and the approval of the establishment of clinics. It was also affected by town of residence. In the capital, Accra, with its more cosmopolitan atmosphere, and in the old capital, Cape Coast, with its long educational tradition, over three-quarters of the respondents in each survey were prepared to use clinics. But in Kumasi, the center of Ashanti, with its high-fertility tradition, and Takoradi-Sekondi, the fast-growing port area of the southwest, the proportions fell to below two-thirds.

Religion showed a significant association at the 5% level to replies only in the case of females over 30 years of age. Among the female respondents, 67% of Protestants and 57% of Catholics would use the clinics, while among the males the proportions were 68% and 59%, respectively. The only significant answers according to educational attainments were a greater disinclination to use clinics among the small group of wives who had never received any schooling. Among female respondents, willingness to use clinics was directly associated with their number of living children, as might be expected. However, among males the relationship, although significant, was an inverse one. This arose, as pointed out in similar circumstances before, because polygamous males tend to have more children. There is certainly a relation among males between adherence to the society's more traditional behavior patterns and reluctance to use family planning facilities. Such a relationship is statistically significant where traditionalism is measured by the practice of unstable marriage or polygamy. A similar relationship was not found among female respondents. It is apparently more a measure of traditionalism for a male to have many wives than it is for a female to be one of many wives. Willingness to use clinics was not associated in either survey with age, occupation, desired number of children, or optimum size of family advised.

A further measure of the strength of the desire for family planning was undertaken in the case of the quarter of female respondents and the third of male respondents who were willing to use even complicated and troublesome methods for preventing pregnancy. They were asked to state the maximum amount that they would be willing to spend per month on contraceptives. The median figures were somewhat over £1.10.0 and just under that amount for the female and male respondents, respectively. This can be compared with the cost of supporting an infant for a month, where the median estimates of these groups were about £2.10.0, and the cost of supporting a child of a few years of age, where the median estimates were around £4. If oral contraceptives could be marketed by family planning clinics for about £1 per month, all but one-sixth of the female respondents in this special group and all but one-eighth of the males say that they would be prepared to pay such an amount. Whether as many would in fact be willing to make outlays of £1 per month or £6 per half-year, if clinics charging such sums came into existence, is quite another matter. It might be noted that there is no evidence that this group is an atypically wealthy cross section of respondents, although there is, of course, evidence that they more strongly desire to prevent conception, and this may well be linked with willingness to pay more for contraception. However, it should be remembered that all respondents in the survey were economically far better off than most Ghanaians.

ABORTION AND STERILIZATION

Questions on abortion and sterilization were less comprehensive than had originally been planned. Modifications were made so as not to jeopardize co-operation in the other parts of the survey, after the government had announced that it intended to introduce heavy penalties for the practice of abortion.

The investigation of abortion was ultimately limited to inquiring whether it was common. Those replying yes made up 35% of female respondents and 45% of male respondents (Table 5). Apart from this sex difference, there were no significant differences in the answers of respondents by personal characteristics, although we had hypothesized that there might be, either by place of present residence or by place of origin.

TABLE 5

VIEWS ON ABORTION AND STERILIZATION[a]

RESPONDENTS' STATEMENTS	FEMALE SURVEY (n = 331)		MALE SURVEY (n = 296)	
	Number	Per Cent	Number	Per Cent
Abortion is common in Ghana..............	116	35	134	45
Ghanaians would favor the availability of sterilization..	124	37	113	38

[a] All percentages are of total respondents in each survey.

After explaining the meaning and implications of sterilization to those not already familiar with the concept, all respondents were asked whether they believed that Ghanaians would favor the availability of such measures. Over a third of the respondents in each survey thought that they would. The only significant association between a yes answer and any characteristic of the respondents was a positive one with education in the case of the female survey. The two most important reasons for replying no were, first, that the method was feared to be irrevocable and appeared to be unnecessary while other methods for preventing pregnancy were available and, second, that the respondents were apprehensive of the operation and felt that it might be dangerous. Very few indeed gave either religious reasons or ones involving the fear of impotence or reduced sexual ability.

THE TOTAL PICTURE

There is no reason to believe that a survey of family planning attitudes among Ghana's urban elite would produce radically different responses than would ones carried out in various other Commonwealth countries in tropical Africa. Admittedly, Ghana, in terms of national income per head, is relatively rich. Its proportion of educated persons is also unusually high, and already a quarter of its population lives in towns with more than 5,000 inhabitants. But these facts are merely indicators of stages in development, and all Commonwealth countries will reach and surpass them in time.

Most of these countries probably contain considerable numbers of urban elite resembling those described in Ghana. These people will be far better educated than most of the community and will have incomes to match their educational attainments. Most will probably be Christians, and perhaps in many of the countries a surprisingly high proportion will be Protestants. They will be members of a class which has undergone very great social change even in their own lifetimes. They will live in countries where it has long been legal for pharmacists and doctors to sell and distribute contraceptives. They will probably have been affected in their purchase and use of such materials by the example of the British colonial class who lived in their own community.

The desire to limit families and the demand for means to do so are likely to grow. Even in a comparatively wealthy African society, the experience of centralized government planning, especially in the field of health services, may channel such demands into pressure for the provision of state-run family planning clinics. Initially, most of the demand for services might be found among the residents of the economically better off suburbs of the towns. However, it is likely that some of these people would continue to purchase contraceptive supplies from pharmacies or doctors. Ultimately the demand from the poor and from the rural population, especially in southern Ghana, should prove more substantial merely because the numbers of such people are so much greater. It would appear that only half the urban elite, and doubtless only a very small fraction of the rest of the populace, would regard oral contraceptives as sufficiently simple to justify persisting with them.

The demand for services and the ability to cope with contraceptives is certainly going to increase. Both factors are positively related to educational levels, the change from traditional family structure, and urban background. All are undoubtedly on the increase. There are no major problems of communication between the spouses in tropical African society, and religious persuasion, at least within the Christian community, does not appear to be of marked importance.

At present the government is not encouraging the establishment of family planning clinics, but it is probable that no final and definite policy on the matter has yet evolved.

Finally, it might be noted, in the light of the impressive success in the last two decades of legalized abortion in reducing high birth rates in some parts of the world, that Ghanaian culture does not appear to be fundamentally opposed to either abortion or sterilization.

49

SOME MISCONCEPTIONS DISPROVED: A PRO-GRAM OF COMPARATIVE FERTILITY SURVEYS IN LATIN AMERICA

CARMEN A. MIRO
Director, Latin American Demographic Center

It has been persistently held in the past among certain sectors of opinion in Latin America, and even outside the region, that it was practically impossible to interview successfully a random sample of women in the general population to gather personal information regarding their reproductive history, their knowledge and use of contraceptives, and their attitudes toward the general subject of family limitation. The Program of Comparative Fertility Surveys, organized by the Latin American Demographic Center (CELADE) with the collaboration of the United Nations Population Branch and Cornell University and with financial support from the Population Council, disproves the validity of the former assertion. The preliminary results so far tabulated and analyzed also give sufficient ground to disavow other misconceptions regarding variables associated with fertility behavior.

BRIEF DESCRIPTION OF THE PROGRAM

The program is to be considered the first step in a co-ordinated effort to obtain in Latin America for different typical areas (rural, urban, and highly urbanized) as complete a picture as possible on: (*a*) levels and trends of fertility, cross-classified by certain demographic and socioeconomic characteristics; (*b*) attitudes and opinions toward desired family size and family planning, as well as certain socioeconomic factors associated with them; and (*c*) the use of con-

Views expressed in this paper are personal and do not necessarily reflect those of the United Nations.

traceptives, attitudes toward their use, and means of communicating about them.

Seven Latin American cities, taken as representative of highly urbanized areas, have been covered in this first phase. Care was exercised to include cities from countries in different stages of development, demographically and otherwise.

This led to the selection of the following cities: Bogotá, Buenos Aires, Caracas, Mexico City, Panama, Rio de Janeiro, and San José, which have the following different characteristics:

1. The three largest cities of the region (Buenos Aires, Mexico, and Rio de Janeiro), two medium-sized (Bogotá and Caracas), and two of the smallest ones (Panama and San José). (See Table 1.)
2. One city (Buenos Aires) belongs to a country quite advanced along the demographic transition, highly urbanized (57.5%),[1] while another (San José) is the capital of a country with one of the highest birth rates and only around 25% urbanized.
3. High, medium, and low levels of literacy, as reported by the surveys themselves. (See Table 1.)
4. The city with one of the most accelerated rates of urbanization in the recent past (Caracas).
5. Cities with an important percentage of foreigners (Caracas and Buenos Aires) and others where this proportion is insignificant (Bogotá and Mexico) (see Table 1), but where an important percentage of the population is of aboriginal descent.
6. Cities highly differentiated in marital status composition. (See Table 1.)
7. Societies with varying degrees of modernization and traditionalism (from Buenos Aires to Bogotá).

Surveys were to be conducted in the seven cities mentioned. In order to insure uniformity of procedures in sampling, content of the questionnaires, instructions to interviewers, interviewing techniques, and processing of the data collected, a workshop was convened at CELADE in July, 1963. This was attended by the national directors of the surveys who were, with one exception (Rio de Janeiro), former CELADE fellows. The Center's staff was responsible for the general organization of the workshop, preparation of a pilot survey in Santiago, and the adoption of the final plans for the execution of the surveys. The director of the International Population Program at Cornell and the assistant director of the United Nations Population Branch collaborated with CELADE in conducting the workshop.

It was agreed in principle that in each participating city a probability cluster sample of about 2,300 women 20–50 years of age of all marital statuses would be selected. This number was fixed assuming

[1]Places of 20,000 or more inhabitants are considered urban.

a loss of around 10%, which would leave at least 2,000 completed questionnaires, deemed representative in the various cities and a large enough number for the different cross-classifications planned. In practice, two cities, Mexico and Rio de Janeiro, selected a larger sample. The surveys were conducted between the end of 1963 and the end of 1964. With the exception of Rio de Janeiro, the loss through refusal, lack of contact, and other reasons in all seven cities was less than 10%. This remarkable result proves that it is possible to conduct interviews to obtain data up to now considered unobtainable. The figures thus far tabulated show that results are in general of good quality. More than 15,000 Latin American women residents of cities (see Table 1) answered more or less freely questions related to their reproductive history, their knowledge and use of contraceptives, and

TABLE 1

SOME PRELIMINARY RESULTS OF COMPARATIVE FERTILITY SURVEYS IN
SEVEN LATIN AMERICAN COUNTRIES, 1963–64

Item	Bogotá	Buenos Aires	Caracas	Mexico City	Panama	Rio de Janeiro	San José
Population (in thousands, around 1960)[a]	1,679	6,763	1,333	4,666	273	3,233	318
Number of women interviewed	2,259	2,136	2,087	2,353	2,222	2,152	2,132
Level of literacy (percentage of total):[b]							
University	2.0	6.5	3.5	5.6	9.5	2.8	6.5
Secondary	29.0	23.7	20.4	24.3	43.8	30.4	25.8
Primary	59.4	67.8	59.3	58.1	45.4	56.1	64.8
No education[c]	9.6	2.0	16.8	12.0	1.3	10.7	2.9
Place of birth (percentage of total):							
In the city	23.6	51.6	26.3	44.0	44.5	48.2	48.8
In another city	15.4	16.2	29.9	26.6	19.3	42.3	19.6
In town or rural area	59.9	15.9	24.6	27.6	30.0	3.4	26.8
Abroad	1.1	16.2	18.9	1.7	6.0	5.7	4.6
Not specified	....	0.1	0.3	0.1	0.2	0.4	0.2
Marital status (percentage of total):							
Single	19.2	19.7	16.1	19.8	17.2	19.2	24.8
Married	63.8	73.9	51.2	61.1	41.1	64.4	55.6
In common-law marriage	4.5	0.9	15.0	7.5	26.7	5.5	7.4
Separated from legal marriage	4.4	2.0	3.5	3.1	3.7	3.3	4.1
Separated from common-law marriage	3.9	0.5	7.9	3.7	8.1	0.4	4.6
Divorced	0.1	0.2	1.5	0.5	1.7	0.8	0.8
Widow from legal marriage	3.6	2.6	3.5	3.7	1.1	5.9	2.3
Widow from common-law marriage	0.5	0.2	1.2	0.6	0.4	0.1	0.4
Not specified	....	....	0.1	....	0.0[d]	0.4	....

[a] As cited by Carmen A. Miro, "La Población de America Latina en el siglo XX," document submitted to the Panamerican Conference on Population, Cali, Colombia, August, 1965.

[b] Refers to the proportion of women completing at least one grade of the indicated level.

[c] Includes "not specified."

[d] This figure is higher than 0, but lower than 0.05.

their attitudes and opinions toward family limitation. The lowest rate of refusal was recorded in Bogotá, precisely the city in which the least success was anticipated by many, because of the more traditional organization of society there.

Under the scheme adopted, each country is responsible for the publication of a report containing the findings of the national survey. A duplicate set of punch cards is to be furnished to CELADE and to Cornell University. The data examined here are based on the sets of cards provided to CELADE.

Some Preliminary Findings[2]

Level of fertility.—The results obtained give clear evidence of differential fertility (as measured by the average number of live births) across the seven cities and within the cities themselves among women of different demographic and socioeconomic characteristics.

Table 2 summarizes, in terms of average number of pregnancies, live births, stillbirths, and miscarriages, the reproductive history of the women interviewed in the seven cities. The figures refer to all and to ever-pregnant women, aggregating all ages.

There are several facts worth noting that relate to this table. In the first place the rate of abortion computed in relation to total pregnancies of ever-pregnant women ranges from 16% in Buenos Aires to about 9% in Bogotá. These rates are considerably lower than those found by Armijo and Monreal (31%)[3] for Santiago, Chile. While the results could reflect different situations, it is not difficult to accept the fact that there might have been some underreporting of this item, since no effort was made in the questionnaire to distinguish spontaneous from induced abortions. Therefore, many of the latter could have been omitted by the women for obvious reasons. The author is not familiar with any study undertaken among Latin American women with the intention of establishing what could be considered a "normal" rate of miscarriages. For other populations, rates fluctuating from 15% to 20% have been so considered. Since in general those recorded in the surveys are below this limit, it is difficult to state that the women of the cities under examination use abortion as a means of reducing their fertility. However, it is interesting to point out that the highest rates of abortion have been recorded in the two cities (Buenos Aires and Rio de Janeiro) with the lowest average number of live births.

[2]Based on the cards supplied by the countries, which are still subject to some internal checks.

[3]R. Armijo and T. Monreal, "Epidemiology of Provoked Abortion in Santiago, Chile," paper submitted to the Conference of the International Planned Parenthood Federation, Puerto Rico, April, 1964.

If one assumes no important omissions in the surveys, the average number of pregnancies, while varying from 4.89 for ever-pregnant women in Mexico to 2.49 in Buenos Aires, suggests that an important proportion of women in all these cities use some means of controlling their fertility.

The difference between the levels of fertility of Buenos Aires and Mexico City is very striking. Inasmuch as they are the two largest cities of the region, with many similarities in their urban development,

TABLE 2

AVERAGE NUMBER OF PREGNANCIES, LIVE BIRTHS,
STILLBIRTHS, AND MISCARRIAGES

City	Pregnancies	Live Births	Stillbirths	Miscarriages
All Women Interviewed				
Bogotá..............	3.60	3.16	0.03	0.32
Buenos Aires.........	1.83	1.49	0.03	0.30
Caracas.............	3.43	2.97	0.03	0.41
Mexico City..........	3.84	3.27	0.06	0.46
Panama..............	3.08	2.74	0.04	0.30
Rio de Janeiro........	2.73	2.25	0.06	0.39
San José.............	3.45	2.98	0.04	0.41
Ever-pregnant Women				
Bogotá..............	4.54	3.99	0.04	0.40
Buenos Aires..........	2.49	2.03	0.04	0.40
Caracas.............	4.35	3.76	0.04	0.52
Mexico City..........	4.89	4.17	0.08	0.58
Panama..............	3.88	3.46	0.06	0.38
Rio de Janeiro........	3.63	2.99	0.08	0.51
San José.............	4.46	3.82	0.06	0.53

one would have expected a closer resemblance in reproductive behavior.

In judging this difference, attention should be paid to the age structure of women in the two cities (see Table 3). In Mexico City the women under 35 years of age number more than 62%, while in Buenos Aires they are only 45%. The higher proportion of women with incomplete fertility in the former city would tend to make the average number of live births smaller in comparison with that of the latter. This can be easily demonstrated if one applies the average number of live births recorded in each age group in Mexico to the Buenos Aires age distribution. This would move the Mexican average number of live births for all women interviewed from 3.27 to 3.91, which is more than two and a half times that for Buenos Aires.

The average number of live births recorded in both cities suggests that urban residence does not automatically imply low fertility and that there must be other factors having a decisive influence upon its level. Buenos Aires is the capital city of a country that has already achieved rather low levels of fertility, while in Mexico the national gross reproduction rate (GRR) is still above 3. If a comparison is made (Table 4) of the GRR's estimated from the survey data and the values of this index estimated for the country as a whole, we find that Mexico City deviates the least from the national average.

More data than are at present available, such as mean age at marriage and duration of marriage, are needed before attempting to formu-

TABLE 3

DISTRIBUTION OF RESPONDENTS BY AGE AND BY CITY

(Per Cent)

Age Groups	Bogotá	Buenos Aires	Caracas	Mexico City	Panama	Rio de Janeiro	San José
20–24....	23.2	13.5	25.1	23.9	26.5	21.4	20.6
25–29....	22.6	13.8	20.8	20.7	19.9	17.6	19.9
30–34....	18.4	18.0	16.6	17.6	16.2	18.0	18.3
35–39....	15.7	19.0	14.2	14.3	14.9	15.9	16.9
40–44....	10.8	17.2	10.4	11.9	11.3	11.7	11.9
45–49....	8.2	15.2	10.7	9.3	9.1	11.4	10.5
50—.....	1.2	3.3	2.1	2.3	2.1	4.0	1.9

TABLE 4

CITY AND NATIONAL GROSS REPRODUCTION RATES

City	GRR as Estimated from Survey[a]	National GRR[b]	Ratio of National to City GRR
Bogotá.............	2.38	....	....
Buenos Aires........	0.97	1.40	1.44
Caracas...........	2.12	3.10	1.46
Mexico City........	2.56	3.10	1.21
Panama...........	1.92	2.70	1.41
Rio de Janeiro......	1.67	....	....
San José...........	2.10	3.50	1.67

[a] A curve was fitted to plotted values of average number of live births by age, from which specific rates were computed by differentiation. From these, GRR's values were calculated.

[b] United Nations, *Conditions and Trends of Fertility in the World*, Population Bulletin No. 7, Table 5.1. Values quoted are for 1960 or years around it. No recent data were available for Colombia and Brazil.

late hypotheses to explain this peculiar behavior. However, some of the data examined below suggest plausible associations.

The second lowest average is that for Rio de Janeiro, which is in keeping with what would be expected if measures of fertility obtained earlier through other methods are accepted as approximating the true situation.[4]

The order in which the other cities appear in terms of average number of live births does not seem to justify any specific comments.

Fertility differentials.—Data so far tabulated for the seven cities allow comparisons of fertility (in terms of average number of live births) by age, marital status, place of birth, educational level, occupational status, and religion of women interviewed. Each of these six aspects will now be discussed.

TABLE 5

AVERAGE NUMBER OF LIVE BIRTHS BY AGE OF RESPONDENTS

Age Group	Bogotá	Buenos Aires	Caracas	Mexico City	Panama	Rio de Janeiro	San José
All women.....	3.16	1.49	2.97	3.27	2.74	2.25	2.98
20–24.........	1.07	0.36	1.15	1.08	1.18	0.69	1.18
25–29.........	2.46	0.99	2.48	2.68	2.33	1.83	2.26
30–34.........	3.85	1.53	3.74	3.66	3.48	2.57	3.22
35–39.........	4.61	1.76	4.25	4.70	3.82	2.80	4.07
40–44.........	4.79	1.95	4.03	5.19	3.72	3.52	4.22
45–49.........	4.27	1.90	4.23	4.62	3.74	3.00	4.17
50—.........	4.89	1.96	3.21	3.83	3.46	3.06	3.71

The differences in fertility between cities, among the various *age* groups, are consistent with what was found when examining the average number of live births for all women interviewed. Misstatements of age and sampling error would tend to affect the values recorded within each age group, but, in general, some valid conclusions appear to be possible (see Table 5).

For example, if the average number of live births for women aged 40–50 is accepted as representative of an index of completed fertility, we find rather high values, exceeding or approximating 5 (Bogotá and Mexico City), others fluctuating around 4.25 (Caracas and San José), one close to 3.75 (Panama), one close to 3 (Rio de Janeiro), and one below 2 (Buenos Aires). In order to appreciate the meaning of these values, it is worth remembering that in 1910 the average num-

[4]The Guanabara Experimental Demographic Survey recorded the following birth rates for the highest, medium, and lowest socioeconomic levels of the population of the State of Guanabara: 18.3, 22.3, and 26.9 per thousand (United Nations, ST/SOA/Ser. A/35, Population Studies No. 35, Guanabara Demographic Pilot Survey [New York, 1964], Table 16, p. 39).

ber of children ever born to women aged 45–49 in the United States was 4.1 for whites and 5.9 for non-whites. The corresponding values for 1950 were 2.3 and 2.7, respectively.[5] It should be stressed that the figures are not strictly comparable, since those for the Latin American cities refer only to children born alive. The differences in reproductive performance between the two populations are therefore larger than those portrayed by the comparison.

The average number of live births already recorded for younger women in most of the cities gives little ground for the expectation that the level they will achieve at the end of their reproductive life will be considerably lower than those cited above, unless some radical changes occur in the near future in their fertility behavior.

Besides age at and duration of *marriage*, for which no data have yet been tabulated, *composition* by marital status has an important bearing on the pattern of fertility in a population. The surveys under examination requested information on the marital status of the women interviewed, making provisions for recording at least one change in this status and obtaining information on duration of the current and the preceding unions for women ever in legal or common-law unions. In addition to the traditional groups of single, legally married, in common-law marriage, and divorced, the separated and the widowed were asked to declare whether they had had a legal or a common-law marriage. The reasoning behind this decision is related to the importance that has been given in demographic literature to the eventual course of fertility in the less developed countries as changes due to modernization occur in marital composition, which in theory evolves from a low proportion of legal marriages and a high proportion of common-law marriages to the reverse. Whether the unorthodox classifications introduced will serve any useful purpose is to be determined when more data become available on the subject. Even granting its utility, it is worth pointing out that unless more information of a sociological nature, such as patterns of mating, should be forthcoming, it is difficult to evaluate the meaning of the differentials in the level of fertility of women in legal and in common-law marriages.

The figures in Table 6 show no definite patterns regarding the reproductive behavior of women in the latter group, as contrasted with those in legal unions. Even recognizing that the figures might be affected by sampling error, it appears that the average number of live births is higher for women in common-law marriages in Caracas, Mexico City, Panama, and Rio de Janeiro, lower in Bogotá and about the same in Buenos Aires and San José. This could be a reflection of

[5]Wilson H. Grabill, Clyde Kiser, and Pascal K. Whelpton, *The Fertility of American Women* (New York: John Wiley & Sons, 1958), p. 46.

a different degree of institutionalization of common-law unions in the several cities, but it could also be due to deficiencies in the data collected regarding marital status or to the lack of uniformity in the definition of these unions or to a different structure of age and duration of union. If the women interviewed are accepted as a representative sample of the female population aged 20–50, the proportion of women in common-law unions in the samples can be taken as a possible indication of the degree of institutionalization of these unions. Of the four cities cited above as having the higher average number of live births per women in a *de facto* situation, three (Caracas, Mexico City, and Panama) have the highest percentages of women in this situation

TABLE 6

AVERAGE NUMBER OF LIVE BIRTHS BY MARITAL STATUS OF RESPONDENTS

Marital Status	Bogotá	Buenos Aires	Caracas	Mexico City	Panama	Rio de Janeiro	San José
All women..................	3.16	1.49	2.97	3.27	2.74	2.25	2.98
Single........................	0.14	0.02	......	0.09	0.27	0.05	0.40
Married.....................	3.96	1.83	3.24	4.10	3.14	2.72	3.92
In common-law marriage......	3.60	1.79	4.45	4.40	3.61	3.18	3.83
Separated from legal marriage..	3.15	1.52	3.60	3.71	3.04	3.07	4.10
Separated from common-law marriage..................	3.37	3.50	3.38	3.17	3.04	1.70	2.66
Divorced....................	2.00	1.50	2.35	2.17	2.18	2.10	1.72
Widow from legal marriage.....	4.18	2.05	4.61	3.78	2.83	3.15	4.25
Widow from common-law marriage.....................	4.00	4.75	3.84	5.31	3.11	1.00	4.44
Not specified.................	......	......	3.00	......	......	......	......
Ever-married women..........	3.88	1.85	3.53	4.05	3.25	2.78	3.83

(see Table 1). Further analysis controlling some of the variables mentioned above is needed before arriving at any definite conclusions.

While comparisons by *place of birth* might be affected by differences in the definitions of rural area, town, and city applied in the various surveys, the differentials recorded leave no doubt that the reproductive behavior of women born in the city results in a persistently lower average number of live births.

Unfortunately, the dichotomy adopted in Table 7 (which puts women emigrating from other cities and those who are international migrants into the group "born outside") tends to blur the differences between the fertility of women born in rural areas and those with city life experience in the same country. As can be seen in Table 1, there are important differences in the distributions by place of birth. The largest percentages of women native to the city were recorded for Buenos Aires, Rio de Janeiro, and San José. The first two have the lowest averages of live births, which in part can be attributed to the downward influence introduced by the lower value of the native women. In San José, the same does not operate, owing to the fact that the difference between the two averages is negligible.

When women "born in city" are compared on average number of live births, the difference which was already noted for all women persists, which can again be taken as an indication that there are factors other than urban residence associated with the level of fertility. One of these follows.

The results summarized in Table 8 confirm the widely held view that there is a strong negative correlation between *educational level* and fertility. The differentials here are much more pronounced than those recorded when place of birth was used as the basis for comparison. While it is not difficult to believe that migrants from rural areas

TABLE 7

AVERAGE NUMBER OF LIVE BIRTHS BY PLACE OF BIRTH

City	All Women	Born in City	Born Outside	Ratio of Born Outside to Born in City
Bogotá	3.16	2.95	3.22	1.09
Buenos Aires	1.49	1.34	1.63	1.22
Caracas	2.97	2.65	3.09	1.66
Mexico City	3.27	2.90	3.58	1.47
Panama	2.74	2.54	2.90	1.14
Río de Janeiro	2.25	1.99	2.50	1.25
San José	2.98	2.86	3.12	1.09

are also less educated, it appears at first sight that level of education has a more important bearing on fertility than area of origin. The distribution of women by level of education is given in Table 1, but not with enough detail to assess the weight of the different groups in Table 8 in determining the average. This information plus level of education cross-classified by place of origin, should help clarify the weight which can be attributed to each variable.

In an effort to establish the socioeconomic correlates of fertility, the questionnaire included questions on the *occupational status* of the woman and of her husband both at marriage and at the time of the interview, as well as on current or last occupation of her father and her father-in-law. Data presently available permit the examination of differentials according to occupation of the husband at the time of the interview and whether the woman was working or not. Table 9 summarizes the figures for the seven cities in terms of the first variable. The classification adopted for the occupational status provided six categories, which were later combined into three broad groups: higher non-manual, lower non-manual, and manual.

The limitations of occupational characteristics of the husband as an index of socioeconomic status has been amply discussed in demographic literature. Wives often do not correctly report their husband's occupation, either because they do not know it or because there is a tendency to overstate the level of it. Also, activities of diverse socioeconomic level are included in each broad occupational group. Whatever the limitations may be, there is no doubt of the utility of the occupational classification as a means of approaching an understanding of the factors associated with changes in fertility. The

TABLE 8

AVERAGE NUMBER OF LIVE BIRTHS BY LEVEL OF EDUCATION OF RESPONDENTS

Level of Education	Bogotá	Buenos Aires	Caracas	Mexico City	Panama	Rio de Janeiro	San José
All women.................	3.16	1.49	2.97	3.28	2.74	2.25	2.98
With no education...........	4.12	2.50	4.27	4.53	4.00	3.33	3.89
With 1–3 primary grades of education....................	3.36	1.55	3.82	4.16	4.18	2.93	3.73
With 4 or more grades of primary education.............	3.17	1.90	2.97	3.83	3.73	2.46	3.74
With complete primary education.....................	3.23	1.74	2.61	3.14	3.14	2.17	2.83
With 1–3 years of secondary education...................	2.89	1.46	1.88	2.20	2.67	1.63	2.26
With 4 or more years of secondary education..............	2.52	1.35	2.16	1.85	2.14	1.43	1.91
With complete secondary education.....................	2.52	1.07	1.71	1.82	1.65	1.38	2.00
With less than 5 years of university education.............	0.68	1.12	0.68	1.41	1.09	1.05	1.59
With 5 or more years of university education.............	1.89	1.03	1.31	1.89	1.22	1.21	1.18
Not specified................	2.00	1.23	6.00	......	3.00	2.00	......

TABLE 9

AVERAGE NUMBER OF LIVE BIRTHS BY OCCUPATIONAL
STATUS OF HUSBAND AT TIME
OF THE INTERVIEW

City	Higher Non-manual	Lower Non-manual	Manual
Bogotá.............	3.40	3.85	4.11
Buenos Aires........	1.91	1.74	1.91
Caracas............	2.89	3.09	3.80
Mexico City........	3.39	3.72	4.58
Panama............	2.66	3.03	3.51
Rio de Janeiro	2.34	2.24	3.15
San José...........	2.99	3.45	4.35

data in Table 9 confirm, as in the case of educational level, the negative correlation of occupational status to fertility.

With the exception of Bogotá and Buenos Aires, the average number of live births of women whose husbands were engaged in the lower occupational classifications differs by more than 30% from those with husbands in the upper classifications. The instance of Buenos Aires is indeed very interesting. There is no difference between the upper and lower groups, and the middle category deviates from these by less than 10%. If, as some authors have suggested, differential fertility according to occupational status is only a phase of the transition from high to low fertility, the figures for Buenos Aires

TABLE 10

AVERAGE NUMBER OF LIVE BIRTHS BY WORKING
CONDITION OF THE WOMAN AT
TIME OF THE INTERVIEW

City	All Women	Working Women	Not Working Women
Bogotá.............	3.16	2.36	3.68
Buenos Aires........	1.49	1.01	1.78
Caracas............	2.97	2.21	3.33
Mexico City........	3.27	2.46	3.72
Panama[a]............	2.74	2.96	3.48
Rio de Janeiro......	2.25	1.79	2.47
San José...........	2.98	1.92	3.68

[a] Refers only to women in legal and common-law marriage.

would suggest that here the declines in fertility have spread to all socioeconomic groups. The instance of Bogotá, with the highest value for the higher non-manual group (3.40 live births per woman), could in the same light be taken as indicative of an incipient decline.

The interpretation of fertility differentials according to the working situation of the woman involves perhaps even more difficulties than the ones that were just discussed. If the data collected, as has been customary in most surveys, refer only to the working condition of the woman at the time of the interview, it is difficult to assess the true influence that her participation in the labor force had had upon her number of children. Only by matching her reproductive and occupational histories would it be possible to determine whether the level of her fertility is a consequence or a determinant of her working record. In the absence of any such data, however, one is inclined to believe that the need or the desire to work acts as a deterrent to high fertility. The figures in Table 10 support this hypothesis. The differentials here are universal, and in one city the average number of live births between working and not working women differs by 91%. Of course, a proper evaluation of the meaning of the differentials would require, at least, knowledge of family organization within each society. In a situation in which the extended family is a common pattern, the women can engage more freely in economic activities, leaving the care of the children to other members of the family. Whether this is true, for example, in Panama and Rio de Janeiro or is due mainly to the difference in the age structure of the two groups of women is something that could be clarified only with further analysis of the survey data, complemented by research of a more sociological nature.

The questionnaire used in the Comparative Fertility Surveys Program included questions on *religious affiliation* and frequency of

TABLE 11

AVERAGE NUMBER OF LIVE BIRTHS BY FREQUENCY OF COMMUNION

Frequency of Communion	Bogotá	Buenos Aires	Caracas	Mexico City	Panama[a]	Rio de Janeiro	San José
Catholic women........	3.16	1.49	2.97	3.27	2.74	2.29	2.97
Once a week or more....	2.93	1.71	2.23	2.39	2.41	1.88	2.47
Once or twice monthly..	2.78	1.06	2.38	2.69	2.89	2.12	2.37
With less frequency....	3.28	1.48	2.69	3.30	3.15	2.15	2.86
Never................	3.27	1.53	3.72	3.68	3.15	2.50	3.52
Not stated...........	3.00	3.00	3.21	....	2.28	1.54	3.50

[a] Refers to *all* women.

Communion. These small samples were not very efficient for measuring differentials due to religious affiliation, inasmuch as more than 90% of the women declare themselves Catholics. The two other variables seem more appropriate to attempt an evaluation of the influence of religion in the reproductive performance of the women interviewed. Table 11 gives, for Catholic women in the samples, the average number of live births by frequency of Communion.

In none of the cities included does there seem to exist a clear and definite association between these two variables. This should not be taken as implying that in fact this association does not exist. It could very well be that the more practicing Catholics are precisely the better-educated women, since in many societies participation in religious services has been considered a form of conspicuous consumption. On the other hand, it has also been suggested that it is among the better-educated groups that secularization of a society proceeds more rapidly. Data on religious participation, cross-classified by education, not available at the time of writing, should help to clarify the issue.

Use of contraceptives.—A section was included in the questionnaire to obtain data on knowledge and use of contraceptives, as well as on initiation of their use, source of information, and the attitude of the woman and her husband toward the general subject of family limitation. As has already been pointed out, no difficulties were encountered in obtaining answers to these questions. The organizers of the surveys are under the general impression that more detailed information could have been obtained on them. The information gathered in these surveys is valuable and could serve as a basis for action by those responsible for the adoption of measures related to the population.

TABLE 12

AVERAGE NUMBER OF LIVE BIRTHS AND PROPORTION OF ALL WOMEN AND OF CATHOLICS IN LEGAL AND COMMON-LAW MARRIAGES WHO DECLARED HAVING EVER USED CONTRACEPTIVES

| CITY | WOMEN IN LEGAL AND COMMON-LAW MARRIAGE | | |
	Average Number of Live Births	Proportion Who Ever Used Contraceptives (per cent)	Proportion of Catholics Who Ever Used Contraceptives (per cent)
Bogotá	3.95	39.5	39.4
Buenos Aires	1.83	77.6	77.1
Caracas	3.50	59.4	59.9
Mexico City	4.16	37.5	36.2
Panama	3.33	59.7	a
Rio de Janeiro	2.75	58.1	55.8
San José	3.91	65.0	65.0

a Figure not available.

The questions on contraceptive practices were addressed to women in legal or in common-law marriages. The proportion of these women who declared having ever used some contraceptive ranges from 37.5% in Mexico City to 77.6% in Buenos Aires (see Table 12). Earlier in this paper it was pointed out that these two cities represent the high and low extremes in levels of fertility. The relationship of these levels to the customs regarding contraception among the female population is that the higher the proportion of women using some means of controlling their fertility, the lower the average number of live births. This also holds true for the other cities, with the exception of San José.

The behavior of Latin American Catholic women in the general field of family limitation has been a much debated question, both within the region and outside it. The data collected by the surveys afford the analysis of some of the relevant factors in this matter. In order to evaluate properly the meaning of the data presented below, it should be pointed out that, in each city except Buenos Aires and Rio de Janeiro, the proportion of Catholics among women in legal and in common-law marriage exceeds 90%. The proportion ranges from 98.6% in Bogotá to 83% in Rio de Janeiro. Furthermore, as can be seen in Table 12, the proportion of Catholic women in the two marital statuses who declared having ever used contraceptives is very similar to that of the group taken as a whole. In summary, then,

TABLE 13

CATHOLIC WOMEN IN LEGAL OR COMMON-LAW MARRIAGES HAVING EVER
USED CONTRACEPTIVES BY LEVEL OF EDUCATION

(Per Cent)

Level of Education	Bogotá	Buenos Aires[a]	Caracas	Mexico City	Panama[a]	Rio de Janeiro	San José
Women in legal or common-law marriages	39.4	77.6	59.9	36.2	59.7	55.8	65.0
With no education	14.6	52.0	38.1	11.0	35.0	40.0	48.3
Some primary education	28.2	74.8	52.5	27.7	46.3	45.5	54.1
Complete primary education	39.7	81.3	71.7	42.9	56.2	60.0	68.4
Some secondary education	59.5	73.9	77.6	54.4	65.0	69.1	78.5
Complete secondary education	74.0	83.4	64.7	63.8	66.7	72.7	50.1
Some university education	70.0	73.5	76.2	50.9	62.7	71.0	77.6

[a] Refers to all women in legal and in common-law marriage.

the behavior of the Catholic woman in this matter is highly representative of all women in legal and in common-law marriages.

The inverse relationship which was observed between fertility and education reverses, as should have been expected, to a positive one when education is cross-classified by use of contraception. Table 13 reveals very neatly that the proportion of Catholic women in legal and in common-law marriages who declared having ever tried to control their fertility goes up with increasing level of education. The lowest percentages of users among women with no education were recorded in Mexico City and Bogotá, the two cities with the highest average number of live births per woman in these marital statuses (4.16 and 3.95, respectively).

The time at which contraceptive practice is started has an important bearing on ultimate size of completed families. In spite of the different levels of fertility among cities and the varying proportions of women who have ever practiced contraception, it is very striking that in all cities a rather high proportion of Catholic women have tried to avoid conception before the third pregnancy (see Table 14).

Again the lowest percentages (at third pregnancy) are found in Mexico City and Bogotá, while in all the other cities they are above 60%, rising to 93% in Buenos Aires. Apparently, among some women there is also present the desire of postponing the birth of their first child, since from 9% in Mexico to 40% in Buenos Aires admitted to the use of contraceptives before the first pregnancy.

From the surveys alone, it is difficult to clarify whether the women included in Table 14 were trying to avoid bearing children or just

TABLE 14

CATHOLIC WOMEN IN LEGAL OR COMMON-LAW MARRIAGES HAVING EVER
USED CONTRACEPTIVES, DISTRIBUTED BY ORDER OF
PREGNANCY WHEN USE BEGAN

ORDER OF PREGNANCY	CUMULATIVE PERCENTAGES						
	Bogotá	Buenos Aires[a]	Caracas	Mexico City	Panama[a]	Rio de Janeiro	San José
Before first pregnancy.........	7.3	40.2	16.2	8.9	12.1	12.0	10.4
Before second pregnancy.......	29.0	79.1	47.6	31.0	42.3	39.6	40.6
Before third pregnancy........	50.3	92.7	65.4	48.7	60.4	60.7	60.8
Before fourth pregnancy.......	66.3	96.2	75.3	64.9	73.9	71.3	74.1
Before fifth pregnancy........	80.0	97.5	82.6	74.4	82.8	77.4	82.8
Before sixth pregnancy........	86.0	98.1	86.1	81.7	89.0	80.0	87.2
Before seventh pregnancy......	90.9	98.4	90.0	87.0	93.8	81.3	89.8
Before eighth pregnancy.......	94.0	....	92.4	88.8	95.6	81.5	93.5
Before ninth pregnancy........	94.9	....	93.8	89.7	96.8	82.0	94.8
After ninth pregnancy.........	96.7	....	96.4	93.4	97.7	83.2	97.7
Not stated...................	100.0	100.0	100.0	100.0	100.0	100.0	100.0

[a] Refers to all women in legal and in common-law marriage.

trying to space their births. How successful they were if they were attempting the first objective could to some extent be determined by reference to the actual number of children they bore. As for the second objective, some indication could be found by examining the women's opinions on what the ideal interval between births should be, as against the actual spacing achieved by them.

If an important percentage of women declared that they were using or had used some means of controlling their fertility and if an important proportion of them admitted that they tried to avoid conception rather early in their reproductive lives, one wonders why the general reproductive pattern is so high. The answer to this could probably be found in the type of contraceptives used and the persistency with which they are employed. There is only one item in the questionnaire that would permit some approximate evaluation of the latter point. It refers to whether the method is used "always, sometimes, or rarely." Unfortunately, these data were not available at the time of writing. As for the type of contraceptive, there is information both on knowledge about each type and on whether it has ever been used. Table 15 gives this for five of the cities covered by the surveys. (The figures for Buenos Aires and Panama were not available.) It should be pointed out that the percentages in Table 14 are not mutually exclusive, since one woman could be counted as using more than one method. This explains why the use percentages if added are completely different from those reproduced in Table 12.

It is quite evident that a considerable proportion of women in the

TABLE 15

CATHOLIC WOMEN WHO DECLARED KNOWING OR HAVING
EVER USED A CONTRACEPTIVE METHOD

(Per Cent)

METHOD OF CONTRACEPTION[a]	USE					KNOWLEDGE				
	Bogotá	Cara-cas	Mexico City	Rio de Janeiro	San José	Bogotá	Cara-cas	Mexico City	Rio de Janeiro	San José
Douche.........	12.3	24.5	14.5	23.0	17.2	56.4	79.2	60.0	81.4	72.0
Sterilization.....	1.0	5.9	1.8	6.1	5.9	36.1	80.2	50.4	63.2	72.0
Diaphragm......	2.0	4.4	3.4	3.5	3.8	23.5	47.2	37.2	42.6	44.0
Jelly............	6.6	2.0	3.8	5.4	4.6	46.2	23.6	23.2	29.4	27.6
Rhythm........	18.5	18.2	14.9	16.0	21.3	48.6	59.8	47.0	62.0	70.8
Condom........	10.5	30.6	8.9	12.4	36.9	39.7	78.9	43.1	62.2	87.7
Coitus interruptus	16.4	22.1	7.1	5.4	23.9	38.8	63.4	32.4	39.9	62.0
Pills............	2.4	1.2	6.1	4.1	1.8	4.9	3.9	20.2	6.8	3.5
Total.........	69.7	108.9	60.5	75.9	115.4	......	......	......	......	......

[a] Methods are listed here in the same order in which they were included in the questionnaire.

cities included in Table 15 use the less effective contraceptive methods. Rhythm appears to be the most popular, followed by the douche, the condom, and coitus interruptus. The Family Growth in Metropolitan America Study found rather high pregnancy rates per 100 years of exposure associated with the use of these methods. As given by Tietze,[6] these rates were: safe period, 38.5; douche, 40.8; condom, 13.8; and withdrawal, 16.8.

If, as can generally be accepted, the use of any of the contraceptives cited by the women is less systematic and persistent in Latin America than it would be in a more developed society, it is not difficult to conclude why the contraceptive practices of the women inter-

[6]Christopher Tietze, "The Use-Effectiveness of Contraceptive Methods," in *Research in Family Planning*, ed. Clyde V. Kiser (Princeton: Princeton University Press, 1962), Table 6, p. 367.

viewed seem to be rather ineffective. The degree of knowledge varies within city and within method. The least-known method seems to be the latest addition to contraception: the progestational compound, popularly recognized as the "pill." The best-known is the douche, followed in second place by sterilization, rhythm, and condom. While "knowledge" about a contraceptive could cover a wide range of acquaintance with it, the reduced proportion of women who ever used a method in comparison with those who declared knowing about it is indeed very striking.

Ideal number of children.—Up to now we have studied the reproductive performance of the women interviewed, as well as how it differentiates when analyzed by age, marital status, place of birth, educational level, religious affiliation, and occupational status of the

TABLE 16

AVERAGE NUMBER OF LIVE BIRTHS AND
AVERAGE IDEAL NUMBER OF CHILDREN

City	Actual Average Number of Live Births	Ideal Number of Children
Bogotá	3.16	3.64
Buenos Aires	1.49	2.88
Caracas	2.92	3.50
Mexico City	3.27	4.20
Panama	2.74	3.54
Rio de Janeiro	2.22	2.66
San José	2.91	3.63

woman herself and that of her husband. We have also tried to examine the possible influence of contraceptive practices upon the ultimate result of this performance in terms of average number of live births. After examination of these data, one question that naturally arises is what is the ideal conception of these women regarding the desired number of children. The surveys included a number of questions on ideals, such as best age for a woman to get married and to have her last child, "convenient" number of children a family should have, what should be the intervals from marriage to birth of the first child and successive births, what occupation she would like or would have liked for her first male child, and so on.

Table 16 compares for all women the actual average number of live births they have borne and the ideal number they declared a family should have. While in all cities the ideals are in the average higher than actual numbers (reflecting the uncompleted childbearing of young wives), there seems to exist a positive correlation between the two variables, as if the ideal has in effect a direct influence on actual reproductive behavior. The only city where the women seem to be currently successful in matching their performance with their ideals is Rio de Janeiro. In all the other cities, the ideals are considerably higher. Before any attempt to judge the meaning of the differentials, a breakdown by age and by marital status should be made. In any case it is evident that, with the exception of Buenos Aires and Rio de Janeiro, in all cities values associated with fertility are those favoring a rather high level, as compared with those prevailing in more developed societies. This seems to be particularly true for Mexico City.

CONCLUSIONS

The preliminary findings of the studies conducted in seven cities, under the Program of Comparative Fertility Surveys in Latin America, have contributed to a sound basis for discarding some misconceptions which have plagued fertility research in the region. In the first place, it has been proved that it is possible to question Latin American women on those matters related to reproduction which have been termed "intimate." More important than this, there are strong indications that, in general, women are not prejudiced against measures addressed to reducing their fertility. Furthermore, the behavior of Catholic women toward this subject does not seem to be very different from that of other women. Knowledge of contraceptives, while not universal, is by no means insignificant, and the concern of the women regarding their use appears rather early in their reproductive lives.

Other concrete results so far obtained from the surveys can be summarized as follows:

1. Fertility, as measured by the average number of live births, exceeds in several cities the level that would have been expected in view of the high degree of urbanization.

2. Buenos Aires appears to be in the last phase of the demographic transition, in which low general patterns of fertility seem to have spread to women of almost every socioeconomic status.

3. Rio de Janeiro seems to be entering the period of declining fertility, followed by Panama.

4. Place of birth, educational level, and working condition of the woman as well as the occupational status of her husband have strong bearing on reproductive behavior in terms of actual number of live children born.

5. Contraceptive practices are very different in the various cities and there seems to be a clear relationship between the prevalence of

contraception and the level of fertility. Even what appears to be the less contraceptive-minded society (Mexico City) shows a proportion of women in legal and common-law marriage who declared having ever used contraceptives which is not low (37.5%).

6. As in the level of fertility, there is a strong correlation between the use of contraceptives and the level of education.

7. Efforts to prevent conception are started rather early in the reproductive lives of the women interviewed.

8. The more widely used methods of contraception in five of the cities surveyed are the less effective ones. This in some way appears to be related to knowledge of the different methods.

9. In most of the cities fertility values continue to be those associated with traditional societies. These values seem to be exercising some influence in the ultimate size of family achieved.

50

ESTIMATING RATES OF POPULATION GROWTH

W. PARKER MAULDIN
Associate Director, Demographic Division
The Population Council

INTRODUCTION

More than two-thirds of the population of the world is poorly housed, poorly clothed, poorly educated, and poorly fed. Hopes for modernization are being strengthened by economic development programs which seek to mobilize the physical and intellectual resources of lands and peoples. The development process requires continuing assessment of results and quantification of achievements. The negative relationship between rapid rates of population growth and economic development is recognized increasingly, and acted upon. But the statistical systems of developing countries are underdeveloped, too. "While nearly all the population in the economically more advanced regions of the world is covered by 'complete' birth registration statistics, such data are available for countries containing only 40 per cent of the estimated population in Middle and South America, 8 per cent in Asia (outside the USSR) and a mere 2 per cent in Africa."[1] Perhaps no more than one-half the births and deaths in the developing countries are registered, and migration statistics are little if any better. Thus rates of population growth often are not known, and frequently are underestimated.

I shall not attempt to catalogue the many uses of data on rates of population growth, but shall cite two examples. Economic development should be measured on a per capita basis, and year-to-year changes, or changes over a 5-year plan period can be quite inaccurate if the rate of population growth is not known with some precision. For example, if gross national product increases at 6% per year, per

[1]*United Nations Population Bulletin No. 7*, 1965, p. 12.

capita change would be one-fourth less with a 3% as compared with a 2% rate of population growth. Such a large difference would be very important for planning purposes. A second important use of population growth data is to determine the effectiveness of a family planning program. In the final analysis changes in fertility rates are the most important criteria of success or failure of a family planning program. But if vital statistics are of poor quality, they may be misleading. For example, if a country has a poor registration system, but one that is gradually improving, the data might show that the birth rate was not being reduced, or even that it was increasing, because a larger proportion of births were being registered—and at the same time the birth rate might be declining.

In the absence of a good registration system which provides accurate information on the number of births and deaths for a country, one can turn to other sources such as censuses or sample surveys for estimates of vital events. In addition, it would be quite feasible to strengthen registration in a sample of areas so as to get good estimates of vital events for the entire country, and this could be done relatively quickly and easily. The purpose of this paper is to review some of the major studies designed to obtain estimates of vital events and to suggest promising approaches to obtaining current vital statistics. I shall concentrate on three promising methods: (1) registration in a probability sample of areas; (2) matching of survey and registration data; and (3) repeated, single purpose surveys, with reconciliation of differences between survey n and $n+1$ and $n+2$. For background purposes, however, it may be well to comment on the use of census and surveys for estimating vital rates.

CENSUS DATA: INTERCENSAL RATES OF GROWTH

In the absence of good vital statistics, census data are very useful in analyzing population trends. The most obvious method of estimating the rate of growth is to compute the average annual intercensal rate of growth. Typically countries take censuses every ten years, and thus intercensal rates of growth become available about six years after the midpoint of the intercensal period, and may be used for several additional years. Thus the intercensal rate of growth represents events of quite a few years ago. During periods of rapid changes in mortality, such figures are misleading. In Pakistan, for example, the average rate of growth between 1951 and 1961 was about 2.2%. By 1962, the year in which this figure became generally available, the rate of population growth in Pakistan was nearer to 3% than to 2%, according to estimates from the Population Growth Estimation Experiment. The commonly accepted rate of growth at 1951 in Pakistan was 1.4%. If one assumes that the actual rate of growth was indeed 1.4%, that fertility remained constant, that mortality decreased linearly so that the average rate of growth for the decade was 2.1%, then the rate of growth at the end of the period would have been approximately 3.0%.

STABLE AND QUASI-STABLE POPULATION ANALYSIS

Many years ago Lotka developed the concept of the stable population, the population which would be produced ultimately by unchanging mortality and fertility rates. A stable population has a constant rate of growth and a fixed age composition. In that past decade it has been found that the characteristics of the Lotka stable population are closely approximated in populations where only fertility, and not mortality is unchanging (if mortality does not change radically). If one is given any two of the following demographic measures, the others are automatically determined: (1) some age measure such as the proportion of a particular age group; (2) a mortality measure; (3) a fertility indicator; and (4) a current growth rate, either of the total population or of any broad age group.

Coale[2] and his colleagues have shown that certain groups of life tables conform quite closely to four distinctive age patterns of mortality, one pattern from each group. Each of these four groups of life tables yields quite distinct estimates of population parameters by quasi-stable methods. Although there are several sources of errors in using the quasi-stable analysis, such procedures are useful where moderately good measurements of two of the four types of measures listed above are available. Data derived in this way serve as a useful check on other estimates.

SURVEYS

Sample surveys have often been used to obtain estimates of births and deaths, but generally with indifferent to poor results. In part this is because the primary purpose of most such surveys is to obtain other kinds of information, such as labor force participation or socioeconomic data. Questions about vital events are often tacked on under the assumption that such important, discrete events will surely be well remembered and can easily be reported. Performance has been so poor,

[2]Ansley J. Coale, "Estimates of Various Demographic Measures through the Quasi-Stable Age Distribution," *Emerging Techniques in Population Research* (New York: Milbank Memorial Fund, 1963).

however, that the French demographer Robert Blanc[3] says that single surveys "should not be regarded as useless because of imperfections but as a step toward better results in later enquiries."

Most industrialized countries have not given serious attention to obtaining current estimates of vital events from surveys, largely because such countries have good registration systems and therefore do not need to use surveys for this purpose. They do use surveys to get information about fertility differentials, but here the important data are ratios rather than precisely calibrated rates. Trends over time do require rates rather than ratios, but emphasis usually is on cumulative fertility performance rather than annual rates.

TABLE 1

UNDERCOUNT OF POPULATION UNDER ONE YEAR OF AGE FROM THE UNITED STATES CURRENT POPULATION SURVEY, BY COLOR, AS COMPARED WITH ADJUSTED BIRTH REGISTRATION STATISTICS, 1960–63

(Per Cent)

Date	All Classes	White	Non-white
March, 1963........	8.8	10.0	2.9
March, 1962........	3.7	1.2	19.1
March, 1961........	7.6	5.6	20.5
March, 1960........	8.2	4.6	33.1

EXPERIENCE IN THE UNITED STATES

The United States Bureau of the Census has pioneered in the use of sample surveys and probably has devoted more attention to sampling and to response problems than any other organization in the world. Matching studies of census and registration data were undertaken in 1940, and since that time a large variety of methodological investigations have been carried out. The Current Population Survey sometimes includes questions about births and deaths. Table 1 gives the ratio of estimates of the population under one year of age based on adjusted birth registration statistics and the estimates from the Current Population Survey, prior to final ratio adjustment, by color, for March of each year, 1960 to 1963. In every instance the sample survey underestimated the population under one year of age. The underestimates varied from about 1% to 10% for whites, and from about 3% to 33% for non-whites. In three out of four years the discrepancy was

[3]Robert Blanc, "L'Analyse des données actuelles sur la fécondité africaine," *International Population Conference, Ottawa, 1963* (Liège: International Union for the Scientific Study of Population, 1964), p. 89.

about 8%–9% for all classes. On the basis of data in Table 1, it seems that even a well-designed and well-executed sample survey may not provide very reliable estimates of children under one year of age.[4]

Data on births and deaths were obtained from the Quarterly Household Survey of October, 1962, covering events of July to October of that year. The sample births consisted of events during the quarter reported by households living in the units at the end of the quarter; the sample deaths consisted of events during the quarter occurring to households living in the units at the beginning of the quarter, but reported by the present occupants of the unit, neighbors, or others. The comparison of estimates of births and deaths obtained from the survey with estimates based on vital statistics (registration data) indicates a survey deficit of 23% for births and 14%–28% for deaths.

These data suggest that the use of single surveys for obtaining estimates of births and deaths is a questionable procedure. Sample surveys tend to undercount vital events, but there is no assurance that the undercount is uniform over time, among different groups, or even that there will always be undercounts.

DEVELOPING COUNTRIES

In developing countries where registration systems are poor, the utilization of sample surveys is rapidly increasing. Several very sophisticated and exciting studies are now under way, notably in India, Pakistan, Thailand, Turkey, and Senegal. Within the past several years a unique inquiry was undertaken in Morocco, and a methodologically interesting study was made in Brazil at Guanabara. The list of areas where other vital statistics studies are being made could be extended, but for those with which I am familiar, one could not use the adjectives sophisticated, exciting, or methodologically interesting.

NSS INDIA

The National Sample Survey of India has conducted multipurpose sample surveys for many years, and much attention has been devoted to estimating vital events. This survey has not always obtained satisfactory data on births and deaths, and because of underreporting of vital events a variety of techniques has been tried to improve the data, and to make better estimates from the existing data. In the seventh round (1953–54) of the Indian NSS the reported number of births was adjusted upward by 20% from 34.3 to 40.9, and the death

[4] J. S. Siegel, "Preliminary Report on Use of Household Surveys To Estimate Birth and Death Rates" (dittoed report), Bureau of the Census, July 30, 1963, p. 2a.

rate was adjusted upward by 45%, or from 16.6 to 24.0. Five years later in the fourteenth round the reference period was increased from one to two years, and reported births were 38.7; this estimate was adjusted upwards by 10% to 42.5. Reported deaths had increased to 19.3, although undoubtedly the true death rate had decreased during the intervening period. Indeed, in 1953–54 the adjusted death rate was 24.0, but in 1958–59 the reported rate of 19.3 was accepted as correct.

In each of the surveys there has been evidence that memory decay increases with time. Som[5] has presented the work of the Indian Statistical Institute relevant to memory decay for vital events. In order to apply the technique, interviews must be carried out monthly (if the events are to be assigned to month of occurrence) among a randomly selected subsample of the total sample population. To cover a reference period of one year, respondents give information for the twelve months preceding the date of the survey, so that twelve monthly consecutive interviews produce a total of 144 observations; that is, each month of the year is represented twelve times, once with a recall period of one month prior to the date of the survey, once with a recall period of two months, and so on up to a twelve-month recall period.

The technique involves averaging the twelve months for which the recall period was one month, two months, and up to twelve months, respectively. If each of these twelve monthly averages is multiplied by 12, twelve annual rates are obtained for recall periods of one, two, and up to twelve months. In the absence of recall lapse, these twelve annual rates would be the same within the range of sampling limitations. As it is, it is usually found that the longer the recall period, the lower the rate. The final step in the technique is to estimate the rate at recall period "zero," (that is, before any recall lapse can set in), on the basis of a smooth mathematical curve fitted to the observed data for the various recall periods. Data from the seventh round of the Indian NSS indicate that if the index for the birth rate at the point of origin is considered to be 100, respondents report decreasing proportions of births each month, with the index being only 83 in the twelfth month. Similarly, the index for reported deaths decreases to 67 for the twelfth month.

An innovation introduced into the fourteenth round (1958–59) of the Indian NSS was to lengthen the reference period from one to two years with a recall period of one year, so that questions were asked about "last year" and "year before last." The results are interesting on two counts. First is the observation that the crude birth and death rates reported for "year before last" were only 82% and

[5]Ranjan Kumar Som, "On Recall Lapse in Demographic Studies," *International Population Conference, Vienna, 1959*, pp. 50–61.

52%, respectively, of the corresponding rates reported for "last year." The second point worth noting is that "last year's" crude rates in the fourteenth round were 12% higher for births and 14% higher for deaths than in the seventh round. It is not likely that these rates did indeed change by these proportions in the five-year interval between the seventh and fourteenth rounds, and in the case of the death rate at least, any real change would probably have been in the opposite direction.[6]

This same innovation was continued in the fifteenth round conducted one year after the fourteenth round, so that what was "year before

TABLE 2

CRUDE BIRTH AND DEATH RATES IN INDIA BASED ON VARIOUS ROUNDS AND
REFERENCE PERIODS IN NATIONAL SAMPLE SURVEYS

NSS ROUND	REPORTED		ADJUSTED	
	CBR	CDR	CBR	CDR
7th round (October, 1953–March, 1954):				
Last year	34.3	16.6	40.9	21.0
14th round (1958–59):				
Last year	38.7	19.3	42.5[a]	....
Year before last	31.6	10.1	....	....
15th round (1959–60):				
Last year	38.7	17.1	....	....
Year before last	28.2	10.0	....	....
Year before last as per cent of last year:				
14th round	31.7	52.3	....	....
15th round	72.9	58.5	....	....
1958–59 data:				
Per cent that "year before last" events from 15th round are of "last year" events from 14th round	72.9	51.8	....	....

SOURCE: Indian Statistical Institute, "The Use of the National Sample Survey in the Estimation of Current Birth and Death Rates in India," *Proceedings, IUSSP Conference, New York, 1961*, Vol. 2 (London, 1963), p. 396.

[a] As reported in M. Majumdar, "Estimation of Vital Rates in the Indian National Sample Survey," paper prepared for the World Population Conference, Belgrade, September 1965, p. 5.

last" in the former was "last year" in the latter. Ideally the rates for the common time period would of course be the same whether collected in the fourteenth or fifteenth round. As it was, crude birth and death rates obtained in the fifteenth round with a recall period of "year before last" were 73% and 52%, respectively, of the levels reported for "last year" in the fourteenth round (see Table 2).

The improvement in coverage for "last year" noted in the fourteenth round compared with the seventh round (when only last year

[6]Murari Majumdar, "Estimation of Vital Rates in the Indian National Sample Survey" (mimeographed), paper prepared for the World Population Conference, Belgrade, September, 1965.

was requested) was maintained in the fifteenth round. Thus it seems that lengthening the reference period from one to two years, with a breakdown into two one-year recall periods, improves coverage of reporting of last year's events by some 12%. Its other advantage is that it affords a comparison of rates, pertaining to the same time interval, from two independent surveys. The limited data available suggest that the shortfall in births and deaths of "year before last" compared with "last year" can be attributed largely to failure to report the births and deaths of those who die in early infancy.

PAKISTAN GROWTH ESTIMATION STUDY

The Pakistan Growth Estimation Study in Pakistan, commonly called the PGE Study, is based on the theoretical work of Chandra Sekar and Deming[7] and the subsequent work of Coale.[8] The major features of this approach are:

1. Births and deaths are collected by two separate systems, continuous registration and surveys.
2. Individual events collected by the two systems are compared and classified as:
    a) counted by R(egistration) and S(urveys),
    b) counted by R only, and
    c) counted by S only.
3. From the above an estimate is made of events that are missed by both R and S. The formula used for this computation is

$$N = C + Nr + Ne + NrNe/C,$$
where N = estimated number of events,
C = events enumerated both by registration and survey,
Nr = events enumerated only by registration,
Ne = events enumerated only by survey, and
$NrNe/C$ = events enumerated neither by survey or registration.

The major theoretical features of this approach are few in number, simple in concept, difficult to apply, but highly rewarding because of their unique self-checking feature. There are other features of the Pakistan experiment which may be of significance. These include:

4. Paid full-time registrars rather than either part-time or voluntary workers. In Pakistan this advantage is strengthened by the requirement that the registrar must routinely visit approximately every tenth house-

[7]C. Chandra Sekar and W. Edwards Deming, "On a Method of Estimating Birth and Death Rates and the Extent of Registration," *Journal of the American Statistical Association*, 44: 101–115 (March, 1949).

[8]Ansley J. Coale, "The Design of an Experimental Procedure for Obtaining Accurate Vital Statistics," *International Population Conference, New York, 1961* (London: International Union for the Scientific Study of Population, 1963, pp. 372–375.

hold, where he inquires about events in the other households. In addition the registrar uses a network of local informants such as doctors, mid-wives, schoolteachers, barbers, and other knowledgeable people in the area.

5. The assigned areas covered by the registrar and the survey are identical.
6. Quarterly single-purpose surveys are conducted in the same areas and therefore basically among the same population, and overlapping reference periods are used in inquiring about vital events.
7. A question whether or not each woman in the reproductive ages is pregnant is included in each survey. The primary purpose of this question is to obtain a better estimate of early infant deaths. There is a tendency for respondents not to report either the birth or death if the infant death occurs within a few weeks after birth; but by following the outcome of a pregnancy one gets a better estimate of such events.
8. *De facto* rather than *de jure* enumeration is used, i.e., all vital events occurring in the area are to be reported but events occurring outside the area to usual residents of the area are not included.

It is clear that this system increases the possibility of an event being counted inasmuch as two investigators using different approaches record events occurring in the area. Also the comparing of individual events not only gives one increased confidence in the results but, equally important, provides a self-check of each set of data, indeed of each event. This approach forces one to evaluate each system. One can no longer hide behind the reassuring phrases that selection of interviewers is carefully done, training is long and rigorous, supervision is thorough, respondent co-operation is excellent, and processing is carefully controlled.

Another advantage of the system is that the so-called boundary effect is practically eliminated. If one asked a respondent to report on events that have occurred during the past year, the respondent may not have a clear concept of what a year is and thus may report events that happened more than a year ago as having happened within the year. Similarly, if one asked about events that have happened "since I was last here," the respondent may remember that an event occurred but thinks that he has previously reported it and fails to report the event. In the Pakistan PGE Study at each quarterly survey the respondent is asked to report on vital events that have occurred during the past year. On the basis of the earlier enumeration of members of the household, as well as previous reports of births and deaths, one is able to determine with greater assurance whether an event properly belongs within a specified year.

It is easy to see that there are many advantages to the system that has been built into the PGE Study in Pakistan. Indeed, this is one of the most promising experiments in the field of vital statistics that has ever been undertaken.[9] A similar study is under way in Thailand,[10] where several important innovations in the procedure have been introduced, notably, smaller sample clusters, a larger number of areas, and inclusion of a question about serious illnesses to strengthen estimates of deaths. Similar studies are also under way in India, also again with important variations. There is much to recommend the PGE approach, but at the same time one should recognize some of the disadvantages that are to be found in this system. Some of these follow.

1. The Chandra Sekar–Deming formula assumes independence on the part of the two systems. With careful controls such as those built into the Pakistan PGE experiment, collusion by the registrars and enumerators need not be a serious problem. Nonetheless, this is a potential problem which must be given careful consideration. More important is the probability that both systems tend to pick up the same type of events and also tend to lose the same type of event. For example, highly mobile populations, single-person households, and the like are more likely to be missed, by both systems, than are regular households among whom migration is relatively low. The tendency to miss the same class of events is a disadvantage that comes to all surveys and registrations and should not be counted as a unique disadvantage of the PGE system.

A more subtle factor may be that the two approaches tend to condition the respondents. The fact that a family member or household head has responded to the registrar about a specific birth or death may influence his reporting the event on the quarterly enumeration. The influence can be in either direction, i.e., he may have the event more clearly in mind or he may miss it because the event has already been reported.

2. Problems of matching are very difficult. There is no adequately developed theory for determining what is a "match," and procedures developed to date in matching studies are not fully objective. If the matching criteria are too rigid (exacting), an event which has been picked up both by the registrar and by the survey will sometimes be counted as two events because the entries about this event differ slightly. If, however, matching criteria are too loose, different events may be considered as the same event. In general, if matching criteria are too rigid, one gets an inflated estimate of the total number of events, and if the criteria are too loose, one gets an underestimate.

[9]For a more detailed discussion of this experiment see Nazir Ahmed and Karol J. Krotki, "Simultaneous Estimations of Population Growth," *Pakistan Development Review*, Vol. 3, No. 1 (Spring, 1963).

[10]Anuri Chintakananda and Patience Lauriat, "Technique To Measure Population Growth: Survey of Population Change in Thailand" (mimeographed), paper prepared for the World Population Conference, Belgrade, September, 1965.

The general procedure used in matching events in the Pakistan PGE Study is to compare events reported to the registrar and to the survey by machine-listing of events arranged in order by characteristics such as name of mother, name of father, name of infant, date of birth, place of birth, and sex of child. All apparent matches are verified by visual inspection of the records. All "possible matches" are visually inspected in the office and divided into three categories—matches, doubtful matches, and non-matches. The doubtful matches are referred to the field for final determination. The steps taken in the matching procedure are much more detailed than I have indicated, and one is partially reassured that such care is taken. Nonetheless, not every event is verified in the field and in practice there are many cases about which there is doubt whether there is or is not a match. The registration procedure, which is very carefully done, gives birth rates in the 40's for Pakistan. An examination of the survey data discloses enough events that were missed by the registrar to make it quite clear that the birth rate in Pakistan is 50 or above.

Matching forces one to compare data gathered by two different systems and inevitably results in one's knowing that neither system is completely accurate. In the absence of a well-developed theory for determining what is a match, we cannot state with assurance whether a given procedure results in an over- or underestimate as a result of the matching process. In addition to the problems of matching, a system such as PGE is time-consuming and expensive both in money and skilled manpower.

3. The number of sample areas in Pakistan is uncomfortably small and the variance of estimates, particularly of the death rate, is larger than would be desirable. The number of areas was determined basically by the decision to employ full-time registrars. The reasoning was that a full-time registrar would do a better job than a part-time registrar, and he would do a better job if he were kept reasonably busy each working day. These considerations led to the selection of areas of approximately 5,000 population each, primarily because of cost but also because of time and availability of personnel. The number of areas in the national sample was held to 20. Sampling theory would indicate that a larger number of areas would be preferable. In Thailand, where a similar study is being conducted, it was decided to select a much larger number of sample areas and to compare survey data with data collected through the regular registration system. In urban areas the registration and survey areas in Thailand are not identical, and special problems arise as a result of this. There has not been sufficient experience in Thailand to judge which of the systems is preferable. It is indeed fortunate that the Thailand plan differs from the Pakistan plan in this important respect; within a year or two

we should have sufficient information to make a meaningful judgment as to which of the two systems is preferable.

4. As was mentioned, vital events are counted (primarily) on a *de facto* basis. It is always difficult to enumerate highly mobile persons, single-person households, events that occurred in institutions, and events that occur to households that are dissolved between visits of enumerators. Some of these problems are heightened by using the *de facto* rather than the *de jure* systems. Also the *de jure* systems would require a follow-up of every individual and household that moved out of the area. It is easy to see that following a moderately large number of people over a considerable period of time would be expensive in both money and personnel.

Identification of the *de facto* universe depends on the accuracy of household listing and identification, the accuracy of reporting the place of occurrence of vital events, and the accuracy with which the PGE area has been delineated and mapped. Since the population is preponderantly illiterate, there is a general problem of how well respondents understand the questions about identification of individuals, characteristics such as age, and the time and place of the occurrence of an event. These factors create difficulties in the decisions on whether or not an event belongs to the universe and whether it matches another event. Obviously, such difficulties cannot be overcome solely by procedural methods.

There are other possible loopholes in the procedure for collecting information on deaths concerning which we have made no comment, because it seems likely that the number of events involved is quite small. It is difficult both in censuses and in sample surveys to obtain adequate coverage of events that happened to households who moved between surveys. Similarly, it is difficult to get a complete count of homeless individuals, of people with no fixed address such as those who sleep on sidewalks, under bridges, and the like.

5. There may be bias due to two systems operating in a single area. One should bear in mind the possibility that vital events will be more completely registered in areas where independent sample surveys are being conducted than in areas where the sample surveys are not being conducted. This differential effect presumably would be due mainly to the fact that sample survey enumerators go to every household and ask about births and deaths, and this in itself could stimulate people to register births and deaths in the regular registration system. Thus a successful matching of the vital events between registration and survey in selected areas will not necessarily mean that registration will also be satisfactory in areas where sample surveys are not being conducted. It is not clear whether on balance this should be listed as an advantage or disadvantage.

The estimated vital events from the PGE study for East and West Pakistan are given in Table 3.

In a separate analysis Melvin Zelnik and Masihur Rahman Khan[11] have estimated the birth rate for East and West Pakistan using the quasi-stable population analysis technique. Their figures for 1962 give a birth rate of 61 for East Pakistan and 48 for West Pakistan. The quasi-stable population technique is presumed to be accurate within four or five points per 1,000 and thus in a general way confirms the PGE results. Zelnik and Khan feel that the quasi-stable population analysis indicates that the death rate is somewhat higher than that shown by the PGE, though in my opinion the evidence for this is tenuous.

TABLE 3

ESTIMATED VITAL EVENTS FROM THE PAKISTAN PGE STUDY

ESTIMATED RATES	1962		1963	
	East Pakistan	West Pakistan	East Pakistan	West Pakistan
Birth..............	57	52	55	53
Death..............	20	19	19	19
Natural increase.....	3.7	3.3	3.6	3.4

THE MOROCCAN SURVEY

Between late 1961 and early 1963 a series of multipurpose surveys were carried out in Morocco.[12] Three surveys were conducted at intervals of six months, and special attention was devoted to birth and death statistics. The sample consisted of 146 primary units, usually villages, stratified by "agro-economic region" and by size. The total sample size (second round) was 63,666 persons. The essence of the method was to determine the base population at survey 1, inquire about vital events at survey 2, compare data from the two surveys, and then verify the data in the field and reconcile the differences at survey 3.

Field procedures consisted of: (1) Independent household enumerations were made on the first and second rounds. These were checked and reconciled on the third enumeration. (2) Retrospective mortality

[11]Melvin Zelnik and Masihur Rahman Khan, "An Estimate of the Birth Rate in East and West Pakistan," *Pakistan Development Review*, Vol. 5, No. 1 (Spring, 1965).

[12]Georges Sabagh and Christopher Scott, "An Evaluation of the Use of Retrospective Questionnaires for Obtaining Vital Data: The Experience of the Moroccan Multi-Purpose Sample Survey of 1961–1963" (mimeographed), paper prepared for the World Population Conference, Belgrade, September, 1965.

reports were gathered on all three rounds. Deaths during the preceding year were requested on the first and third rounds; deaths during the preceding seventeen months were recorded on the second round, and date of death plus age at death was noted.

This procedure resulted in complete agreement for 85% of births but for only 59% of deaths. The checking procedure disclosed that the single inquiry about vital events resulted in about 10% overreporting and 7% underreporting of births. Similarly, the single inquiry gave 26% over- and 15% underreporting of deaths. The adjusted or corrected birth and death rates were not greatly different from those obtained from the single inquiry: 44.8 versus 46.2 for births, and 21.0 versus 23.3 for deaths. The authors point out, however, that single surveys contain many errors, and indeed the figures just presented show that there was considerable over- and underreporting of vital events. The fact that the over- and underreporting more or less canceled each other in this particular case should not lead us to relax the skepticism that has developed regarding single surveys.

Promising though this procedure appears to be, difficulties of implementation are considerable. First, the "corrected" figures include arbitrary additions of 2% of births and 8% of deaths. The rationale for the additions is clear enough. Infant mortality was assumed to be 170, and both births and infant deaths were added to reflect this rate. Reported mortality among inmigrants was lower than seemed reasonable, and a number of deaths were added to bring these figures into line. Second, 10% of the sampling units containing about 12% of the population were dropped from the analysis because 15% or more of the population found at the second round could not be matched with that of the first. We are not given information about matching of populations in the remaining sampling units, although it is a fair inference that varying proportions up to 15% of the population could not be matched in the two surveys. In addition to the problem of coverage, or counting the population, characteristics such as age, occupation, and the like undoubtedly were reported differently in different surveys. Third, such a procedure assumes that in-migration balances out-migration, both in volume and kind. This assumption probably leads to an undercount of deaths. For example, single-person households which are terminated by death tend to be counted as outmigrants rather than as deaths. Fourth, if a *de facto* procedure is used, events occurring in institutions are difficult to estimate with accuracy. A sufficiently large sample of areas would include a representative sample of such institutions, but in practice a special count of such events probably is needed. If the country in which the study is being conducted is very underdeveloped, relatively few births and deaths occur in institutions, but as economic development increases this problem becomes increasingly important. Fifth, this procedure shares with other surveys the problem of underenumeration of infants. Some infants born shortly before the first round are missed at the first round. If the infant dies before the second round there is a high probability that he will be missed. If he survives until the second round he is likely to be enumerated and to be counted as a birth that occurred between the two surveys. This particular procedure leads to some overcounting. On the other hand, infants born between the two rounds who were missed at the second round were not counted at all. The latter two types of errors would be largely eliminated if the surveys were to continue year after year.

These are formidable difficulties, but there are advantages to the system. By taking more than one survey, one can largely eliminate the so-called boundary effect. This is possible by using the first survey as the starting point, counting the population living in a specified area, and then recording changes in the households. With minor exceptions one can determine whether a given event occurred before or after the first survey even if the respondent misplaces the event in time. One must use an overlapping reference period, that is, ask about events that occurred during the survey interval plus some longer period. For example, if the surveys were taken six months apart, one could ask about events during the past twelve months. Similarly, if the surveys were twelve months apart, one could ask about events for the past eighteen months. A second advantage of this approach is that vital events can be included as part of a multipurpose survey, thus keeping costs down. It must be admitted, however, that one does not know whether the data will be of as high quality as might have been the case if the survey had attempted to obtain only the base population, a few characteristics such as age, sex, and relationship to head of the household, plus births and deaths.

REGISTRATION AREAS

An obvious though untried method of estimating vital events for a country is to set up a probability sample of registration areas, taking special steps to insure that registration is of high quality in the sample areas. One would need to conduct annual or biennial censuses in such areas in order to obtain a good estimate of the total population which is required in order to obtain birth and death rates. At the same time the censuses could ask about vital events during the preceding year and matching could be performed if desired for a subsample of such events. This latter approach would provide a check on the quality of registration and insure that the system was operating properly.

Persons responsible for registration of vital events by and large have taken the view that registration systems must be extended throughout the country as rapidly as possible. They have not been sufficiently concerned with the possible demographic uses of registration data to institute a system such as that described above. Registration data are needed for individual records, but at the same time they are useful for demographic purposes. It takes decades rather than a few years to set up a good registration system. In the meantime imaginative registration officials could provide useful national data and strengthen their case for registration statistics if they were to set up a probability sample of registration areas for the purposes of providing current estimates of vital events and of establishing model registration areas.

OTHER MAJOR STUDIES

We have already mentioned the main features of studies in Pakistan, Thailand, Morocco, and India (the National Sample Survey). There are several other studies and techniques that deserve special mention.

Guanabara Demographic Pilot Survey.[13]—This was a joint project of the United Nations and the government of Brazil undertaken in 1961. A careful sample was drawn and a sophisticated actuarial accounting procedure used to determine the period of observation. A relatively small sample of 2,411 households, and 11,438 persons were observed for a total of 6,750 person-years. Dwellings that came into the sample were visited four times during the year, and on the fourth visit inquiry was made about all vital events during the period of observation, thus affording a check on data gathered between rounds 1 and 3. Omissions discovered during the fourth round increased the birth rate from 15.5 to 22.8 and the death rate from 6.0 to 7.3. The report on this study does not give details of the forms that were used, the questions that were asked, or how certain concepts were applied. For example, it is stated that the period of observation was defined as the time between the moment at which a person was registered for the first time to the date of his last interview unless he had ceased to live in the particular dwelling or had died before this last visit. In either of these cases the period of observation was considered to be terminated on the day when the person left the investigated dwelling or died. The problem of follow-up for a household that migrated during the period, or of the dissolution of a household, is not discussed.

[13]United Nations, *Guanabara Demographic Pilot Survey: A Joint Project of the United Nations and the Government of Brazil* (New York: United Nations, 1964).

Senegal: The Sine Saloum Study.[14]–Two homogeneous political districts were selected for a study of vital statistics, one containing a population of about 33,500 and the other a population of 17,500. An individual card index was established for each person, and this is brought up to date annually by visiting each family and recording the events that have occurred since the original census. Cantrelle states that the data collected by this procedure are much better than those provided by the official register of births, marriages, and deaths. Also, according to Cantrelle, the method used seems to be preferable to the surveys based on a single retrospective questionnaire, which had previously been used in Senegal. Field workers carry with them at each survey information collected during the preceding visit. Special attention is given to recording live births resulting in a death between censuses. This is done by intensive questioning of women aged 15–49 who are recorded as not having borne a child during the study period. In a one-in-four sample of villages, retrospective fertility records were collected.

Data from the studies for 1963 and 1964 show birth rates of 54 and 51 for 1963, and 47 and 44 for 1964. Death rates were 25 and 34 for 1963, 28 and 35 for 1964.

United Arab Republic.[15]–A study conducted by the North African Demographic Center, with financing from the United States National Center of Health Statistics, is designed to obtain an estimate of the birth rate and the death rate, initially in lower Egypt. Three censuses will be taken at six-month intervals in order to provide estimates of the population at risk. The censuses will ask about the number of children ever born, but will not attempt to obtain estimates of births and deaths. Instead, these data will be obtained from a special registration system utilizing part-time local personnel, with each registrar covering 200 households, about 1,000 people. He will make five calls a day, thus completing a round every forty days, with more frequent calls on known pregnant women. In addition, the registrar will talk frequently with knowledgeable people, but information is to be obtained by observation and from informal conversation rather than by structured interviews.

The Turkish Demographic Survey.[16]–The Turkish Demographic

[14]Pierre Cantrelle, "Repeated Demographic Observation in a Rural Area in Senegal: Method and First Results" (mimeographed), paper prepared for the World Population Conference, Belgrade, September, 1965.

[15]G. Vukovich, "The U.A.R. Project for Measuring Vital Rates in Rural Areas" (mimeographed), paper prepared for the World Population Conference, Belgrade, September, 1965.

[16]Nusret H. Fişek, Yasar Heperkan, Zeki Avralioglu, and John Rumford, *The Turkish Demographic Survey* (Ankara: School of Public Health, 1964).

Survey is an annual household sampling program designed to provide estimates of vital statistics for all of Turkey, for five major geographic areas, and for rural and urban populations in each of these areas. Within the urban areas blocks of 100 households will be taken and in the rural areas 150 villages averaging about 100 households will be included. The basic procedure is to take annual censuses asking about births and deaths during the preceding one year. In one-fifth of the areas a subsample will be taken and a part-time registrar who lives in the area will record births and deaths throughout the year. Data collected under the two systems are to be compared on a gross basis, and in a subsample of areas individual events will be matched. The survey was undertaken in the Ankara area early in 1965, and it was planned to extend the program to another area before the end of the year. Additional areas will be included in subsequent years.

CONCLUDING REMARKS

The above listing of studies in the field is not complete. For example, several studies are under way in India which are patterned on the Chandra Sekar–Deming approach, but the supervisor, who takes censuses semiannually and inquires about births and deaths, reconciles information he obtains with that of the registrar while still in the field. A very important methodological study is being undertaken by the United States National Center of Health Statistics with the co-operation of the Triangle Institute in North Carolina. This study is very carefully designed and basically attempts to determine whether single retrospective questionnaires can obtain accurate estimates of vital events even under ideal conditions in a developed country. Another recent development is a specialized method of analyzing "poor" demographic data. The so-called Brass technique assumes that younger women are less likely to forget recent vital events, and less likely to misplace such events in time than are older women. Given data on total number of children ever born—say, from a census—and recent data on children born, both by age of mother, the Brass technique provides a method of analyzing and of adjusting the data in order to arrive at better estimates of births. A similar procedure has been developed for estimating deaths.

The burden of this paper is that:

1. Single retrospective surveys cannot be depended upon to provide valid or reliable estimates of births and deaths.

2. Multipurpose surveys tend to carry such a heavy load of questions that both interviewers and respondents perform poorly in asking about and providing information on vital events.

3. Repeated surveys among the same population, or with a relatively small proportion of the sample being rotated in and out at each survey, is a promising technique, though the difficulties of carrying through such an operation are formidable.

4. An important loss is failure of respondents to report births that terminate in early infant death. A partial solution to this problem is to ask about pregnancies in each survey, and to determine outcome of the pregnancy in a subsequent interview.

5. Another source of error is failure to use overlapping reference periods. The result is that respondents sometimes fail to report a remembered event because they think they have already reported it.

6. Matching studies such as the Pakistan PGE provide a unique self-checking feature which forces recognition of the fact that each procedure is missing significant numbers of events. The procedure is difficult to police, is moderately expensive, and requires skilled, dedicated, and patient personnel, but at the present time it appears to be the best procedure available.

7. A probability sample of registration areas probably would provide good data at relatively low cost and relatively small input of professional personnel. During the initial years of installing such a system, checks on a part of the sample should be undertaken with surveys, including individual matching of events.

51

KAP STUDIES ON FERTILITY

BERNARD BERELSON
Vice-President, The Population Council

If there is one theme that characterizes the field of family planning, it is recency. Several national programs to implement family planning have been initiated or largely expanded in the past few years, and a major innovation in contraceptive technology was brought to world-wide attention and use in the same period. Similarly with respect to the present subject: over twenty so-called KAP studies of some substance have been done in as many countries since the 1960 conference on research in family planning[1]—for example, in South Korea, Taiwan, Turkey, Tunisia, Thailand, the Philippines, Ghana, seven Latin American countries, and, again in the fall of 1965, the United States. Accordingly, it seems appropriate to take stock, particularly with regard to these recent endeavors.

By "KAP studies" we mean sample surveys of knowledge, attitudes, and practices with regard to fertility matters. I shall restrict myself here to those surveys primarily KAP in character, and shall not speak of surveys designed mainly to get at vital rates or of surveys designed mainly to get at a specific matter like, for example, a follow-up study of IUD practice (both of which are dealt with elsewhere in this volume). Moreover, I shall concentrate, as fits the occasion, on the place of KAP studies in furthering family planning programs—that is, on their applied or professional contributions rather than their basic or academic ones.[2] Finally by way of introduction, I

---

[1] Clyde V. Kiser (ed.), *Research in Family Planning* (Princeton: Princeton University Press, 1962).

[2] I am encouraged to do so not only by the nature of the Conference but also by the appearance in *Studies in Family Planning*, No. 7, June, 1965, of a thorough review of such surveys by my colleague at the Population Council, W. Parker Mauldin, Associate Director, Demographic Division.

shall speak to three questions: What do KAP studies cover? What do we learn from them? How are they used?

WHAT COVERED

Analysis of the major KAP questionnaires of recent years reveals a common subject matter that can be summarized under six main headings. This, then, is what KAP studies tend to cover—"tend to" because not every study covers the same items, certainly not in the same way, though there does appear to be a growing standardization among studies.

Coverage of KAP Studies[3]

Vital data: marriage age and duration, pregnancy history, live births, living children, fecundity

Attitude on family size: desired family size, expected family size, ideal number of children, ideal pregnancy interval, desire for more children, discussion of family size with spouse and others, perception of others' attitudes on similar questions

Attitude on family limitation: approval or disapproval of family limitation in general, of contraception, of sterilization, and of abortion; reasons for approval or disapproval, readiness to practice family planning, willingness to learn methods of family planning, approval or disapproval of government program for family planning, attitude toward national population growth, source of influence on fertility attitudes, perception of others' attitudes on similar questions

Knowledge: information about reproductive physiology, including time of conception; knowledge of contraceptive methods, general and specific; perception of recent trends in mortality, especially infant mortality

Practice: ever, now, and expected practice of family planning by method, when started and sequence, sterilization of either spouse, experience of abortion

Background characteristics: not only the usual demographic items such as age, education, literacy, religion, and occupation, but also rural-urban origin, household composition and facilities, family structure, interest in education, mobility, and other indices of modernized attitudes

This may seem simple enough—but only to someone who has never tried to frame a manageable questionnaire along these lines or to administer it in the field. In fact, it is by no means easy to construct a valid instrument to measure these items, as is perhaps indicated by the number of separate questions utilized and the interview time required in some recent surveys (Table 1). Not every question is asked of every

[3]From analysis of the recent KAP questionnaires listed in Table 1.

respondent—some questions are dependent upon earlier answers—but as the time column shows, it still takes at least half an hour for a short version and over an hour for the full exercise.

What Learned

It is easy to make technical criticisms of such studies, but it is not easy to do better. We need not go into the technicalities here, but in my opinion, the sampling has been fairly good, the formulation of questions acceptable or better, the interviewing at least adequate, and the analysis if anything overdone (again, from the standpoint of administrative requirements). The main question probably goes to validity of response: do people really mean what they say? Probably

TABLE 1

QUESTIONS AND DURATION IN RECENT KAP INTERVIEWS
(Approximate)

Country	Number of Questions	Average Duration of Interview (in minutes)
Taiwan (1962): long version	309	80
(1963): short version	107	30
Turkey (1963)	140	45
Tunisia (1964)	162	40
Latin America: 6 cities (1964)	130	45
Thailand (1964)	241	40
United States (1965)	251	75

not, literally and fully. But that does not imply that the responses are capricious—far from it. My own view is that the surveys are indeed valid as indications of broad tendencies within groups, though not for every specific item in each individual case, and that their substance can be taken seriously in administrative calculations.

The results of such studies are, in good time, written up in several hundreds of pages. Accordingly, it is difficult to present such complex matters in capsule review but perhaps the effort can be made so long as it is appreciated for what it is. Without all the necessary qualifications for particular cases, here are what seem to me to be six major sets of findings from KAP surveys, viewed primarily from the administrative standpoint.

1. On the whole, married couples in the developing countries want fewer children than they will have under present fertility conditions —enough fewer to make a demographic difference if actuality were

made equivalent to desire (Table 2). The size of the difference varies: of the order of 25%–30% in Asian and African countries, about 15% in Latin America (though all of the latter samples are urban, where the differential is smaller than in the rural areas). In other words, if couples were able to do what they said they wanted to do, and if all other conditions remained the same, this would mean a decline of, say, ten points in the birth rate of the typical developing country and a decline of one point in the growth rate. (In the developed countries, incidentally, the "ideal" is much closer to completed family size, e.g., 97% in the United States.)

TABLE 2

COMPLETED AND "IDEAL" FAMILY SIZE[a]

(Approximate)

Country	Completed Family Size	"Ideal" Family Size	"Ideal" of Completed (per cent)
Ghana (urban).........	7.0	5.3	76
Tunisia (national).......	5.9	4.3	73
Korea (national).......	5.4	4.2	78
Taiwan (urban).........	5.5	3.9	71
Thailand (rural)........	5.2	3.8	73
Turkey (national).......	5.8	3.5	60
Colombia (urban).......	4.8	3.6	75
Venezuela (urban).......	4.3	3.5	81
Mexico (urban).........	5.0	4.2	84
Panama (urban)........	3.8	3.5	92
Brazil (urban)..........	3.3	2.7	82
Costa Rica (urban)......	4.3	3.6	83

[a] Data taken from the Mauldin article and the more recent surveys, as reported in this volume, e.g., Tunisia, Thailand, Latin America. Completed family size is usually number of living children for women of highest age group, e.g., over 40. Here and elsewhere, my thanks to the various investigators for making these data available.

Note too the relationship of actual (completed) and desired family size: the lower the one, the lower the other (Fig. 1).[4] This may seem almost a truism—if people want fewer children they will have fewer—but it is more than that in two ways. First, as we have just said, many couples in the developing world (and the developed too, for that matter) will have more children than they want because of lack of

[4]In addition to the countries listed in Table 2, the following are included in Figure 1:

	Completed Family Size	"Ideal" Family Size
Japan (national)................	2.0	2.8
Hungary (national)..............	2.5	2.4
France (national)...............	2.8	2.7
United States (national).........	3.4	3.3
Philippines (urban/rural)........	5.9	5.0

information, services, and supplies. Thus, almost all the countries have larger completed families than the ideal—that is, lie on that side of the equivalence line in Figure 1. Only Japan is on the other side.

Beyond that, however, the fact comes to have an influence upon the ideal: there is an effect from behavior upon attitude as well as the other way around. What this suggests is that as the size of completed family declines in the developing countries, with the successful implementation of family planning programs, the "ideal" family size will

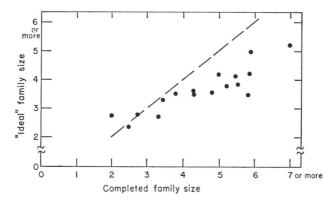

Fig. 1.—Completed and "ideal" family size (approximate), by country

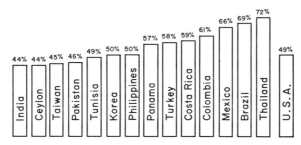

Fig. 2.—Percentage wanting no more children (approximate)

decline too. Thus the "ideal" does not have to be attacked directly via educational programs, or at any rate not solely that way, in order to bring it down; the indirect influence of an actual decline in completed family size may actually be the best way to achieve that objective.

2. As corollary, substantial proportions of people in the developing world want no more children now—from nearly a half to three-fourths (Fig. 2). And everywhere, the main reason for this interest has to do with the economic welfare of the family, including the pro-

vision of educational and occupational opportunities for the children. Thus, the very circumstances of life have produced what may be called a natural motivation toward family planning as distinguished from the contrived motivation that may result from informational campaigns if perceived as artificial—and the former are far more durable and consequential than the latter. In short, if one takes these responses at their face value—and if one believes in the personal freedoms at stake, quite aside from the population problem—these data seem sufficient warrant in themselves for remedial administrative action wherever necessary.

3. Furthermore, whenever asked, substantial proportions of married couples approve family planning in principle, express interest in learning how to control their own fertility, say they would do something if they had appropriate means, and want the government to

TABLE 3

INTEREST IN LEARNING FERTILITY CONTROL

Country	Interested in Learning (per cent)	Want Government Program (per cent)
Taiwan (1963)	66	....
Thailand (1964)..........	66	57
Tunisia (1964)..........	66	....
Turkey (1963)............	68	75
Korea (1964).............	73	....

carry on a program along these lines. In Table 3 are illustrative data from studies done in the past few years. The essential equivalence of interest in learning, in these countries of the developing world, is quite remarkable. And almost everywhere, women strongly disapprove of induced abortions but, under the pressure of circumstances, many have them.

4. When it comes to knowledge, the picture is rather different. The level of information about the physiology of reproduction is low indeed: for example, fewer than 10% of Turkish and Thai women correctly know the days of the cycle when conception is possible. Substantially more people know, at least in an elementary way, that fertility control is possible and that one or more contraceptive methods are available. But the proportions who do not know any contraceptive method range from over 40% in Turkey to 65% in rural Thailand to 85% in Tunisia. At the same time, large proportions know that child mortality is down in their areas as compared with their own and their parents' generations (e.g., 40% in Turkey and 76% in Thailand). In

general, on this as on most other matters, people tend to believe that others think as they do; thus perception and observation come to reinforce one another.

5. The practice of family planning varies: in the developing world from very low to moderately low (for example, under 10% in rural India, Pakistan, and Thailand; 15%–20% in Taiwan, Korea, and Tunisia; 25% in Turkey); in the developed world from moderately high to high (over two-thirds in Japan, 80% in the United States). And the more general the practice, the earlier it tends to begin: before the first child in the developed countries; only after the third or fourth child, if at all, in the developing countries. Going beyond available data, one might conjecture that early use of contraception, for spacing purposes, will not take hold until something like 25% of the married population practices family planning with some regularity (or until popular education reaches large proportions of the young women), and that a mass program to spread family planning can make substantial headway if as many as 15%–20% of the people are already practicing contraception, as a base of acceptance.

6. Finally, the social differentials correlated with fertility attitudes and behavior are essentially the same across societies.

To begin with, there is one important characteristic that does not seem to have a major differential effect in these matters: husbands and wives have essentially the same attitudes. True, in most countries the men want more children than the women, but not by much. On most attitude questions, husbands and wives give similar answers. So even if they have not talked much about these issues—and that is what the evidence suggests—they nevertheless tend to agree.

But there are some things that matter a great deal. A major determinant of the desire for more children, probably *the* major determinant, is the number of children the parents already have. The picture is remarkably consistent, and everywhere the same. By the time the parents have had two children, substantial proportions say they are ready to stop; by the time they have had three or four children, over two-thirds of them are ready to stop (Fig. 3).[5] Here again, the distinctiveness of the urban samples in Latin America stands out: the city people are ready at an earlier stage, and those curves are on the high side (particularly the top one for Brazil).

[5]Again the data, in a few cases approximated from different samples, are from the Mauldin article and the later surveys, and for the following countries: Ceylon, India, Pakistan, South Korea, Taiwan, Thailand, The Philippines, Turkey, Tunisia, Brazil, Colombia, Costa Rica, Mexico, and Panama. The dotted line is for the United States (based on data kindly provided by Arthur Campbell, from the 1960 "growth of American family" study reported in Pascal Whelpton *et al.*, *Fertility and Family Planning in the United States*, Princeton University Press, 1965.) The detailed data are given in Table 4.

In addition, literacy and education matter, as well as income and urbanization (the last partly reflecting the higher educational levels of the cities). In every survey comparing rural and urban residents, the urban are farther along the road to effective contraception, in both attitude and behavior. And the more education, the more modern in regard to family planning too. Figures 4–7 illustrate the situation, with

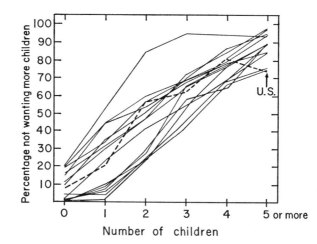

Fig. 3.—Percentage not wanting more children, by number of children

TABLE 4

PERCENTAGE NOT WANTING MORE CHILDREN BY NUMBER OF CHILDREN

COUNTRY	NUMBER OF CHILDREN					
	0	1	2	3	4	5 or more
Ceylon............	2	8	29	57	69	88
India.............	2	7	25	43	74	88
Pakistan..........	4	5	25	42	67	74
Taiwan...........	0	1	24	54	76	88
Thailand..........	12	30	48	71	85	96
Turkey...........	19	34	58	68	67	76
Philippines........	3	24	42	56	68	85
Korea............	1	8	28	65	81	94
Tunisia...........	1	9	26	44	68	87
Brazil............	21	53	85	95	93	93
Colombia.........	15	45	55	67	79	93
Costa Rica........	20	45	60	67	78	86
Mexico...........	16	30	48	64	76	86
Panama..........	11	35	51	70	86	94
United States......	8	20	57	62	81	74

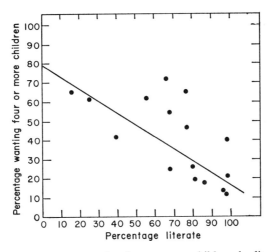

FIG. 4.—Percentage wanting four or more children, by literacy

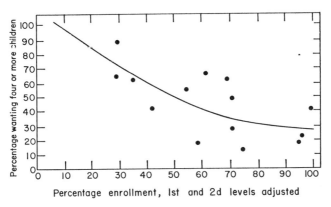

FIG. 5.—Percentage wanting four or more children, by educational enrollment

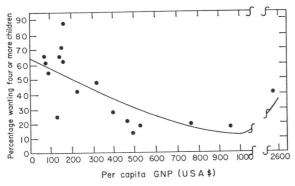

FIG. 6.—Percentage wanting four or more children, by income

countries as units.[6] Note, for example, that of the countries with more than 70% literate, only three (Korea, Jamaica, and the United States) are 40% or above in wanting four or more children; and of those with less than 70% literate, only one (Ceylon) is below 40%. The differentiation is even stronger in the case of per capita GNP (at the break of $400)—which is, of course, a direct indication of national development. (For these data, incidentally, the minimum value for "wanting four or more children" comes at a per capita income of about $1,500.)

Two further points should be made. In the first place, illiterate women of no education are today practicing effective contraception and have been brought to that practice by deliberate programmatic

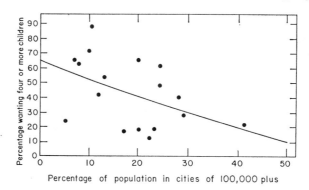

Fig. 7.—Percentage wanting four or more children, by urbanization

effort—for example, in Taiwan where 40% of recent acceptors were women of no education or in Korea where the illiterate participated in the program almost as fully as the literate (i.e., in a rural area with 47% of the women illiterate, 40% of the acceptors were illiterate; and in an urban area, the corresponding figures were 19% and 15%). The importance of this point is worth stressing: at least some measure of family planning need not wait upon the long, slow process of modernization.

The second point is that in the developed countries, where contraception has been in effect much longer, the filter-down process is not yet complete—for example, in Japan, where perhaps one-quarter of the people are not yet effective contraceptors, or in the United States,

[6]The data on literacy (reversed from illiteracy), education, and urbanization in Figures 4–7 come from the United Nations, *Compendium of Social Statistics: 1963*, Tables 59, 61, and 5, respectively. The data on gross national product are from the U.N.'s *Yearbook of National Accounts Statistics, 1962*, Table 3. The data refer to different years and are probably not strictly comparable or equally valid, but they do provide the rough picture. The detailed data are given in Table 5.

where a recent report of the National Academy of Sciences, "The Growth of U.S. Population," estimates that 10%–12% of the population, the poorer segment, are similarly uninformed and unprovided for.

How Used

KAP studies are used for three purposes—the descriptive, the evaluative, and the directive.

By descriptive, I mean their use to secure a reliable picture of the

TABLE 5

PERCENTAGE WANTING FOUR OR MORE CHILDREN, BY EDUCATIONAL
ENROLLMENT, LITERACY, INCOME, AND URBANIZATION

Country	Percentage Wanting 4 or More Children	Enrollment, 1st and 2d Levels (adjusted)	Percentage Literate	Per Capita GNP (US$)	Percentage of Population in Cities of More than 100,000
Ghana............	88	30	....	172	11
Korea............	65	62	77	144	20
Taiwan...........	62	69	54	161	24
Thailand..........	54	55	68	96	13
Turkey...........	42	42	39	220	12
Pakistan..........	65	29	17	70	7
India.............	62	35	24	75	8
Philippines........	71	....	65	153	10
Hungary..........	13	74	97	490	22
France...........	17	94	96	943	17
Japan............	22	96	98	464	41
Italy.............	18	58	86	516	20
United States.....	40	100	98	2,572	28
Ceylon...........	25	....	68	128	5
Chile.............	27	71	80	400	29
Jamaica..........	48	71	77	316	24
Puerto Rico.......	19	....	81	761	23

present situation for the enlightenment of everyone concerned. And by "everyone concerned," I refer not only to the professional people directly involved, but also, and perhaps particularly, to governmental and political officers, the medical fraternity, the press, the business community, and other professional and lay groups whose support is important for family planning programs. It is probably fair to say that such groups tend to believe that the mass of their own people, those low in status and life position, are uninterested in fertility control; and it is important to correct that impression. As an example, the KAP survey done in Turkey in 1963 was given wide attention and contributed to bringing about the recent change in national population policy. It may even be, contrary to the typical impression of national elites, that there is more political potential in this issue than political risk.[7] In any case, the KAP survey performs a useful service in setting forth, in objective and scientific manner, what people now know, believe, and do with regard to fertility.

By evaluative, I refer to the use of KAP surveys as part of the battery of instruments to measure the outcome of a family planning program. In fact, it is one of three such tools, along with the day-to-day system of records and the registration of vital data (or a substitute therefor). As an evaluative instrument, an initial KAP survey can provide the baseline against which progress in information, attitude, and practice can be measured by subsequent surveys of similar character. For example, surveys done only a year apart in Korea showed that even in that brief period, but with a vigorous effect, the results shown in Table 6 can be attained. Where good vital data are available,

TABLE 6

EVALUATION OF KOREAN PROGRAM, OVER
A ONE-YEAR PERIOD[a]

(Per Cent)

	April, 1964	April, 1965
Knew a contraceptive method..........	55	64
Knew the IUD	11	71
Currently practicing family planning....	10	16
Methods practiced (of all methods)		
Rhythm.........................	39	17
Condom.........................	36	54
IUD.........................	4	24

a Data from chap. 2 in this volume.

they are the court of final appeal, since they are what the whole exercise is about. (In this connection, the KAP question about current pregnancy is in my opinion a useful substitute for trend measurement of over-all success). Where a good record system is available, it can yield a great deal of data useful for evaluative purposes. The KAP survey takes time and, in order to measure small changes in behavior reliably, rather large samples; and hence it may be costly in money and personnel.

Finally, by directive I mean the use of such surveys to guide programmatic decisions. Take, for example, the promising analyses of Korean and Taiwan data shown in Table 7. In the Korean case, a single question differentiates sharply between those who do and do not subsequently accept family planning; and the two questions jointly dif-

[7]Since this was written, for example, the availability of oral contraception was made a political issue in France, and opposition candidates for the presidency appealed to the women's vote on that basis.

ferentiate from over 50% down to 2%. Thus, if he is able practically to take advantage of the information, the administrator is told, for example, that over half of those people who *both* say they want contraception *and* had a child within the past two and a half years will indeed become family planners, whereas their opposites are hardly worth pursuing at all; and those with one characteristic but not both are in the middle, with one chance in four of accepting. The Taiwan data are not so dramatic, but there too one sees some differentiation

TABLE 7

PERCENTAGE ACCEPTING FAMILY PLANNING[a]

KOREA: KOYANG AND KIMPO

Months since Latest Birth	Want Contraception?		Total
	Yes	No	
29 or fewer.........	53 (281)[b]	25 (164)	42 (445)
30 or more.........	23 (51)	2 (147)	7 (198)
Total...........	48 (332)	14 (311)	31 (643)

TAIWAN: TAICHUNG

Months since Latest Birth	Has Son?		Total
	Yes	No	
23 or fewer.........	17 (1,128)	3 (311)	14 (1,439)
24 or more.........	8 (841)	2 (163)	7 (1,004)
Total...........	13 (1,969)	2 (474)	11 (2,443)

[a] Data kindly made available by my friends at the Population Studies Center, University of Michigan: Ronald Freedman, John Takeshita, and John Ross (now with Population Council).

[b] Base figures in parentheses.

on the basis of only two questions. However, it must be added that such information is not readily capable of exploitation by administrative action: that is the problem.

These are only the briefest indications of how KAP surveys are utilized, with an illustration or two. It is perhaps fair to say that their utility to date has been roughly in the order given. As description, they have helped to dispel several myths that have characterized this field, and to bring some influential people to a clearer recognition of the present state of things. As evaluation, their use has thus far been infrequent. As direction, only the first beginnings have been made.

If there is one key recommendation that emerges from this quick review of the KAP survey as a servant of family planning programs, to my mind it is that we must find quicker and more efficient ways to tie KAP studies into administrative actions. That probably means shorter interviews and faster analysis and reporting of central findings: in administrative work, at least, there is such a thing as misplaced precision. It may also mean more standardization of questions, though a good start has already been made.

Beyond that, however, it will require deliberate focusing of KAP surveys on administrative questions. The problem is that the scholar is after valid conclusions, the administrator after workable decisions— and the two are not the same. How to improve the contribution of conclusions to decisions—that is the question that now faces scholars and administrators engaged in this common enterprise.

52

RECORDS AND RECORD-KEEPING IN FAMILY PLANNING PROGRAMS

CHRISTOPHER TIETZE, M.D.
Director of Research
National Committee on Maternal Health

Quod non apparet non est is a time-honored juridical maxim: That which does not appear in the record does not exist, at least not in the eyes of the law. While bitter experience has taught demographers to adopt a less formalistic attitude vis-à-vis the sometimes baffling relationships between recorded, registered, or reported "facts" and the underlying realities, they cannot escape the imperatives of a culture which exalts the written word and the written number. In olden days the adherents of three great religions—Jews, Christians, and Muslims—were collectively referred to as the People of the Book. There are also "professions of the book" and one of these is the demographic profession. We reserve our highest esteem for what we call, not infrequently with considerable self-deception, hard data, and we hold in suspicion and even in contempt the medical practitioner's clinical impressions and the social reformers' self-evident relationships of cause and effect.

When our chairman asked me to prepare a paper on records and record-keeping in family planning programs, he did not specify the scope of my paper. He did not need to do so since I knew I would be addressing a group ready, willing, and able to assign to this subject the importance it deserves.

In theory, my discussion could include at least three major types of records: (*a*) Records primarily designed for research purposes, including the forms used in surveys of knowledge, attitudes, and practices; (*b*) records primarily designed for providing service to individual patients or clients; and (*c*) records used in large-scale family planning programs and designed to provide the administration with information required for evaluation and policy-making.

It became quickly apparent, however, that it would be necessary to sidestep the entire area of records for research purposes. There are as many types of research records as there are problems to be studied. Moreover, there is usually more than one good way to record a particular set of data and it would be utter folly on my part, as well as *hubris,* to try to spell out what I consider the best approaches to some of the research problems in which this group is interested. I recognize that our principal concern is not pure research, but action-oriented research. I believe, however, that this distinction is more important from the point of view of choice of subject than from the point of view of methodology and, therefore, of records and record-keeping.

Nor do I want to discuss records primarily designed for service to the individual patient or client or, in the context of family planning, to the individual couple. Prototypes of such records appear in the *Medical Handbook* of the IPPF. If they are well designed and well kept and if the follow-up is reasonably complete, they may occasionally serve as a basis for research, but because they remain in the clinic or in a doctor's office, they cannot easily be used for the day-to-day tasks of evaluation and policy-making.

The remaining portion of my report is concerned with records designed to provide the administrator with the information he needs for the evaluation of a family planning program and for making policy decisions. Since the kind and amount of information required are obviously predicated upon the nature and scope of the program, I shall boldly assume that the program involves, among its major features (*a*) educational activities on the local level, such as home visiting or neighborhood meetings, and (*b*) the insertion of intra-uterine contraceptive devices (IUD's) by physicians in private practice or in special clinics. Nationwide programs of this type were launched in Taiwan and Korea in 1964 and are moving successfully toward their targets.

The key document in this type of program is the "coupon" which is issued by local family planning workers to those women who wish to have an IUD inserted. The woman surrenders the coupon to the physician at the time of the insertion. At the end of the month, the physician transmits the accumulated coupons to the appropriate authority and receives an honorarium based on the number of insertions he has reported.

A typical coupon is shown in Figure 1, based on those now being used in Taiwan and Korea. The upper portion is filled in by the family planning worker. It serves to identify the woman being referred, as well as the person making the referral. In addition, it provides space for the recording of basic demographic and social information about the woman requesting insertion. The details of this section are, of course, tailored to the requirements of the program.

The lower part of the coupon is filled in by the doctor who certifies the fact and date of insertion and claims the stipulated fee. The question relating to type and size of IUD may be modified or omitted if only one size or type of device is used in the program.

The coupon is a most cleverly designed instrument for the collection of up-to-date information on the progress of the family planning program and has already demonstrated its usefulness in Taiwan

REFERRAL COUPON

Coupon number.......................................

Name...

Address...

Date of birth...........................Age...........................

Living children: Male..............Female..............Total..............

Source of referral:

Name...

Address...

Circle one: FP field   Visiting   Health

                 worker   nurse   station

                 Other (specify)...

Name of physician.......................................

Address...

Type and size of IUD..................................

Date of insertion..

Fig. 1.—Typical coupon issued to women who wish IUD

and Korea. I can make this statement without embarrassment, since I had nothing to do with the design. Consider the advantages and potentialities of the coupon:

1. Underreporting and late reporting are minimized by the fact that payments are made to the inserting physicians on the basis of the number of coupons returned by them. According to some accounts, it has been more difficult, on occasion, to arrange for prompt payment than to obtain timely reporting. Overreporting is possible if some doctors try to claim compensation for insertions not actually performed. However, detection of fraud can be avoided with certainty only by the collusion of three individuals—the physician, the field worker, and the woman alleged to have been fitted with an IUD. Since coin of the realm is involved, one may expect the fiscal authorities to be alert to gross overfulfillment of quotas in particular localities.

2. The coupons returned each month can be hand-sorted quickly by residence, age, number of children, and so on. Almost complete information on the number and geographic distribution of insertions and on the characteristics of the women can be available to the administrator within weeks after the end of the month during which the insertions took place. Moreover, the tabulation of returned coupons by source of referral may reveal variations in performance between individual family planning workers and thus furnish guidance for such administrative actions as promotion, further training, admonition, or dismissal.

3. At a later date, a suitable sample of coupons may be drawn and the women in question visited by trained interviewers. This procedure is likely to furnish more complete and more representative information on pregnancies, expulsions, removals, and retention of and satisfaction with the IUD than could be obtained by any other means.

4. If a carbon copy of the coupon is retained by the family planning worker or at least the name and address of the recipient is recorded, the returned coupons may be matched against the list of women referred for insertion. Persons who requested or accepted a coupon, but did not have an IUD inserted, can thus be identified. Follow-up studies of samples of these women may serve to ascertain the reasons for their failure to implement their avowed intention and thus facilitate necessary changes in educational procedures and other aspects of the program.

Coupons may also be used—and are in fact so used in Korea—for the referral of men for voluntary vasectomy and for the reporting of these operations. With certain modifications of procedure, they could also be used for the reporting of sterilizing operations on women. Tubal ligation is always done in a hospital, as a rule immediately after confinement. The decision is probably made in many cases after admission. Since no special referral would be involved in these cases, the upper portion of the coupon would have to be filled in by hospital staff.

The use of the coupon for the recording and reporting of insertions of IUD's and of sterilizing operations is a comparatively simple procedure because these methods of fertility control require the participation of medical personnel who have to be paid and may be suitably compensated on a fee-for-service basis. The use of the coupon is also meaningful because the methods involved are quasi-permanent or permanent. Acceptance is, therefore, closely correlated with continued use.

The situation is quite different in regard to the so-called traditional methods, such as condoms and foam tablets, which play an important role in the family planning programs of a number of countries. The use of these methods does not require individual instruction, let alone the services of a doctor, and the necessary supplies can easily be distributed by paramedical or lay personnel. Experience has shown that willingness on the part of prospective users to accept initial supplies does not necessarily indicate willingness to try them and certainly does not justify any predictions as to continued use over a protracted period. The number, distribution, and characteristics of "new users" are, therefore, poor indicators of the success of a family planning program relying on traditional methods.

A more meaningful measure would be, in my opinion, the volume of contraceptive supplies flowing to consumers, especially if the latter have to make even a small financial contribution. It would not be difficult to design a form on which the basic demographic and social characteristics of the recipients or purchasers could be recorded, but I do not believe that it would be a useful exercise. There is a growing conviction among us that the success of a family planning program depends, in part, on the extent to which contraceptive supplies are made available through ordinary trade channels, along with salt, matches, kerosene, and other necessities. It is certainly futile to expect that the small tradesmen who handle these goods in the villages and in the bazaars will spend five minutes in filling out a statistical form each time they sell a package of condoms. Even within the official channels of the health agencies, the dispensing of contraceptive supplies should be a simple procedure not burdened with what must appear to most applicants as a useless bureaucratic rigmarole.

The flow of contraceptive supplies through health channels, including local family planning workers, to consumers can and should be recorded, of course. This can be done, with a minimum loss of time, in a variety of ways adaptable to the local situation. Transactions may be entered in a notebook and toted up at the end of the month. Supplies may be issued against simple chits, showing the kind and amount issued and, if necessary, signed, sealed, or thumb-marked by the recipient. Or, if the fiscal authorities permit it, the outflow may be determined by periodic inventories at the lowest level of the distribution system.

Oral contraceptives, because of their relatively high cost and the need for subsidy payments, may lend themselves to a system of record-keeping by means of coupons which would have to be channeled through drugstores or other outlets, rather than through physicians. In the case of the orals, the correlation between supplies issued and number of users is, of course, much closer than with any of the traditional methods.

Changes in the over-all pattern of family planning practices, including all methods and all sources of supplies and services, cannot be determined, in my opinion, by any feasible system of administrative records and record-keeping, but only by periodic sample surveys, preferably at annual intervals. Such surveys should, therefore, be an integral part of every large-scale family planning program.

53

EVALUATION PROCEDURES FOR A FAMILY PLANNING PROGRAM

L. P. CHOW, M.D., Dr.P.H.
Senior Specialist, Joint Commission on Rural Reconstruction
Associate Director, Taiwan Population Studies Center

INTRODUCTION

This paper describes the evaluation of a family planning program involving primarily the Lippes loop in Taiwan, Republic of China. The program, preceded by a pilot action-study program in Taichung City in February, 1963, began to expand to the whole province in January, 1964. By the end of June, 1965, there were a total of 104,112 acceptors recruited by the program, some 8.1% of the total married women 20–39 years old in the province.

There are presently 400 specialists in obstetrics and gynecology (OBG's) and about 100 general practitioners (GP's) participating in the insertion of loops throughout the province—all private practitioners. Two types of workers are referring cases: the pre-pregnancy health workers (PPHW's) and the village health education nurses (VHEN's). The former now number 240, are employed exclusively for family planning, and are assigned one to each township. The VHEN's, numbering 100, are multi-purpose health workers devoting about half their time to family planning and moving monthly in teams of three from one village to another.

The author is deeply indebted to the assistance and guidance he received from Dr. T. C. Hsu, Commissioner of Health, Taiwan Provincial Department of Health, and Dr. S. C. Hsu, Chief, Rural Health Division, Sino-American Joint Commission on Rural Reconstruction. Mr. S. M. Keeny and Mr. George P. Cernada, both of the Population Council, kindly edited the draft of this paper. Thanks are also due to the technical and secretarial staff of the Taiwan Population Studies Center, whose contribution has been invaluable for the implementation of the over-all family planning health program. In the current paper the author simply summarizes and reports their past accomplishments.

Government health organizations assume responsibility only for education and motivation of the people. Service is provided by the Maternal and Child Health Association (MCHA), a non-governmental voluntary organization. The MCHA provides supplies and pays half of the cost of insertion, which is fixed at NT$60 (US$1.50).

This program is unique in having an evaluation unit, the Taiwan Population Studies Center, which continuously evaluates progress in order to insure as far as possible the effective and efficient use of money and man power. The following are the procedures adopted by the Center in evaluating the program, some of which, it is hoped, may be applicable to family planning programs outside Taiwan.

OBJECTIVE AND TARGET

Evaluation begins with the formulation of an objective. In other words, the changes desired by program implementation should first

TABLE 1

PROJECTED DECLINE IN FERTILITY RATES, TAIWAN

Rate	1963	1973	Decline 1963–73 (per cent)
Crude birth rate........	36.3	24.1	33.6
Natural increase........	30.2	18.7	38.1
Total fertility..........	5,220	2,935	43.8
General fertility........	170	98	42.4

be made explicit. In a family planning program the general over-all objective is to help promote the welfare and happiness of the family by helping couples have the number of children they desire. This objective is usually attained in most developing areas where fertility rates are high through helping to reduce the rate of natural increase of the population and the fertility rate.

The program in Taiwan intends to lower fertility rates, as indicated by the projected percentages of decline in Table 1.

To attain this objective, it has been roughly estimated that 600,000 loops must be inserted in six years, 1964–69. This number is equivalent to about 45% of the total married women aged 20–39 in the province now. This over-all target of 600,000 is allocated over a period of six years as follows: 50,000 in 1964, and 100,000, 150,000, 150,000, 100,000, and 50,000, respectively, for the subsequent years.

The annual targets are again divided into monthly targets with a specific breakdown for each township based on the number of married women aged 20–39 in that township. These targets, then, serve as guideposts for measuring progress of the on-going program.

ANTICIPATED PROCESS OF CHANGES

A series of anticipated changes due to the implementation of the program may be carefully analyzed for the purpose of evaluation.

Assuming that a family planning program is implemented, the first accomplishment expected of the program will be improvement in knowledge about, and changes in attitudes toward, family planning among married women. Given an increase in knowledge and change in attitude, it is likely that more people will practice family planning, thus contributing to attaining the program objective.

Reduction of fertility is directly related to the number of people who have been practicing family planning. The latter, again, is directly related to the number of people who have a favorable attitude toward and improved knowledge about family planning. The progress of a family planning program may be measured at any of the above stages. For convenience this evaluation may be divided into three stages: immediate, intermediate, and long-term. The following actual steps have been adopted by the program for the purpose of evaluation:

A. Evaluation of the immediate effect
    1. Analysis of the returned coupons
    2. Evaluation of the accomplishment of field workers
B. Intermediate evaluation
    1. Collection and analysis of basic data
    2. Fertility surveys—annual or biannual
    3. Follow-up interview of the IUD acceptors
    4. Sampling survey of clinical records
    5. Follow-up interview of coupon-holders
    6. Survey on family planning of medical practitioners
    7. Evaluation of administrative procedures of the program
C. Evaluation of the long-term effect
    1. Measurement of decline in fertility rates

We shall now discuss each of the points in this outline, and then turn to other aspects of evaluation.

EVALUATION PROCEDURES

EVALUATION OF IMMEDIATE EFFECT

Analysis of returned coupons.—Evaluation of the immediate effect of the program is made by analysis of returned coupons (see Fig. 1). The coupon is filled out by the person who refers the woman to the doctor and entitles the holder to a 50% discount on the cost of insertion. The MCHA pays a subsidy of NT$30 (US$0.75) to the doctor per coupon returned. The coupons are collected by the local nurse-supervisors and finally sent to the Taiwan Population Studies Center for analysis.

The following tabulations are presently being made, using the information on the coupons.

1. Acceptors by month by administrative unit (county, city, township)
2. Acceptors by source of referral
3. Acceptors by age groups
4. Acceptors by number of living children
5. Acceptors by number of living sons
6. Acceptors by level of education
7. Acceptors by type of clinic inserting the device

Cross tabulations are also made for the following characteristics of the acceptors:

1. Number and rate of acceptance by age groups and number of living children
2. Number and rate of acceptance by level of education and number of living children
3. Number and rate of acceptance by age groups and level of education

From present tabulations the Population Studies Center has been able to isolate the following certain findings concerning the program.

The highest rate of acceptance in a single township by married women aged 20–39 at the end of June, 1965, was 26%. Of 361 townships in the province, there were 4 where the rate of acceptance exceeded 20%, 17 fell between 15% and 20%, 66 from 10% to 15%, and 169 from 5% to 10%. In the other 105 townships, the rates were less than 5%.

The modal acceptors are women aged 30–34, of primary education, who have four living children and two living sons. The number of living children and level of education seem to be two important factors in acceptance because, keeping other characteristics constant, the rate of acceptance increases with an increase in these two. Another similar but less significant characteristic is the degree of urbanization.

Most cases are referred by the pre-pregnancy health workers. Female private OBG's insert more per person than the males. The mobile clinics run by the local health departments are also proving efficient because more than twenty insertions can usually be made during one clinic session of three hours.

In addition, it seems that the program is first recruiting older women of higher parity. If the over-all objective is to be attained, the program must soon move to younger women who have fewer children. In other words, not only limitation but also child spacing must be practiced.

Evaluation of the accomplishment of individual workers.—As the number of field workers increases, their supervision becomes more difficult. To help solve the problem, each field worker has been given a monthly target based upon the number of married women

---

The following items will be filled out by the person who refers the case

Name	Age
Level of Education	No. Living Children M ( ) F ( )
Address	
Name of village	
Name of person referring case	
Type of person who referred (check one). PPH worker ( ) VHEN ( ) Military Hospital ( ) Farmers' Association ( ) Health Bureau/Station ( ) China Family Planning Association ( )	Practitioner ( ) Private Midwife ( ) Provincial Hospital ( )
Others (specify)	
Date of Issue	

The following items will be filled out by the doctor who inserts the device

Date of Insertion			
Type of Loop I ( ) II ( )		III ( )	IV ( )
Name of Clinic	Name of Doctor		
Address of Doctor			
Area Representative			

(NT$30 will be paid by MCHA upon receipt of this coupon.)

FIG. 1.—The coupon used for IUD program

---

aged 20–39 in her area. Evaluation is made of her accomplishment according to two factors, the total acceptors from the township and the number of cases referred by the worker.

A monthly evaluation sheet is prepared and distributed to each worker before the end of the next month with a brief comment by the Population Studies Center. The names of the best workers of the month are advertised in a health bulletin. In addition, an individual card is made for each worker and placed at the Center to record her personnel status and monthly accomplishment. These methods seem to be effective in stimulating working morale and efficiency.

Further analysis has shown that the single-purpose type of workers who are married with a couple of children of their own, have senior high school education or above, are emotionally mature, and can speak to the people in a common language are more successful workers. The length of work experience is another important factor.

The number of acceptors is also correlated with the number of OBG's available in the area for insertion.

INTERMEDIATE EVALUATION

Collection of basic data.—Determination of a program baseline is a prerequisite for evaluation of subsequent change. One way of accomplishing this is by collection and analysis of available data and by conducting *ad hoc* surveys. These data should include demographic information such as population and registered number of births, medical and health information such as the number and type of medical and paramedical personnel; attitude and practice of medical personnel on family planning; medical and health facilities available for the program; and various essential data concerning the public's knowledge of, attitude toward, and practice of family planning.

Fertility survey.—Undertaking a series of *ad hoc* surveys to assess the changes occurring because of the program is another way to evaluate progress.

The first of a series of annual fertility surveys, using a standard questionnaire, is planned for September, 1965. The total sample size will be 4,000 drawn from 1.6 million married women aged 20–44 in the province. A stratified three-stage area-sampling technique was applied. The township is the primary sampling unit. Fifty-six townships have been chosen from 331, excluding 30 in the aboriginal areas.

The result of the province-wide fertility survey will be compared with that of the survey of IUD acceptors drawn from the same townships. Major items of interest in making this comparison are:

1. The characteristics of acceptors and non-acceptors
2. The knowledge, attitude, and practice of family planning by acceptors and non-acceptors
3. The difference in reproductive behavior and change in fertility of acceptors after insertion of the IUD

The proportion of married women who are currently pregnant appears to be a good index for measuring the success of a family planning program, but experience here in Taiwan shows that respondents are not consistent in answering this question. Women are not certain about pregnancy at an early stage.

Two fertility surveys were undertaken in the past, one in Taichung City in 1962 and another in 82 other townships in 1964. Both surveys showed that people were ready to accept the idea of family planning and that one-fourth of the married women would show interest in the loops.

Follow-up interview of the IUD acceptors.—Our next interest is to evaluate the rates of removal, expulsion, accidental pregnancy, and frequency and type of side effect, as well as the degree of satisfaction among the IUD acceptors. In Taichung City, where a medical follow-up studies program is underway, cases are examined by OBG specialists every six months. Most insertions are by private practitioners, and although women are told to come back for a regular check-up, most of them do not unless they have some trouble. It is obvious that the scope of the program makes it impractical to bring every woman to the clinic for a follow-up examination.

A follow-up interview by public health nurses on a sample of acceptors was decided upon, and 1,034 cases were drawn from 46,600 acceptors in 1964 for such an interview. The results showed that in general 79% of the users were satisfied with the loops, although some had had mild side effects. A total of 211 complaints were made by 118 women who had had the loops removed because of side effects. Of these 211 complaints, 46.4% were said to be mild and 40.3% moderate, with severe complaints accounting for only 13.3%. The pregnancy rate per 100 woman-years was 3.8 after an average of 4.3 months of use.

The results of the follow-up interview compared favorably with the medical examination by OBG specialists. In view of its low cost, (US$0.50 per case), interviewing is a suggested method to evaluate an action program on a larger scale. The plan is to conduct interviewing on more carefully drawn samples and repeat it every year. This procedure will enable us to compare rates of acceptors and non-acceptors with regard to certain characteristics, fertility, and other relevant factors.

During the follow-up interview the question was asked who most influenced the woman to have the insertion. The answers showed that satisfied users were most influential in terms of referrals.

Sample survey of the clinical records.—The IUD acceptors are being followed up by a sample survey and by an analysis of the clinical records of the OBG's. Information on the clinical records is coded on the survey form for analysis. The results indicate that most of the satisfied users do not come back for regular check-up by the doctors, although they were told by the doctors to do so.

Of a total of 1,474 insertions by the private OBG's, 66% had never come back for follow-up, 24% were followed up and examined once;

7.5%, twice; and only 2% of the cases were followed up and examined more than three times.

Sixty-four per cent of the follow-up exams were for regular checkup and 36% for other reasons, mainly because of side reactions. The expulsion rate was 3%; removal rate, 8.4%; and reinsertion rate, 2.3%. This method will underestimate various rates; e.g., removal made by other doctors probably will not appear in the clinical record.

Follow-up interview of coupon-holders.—During 1964 a total of 275 coupon-holders (women who had asked for and had been given coupons but had not had the loop inserted) were sampled and interviewed to find out why they had not taken action. More than one-third (42.5%) did not really mean to use the coupons. Lack of confidence (27.5%) was the second major reason given, followed by influence of others (17.4%), inadequate motivation (11.5%), and miscellaneous reasons among the remaining 1.1%.

The workers have therefore been instructed to be more careful in issuing the coupons and to work toward improving and strengthening health education methods.

Survey of medical practitioners.—A series of surveys has been initiated to measure change in attitude toward, and participation of medical practitioners in, family planning, as well as their practice in contraceptive guidance and performance of induced abortion and sterilization. This is being done by a self-administered questionnaire addressed to all participating doctors. A preliminary analysis of this survey revealed that in a month the average OBG inserted six Ota rings, performed two tubal ligations and 0.4 vasectomies, had eleven cases for consultation on induced abortion, and twelve cases for consultation on other contraceptive methods.

Evaluation of the administrative procedures.—Occasional checking on the efficiency of the administrative channel is important to insure success of the program.

The degree of satisfaction and co-operation of the practitioners with the program is of major interest. A systematic evaluation of these particular topics is being made in conjunction with the survey of medical practitioners by sending out a self-administered questionnaire to all the participating doctors.

EVALUATION OF THE LONG-TERM EFFECT (FERTILITY)

Taiwan is fortunate in having a unique system of household registration through which population, births, deaths, and all other relevant demographic information can be obtained. The quality of the registration system in Taiwan compares favorably with that of most industrialized countries, although underregistration of births and neo-natal deaths still exists.

The pattern of fertility decline is as important as its extent. Experience in Taiwan indicates that in the past the decline in fertility has almost exclusively occurred among women over 30 years old. This has been taken as an indication that birth control, rather than child spacing, has been generally practiced by Taiwanese women. In Taiwan by the time a woman is 30 years old, she will have an average of three to four living children, which is considered to be a desirable number by most women.

The IUD program started in Taichung City in early 1963 has begun to show its effect. In the city between 1963 and 1964 the crude birth rate declined by 6.2%, the general fertility rate by 7.0%, and the total fertility rate by 6.4%, compared with 2.7%, 3.4%, and 3.1%, respectively, for four other major cities combined.

To eliminate the effect of differences in age composition, the total fertility rate is used as an index to measure the change in fertility. In view of the fact that most women in Taiwan will start practicing birth control after 30 years of age, cumulation of the age-specific fertility rates of age groups above 30 years old will be more "sensitive" in detection of the effect of the family planning program. This index is tentatively designated as "fertility rates above 30"; its decline during 1958–63 and 1963–64 is shown in Table 2. The decline in fertility in Taiwan expressed in other indices is shown in Table 3.

EVALUATION OF EDUCATIONAL METHODS AND COST

A comprehensive study on the method of health education to get the most loops in with the least cost was undertaken by Drs. Freedman and Berelson in Taichung in 1963. Four different "treatments" were used: nothing, mailing, mailing plus home visit to wives, and mailing plus home visit to both wives and husbands. The results show that considerable numbers of acceptors were registered from the "nothing" area, indicating a circulation effect. Mailing added very little. Home visits seemed no more effective when both wives and husbands were visited than when the wife alone was visited. A subsequent analysis of the "density" of home visits revealed that it is more efficient to home-visit every fifth *lin* (neighborhood), rather than any higher proportion.

The program is conscious of the cost. Although the total estimated cost to insert 600,000 loops is US$1.5 million, which averages US$2.50 per case, at the initial stage of the program, the cost will be much higher.

Cost analysis has been made by type of workers. For instance, during January–June, 1965, single-purpose workers recruited an average of 18.2 cases, costing US$1.25 per case. The multi-purpose workers cost more, each person recruiting an average of 9.1 cases at an average cost per case of US$5.40.

In order to reduce cost further, studies of methods of reaching the population regarding loops are being conducted in various townships. In one case, three "treatments" were assigned to a total of thirteen townships: mailing, home visiting, and group meeting. Each treatment was again divided into two "factors": "free insertion for a limited time" and "insertion at regular cost of US$.75." The rates of acceptance by "treatments" in three months are shown in Table 4; the average cost to recruit a case by "treatments" is given in Table 5.

TABLE 2

DECLINE OF "FERTILITY RATES ABOVE 30"

Fertility Rate	1959	1963	1964	Decline 1959–63 (per cent)	Decline 1963–64 (per cent)
Total fertility:					
All women............	5,990	5,355	5,096	10.6	4.8
Married women........	9,050	8,315	8,010	8.1	3.7
Fertility rates above 30:					
All women............	2,800	2,205	1,970	21.2	10.7
Married women........	3,130	2,425	2,165	22.5	10.7

TABLE 3

DECLINE IN FERTILITY BY OTHER INDICES

Rate	1959	1963	1964	Decline 1959–63 (per cent)	Decline 1963–64 (per cent)
Crude birth rate.........	41.2	36.3	34.5	11.9	5.0
General fertility.........	184	170	162	7.6	4.7

TABLE 4

RATES OF ACCEPTANCE, BY "TREATMENTS"

(Per Cent)

Treatment	Free	Regular	Total
Mailing...............	3.3	1.2	2.3
Home visiting..........	6.8	4.3	6.2
Group meeting.........	2.4	0.8	1.8

It will be noted that home visiting and mailing are more efficient than the group meeting. "Free insertion for a limited time" will be cheaper within a short period, even though the total cost of US$1.50 is paid by the program. This does not mean that the program should have been made completely free. Rather, it indicates that because the program was not made free, "an offer of free insertion for limited period" was an incentive for women to accept the device within the limited period.

Studies of similar kind are also being done on the effect of paying for referral, whereby US$0.25 is offered to anyone who refers an accepted case. A study in three military dependents' villages showed a rate of acceptance of 18.6% in one of the three villages in three months.

TABLE 5

AVERAGE COST TO RECRUIT A CASE BY "TREATMENTS"

Treatment	Free	Regular
Mailing................	$0.75	$2.02
Home visiting...........	0.75	2.00
Group meeting..........	$1.70	$4.00

TABLE 6

RESULTS OF USE OF MATCHING TECHNIQUE

Birth Rate	Cases	Matches
In 5 years preceding entry into program (per 100 person-years).....	38.0	34.2
From entry into program to June 30, 1962 (per 100 person-years)...	10.4	13.1
Per cent reduction...	73	62

METHOD TO CONTROL EXTRANEOUS FACTORS

The desired changes may be in part due to other, unrelated factors. In evaluating the effect of a family planning program, this is particularly important because fertility may decline owing to such factors as improvement in education, the standard of living, industrialization, and urbanization.

The classic "control-group design" is one way to eliminate the effect of extraneous factors. Evaluation by the "matching" technique is another method used. In 1962 the Taiwan Population Studies Center used the matching technique to evaluate the effect of an action program using mainly the traditional methods, foam tablets and condom, with results as shown in Table 6.

"Matches" were selected from the registers so that for every PPH case there was a matching couple who, at the time the case entered the program, had similar characteristics with respect to wife's age, duration of marriage, number of living children, and number of living sons. It was further stipulated that the matching case not have a live birth within nine months of the corresponding entry of the PPH case into the program. The latter restriction was necessary inasmuch as women were selected for the program because they were not then pregnant. "Matching" is a useful technique but has the disadvantage that selecting adequate "matches" is a rather tedious job.

Another device for eliminating the influence of extraneous factors is regression analysis. The percentage decline in the general fertility rates across townships will be regressed on the total person-years of

TABLE 7

WEIGHTS COMPUTED BY AGE-SPECIFIC
FERTILITY RATES

Age Group	Marriage Fertility Rate, 1963	Weight
20–24........	426	10
25–29........	374	9
30–34........	247	6
35–39........	149	3
40–44........	68}	1
45 and over...	12}	

use of IUD per 1,000 married women in the respective townships. The slope thus obtained may reflect the real effect of the IUD program.

THE "QUALITY" OF ACCEPTANCE

In evaluating the IUD program it is of interest also to see the change in the "quality" of acceptance. Age, parity, and educational level are three significant characteristics in observing the changes. The hypothesis is that as the program progresses, more younger women who are of lower parity, and less educated women, should be recruited.

Changes in the composition of acceptors with respect to these characteristics may be expressed in terms of the percentage distribution of acceptors. The need is felt, however, for a single index which will summarize the changes and will reflect the "quality" of acceptance. This is done by assigning a series of weights to the respective categories. For instance, age-specific marriage fertility rates in 1963 were used to compute the weights by age group as shown in Table 7.

Similarly, based upon the 1964 fertility survey and the total fertility rate in Taiwan, the weights for educational levels and numbers of living children are given as follows:

Education: no formal education(10), primary education(9), junior high school(8), senior high school and above(7).
Number of living children: none(6), one(5), two(4), three(3), four(2), five and above(1).

With these weights the changes in the monthly acceptors since January, 1965, standardized with respect to the acceptors in 1964, are shown in Table 8. From Table 8 it is evident that it is still too early to expect remarkable changes in the "quality" of acceptance.

TABLE 8

MONTHLY ACCEPTORS IN 1965 STANDARDIZED WITH RESPECT TO 1964 ACCEPTORS

STANDARDIZED WITH RESPECT TO:	1964	ACCEPTORS IN: 1965					
		Jan.	Feb.	Mar.	Apr.	May	June
Age	1,000	1,028	1,014	997	997	1,001	1,006
Education	1,000	1,003	1,001	998	1,001	1,008	1,007
Number of living children	1,000	1,037	1,029	1,016	1,030	1,024	1,030

COST OF EVALUATION

The Taiwan Population Studies Center now has sixteen full-time staff members who not only undertake evaluation but also conduct various demographic studies. The annual expenditure is about US$25,-000, which is equivalent to 7% of the total budget for the family planning health program.

CONCLUSION AND SUMMARY

The importance of program evaluation is being given increasing recognition. Although more administrators are now aware of the significance of evaluation to guide the program's operation, the general evaluation procedures for the family planning program will still have to be worked out. The present paper describes the experience in evaluating a family planning health program in Taiwan. Some of the major lessons learned are:

1. Although the monthly IUD acceptors are sharply increasing, so far mainly older women of higher parity have been recruited. In order

to attain the objective of reducing the natural increase rate from 3% now to less than 2% within ten years, younger women of lower parity will have to be recruited.

2. Although we have been concerned with three stages of evaluation, immediate, intermediate, and long-term, immediate evaluation is of particular importance in safeguarding the use of money and man power and cannot be stressed too heavily.

3. The coupon is a device particularly adapted to immediate evaluation. This scheme seems suitable for adoption in other countries for a similar purpose.

4. Evaluation of the accomplishment of individual workers by preparing and distributing a monthly evaluation sheet proved to be an effective way to stimulate workers to work harder and more efficiently.

5. Taiwan is fortunate in having a household registration system, from which most of the relevant demographic and vital statistical data can be obtained for the purpose of evaluation. In other areas where the registration system is grossly inadequate, *ad hoc* surveys may have to replace this.

6. Follow-up interviews of IUD acceptors by trained public health nurses have proved to be a cheap and effective method of evaluation.

7. By interviewing women who asked for and had been given coupons but had not taken action to insert loops, barriers to taking action were found.

8. Evaluation of the relative efficiency of various health education methods has indicated that home visits made to one-fifth of the women in an area seems to be most efficient.

9. The Taiwan program expended about 7% of its total program funds for the purpose of evaluation and related studies. It is felt that this expenditure will provide future guidelines for program operations which will insure more savings in terms of both money and man power. The importance of on-going evaluation and immediate application of findings to program operation cannot be overemphasized. This sort of evaluation is proving most valuable when incorporated into the over-all plan of action for the program at the initial planning stages. With a built-in evaluation system, the enormous difficulties of "midstream" evaluations in the latter stage of a program's activities are often completely avoided and totally unnecessary.

10. It is often noted that when a program is being evaluated, the quality of related data will gradually be improved because of increased consciousness of the value of data. It should be noted also that reporting of births may improve, which will tend to underestimate the real effect of a family planning program.

REFERENCES

1. Hsu, T. C., and Chow, L. P. "Family Planning Health Program in Taiwan, Republic of China" (mimeographed).
2. Chow, L. P. "Evaluation of Family Planning Program of Taiwan" (mimeographed).
3. Berelson, B., and Freedman, R., "A Study in Fertility Control," *Scientific American*, May, 1964.
4. Taiwan Population Studies Center, Annual Reports, 1962–1963, 1963–1964.
5. Taiwan Population Studies Center, Semi-annual Report, 1964.
6. Chow, L. P. "A Program To Control Fertility in Taiwan—Setting, Accomplishment, and Evaluation" (mimeographed).
7. Chow, L. P., *et al.* "A Fertility Survey in Taiwan," *China Medical Journal* (in press).
8. Chow, L. P., *et al.* "Evaluation of IUD Program by Follow-up Interview," *Formosan Medical Journal*, Vol. 64(7) (July, 1965).
9. Family Planning Health Program Monthly Reports.

54

LESSONS LEARNED FROM FAMILY PLANNING STUDIES IN TAIWAN AND KOREA

JOHN Y. TAKESHITA
University of Michigan Population Studies Center

This paper summarizes some of the important results and lessons learned from two of the research projects on family planning in which the author has been closely involved since 1962: the Taichung Family Planning Study in Taiwan, as field director of evaluation, and the Seoul Urban Project on Family Planning in Korea, as adviser. The former was undertaken in 1963; the latter, started in July 1964, is currently underway and is scheduled to be continued to mid-1966. These studies, though undertaken in two different countries, are not unrelated. As a matter of fact, the current study in Seoul can be regarded in some respects as an extension of the Taichung Study. This is not by accident. The directors of the Seoul project had in mind testing some of the things that could not be adequately tested in Taichung.

STUDY DESIGNS

By way of introduction, a brief review of the designs of these studies, indicating their similarities and differences, is in order.

The author is indebted to many organizations and individuals for making this report possible. Grateful acknowledgment is made, though far from adequately, by listing just a few of them here: The Population Council, The Taiwan Population Studies Center, The Taiwan Maternal and Child Health Institute, Seoul National University Urban Population Study Project, and The Michigan Population Studies Center; Dr. Bernard Berelson of the Population Council; Dr. T. C. Hsu, Taiwan's Commissioner of Health; Dr. S. C. Hsu of the Sino-American Joint Commission on Rural Reconstruction; Dr. L. P. Chow, Associate Director of the Taiwan Population Studies Center; Dr. C. L. Chen, formerly director, and Dr. C. H. Lee of the Taiwan Maternal and Child Health Institute; Dr. J. Y. Peng, formerly deputy director of the Taiwan Maternal and Child Health Institute and now in Thailand for the Population Council; Dr. E Hyock Kwon, Director of the Seoul National University Urban Population Study Project; and Dr. Ronald Freedman, Director of the Michigan Population Studies Center.

691

Taichung Study[1]

Taichung, the capital city of the Province of Taiwan, Republic of China, had a population of about 320,000 in 1963 in an area of about 63 square miles, or a density of about 5,000 per square mile.

There were other activities to promote family planning in the rest of the province during the study period from February through October, 1963, but the new IUD was offered in Taiwan for the first time in this experimental program.

The new IUD—the Lippes loop, for the most part—was offered along with oral pills and several varieties of traditional methods. Both the IUD and the oral pills could be inserted or prescribed only at special clinics, of which there were nine half-day or one-day sessions per week in various parts of the city and one daily session at a central location. Other methods were also available at these clinics; but, in addition, they could be obtained directly from field workers who made home visits and conducted group meetings during the course of the study.

The charge was 75 cents for an IUD insertion or a month's supply of oral pills. Nominal charges were made for the others also.

Taichung's neighborhood units (*lins*) were allocated to four different treatments by which the married residents were informed about the program's family planning services. The target of the program was the 36,000 or so married couples with wives aged 20–39. Posters were displayed throughout the city and mass meetings held in various public halls. In all but a third of the neighborhoods, where nothing more was done, letters and pamphlets about family planning were sent to married couples with at least two living children and to newly-weds. In about half of these neighborhoods, in addition to letters, trained field workers visited every married woman aged 20–39 in her home. For further variation, in one-half of the neighborhoods where home visits were scheduled, the field workers visited the husbands as well. Small group meetings were also scheduled in the neighborhoods receiving home visits, although only a little more than half of these were actually held. As summarized in Table 1, treatment went cumulatively from little (*nothing* but posters and mass meetings) to much effort (posters, mass meetings, letters, small group meetings, and home visits). Our purpose was to discover the differential effect of these varying treatments.

These treatments were mixed in different proportions in three more or less similarly constituted sectors of the city. In the first sector, one-

[1]For a full description of the Taichung Study, see Bernard Berelson and Ronald Freedman, "A Study in Fertility Control," *Scientific American*, 210: 29–39 (May, 1964).

half of the neighborhoods received home visits; in the second sector, one-third; and in the third sector, only one-fifth. "Mail" and "nothing" treatments were distributed equally in the remaining neighborhoods in each sector. Measured by the proportion of neighborhoods receiving the "everything" treatment, which included the home visit, these sectors were referred to as "heavy," "medium," and "light" density sectors, as shown in Table 1. We wanted to discover the differential play of diffusion when the density of effort was varied in this way.

For political reasons, the use of the mass media was kept to a minimum and the posters and letters made no reference to the IUD.

TABLE 1

ALLOCATION OF TAICHUNG'S NEIGHBORHOODS BY
TREATMENT AND DENSITY SECTOR

TREATMENT (cumulative)	ALL SECTORS	DENSITY SECTOR		
		Heavy	Medium	Light
Nothing	767	232	243	292
Mail	768	232	244	292
Everything: wife only	427	232	122	73
Everything: husband and wife	427	232	122	73
Total	2,389	928	731	730
Per cent "everything"	36	50	33	20

SEOUL STUDY[2]

Seoul is the capital city of the Republic of Korea. The study is confined to one of its nine districts, the Sungdong Gu, which has a population of about 370,000 in an area of about 39 square miles, or a density of about 9,500 per square mile. Compared to Taichung, the study area in Seoul is much more compact, although the size of the target population is nearly the same in the two places. In Sungdong Gu, the program has been directed to the estimated 45,000 married couples with wives aged 20–44.

The national program involving the IUD, vasectomy, and traditional methods had been in full swing since May, 1964, two months before the start of the study, so that there was already a favorable climate for this kind of activity.

2For a full description of the Seoul Study, see E Hyock Kwon, *Seoul National University Sungdong Gu Action-Research Project on Family Planning: A Progress Report (for Period 10 July–31 December, 1964)* (Seoul, Korea: School of Public Health, Seoul National University, April, 1965).

The IUD and vasectomy are offered along with condoms, foam tablets, and jelly—all free of charge.

There are four service stations, or family planning consultation offices, set up at convenient locations in the district. All persons interested in receiving contraceptives must come to these places. Traditional methods are dispensed there. The IUD and vasectomy operation are available at clinics established near these offices from which interested persons are referred with coupons. Unlike Taichung, traditional methods are not available from field workers on home visits or at group meetings. The consultation offices and the clinics, however, are open throughout the week.

The neighborhood units (*bans*) in the district have been allocated also to four different treatments: mass media only, mailings, group meetings, and home visits (see Table 2). The design, however, differs from that of the Taichung study in several respects:

TABLE 2

ALLOCATION OF SEOUL'S (SUNGDONG GU)
NEIGHBORHOODS BY TREATMENT

Treatment	Number of Neighborhoods	Per Cent
Mass media only........	2,145	55
Mailings..............	585	15
Group meetings.........	585	15
Home visits............	585	15
Total...............	3,900	100

a) Except for the mass media treatment, which extends across the board, each treatment is confined to a given set of neighborhoods. There is no cumulating of treatments as was done in Taichung. This permits easier measurement of the separate effects of each of the treatments than in Taichung.

b) Mass media are given full play with sanction from the government. Radio, television, and newspapers have been used extensively to advertise the program and the locations of the service centers; and leaflets discussing the various contraceptive methods and the IUD in particular have been distributed through the neighborhood leaders.[3]

c) Letters too were distributed through the neighborhood leaders and also included specific reference to the IUD and the locations of the service centers—quite in contrast to those used in Taichung. But

[3]There is some question whether these should be regarded as "mass media"; they are not easily distinguished from the "mail" treatment except in the volume of materials distributed.

because these were distributed by the neighborhood leaders, no test is made of the utility of the existing postal system as a way to reach the eligible couples.

d) Only 15% of the neighborhoods and there only the wives receive home visits. On the other hand, more than half (55%) of the neighborhoods are given only the mass media treatment.

e) The design does not include a variation in density of treatment. Diffusion has been measured so far by the acceptance in the "mass media only" neighborhoods and in the other neighborhoods before the special treatments reached them.

The program is scheduled to run for two full years to learn the effects of repeated treatments of the kind described.

BRIEF REVIEW OF FINDINGS

TAICHUNG STUDY[4]

Over-all effects.—From its start in February, 1963, to April 1, 1964, 5,454 couples accepted family planning guidance in the program. Nearly 80% chose the new IUD; less than 2%, the oral pills; and about 19%, traditional methods (mostly condoms).

The 4,027 acceptors coming from within Taichung itself represented about 11% of all the married women aged 20–39 there. When the various categories of couples who were not eligible, either permanently or temporarily, are excluded, the rate of acceptance comes to more than 40%.

Current users of contraception (including sterilization) in Taichung increased from 28% before the program to 36% just at the close of the program, the largest increase occurring in the proportion of IUD users—from less than 1% to 8%.

The increase in contraceptive practice and of a more effective method in Taichung following the intensive program has depressed fertility, as it was hoped, to a significant degree in a brief span of time. The data from the population register show that between 1963,

---

[4]A more detailed discussion of most of the findings from the Taichung study presented here is available in John Y. Takeshita and Ronald Freedman, "Important Results of the 1963 Taichung Family Planning Study," Paper No. 7 read at the First Regional Conference of the International Planned Parenthood Federation, Western Pacific Region, May 26–29, 1965, Seoul, Korea, and to be published in the conference proceedings. Other reports of relevance are: R. Freedman, J. Y. Takeshita, and T. H. Sun, "Fertility and Family Planning in Taiwan: A Case Study of the Demographic Transition," *American Journal of Sociology*, 70: 16–17 (July, 1964); and R. Freedman and J. Y. Takeshita, "Studies of Fertility and Family Limitation in Taiwan," in *Public Health and Population Change: Current Research Issues*, ed. Mindel Sheps and Jeanne Clare Ridley (Boston: Schenkman, 1965).

the year of the program, and 1964 the total fertility rate declined 6.3% in Taichung as compared to 3.1% in the other major cities.[5]

The influence of home visits and density of effort.—The "everything" treatment, which included the home visit, yielded higher rates of acceptance than the "mail only" and "nothing" treatments, as might have been expected, but much of the advantage of the intensive effort was confined to acceptance of traditional methods. Even the advantage of the heaviest density of effort over the lighter densities was confined largely to acceptance of traditional methods.

The acceptance of traditional methods occurred almost entirely in connection with home visits and diffused but little into the non–home-visit neighborhoods, the overwhelming majority of the acceptances in the latter places involving the IUD. Table 3 summarizes these findings in detail.

Additional visits with the husbands made little difference. This is probably due in part to the fact that there was already considerable consensus among many husbands and wives about the need for family planning and also in part to the fact that the crucial element in the Taichung program was the IUD, a female method.

The letters, which, among other things, invited the recipients to request home visits, also made little difference. As mentioned earlier, they did not include any statement about the new IUD; they mentioned only that family planning guidance could be obtained from a field worker upon request or by going to the nearest health station. Less than 2% of those to whom letters were sent actually requested a home visit. We do not know, of course, what the effect would have been had the letters been keyed specifically to the IUD.

The influence of group meetings.—Group meetings were conducted in only about 500 of the 850 or so neighborhoods in which they were scheduled. Although not planned this way, this provided us an invaluable opportunity to measure the influence of the group meetings. The meetings, if held, were rated as "effective," "somewhat effective," or "not effective" on the basis of the field workers' own evaluation immediately after the meetings (which they conducted) before they could know what the response in acceptance would be. We find that the neighborhoods in which group meetings were held yielded more acceptances only if they were "somewhat effective" or better. Furthermore, this advantage was only in the higher yield of IUD cases; they did not influence the acceptance of traditional methods. It now appears that the somewhat greater yield of IUD acceptances in the

[5]For a full report on the fertility trends in Taiwan before and after the Taichung study and the start of the national program, see Ronald Freedman, Lienping Chow, and Julia Ann Smith, "The Accelerating Fertility Decline in Taiwan," to be published in a forthcoming issue of the *Population Index*, Office of Population Research, Princeton University, and Population Association of America, Inc.

"everything" neighborhoods was due to "effective" group meetings. If the group meetings were "ineffective" or not held at all, these neighborhoods, although home-visited, did not do any better than the "mail only" and "nothing" neighborhoods. Table 4 summarizes these most interesting results, which are unique in demonstrating the influence of group meetings.

TABLE 3

ACCEPTANCE RATES PER 100 MARRIED WOMEN AGED 20–39 IN
TAICHUNG UP TO APRIL 1, 1964, BY TYPE OF METHOD,
BY TREATMENT, AND DENSITY SECTOR[a]

TREATMENT	All SECTORS	DENSITY SECTOR		
		Heavy	Medium	Light
All Methods				
Everything: husband and wife....	17	20	12	14
Everything: wife only...........	16	18	14	14
Mail.........................	8	8	7	8
Nothing......................	7	9	6	7
Total.....................	11	14	9	9
IUD Only				
Everything: husband and wife.....	10	10	9	10
Everything: wife only...........	10	9	10	11
Mail.........................	7	7	6	7
Nothing......................	6	8	5	6
Total.....................	8	9	7	7
Other Methods				
Everything: husband and wife....	7	10	3	4
Everything: wife only...........	6	9	4	3
Mail.........................	1	1	1	1
Nothing......................	1	1	1	1
Total.....................	3	5	2	1
Per Cent of Acceptances IUD				
Everything: husband and wife.....	59	52	72	74
Everything: wife only...........	60	50	72	78
Mail.........................	88	87	88	90
Nothing......................	90	91	90	90
Total.....................	73	63	80	85

[a] The rates are rounded to the nearest per cent for ease of reading and therefore the component parts do not always add up exactly to what is given in the first panel. The "per cent of acceptances IUD" was computed on the basis of the original rates, which were given to the nearest 0.1%.

TABLE 4

ACCEPTANCE RATES PER 100 MARRIED WOMEN AGED 20–39 IN TAICHUNG UP TO APRIL 1, 1964, BY TYPE OF METHOD, BY SECTOR, BY TREATMENT, AND BY WHETHER A GROUP MEETING WAS HELD AND WAS EFFECTIVE OR NOT

TREATMENT	ALL SECTORS			DENSITY SECTOR Heavy			Medium			Light		
	All Methods	IUD	Others	All Methods	IUD	Others	All Methods	IUD	Others	All Methods	IUD	Others
Everything, with:												
Effective meeting	21	13	8	20	11	9	30	23	7	14	12	2
Somewhat effective meeting	17	11	6	19	9	10	16	12	4	16	12	4
Ineffective meeting	14	7	7	18	7	11	11	7	4	12	8	4
No meeting	14	8	6	17	8	9	11	7	4	12	8	4
Mail	8	7	1	8	7	1	7	6	1	8	7	1
Nothing	7	7	1	9	8	1	6	6	1	7	6	1
Total	11	8	3	14	9	5	9	7	2	9	7	1

The diffusion effect.—Evidence is abundant that diffusion played a key role in the success of the Taichung program. This is extremely important, since it indicates that it is unnecessary to approach each couple in expensive individual contacts. Systematically spaced efforts have considerable effect on population not approached directly.

For example, 26% of all acceptances to April 1, 1964, came from outside Taichung, where no formal effort was made to recruit them. This proportion exceeded 40% in the last month of the program and in every subsequent month to date.

Also, the number of acceptances in Taichung from other than the "everything" neighborhoods was unusually high throughout the program period but especially after its formal close. During the program 66% of all acceptances in Taichung came from the "mail only" and "nothing" neighborhoods; during the five-month period after the program 76% came from these neighborhoods.

Finally, even in the "everything" neighborhoods, where home visits were scheduled, about 16% of their acceptances came before the home visitors could reach them.

The most important media of diffusion were the word-of-mouth messages of neighbors, friends, and relatives. These informal channels were particularly important in the diffusion of program information into areas outside of Taichung. More recent studies in Taiwan show that "satisfied users" of the IUD are the best source in this respect.[6] However, not to be ignored are the regular health station personnel who presumably already have the confidence of the public; not a few of them served as active recruiters of new cases as well as messengers about the program.

The role of the new IUD.—The appeal of the new IUD in Taiwan is unmistakable. This is certainly demonstrated in the subsequent development of the province-wide program in which the Lippes loop, now locally manufactured, is its mainstay. In the Taichung study, where all kinds of methods were offered, nearly 80% chose the IUD. It is clear in reviewing the progress of the program that this device played a crucial role in the diffusion effect we noted. From the very beginning acceptances from areas either in or outside the city where no direct face-to-face contacts were made for purposes of recruitment involved the new IUD almost entirely. Furthermore, even in the neighborhoods where home visits and group meetings were held, once these activities were completed, acceptances that continued to come forth also involved this device for the most part.

A cost analysis recently completed shows that it cost more than five times per case to produce an IUD acceptance rate in the "every-

[6]See T. C. Hsu and L. P. Chow paper on Taiwan program, chap. 4 in this volume.

thing" neighborhoods that was only about 1.5 times higher than in the "mail only" and "nothing" neighborhoods.[7] The economic advantage of allowing diffusion to have its play is clearly demonstrated.

Demographic characteristics of acceptors.—The program has had a special appeal to couples who already feel they have a problem of family limitation and who have made unsatisfactory attempts to do something about it. This generalization is based on the data summarized in Table 5, which shows the acceptance rates by several characteristics of those receiving home visits in the program (but ex-

TABLE 5

ACCEPTANCE RATES PER 100 HOME-VISITED MARRIED
WOMEN AGED 20–39 (EXCLUDING STERILIZED AND STER-
ILE) IN TAICHUNG UP TO APRIL 1, 1964, BY SELECTED
DEMOGRAPHIC CHARACTERISTICS

Characteristics	Per Cent Accepting to April 1, 1964	Number of Married Women 20–39 Not Sterilized or Sterile When Home-visited
All women......................	22	9,554[a]
Wife's age:		
20–24.........................	15	2,145
25–29.........................	21	3,124
30–34.........................	26	2,621
35–39.........................	27	1,661
Number of living children:.........		
None.........................	2	375
1.............................	8	1,342
2.............................	16	1,809
3.............................	24	1,865
4.............................	28	1,712
5 or more....................	32	2,448
Number of living sons:		
None.........................	8	1,761
1.............................	17	2,979
2 or more....................	30	4,811
Experience of birth control:		
Currently using contraception but never had abortion...........	21	1,367
Currently using contraception and had abortion.................	25	738
Past use of contraception but never had abortion..................	36	271
Past use of contraception and had abortion.....................	43	176
Abortion only..................	40	334
Never used anything...........	18	6,523

[a] "All women" includes "not ascertained" on these characteristics.

[7] For the full report, see John A. Ross, "Cost Analysis of the Taichung Experiment." *Studies in Family Planning* (The Population Council), No. 10 (February, 1966).

cluding those who were already sterilized or thought themselves to be sterile at the time of the home visit). In short, the acceptance rate: (*a*) rises with age and is particularly high for those past 30; (*b*) rises also with parity and the number of sons present at the start of the program and is especially high after three children or two sons; and (*c*) is especially high if they had tried something in the past, either contraception or induced abortion, but were not using anything when they were visited by the field workers.

Even more convincing is the set of data in Table 6, which shows

TABLE 6

RATES OF ACCEPTANCE IN THE TAICHUNG PROGRAM UP TO APRIL 1, 1964, BY WHETHER FAMILY LIMITATION HAD BEEN USED BEFORE THE PROGRAM, AND BY NUMBER OF MONTHS SINCE LAST BIRTH AT THE BEGINNING OF THE PROGRAM

(Married Women Aged 20–39)

NUMBER OF MONTHS SINCE LAST BIRTH	ALL WOMEN		USED CONTRACEPTION AND/OR ABORTION BEFORE THE PROGRAM		NEVER USED ANY FORM OF FAMILY LIMITATION BEFORE THE PROGRAM	
	Per Cent Accepting	Number in Base Group	Per Cent Accepting	Number in Base Group	Per Cent Accepting	Number in Base Group
Less than 9.....	16	597	29	69	14	528
9–11..........	13	205	20	35	12	170
12–23..........	13	588	17	156	12	432
24–59..........	10	521	14	256	7	265
60 or more.....	5	262	8	146	0	116
Total........	12	2,173[a]	15	662	11	1,511

[a] Excludes the 220 "sterilized" cases among whom 3 cases still accepted in the program.

that acceptance was highest among those who had most recently demonstrated their fecundity. The acceptance rate was higher the shorter the period since the last birth, and this was especially accentuated when the previous use of some family limitation method (other than sterilization) was taken into account. The higher acceptance rates were found among those who had recently had a live birth *and* had tried to limit family size previously.

It needs to be pointed out, however, that the program did succeed in getting a sizable proportion of even the *current* users of contraception and those without any previous experience of birth control. Also, it appears that the social support for family limitation generated by the intensive program resulted in more acceptances among lower-parity women and those with fewer sons in the city than from outside the city. The proportions of acceptors with fewer than three children and with fewer than two sons were directly related to intensity of program effort. Eighteen per cent of all acceptors from the "everything" neighborhoods, 16% from the "mail only" and "nothing" neighborhoods combined, and 11% from outside Taichung had fewer than three children. Similarly, 30%, 29%, and 20% of all acceptors from these areas in descending order of intensity of effort had fewer than two sons.

Social and economic characteristics of acceptors.—While the practice of contraception before the program was definitely more frequently reported among the better educated, the higher income, and the more "modern" groups, acceptance in the program was as likely

TABLE 7

RELATIONSHIP BETWEEN WIFE'S EDUCATION AND LITERACY AND THE USE OF ANY FORM OF FAMILY LIMITATION (CONTRACEPTION, ABORTION, AND STERILIZATION) BEFORE AND AFTER THE PROGRAM IN TAICHUNG

(Married Women Aged 20–39)

FREQUENCY WIFE READS NEWSPAPER	WIFE'S EDUCATION	No. OF CASES	BEFORE PROGRAM, PER CENT EVER USING ANY FORM OF FAMILY LIMITATION	IN PROGRAM	
				Per Cent Becoming Acceptors	Per Cent of Acceptors Never Used Before
Never.............	Less than primary grades	981	21	10	80
Never.............	Primary grades or more	391	29	15	67
Less than once a week..	Primary grades or less	279	41	12	50
Less than once a week..	More than primary grades	56	59	12	58
Once a week or more..	Primary grades or less	286	45	8	38
Once a week or more..	Junior high school	248	58	11	27
Once a week or more..	Senior high school	200	72	12	50
Total.............		2,441	36	11	61

among the less educated, the lower income, and the less "modern" group as among the former. Furthermore, the proportion of acceptors who previously had no experience of birth control was higher by a wide margin among the latter. Table 7 illustrates these findings for wife's education and literacy, only two of several characteristics considered in our analysis.

Clearly the program served to bring family planning to those in the population who for various reasons had been slow to take up the practice on their own. Multivariate analysis with more than ten demographic and socioeconomic variables has shown that acceptance in the program is best predicted by the demographic variables, most notably recency of childbirth, previous use of family limitation methods, and parity. We are led to the gratifying conclusion that the program served to help those who were most hard-pressed with the problem of growing family size, whatever their station in the community.

Follow-up of IUD cases.—While the program in Taichung has shown impressive results in terms of IUD acceptance and subsequent fertility decline, the follow-up study of nearly 3,000 IUD cases for one year and of about 1,700 for two years reveals certain problems (see Table 8). For example, in the two-year period 16% of all the insertions were expelled spontaneously and 33% were voluntarily removed. Fortunately, many women requested reinsertions so that the proportion of cases still wearing an IUD at the end of the first year was 72% and at the end of the second year, 62%. The failure rate was 4.0 pregnancies per 100 woman-years of use in the first year and 7.4 pregnancies per 100 woman-years in the entire two-year period. While both the continuation rate and the failure rate are considerably more favorable than those involving traditional methods,[8] they are not as favorable as most of us hoped at the start of the program. There is evidence in the study, however, that improvements may be possible. For example, the larger loop, which is now being introduced in Taiwan, appears to have much lower rates of both expulsion and pregnancy. Also, comparison of the removal rates (as distinguished from the natural expulsion rates) after one year among groups of women who had their insertions in different months of the program period shows that they declined with fair regularity from a high of 27% among the earliest group to 14% among a later group. It is suggested that voluntary removal is affected by how much public confidence there is in the new device. It appears that such confidence was gradually built up with the progress of the program in Taichung.

SEOUL STUDY[9]

The results available to date from the Seoul project tend to confirm our findings from Taichung, but there are some important differences

---

[8]In Taiwan, a recent experiment with free distribution of traditional methods showed that only 36% of the takers had actually used the methods when reached from eight to eleven months after their "acceptance," and the pregnancy rate among those who reported use was as high as 36 per 100 woman-years. For details, see "Monthly Report June 1965: Family Planning Health Program, Provincial Department of Health, Maternal and Child Health Association, and Taiwan Population Studies Center, Republic of China, July, 1965, (mimeographed). In rural Korea, free distribution of traditional methods resulted in an acceptance rate of as high as 45% of all married couples with wives aged 15–44 but the pregnancy rate after 18 months of the program was 23 per 100 woman-years. For details, see Jae Mo Yang, Sook Bang, Myung Ho Kim, and Man Gap Lee, "Fertility and Family Planning in Rural Korea," *Population Studies*, 18:237–50 (March, 1965).

[9]Based on E Hyock Kwon *et al., Seoul National University Sungdong Gu Action-Research Project on Family Planning: A Progress Report (for Period 1 January–30 June, 1965)* (Seoul, Korea: School of Public Health, Seoul National University, September, 1965), and the bimonthly mimeographed reports of the project.

TABLE 8

One-Year and Two-Year Follow-up of IUD Cases in the Taichung Study, 1963[a]

Month of Initial Insertion	Number of Cases	Cases Followed Up After 1 Year		Cases Followed Up After 2 Years		Total Insertions[b] Followed Up at End of:		Per Cent of All Insertions Expelled at End of:		Per Cent of All Insertions Removed at End of:		Per Cent of All Followed-up Cases Continuing at End of:		Pregnancy Rate[c] per 100 Woman-Years in:	
		Number	Per Cent	Number	Per Cent	1 Year	2 Years	1 Year	2 Years	1 Year	2 Years	1 Year	2 Years	1 Year	2 Years
February	255	243	95	230	90	269	288	12	17	27	40	68	56	6.2	8.7
March	304	291	96	283	93	314	352	11	16	25	36	69	60	6.5	8.7
April	400	371	93	381	95	389	445	12	14	26	34	66	61	5.2	5.5
May	509	493	97	476	94	540	589	13	17	18	28	76	67	4.1	7.3
June	331	316	96	318	97	346	376	14	17	19	33	73	59	4.1	7.4
July	293	293	100	.....	.....	328	.....	16	.....	16	.....	76	.....	4.0	.....
August	378	375	99	.....	.....	413	.....	15	.....	19	.....	72	.....	1.0	.....
September	255	253	99	.....	.....	280	.....	15	.....	14	.....	78	.....	1.4	.....
October	296	260	88	.....	.....	282	.....	11	.....	21	.....	74	.....	2.0	.....
Cumulative Total	3,019	2,895	96	1,688	94[d]	3,161	2,050	13	16	20	33	72	62	4.0[e]	7.4

[a] Based on data from monthly reports of the medical follow-up study prepared by Dr. C. H. Lee, Provincial Maternal and Child Health Institute, Taichung, Taiwan.
[b] Total insertions exceed the number of cases because of reinsertions.
[c] Pregnancies with device in situ or position of device unknown.
[d] Refers to 94% of the cases with insertions from February through June, 1963.
[e] Based on the aggregate months of exposure of the cases that had insertions from February through September, 1963.

and new insights. We summarize here the most salient findings to date.

Altogether 7,699 new cases have come to the family planning consultation offices in about twelve months since the start of the program. The 6,703 cases known to have come from the experimental area represented about 13% of the approximately 45,000 married couples with wives aged 20–44 living there.

Of these new cases, 37% accepted coupons for the IUD; 48%, supplies of condoms, foam tablets, or jelly; and 2%, coupons for vasectomy. Fourteen per cent merely sought advice without accepting anything.

That all contraceptives are available free of charge probably accounts for the unexpectedly high rate of acceptance of traditional methods in Seoul, where the IUD was far less dominant. In Taichung the *relative* cheapness of the IUD, given its advantages, was apparent to the prospective cases, who had to pay for any method they chose. There is also evidence that the older Ota ring, while widely known and used in Taiwan, was neither widely known nor used in Korea in the past. The loop probably represents a greater innovation in Korea than in Taiwan.

There is striking evidence, however, that the IUD has gained in popularity since its introduction. The proportion of acceptors choosing the IUD on first visit to the consultation offices has risen steadily from 25% in the first month of the program to 57% in May and June, 1965.

Including those who originally accepted traditional methods and subsequently switched, altogether 4,192 cases have now accepted IUD coupons, and nearly all (96%) have turned them in for insertions.

The 4,000 or so IUD insertions to June 30, 1965, constitute about 9% of all the married women aged 20–44 in Sungdong Gu, or about 27% of the approximately 14,800 "immediately eligible" women (defined as those who are free of known fecundity impairments, do not want any more children, are not using a method that satisfies them, and are neither pregnant nor experiencing post-partum amenorrhea).

Nearly 80% of all the visitors to the family planning consultation offices to the end of 1964 came before the special treatments—other than the mass media—reached them. Or, to put it in another way, nearly 80% came in response to mass media and whatever circulation effect that was generated from the special treatments completed to the end of 1964.

The indirect influences of the program in Seoul have also been mediated for the most part by neighbors, friends, and relatives—particularly satisfied IUD users among them—and the neighborhood leaders who were given special briefings on the program.

The rates of acceptance to date vary by treatment in such a way as to indicate that the group meetings and home visits do have added influence above and beyond the mass media, though perhaps not so much as one would have expected. Mailings, on the other hand, have hardly had any influence (see Table 9).

As in Taichung, the program has had special appeal to women in their 30's, those with three or more children or at least two sons, and those who have already tried contraception on their own. In Korea not only those who had used a method in the past but also current users have responded well, presumably because supplies can be obtained free by registering in the program.

TABLE 9

ACCEPTANCE RATES PER 100 MARRIED WOMEN AGED
20-44 IN SUNGDONG GU, SEOUL, TO JULY 1, 1965,
BY TYPE OF METHOD AND BY TREATMENT[a]

Treatment	All Acceptances	IUD Coupons	Other Methods
Mass media only....	11	4	7
Mailings............	12	5	7
Group meetings.....	15	7	8
Home visits.........	18	8	10
Total.............	13	5	8

[a] Excludes 750 cases whose treatments could not be ascertained.

There is evidence, however, that the IUD has had somewhat greater appeal to those without previous contraceptive experience than have the traditional methods. Seventy-six per cent of the IUD acceptors as against 61% of the traditional methods acceptors had not used any method before.

While the program generally does have greater appeal to those with the demographic characteristics mentioned above, with the passage of time it has brought in more and more of those under 30 years of age, those with fewer than three children or two sons, and those without previous contraceptive experience. For example, from the first month of the program to the most recent months (May–June, 1965) the proportion of acceptors under 30 increased from 28% to 33%; those with fewer than three children, from 18% to 25%; those with fewer than two sons, from 28% to 32%; and those without previous contraceptive experience, from 43% to 68%.

LESSONS LEARNED

Many lessons have been learned from these studies and already applied in the national programs of these countries. Some of the specific lessons applied and found fruitful are summarized in the background paper by the participants from Taiwan and need not be repeated here (see chap. 4 in this volume). I would prefer to address myself to the lessons learned in more general terms. We must be forewarned, however, of at least two things. In the first place, the lessons apply mostly, though probably not exclusively, to those societies or communities of incipient fertility decline in which all or most of the conditions Professor Freedman has recently specified[10] obtain: (*a*) where significant social development has already occurred; (*b*) where mortality has been relatively low for some time; (*c*) where there is evidence that many people, wanting moderate-sized families, are beginning to try to limit family size; and (*d*) where there are effective social networks transcending local communities through which family planning ideas and services and other modernizing influences can be disseminated. It follows that what we can learn from these studies is not so much how to start a movement toward family planning and fertility decline as how to accelerate what is already underway. In the second place, these studies raise more questions than they answer. Our discussion to follow, then, is presented in this frame of mind.

The method offered makes a big difference. A method such as the IUD that is infinitely more advantageous than what has generally been available can accelerate the movement by meeting the prospective users half-way, as it were. Its acceptance diffuses quickly from the highly motivated even to those who are not sufficiently motivated to seek out methods on their own, such as the younger women with few children and sons, those with little education, and the more traditional in several respects. What is more, a method like the IUD has the advantage that once accepted its effect on fertility is decisive and for the most part is influenced very little by the users' strength of motivation. Traditional methods have been offered free experimentally in Taiwan and regularly in Korea and acceptance rates have been high, but the continuation rate has been very low and the failure rate inordinately high.[11] Besides, in Taiwan at least, only the IUD has diffused with little direct effort.

[10]Ronald Freedman, "The Transition from High to Low Fertility: Challenge to Demographers," presidential address for the Population Association of America, presented at the annual meetings in Chicago on April 23, 1965, and to be published in a forthcoming issue of the *Population Index*, Office of Population Research, Princeton University, and Population Association of America, Inc.

[11]In Taiwan, a recent experiment with free distribution of traditional methods showed that only 36% of the takers had actually used the methods when reached from eight

Because we can count on informal channels to carry the message about the IUD and to elicit cases for insertion, direct face-to-face contact (whether by home visit or group meeting) for recruitment purposes need not be highly concentrated. It can be interspersed with some distance between contacts. Random assignment, however, probably is not the most efficient approach, but it is difficult to determine the most efficient spatial distribution of direct effort without further study. What we do know and can do in a direct way is to approach certain couples first—for example; (*a*) the high-parity (say, at least two or three children) with at least one or two sons; (*b*) especially those who were recently pregnant, proving their fecundity; and (*c*) those who have already tried to limit family size either by contraception or by induced abortion, showing their concern. Once these couples have become satisfied users of the new method, they are likely to serve as the most effective promoters of the program to others in the population.

The implication of the foregoing is that field workers should be recruited from the local communities in which they work so as to facilitate the identification of these more susceptible couples. Also, midwives and doctors who have contact with women at psychologically ripe moments as far as receptivity to family planning practices goes should be made active participants in a program. While the private physicians have been successfully brought into the programs in both Taiwan and Korea, the private midwives have not always responded well, if they have been recruited. To gain the latter's commitment, not only economic incentives but also a redefinition of their occupational role probably is needed.

In both studies, there has been very little exploration of the timing of the treatments when they have been combined. We learned from

---

to eleven months after their "acceptance," and the pregnancy rate among those who reported use was as high as 36 per 100 woman-years. For details, see "Monthly Report June 1965: Family Planning Health Program," Provincial Department of Health, Maternal and Child Health Association, and Taiwan Population Studies Center, Republic of China, July, 1965 (mimeographed). In rural Korea, free distribution of traditional methods resulted in an acceptance rate of as high as 45% of all married couples with wives aged 15–44, but the pregnancy rate after 18 months of the program was 23 per 100 woman-years. For details, see Jae Mo Yang *et al.*, "Fertility and Family Planning in Rural Korea" (n. 8 above). Based on data from the medical follow-up study of IUD acceptors in Taichung by courtesy of Dr. C. H. Lee of the Taiwan Provincial Maternal and Child Health Institute, we learn that the proportion of women still wearing an IUD at the end of the first year after their initial acceptance in the experiment was 72% and at the end of the second year, 62%. The failure rate was 4.0 pregnancies per 100 woman-years in the first year and 7.4 in the entire two-year period since initial insertion.

Taichung that when effective group meetings were followed by home visits, the acceptance of the IUD increased. The group meetings in which participants show active interest in the new device probably provide the social support that is often needed to move the interested to try it out. In Taiwan, the home visit by itself could not raise the acceptance of the IUD above the level of the "mail" and "nothing" treatments. We do not know, of course, the effect of a group meeting when it follows home visits in a given neighborhood. A more efficient approach than heretofore attempted is to combine the various treatments—and letters are not necessarily ruled out—in different ways to maximize the reinforcing effect of each upon the other. We know from a follow-up study in Taichung that not only acceptance but also continuation of the IUD is affected by the public's confidence in it.[12] Strategically timed publicity through the mass media and group meetings probably can *facilitate* the growth of this confidence, especially if the prevailing notions that are interfering with wider acceptance are countered in specific and authoritative terms.

The studies to date have in the main emphasized efficiency of results at a given cost. In the two studies reported here, no targets were set. The national programs in both Taiwan and Korea, however, have set specific targets to be reached within the coming decade both in terms of the level of fertility to be attained and the number of IUD insertions required. Answers are needed to the question, How much of what kind of effort is needed to reach a given goal most economically? The studies so far have answered the question, What results follow from what kind of effort? They have provided only indirect answers to the more urgent, former question.

To conclude, we have learned much about the relative effectiveness and efficiency of various approaches to promote contraceptive use—and this is an advance. However, the most efficient combination of the several approaches is yet to be discovered. It probably differs considerably, depending on the character of the target population, such as, for example, their readiness for family limitation generally and the IUD in particular and their level of education. The most efficient combination, however, cannot be predetermined rigidly even for a given population. It should emerge in adaptation to the particular course the program takes. In other words, a given approach should be

[12]In support of our observation that continuation of the IUD may be affected by the public's confidence in it is the fact that during the first year since the program in Taichung voluntary removal of the device declined with fair regularity from 27% among the earliest acceptors to 14% among the latest acceptors, while spontaneous expulsion of the device remained relatively constant at about 11%–15% of all the insertions made throughout the program period.

adapted to the situation at hand, which may differ in place, in time, and for different segments of the population. This calls for constant evaluation of the program and flexibility in program planning, even allowing for local variations within a given national program and variations for different population segments, if only to maximize the results vis-à-vis the over-all goal set and the budget that can be won for the program.

55

DEMONSTRATIONS, EXPERIMENTS, AND PILOT PROJECTS: A REVIEW OF RECENT DESIGNS

FREDERICK F. STEPHAN
Senior Demographic Consultant, The Population Council

The background papers and discussion in this volume report remarkable progress in family planning during the past five years or more. Formal research projects, demonstrations, and pilot studies have contributed greatly to this record of progress. They have provided important information; they have served as training centers; and they have exposed family planning programs to the test of actual practice, thereby revealing many of the difficulties to be overcome when a large-scale program is launched. They have been conducted under a variety of circumstances around the world and for a sufficient period of time to establish the practicality and effectiveness of family planning programs when such programs are conducted competently and supported adequately.

The need for formal research has not diminished. Family planning pioneers surely find recent progress very gratifying, but they are likely to be the first to point out that far greater advances must be made in the future than have been made in the past. While several countries have national programs well underway, most of the world lacks effective family planning. The results of research and the developing experience of these leading countries will be a great asset to other nations when they come to consider various actions to cope with their population problems. It remains to be seen, however, how adequately previous research and even the experience gained in established national programs can take the place of new pilot projects in countries that are not as yet committed to such programs. Moreover, even in countries that now have national programs many important problems remain, some of which require further experimentation, and research for their solution.

Therefore, in preparation for future research efforts, it is well to consider the ways in which family planning studies have been conducted in the past and the stage of development they have reached at the present time, with emphasis on how the approach and design of such studies can be strengthened.

LESSONS FROM THE PAST AND QUESTIONS FOR THE FUTURE

Pioneering projects in Hong Kong, India, Korea, Pakistan, Taiwan, and other countries contribute information and encouragement to countries now at the threshold of family planning, such as Thailand, Tunisia, and Turkey. Somewhat different information comes from European countries, Japan, and the United States, whose social and economic development has been accompanied by a more gradual evolution of population policies and contraceptive programs. With all this past experience, are further trials needed? The answer is clear. Not only are additional pilot studies and demonstrations needed but they should be more carefully planned and more scientifically designed, since they must carry to a more advanced stage the research that previous studies initiated. If these new projects and experiments seem strange or excessively technical to pioneers who launched simpler demonstrations, this should not cause dismay. Indeed, progress necessarily leads to novel and unexpected developments. It is part of the fulfillment of the long-range objectives of pioneering programs.

The published reports of recent pilot studies and demonstrations are helpful, but they do not suffice to guide present and future programs. In fact, one cannot always know precisely what they have demonstrated and what they have proved about effective ways to conduct a family planning program. For example, in a discussion of one major project it was reported that country X "with one of the most extensive birth control programs in the world, has been unable markedly to affect fertility largely because cultural factors have not been taken sufficiently into account." This summary of experience raises more questions than it answers. What cultural factors were neglected? How was the program conducted? When and where? What methods were favored? Was there a well-trained staff? What was its relation to the medical profession? Were there any unusual difficulties? These and other questions must be answered before one knows what the reported experience can tell him about how a family planning program should be conducted in his own area.

Similar questions have to be answered for those pilot studies and demonstrations that appear to be successful. Was the study made under unusually favorable conditions? Were the women who came to the clinics, or otherwise adopted contraception, typical in their social customs, literacy, education, and previous contact with other health programs or were they different from the women now about to be approached? In either case, disappointing failure or encouraging success, what dependable evidence is there that repeating the pilot study in a new location will result in the same results as before?

THE NEED FOR EXPERIMENTS

Because such questions are difficult to answer, it is highly desirable to conduct experiments in which we attempt both to reduce the interfering and confusing effect of unusual conditions and to strengthen and increase the effect of the program we are testing. Fundamentally, experimentation is an attempt to reveal more clearly what is being studied. It does this by eliminating as much as possible the obscuring factors or influences and reinforcing the essential facts which are to be discovered and demonstrated.

Experiments are only special kinds of experience. They are more deliberately organized and conducted than are the simpler types of action programs. They are planned with the particular purpose of contributing dependable knowledge for larger programs. To fulfill this purpose, they include special provisions for observing and recording. They are conducted and controlled so as to yield good data, to permit effective analysis of these data, and to produce conclusions that are both valuable and dependable. Hence they must be well planned and designed to fulfill these purposes. They must be conducted with care and competence. The analysis of their results must be done in accordance with sound scientific principles and related properly to the objectives of the program.

VARIETY OF STUDIES AND TRIALS

There is no standard pattern for family planning pilot studies and experiments. They may promote the use of one or several methods of contraception, emphasizing in some instances "traditional" methods, in others rhythm, sterilization, oral contraceptives, or intra-uterine devices. In the future there may well be entirely new methods based on immunological processes or other biochemical principles. Some findings probably apply to other contraceptives, some do not. Some projects are concerned primarily with the effectiveness of a particular kind of educational program, some with measuring the response to various media of communication, some with training personnel and organizing a system of family planning centers, some with overcoming the obstacles that retard establishment of a successful family planning program in a particular area.

If, then, there is no single pattern for a family planning experiment, are there distinguishable types? Not yet. Perhaps two or three can be found that are very similar in their principal features but no clear concentration around a few typical varieties appeared in my attempts to classify the studies for which I had descriptions. In addition to the methods emphasized and the phases of a program that were stressed, no consistent grouping was evident with respect to (a) the auspices (Ministry of Health and Welfare, provincial government, family planning association, or other governmental agency or voluntary group), (b) geographic location (concentrated in one locality, spread over a province or large district with several service centers, mobile units), (c) mode of operation (separate family planning clinic, combined clinic with maternal and child health programs, extension program of community meetings, home visits, use of commercial and other distribution systems), (d) use of surveys and follow-up (knowledge, attitudes, and practice regarding contraception at the initiation of the program, changes in these fundamental conditions during the experiment, study of subsequent experience of participants served by the program, study of eligible women who do not respond to the program), and (e) efforts to determine effect of the project on family health or welfare and on population growth.

It seems likely that several principal types of studies and trials will emerge in the future from our continuing efforts to test family planning programs and discover how to improve them. They will probably be conducted as part of the development of national programs and will in some cases be indistinguishable from regular administrative planning and supervision. If they are absorbed into these operating functions, however, they are likely not to include an adequate range of variations in the program or give sufficient attention to all important factors.

DESIGN OF PILOT PROJECTS AND EXPERIMENTS

If there are no standard or typical patterns for family planning experiments, how should one proceed? It is easy, but also at times fruitless, if not foolish, merely to pick some previous study that looks interesting and imitate it in a new situation. There is good reason to repeat important studies to test their findings, but one should first ascertain whether the new situation is an appropriate one in which to make this further test. For example, a test of mailed leaflets originally conducted on a literate population (with at least implicit recognition that a high degree of literacy was a necessary condition for the use of this means of communication) could not be repeated usefully on an illiterate population. Hence repetition of a study should be preceded by investigation of the appropriateness of the new location and circumstances. Even when there are no conditions in the new location that make it inappropriate, there are likely to be some circumstances which force modifications. The report of the new trial should then include adequate description of the changes made and the reasons for making them. If the results of the new trial differ from those of the original experiment, there will be lively discussions of whether the differences are due to changes in the way the trial was conducted and whether the findings of the original experiment should be corrected.

Of course, changes may be made unwittingly in the repetition of the experiment and important factors or conditions may escape notice or fail to be described precisely in the records and reports. This may also be true of the original experiment. Hence every care should be taken to identify and describe adequately in the reports those factors and conditions that may have an important relation to the outcome of the experiment.

An interesting example is provided by the Family Planning Extension Program in Taiwan. Special surveys, aimed at determining significant facts about the population before the intensive promotion of intra-uterine devices, showed that the Ota ring was well known and highly acceptable among married women. In fact it was being worn by approximately one woman in twelve to fourteen of the married women between 20 and 40 years of age. Recognizing how important is the effectiveness of word-of-mouth communication from satisfied users, one must consider this factor very carefully in any attempt to repeat the Taiwan experiments elsewhere without the influence of twenty years' previous exposure to an earlier form of intra-uterine device.

Likewise, if there had been a severe epidemic or some other major adverse influence on the Taiwan experiments, that would have been essential to the record and to an understanding of the results of these studies. Or if such major disturbances arise in a repetition elsewhere, they should be taken into account in comparing the findings of the new study with those reported for Taiwan.

To improve the dependability and comparability of research findings it is common to protect experiments from interference by outside influences. This is easier to do in a laboratory than in a trial that of necessity must be conducted under actual field conditions. A second line of defense, then, is to carry on in spite of the interference but to measure its effect, or at least to balance it out, through a comparison of the experiment with a similar situation in which the experiment was not conducted. This is the familiar procedure of designing an experiment so that it has a "control group" or "controls." An example of both principles of design is offered by the Koyang Family Planning Study in Korea. Koyang was selected as a rural area judged to be far enough from Seoul to escape the disturbing influences of a dominant urban center. However, other influences were operating to reduce the birth rate in Koyang from year to year. Hence, a similar area, Kimpo, was selected to serve as a control without the special family planning services and program that was being tried in Koyang. The effect of the program would be revealed, therefore, by the degree to which the birth rate dropped more rapidly in Koyang than in Kimpo.

Here again it is essential to recognize important circumstances, describe them in reports and take account of them in explaining the findings. Koyang had been used as a training center for students at Yonsei University Medical School. Kimpo is the site of the Seoul International Airport. Hence they were not strictly comparable before the experiment and they may have been affected differently by various influences during the period of the study.

Other well-established principles of experimental design can be applied to family planning pilot studies and demonstrations. They include replication (repeating many small experiments of the same kind within one large experiment), special instruments for observation and measurement, special means to intensify effects of what is being studied and to reduce all other effects, and accurate, dependable procedures for analyzing data. Some recent family planning experiments, notably the Taichung study, have used some of these principles. Future experiments should progress even further in control and in improvement of their effectiveness for providing sound information to guide the development and administration of family planning programs.

How Much Experimentation?

Much of the progress of rapidly developing countries is a consequence of research and experimentation, either their own or what they borrow from more advanced nations. Some industries devote as much as 5%, and in special cases twice as much, of their budget to research. How much family research and experimentation should be done is debatable. Inadequate or poorly executed pilot studies may dissipate resources and delay full-scale family planning programs.

Excessively elaborate and poorly designed experiments can also be a net loss. Erroneous findings can be detrimental to the success of the larger program. Hence it is important, in answering the question of how much experimentation, to emphasize quality and dependability.

But if poor research can be wasteful, so too can action that is guided by poorly informed judgments or incorrect assumptions. The detrimental effects of decisions made without the benefit of good research can be vastly greater than those likely to be made on the basis of poor research. The development of family planning programs need never be impeded by experiments; sound use of experiments and special pilot studies should contribute substantially to the ultimate success of these programs.

Future Progress in Experiments and Pilot Studies

In recognizing the great contribution that pilot studies and experiments have made to family planning, we do not imply that they have solved all problems successfully. Here are some examples:

1. How can we project from the early response to a family planning program what its degree of success will be in the long run? At first the women who adopt family planning will be more favorably disposed to it than other women, even those of the same age and parity. Will the rate of new acceptances decline after the most responsive part of the eligible population have become old acceptors? How resistant are the women who do not respond immediately? In one survey of women who accepted coupons entitling them to an IUD insertion without cost but did not use the coupons, it was found that 40% of them said they were "too busy" to do so. Will they use the coupons later when they are not so busy or did they accept them with no intention of using them? If the latter, why did they refrain from accepting the IUD, and will they change their minds and accept it at a later date? The findings of this pilot study will not be clear until such questions have been answered through further research.

Likewise, the introduction of new types of contraception raises questions about the extent to which they increase the effective practice of family planning and the extent to which they replace other methods. We still do not know how accurate are the data obtained by asking men and women about their use of various methods and their intentions to continue in the future. Experience in other fields of research gives us reason to use such data cautiously. Certainly more should be known of those aspects of the operation of family planning centers which prove unsatisfactory or ineffective to important fractions of the eligible population. Is it too difficult to travel to the center? Is the center too crowded? Are the hours it is open suitable for women who are employed during the day? Are many women misinformed about how they will be treated? These and many other practical questions should be investigated to improve the effectiveness of the program and determine the level it will attain when it has been fully established.

2. What influence does the social environment of a woman have on her response to a family planning program? It is recognized that the broader social and cultural environment in some countries strongly favors large families, and that legal, religious, and other influences prohibit contraceptive practices or discourage parents from taking action to regulate the number of children they have. However, relatively little attention has been given to the immediate social influences exerted on husbands and wives by other members of their households and by their neighbors. These influences differ from one household to another, even within the same village or urban neighborhood.

In the early stages of a program, acceptors are likely to come primarily from households in which these immediate social influences are favorable. Whether the program will succeed in overcoming unfavorable influences and thereby find many acceptors in the other households depends on several factors. For example: (a) The experience of the early acceptors, by word-of-mouth communication and by example may change the social environment. (b) Less favorably disposed women may become acceptors after a longer period of exposure to the educational and promotional activities of the program. Their reaction is merely slower and more deliberate. (c) The progress of the program may accentuate the differences of belief and action between households, thereby increasing resistance and hardening the opposition to family planning. (d) Rumors may be circulated and false information spread as some acceptors become dissatisfied or report trouble. Therefore studies are needed of the influences exerted by husbands, mothers-in-law, other relatives, and neighbors to determine how the program can utilize favorable influences and change or offset unfavorable influences. Then trials and experiments will be needed to test the effectiveness of these new developments in family planning activities. Already in Taichung and Seoul, experiments have been conducted on the relative effectiveness of mass media communication, home visits, and group meetings as ways to stimulate favorable influences. Future research will surely go further in analyzing the immediate social environment and testing ways to make it more favorable to family planning.

3. Perhaps the weakest aspect of current family planning is the use of contraceptives and rhythm to *space* births for the benefit of the

mother's health and welfare as well as that of the children. To help make the program more effective with young mothers, further research and pilot projects are needed. The effectiveness of special programs for men in the armed forces and for older girls in the schools, for example, is still to be determined. With the development of antenatal and postnatal care as well as hospital deliveries, increasing opportunities are available for special programs centering on women at the time of giving birth. More serious are the problems and opportunities for special programs centering on women who have just had an abortion. For such special programs improved methods of conducting the program must be found by suitable studies, pilot projects, and experiments.

For the study of such problems and for the improvement of family planning programs wherever that is possible, it is essential that the necessary studies and experiments themselves be conducted on an increasingly higher level of scientific research. At the same time, they must be closely related to the day-to-day work of family planning programs, coming to close grips with the actual conditions and important influences under which their findings will be applied. There need be no conflict of action programs and research activities; indeed, they are interdependent and should contribute much to each other.

Advances Needed in Research and Practical Trials

There is a widely recognized progression in scientific research from basic research to applied research to development and field trials to monitoring fully developed applications to operational studies and systems analyses. Without basic research, we would have no oral contraceptives or IUD's and, without more of it, there will be no further advances in family planning methods. (Even the rhythm method would be less effective.) Without development and pilot studies, neither the pills nor the IUD's would have left the laboratory. Without good research on the operation of family planning programs, they will fall far short of their possible accomplishments.

The pilot studies and experiments of the future will have problems of their own to solve: the selection of the sites for demonstrations, the choice of controls, the reduction of response error in surveys, the difficulty of follow-up studies, the improvement of measurement, the avoidance of grossly incorrect conclusions, the problems of projecting or anticipating long-term changes, the fuller utilization of scientific findings from other fields, the obstacles set by the varieties of language, culture, class differences, and other socio-cultural differences, the difficulty of obtaining adequate data on family life and personal choices as well as interpersonal influence and community relations. In comparison with what is needed, the research that has been done in family planning has been spread quite thin, often with populations and samples too small to warrant any precise or general findings. Where the studies have covered larger populations, they have tended toward the superficiality of one-time surveys and have been weak either in tracing changes or in reconstructing past events. They present an incomplete picture of the interplay of important influences.

Nonetheless, though every effort should be made to eliminate these shortcomings from future research, this is not a discredit to past studies. They were made under extraordinarily difficult circumstances. Apathy or even active opposition was common. Budgets were meager, staff limited, and travel arduous in most instances. The pioneers who made these studies and conducted early pilot studies opened up the opportunities for larger, better family planning programs in many countries. And they are still at work. They are being joined by new researchers with more advanced methods and more ample resources. With new strength and skill, their work will lead to the improvement of family planning programs and contribute to the accomplishment of the ultimate purposes to which the papers in this volume are devoted.

56

FAMILY PLANNING RESEARCH: AN OUTLINE OF THE FIELD

DONALD J. BOGUE
Community and Family Study Center
University of Chicago

INTRODUCTION

Research is playing a most important role in the world-wide program to slow the rate of population growth. Although the two are interrelated, it is possible to subdivide this research activity into two major types:

1. *Demographic research*—the study of population size, composition, and growth and the implications of these phenomena for economic development and other academic disciplines. By revealing the detailed population processes involved in the growth of the labor force, in educating oncoming generations, in providing housing, and in striving to increase per capita income, it furnishes the broad perspective which makes it evident that fertility control is necessary and urgent for national and world welfare. This branch of study usually concentrates on the analysis of national census and vital statistics data or of population data derived from national sample surveys.

2. *Family planning research*—the systematic study of the phenomenon of family planning among populations, of the processes by which the practice of family planning diffuses throughout a community or nation, and of the forces that retard or facilitate such diffusion and adoption. Such studies may be investigations of contemporary conditions or they may be linked to experiments designed to accelerate the adoption of family planning. One of their outstanding traits is that official census and vital statistics are seldom sufficient for their purposes; family planning research usually involves going into the field and collecting data in a comparatively small local area, either to test a hypothesis or to evaluate a proposed action program.

The principal reason for making this distinction is to emphasize that the upsurge of family planning action has created new research demands and avenues of inquiry that previously had not been of great interest to demographers, and which previous demographic research could not satisfy. Whether the field of demography will expand its scope to include all of what is here called "family planning research" remains for history to determine. The purpose of this paper is to outline the content of the new field of "family planning research" and to attempt to lay down some guidelines for its future development.

CONTENT OF THE FIELD OF FAMILY PLANNING RESEARCH

The subject matter with which family planning research is concerned may be classified into four categories, as follows:

1. *The study of motives favoring and opposing family planning.* Consciously or unconsciously, populations which have high fertility are striving to satisfy certain needs by having large families. Similarly, populations that adopt family planning do so in order to satisfy certain needs. What are these needs? How prevalent is each motive among the population? How easily can new motives be acquired by illiterate populations? To what extent does population pressure and its attendant hardships cause motives to change? Motivation research is a foundation upon which scientific family planning programs must be founded. Programs intended to stimulate family planning adoption cannot succeed if the motivational need-structure of the population is only surmised.

2. *The study of attitudes with respect to family planning.* Attitudes are predispositions toward taking (or not taking) a particular course of action in response to situations where a need is experienced. Is the population favorably or unfavorably disposed toward smaller families? Does it approve or disapprove of the abstract idea of fertility control? Does it accept or reject each of the particular methods of family planning that currently is available? What is the nature of the objections? What is the basis for the attraction of the more popular methods?

3. *The study of popular knowledge about family planning.* How much does the population know about each of the modern methods of family planning? How much does it know about the physiology of reproduction? How much incorrect information and folk beliefs are extant? How much does the citizenry know about the availability of family planning service: where to go, what to ask for, how to use each method, how much each costs?

4. *The study of actual behavior with respect to family planning.* What share of the population has actually tried a family planning method? When in its reproductive career did this begin? What were the methods tried? What has been the degree of success? What situations precipitated the effort to make a first trial? What are the conditions of failure? What effect upon the birth rate did this use have?

These four classes of inquiry may be termed the *subject matter,* or the subfields of family planning research. In order to specify fully the content of the field we must state the principal ways in which these variables are used in research. There are three different research contexts in which these subjects can be studied:

1. To *inventory* a situation, perhaps just before undertaking a family planning action experiment. The objective of such an inventory may be to establish a baseline against which to measure progress or change as the result of the experiment.

2. To *explain* fertility motives, attitudes, knowledge, and behavior in terms of other variables that are hypothesized as being "causal" or "fundamentally interrelated." The explanatory variables that are invoked for this purpose may be psychological, sociological, anthropological, or economic in nature. Each variable that is admitted as an explanatory variable must be justified not only by an empirical demonstration of relationship but also by a theoretical formulation of how and why the relationship exists.

3. To *evaluate* the effectiveness of family planning action experiments, by determining whether there has been a significant change in motives, attitudes, knowledge, or behavior in the direction of accepting family planning.

SUBFIELD OF FAMILY PLANNING RESEARCH	RESEARCH CONTEXT		
	Inventory (Baseline studies)	Explanation (Testing of hypotheses)	Evaluation (Measurement of change)
Motives for adopting or rejecting family planning..............	Inventory of motives	Explanation of motives	Change in motives
Attitudes toward family planning	Inventory of attitudes	Explanation of attitudes	Change in attitudes
Knowledge of family planning methods and services	Inventory of knowledge	Explanation of knowledge	Change in knowledge
Behavior: adoption or rejection of family planning	Inventory of behavior	Explanation of behavior	Change in behavior

FIG. 1.—Schematic outline of the field of family planning research

Figure 1 illustrates graphically the content of the field of family planning research, as outlined above. This diagram makes it clear that each of the four subfields of family planning research may be meaningfully studied in each of the three research contexts. This yields twelve types of family planning research problems (four subfields × three contexts), as exemplified by the twelve interior cells of Figure 1. It is our contention that every research problem in the field of family planning research may be classified in one of these twelve cells; and that together these twelve cells exhaust the field.

The assertion made above that family planning research lies outside the field of demography as it has been defined in the past, is more understandable and defensible when the content of the field is listed in this fashion. Only one of the twelve categories, "change in behavior," appears to overlap one subfield of demography, "change in birth rates." As we shall attempt to demonstrate below, the field of family planning research requires its own special methodology for this category, and uses measures that are essentially non-demographic, although they may be translated into demographic measures if desired.

ORIENTATION OF FAMILY PLANNING RESEARCH

It has sometimes been claimed that a distinction between family planning research and demographic research is that the former is concerned with immediate action even if knowledge is incomplete, while demography is intent upon developing the knowledge upon which action should be based. The implication is that family planning research hopes to "learn by doing"; we start out by trying something that sounds reasonable and modify our actions as we gain experience concerning what "works" and what doesn't. This is an incorrect interpretation. Family planning research, as defined here, has none of the trial-and-error component implied in the term "operations research." It is no less scientific, no less rigorous, no less intent upon developing basic knowledge than any other branch of social science. In fact, family planning research identifies explicitly the sociological and psychological knowledge that is needed in order to "solve" the world's population problem and sets out on the long trail of producing it.

The *raison d'être* for family planning research is the recognition that none of the theories or hypotheses being explored by traditional demography can provide the basis for a stepped-up "crash" program for fertility reduction. Most of such theories are based upon correlations between fertility and other variables that are incapable of being manipulated rapidly, such as the educational level of the population, the degree of urbanization, changes in real per capita income, experience with other aspects of modern technology, and fundamental changes in culture. Family planning research does not deny the existence of these relationships. It begins with the assumption that by the discovery of new principles we may be able to devise programs that can accomplish the desired results more quickly than would be possible if we waited for the solution along the lines of increased literacy–rising urbanization–improved level of living–increased contact with technological-cultural change.

Once it makes this assumption, family planning research is forced to become experimental. If a hypothesis is developed concerning a principle that might speed up family planning adoption (such as the recruitment of "opinion leaders" in favor of family planning), the only way to test that hypothesis is to devise an experiment and see if it has any measurable effect upon motives, attitudes, knowledge, or behavior with respect to family planning. Since there exists nowhere in the real world a situation where this event is taking place spontaneously, we must create such a situation and then observe the result.

Such experiments should not and must not be of the informal and muddling type implied by the term "action research." They must be experiments in the highest tradition of science. They must conform to the principles of sound experimental design to the maximum extent possible. (It appears that some experimental designs that are standard in other branches of experimental work are inappropriate for family planning research because they permit contamination, and that innovations will be needed.) Thus, instead of being a drive to "do something quickly, even if sloppily," family planning research is a movement from *ex post facto* research of the type with which most social science must be content to the conduct of *experiments*, where conditions are at least quasi-controlled. It could even be claimed that this shift is in the direction of becoming *more* scientific, rather than less, in comparison with the other fields of social research, including traditional demography.

THE "DEPENDENT VARIABLES" OF FAMILY PLANNING RESEARCH: NEED FOR STANDARDIZATION

The four subfields of family planning research can be expressed as a list of specific "family planning variables," or "dependent variables for family planning research." Therefore, it behooves those who are doing work in this field to pool their ideas and develop the list. With the list once established, researchers should then pool their knowledge and proceed to arrive at standard operational definitions of each variable and devise standard procedures for collecting and categorizing data. This will promote comparability of findings among nations and the more rapid cumulation of knowledge. Such a program aimed toward standardization should not be designed to destroy originality and fresh thinking but should have as its objective the integration and codification of the vast amount of experience that has already been accumulated, in order to eliminate needless non-comparabilities caused by incomplete communication and discussion. Sufficient research has already been completed to permit this process to begin.

As a first step toward promoting this standardization, a list of the dependent variables for family planning has been prepared with operational definitions and proposed procedures for collecting, coding, and tabulating data.[1] Because of space limitation it is possible here only to list these variables; the interested reader is referred to the full report for the detailed exposition of each.

I. Motives for adopting or rejecting family planning
   a) Health
   b) Economic
   c) Family welfare
   d) Marriage adjustment
   e) Personality needs
   f) Community and national welfare
   g) Moral and cultural needs
   h) Aesthetic enjoyment of sex
   > Note: In the report, these are only general categories which are in turn subdivided into more specific motives.

II. Attitudes toward family planning
   A. Ideals of reproduction
      a) Ideal family size
      b) Ideal age at first marriage
      c) Ideal time to have first child
      d) Ideal interval between pregnancies
      e) Ideal age to terminate childbearing
   B. Attitudes toward childbearing
      a) Attitude toward having more children
      b) Feeling that children are a handicap
      c) Attitudes concerning opportunity costs of having children
      d) Realization of excess fertility
      e) Respondent's definition of a "large" and a "small" family
      f) Worry about getting pregnant
      g) Tolerance of family size
      h) Expectations of family size
   C. Attitude toward fertility limitation
      a) Attitude toward use of particular methods
      b) Acceptance or rejection of abortion
      c) Acceptance or rejection of sterilization

III. Knowledge of family planning
   A. Awareness of family planning

[1] Donald J. Bogue, *Inventory, Explanation, and Evaluation by Interview of Family Planning Motives, Attitudes-Knowledge-Behavior*, prepared for discussion at International Conference on Family Planning Programs, Part I (Chicago: Community and Family Study Center, 1965).

B. Familiarity with individual methods of contraception
C. Number of different methods known
D. Respondent's knowledge of reliability of individual methods of contraception
E. Summary index of contraceptive knowledge
F. Index of ignorance and misinformation about contraception

IV. Behavior with respect to family planning
    A. Use of individual methods of contraception—methods ever used
    B. When first use began
    C. Number of different methods ever used
    D. Method of contraception currently being used
    E. Index of reliability of method being used
    F. Frequency of "taking a chance"
    G. Summary index of contraceptive protection
    H. Family planning use status

This list is submitted for review by researchers around the world, in the hope that additional variables will be added and that standardized procedures for collecting data for all of the subject-matter variables in family planning research may be developed quickly.

THE "INDEPENDENT" (EXPLANATORY) VARIABLES OF FAMILY PLANNING RESEARCH

If experiments are to be designed that successfully reduce fertility at a rate faster than would be expected, it will require the application of new principles or theories. Such principles and theories can be developed only on the basis of a test of a hypothesis concerning the relationship between one of the family planning variables and some "explanatory" variable. The family planning programs now underway, for example, place great emphasis upon the "knowledge and service" theory: If you inform people about the methods and give them good service, a significant number will accept. If we hope to devise even better programs, we must develop more sophisticated theories. This calls for the testing of a wider variety of hypotheses, which in turn calls for the quantification of a large number of independent variables.

In Part III of the report cited above, an effort was made to list the explanatory variables that have the greatest potential for testing at the present time. Each was discussed in abstract terms; and a standard procedure for obtaining data and classifying data was proposed. A list of these variables follows; for a detailed discussion of each the reader is again referred to the full report.

    I. Social security: Does having many children provide security in old age?

Do people have many children in order to provide security in old age?

II. Religion: Do people have many children because of religious beliefs?

Do highly religious people reject contraception more frequently than people with low interest in religion?

III. Perception of the population problem
IV. Communication variables
    A. Sources of information about family planning
    B. Age at first learning about family planning
    C. Inter-spouse communication about family planning
    D. Conversations about family planning with relatives, friends, neighbors
    E. Participation in group discussions of family planning
    F. Reading about family planning
    G. Response to mass media communication about family planning
   V. Desire to learn more about family planning
  VI. Fatalism-hopelessness-powerlessness syndrome and family planning
 VII. Aspirations for children and family planning
VIII. Traditionalism-modernism and family planning
  IX. Equality of the sexes and family planning
   X. Companionate marriage and family planning
  XI. Personality traits and family planning
 XII. Sex behavior and family planning
XIII. Happiness in marriage and family planning
XIV. Influence of the extended family and family planning
 XV. Economic status and family planning
XVI. Sociological and ethnic characteristics and family planning
XVII. Demographic and ecological characteristics and family planning

It is known that this list is not complete. It is submitted for consideration in order that additional explanatory variables may be added and that all variables may be reviewed with the intent of standardizing definitions, data collection procedures, and categories for analysis.

EVALUATION OF FAMILY PLANNING PROGRAMS:
THE MEASUREMENT OF CHANGE

One of the major developments in family planning in recent years has been the recruitment of experts to help devise new programs. Experts in communication, adult education, public health, education, medical sociology, family life, and group dynamics have become interested in family planning and are lending their skills to the development of new programs. Action programs that incorporate very advanced ideas from these various disciplines are now underway or on the drawing boards in many parts of the world.

One of the most important tasks of family planning research is that of *evaluating* what effect, if any, these programs will have in promoting the cause of fertility reduction. This is a branch of family planning research which, as yet, is only embryonic. The comments made here are intended more to promote discussion of the problems rather than to summarize established principles.

The evaluation of a family planning program involves two lines of inquiry: (*a*) Can any change be attributed to the program; if so how much? and (*b*) If change occurred, how did it exert its impact: upon whom, by what means, and at what expenditure of effort? The first of these is discussed below; the second will be treated in the next section.

We need to set up a criterion of what constitutes "success" in a family planning program. The following is proposed:

There are two kinds of success—"relative success" and "absolute success." Relative success may be defined as any statistically significant change in motives, attitudes, or knowledge in a direction more favorable to the eventual adoption of family planning that can be attributed to a family planning action program. Specifically, if a population can be induced to experience the motivational needs that fertility reduction satisfies; if it can be induced to relax attitudes of hostility or indifference and accept attitudes favorable to the practice of family planning; or if it can be taught more about family planning methods—how they work and how to get started—it is possible to claim "relative success" for an experiment or program.

Absolute success may be defined as a statistically significant reduction in the pregnancy rate: the number of pregnancies per 100 woman-years of exposure to pregnancy.

It is customary to assert that a family planning program is succeeding only if it brings about a reduction in the birth rate. In most countries of Europe and North America, such a criterion would be equivalent to the criterion of absolute success stated above. Changes in the pregnancy rate are almost perfectly associated with changes of identical direction and magnitude in the birth rates. This, however, is not necessarily true in many developing nations. In fact, in many of these nations there are strong forces at work to increase the birth rate—for example, the conquest of malaria and other diseases that frequently kill pregnant women or induce abortions, the reduction in widowhood, the reduction in pregnancy wastage due to improved prenatal care and medical care at time of delivery, the reduction of sterility due to venereal disease, poor post-partum care, and untreated disorders of the reproductive system. Since 1945, a genuine rise in birth rates has been registered in several nations of Asia and Latin America, and if trustworthy data could be had, it is probable that there are strong forces acting to reduce pregnancy wastage in all. For evaluating family planning programs, therefore, it is good to think in terms of pregnancy rates. However, there need be no strong objection to the use of falling birth rates as the criterion of success if it is understood by all that this is a very conservative test, biased in the direction of declaring that a family planning program has produced no effect when, in fact, it may have done so.

How should we determine whether a family planning experiment has been a success? The most unambiguous way of testing whether it has been a success is the scheme outlined in Table 1.

In this scheme, a and c could be the initial and the follow-up measurements of motives, attitudes, knowledge, or conception rates. Any

TABLE 1

SUCCESS $= (c - a)$ is greater than $(c' - a')$

Time	Treatment Group	Control Group (No Treatment)
Baseline status...........	a	a'
Treatment...............	b	b'
Follow-up status.........	c	c'
Differences............	$c-a$	$c'-a'$

value of $(c - a)$ which is greater than zero is either an implied success, a random event, or a secular change that is occurring in the universe irrespective of the experiment or intervention taken. In this design, if a larger success is observed in the treatment group than in the control group, and if extraneous factors have been controlled, then there is evidence which most statisticians would accept that there has been a positive effect of the treatment program.

A less convincing procedure, which makes it look plausible that an effect has occurred, is the scheme suggested in Table 2. In this case, no baseline measurement is taken before the treatment is given. But if it is observed that among the group with the most treatment there is a greater amount of change in motives, attitudes, knowledge, and pregnancy rate than in the group with no treatment, with the "small amount of treatment" group falling in between (and if this difference cannot be shown to have resulted from extraneous factors), it is plausible that the greater amount of outcome in the "large amount of treatment" group has been induced by the program. Where this type of design is employed, the researcher is implicitly assuming that if a baseline survey had been taken it would have been found that $a=a'=a''$, or that differences between a and a' and a'' were smaller than those between c and c' and c''. He must bear the burden of supporting this claim. If he can make out a convincing case for this assumption, then his findings may be given tentative credence.

If no baseline data were taken at the start of an experience, it is possible to reconstruct baseline estimates by asking the respondents to report their status *before* the start of the experiment or by estimating this status from other sources of data. This procedure is subject to errors of recall and estimate. The bias of recall should run in the direction of failing to report change when it has in fact occurred, so that it is conservative in that it is likely to claim less "success" than was actually achieved.

TABLE 2

SUCCESS $= c$ is less than c' is less than c''
$= d$ is less than d' is less than d''

(retrospective measurement of a, a', and a'')

Time	No Treatment	Small Amount of Treatment	Large Amount of Treatment
Baseline not taken....	(a)	(a')	(a'')
Treatment..........	b	b'	b''
Follow-up..........	c	c'	c''
Difference........	$d=c-a$	$d'=c'-a'$	$d''=c''-a''$

CONTAMINATION AND EVALUATION

If a baseline survey is to be made, great care must be taken so that the process of obtaining the information for evaluation does not itself constitute a communication or motivation treatment. Practitioners of non-directive interviewing have emphasized the very powerful effect which can be produced by asking a chain of related questions which call only for a reporting of facts, in getting people to re-examine their own motives and attitudes deeply. Indeed, this very procedure is the basis of one of the most widely used procedures of counseling by clinical psychologists, so-called non-directive therapy. A baseline survey that collects attitudes about fertility and contraception may easily perform the function of a clinical interview. It could cause the respondent to rethink entirely the problem of family size, and cause him to decide to begin family planning.

It is the essential nature of most family planning experiments that they give a mild stimulus to many hundreds or thousands of individuals, in the expectation that a small but significant fraction of sensitized persons will respond. A baseline interview can contaminate an experiment in two ways. (1) It can be a far more powerful stimulus to the individual who receives it than the weak mass communication stimulus, and can lead to a confounding of interview-effect with communication-effect. (2) It can so sensitize the respondent that he discusses the topic extensively with his friends and neighbors and sensitizes them also, thereby promoting a greater response. Both of these types of contamination could lead to an exaggeration of the true effectiveness of a particular type of communication. It is imperative, therefore, that for attitude studies, the sample of persons for whom the follow-up is taken should be different from the sample of persons for whom the baseline is taken, unless the baseline interview is itself a part of the communication treatment. This consideration may cause an evaluator to employ the second of the above study designs.

Experience to date has shown disappointing results in the use of control groups. The setting-up of an independent population for purposes of comparison in an experiment requires three assumptions:

1. The control population is identical in composition (motives, attitudes, knowledge, practice) to the treatment population.
2. There will be no stimuli toward the adoption of family planning in the control population, or if any such stimuli occur they will also affect the treatment population by an equal amount in addition to the stimuli of the family planning program being evaluated.
3. There will be no communication between the control and the treatment populations that would affect the adoption of family planning.

In actual practice one or more of these conditions tends to break down. A period of at least two years must elapse between the start of a family planning program and the start of the follow-up evaluation, and a period of three or four years is desirable. This is a very long time to "hold things constant"; the very fact that an experimental "family planning vacuum" has been set up for control purposes is an invitation for a great many forces to rush in to fill the gap. The researcher who is designing an evaluation program should not hesitate to set up control groups, but he should not gamble his entire evaluation experiment on this design alone. Instead, he must set up a "second line of defense."

One such second line of defense is to measure, in the follow-up data, exactly how much the action program succeeded in penetrating the consciousness of individuals, either directly or indirectly, and then to compare the fertility behavior of persons who were reached with that of persons who were not reached.

Procedures for measuring change in family planning motives, attitudes, knowledge, and behavior are discussed at some length in Part II and in Part IV of the full report mentioned above. In this area a kit of tools that produce valid and reliable results has not as yet been assembled, in my judgment.

EVALUATION OF FAMILY PLANNING RESEARCH: COMPONENTS OF THE PROGRAM

It is most encouraging to demonstrate, by an evaluation research program, that a family planning action program has succeeded in bringing about relative or absolute success; yet if the evaluation stopped at this point, it would be inadequate. There are many other questions to be answered. The evaluator must try to trace the impact of his program upon individual couples in the population. What kinds of persons responded and what kinds did not? Which particular aspects of the program were most effective in promoting change, and which ineffective? Of the persons who did not respond, was the non-response due to failure to receive the stimuli or failure to change even though reached? Was the effect achieved as a direct result of the program, or was it an indirect result of some unanticipated chain of events? What part was played by the formal program and what part by informal spontaneous interaction among persons as a response to the formal program? In other words, the evaluator must not only determine whether success was achieved, but he needs also to explain *how* and *why* success or failure occurred.

In order to obtain answers to questions of these types, the follow-up analysis must adopt the viewpoint of studying individual couples, rather than treat the entire group as an entity. The follow-up analysis should try to reconstruct, in historical sequence, the family planning stimuli which each couple in the sample experienced, and the sources from which they came. Then an effort must be made to correlate the number, content, and source of these stimuli with changes (if any) in family planning motives, attitudes, knowledge, or behavior manifested by the couple. This type of inquiry requires the evaluator to collect a great deal of information by respondent recall and subjective evaluation. The techniques for carrying this out are as yet comparatively undeveloped. The analytical process, of course, is simple and straightforward, as illustrated by the scheme in Table 3. This scheme can be used for measuring rates of change in motivation, attitudes, knowledge, or action. In addition to components of a family planning program, the stub of the table may contain variables measuring characteristics of the couples, the types and amounts of informal interaction they have had with opinion leaders and peers with respect to family planning, or other variables expressing hypotheses concerning how and why individual couples in a population move toward family planning and others remain unaffected by action programs. In addition to taking each component or category one at a time, they may be studied in combinations. The major problems are associated with obtaining valid and reliable data.

CONCLUSION

It is hoped that the above exposition helps to establish a greater awareness that there is a very large area of research, here called simply "family planning research," that is not as yet adequately covered by the methodology and span of interest of demography, as it has been

TABLE 3

TABULAR OUTLINE OF PROCEDURE FOR ANALYZING IMPACT UPON COUPLES
OF PARTICULAR COMPONENTS OF FAMILY PLANNING PROGRAMS

Component of Family Planning Program Experienced by the Couple	Number of Couples Not Practicing Reliable Family Planning at Start of the Program (1)	Number of Couples Starting To Practice Family Planning Reliably during the Course of the Experiment (2)	Rate of Improvement in Adoption of Family Planning (2)/(1)×100
Component 1 Component 2 Component 3 Component 4			

defined in the past. This area of study has four major topics for research: motives, attitudes, knowledge, and behavior with respect to family planning. Each of these four may be studied in three different contexts: inventory, explanation, and evaluation. It is possible now to outline, in schematic form, the types of study design that are appropriate for use in each context. It is possible to identify explicitly and define operationally the leading dependent and independent variables involved. A great deal of experience has already been accumulated around the world in various aspects of this field of research. Yet there are several difficult problems that are now unsolved but solvable.

Family planning research has been in existence as a major activity for about ten years. It would appear that the time has arrived for those who are most interested and most involved in this endeavor to begin systematically to pool their experience, with the goal of standardizing and codifying procedures that are widely valid and useful and of clarifying and exchanging hypotheses about problems that are as yet unsolved. Until this development takes place, the results of particular action programs undertaken in particular localities will continue to be ambiguous, those who design new family planning programs will not know how and why they succeed, even if they do have unmistakable success, and the results of one action program cannot be easily compared with those of another. Family planning researchers must somehow invent a procedure for making their knowledge more cumulative and systematic without destroying originality, fresh thinking, and inventiveness.

57

THE IMPACT OF BIRTH CONTROL PROGRAMS ON FERTILITY

BYUNG MOO LEE

Research and Training Department, National Institute of Health
Ministry of Health and Social Affairs, Korea

and

JOHN ISBISTER

Graduate Student in Economics, Princeton University

The relationship between birth control programs and economic development can be studied by taking fertility reduction as the intermediate link. A birth control program of a given size will produce a certain fertility reduction. This fertility reduction will then affect the course of economic development. The latter connection is the more dramatic and the more complex; it has been studied in considerable detail by many demographers and economists.[1] The first connection, between a birth control program and the fertility reduction which ensues, has been given little attention, if only because the possibility of effective birth control programs is such a recent phenomenon.[2] The importance of a better understanding of this relationship is obvious,

The first draft of this article was written by Lee as a workshop project, while participating in the program for visiting students at the Office of Population Research, Princeton, 1964–65. It was revised and completed by Isbister during the summer of 1965. The authors are greatly indebted to Professor Ansley J. Coale for his guidance and suggestions. They would also like to thank the Population Council for its most generous financial support, and Dr. John Ross for his critical comments.

[1]For quantitative estimates of the effects of different fertility patterns on economic development, see Ansley J. Coale and Edgar M. Hoover, *Population Growth and Economic Development in Low Income Countries* (Princeton: Princeton University Press, 1958).

[2]See, however, Christopher Tietze, "Pregnancy Rates and Birth Rates," *Population Studies*, Vol. 16 (1) (July, 1962), for a discussion of the relationship between contraceptive effectiveness and fertility rates.

737

both as an instrument of efficient planning and administration and as a part of the development of demography.

To analyze this relationship, we shall develop some general formulas. These formulas enable one to estimate (1) the effect of a given birth control program on the fertility of a particular future year, (2) the total effect that IUD's will have during all the years they remain in use, and (3) the scale of an IUD program required to achieve specified objectives. In order to illustrate the methods we have examined the family planning program of the Republic of Korea. Korea, with a population of almost 30 million growing at 2.9% a year, has launched an ambitious government-sponsored program, and its experience is of great interest to many other low-income countries with high fertility.

EFFECT OF A BIRTH CONTROL PROGRAM

As a first step, we shall estimate the effect of a given program on the age-specific fertility schedule. For each future year in which we are interested, the number of live births to women in each age group and the total number of women in each age group must be calculated.

The births in a given year can be thought of as equal to (a) the births which would have occurred during that year in the absence of a family planning program minus (b) the births prevented by the program.

a) The "potential births," or births which would have occurred without family planning, are easily calculated provided it can be assumed that age-specific fertility would remain constant if there were no birth control program. Then the fertility rate of the ith age group in the base year is simply multiplied by the number of women projected to be in the ith age group in year t. If it is suspected that fertility would change for some independent reason, such as a change in the proportion married or an improvement in maternal health, the fertility figures used in estimating potential births should be adjusted accordingly. (We shall, however, make no such correction in the exercises reported herein.)

b) To find the births prevented by family planning in the ith age group in year t, one estimates the number of women of that age who are making effective use of contraceptives, and the fertility rate which those women would have had were they not using contraceptives.[3]

---

[3] A birth control program can have many indirect effects on fertility, through stimulating greater use of commercially obtained contraceptives, through a higher abortion rate of accidental pregnancies, through the intangible effects of raising the status of women, and so on. We neglect all such effects in this paper, not because they are necessarily unimportant, but because we have no way of predicting them. This analysis concerns direct effects only.

Discovery of figures for this rate of "fertility foregone" naturally presents a problem. It can probably be assumed that women coming to a birth control clinic would have had higher fertility than the average of all women of that age (provided they are not merely changing to mechanical methods of birth control from other methods, such as abortion). If being married were the only factor separating acceptors from all women, then the age-specific marital fertility rates of the base year might be sufficient to estimate births prevented. But the acceptors probably have even greater proneness to fertility than the average of married women. Few of them (or their husbands) are sterile or seriously ill; and women who know themselves to be quite fertile may be naturally more interested in family planning than other married women. Of course this "potential fertility foregone" cannot be known with certainty, but research can indicate whether acceptors have had higher than average fertility in the recent past, before they entered the program. If they have, then rates somewhat higher than the marital fertility rates should be used. (We shall assume below, based on Taichung data, that without the program, acceptors' age-specific fertility rates would have been 20% above marital fertility rates in the general population during the base year.)

Births do not occur at the same time as conception; there is a gestation period of nine months. So, approximately speaking, it is the contraceptives in use in year $t-1$, not year t, those which are used by women who will be in age group i in year t, which will affect the fertility of the ith age group in year t. In other words, to predict the fertility of women aged 20–24 in 1971, one must estimate the contraceptives in use by women aged 19–23 in 1970. The formula used in estimating future age-specific fertility is:

$$f_{i,t} = \frac{F_{i,t} \cdot f_{i,0} - Q_{i,t} \cdot g_i}{F_{i,t}}, \tag{1}$$

where $f_{i,t}$ = the fertility rate of women in the ith age group, in year t;

$f_{i,0}$ = the fertility rate of women in the ith age group in the base year, before the program is begun;

$F_{i,t}$ = total women in the ith age group, year t;

g_i = "potential" fertility, which contraceptive users in the ith age group would have experienced, were they not using contraceptives;

$Q_{i,t}$ = number of women in the ith age group in year t who were practicing totally effective contraception in year $t-1$; and . . . .

$i = 1 \ldots 7$, referring to age groups 15–19 . . . 45–49.

In using this formula, four magnitudes are required for each age group: fertility of the base year, total women in year t, "potential" fertility of women using contraceptives, and number of women practicing effective contraception. The first, $f_{i,0}$, can sometimes be taken from the census or vital statistics. The second, $F_{i,t}$, can be projected, given the census of the base year and suitable life tables. The third, g_i, can equal the marital fertility rates of the base year (or, if appropriate, rates drawn from research on acceptors). A method of estimating the fourth, $Q_{i,t}$, is developed next, a rather lengthy task.

Estimation of Effective Contraceptives in Use (Q)

For traditional contraceptives such as condoms, one simply estimates the number of users and then subtracts some proportion of these, to account for failures in use and wastage. In our calculations we have assumed that only 60% of traditional contraceptives are used effectively. While this figure may seem low to those who are familiar with contraceptive effectiveness in Western countries, it should be remembered that such poor performance is precisely the reason that traditional contraceptives are of limited use in illiterate, low-income populations. Our figure of 60% should, of course, be replaced by the results of field studies where available, but it is doubtful whether the true proportion for an Asian or Latin American population would be much higher than this. The contraceptives which are used effectively are then assigned to the respective age groups, according to proportions discovered by surveys or adapted from the records of other countries.

The process of estimating the number of intra-uterine devices (and vasectomies) in use in a given year is more complex. Unlike traditional methods, IUD's are continuous in their effect; an IUD inserted this year may continue in place for ten or more years to come. During this time, it will be subject to a certain probability of removal, and the woman wearing it will be subject to a certain probability of dying and of widowhood. Even if the IUD remains in effective use, the woman will be growing older and will belong to a succession of different age groups.

The Taichung study indicates that about 30% of IUD's inserted are removed within the first year, and 40% by the end of the second year.[4] As a rule of thumb, we have assumed that 70% of all IUD's are effective. Thus we assume that 30% come out immediately upon in-

[4]Michigan Population Studies Center, Taichung Project, Taiwan, "One-Year and Two-Year Follow-up of IUD Cases in the Taichung Experiment," report, July 30, 1965. It is quite possible that the introduction of larger IUD's in Taiwan will improve substantially upon past performance.

sertion and so are worthless. Actually, some stay in long enough to do some good; but more than 30% come out in the first few years. If on balance the 70% assumption seems high, it is hoped that, with more experience and improved design, IUD's will become serviceable for a higher proportion of women.

Since IUD's have been in existence for such a short time, there are almost no data available on the extent to which women intentionally discontinue using them after several years. In the absence of such data, we have supposed that women under the age of 29 use IUD's primarily in order to space their babies rather than to prevent them altogether, and so every five years one-half of these women will remove their IUD's. This consideration alone would bring the initial 70% down to 35% over five years. We have further assumed that women over 29 do not remove IUD's, after the initial loss of 30%. The only reduction in the number used by these women occurs through mortality and widowhood, factors which also act on women below age 30. Mortality can be estimated with the appropriate female life table, and widowhood with the appropriate male life table.

Suppose that we are given the number of IUD's to be inserted each year; our task is then to estimate the number in place in each age group in a given future year. First the number of insertions is reduced, to account for the 30% initial loss, for mortality, and for widowhood, and then the remaining insertions are allocated to the different age groups. Since the Q_i figures must represent contraceptive users in age groups one year younger than the conventional ith age groups, it is convenient to allocate the contraceptive acceptances to these younger age groups also. On the basis of the Korean experience in 1964, the distribution shown in Table 1 was used in the computations for insertions made from 1962 to 1965.

In some of the calculations for years after 1965, we have employed a different IUD insertion distribution which is more heavily weighted in the younger age groups; this distribution is more effective in lowering fertility, as shown in Table 2.

Distribution C was used for vasectomies throughout, and traditional contraceptives were always assumed to be distributed by age in the same manner as the current IUD insertions.

To estimate $Q_{i,t}$, the number of effective contraceptives in use in mid-year of year $t-1$ (mortality of contraceptive users between years $t-1$ and t is neglected), it is assumed that acceptances occur at a constant rate throughout each year of the program, and that the contraceptives are distributed evenly to all ages within each age group. To the extent that these assumptions do not hold, small errors will be introduced into the calculations. It follows that, of the IUD's inserted in an age group last year, 80% will remain in that age group this year, and 20% will pass on to the next age group. Of those inserted two years ago, 60% will remain, and 40% will pass on, and so forth. If the IUD's of this year are inserted evenly throughout the year, they will be in place for an average of only six months, so that only 50% of them can be counted as in place. Of these, one-fifth will spend on the average one-half of their time this year in the next age group. So of the effective IUD's inserted this year, 45% can be counted as in place in the same age group this year and 5% as having passed on to the next age group. The total effective IUD's in use in year $t-1$, by

TABLE 1

DISTRIBUTION, BY AGE, OF CONTRACEPTIVE ACCEPTANCES[a]

(Per Cent)

Age Group	IUD Insertions (Distribution A)	Vasectomies (Distribution C)[b]
2: 19–23	2	0
3: 24–28	17	5
4: 29–33	37	25
5: 34–38	32	35
6: 39–43	12	35
	Mean age: 33.3	Mean age: 36.5

[a] From Youn Keun Cha's paper on the Korean program (chap. 2 in this volume). The actual reported distributions for 1964 were (per cent):

Age Group	IUD's	Vasectomies
20–24	2.23	0.14
25–29	20.31	5.06
30–34	38.00	23.23
35–39	30.00	35.26
40–44	8.40	25.15
45–49	0.95	8.53
50–		2.63

The vasectomies reported in these figures were distributed according to the age of the male.

[b] The vasectomies should be assigned to age groups according to the age of the wife, not the husband.

TABLE 2

Age Group	IUD Insertions (Distribution B) (per cent)
2: 19–23	15
3: 24–28	33
4: 29–33	33
5: 34–38	15
6: 39–43	4
	Mean age: 29.5

women who will be in the ith age group in year t, is therefore given by:

$$Q_{i, t} = 0.45 q_{i, t-1} + 0.05 q_{i-1, t-1}$$
$$+ 0.80 q_{i, t-2} + 0.20 q_{i-1, t-2}$$
$$+ 0.60 q_{i, t-3} + 0.40 q_{i-1, t-3} \qquad (2)$$
$$+ 0.40 q_{i, t-4} + 0.60 q_{i-1, t-4}$$
$$+ 0.20 q_{i, t-5} + 0.80 q_{i-1, t-5} ,$$

where $q_{i,t-1}$ is the number of effective surviving contraceptives inserted in the age group one year younger than the conventional ith age group in year $t - 1$. This procedure gives us $Q_{i,t}$, the number of

TABLE 3

PROGRESS AND GOALS OF THE KOREAN
FAMILY PLANNING PROGRAM

Year	IUD Insertions	Vasectomies	Traditional Methods
1962............	....	3,413	54,000
1963............	1,600	19,559	130,000
1964............	111,883	26,095	250,000
1965............	200,000	25,000	300,000
1966............	300,000	25,000	300,000
1967-70 (each year)	200,000	25,000	300,000

women practicing effective contraception in year $t - 1$. This can be used in equation (1), along with the other three quantities, to estimate age specific fertility in year t.

AN ILLUSTRATION: THE KOREAN FAMILY PLANNING PROGRAM

The techniques of this section can be illustrated with examples from Korea.[5] Each quantity in equation (1) will be considered.

The Korean birth control program was begun in 1962 and is to reach its full momentum in 1965. Its goal is to lower the population growth rate from 2.9% to 2.0% by 1971. According to various publications,[6] it appears that the Korean family planning program can be summarized as shown in Table 3.

[5]The Korean demographic data are taken from *The 1960 Population and Housing Census of Korea*, Vol. 1, p. 11-1 (Seoul, 1963); and *The New Population Projections for Korea, 1960–2000* (Seoul, 1964, both published by the Economic Planning Board of Korea).

[6]Youn Keun Cha, chap. 2 in this volume, and *Family Planning*, Vol. 1, published by the Ministry of Public Health and Social Welfare, Korea, 1963 (in Korean only).

Korean age-specific fertility rates for 1960, the $f_{i,0}$ values, were estimated from the census data of that year,[7] with a correction for memory error. (Total fertility was 5.99, and the crude birth rate 42.0 per thousand. There were about 1,065,000 births.) The population of Korea after 1960 was projected, to obtain the $F_{i,t}$ values, using the Model Life Tables of Coale and Demeny,[8] Region East, with life expectancy rising from about 54 years in 1960 to about 60 years in 1971, owing to probable improvements in public health and sanitation. For the g_i values, the potential fertility of contraceptive users, we used figures 20% higher than the 1960 marital fertility rates. An adjustment of this magnitude seemed to be indicated by data gathered in the Taichung study, Taiwan, from 1962 to 1964.[9] Finally, the $Q_{i,t}$ values were computed as shown in the discussion above explaining that quantity (Table 4).

TABLE 4

$Q_{i,t}$ VALUES

Age Group	Marital Fertility, 1960	g_i[a]
15–19	.529	....
20–24	.437	.524
25–29	.354	.425
30–34	.280	.336
35–39	.223	.268
40–44	.098	.118
45–49	.019	.023

[a] Assumed potential fertility of contraceptive users.

RESULTS

The numerical estimates which are presented now and in the following sections are only approximations, since the assumptions lying behind them are by no means exact. They do, however, show the orders of magnitude involved.

It is estimated that by 1966 the family planning program will have reduced age-specific fertility rates sufficiently to lower total fertility from 5.99 to 5.33, and by 1971 to 4.56, if the present insertion distribution of IUD's is maintained (Table 5). However, this reduction in fertility, substantial though it would be, would reduce the popula-

[7] See the appendix to this chapter for a description of the method used.

[8] Ansley J. Coale and Paul Demeny, *Regional Model Life Tables and Stable Populations* (Princeton: Princeton University Press, 1966).

[9] John A. Ross paper, chap. 58 in this volume. See Table 3.

tion growth rate to only 22.8 per thousand in 1971, not 20 per thousand as desired.

It is unlikely that the insertion distribution of IUD's will remain constant. The experience of family planning programs so far has been that the first participants in a program are generally older women, most of whom have already achieved the family size they desire.[10] As

TABLE 5

FUTURE KOREAN FERTILITY, WITH THE CURRENT BIRTH CONTROL
PROGRAM AND THE IUD INSERTION DISTRIBUTION OF
1964 (A) MAINTAINED TO 1970

	1960	1966		1971	
	f_i	f_i	Per Cent Change from 1960	f_i	Per Cent Change from 1960
Age group:					
15–19........................	.037	.037	0	.037	0
20–24	.283	.280	− 1.1	.279	− 1.4
25–29........................	.330	.308	− 6.7	.293	−11.2
30–34........................	.257	.212	−17.5	.167	−35.0
35–39........................	.196	.148	−24.5	.086	−56.1
40–44........................	.080	.067	−16.3	.039	−51.3
45–49........................	.014	.014	0	.011	−21.4
Total fertility........	5.99	5.33	−11.0	4.56	−23.9
Births....................	1,065,000	1,092,000	+ 2.5	1,084,000	+ 1.8
Potential, if no program...	....	(1,210,000)	....	(1,368,000)	....
Per cent reduction from potential.................	....	....	− 9.8	....	−20.8
Crude birth rate..........	42.0	36.7	....	32.3	....
Growth rate (per thousand).	29.0	25.5	....	22.8	....
Contraceptive acceptances/ births prevented in target year[a].....................	....	5.8	....	6.7	....

[a] Total IUD insertions and vasectomies from 1962 through the year preceding the target year plus traditional contraceptives in the year preceding the target year, divided by births prevented in 1966 and 1971, respectively.

the population becomes accustomed to the idea of family planning, younger women may begin to participate, and the use of contraceptives for the spacing of children may become more prevalent.

If the younger insertion distribution, B, given above, were achieved during the years 1966–70, total fertility in 1971 would be further reduced to 4.36 (Table 6). This time the growth rate would fall to 21.1 per thousand. This is very close to the desired growth rate of 20.0 per thousand; there is enough uncertainty in all the assumptions we have

[10]Bernard Berelson, "National Family Planning Programs: A Guide," *Studies in Family Planning*, No. 5 (supplement) (New York, The Population Council), December, 1964.

made to allow us to say that the growth rate may fall to 2.0%, provided younger women accept the contraceptives.

A family planning program is made much more effective by securing younger participants. This is so because the potential fertility of contraceptive users falls with age (provided it follows the same pattern as marital fertility). The estimated "potential" fertility of users falls from a level assumed to be .524 in age group 20–24 to .118 in age

TABLE 6

FUTURE KOREAN FERTILITY, WITH A MORE FAVORABLE IUD
INSERTION DISTRIBUTION (B) FROM 1966 TO 1970

	1960	1966	1971	
	f_i		f_i	Per Cent Change
Age group:				
15–19	.037		.037	0
20–24	.283		.253	−10.6
25–29	.330	Same as	.245	−25.8
30–34	.257	Table 5	.156	−39.3
35–39	.196		.114	−41.8
40–44	.080		.045	−32.5
45–49	.014		.012	−14.3
Total fertility	5.99		4.36	−27.2
Births	1,065,000		1,022,000	....
Per cent change from 1960	....		....	− 4.1
Potential, if no program	....		(1,368,000)	....
Per cent change from potential	....		....	−25.3
Crude birth rate	42.0		30.6	....
Growth rate (per thousand)	29.0		21.1	....
Contraceptive acceptances/births prevented in target year	....		5.5	....

group 40–44 (see g_i values above). This fall is typical of patterns summarized by Henry in an article on populations not practicing birth control.[11] So a given number of contraceptives in use in a particular year in the age group 20–24 prevents in the next year more than four times the number of births that are prevented by the same number of contraceptives in age group 40–44. This relation can also be seen if the average interval between births is considered; this interval is given by the inverse of the fertility rate. Contraceptive users in Korea aged 20–24 would have had a child every two years, while contraceptive users aged 40–44 would have given birth only every eight years. So

[11]Louis Henry, "Some Data on Natural Fertility," *Eugenics Quarterly*, Vol. 8 (2), (June, 1961).

it requires eight IUD's in place to prevent one birth to the older women the following year, but only two IUD's in place to prevent one birth to the younger women that year. Another advantage to be gained by achieving a younger insertion pattern is that, if the IUD's remain in place, they will affect women in the reproductive ages for a longer period of time. We have heavily discounted IUD insertions among young women by assuming that, every five years, half of the women under 29 remove their IUD. Nevertheless, the figures show that this discounting is more than offset by the other effects in our illustration.

The change to a younger acceptance pattern may occur autonomously, but a comparison of Tables 5 and 6 shows that it is definitely worth the trouble to encourage such a change if it does not appear to be happening on its own. In Korea, the success of the entire program may depend upon the achieving of a younger insertion pattern. Of course an intensive publicity campaign to persuade younger women to accept IUD's might be expensive, but the figures here suggest that considerable expense would be justified.

The bottom row of Tables 5 and 6 gives the ratio of contraceptives accepted throughout the program to births prevented in the target year. The discussion of this ratio is postponed until a later section of this paper.

ESTIMATION OF TOTAL BIRTHS PREVENTED PER IUD ACCEPTANCE

In addition to analyzing the effect of contraceptive acceptances on the fertility of a certain year, we can also examine the effect that IUD's will have in preventing births throughout their entire duration in place. The calculations are simple, provided the necessary assumptions concerning survivorship, potential fertility, and insertion pattern can be made.

IUD acceptances by women of different age groups are considered separately. Using the survivorship assumptions (the combined effects of the proportion of IUD's removed, female mortality, and widowhood), one can estimate the average number of years to be spent in each age group by a woman wearing an IUD which was inserted while she was in the *i*th age group. For example, of the women accepting IUD's in the age group 29–33, we may assume that only 70% will retain them for any length of time, and of these, 99% will wear the IUD for an average of 2.5 years in age group 29–33 (1% die or are widowed), 96% will wear it for five years in age group 34–38, 90%

for five years in age group 39–43, and so on.[12] The years spent in each age group are multiplied by g_1, the potential fertility of contraceptive users in that age group: these products, when totaled, give the number of births ever to be prevented by IUD acceptances of women in the ith age group. The operation is repeated for acceptances by women of each age group; the results are then weighted according to the insertion distribution and averaged. Table 7 shows the results of such calculations, using the IUD-removal assumptions described in the first section of this paper and the "East" Model Life Table of Coale and Demeny, level 17, for female mortality and widowhood.

TABLE 7

TOTAL BIRTHS EVER TO BE PREVENTED PER IUD ACCEPTED

Age Group of IUD Acceptor (1)	Total Births Prevented per IUD Accepted (2)	Insertion Pattern A (3)	Total Births Prevented per IUD Distributed According to Pattern A $\Sigma(2)\times(3)$ (4)	Insertion Pattern B (5)	Total Births Prevented per IUD Distributed According to Pattern B $\Sigma(2)\times(5)$ (6)
19–23	2.68	.02	. . . .	.15	. . . .
24–28	2.21	.17	. . . .	.33	. . . .
29–33	1.91	.37	. . . .	.33	. . . .
34–38	0.92	.32	. . . .	.15	. . . .
39–43	0.28	.12	. . . .	.04	. . . .
			1.5		1.9

Again it is found that the contraceptives are more effective if younger women accept them. Not only does a younger insertion pattern imply contraceptive users of greater potential fertility, but the users stay in the reproductive ages for a longer time. Of course a change in survivorship of IUD's would affect the average births prevented per acceptance; for example, we calculated that if all of the IUD users aged 19–28, and in addition, half the users in the next higher age group (29–33), were assumed to remove their IUD every five years, then the total births prevented per IUD insertion according to pattern A would be only 1.1, and according to pattern B would be only 1.3.

A "STEADY STATE"

One can imagine a "steady state" in which the fertility rates remain constant over time, and the births prevented each year are a constant multiple of the IUD insertions of that year.

Consider first what would happen if a constant number of IUD's

[12]These figures are derived by multiplying the average survivorship of females in the childbearing ages for 2.5 years, 7.5 years, 12.5 years, etc., times the respective average male survivorship (to account for widowhood).

were inserted each year, always with the same insertion pattern by age. After about thirty years, when the youngest women who had accepted IUD's in the first year of the program had passed out of the childbearing ages, a constant number of births would be prevented each year. This can be seen by analogy to a "life-table population"; it is known that, if mortality risks do not change and there is a constant annual number of births, eventually the age distribution of a population will be given by the L_x column of its life table. The L_x column can then be thought of as representing either a single cohort, over time, or an entire population at a point of time. Similarly the number of years spent by women wearing IUD's in each age group, which was calculated above, can refer either to the IUD acceptors of a single year, as they grow older, or to all the IUD users in a given year, if there has been a past history of a constant annual number of IUD acceptances. Hence the total births prevented per IUD accepted can refer either to the results of the IUD acceptances of a single year as the acceptors grow older, or to the births prevented in a single year expressed as a ratio of the IUD acceptances of that year. For example, if insertion pattern B were achieved and if our survivorship assumptions held, a constant annual number of insertions would result, after about thirty years, in 1.9 times as many births being prevented each year. This would not produce a "steady state" as defined above, however, unless a zero rate of natural increase happened to be achieved. Otherwise, with a growing population and a constant annual number of births prevented, the birth rate would rise (or fall if the growth rate were negative).

To achieve a steady state in which the birth rate remains constant, the number of births prevented each year must grow at the same rate the population is growing; and so the IUD's inserted each year must also grow at this rate. This will again result in the births prevented each year being a constant multiple of the IUD insertions of that year. However, with a positive growth rate, the ratio of births prevented to IUD insertions of a given year will be smaller than if a constant number of insertions were made each year, since fewer insertions will have been made in past years than in this year. To find this new ratio, one must estimate the average number of years that IUD's have been in place when they prevent births: this will not be more than about six or eight years. So the births prevented in a given year can be thought of as resulting from the IUD insertions of, say, six years before. If the insertions are growing at an annual rate of 2%, the number of insertions of six years ago will be .89 of the number for this year. Therefore in a steady state, with our insertion distribution B, and population and insertions both growing at 2% a year, the births prevented each year would be .89 × 1.9, or 1.7 times the number of

IUD insertions made that year. A constant *proportion* of births would be prevented, and the birth rate would be constant, although the absolute number of births per year would grow.

THE ECONOMIC VALUE OF AN IUD ACCEPTANCE

One can estimate the economic value of an IUD acceptance. Several studies have examined the benefits to be gained by preventing births in an underdeveloped country. Demeny suggests that, in a country with a per capita income of $100, the prevention of each birth is worth at least $125 and perhaps several times this sum.[13] In other words, a country could afford to spend anything less than this amount in order to prevent a birth, and still obtain higher per capita incomes than if birth control were never attempted. Now if each IUD insertion will eventually prevent an average of 1.9 births, then the value of an IUD insertion would be at least $125 and perhaps more (the exact value would depend upon the rate of discount used to find the present value of future births prevented). If a steady state were reached with a growth rate of both population and insertions of 2% a year, it would be possible to pay up to $1.7 \times 125, or $213, for each insertion, under the above assumptions. The experience of national family planning programs so far has been that the cost of securing an IUD acceptance is much smaller than this—in Taiwan, for example, it is estimated that each IUD insertion costs $3.20.[14] So the benefits to be gained by instituting this type of birth control are very large indeed.

ESTIMATION OF THE SIZE OF BIRTH CONTROL PROGRAM REQUIRED TO ACHIEVE A SPECIFIED GOAL

We now reverse the estimation process of the first section of this paper. Instead of taking the number of contraceptives as the given data, and then estimating their effect, we start at the other end by stating a particular goal for a certain year, and then estimating how large a program will be necessary to achieve this goal. We shall suppose that the program will use only IUD's, not vasectomies or traditional contraceptives.

The number of births prevented by family planning in year t in age group i is:

$$BP_{i,t} = Q_{i,t} \cdot g_i. \tag{3}$$

[13]Paul Demeny, "Investment Allocation and Population Growth," *Demography*, Vol. 2 (1965).

[14]John A. Ross, chap. 58 in this volume.

As before, $Q_{i,t}$ is the number of women in the *i*th age group who were practicing completely effective contraception in year $t - 1$, and g_i is the potential fertility rate of these women. The total number of births prevented in year *t* is therefore:

$$BP_t = \Sigma_i Q_{i,\,t} \cdot g_i \,. \tag{4}$$

Equation (4) can be used to determine the annual number of IUD insertions required. To employ this equation, the goal of the program must be restated in terms of births to be prevented. In some cases this is simple; in other cases it is more complex. One fact which helps in translating the program goal into births to be prevented is that the number of women in the childbearing ages, 15–49, is not affected by the family planning program until fifteen years after the program is begun. Even up to twenty years later the difference is hardly significant. Suppose then that the goal of the program is to reduce general fertility (the number of births in a year divided by the number of women of childbearing age) by one-half in the fifteenth year after the program is begun. We must calculate the number of births in year 15 (*a*) with the program and (*b*) without it, as follows.

The present female population aged 0–34 is projected to year 15 by use of appropriate life tables, and the present age-specific fertility rates are applied to this population to give the number of births which would occur in year 15 in the absence of family planning. Since the denominator for general fertility (total women of childbearing age) is the same regardless of whether the program is instituted, the number of births *desired* in year 15 is found by multiplying the number of women by one-half the original general fertility. There are now two figures for births in year 15, and the difference between them is the number of births to be prevented.

Our aim now is to discover the number of IUD insertions required each year, if a certain number of births are to be prevented in year *t*. In equation (4) we are given both BP_t (derived from the program goal) and g_i. So what is needed is a way of expressing $Q_{i,t}$ (the number of IUD's in place in year $t - 1$) in terms of the number of IUD's to be inserted each year (represented by I). To do this we merely rearrange equation (2).

Let us begin with a program which is to last only five years. It will be recalled that the q_i's in equation (2) represented not the number of IUD's inserted but rather the number of insertions which *survived* in place until the target year. Since we are now interested in the total number of insertions, we must break q_i into its component parts:

$$q_i = I \cdot S_i \cdot D_i \,, \tag{5}$$

where I is the total number of IUD's inserted in the year, S_i is the proportion of IUD insertions which survive in place to year t, and D_i is the IUD insertion distribution, or the proportion of insertions allocated to the ith age group (when attached to S and D, as well as to q, the subscript i refers to age groups one year younger than the conventional ith age groups). For a five-year program, with a constant number, I, of IUD insertions each year, equation (2) can be rewritten as follows:

$$Q_{i,t} = [I \cdot S^{1-5}][(D_i)(.45 + .80 + .60 + .40 + .20)$$
$$+ (D_{i-1})(.05 + .20 + .40 + .60 + .80)]. \tag{6}$$

For a five-year program, survivorship of IUD's, S^{1-5} (the superscript refers to the number of years between insertion and year t) is taken to be independent of the age group; it is simply the proportion of IUD's which are accepted, in our calculations .70, times a female mortality survivorship factor, in our case .99, times a male survivorship factor (to account for widowhood), also .99, giving an S^{1-5} of .69.

For a ten-year program, the expression is longer:

$$Q_{i,t} = I \cdot S^{1-5} \cdot D_i \ (\ .45 + .80 + .60 + .40 + .20)$$
$$+ I \cdot S^{1-5} D_{i-1} \ (\ .05 + .20 + .40 + .60 + .80)$$
$$+ I \cdot S_{i-1}^{6-10} D_{i-1} (1.00 + .80 + .60 + .40 + .20) \tag{7}$$
$$+ I \cdot S_{i-1}^{6-10} D_{i-2} (\qquad .20 + .40 + .60 + .80).$$

Survivorship, S, for over five years before t is age specific; we are using the same survivorship assumption that was made in the first section, with one-half of the women under 29 who were using an IUD at a given date discontinuing its use within the next five years. Similar expressions can be derived for programs lasting fifteen years or longer.

It is not necessary to confine ourselves to the assumption that a constant number of IUD's is inserted each year. Any assumption can be made, provided the insertions each year are so related that, if the figure for one year is found, all the others can be found. For example, one might state that the insertions would increase by 10% each year. In this case, I would denote the number of insertions in the first year. For a five-year program the formula would be:

$$Q_{i,t} = \{I \cdot S^{1-5}\}$$
$$\times \{[D_i][.45(1.1)^4 + .80(1.1)^3 + .60(1.1)^2 + .40(1.1) + .20] \tag{8}$$
$$+ [D_{i-1}][.05(1.1)^4 + .20(1.1)^3 + .40(1.1)^2 + .60(1.1) + .80]\}.$$

By use of an equation such as (6), (7), or (8), $Q_{i,t}$ can be expressed in terms of I. Now equation (4) can be solved for I, the number of IUD's to be inserted a year.

ILLUSTRATIONS

In order to illustrate the method, we have supposed the Korean birth control program to begin in 1966, and to consist only of IUD insertions. In each example we postulate a goal of reducing by half the births which would have occurred in the target year in the absence of family planning. Table 8 summarizes the results.

The table shows programs lasting five, ten, and fifteen years. In all programs it is assumed that the insertion distribution of IUD's for the first five years is pattern A, the actual distribution of Korean insertions in 1964. After five years, some of the programs (nos. 3, 4, and 6) switch to a younger insertion distribution, pattern B. Just as it was found in the first section of this paper that a younger insertion pattern would lower fertility further, given the number of IUD's, now we find that, given the reduction in fertility to be achieved, fewer contraceptive users are required if younger women enter the program. For a ten-year program, almost a million fewer insertions are needed with the younger acceptors, a difference of 15%, and for a fifteen-year program the difference is almost two million or 19%.

Table 8 shows that the task of achieving a certain goal in terms of a fractional reduction in the number of births becomes more difficult with the passing years. A program to cut fertility in half by 1976 (no. 2) actually requires somewhat *fewer* annual insertions than does a similar program with a fifteen-year horizon (no. 5). This is so because, as mentioned earlier, the number of women of childbearing age will increase for many years into the future, regardless of whether birth control is instituted. It follows that the absolute number of births which would occur, under constant fertility and in the absence of family planning, increase. Therefore the births to be prevented by family planning increase with time (col. 4) and the IUD's required to be in place increase (col. 9).

Column 10 gives the ratio of total insertions during the program to births prevented in the target year. This is not merely the inverse of the ratio of total births prevented to each IUD acceptance, as noted above. Here we examine only the births prevented in a single, given year. This ratio is of interest because it may help predict the fertility rates of a given future year (for this reason, the following paragraph should be considered together with the first section—we have postponed our discussion until now so that Table 8 could be used as an

TABLE 8

FAMILY PLANNING PROGRAMS IN KOREA, USING IUD'S ONLY, REQUIRED TO REDUCE BY HALF THE NUMBER WHICH WOULD HAVE BEEN BORN WITH CONSTANT FERTILITY IN THE TARGET YEAR

Program (1)	Duration (Years) (2)	Target Year (3)	Births To Be Prevented in the Target Year (4)	IUD Insertion Distribution (5)	Time Sequence of Insertions (6)	Insertions Required Each Year (I) (7)	Total Insertions (8)	IUD's in Place, Target Year − 1 (9)	Ratio of IUD's Inserted to Births Prevented in Target Year (10)
1........	5	1971	684,000	A mean age: 33.3	Constant number of insertions each year	845,000	4,225,000	2,623,000	6.2
2........	10	1976	794,000	A	Constant	619,000	6,190,000	3,742,000	7.8
3........	10	1976	794,000	A (1966–70) B mean age: 29.5 (1971–75)	Constant	527,000	5,270,000	3,190,000	6.6
4........	10	1976	794,000	A (1966–70) B (1971–75)	Insertions increase by 10% each year	306,000 (1966) to 723,000 (1975)	4,885,000	2,932,000	6.2
5........	15	1981	940,000	A	Constant	646,000	9,690,000	5,230,000	10.3
6........	15	1981	940,000	A (1966–70) B (1971–80)	Constant	523,000	7,845,000	4,098,000	8.3

illustration). For comparison, the ratios found in Tables 5 and 6 were 5.8, 6.7, and 5.5. These ratios would probably be of about the same magnitude in any low-income country, since fertility in the absence of family planning is not sufficiently variable to change them seriously.

Planners of birth control programs often use rough rules of thumb for the ratio of total insertions to births prevented in a year; it is frequently heard that five IUD's will prevent one birth a year. It may well be true, in a typical program, that for every five IUD's inserted this year one or even more births will be prevented next year. For example, in our illustrations, if the IUD's were inserted according to pattern A, 4.7 insertions in a given year would prevent one birth the following year; if the younger pattern B were achieved, 3.9 insertions one year would prevent one birth the next year. As the program continues for several years, however, the ratio of total contraceptive acceptances throughout the entire period to births prevented in the next year will rise. This is so because progressively more of the early IUD's come out, and the women accepting IUD's near the beginning of the program grow older, entering less fertile age groups.[15] Note, however, that the proportionate impact of the early insertions depends on the subsequent time curve of acceptances. Of course the older the insertion distribution is, the higher will be the ratio, since the older women have lower potential fertility and tend to pass out of the childbearing ages sooner.

CONCLUSIONS

We have described one approach for estimating the effect which a birth control program has on fertility. An adaptation of the same method can provide an estimate of what size program is required to accomplish a given reduction in fertility. Korean data are used to explore how well the method works when applied to a major family planning program. The results, though on the optimistic side, are not unreasonable, and happen to square relatively well with current rules of thumb. We would recommend that, before the institution of a birth control program, similar calculations be made, incorporating as much specific data for the country concerned as possible. As an aid we list here our key assumptions (which others may wish to revise or vary in their own calculations):

1. Survivorship of contraceptives in use:
    a) 30% of IUD's come out immediately upon insertion.

[15]The fact that this ratio rises without limit over time should not be taken to mean that a program must become less efficient the longer it lasts. In fact, as shown above, it is possible to reach a steady state in which "efficiency" is constant: the annual births prevented are a constant multiple of the IUD insertions of that year.

  b) One-half of the IUD users under age 30 take out their IUD every five years.

  c) 60% of the acceptors of traditional contraceptives use them effectively.

  d) Female mortality and widowhood are estimated from the life tables chosen.

2. Age-specific fertility would remain at a constant level in the future if a birth control program were not instituted.

3. Without the program, acceptors' fertility would run 20% above age-specific marital fertility rates in the population at large (if over-all fertility were expected to fall independently of the program, contrary to assumption 2, then this "potential fertility" of contraceptive users should also be adjusted downward over time).

4. Contraceptives are accepted at a constant rate throughout each year, and are spread evenly within each age group.

5. Acceptances of IUD's, vasectomies, and traditional contraceptives follow age-distribution patterns A, B, or C.

6. Future Korean mortality is accurately predicted from the life tables of Coale and Demeny, Region East, with life expectancy rising from 54 years in 1960 to 60 years in 1971.

If it is felt that the available data do not support such involved calculations, or if a quick, rough estimate of the fertility reduction in a future year is desired, we suggest (with the qualifications below) the following ratios of total IUD's ever inserted to births prevented in that year: for a program that has run during the previous year only, 5; for a five-year program, 6; for a ten-year program, 7; for a fifteen-year program, 9. These figures assume a relatively level time curve of acceptances, as in the Korean program. To estimate the total effect of an IUD program, we suggest that each IUD inserted will prevent an average of 1.5–2 births during its duration in use. It should be remembered, however, that the lower the age of the contraceptive acceptors the greater will be the effect of the program.

APPENDIX

AGE-SPECIFIC FERTILITY IN KOREA, 1960

To employ the methods outlined in this article, the age-specific fertility and marital fertility of the base year must be known. The Koreans census of 1960 did not report current fertility, only the number of children ever born to women, tabulated by single ages of mothers. From this information we have estimated the fertility rates of 1960.

If fertility has not changed significantly in the past few decades, then age-specific fertility rates can often be derived by successive subtraction of the figures for children ever born. In performing this operation, the concepts of census age (or age last birthday) and exact age (exact time elapsed since birth) must be kept clearly in mind. If the age-specific fertility rates for *census* age groups of 15–19 and 20–24 are added and multiplied by 5, they give only an estimate of the mean of the children ever born to women of *exact* age 25. Therefore the census reports of children ever born to women of different census ages must be adjusted to obtain estimates of children ever born to women of different exact ages. To find children ever born to women of exact age x, we took the average of children ever born to women of census[16] ages $x — 1$ and x (since the average exact age of women in their $x — 1$ year is $x — 0.5$, and of women in their xth year is $x + 0.5$). Now our estimate for age-specific fertility of women aged 20–24 (census age) is found by subtracting the mean of children ever born to women of exact age 20 from children ever born to women of exact age 25, and dividing by 5.

Certain conditions must be met before this procedure can be used. (1) Fertility must have been reasonably constant in the recent past; in fact what fluctuations there have been in Korea have probably not been strong enough to cause large errors in our estimates. (2) Women who have died must not have had a different childbearing experience from those who have lived: we have simply assumed this to be true. (3) The census reports of children ever born must be accurate: this does not hold true, and adjustments are required to obtain acceptable estimates.

If the mean of children ever born were accurately reported, then the figure should remain constant after about age 45, when childbearing ceases. In fact, in the 1960 census, the figure *declines* after age 45, owing probably to "recall lapse." Accordingly we had to make some estimate, however crude, of the number of children ever born who were forgotten at each age.

It was assumed that childbearing ends at about age 45. Then, by examining the decline in the figures for children ever born between exact ages 45.5, 47.5, and 51.3, we were able to estimate the average number of *additional* children forgotten every year at the end of childbearing. Our conclusion was that, by census age 48, every 1,000 women were forgetting an additional 47.5 children each year.

It was assumed, following Brass,[17] that there was no recall lapse at age 22. We then postulated, admittedly arbitrarily, that recall lapse

[16]The 1960 Korean census was based on several Eastern methods of reporting ages, not the Western system used here. Estimates for Western ages were made from the census, using the method recommended by the Economic Planning Board in *The New Population Projects for Korea* (see n. 5 above).

[17]For a description of Professor William Brass's technique of estimating fertility see *The Demography of Tropical Africa*, chap. 3, to be published by the Office of Population Research, Princeton University.

increased linearly by age. Thus, if Y denotes the additional children forgotten by every 1,000 women at an age, and X denotes the census age, $Y = aX + c$. Given that when $X = 48$, $Y = 47.5$, and that when $X = 22$, $Y = 0$, then $Y = 1.8X - 40$. Using this equation, we estimated the additional children forgotten at each age and, cumulatively, the total children forgotten at each age.

TABLE 9

AGE-SPECIFIC FERTILITY AND MARITAL FERTILITY FOR KOREA, 1960

AGE GROUP	FERTILITY	PROPORTION MARRIED	MARITAL FERTILITY[a]	TAIWANESE FERTILITY	
				1958	1961
15–19..........	.037	.070	.529	.043	.045
20–24..........	.283	.648	.437	.248	.248
25–29..........	.330	.931	.354	.336	.341
30–34..........	.257	.917	.280	.281	.246
35–39..........	.196	.882	.223	.199	.156
40–44..........	.080	.821	.098	.090	.071
45–49..........	.014	.760	.019	.014	.010
Total fertility..	5.99	....	....	6.06	5.59

[a] Marital fertility does not always exactly equal over-all age-specific fertility divided by proportion married, because of rounding.

These figures were then added to the census reports of children ever born, and the corrected estimates were used in the manner described above, to derive age-specific fertility rates for 1960. These, together with proportions married from the census, gave the marital fertility rates, The results are set out in Table 9; for comparison the Taiwanese age-specific fertility schedules for 1958 and 1961 are given. While some aspects of our procedure may seem quite arbitrary, it is reassuring that our results are so close to the fertility pattern of Taiwan, a country of roughly similar demographic and social conditions.

58

COST OF FAMILY PLANNING PROGRAMS

JOHN A. ROSS
Demographic Division
The Population Council

In its rush to get something done quickly, the family planning field has paid very little attention to cost records. Consequently, program evaluation is seriously impeded. But by reviewing the fragments of information now available, we can take a first step toward correcting this deficiency. This survey of cost is necessarily quite preliminary: perhaps it will suggest categories to which more systematic effort can be subsequently applied.

The method behind this survey was to study each conference paper distributed in advance, excerpting all reference to cost topics. To this material was added the Keeny *Newsletter*, the Taiwan monthly reports, the *Studies in Family Planning* series, unpublished documents in the Population Council files, and miscellaneous other items. This purely empirical approach to cost information suggested the subheadings which follow.

MAGNITUDE OF BUDGETS BY PER CAPITA EXPENDITURES

Sufficient experience has now accumulated to fix the range of expenditures for large-scale family planning programs. This range stands at a low level: 3–6 cents (U.S.) per capita per year in past efforts (see Table 1). A program often starts below this, building up to the indicated range over a few years (Korea). Hong Kong records actual expenditures of 4.2 cents in 1964 but states that volunteers made a substantial contribution not reflected in its figures. The Taiwan program is spending at the rate of 2.5 cents, but its clients carry about one-

I wish to thank W. Parker Mauldin for many helpful suggestions in preparing this paper.

fourth of the total cost. In Taichung City, more was spent, but that was a high-impact experimental program.

Anticipated future expenditures agree with the range of 3–6 cents except for India and Pakistan. Their high figures of 8.3 and 12 were not chosen lightly; yet their past spending has fallen well below the amounts budgeted. It may be argued that India and Pakistan will find it much more difficult to reduce fertility than the other countries listed. If this is so, their spending may need to exceed 5–6 cents.

TABLE 1

PER CAPITA EXPENDITURE PER YEAR BY FAMILY PLANNING
PROGRAMS, BY YEAR AND PLACE

(In U.S. Cents)

PLACE	YEAR					
	1961	1962	1963	1964	1965	Planned
Korea		1.2	2.2	4.8	?	5.0
Hong Kong[a]	1.6	1.7	2.8[b]	4.2	?	
Taichung			7.0[c]			
Taiwan				?	2.5[d] (1965–69)	
Turkey				(1.7)[e]	2.2	4.0, rising in 3 years to 5.5
Tunisia				4.1[f]	4.1[f]	4.1[f] (1966–67)
Pakistan			0.6[g]		?	12.0
India .02,[h] .26[h]	.8	1.2		2.6[i]		8.3

[a] Based on Table 4 of Daphne Chun's paper (chap. 5 in this volume), using 3,800,000 as the Hong Kong population, and an exchange rate of HK$5.7 = US$1.

[b] The figure is 3.3 for the fiscal year ending March 31, 1964.

[c] The response to this high spending was excellent, producing a low cost per loop inserted and per case.

[d] Central funds only—excludes client charges.

[e] Appropriated in late 1963, but largely unspent owing to delayed repeal of an old law prohibiting family planning.

[f] Approximately $370,000 was spent over the two-year period, 1964–65. A similar amount was budgeted for 1966–67.

[g] 1.3 cents per capita had been budgeted for the five-year plan, but only 0.6 cents per capita was used. Figures drawn from Enver Adil's paper (chap. 10 in this volume); they include the Rs. 1.2 million outside grants he mentions.

[h] Spent during the 1951–55 and 1956–60 five-year plans, respectively. Considerably more had been budgeted.
[i] Budgeted.

Per capita figures are useful, but one must bear in mind what stands behind them. Table 1 refers to money actually spent (unless noted differently, or unless the years are future ones). The figures refer only to money channeled through the dominant action program in each place; and no attempt was made to include such items as fellowships, specialized research projects in selected locations under independent grants, and the like. No allowance was made for informal subsidization of space and so on from such allied agencies as maternal and child health centers or for volunteer help. Thus the table entries are if anything underestimates; nevertheless they are of the correct order of magnitude, and they show rather accurately the sums being spent by those agencies intervening seriously in fertility levels. (See the appendix to this chapter for a comment on per capita indicators.)

Cost per IUD Insertion

This cost has been variously estimated between $1.00 and $10. Careful cost records kept during the Taichung experiment of 1963 put the clinic cost at $1.30 to service one IUD acceptor. This is largely a salary expense, since IUD's, space, and much of the equipment were donated. If solicitation costs are added to this, the cost was $5.00 to $9.00 depending on which sector of the city is considered. In October, 1963, the intensive field work ended, and for some time the solicitation costs were zero. In April, 1964, field activity was resumed, but even so, the average IUD cost has fallen, perhaps to as low as $3.50. Monthly reports from the enlarged Taiwan program formed the basis for a figure of $3.20 per IUD insertion (including the $1.50 paid to the doctor, half by the program and half by the client), used in a recent Population Council mission report.

Daphne Chun's paper in this volume (chap. 5) indicates that with the introduction of the IUD, Hong Kong's cost per patient may drop drastically from $2.60 to as low as $0.86. This implies a very low IUD insertion cost, perhaps due largely to volunteered time of M.D.'s.

In Korea's 1964 experience, the cost per loop inserted was only $12.20 even if the 110,000 loops are given responsibility for the entire year's budget ($1,357,900) and with no allowance for the tooling-up that will pay off in future years.

It is estimated that if Korea's five-year program just started goes as planned, each IUD inserted will cost $4.67. The Korean national government is expected to pay 72%, provincial and local governments 21%, and other sources 7%.

How May Costs Be Predicted?

Certain rules of thumb have gained currency, as more nations have planned extensive programs. Three of these are especially noteworthy:

1. Of five IUD's inserted this year, two will come out before they have time to do much good. The others will stay in at least five years.
2. The marital fertility rate among *acceptors* would be about 333 in the absence of a program. Consequently:
3. Five IUD's inserted this year will prevent one birth next year and

another birth each year for at least four more years. Thus, each IUD inserted this year prevents one birth within five years, on the average.

The reasoning is that the three women retaining the IUD have a new fertility rate of zero, and thus the one birth among three women (marital fertility, 333) is prevented each year.

Each of these rules can be debated, but the point being made here is simply that they are being used. The first rule is not unreasonable; follow-up in the Taichung experiment, for example, shows a 60% (3 in 5) retention rate at two years after insertion (72% at one year). Rule 2 may appear more questionable. Age-specific fertility rates do not run as high as 333, even where all women marry. The main imponderable, however, is the fertility of *acceptors*, as opposed to all women.

Clearly, acceptors have unusually high rates, but until recently no data were available to measure the differential. Tables 2 and 3 show

TABLE 2

MARITAL FERTILITY RATES, BY WHETHER RESPONDENT WAS "IUD ACCEPTOR," "OTHER ACCEPTOR," OR "NON-ACCEPTOR," BY AGE, FOR TAICHUNG WOMEN MARRIED AT LEAST FIVE YEARS[a]

Age	Birth Rate in 3 Preceding Years (per annum)	Birth Rate in 5 Preceding Years (per annum)	Number of Women
All ages:			
IUD acceptors.........	345	405	154
Other acceptors.........	331	358	63
All acceptors..........	341	392	217
Non-acceptors.........	272	304	1,689
Total (all women).......	279	314	1,906
25–29:			
IUD acceptors.........	401	468	52
Other acceptors.........	400	473	15
All acceptors..........	401	469	67
Non-acceptors.........	335	399	488
Total (all women).......	343	407	555
30–34:			
IUD acceptors.........	329	391	66
Other acceptors.........	349	377	27
All acceptors..........	335	387	93
Non-acceptors.........	285	305	574
Total (all women).......	292	316	667
35–39:			
IUD acceptors.........	285	335	31
Other acceptors.........	243	236	20
All acceptors..........	269	295	51
Non-acceptors.........	189	195	536
Total (all women).......	196	204	587

SOURCE: Provided by courtesy of the Population Studies Center, University of Michigan.

[a] Respondents are all women married five years or more, out of a representative sample of all married women aged 20–39 in Taichung City, 1962. The survey is described in Ronald Freedman, John Y. Takeshita, and T. H. Sun, "Fertility and Family Planning in Taiwan: A Case Study of the Demographic Transition," *American Journal of Sociology*, 70(1): 16–27 (July, 1964).

TABLE 3
EXCESS OF ACCEPTORS' FERTILITY RATES[a] OVER OTHER FERTILITY RATES
(Per Cent)

ACCEPTORS[c]	FOR 1960-62[b] RATES PER ANNUM			FOR 1958-62[b] RATES PER ANNUM		
	Excess over Age-specific Rate for All Women Married 5 Years or More, in the Taichung Sample[d] (1)	Excess over Official Register[e] Age-specific Rate for Married Women in Taichung (2)	Excess over Official Register Age-specific Rate for Taichung (3)	Excess over Age-specific Rate for All Women Married 5 Years or More, in the Taichung Sample[d] (4)	Excess over Official Register[e] Age-specific Rate for Married Women in Taichung (5)	Excess over Official Register[e] Age-specific Rate for Taichung (6)
All ages, 25-39:						
IUD acceptors	24	34	50	29	54	69
Other acceptors	18	29	44	14	35	49
All acceptors	22	32	48	25	48	63
25-29:						
IUD acceptors	17	9	27	15	29	49
Other acceptors	17	9	26	16	31	51
All acceptors	17	9	27	15	30	49
30-34:						
IUD acceptors	13	38	52	24	57	69
Other acceptors	19	46	61	19	52	63
All acceptors	15	41	54	22	56	67
35-39:						
IUD acceptors	45	98	119	64	112	120
Other acceptors	24	68	87	16	50	55
All acceptors	37	86	107	45	87	95

SOURCE: Basic data provided by courtesy of the Population Studies Center, University of Michigan.

a During the years immediately prior to acceptance. Table figures are obtained by dividing acceptors' rates by the other rates and subtracting 100%.

b For the Taichung sample (cols. 1 and 4) and for all acceptors, rates are calculated on a basis of 3 years, and 5 years, prior to the interview date. Interviews occurred throughout the last three months of 1962; and the acceptances considered here occurred February 1, 1963–March 31, 1964. More precise calculations, by calendar years, will be done soon.

c Excluding those married less than 5 years at acceptance.

d See note to Table 2 describing the sample.

e The register is thought to underestimate the true rates by about 10%. Since Taiwan's register is unusually accurate, the table figures in columns 2, 3, 5, and 6 would be much higher for most developing countries with registers.

that acceptors in Taichung had recent fertility rates about 20% higher than non-acceptors (cols. 1 and 4, Table 3). Moreover, among women aged 35–39 (bottom panel of Table 3), where anti-fertility motivation is strongest, IUD acceptors are those with especially high past fertility, suggesting that really determined women will seek out surer protection. These results clearly imply a selective response to the Taichung family planning program: the fertility rates of acceptors are, in fact, substantially above the assumption of 333 in Rule 2 above.[1]

Far more striking is the gross error that can result when conventional rates are used to estimate acceptors' fertility. Table 3 shows the excess of acceptors' recent fertility rates over other rates. First (cols. 1 and 4, based on Table 2), sample survey data are used to show the "best estimate" of acceptors' advantage in fertility. This survey used a full pregnancy history, with subsequent checks on many respondents. The excess is 20%–25%, implying an underestimate of that magnitude where excellent data on married women are used. Next (cols. 2 and 5), acceptors' rates are compared to register rates for all married women in Taichung, showing an over-all underestimate of over a third. Finally (cols. 3 and 6), acceptors' rates are compared with ordinary age-specific rates from the register, and the over-all underestimate becomes about 50%. The differential tends to rise steeply with age, which is especially important, since most acceptors are in their 30's. All this suggests that the fertility rates provided even by a good register like Taiwan's may, if taken as an index of births prevented, seriously understate program impact.

The above discussion represents of course only one consideration. An accurate over-all assessment of the 1 in 5 ratio of Rule 3 gets into numerous complexities, especially the problem that in some areas fertility rates for women over age 30 are falling rapidly without any program at all. Allowance should be made for this trend in assessing program impact. There are other difficulties associated with assessing the 1 in 5 conclusion: the age distribution of acceptors, voluntary removals of the IUD for spacing purposes, five-year removal rates of the IUD, and so on. None of these is discussed further here.[2]

Assume now that country X decides to undertake a national family

[1]To this evidence may be added results from the Koyang-Kimpo experiment, which show that acceptors have higher recent fertility. The elapsed time from their last birth to the introduction of the program is usually much less than that of non-acceptors. This implies that acceptors are acutely aware of their own fecundity, having just demonstrated it. This finding is consistent with responses to interview questions about fecundity.

[2]A more exacting method which can take account of these factors has been developed by B. M. Lee and J. Isbister, Princeton University (see chap. 57 in this volume).

planning program. Its growth rate is probably 2.5%–3.5% per annum, or soon will be, and this is to be cut in half over ten years. If we suppose the birth rate to be 50, a standard population of one million will have 50,000 births per year. If mortality is about 15 and is dropping, then the growth rate will be cut in half by reducing the birth rate from 50 to 30. Traditional contraceptives and vasectomies are assumed to play a minor role; so the program must grow rapidly to the point of preventing 20,000 births per year through IUD insertions. A schedule must now be developed for the target number of insertions each year and the overlapping waves of future births prevented which result. Calculations for Turkey cumulate the number of adopters expected each year and assume that for every five women wearing the IUD in a given year, one birth is prevented during the next year. This produces a column of births prevented by year. This is quite workable for a five-year period, before acceptors begin passing out of the fertile years. It is a rapid way of exploring the consequences of differing schedules of number of adopters by year. By continuing adjustments, one can work out a five-year program that is realistic and promises to be effective.

In the illustration under discussion, one might very tenuously accept 15,000 IUD's per year as the required target, to be reached soon after the program is established. This would be a demanding target for a population of one million, but it corresponds to the objective of halving the growth rate. Taiwan is now inserting 10,000 IUD's per million population per year; Korea almost the same. Their objectives are to reduce growth, over five years, from about 3% to 2% per year, a one-third reduction. In Taiwan, this was translated to mean a five-year goal of 600,000 loops for the population of 12 million. This is 5% of the total population (1% per year), and more than one-third of all married women aged 20–39.

Cost.–In a recent exercise of the type just described, three separate cost estimates were used. Based again on a standard population of one million they use:

1. The average cost (estimated) of $3.20 per IUD insertion experienced in Taiwan. This, times the 15,000 IUD's, would come to $48,000 per year after the program is established.
2. Computations based on local salaries together with careful estimates on new staffing required by the program. This happened to produce figures close to $30,000. To this must be added supplies and routine travel, but they are minor compared to salaries.
3. The per capita figure of 3–5 cents per year registered in Korea. The program there, in the years 1962–64, cost per capita 0.012, 0.022, and 0.048, and is expected to level off at about 5 cents per capita. (Local government contributes one-quarter of total costs.) In Taiwan the per

capita figure is now 2.5, but it would be well above 3 if patient charges and other hidden items were added. For a population of one million, this gives a range of $30,000–$50,000.

Thus the three methods agree, within the $30,000–$50,000 range. This stability of the estimates must not be taken too literally, however. Methods 1 and 3 are based on experience in only two countries. The new five-year plans for India and Pakistan anticipate spending 8.3 and 12 cents per capita, respectively. Illiteracy in India and Pakistan requires larger expenditures for family planning education, and more extensive incentive payments have been included there.

COST OF INDIAN VASECTOMIES AND OF THE CONSEQUENT BIRTHS PREVENTED

S. N. Agarwala[3] has compiled a summary of various Indian reports on vasectomy costs. He says (references to footnotes renumbered),

There are various estimates of the cost of a vasectomy operation, and they range from rupees ten to rupees thirty-two. For instance, Dr. K. T. Chitre found that a sterilisation operation costs in Maharashtra rupees eighteen, "without of course taking into consideration the salaried staff employed otherwise by the State for other functions."[4] Dr. C. M. Phadke mentions that the cost at a vasectomy camp recently held in the State of Maharashtra, where 2224 operations were performed during a period of six days comes to rupees 19 per patient. This includes Rs.10 given to each patient for incidental expenses.[5] According to Dr. P. Laxmi the cost of professional and ancillary services for vasectomy in Madras is rupees 10 per operation.[6] In Madras, rupees 30 are paid to the person getting sterilised to meet his incidental expenses and rupees 10 to *Panchayats* to meet transport cost of the patient. In the vasectomy camps organised in Satara and Jalgaon, the cost per vasectomy operation came to Rs.32 and 17 respectively.[7] Since the various estimates of the cost do not always include

[3]S. N. Agarwala, "Sterilisation as a Population Control Device: Its Economics," *Economic Weekly*, July 4, 1964.

[4]Dr. K. T. Chitre, "Sterilisation as a Method of Family Limitation and Its Implementation in the Family Planning Programme," *Maharashtra Medical Journal*, 11 (2): 288 (May, 1964).

[5]Dr. G. M. Phadke, "Sterilisation as a Method of Family Limitation," *Maharashtra Medical Journal*, 11 (2): 244 (May, 1964). "We are unable to find the cause of difference between the estimates of Dr. Phadke and Dr. Chitre."

[6]Dr. P. Laxmi, "Family Planning Programme in Madras State: The Role of Sterilisation as a Method of Family Planning," *Maharashtra Medical Journal*, 11 (2): 271–72 (May, 1964).

[7]*Family Planning News*, February, 1962, p. 42, and April, 1962, p. 82. "In Satara 1400 operations were performed at a cost of Rs. 44,682 and in Jalgaon 1071 operations at the cost of Rs. 1,845,460."

the same items, it is appropriate to break up the total cost and compare different items of the cost. Table 4 gives details.

It thus appears that approximately rupees 10 is the cost of professional medical service per vasectomy operation; rupees 10 transport cost; rupees 4 cost of meals, petrol and printing; rupees 2.5 cost of *dhobi* and miscellaneous items and rupees 10 to 20 incentive cost for loss of wages which is paid to sterilised persons. The approximate cost per vasectomy operation thus works out to between rupees 36 and 46.

TABLE 4

COST PER VASECTOMY OPERATION

(In Rupees)

	Satara	Jalgaon	Maharashtra	Madras	Estimated Cost (average)
1. Meals, petrol, printing, and propaganda..............	4.1	N.A.	N.A.	Nil	4.1
2. Dhobi and miscellaneous.....	2.5	N.A.	N.A.	Nil	2.5
3. Medical............ }			8–9	10	10.0
4. Incentive charges for loss of labour............. } ...	25.3	17.2	10	30	10–20
5. Transport cost............	....	....	....	10	10.0
Total..................	31.9	17.2	18–19	50	36.5–46.5

NOTE: one rupee equals 21 U.S. cents.

Agarwala then estimates from age data on previous vasectomies that the average male sterilized has four children and would have had two more. Rs. 36–46 was spent to prevent this; so each birth prevented costs about half of the mean, or Rs. 20 (US$4.20). Any incentive payments (beyond those already mentioned for work lost and transport) must be added.

Agarwala's breakdown of costs may be of particular interest for such plans as the IUD camps in India. Medical costs should remain about the same; payments for work lost would be smaller.

COST ANALYSES

The imperatives of funding lead to multiple sources of support, making cost analysis difficult. Space and personnel may be partially contributed by a health program; supplies, equipment, and education materials may come from numerous sources. The Korean national program, as an example, involves three levels of government, collaboration with Korean universities, and various kinds of co-operation with five private foundations. These complexities are not as troublesome as they might seem, however, since usually the major financing comes from only two or three sources.

Cost analyses must be used judiciously even when they are feasible. Certainly they shed some light, and in general they are highly desirable.[8] They are almost impossible unless proper accounting procedures are used from the start of the project, so as to break up the usual gross categories and force the cost data to match actual program components. The figures which come out of even the best analyses are, however, not necessarily useful in other settings. The appropriate personnel may not be the same in another culture, and this may permit salaries to be lower. Research costs, on the other hand, may be higher. The nature of the program may be different, depending on what infrastructures already exist and how amenable they are to the addition of family planning. The relative importance of budget items may shift: for example, some African populations are dispersed; consequently more mobile clinics may be required, and the supply lines must be more elaborate.

All this says that the best cost predictions are based not simply on figures produced by other projects, but on close *descriptions* of those projects. Precisely what are the characteristics of field workers, how are they trained, how equipped, how much are they paid, what incentives are given them, and so on? If the program is integrated with a prior MCH structure, is this achieved via inserting new workers at each level to handle family planning functions or by asking MCH staff to learn new duties? And how well is the arrangement working? Most family planning programs use several stimuli—home visits, group meetings, propaganda. How is the proportion set? What aspects of the particular culture involved deserve special note? All these questions are vital if the *budget* which is borrowed from a neighboring program is to be accompanied by the *effectiveness* of that program.

Finally, precision in analysis of costs is often not needed to decide which of two programs is superior. In a Taiwan experiment on the optimum ratio of group meetings to home visits, the only thing at stake was field worker time. A decision was reached with no cost data at all.

CLIENT CHARGES AND INCENTIVE PAYMENTS

Where funds are scarce, client charges can make all the difference. In Taiwan they offset about 30% of the program's total cost, mainly

[8] A cost analysis of the Taichung City experiment has been completed by the present author. See *Studies in Family Planning*, No. 10 (February, 1966).

by charging 75 cents to each woman accepting a loop. In areas of lower standards of living, however, and in rural economies that are largely non-monetized, patient charges may not be feasible.

There is wide variation in client charges. Korea is providing almost all its loops and traditional contraceptives free. Taiwan patients pay the 75 cents per loop and the entire cost of supplies for traditionals, but the indigent (10% of acceptors) are exempted. In Tunisia's two-year experimental program (1964–65), there are no charges whatever. The new Pakistan five-year plan will insert loops free but will charge Rs. 0.10 per dozen for condoms or foam tablets and Rs. 1 for contraceptive jelly, Emko, and diaphragms. In the UAR, all devices are given for the nominal charge of 7 cents, to conform with the governmental policy of that charge for medicines in health units. Even this is sometimes foregone. In the United States, Planned Parenthood fixes charges according to ability to pay, and for all affiliates aggregated, patient charges cover 36.2% of all costs.

Throughout such variations, the principles appearing seem to be: (*a*) consistency with fees for other services given through the same outlets, (*b*) the program's need for funds, (*c*) ability to pay, and (*d*) effect on patients, both their willingness to buy and their evaluation of the service.

Patient charges are good in that they ease the budget, but what do they do to patient motivation? Some argue that they dramatize value-received and thereby heighten personal commitment to contraception. Some women are intensely motivated already, however, as the abortion rates show; for them a fee may only irritate. We know of no studies exploring patient reaction to fees, except that in Taiwan a coupon "good for a limited time only" seemed to trigger many acceptances.

The coupon episode raises the reverse question, that of monetary incentives. These are of two types, those paid to clients, and those paid to people who refer or service clients. Pakistan's new plan includes a monetary incentive designed to make the IUD popular; it will pay an IUD fee to doctors, lady health visitors, and trained midwives. A referral fee will be paid the village dais and others who refer cases. Taiwan pays a 25-cent referral fee. India's experience with incentive payments is well known. (Consult the Enke references in note 9 for part of this literature.)

Funding

Funding practices vary considerably, but in no case is the total expenditure borne by a single agency. Where the program is governmental, it typically receives contributions from national, provincial, and local budgets. Such a program works through the entire administrative hierarchy, from central planners to local health officers. In several countries (Hong Kong, Singapore, Chile, and Egypt until 1965) government simply furnishes funds to a private family planning organization and stays clear of administration. The private organization is then free to seek additional support from local donors, from the IPPF, or others.

Taiwan finances its program from interest accumulated on United States counterpart funds. This "second generation" money is not subject to United States control, nor does it enter the official Taiwan annual budget. The Economic Planning Board there controls it. Thus the central government does not officially sponsor or pay for the program, though the established MCH network is intimately related to it.

Foreign sources of support, though they may be helpful for selected purposes, are not likely to participate significantly in direct operational costs. Private foundations are involved somehow in most family planning programs, but they are hesitant to underwrite day-to-day items like salaries, supplies, and routine travel. This is partly due to balance-of-payments considerations, but it also reflects a desire to see the major responsibility for the program fixed indigenously. No program can succeed unless the main force is local; and nothing suggests that as well as the commitment of major funds. In addition, outside agencies simply do not have resources to carry operational costs for the numerous programs now established. They really have "seed money" only, and their willingness to direct portions of it to a particular program is closely related to the priority already given it by the government there.

Seed money is good for such non-recurrent items as consultants, research, demonstration and pilot projects, fellowships and foreign travel, and initial equipment and supplies. These are non-recurrent expenditures. It is clear that for funding purposes, recurrent and non-recurrent items should be separated. Funding which recognizes distinctions of these general types will probably be more efficient.

It is noteworthy that international agencies and certain of the developed nations are increasing their support of family planning projects. In the United Nations, WHO and the Economic and Social Council have just decided to furnish assistance. The Swedish International Development Authority has long been active. The Ministry of Overseas Development of Great Britain has announced its interest. United States AID is giving serious consideration to provision of vehicles in a few areas where family planning activities are present.

Further comments on funding appear under the later heading, "Financing of Private Family Planning Associations in Asia."

SAVINGS INDUCED BY FAMILY PLANNING PROGRAMS

That family planning programs, if effectively administered, can pay their way has been thoroughly demonstrated. The economic analyses by Demeny, Enke, Coale and Hoover, and others[9] present the case for demographic investments by economic planning boards. Recent papers are clarifying the actual linkages between reduced fertility and such economic factors as saving and employment.[10] Lee and Isbister's background paper (chap. 57 in this volume) uses Korean data to offer interesting new illustrations of the economic gains from a reduced birth rate. Undoubtedly, returns to investment in family planning can be very much greater than in other kinds of economic development projects, especially so long as the latter continue at a high level.

But just as vital are other kinds of evidence. Where the abortion rate is high under enforced laws prohibiting it, the immediate economic gains in substituting inexpensive birth control for expensive medical care of septic abortions will go far toward covering program costs. Especially with a program that involves a medical examination, as the IUD programs do, the immediate savings can be substantial from medical care avoided and from lessened debility. Social and psychological dislocations from excessive childbearing are severe. Though difficult to measure, their costs are nonetheless real. Their diminution follows immediately upon the introduction of a family planning program.

[9]A. J. Coale and E. M. Hoover, *Population Growth and Economic Development in Low-Income Countries* (Princeton: Princeton University Press, 1958); P. Demeny, "The Economics of Government Payments to Limit Population: A Comment," *Economic Development and Cultural Change,* 11: 641–44 (1961), and "Investment Allocation and Population Growth" (Ph.D. diss., Princeton University, 1961); S. Enke, "The Gains to India from Population Control: Some Money Measures and Incentive Schemes," *Review of Economics and Statistics,* 42: 175–81 (1960), "The Economics of Government Payments to Limit Population," *Economic Development and Cultural Change,* 8: 339–48 (1960), "Government Bonuses for Smaller Families," *Population Review,* 4: 47–50 (1960), "A Rejoinder to Comments on the Superior Effectiveness of Vasectomy–Bonus Schemes," *Economic Development and Cultural Change,* July, 1961, "Some Reactions to Bonuses for Family Limitation," *Population Review,* July, 1961, and *Economics for Development* (New York: Prentice-Hall, 1963); H. H. Villard, "A Note on the Economics of Birth Control," *Review of Economics and Statistics,* February, 1958, pp. 78–79.

[10]P. Demeny, "Demographic Aspects of Saving, Investment, Employment and Productivity," United Nations World Population Conference, Belgrade, August 30 to September 10, 1965; Simon Kuznets, "Demographic Aspects of Modern Economic Growth," United National World Population Conference, Belgrade, August 30 to September 10, 1965.

Recent projects have added further illustrations of the economic returns from family planning programs.

1. The cost per birth prevented in the island-wide Taiwan program is considered below $5.00, even with the most conservative estimates on how long the loops will stay in. This is below the cost to the government for education alone ($135 for six years of primary school). It is also below the cost to the parents for food alone ($547 if the food costs 10 cents per day for 15 years) (see chap. 28).

2. In one developing country, central government expenditures for maternity care, if averaged over all births in the population, run about $6.00 per birth. That alone is the approximate local cost of preventing one birth. Potential savings to the government in reduced expansion of maternity care services alone would pay for the fertility reduction program.

3. In the same country, government expenditures for education in a recent year ran at $86 per child in the primary grades. For 100 infants born, after mortality and non-attendance are subtracted, the educational expenditures were then estimated at $27,200 over the seven years of primary school, or $272 per child (using 75% survivorship and 60% attendance, so that 45 children attend school). The first grade of schooling alone, by this accounting, costs $38.

4. For a United States example, see the Appendix to this chapter.

AFRICA

Attacking the cost question on an area basis has no particular merit, but in the case of Africa our information is too fragmentary to do anything else. Caldwell's paper on Africa (chap. 14 in this volume) is the best survey now available. His research will assume even more importance as data from additional countries come into his project.

In the first place, family planning activity is sparse in many or most African polities. Partly because of this, and partly because few people have tried to find out, we know little about what is going on. Caldwell has performed a valuable service in his African survey, and has included in his paper a few summary paragraphs on what he turned up on costs. Caldwell made a point of investigating government policies on overseas funding of family planning. The results imply that areas with a history of British influence feel no opposition to the entry of foreign monies, whether governmental, private, or international. Former French tropical Africa, however, seems to have reservations.

Leaving Caldwell's material, we should note three specific African countries. Tunisia is just ending a $370,000, two-year experimental program, financed jointly by the Tunisian government and the Ford Foundation. It is being followed by an official national program, starting January 1, 1966, with about the same magnitude of cost. The aim there is to insert 120,000 IUD's over the two years 1966–67, toward reducing the birth rate an additional 5% each year, after the first year of tooling up. In the meantime, extensive groundwork will be laid by training almost all doctors in IUD insertion, making family planning services an integral part of all medical installations, obtaining proper equipment including vehicles, and extending health education. The largest hidden cost is the contribution of hospitals for IUD services.

Kenya has recently shown strong concern over its growth rate by requesting a visit by an expert commission to examine the situation and make recommendations. Initial figures indicate that the birth rate there might be halved in ten years or so by an annual expenditure of about $300,000, rising to $500,000 by the fifth year. Substantial portions might of course be funded from various sources other than the Kenyan government.

The Mauritius government has recently granted well over $55,000 to the two family planning associations on the island. This represents over 8 cents per capita. If spent, this will be a very high per capita figure, especially since it is an underestimate.[11]

Financing of Private Family Planning Associations in Asia

A recent paper by M. C. Balfour[12] reviews the entire financing question for Asian family planning associations. The pattern he finds has these traits: that in most countries the associations receive their major support from government grants or subsidies; that dues and subscriptions make only a negligible contribution; and that response from individual donors, businesses, and industrial sources has been disappointing. So far, family planning organizations have not been able to tap private sources of funds in the manner of the Red Cross, tuberculosis societies, and the like. Tax policies in certain countries discourage private giving, and, in general, the picture is a dark one. Balfour concurs with Caldwell's African report that poor financing is the major bottleneck to expanded activity.

Tight budgets have been relieved to some extent by IPPF funds and by assistance from certain private foundations. In Japan and Hong Kong, sports organizations have made regular contributions. Some family planning associations obtain small sums from the sale of supplies and educational materials and from miscellaneous other efforts. Balfour

[11]Personal communication from J. C. Caldwell, August 19, 1965.

[12]Marshall C. Balfour, "The Role and Financing of Family Planning Associations in Asia," International Planned Parenthood Federation, Western Pacific Region, First Regional Conference, Seoul, Korea, May 26–29, 1965.

supplements his review with brief cost figures for eight associations. He stresses that "the great weakness of the family planning movement in Asia . . . concerns its finances," and suggests ways of strengthening it.

COMPARISONS WITH THE COSTS OF MALARIA ERADICATION

The cost of malaria eradication serves as a useful standard of comparison, since it too concerns the mass of developing countries, tries to reach practically every household, tries to maintain continuous effectiveness, and has been an urgent campaign centrally administered but dependent on local co-operation.

The cost of malaria control has been decidedly above that of family planning programs. In 1963, 704 million people were covered by malaria programs in the "attack and consolidation" phases. The costs of these operations averaged approximately 23 cents per capita. The comparable cost in 1967 for an anticipated population of 531 million is 45 cents per capita. Regional variation is large, ranging in 1963 from 7.4 cents in India to 18 cents in Asia as a whole, to 21 cents in Europe and 51 cents in the Americas.[13] A 1958 estimate ranged from 11 cents in Southeast Asia to 46 cents in the Americas. Africa is thought to experience costs even higher, at least 80 cents per capita as of 1962. In general, we may say that the lowest cost estimates for malaria control are well above the highest estimates for family planning programs. We may also say that an effective national family planning program will cost one-fifth or less of a malaria-control program, roughly speaking (taking family planning at 5 cents per capita and malaria control at 25 cents per capita).

SOME EXPECTATIONS FOR THE FUTURE COST OF FAMILY PLANNING PROGRAMS

1. Expenditures will rise. As the urgency of fertility reduction becomes progressively clearer, governments will continue to step up

[13]For these figures and all other malaria cost information given here I am indebted to Dr. L. J. Bruce-Chwatt, Chief, Research and Technical Intelligence, Division of Malaria Eradication, WHO, Geneva. The 1958 estimate is drawn from the WHO pamphlet, *Malaria Eradication: A Plea for Health*. The African figure was reported to the Third Malaria Conference in Africa. For general information and references see E. J. Pampana, *A Textbook of Malaria Eradication* (New York: Oxford University Press, 1963). For cost details in Greece and Spain, respectively, see articles by G. Livadas and D. Athanassatos, *Rev. Malaria,* 42: 177 (1963); and by J. J. Fernandez Maruto, *Rev. Sanid Hig. publ. (Madr.),* 38: 89 (1964). For a 1960 costing exercise by the International Cooperation Administration Expert Panel on Malaria, see "Report and Recommendations on Malaria, a Summary," *American Journal of Tropical Medicine and Hygiene,* 10: 451 (1961).

their family planning programs. (The only exception seems to be Japan, which is terminating its national support of about $170,000 per year.) Expenditures will probably stabilize at no more than 5–10 cents per capita, since a vigorous program apparently does not need more than that.

2. Increased assistance will become available from international agencies, governments of certain developed nations, and private foundations. Other agencies will increasingly participate which, though small, may nevertheless be important catalysts, e.g., the American Friends Service Committee.

3. Certain kinds of costs may be expected to decline. More countries are starting local manufacture of IUD's and other contraceptives. Given adequate equipment, this produces benefits from lower wage scales, reduced foreign exchange problems, and increased commercial activity. In addition, some countries are past the costly early stages of program development, i.e., the extensive training of physicians, nurses, field workers, and the winning of the basic confidence of the populace.

4. Efficiency will rise, in terms of both time and money.

a) Much less time need be spent in the future on preliminary research topics. Each country initiating a program will of course want data on its own population; but future decisions will have the advantage of reduced uncertainty. Much of the unavoidable fumbling and risk inherent in early intervention can be avoided. We have learned a great deal from the many experiments, KAP studies, and demonstration and pilot projects already completed. It has been noted that this is the largest cross-cultural body of data ever gathered on one aspect of behavior. This does not minimize the desirability of basic demographic inquiries, nor does it apply to the testing of new contraceptive methods. New programming ideas will also arise, requiring field tests. Large-scale programs will need a series of *ad hoc* studies to answer practical questions, e.g., the small experiments in Taiwan, summarized in the Hsu-Chow paper in this volume (chap. 4).

b) Effective international communication is well begun and will spread to new areas. Advances in contraception and programming can disseminate with increasing ease. The family planning field has relatively low friction in the exchange of skills and knowledge, and only moderate friction in the flow of supplies and equipment. The IUD especially illustrates this; indeed, its diffusion rate must rival that of the antibiotics.

c) Program structuring has been improved greatly: first, by simplifying supply lines through use of the IUD; second, by directing programs specifically to high-parity women; third, by such tactics as contacting only *n*th household or precinct; fourth, by discovering a good balance between group meetings and home visits. Strategies not yet fully explored are post-partum programs and the insertion of IUD's at any time of the month. A careful examination of what mass media can do, acting either alone or nearly so, has yet to be done. Finally, no rural program has yet tested systematically the plan of contacting every *n*th village. Although it is quite plausible that this plan would increase efficiency, it is not clear whether it would work in the same manner as visits to every *n*th household.[14]

APPENDIX

UNITED STATES DATA ON CLINIC COSTS

Certain cost data from all United States Planned Parenthood chapters are submitted regularly to a central research office (Table 5). Because of higher costs in the United States, these figures are a kind of

TABLE 5

COSTS INCURRED BY CLINICS OF SELECTED UNITED STATES
PLANNED PARENTHOOD CHAPTERS, 1964[a]

PP Chapters	Average Cost per Patient	Average Cost per Visit
Washington, D.C.	$12.39	$6.18
Cincinnati	20.65	6.98
Oklahoma City	10.57	2.75
Chicago	24.61	5.72
New York City	19.37	6.23
Manhattan and Bronx	22.17	6.86
Brooklyn	15.73	5.27
Far Rockaway, Queens	18.14	3.58
Jamaica, Queens	13.44	6.69
United States	$22.02	$6.26

SOURCE: George Varghese, Planned Parenthood–World Population Research Office, New York City, personal communication.

[a] No corrections are included for variations in volunteer help, in salary scales, cost of living, and so on. Planned Parenthood clinics typically must furnish all their own administrative services. Their budgets will reflect this item, unlike many government-related programs. The denominator in the first column is only those patients who actually visited a clinic one or more times during the year.

[14]Donald Bogue's Chicago experiments imply that reaching every person would be a serious mistake. When only a limited number of persons possess information of high interest to everyone, they occupy a special status. This status, however, can be realized only by spreading the news. If everyone already knows it, however, there is little to talk about. Pluralistic ignorance remains undiminished, and the social legitimation of birth control which discussion might have created is lost. No one knows as yet whether social-psychological dynamics of this kind would appear by omitting entire villages. See Donald J. Bogue and James A. Palmore, Jr., "The Chicago Fertility Control Experiments: Some Preliminary Findings," also Bogue's mimeographed manuscript, "West Side Fertility Report," both available from Community and Family Study Center, University of Chicago.

maximum, although United States Planned Parenthood activities rarely include the field solicitation contained in numerous programs elsewhere.

Chicago Planned Parenthood has one of the largest case loads of any chapter anywhere and is one of the most vigorous. A recent cost analysis of its operations was conducted with great care for reasons associated with the State of Illinois public assistance program. This yielded a cost per visit of $7.22 (calendar year 1962). Among the fourteen or so clinics involved, this figure ranged from $3.86 to $10.10, and was $14.90 for a mobile unit. Salaries were by far the largest cost, representing 77% of the total. Medical supplies were 9%. The mean number of visits per patient per year runs about 4.3.

Chicago Planned Parenthood in 1962 serviced 4,200 mothers who were also under the state Aid to Dependent Children program. Assuming that the one year's birth control for the 4,200 mothers has an ultimate effect of 3,360 prevented births, a calculation is possible of savings from the program. Delivery costs, ADC costs, and school costs, cumulated through 1974, would total $19,300,000, or an average of $4,600 per mother. This may be contrasted with the cost of the year's birth control service, put at $40 (about $10 a visit and four visits per year).[15]

NOTE ON PER CAPITA INDICATORS

Since per capita indicators promise to be widely used in cost discussions, a note on them is perhaps in order. They seem to have at least two drawbacks:

1. The denominator does not correspond to the target population. The program is typically directed only at women of childbearing ages. Even more restrictive definitions of the "eligible population" have been proposed. This kind of objection, when relevant, can sometimes be handled by correcting the denominator.

2. The per capita figure implies even spending over the entire population, when in fact some national programs spend most of the money in a few particular areas. Selective overspending of this kind is concealed by the per capita figure. One correction is to restrict the denominator to the subpopulations immediately affected by the program. A more subtle difficulty is that initiating the program in selected areas may be a deliberate strategy in a truly national program. The belief may be that early successes in a few locations are the fastest path to general acceptance. The Taiwan case illustrates this.

[15]Chicago data provided by courtesy of Mrs. Jane C. Browne, Executive Director of Chicago Planned Parenthood.

Korea is a counter-example: the national program there began with almost the entire nation and has developed rapidly.

Other points may be raised which apply universally to cost comparisons, e.g., devaluation, inflation, real versus actual cost. In addition, it is important to specify, where possible, what items enter the numerator—the national budget only, or the national budget plus grants, and so on. Other points relate not to the indicator itself but how it is used. It may represent either the amount budgeted or the amount actually spent, and where the gap between the two is great, one may suspect an absence of program vitality. The per capita indicator may also reflect differences in the standards of living between two areas—Taiwan spends less per capita than Korea, but that may mean that Taiwan has an easier job of it. It is not a criticism of the indicator per se.

Per capita measures of family planning programs have certain advantages. They are simple, of course, since the denominator is widely published. They also reflect the tax base. Their utility is not affected by size of country, for no economies of scale seem to exist in the family planning industry. A small factory run by fourteen technicians can produce enough IUD's for all of India. Condoms are purchasable about as cheaply as they can be manufactured locally (though local manufacturing may ease foreign exchange problems and stimulate commercial sales, as in Korea). Supplies in "small quantities" are often available free or are sold at about the same rates as in large quantities. The same may be true of vehicles. Educational materials need not be developed specially for each new program; borrowing from other cultural settings has proved feasible. Expert consultants need not be trained indigenously, and even local M.D.'s, nurses, and midwives can be trained rather quickly after the first links are established with foreign centers.

59

RESEARCH AND EVALUATION: NEEDS FOR THE FUTURE

LYLE SAUNDERS
Program Associate, The Ford Foundation

Research, like virtue, seems to be in perennial short supply. Research is one of the great positive values of our time, and there is always likely to be less of it and its fruits than somebody wants. In any academic or professional field, it is easy to obtain consensus around the proposition that more and better research is needed. Disagreement tends to appear only when we begin to talk about specific priorities and emphases.

Those interested in programs aimed at limiting fertility are no exception to the generalization. At the 1954 World Conference on Population in Rome there was grumbling about how little was known on what was happening to population and how few effective means there were of reducing fertility, and more research was proposed to improve the situation. Five years later, in New York, at the Milbank Memorial Fund conference on family planning programs, the current state of family planning research was characterized as "disgracefully inadequate," the biological and the social sciences were scolded for their relative lack of interest, and there was mention of an urgent need for immediate and intensive concern with "practical problems of social engineering," especially through action research.

Viewing research broadly for a moment, it is probably fair to say that there has not been any dramatic change in the situation since 1959. A great deal of research has been mentioned in this volume. But these papers were written by a special group for a special occasion.

The help of David Radel, Research Assistant, The Ford Foundation, New York, in gathering materials for the paper is gratefully acknowledged, as are the helpful critical comments of an earlier draft made by Oscar Harkavy, Director, Population Program, The Ford Foundation.

779

Much more typical of the general level of interest, I think, was the program of the World Conference on Population at Belgrade which during two weeks of discussion on population devoted part of a half-day session to family planning. In medicine, public health, the biological sciences, and the social sciences there has been a noticeable increase in research activity directly related to family planning. But in none of these areas is there yet a professional commitment proportionate to the importance of fertility control for human welfare.

Social scientists in particular seem to be missing opportunities for both basic and applied research that might not only contribute toward the amelioration of a pressing social problem but also lead to important theoretical and methodological contributions to the social sciences. When an experimental rocket is sent off anywhere, it generally goes loaded with instruments, plants, and animals put aboard by physical and biological scientists to bring back information about conditions in space and their effects on living organisms. But when a government inaugurates a national family planning program designed to bring about extensive changes in one of the fundamental areas of human behavior, the event goes practically unnoticed in the social science community.

Family planning programs include such a range of activities, draw upon such a broad spectrum of knowledge, and involve such a variety of talents and skills that it is difficult to make any meaningful summary statement about the research that underlies their development. But several streams of both basic and applied research activity do seem to have been especially influential in their contributions to more effective program efforts. One has been the continuing and expanding research in reproductive biology that is providing basic biological and biochemical knowledge from which further improvements in contraceptive methods may be expected. It has already given us two methods that seem to give effective results with couples whose motivation to limit or space their children is relatively low.

A second influential stream of research activity has been that concerned with clinical trials of contraceptives, especially orals and IUD's. The extensive information that has accumulated about the safety, acceptability, and reliability of various contraceptive procedures and materials has served to stimulate and orient recent developments in family planning programs and has contributed to a shift in emphasis toward increasing use of the newer methods.

Demographic research has included efforts toward more complete analyses of census data, the development of improved methods of estimating fertility rates from incomplete data and from age distributions, the search for more meaningful indices of fertility change, and the beginnings of computer simulation of population dynamics. All this has contributed to better understanding of population phenomena and to more precise measurement of the effects of programs intended to reduce the growth rate.

Communications and motivation research, as illustrated by the "planned diffusion" experiment that Dr. Samuel Wishik reported from Pakistan and Donald Bogue's postcard system for reaching and recruiting people over long distances, has contributed both directly and indirectly to improvements in handling one of the persistent problems of family planning programs.

Useful information has also come from the new large series of fertility surveys that have explored in many countries people's knowledge about reproduction and contraception, their notions about ideal family size, their sexual practices, and their expressed receptivity to contraceptive innovation. The survey technique has also been effectively used to compile information about the incidence and prevalence of induced abortion, the population groups that resort to it, the circumstances that lead to it, and its social, medical, and economic costs. Much of this information has direct relevance for operating family planning programs.

There has also been action research. Since the mid-1940's, there has been a long series of pilot projects, demonstrations, and experiments, most of them on a relatively small scale and dealing with populations in the thousands, rather than in the hundred thousands or millions, and directed toward getting answers to questions that are basic to family planning programs: Can sex and human physiology be publicly discussed? Do people want contraceptive knowledge? Will they use contraceptives if made available? Who is most likely to use them? Under what circumstances and to what extent? Which methods are likely to be acceptable? How does information spread? What services are needed? How are they best organized?

In the most general statement, the contributions of these several streams of research to family planning action programs seem to be three.

1. They have helped to make family planning respectable and to bring about a climate of opinion in which it can be freely discussed.

2. They have provided two safe, acceptable, highly effective contraceptives that seem to promise better results with low-motivation populations than anything previously available.

3. They have helped to accumulate a body of knowledge on which to base the ambitious efforts of emerging programs. Almost none of this knowledge is in the form of tested scientific propositions, nor could it be expected to be. Rather, it consists of an accumulation of

what the Population Council likes to call "lessons," bits of professional wisdom acquired through "critically viewed experience," that are more or less appropriate and valid from one situation to another. These lessons still leave a great many operational questions unanswered, but on the other hand they do provide useful and workable guidelines for organizational forms and action alternatives such as those embodied in Berelson's guide to national family planning programs[1] and Bogue's new manual on evaluation.[2] A great many new "lessons" have been added by the papers and discussions of this conference.

There are obviously many things that we don't yet know about family planning programs and their outcomes. One is the answer to the pay-off question that underlies the population control aspect of family planning efforts: Is it possible through a deliberate policy and program to reduce fertility to a predetermined level and keep it there? I think it is correct to say that no country that has achieved sustained low fertility has done so as a result of a deliberate, planned population control program. The encouraging progress in countries like Korea and Taiwan in the past year and a half provide a basis for hope that it can be done. But the convincing demonstration is still in the future.

If it should be demonstrated that fertility can be brought under rational control, there remains the question, What are the necessary and sufficient conditions for it? And such corollary questions as, Is there a set of such conditions common to all countries? Are there certain types of family structure that are compatible or incompatible with such control? Is the proportion of urban population significant? Or the type of urbanization? Are modes of economic relationships involved? Is a given level of literacy necessary? Or a given level of infant survival? Can fertility be effectively reduced in developing countries in the absence of profound changes in the domestic and community roles of married women?

Still unanswered, too, is the question of whether rapid acceptance of an effective, convenient, inexpensive method, such as has occurred in Taiwan and Korea, can develop its own motivating influence capable of generating new acceptors in sufficient numbers to maintain a high level of protection in the population, or whether the ready

[1]Bernard Berelson, "National Family Planning Programs: A Guide," *Studies in Family Planning*, No. 5 (supplement) (New York, The Population Council), December, 1964.

[2]Donald J. Bogue, "Inventory, Explanation, and Evaluation by Interview of Family Planning Motives–Attitudes–Knowledge–Behavior," document prepared for discussion at International Conference on Family Planning Programs, Geneva, Switzerland (August 23–27, 1965), available at Community and Family Study Center, University of Chicago.

acceptors represent a kind of "cream" that once taken off will bring us to the hard task of developing motivation for the "skimmed milk." There is also the related question of whether the present acceptors represent new converts to family planning or whether they are largely people who are shifting from one method to another and thus represent little or no total gain.

The immediate future for family planning programs is likely to see continuing rapid change and expansion, with a wider base of public information and interest and more professional commitment and support then we have had in the past. It will be a time of increasing involvement of international agencies in fertility action programs, with the first steps already having been taken by WHO. It will be a time characterized by development of national programs with government commitment and support, and by attempts to bring total national populations down to manageable rates of growth. It is likely to be a time of much experimentation with organizational arrangements and with programs for public information, service, and training. India and Pakistan have already extensively revised their programs in an effort to make them more effective. Korea and Taiwan are experimenting with government-voluntary association collaboration, with ways to use private physicians to carry the major load of IUD insertions, with a variety of methods for disseminating information, and with several forms of incentive payments. An experiment suggested for Ceylon would test whether a program without paid field workers, relying on the mails and mass media for information diffusion and on volunteer workers for personal contact, can produce satisfactory results with lower costs per acceptor than either the Korean or Taiwan programs. Dr. Howard Taylor has suggested a promising program innovation that should be tested in an action situation to see if it will give the improved results and the lower costs that he predicts (see chap. 35). The new international comparative post-partum program announced by Bernard Berelson represents an experiment that may demonstrate a model balance between research and program accomplishment (see chap. 51). The project reported by Dr. G. T. M. Cummins, exploring the use of midwives for IUD insertions in Barbados, may open new possibilities and provide valuable new lessons for future programs (see chap. 37).

The near future will probably also be a time of improvement in familiar contraceptives—cheaper, low-dosage orals, plastic condoms, new IUD designs—and a time when the introduction of new contraceptives may require new approaches, new arrangements, different program emphases.

Broadly viewed, the role of research in the immediate future will probably not differ greatly from its role in the recent past. I found it of some interest that relatively few of the "problems" identified in the country papers prepared for this conference were of such a nature that they could best be approached through systematic research. They seemed to be more the kinds of matters that could be handled through administrative tinkering or that would tend to disappear if some means could be found to get more funds, more staff, more support from governments, and less opposition from political and religious groups.

Some clues to the future role of research may perhaps be found in what might be called the non-research uses of research. In Taiwan, a program that is rapidly becoming national in scope grew out of a social research experiment, and research techniques have been used to provide corrective feed-back information to the program. In both Korea and Taiwan, research techniques were used for pre-testing program approaches before making large-scale commitments to program alternatives. A case in point is the field experiments reported by the Taiwan program which were designed to provide comparative information on how to get the most loops inserted at the least cost. In Colombia a research program is being used as a vehicle for developing an institutional basis for a national program, as a way of getting ready for the time when a wider range of more effective contraceptives can be used, and (as in Chile) as a means of influencing public and official opinion. In Peru research is likely to provide the opening wedge in broadening the base of knowledge and interest in problems related to high fertility, after which something may be done about them. In the UAR an interest in research, combined with a desire to improve medical and public health training programs, may provide the first opportunity to bring contraceptive service to two large populations that together include almost 10% of the people of the country. And in many countries, research—in the form of the fertility survey—has been a means of overcoming apathy, winning public and official support, and demonstrating to skeptics that there is more readiness for family planning than almost anyone supposed.

NEW EMPHASES

Present trends in family planning programs would seem to call for continuation of much of the research activity that is now going on and for some new emphases.

Certainly there is a need to continue and expand biological research. We are a long way from knowing as much about reproductive processes as we do about some other biological processes; and we are a long way from the ideal methods of contraception. Fortunately, both research itself and the training of people for research in this area are expanding.

We will probably need to continue clinical trials—of new contraceptives as they come along and also of the old ones as new countries become interested in having family planning programs. Particularly important will be the development of programs to follow up acceptors in mass programs. One of the "lessons" of past experience is that there is probably nothing as unconvincing as someone else's clinical results. It may be that for the oral contraceptive in its developing forms and for the IUD there is still something to be learned from large-scale trials, repeated from one area to another. But even if there were not, we should probably still require such trials if for no other reason than that they seem to be politically necessary to win the approval of medical and government decision-makers.

For the same reasons we shall probably continue to have fertility surveys. Such studies do not promise many surprises anymore, but they do provide clues that are useful in designing programs, they are necessary for some types of evaluation, and they help build a broad base of interest in fertility and support for programs.

There is no question about the need for continued demographic research and for the improvement of demographic techniques. Better techniques are basic to any improved understanding of fertility and to any efforts that may be made to control it. Particularly thoughtful suggestions for demographic research have been offered by Ronald Freedman in his presidential address to the American Population Association earlier this year and in his penetrating analysis, "The Sociology of Human Fertility," published in 1963 in *Current Sociology*.

We have had much opportunity to observe that family planning programs are highly varied in format, goals, and procedures. And perhaps even more diversity will be desirable in the future. We need operations research that will permit comparisons among a variety of organizational forms; explorations of new ways of making use of the skills of private medical practitioners; more imaginative schemes for recruiting, training, and using non-professional workers; and more trials of schemes to provide direct incentive benefits to those who use or recruit others to use effective contraception. We also need more long-range comparative studies similar to those Dr. Christopher Tietze has been carrying on and to the international post-partum IUD experiments that the Population Council is starting.

Our techniques for estimating the value of postponing or preventing

786 /   RESEARCH AND EVALUATION

a birth[3] in a given economy are not highly developed. With a growing emphasis on family planning as an aid to economic development, such estimates are useful in helping to convince government decision-makers of the value of investing scarce resources in fertility-limitation schemes. More work is needed in this area, possibly along the lines that have been pioneered by Stephen Enke or of the type used in the Lee and Isbister paper (chap. 57). We also need more refined comparative techniques for calculating the costs of preventing a birth, and improved ways of estimating the effects on fertility of mass IUD insertions and other contraceptive programs.

Many people have pointed out that it would be useful to know more about ways in which family planning information diffuses through a society and about how contraceptive practices are legitimized and social support created. There is already a useful body of both basic and applied research results in communications and in the field of innovation diffusion. Research on processes of information diffusion have been incorporated as part of several recent programs reported in this volume. Such studies will surely be continued and expanded.

There are innumerable problems relating to the organization and operation of family planning programs that require investigation. In an ongoing program, decisions have to be made constantly; facts and "lessons" are not always available to guide sound choices among alternative courses of action. It is probably desirable that new country programs include operations research units that can do baseline and evaluation surveys; that can help choose evaluation indices and provide a continuing input of data relating to them; that can observe operations and suggest corrective controls that will move the program toward more efficient and effective operation; that can help design, study, and assess the effects of different approaches to service, supply, training, and public information programs; that can generate data necessary for continuing public and government support; and that can provide something resembling an intelligence service concerned with relations

[3]Parenthetically, I find the concept of a prevented birth a most fascinating one. It has all the abstract purity of a mathematical symbol. For some reason, it reminds me of a bit of fugitive culture from the United States that my fellow countrymen will all remember from a few years ago:

> "The other day upon a stair
> I passed a man who wasn't there.
> He wasn't there again today.
> I really wish he'd go away."

In similar vein we might now say:

> "Yesterday from dark to morn
> Ten thousand babies were not born;
> Like autumn leaves the non-born fall;
> I wonder where we'll put them all?"

between the program and its public, the program and its sponsors, the program and its collaborators and rivals, and among the components of the program itself.

Illustrative of the kinds of broad general questions for which we need administrative "wisdom" based on carefully observed experience are these: What is the simplest organizational form for a workable program? What is the optimum size population unit for a single program? Should nations with large populations perhaps have a series of relatively independent programs? What is the most appropriate role for voluntary organizations in nations with government programs? How many workers and of what types are needed for a population of, say, one million? How many births are likely to be prevented by a program with a given rate of IUD insertions? How can indigenous midwives be used effectively? Questions such as these are not best approached by independent research activity; the information needed for answering them will be found in the accumulating experience of a variety of operating programs. It is thus likely that the future will bring some reversal of emphasis between research and program objectives. Where there was a tendency in the action-research programs of the recent past to subordinate action to research and to use action mainly as a means of generating data for research analysis, the trend of the future is likely to be more the reverse, toward using research as an adjunct of action programs to provide analytical and evaluative information immediately useful to the program.

A final need is that of devoting increased attention to non-contraceptive ways of reducing fertility. Sloan Wayland has discussed one such line of activity (see chap. 27). There are many who believe that family planning programs will never reduce fertility significantly without prior change in other social arrangements and relations. If they are right—and there is not yet any conclusive evidence that they are not—it is essential that we begin to identify factors that may be casually related to fertility, to assess the nature and the extent of the relationships, and to devise and apply ways of modifying them in desired directions. Colonel Raina, in his paper in this volume (chap. 9), has indicated that India is planning action research in these areas.

The focus of these very general comments has been strictly on the research needed by and for family planning programs. This of course is only a tiny segment of the total spectrum of research needed to give us a better understanding of human fertility and its correlates. Broad areas of demography and the biology of reproduction have been barely mentioned. It may be appropriate to recall that we also need greatly expanded basic research in such areas as the sociology of fertility, the psychology of fertility, the economics of fertility, the politics of fertility, and—closer to our topic—the management of fertility.

Human reproduction is a complex phenomenon that cross-cuts the interest areas of a great many disciplines and professions. It is activated through some of our strongest biological drives and fundamental social institutions. The idea that we may be able to bring it under rational control is as audacious and improbable as the notion that we can visit the moon. But somebody will visit the moon in a few years; and perhaps we will learn how to control fertility. In either instance, research, both formal and operational, will provide the light that guides our steps as we move into the unknown.

PART FIVE

Summary

The International Conference on Family Planning Programs, 1965, concluded with brief summary statements representing the planned parenthood community, the international assistance agencies, and several national programs. They were followed by an over-all review of the present situation, focused on the major themes of the Conference. Then came the "Closing Remarks."

60

IMPLICATIONS OF THE CONFERENCE

FROM THE PLANNED PARENTHOOD COMMUNITY

SIR COLVILLE DEVERELL, Secretary-General, International Planned Parenthood Federation

Mr. Chairman, I like to think that your invitation to those of us from IPPF was in some part a recognition of the vital pioneering work that the voluntary movement has performed all over the world. Without this work, carried out in a climate of opinion that would have daunted many of us professional people in this room, it would not have been possible for a scientific, objective, and professional approach now to be made to the individual and collective problems of population control.

I have been asked to speak on the implications of the Conference from the IPPF standpoint. This is a tall order and I can only attempt to comply in extremely general terms. It seems to me that the most significant feature at the present time is that we are meeting at what is really a turning point of our whole movement. All over the world there is now a general acceptance of the rightness of the principle of family planning, and the only remaining arguments of any significance are the Roman Catholic reservations about the permissibility of artificial methods and the Communist rejection of what they term neo-Malthusianism, which is sometimes wrongly identified with family planning.

In this new and surprisingly genial climate, the voluntary organizations are being reinforced and to some extent replaced by the activity of their domestic governments, the technical aid from other interested governments such as the Swedish government, the United States AID, and the British Ministry of Overseas Development, and by the assistance of the foundations. And at last we have the most welcome appearance of the United Nations agencies. We are in fact in a state of

791

welcome flux and at a stage when it seems to me that some reappraisal of our respective roles will soon be desirable, so as to ensure that our combined efforts are sensibly co-ordinated to produce the optimum result.

For a number of years now the IPPF, which was the first to concert work in this field internationally, has set itself the aim to try to establish family planning associations in all countries. Broadly, the objective has been twofold: first, to provide family planning facilities for those who wanted them, simply to meet a human need; and, second, to create a climate of opinion that would enable or impel governments to include family planning in maternal and child health services and, incidentally though most importantly, to make it possible for outside assistance to be imported at governmental instance.

These are still our objectives, and though the process of handing over to governments responsibility for clinical services long provided by devoted volunteers can be personally distressing and painful, we have no doubt that, by and large, full government acceptance of responsibility to provide family planning services is a consummation devoutly to be wished. This process of reorientation of ideas about our functions is not, I suggest, something that the voluntary organizations alone face, and I hope that corporate bodies will not find change as difficult to contemplate as some individuals inevitably and naturally do.

A number of the papers presented at this Conference, and a number of the speakers, have referred to the role of the family planning associations, and voluntary agencies generally, after governments have decided to incorporate family planning in their health services. (Frequently, of course, governments do in fact prefer the alternative course of subsidizing family planning associations.) Most of those who have commented—in fact, I think, all of them—have agreed that there is indeed a continuing need for voluntary organizations.

The classical example of a fruitful combined effort must surely be Korea, where the government, the Population Council, and the family planning association combine so effectively that if something has to be done, one or the other agency will find the means to do it.

There is in the very interesting report of the first Pan-American Assembly on Population, just held, a description of the role that private national organizations should play before and after governments have adopted family planning programs. I agree with this statement, and would summarize my own views on this matter as follows: (1) to provide an informal pressure group to keep the governments up to the mark; (2) to assist in the education of public opinion at all levels in the community, using every form of mass media, and personal channels of communication and influence; (3) to assist in the training of voluntary and part-time workers; (4) to keep up a continuous process of expanding the number of social units organized to take care of their own contraceptive needs—for example, the staffs of factories, government departments, large agricultural estates, and big stores; (5) in urban areas, to assist in the organization of a reporting system that will locate and link post-partum cases with appropriate contraceptive services; and (6) to run a modest number of clinics to provide opportunities to try out new methods and procedures that governments naturally enough might be hesitant to do. Now obviously the emphasis that should be placed on these various functions will differ from country to country, particularly in relation to the strength of the government health structure.

At the same time as we reconsider all our various roles, in the light of governmental and international intervention in this field, I suggest that it would be wise to reconsider the substance of the general presentation of the case for governmental family planning programs. My suggestion is that we should rest our public case on the following self-evident propositions: (*a*) that parents have a human right to decide the size and spacing of their families, and (*b*) that governments have a right to encourage family planning so as to relate the population's size and the rate of growth to optimum economic and social requirements, whatever those may be.

Regarding the economic argument, I personally like the balance struck in the Pan-American report to which I have just referred, making quite clear the complementary nature of the need to curb growth rates in developing countries.

Though all of us, naturally, accept the fact that other essential social, agrarian, and economic reforms must accompany the reduction in population growth rates, if countries are to develop satisfactorily, we often do not mention this; and so, in default, we expose ourselves quite unnecessarily to the mistaken charge that we regard population control as a sort of independent, self-sufficient panacea. I should like to see more frequent reference to our basic aim of improving the quality of human life, and a more insistent assertion of the basic, essential right of women not to bear children against their will.

Now I should like to refer briefly to a point that was debated at some length yesterday, arising from Dr. Howard Taylor's powerful pleas. We in the IPPF believe with him that ideally family planning should be an integral part of maternal and child health services, for every conceivable reason. But you cannot integrate with something that does not exist; and unfortunately in many developing countries there are virtually no maternal and child health services in many parts of the rural areas, where the bulk of the population is. The practical alternative, then, is whether to try some other method of supplying family planning in the interval or to do nothing until a maternal and child welfare service is forthcoming. Now this is not purely a question of priority in the allocation of scarce financial resources. It is not purely a question of training sufficient doctors and paramedical personnel. It is also, and sometimes crucially, a question of finding ways to induce doctors and paramedical personnel to serve in rural areas. I do not personally believe that these problems are insoluble in the long run but I believe they may often be in the short run, and that we cannot afford not to improvise in the interval. I suggest this is an area for investigation that deserves the urgent attention of us all.

It now seems likely that the IPPF can make its most significant contribution in the immediate future by trying to introduce and develop family planning by the formation of indigenous units in Latin America and Africa. Dr. Delgado's and Professor Caldwell's papers throw a most useful light on the situation and prospects in each of these enormous areas, and it is clear that the prospects generally are promising. It is, however, also clear from Professor Caldwell's exposition that a special effort is needed to bring the former French territories south of the Sahara into the movement. We ought clearly to plan how best this can be done, and preferably with the support of our French colleagues.

I should like to add a word on the financial implications. If the IPPF and the other voluntary agencies are adequately to serve these two vast awakening continents, they must be prepared initially to give the fledgling associations recurrent financial support. Now the provision of recurrent aid is of course very difficult for voluntary organizations not supported by fixed, assured endowments. I hope that this predicament will be sympathetically understood by those agencies, whether government or otherwise, that believe the voluntary organizations have a vital role to play.

And now, finally, may I make a hazardous incursion into the question of attitude research that was discussed in such an entertaining and lively manner this morning? I agree that it would be most useful if we knew why people, though undoubtedly strongly motivated and with ready access to convenient and efficient methods, yet fail to use them. But I fear that it will be difficult to find the right questions to produce the right answers if we base the questions on the presupposition that in this field of human relations reason prevails. Personally I have never found this to be the case.

ALAN F. GUTTMACHER, M.D., President, Planned Parenthood–World Population, United States

Before I can analyze the impact that this Conference and the developments so graphically told us will have on the American Planned Parenthood movement, I had best describe the current American situation.

Studies by the social research staff of Planned Parenthood–World Population (PP-WP) demonstrate that five million women in America of childbearing age must get their birth control help either from a voluntary agency or from a public facility. Last year, Planned Parenthood served 282,000 of the five million. According to a statement by Mrs. Oettinger, Director of the Children's Bureau, tax monies in the order of $1.75 million were spent last year to give birth control to people of this group. On the basis of $17.50 per case, a modest amount, we calculate that these expenditures covered perhaps another 100,000 women. Add to these another 100,000 served by the birth control facilities of voluntary hospitals; then in round numbers we find that a half-million American women of the five million are now receiving contraceptive help. Therefore, if our analysis is correct, there remain approximately 4.5 million American women still not getting adequate contraceptive advice and service. Hence I can assure those from the developing countries that in America we have problems not wholly dissimilar to theirs. And some of the developing countries possess an advantage that we lack—that is, their governments are strongly of the opinion that efficient contraception has a significant contribution to make to the welfare of the people and the state.

As many know, our government is warming up to this attitude. We are quite heartened by the recent statements of President Johnson in his State of the Union message (1965), and in his United Nations address in San Francisco. There are also bills before the United States Senate and the House of Representatives which in effect would mobilize a more forthright expression of interest by the United States government. The bills call for an Assistant Secretary of State and an Assistant Secretary of Health, Education, and Welfare for Population; for a White House conference on population in 1967; and for an increase in research funds for the general area of human reproduction. The sponsors of the bills believe that they may bring forth on the floors of the Senate and the House of Representatives favorable expressions of opinion which in turn might then invigorate the government to a more positive stand. At present, thirty-three of the fifty states have programs of family planning, but the birth control efforts are extraordinarily varied. In some states it is practically lip-service to a virtually dormant situation, while in other states very active programs are already in operation.

With the expansion of governmental interest and activity, the question for private agencies is whether they can live with the success they have helped bring about—to be sure, governmental participation has been their aim for the past twenty years. The fact that PP-WP served 22% more patients in 1964 than in 1963 makes one feel that there is still a real place for privately operated clinics. We shall continue to operate clinics, at least as long as we find that attendance is increasing. At the same time, voluntary birth control agencies have to be careful lest their operations reduce the pressure on the county, city, state, and federal governments to provide birth control services. In other words, we should not operate clinics too long. And therefore, I foresee the time when eventually the three hundred clinics operated by Planned Parenthood throughout America will be reduced to a relatively small number. This will be no tragedy, but a highly desirable result.

When and if this happens, the question naturally arises whether voluntary agencies still have a function in this field. In the first place, they should continue to maintain some clinics to carry out clinical research free of the constraint imposed by the red tape that is so likely to thwart such work in government clinics and also to establish a standard of clinical excellence for government to emulate. In the second place, we must maintain constant pressure on the government so that it will wholly fulfill its obligation to make contraception an integral part of normal public health procedures.

I am deeply interested in many of the suggestions made at this Conference, and I am particularly heartened by everyone's concern over the problem of illegal abortion. I think that the World Health Organization could make a significant contribution to the health of the world if they would make abortion the number one problem for study, because it is so universal, so destructive, and because we know so little about it. I can think of no agency better equipped to make such a study than the World Health Organization. I further feel that we ought to try, if possible, to approach the abortion problem more realistically, less from the religious and more from the ethical angle. I do believe that we in the medical profession—and I hope that many of you share my opinion—must re-examine our fixed and frozen attitudes toward a problem that requires careful, tolerant, unemotional investigation—an investigation slanted toward finding a solution.

FROM INTERNATIONAL ASSISTANCE AGENCIES

LEONA BAUMGARTNER, M.D., Agency for International Development, U.S.A.

Technical "assistance" is not the right word to describe our joint efforts. What we are really engaged in is technical *co-operation*—a give-and-take exchange of ideas, techniques, and information among people of related professional backgrounds in different technologies. The kinds of technical co-operation most needed in the operation of family planning programs were admirably summarized this morning by Lyle Saunders. I shall repeat something of what he said, and give a few practical examples of my own.

First, every country I know needs to improve its recording and analysis of vital statistics, so that the effects of family planning programs can be seen and measured.

Second, it should be part of technical co-operation to help develop an understanding of the interrelationships between economic growth and population growth. The investment of effort and funds that any country puts into family planning depends on the recognition, at the planning level, that economic and population growth are interdependent. Hence planning commissions should have the expert assistance of both economists and demographers.

Third, in the actual operation or initiation of family planning programs, there is great need for what Saunders called "operational research and administrative help." It is also called "evaluation," as well as a host of other terms.

For example, we need to exchange ideas on how to improve the administrative machinery, so that vehicles run and supplies get to where they are needed. The simple business of keeping an automobile on the road can make or break a family planning program. We need to know how to maintain local manufacture of loops and other contraceptive supplies. We need to find the best ways to put services where they are needed, and in ways that are easy for people to accept.

We need to know how to communicate across the barriers that exist between different groups. Almost everyone in every family planning program, and almost everyone at this Conference, is a city-bound professional who knows very little about how villagers think, feel, and act. We need to pay a great deal of attention to communication with village families, village leaders, health visitors, and indigenous midwives. On another level, we also need to know how to communicate with government planners and with business, labor, and other groups.

We need to know how to use research studies that have been made, and how to decide what further research is needed and what is not needed. We need to be able to decide what record-keeping is essential, and how to supervise daily work. We need to know how to build evaluation into action programs, and put results into action without delay. In short, we need good operational research.

Given the needs, who can fill them? There is the United Nations itself, and its many branches and multilateral agencies—UNICEF, WHO, UNESCO, FAO, ILO, and the various regional organizations of the United Nations. WHO has entered the field; there is the World Bank; ILO has a Population Branch; so does FAO. There is the multilateral Organization of American States with its excellent policy statements. We have heard today about family planning in Chile; there is a good deal of potential technical assistance developing in that country, as well as in Colombia. There is the Colombo Plan, in which "everyone is a donor country." ECAFE gives technical assistance to countries in its area. There is the International Planned Parenthood Federation and its various affiliates. There are bilateral efforts operating between the governments of two countries: Israel, Japan, Sweden, the United Kingdom, and the United States are all parties in bilateral co-operation in family planning programs.

We have heard a great deal about what is being done by that peculiarly American institution, the foundation, with the Population Council, the Ford and Rockefeller Foundations, the Milbank and Pathfinder Funds already in the family planning field. We sometimes overlook the many other philanthropic organizations and churches, and the international activities undertaken by universities. Big business firms, with their tremendous stake in economic growth, are also a logical potential source of help in family planning.

The very fact that there are so many different sources of technical co-operation creates another problem—the problem of getting them to co-operate among themselves without getting in each other's way. I suggest that family planning leaders should co-ordinate their activities with those already existing within their country. I have been struck, for example, by the lack of attention paid in Asia to all the local mission hospitals and clinics; yet they are continuously in touch with a large number of pregnant women. Labor unions and military groups might profitably be brought into the picture as well.

As Carmen Miro pointed out, geographical and cultural differences have important implications for technical co-operation. Here it may be useful to look at the past experience of different countries. For example, the United Kingdom and British Africa have a common tradition; they have the same governmental structures, and they understand each other. Or Latin America, where Chile and Colombia have a great deal to give to the other countries in that region. Or Moslem countries could get together to share their common experience. Then again, some countries are outstanding in particular skills: the United Kingdom, for example, was the first to bring together an outstanding group of operational research specialists. We might think of them as the group to call on for operational research.

The problem of foreign exchange has been brought up several times, but I cannot see that clinical supplies are a very great problem at this stage of the development of family planning programs. Vehicles are one of the big items needed, and I applaud the decision of the United States and United Kingdom governments and UNICEF to provide them. However, every country has foreign exchange; the question is, what is to going to be used for? Perhaps family planners need to persuade their governments that some small part of the foreign exchange available should be used to buy the supplies and equipment that have to be imported.

There is a great deal of experience accumulated on how to get family planning programs started, and there is need for continuing exchange, both internal and international, of information and experience on that subject.

However, I can see no evidence that any mass programs are really off the ground. There it seems to me that one of the greatest challenges for technical co-operation is to develop a variety of mass solutions. Although I doubt that many here would agree with me, I think there is a great deal to be learned from the malaria eradication program. Here is a successful mass program that has worked out techniques, learned how to apply those techniques widely, and has reached every home in many parts of the world. They learned how to use the improvements as they came along (as improvements will surely come in family planning techniques) and put them into the administrative machinery.

It has been said that all that was needed to make the malaria program a success was intelligence and perspiration. These are both needed in family planning programs. But I would add a third, and put it first—what we all need now is *in*spiration. We need to believe that something can and will happen. We need to care much more that it *does* happen. And we need to devote ourselves to seeing that it does happen.

MALCOLM TOTTIE, M.D., Senior Medical Officer, National Swedish Board of Health

In his opening remarks, John D. Rockefeller 3rd said that discussion on population problems could now proceed in a warm and sunny climate. I would like to remind you of the hurricane provoked by the delegate of Sweden in the United Nations when the question of the effect of population growth on social and economic development was raised only a few years ago. Within that short time we are now challenged, all of us, by the opportunity to do serious work on the problem and to find ways to tackle it. And those who witnessed the development in the World Health Organization Assembly last year surely will agree on the currently favorable trends.

What are the implications of this Conference from the point of view of the technical assistance community? You will note the word "community." That means that we are all, as we say in Swedish, in the same boat or perhaps on the same globe, and that we are all forced to work together. Experiences gained in different countries are of value to us all.

One type of technical assistance that is of extreme value is the development of different types of programs of evaluation. When we are assisting each other in a plan for a specific country, this gives us a challenge to review our own problems, procedures, and administrative systems. As another example, Dr. Taylor's statement on how to use the post-partum period provides a new impetus to re-evaluate what we are doing at home. Several speakers in this Conference have underlined the fact that family planning must be looked upon as part of an over-all health problem and be located within the health services of any country, as appropriate to the organizational structure. I would perhaps dare to say that it should be an integrated part in the health services of all countries. An expenditure on family planning is a good investment when distributing available funds. All of us on the health team are important: the public health man, the pediatrician, the obstetrician, the public health nurse, the midwife. We all must feel our responsibilities.

We must not forget what has happened since planning for technical assistance in this direct sense started. I had the honor of participating in the planning for Swedish technical assistance in Ceylon, only eight years ago, and at that time we had just heard about the pill and knew nothing about the loop, and still we tried to plan. And now the development on the technical side has been fast, rocket-like, and this gives us still better facilities to co-operate.

In a way, it is a pity that special films are still necessary to start and promote interest in population problems among medical students. [Such a film was shown at the Conference.] I can understand why it is so, but it is our fault that medical people are not sufficiently interested. It seems to me that doctors should work with human beings in their society to the utmost extent; and the society of today means, to my mind, more or less the entire globe. A conference like this, where people devoted to these problems come together to exchange experience, should serve as a base for raising the interest in all our countries, for making us all into a global technical assistance community.

I would like to add two specific comments. We must not forget that we are working with human beings. I was glad that Colonel Raina mentioned yesterday that it was a good idea to have the husband participate in the post-partum training in the maternity wards. For the long-term planning we should remember that the family consists of at least two persons, and we must have lasting motivation on the part of both partners, wherever possible.

Second, I was surprised that when we discussed conventional methods of contraception, hardly a word was said about coitus interruptus, one of the popular methods in many countries. This is perhaps because we physicians have said that this could be a dangerous method, or perhaps that people feel that they are up to date only when they are speaking of the more sophisticated methods.

This Conference marks another step forward in our goal toward healthy children and healthy parents. We do hope that the next time we meet—and I do hope we shall—we shall be able then to hear that in many parts of the world modern technology has increased not only the number of cars or television sets or moon rockets but also of families in which the situation complies with the human rights so admirably stated in the constitution of WHO: "Health is a state of complete physical, mental and social well-being and not merely the absence of disease"—in a world where the needs of the population are balanced and covered by existing resources.

FROM NATIONAL PROGRAMS

INDIA

LIEUTENANT-COLONEL B. L. RAINA, Director, The Central Family Planning Institute, New Delhi

The implications of this Conference are varied, and of far-reaching consequence. I have jotted down ten points that struck me as the major issues in the discussions.

First, I am left with the impression that national programs in different parts of the world are now getting into high gear. I am not disturbed by assertions that programs are still not off the ground. Some of us have been in this effort a very long time and for us this Conference is a matter of great encouragement. I have the feeling that several countries have gone beyond the planning stage and are now entering the action phase with a sense of urgency.

Second, the enthusiasm and the objective reporting that I have heard about the IUD has dispelled my anxiety, and the anxiety of many people, about its possible side effects. It is rare indeed that one finds such unanimity in the use of a device.

Third, there seemed to be a general feeling for the need for a strong, flexible, fast-moving organization and administrative machinery, as so carefully prepared and brilliantly brought out by Mr. Keeny with regard to budget and timetable. Such an organization should keep in view the personal problems of the workers in the field—their personnel management, their own problems, their pay scales, accommodations, facilities, etc.—so that they are able to deliver the goods.

The concepts of operational approach, target-bound and time-bound, and promotional-professional approach, have been the subject of some discussion. I feel after the discussion here that these two are not irreconcilable. It is a prerequisite to have a promotional-professional effort, but in many parts of the world now the stage has been reached for a time-bound, target approach to the problem. But even there the promotional-professional approach should continue. Even in countries where you have target-bound areas, there may be pockets where targets cannot be set up, and where promotional-professional efforts must proceed.

I also think there is general agreement that the administrators, the social scientists, and the technologists must work together. A social scientist who does not appreciate administration and technology is in an illusory world. Similarly, a technologist who does not consider social conditions is seeking to become a technical dictator.

The discussion at the Conference has reinforced the experience in many countries that maternal and child health and family planning should move together. I am quite certain that all students of medical history believe that the one medical discipline that has existed since the period of Adam and Eve is maternity and child health. I don't believe that a child is born without any maternal skill. Everywhere in the world there is at least an indigenous midwife. What we should aim at, as family planners, is to improve capability of this indigenous midwife, to give her training, to raise her status, to see that we utilize her to the maximum. I have not the slightest doubt, borne out by the experience of others too, that if the family planners are neglecting the indigenous midwife, if they are not making use of these people and not co-ordinating their efforts with family planning, then maximum success will not be attained. To me, it is not rational to see 200 or 500 women sitting in an MCH center, and four people sitting in a family planning clinic, because the two are not trying to work together. We should carry with us two operational concepts: (1) the period of pregnancy is the period of preparation par excellence, and (2) the post-partum period is the period of decision and action. Let us not divorce the midwifery service or the MCH service from family planning.

I agree with Dr. Guttmacher that we must have a "new look" everywhere, even at the international level, at the problem of abortion. It was very heartening to hear that WHO is already working on that delicate matter. In addition, besides the IUD and sterilization, other methods including coitus interruptus or rhythm still continue to play an important role. Moreover, in the process of integrating maternal and child health and family planning, with focus on the mothers, we should not lose sight of the fathers. Finally, administration and organization is important, very important, but it is only a part of the total key to the success of the program. Any planner who devotes his entire attention, or 90% of his attention, just to administration or organization, who thinks that if he just puts a few people here or there success will be achieved, will not reach his goal.

Fourth, steps are required to develop our program in formal education. In India we have no definite model to test out; so it will be necessary to experiment with processes and materials that may in time be of value. We have hardly begun. It may now be necessary to designate professional educators and family planning workers as a working group to initiate pilot projects in teacher-training institutions, to discuss the experience so gained, and then move quickly to the stage of syllabi, textbooks, and teacher training.

Fifth, we should rapidly advance, of course, in the field of training. Programs for short-term and long-term training, revision of training manuals, programmed teaching materials, teaching techniques, the development of university programs, family planning content for basic courses of doctors, nurses, and students of the social sciences—all these are needed.

Sixth, a great deal of valuable experience has been collected in the field of communications, and the material on exhibit at the Conference was most valuable. However, we do need systematic study of our impressions—are they correct? We are relying on the major combination of IUD and extension work. We should measure how far that will be sufficient to do the full job.

Seventh, in the field of research, we need to continue with biomedical inquiry. Various figures were given to the effect that a very appreciable number of women are still beyond the effective control of conception. So the search for new methods should not be relaxed. Basic research is an essential forerunner of any advances in applied technology. Nor should we relax our efforts to investigate the difficult questions of qualitative development.

Eighth, in the field of evaluation, we should evolve some standards, with regard to cost studies, more sensitive indices of changes in fertility, and the like.

Ninth, this Conference has shown a great spirit of mutual help in the area of international co-operation. The statement of the WHO representative and the fact that he and his two colleagues attended the Conference repeatedly are of great significance. There should be more free flow of information, and we may try regional workshops on specific aspects of the population problem. International co-operation can operate in many fields—in education, training, capital outlay, and other areas in which foreign assistance is required.

Lastly, one area gets bogged down because people say: "Well, it won't have immediate effects." Social legislation and social policy needs more attention. What would be useful? Improvement of the status of women, the employment of women, formal education, taxation policy—such matters are not really touched yet. I would hope that social scientists will help to identify areas where the forces of social policy can considerably strengthen the family planning program.

Man has been striving for thousands of years to enrich daily living. There have been ups and downs, revolutions and evolutions, development and disintegration. Out of twenty-six great civilizations, sixteen have died, nine broken down, and the current civilization is faced with serious threats. I am quite certain in my mind that this Conference has been a major contribution toward postponing that threat. As Mr. Asoka Mehta said only the other day in New Delhi, it is not the resources, it is not the number of people, it is not the technology, it is really the spirit of crusade that counts. And it seems to me that the sense of urgency that is witnessed in this Conference will gather up into a crusade for moderating fertility.

PAKISTAN

ENVER ADIL, S.Q.A., C.S.P., Family Planning Commissioner

Mr. Chairman, Ladies and Gentlemen: May I briefly recapitulate what has emerged during this Conference. Let me say at once that it is all very helpful. The ground is either ready, or fast getting ready, for national programs of family planning in many countries. In all countries the beginning is made by private effort. Government steps in at a later stage, after the climate is prepared.

Motivation is the most important ingredient of such a program. Person-to-person dissemination catalyzes the diffusion process. A high degree of organization is required to make the services and the availability of supplies go hand in hand. This organization must project itself in terms of local culture and requirements. Exchange of information is indispensable. A program of family planning must be flexible, pragmatic, and progressive. A drastic reduction in birth rates should not be sought for in a short time. There are no psychological breakthroughs. Family planning is a fashion of life that can be incorporated in a given value system by gradual stages. Evaluation should have a functional bias. The results of evaluation will have to be carefully sifted and processed before they yield informative end results. Funds and supplies needed for the program must maintain an uninterrupted flow. The program should not suffer from looseness, lacunae, or lack of perseverance. It is in some places unavoidable to employ trained paramedical personnel for IUD insertions, but medical supervision must be ensured in all such cases. It is necessary to emphasize the mechanics of how contraception works so that public opinion does not identify it with the taking away of life. It is not possible to do away with governmental co-operation; on the contrary, to make a program of family planning successful and effective governmental participation is necessary. Close co-ordination must be maintained between the different ministries or departments that represent the different specialties involved in the program. Transportation difficulties need to be overcome and a system devised for this purpose must be efficiently administered.

There is diversity of details both in nature and extent so far as the solution to the population problem is concerned. The details of the solution or of the scheme planned for this purpose must therefore vary in different areas, maybe even within the same country. Maternity services need to be distinguished from family planning services in point of time and in approach. The experience of the period during which a mother is based at a maternity center is certainly a great motivation for family planning. But this sort of motivation is a passing phase and, while it is there, contraception cannot be practiced. The mother then gets busy nursing her new baby and forgets all about what she has passed through in giving birth to it. Effective motivation must therefore synchronize with the right time to practice contraception and also with the availability of contraceptive services and supplies. The emphasis therefore shifts to the synchronizing of motivational, clinical, and supply agencies during the normal life of the female, when she is not pregnant. While motivation should be concentrated and constant in nature, supply channels must be extensively spread out. In Pakistan we have almost 200,000 commercial points, shopkeepers, retailers, grocers, and so on, dispensing contraceptives as a part of their normal merchandise, backed by 53,000 personnel—50,000 operational and 3,000 supervisory—to motivate and bring clients for contraceptive services and supplies.

Supervision of paramedical by medical personnel involves a certain amount of administrative co-ordination in the field of transport and personnel posting, so that the various lady health visitors under the charge of a medical doctor, are located equidistant from the doctor and at the same time evenly spread out through the population. At the village level the "dais," or midwives, should be sufficiently compensated for family planning services so that lowering the birth rate does not mean monetary loss to them.

There are common characteristics, common difficulties, and common interrelationships operating in family planning programs in different countries and there is therefore a large area for which common approaches can be devised by mutual consultation. Overpopulation is not merely an economic problem; it is more gravely a social problem. Legislative provisions can be permissive in enabling the program to be executed and to streamline the administrative procedures wherever required for this purpose. Legislation also legitimizes the concept of family planning in the eyes of the public. Monetary incentives are useful to mobilize adequate interest for the program among medical and paramedical personnel whose services for family planning can be obtained only on a part-time basis. It is not feasible to have full-time family planning doctors in sufficient number. Rather, it is preferable to have as many full-time family planning functionaries in the non-clinical field as possible. Religious and social prejudices can best be overcome by the rising tide of progressive living and the practical acceptance and practice of the concepts of progressive life in allied fields of social-economic activity. Documentation is important but it should be simple and kept at the barest minimum. The action workers entrusted with documentation should not feel it an encumbrance but an asset. The content of training and research material should be kept under constant review. What is needed is an action program and a bold, imaginative, and earnest effort to implement it and above all, perseverance in such an effort.

Mr. Chairman, this Conference has been a tremendous success in every way. No aspect has been left untouched and what has been established by this Conference is the workability of family planning on a world-wide basis. The Conference has proclaimed internationally that family planning is a legitimate and laudable concept. It has found that the future destiny of mankind will depend on the extent to which this concept is realized in practice.

TURKEY

NUSRET FIŞEK, M.D., Under-Secretary of State, Ministry of Health and Social Assistance

It is difficult to predict what the ultimate influence of this Conference will be. I can only discuss the information received here which is potentially helpful to our program in Turkey. We are at the beginning of the family planning effort in Turkey. Since we are awaiting the decisions of the scientific board on family planning methods to be authorized, the papers and discussions on contraceptive methods are particularly useful to us. We have submitted the excellent and very complete studies done by Dr. Tietze to the scientific board. However, many members were still hesitant to accept the IUD for immediate nationwide use even after reading these studies. The question raised was that inasmuch as these studies were done in the United States, in well-equipped and well-staffed clinics, the scientific board did not really know what would be the results of mass application in developing countries where the application environment would be quite different. Consequently what we have learned here about such mass programs will be extremely valuable for our program in Turkey.

Another point of significant interest is the use of paramedical personnel for IUD insertions. It is difficult to expect this in my country because the medical profession is very conservative. But the fact that paramedical personnel are being allowed to insert IUD's in some countries will make it easier for us to establish the role of the general practitioner in an IUD insertion campaign, as against the concept of insertions being done *only* by OBG's. A most valuable adjunct to this is the definitive material on perforations and the information on the times of the cycle when IUD insertion may be done.

The discussions on the use of oral contraceptives are also valuable for us. I have been personally reluctant to accept the idea of pills in a nationwide program, considering the cost and probable low acceptability to illiterate women. However, the reports we have heard here are quite encouraging. The knowledge about medical effects on liver function and lactation plus the figures provided by Mr. Levin about the numbers of women using pills throughout the world will be important to our scientists who are presently reviewing the situation in Turkey. In addition, the report by Dr. Klinger on Hungary is most important to Turkey. Many of our people have always thought that the legalized system of abortion in Hungary and the low rate of population increase there represent an example of an overpowerful effect of a population control policy. But the important thing that emerges from this report is that actually abortion in Hungary is permitted not as a means of population control, but simply to prevent non-medical abortion.

Finally, I have some comments on the administrative (operations) and research aspects of a family planning program. I personally feel we should have had more discussions about the administrative elements of population control in this Conference. In reality, this is the most difficult part of any program. Research on a continuous basis must go hand in hand with the administration of the program. Without good data, and timely data, the administrator is in the dark. So I appreciated the presentation of Dr. Saunders. If a man works in research he is usually thought to be smart because his function is to criticize and provide ideas. But the administrator must shoulder the total burden, and he is always subject to criticism for mistakes, no matter how trivial. Let us add a note of caution at this point: promote research, but be sure to keep a balance between research and the action efforts. What we need, therefore, is to find that rare category of man, the research-minded administrator in the action programs who will encourage researchers to accept administrative responsibility. In this manner we can develop the ablest type of person for what is most urgently needed now—action.

SOUTH KOREA

TAEK IL KIM, M.D., Chief, Maternal and Child Health Section, Ministry of Health and Social Affairs

1. Population control is one of the most important responsibilities of a government, whether a country is overpopulated or not. The answer is successful family planning in mass programs.

2. Most of the people in the world are demanding information and service for birth control. Every government should provide family planning programs to meet people's demands through the mobilization of money, man power, and material within their present capacity—and immediately.

3. It is not wise to wait until the academic people agree on a method or a measure that is 100% acceptable. There will be endless arguments about advantages and disadvantages on many topics. If we consider that family planning is a public health measure, the public health staff should make every possible effort, utilizing the soundest methods available to provide benefit to the majority of people. The role of the public health officer is a key factor in initiating a national program, as well as in conducting and evaluating the program.

4. The IUD is one of the soundest methods of family planning in

the mass, because it is cheaper, safer, more effective, and has a high acceptance rate.

5. It will be wise to adopt several contraceptive methods, with emphasis on the IUD, for comprehensive implementation in national programs, especially in the developing countries. This is also a way to prevent induced abortions.

TAIWAN

S. C. HSU, M.D., Chief, Rural Health Division, Joint Commission on Rural Reconstruction

Since our program was among the first to utilize the newly developed IUD, we had the good fortune to help demonstrate its applicability in mass programs of family planning. However, we have recently reached a plateau that may also be indicative of what will happen in other national programs, and hence we are becoming more and more conscious of the need for new strategy, new tactics in dealing with this problem. We need more ideas and better information, and this Conference has provided some that we may consider in our own situation.

For example, I was particularly impressed with Dr. Taylor's suggestion that the ideal time for family planning education is the antenatal and parturition period and the ideal time for contraceptive service is the post-partum period. This is in principle a very good guide, but it will take a great deal of organization to implement it in our situation. Our doctors do not like to insert the IUD within two months of delivery, and after that they like to have a clear indication, by blood test, that the patient is not then pregnant. This means at least two visits to the doctor, and it complicates the program in other ways as well. It would be very helpful if we could persuade the doctors to do insertions about a month after delivery, for there would be no problem of pregnancy at that time. Perhaps we shall recommend that after further consideration of this important idea.

I was also interested to learn that in the very rare cases of perforation of the uterus, the best thing to do often is to leave the condition alone, but under close medical surveillance. That may indeed be preferable to more substantial remedies that we are now inclined to follow.

Moreover, we now recommend the insertion of IUD's only after the menstrual period. So far as unintended pregnancies are concerned, as well as lengthening the time in which insertions are possible, it would be useful to be able to do insertions during menstruation as well. I was glad to learn here that such insertions have as good results as the others. With further regard to insertion technique, it is always helpful to be able to cite the judgment of the distinguished obstetricians here, and not simply that of public health doctors, to the effect that the thread should not be cut too short, and similar matters.

We were also interested to learn of the Latin American experience in connection with the successful use of the rhythm method by means of abstinence during the pre-ovulatory stage. We are always concerned about those for whom the IUD is not appropriate, and although we see considerable difficulty in implementing such an effort, it is good to know that work is going forward along that line. Similarly, it is interesting to hear of the experience of controlling induced abortions through legalizing the matter.

Finally, we still have with us the problem of developing more interest and action among the low-motivated people. For certainly our effort must be toward more efficient programs. On this problem more perhaps than any other, time is important. In the long run, the birth rates will of course fall. But we are seeking to telescope twenty-five years into ten years or even five—to demonstrate that money and effort can buy time. And when we are dealing with rates of increase, time is critical.

It is in this connection that I make my last observation, with regard to research and operations. Researchers are typically very articulate and hence always receive a certain amount of attention. But the operational people are very important for this entire enterprise, and we should find ways to develop balanced programs in which both kinds of contributions receive their due credit.

61

FAMILY PLANNING PROGRAMS TODAY: MAJOR THEMES OF THE CONFERENCE

RONALD FREEDMAN
Director, Population Studies Center
University of Michigan

In historical perspective, we may be at a turning point in world demographic trends. If we believe what we say about the importance of population trends, the next several decades may mark also an important turning point in world history. Such grandiloquent statements seem a little pompous, but I believe they are justified by the facts today and by what seems plausible, if not probable, for the next five to twenty years.

I base this rather sweeping assertion on two observations. First, there is reason to expect that in the next five years we shall see for the first time in history[1] in at least several small but significant populations really major national fertility declines induced, or at least accelerated, by organized family planning programs. Second, in many other larger countries there are likely to be significant beginnings of fertility decline with new vigorous organized programs, although whether these efforts in other countries will be as successful as needed to accomplish their objectives is still very problematic.

In Taiwan and in Korea such major induced fertility declines are

This statement was the final summary address at the Conference. It represents the author's views, at the time, of the major themes and implications of the Conference papers and discussions rather than any attempt to summarize, in the fashion of a rapporteur, the large body of important, detailed material presented at the meeting.

[1] There have been previously organized efforts which have affected the course of fertility, but these were not efforts specifically to reduce birth rates. For example, the legalization of abortion in Japan and in the Eastern European countries resulted largely from attempts to replace a large volume of illegal induced abortions with abortions under safer medical auspices.

likely to begin this year or next. In Taiwan, and probably in Korea too, the cumulative effect of the new IUD and related programs should accelerate gradual fertility declines already underway. By the end of this year about 10% of the married women in the childbearing years in Taiwan and perhaps a similar proportion of those in Korea will have become at least initial users of the effective IUD in the official programs. This does not take into account the even larger numbers of additional couples who are and will be practicing other forms of family limitation—contraception and abortion—as a result of trends preceding the organized program and as a result of the important indirect effects of the present organized programs.

In Singapore and in Hong Kong, too, the privately organized programs, with some government support, are now reaching a significant number of women, with a notable quickening of the response after the introduction of the IUD.

We must recognize that the fertility declines in these four populations, if they materialize as expected, will only demonstrate initially that organized programs can make a difference in small populations in which conditions are relatively favorable.

I have elsewhere[2] defined the situations that seem especially favorable to a fertility decline in developed societies as those:

1. Where mortality has been relatively low for some time.
2. Where significant social development is underway so that many people are linked to groups and institutions outside their extended family and local community for both the definition and achievement of their life goals.
3. Where there is evidence that many people wanting moderate-size families are beginning on their own to try to limit family size.
4. Where there are effective social networks transcending local communities through which family planning ideas and services and other modernizing influences can be disseminated.
5. Where there is an effective organization to provide family planning information and services.
6. Where such newer contraceptive devices as the IUD and oral contraception are available.

We do not know what combinations of these several factors will produce a given fertility decline. It is plausible that the more of each present in a situation, the greater the potential for fertility decline. We urgently need data from action studies to tell us more about necessary minimal and optimal combinations. Such studies need not delay vigorous action. On the contrary, they are possible only with such action.

[2] "The Transition from High to Low Fertility: Challenge to Demographers," *Population Index*, October, 1965.

I hazard the prediction of really major fertility declines in the next five years in at least the four populations mentioned, because they seem to have, in substantial measure, the six conditions specified. The fact that the probable success of organized programs in these four countries comes under unusually favorable conditions does not diminish the historic importance of the event. In the 1960 Milbank–Population Council Conference,[3] only five years ago, there were doubts that organized efforts could make a difference on a large scale anywhere soon. The four populations to which I refer were not even represented by scholars or reports at the 1960 conference. They were hardly mentioned. These places where early successes are possible offer an important opportunity for research and evaluation which will help the programs in other countries.

What about the rest of the developing world? Obviously, I cannot either survey the detailed situation in every region or make a single generalization that will cover the whole world. However, I believe the accumulating evidence is that in almost every major region and country there are at least significant minority strata of the population in which the conditions are favorable. Even if fertility decline is less likely in the less developed and isolated village areas, there are enough people in the more favorably situated sectors in most countries to make at least modest over-all fertility declines plausible in such large populations as those of India and Pakistan. A few years ago I was more pessimistic. The possible grounds for my cautious optimism now for the larger world arena are, first, that there are signs of success in populations and areas that most of us thought not very promising a few years ago. Second, there is much more evidence that there is a real determination in such areas as Pakistan, India, Turkey, and Tunisia to "do it now," really to implement reasonable plans with massive systematic action.

The fact that there are at least initial signs of success in places previously considered unpromising may mean either that conditions were more favorable than we had imagined or that our assessment of the necessary conditions was incorrect. For example, five years ago at the 1960 conference, Africa was neither represented nor mentioned, apart from Egypt. The initial reports here from Tunisia are most promising. Caldwell's assessment of the favorable possibilities in the modernizing sectors of major parts of sub-Saharan Africa and of the possibility of fairly rapid diffusion of social change indicates at least favorable initial possibilities in an area in which I, at least, had expected no beginnings for some decades.

3 The proceedings of that 1960 conference are reported in Clyde V. Kiser (ed.), *Research in Family Planning* (Princeton: Princeton University Press, 1962).

The reports from Thailand are another example of success under conditions that would have led many of us to expect failure a few years ago. We must recognize as remarkable the achievement of a 20% acceptance rate for IUD's in less than a year in the rural area of Photharam, where many women are illiterate, where previous knowledge and practice of family planning were almost non-existent and where parts of the population are accessible only by riverboat.

In Latin America also there is evidence that, at least in urban areas, there was a desperate resort to abortion and now other forms of family planning are beginning to move forward under the same cross-pressures of lower mortality and rising aspirations that set off the fertility part of the demographic transition elsewhere.

Many other specific examples could be cited to illustrate the basis for more optimism and a greater expectation of fertility decline than we anticipated a few years ago. But these would at best be only pilot or isolated examples.

To be realistic, we must remember that even the really major induced fertility declines that seem plausible and probable for Taiwan, Korea, Hong Kong, and Singapore are in the future. The lesser and rather later fertility declines that seem plausible for such other countries as Pakistan, India, and Turkey depend in part on whether the remarkable and promising plans which have been made really are carried forward to completion in systematic detail with the imagination and energy of which there is present evidence. Moreover, while modest fertility declines in the next decade in the larger developing countries seem plausible to me, whether they will be great enough to meet the apparent need and goals is still highly problematic.

Success will come only over some time with systematic implementation of the specifics of many particular programs. This Conference and the rapidly accumulating literature of the field offer some possibility of very tentative generalizations about current experience and future possibilities. The evidence is so uneven, recent, and complex that I really cannot offer a summary of what we know scientifically. The list of observations I am about to present is really only one man's personal assessment of what seems plausible.

1. In the last five years, we have learned in many places that a significant minority and often a majority of the population are interested in family limitation. These results emerge from studies on every continent and in many regions and countries. The few studies like that from Indonesia, reporting lesser interest, appear to be exceptions. What is remarkable is the rough similarity of survey results from such a wide variety of cultural settings. I take this to mean that there will be a rough similarity of response as changes in mortality and social condi-

tions put various peoples in a new and similar socio-demographic position.

These survey results indicating verbal assent and interest in family limitation certainly are more widely available than a few years ago, but we know that such verbal assent is not necessarily followed by widespread adoption of family limitation practice. Does this mean that the responses are not based on conviction or are only intended to please the investigator? Although this may be true to some extent and in some places, the fact that a population perceives that family planning ideas are held by such respected "others" as the investigators is in itself a significant basis and reinforcement for social change. The small family idea, at least, must be there.

In any case, I would accept the responses on such surveys as valid initially until they are tested by a really effective, persistent, all-out service and information effort. Devious psychological explanations of why the respondents really did not mean what they said may be too easy a rationalization for a feeble or insufficiently thorough effort.

2. There is much evidence that very large numbers of couples in developing countries are ambivalent about family planning. In the early stages of the fertility phase of the demographic transition we cannot expect the couples to be rationally and unambiguously for or against small families or family planning. They are under cross-pressures between traditional values and the persistence of traditional life conditions, on the one hand, and newer values and their partially changed situation, on the other. The resulting ambiguity and internal conflict probably account in large part for inconsistencies in survey responses and for the fact that significant numbers of couples who say they will adopt family planning do not, and that others who say they will not practice actually do so. In such conditions of ambiguity the couples are more likely to be moved to favorable action if their already positive feelings are strengthened by messages and stimuli from a variety of different trusted sources which make them feel that family planning is generally accepted and practiced by others. As I will shortly indicate on other grounds, I believe this argues for staged concentrated efforts in selected areas rather than for spreading the effort thinly over the whole population.

3. Some population sectors are readier than others to adopt family planning. Large-scale adoptions so far are reported from places where mortality declines and some socioeconomic change has been great enough so that a significant number of young parents are under the cross-pressures of large numbers of living children and rising aspirations for them. The strata and countries that are most ready may be defined briefly as better educated, urban, and in the modern sector of

the economy. At least these are the sectors in which family planning is adopted independently of organized programs. But there are now some significant exceptions.

4. Very significant proportions of the less literate, more rural, and less advanced sectors of the population are adopting family planning, at least in the Korean and Taiwanese programs and perhaps now in some parts of India and Pakistan, where they have as a model a significant elite which has learned to practice family limitation (even if ineffectively) on its own. The elite groups appear to be able to adopt family planning on their own, but given the continuing support and reassurance of the organized programs the less advanced strata accept family planning in proportions that are lower than those of the elite but very significant because the disadvantaged strata are so large.

We do not know yet whether a large-scale organized program can be equally successful in parts of the population where there is no leading model elite or where mortality is still relatively high with little social development. We still have not observed the results in a very disadvantaged population of the same kind of all-out persistent program effort using the best of methods and personnel.

At the 1960 conference there were a number of suggestions that experimental tests should be made using equally vigorous efforts in selected areas varying in mortality and in social development. My personal view is that this is still not only possible but very desirable in such large-scale programs as those of Pakistan, India, and Turkey in order to learn something of the threshold mortality and development levels at which a significant fertility decline is possible. Probably, success will be much greater in the more advantaged parts of the population and will diffuse from there to the rest. I would concentrate disproportionate efforts there, but I would allocate a significant minority of the resources to the best possible programs in selected less advanced parts of each country. This is controversial and the stakes are high; so "all the eggs should not be in one basket." Whatever the distribution of effort between more and less advanced areas of a country, it is very desirable that an evaluation be made from the beginning to study this question. Since resources at least of personnel are initially limited, some decision about priorities is essential. An effort at systematic scientific evaluation of this crucial question need not retard action. It may accelerate it.

5. The power of indirect diffusion in spreading information about family planning is being demonstrated in one study after another in various countries. This suggests that serious consideration should be given to plans for systematically and deliberately spacing the maximum organized efforts to reach every second or third village or area

rather than to try to blanket all areas more thinly. In the Taichung study, for example, where neighborhoods were the basic unit, the acceptances were highly clustered by group. Despite reasonably significant over-all success, 30% of the neighborhoods had no acceptances at all. There was apparently greatest success where group reassurance was possible.

It seems likely, as Moye Freymann has indicated in this Conference, that discussion and diffusion of family planning ideas is more likely to occur where there are numbers of people in significant groups practicing and discussing family planning.

Some have suggested that it is desirable to get at least one couple in each village practicing family planning. Quite to the contrary, I would argue that it is better to have ten couples in each of ten villages than one in each of a hundred villages. With nucleation and concentration of effort and practice the couples will reinforce each other, the limited program personnel can provide services and further reassurance. The "good word" will spread then by diffusion to the other places as a basis for organized programs there in the next phase.

There is some concern that such diffusion can spread bad news as well as good. I would have faith that the message in this field is fundamentally so good and so much needed that any unfavorable rumors will be only temporary and will be countered by the overwhelming weight of the truth.

6. The IUD appears greatly to increase the success of both private and public programs. Almost all the success stories to date involve major reliance on this device. These results are certainly consistent with the reasonable view that at any given level of motivation, and especially in an ambivalent population, acceptance will be greatest with a method that is long-lasting, without any further action, cheap, unconnected with the sexual act, and relatively effective and trouble-free.

But apart from the continuing need for medical studies, the evidence from this Conference is that it would be well to avoid total reliance on the IUD.

First of all, we have heard evidence for the United States and from Taiwan that 40%–50% of the women expressing an interest in the IUD will either be advised not to use it initially or will not be using it two years after insertion for various reasons.[4] It is likely that no other

---

[4] As Dr. Tietze pointed out at the Conference, these continuation rates may be too low, because they do not take into account the women who gave up the IUD for reasons not related to the method itself (e.g., to have another baby). However, even if we were to adjust the continuation rate upward to 65% or 70%, the discontinuance by 30% or 35% still poses a major problem.

contraceptive (with the possible exception of the contraceptive pill) can claim even this level of effective use over a two-year period. Nevertheless, this still leaves a very large group for whom other methods must be available.

Second, we must remember that the initial success with the IUD still involves a very small proportion of any population, reaching 25% in only a few places. What will happen in the necessary second and third and succeeding rounds still remains to be seen. Reasonable optimism is justified and necessary, but proof will be even better.

While there are reports of promising success with the use of paramedical personnel for IUD work, it seems likely that there are places and groups for whom the traditional non-clinical methods or oral contraception may still be most appropriate because of the lack of needed clinical personnel or for other reasons.

The fact that the IUD may not do the whole job should not be a basis for discouragement. After all we have only presumptive evidence that the recent major successes depended entirely on the IUD. For example, the Korean and the Taiwanese programs exemplify not only the use of the IUD but also very well organized programs carried out systematically and thoroughly, with good leadership and under relatively favorable conditions. What would have happened if a similar organized effort went into a program based on the traditional methods? I would guess that the response would have been considerably less but we do not know by how much. A significant, if lesser, success with traditional methods may be possible.

At the 1960 conference it was suggested that a mass media campaign might be successful in Calcutta in view of the favorable conditions including the considerable number of people already interested and practicing traditional methods of contraception. Nothing was done then, but I understand that this year a mass media program involving the IUD has had very successful beginnings. Do we know that a similar program based on the traditional methods might not have succeeded, if in lesser degree, some years ago?

I think there is a general consensus at this Conference that the IUD may have revolutionary significance in fertility control. This need not lessen a continuing concern with knowing more about the conditions under which the traditional methods or other new methods will be acceptable. In this connection, the Western countries may make a contribution by additional research to understand why their populations continue to rely more or less successfully on more traditional and even primitive methods.

7. Family planning programs today, whether successful or not, are

still predominantly female-oriented. The workers are mainly female, the approach is mainly to wives, and the IUD (which is sweeping the field) and the available orals are female methods. A dominant theme of the 1960 conference was that the limited success of organized programs to that date resulted from reliance on female clinical methods. There was considerable emphasis on the idea that new efforts should involve male workers approaching husbands with male and especially non-clinical methods. The spectacular rise of a female method, the IUD, has eclipsed this line at least temporarily. Again let us remember that so far we are reaching with the IUD's only 5%–25% of the eligibles in the more successful programs while the goal is 50%–75%. How will the larger goals be attained? Surely the IUD may reach many more in succeeding rounds and with diffusion, but it is not implausible that there may be significant parts of the population who can be reached most successfully by male workers and male methods. It has been suggested in the Conference that the role of the male in the discontinuances of the IUD should be investigated too.

My personal view is that the overwhelming dominance of the male in developing societies is one of a large number of ideas that may be more myth than reality and that it should be tested. The idea, for example, that only female doctors can serve the women in any given country should be tested before being accepted, if acceptance of the idea poses real problems in a particular place. "Let's try it" is a policy that has eliminated a number of imagined barriers in similar situations. In the end, whether more attention should be given to husbands seems to be an empirical question in which the necessary and desirable tests have not been made. It is plausible that the male non-clinical methods used successfully in the West have some significant place in the developing countries too.

8. Abortion is a very important method of family limitation in many places. It well may be the most widely used single method in the world today. Large increases in illegal induced abortion rates are reported from many places in the period when families feel the pressures between the large numbers of surviving children and rising aspirations for them. Legalized abortion under medical auspices as the leading method now is a major mass phenomenon in countries with combined populations of more than 400 million.[5] In addition, illegal abor-

---

[5] We are here counting Japan, the Soviet Union, and the Eastern European socialist countries, excluding Albania. Although we have no actual data on the number of abortions in the Soviet Union, it is likely that there are a very considerable number. Reports from visitors to mainland China indicate that a considerable number of abortions are being performed, at least in urban hospitals. This large population is not included in the count of 400 million.

tion probably is a leading method if not the most important single method used in many other countries.[6]

This massive world phenomenon has a number of implications. In the first place it appears that in Taiwan and Korea, at least, many of those adopting the IUD formerly have used illegal abortion. For such couples, the new practice may be more important for family health and welfare than for the effect on the birth rate. Certainly the former goal is at least as important as the latter, but this should warn us that in assessing the effect of the adoption of IUD on demographic trends we must know the former fertility and fertility limitation practices of the acceptors. We must also know the later history and practices of the significant minority who give up the IUD.

A second implication is that we need to know much more about this massive world phenomenon. Our colleagues in Japan and in the Eastern European countries are in the best position to answer pressing questions here. Apart from the moral issues involved, there is yet relatively little hard data to support the easy generalization that repeated abortions under medically sound auspices are harmful. Mr. Klinger has provided us illustrations of the kind of data we need, in his report showing that prematurity is associated with repeated legal abortions in Hungary.

I suspect that in the next few years we may even begin the difficult, but I think feasible and necessary, task of studying the incidence, characteristics, and consequences of illegal abortions in Western countries.

Over-all, it is clear that we have not yet faced squarely and honestly the moral, medical, and social issues involved in this phenomenon. There is already a trend for liberalization of abortion laws in some countries, at least as a transitional measure and in special circumstances, and the issue is alive in other places. Whether there should be further liberalization and of what character in any particular country is a matter for internal decision, but it is unlikely to be made intelligently without a greater willingness to study the facts about it dispassionately.

9. Women who have demonstrated their fecundity to themselves by a recent pregnancy or birth are most interested and concerned about family planning. This is plausible, of course. But we are getting increasing empirical evidence about the actual importance of this group, for example, from the abortion studies, from the very significant postpartum programs in hospitals, and from the data in the Taiwan and

[6] We know, for example, that in Korea, Taiwan, and Chile there are a considerable number of illegal induced abortions on the basis of specific empirical evidence. For many of the Western European countries and the United States there are no specific data but there is indirect evidence that the number of illegal induced abortions must be very considerable. In such countries as Greece, for example, it is probable that abortions may be as important as any other single method.

Korean programs on the relation between acceptance rates and months since last birth.[7] Increasing ingenuity is needed to devise ways of using village midwives and others with local intelligence to identify this minority of high-risk women for special programs. Lists of women who are currently pregnant and classifications of the others by months since last birth may furnish the best priority lists for family planning programs.

10. There is a growing recognition that important existing social and economic networks may be used to implement and strengthen family planning programs. These include pre-eminently the established commercial networks which penetrate into almost every village today. They also include the schools, the armed forces, and various occupational and other special groups. Such a list should also include the networks of private medical and health personnel which have been only lightly involved in many countries by the much smaller medical contingent engaged in the formal family planning programs.

These various natural social networks in their massive totality make up the society as a going concern. The more the family planning message and services can be carried by them in their well-tested channels, the less reliance will be placed on special family planning organizations, necessarily artificial and clumsy, created *de novo*. Such existing networks as retail and wholesale distribution systems connect at many points with the underlying basic structure of small groups of friends, relatives, and neighbors in which patterns of norms and behavior are shaped and maintained.

Several of the national plans for family planning rely on independent action by individual couples to accomplish a major part of the national planning goal. All of them probably have as an objective an eventual "take-off" point where the formal organized programs will have done their major work and most family planning practice will be carried on independently of them. How much of this happens depends on how soon family planning ideas and services and information are brought into the existing natural social networks. So far these promising possibilities have been tried only on a small scale. They have not been given the large-scale mass trial they deserve.

This is one of a number of areas in which only a large-scale effort can succeed.[8] For example, using a small number of storekeepers in a

---

[7] In Taiwan, one study indicates that the variations in fertility between major social and economic groups related more closely to the interval since the last birth than to the intervals between births.

[8] The issue here is whether it is necessary to have a program reach a minimum "critical mass" before success is likely. I would argue that small isolated pilot programs are likely to fail, because they will not have the mutually reinforcing stimuli from a

limited area as depot-keepers for supplies does not mobilize either the ingenuity or resources of the marketing organizations behind them. It does not build up the perception among the storekeepers that selling contraceptives is regarded as normal and profitable by their peers and superiors from whom they derive their commercial norms and ideas.

11. Research findings and procedures—both basic and applied—are providing essential information to guide and direct family planning programs at various levels. While there are some differences of opinion about priorities and emphases in research, there appears to be a general consensus in the Conference that we know enough to launch and guide major action programs while the research continues. Although there is much that we do not know, much of it can best be learned if research—both operational and basic—has an integral connection with the action programs.

My personal impression is that, in close contact with action programs, basic and applied research are interpenetrating. Whatever is lacking in present action programs, I doubt that the problem anywhere is too much research. I would recommend that every national program have a strong central research and evaluation unit close to the top administration so that administrative and research ideas can continually interact.

I have enough faith in the value of research to predict that necessity will lead administrators to ask for more rather than less research in successful programs. In various places, of course, there will be the essential laboratory work in developing new contraceptives. These must be tested ultimately in the clinics and then in field settings. For example, the efforts at mass IUD programs will be drawn by necessity to utilize field samples of continuing IUD users, of those who discontinue, and of non-users, to determine not only retention, expulsion, removal, and pregnancy rates but also to determine prior and subsequent fertility rates of these various groups in order to assess effects on the birth rates.

Promising methods of measuring the birth rate in countries with poor vital records have been described. Work in this direction undoubtedly will continue, since it may be decades before routine vital registration systems can provide the needed data. My impression is that administrators are insufficiently aware that this still is a technical and difficult job which cannot be done by inexperienced personnel as an adjunct to other types of survey work. A serious present problem is that most of the experiments in this field provide only birth rates for

variety of sources or the legitimation that comes from the perception that family planning is being discussed over a wide area.

an entire country. To be of maximum value for either administrative decisions or basic research it is necessary that sample size be expanded or other means be used to derive estimates for local areas. It is very desirable that there should be means for estimating age-specific birth rates as well as crude birth rates, since the crude rates may be quite misleading in some cases. There are now a number of countries in which age distributions are so distorted that crude birth rates may decline without any fundamental change in the underlying fertility rates or family planning practices. Conversely, there could be increases in crude birth rates temporarily even while family planning is spreading and age-specific birth rates are falling. Besides, knowing age-specific fertility rates permits a much more informed evaluation of just where in the family life cycle the programs are succeeding or failing.

Sample surveys have been and will be used not only to assess changes in the fertility and family planning atttitudes and practices in the population of couples but also to assess their contact with and evaluation of the actual programs. Such surveys if properly done at regular intervals can serve a wide variety of research and evaluation needs. In this respect, my impression is that we are *not* doing what can be done with competent use of the best-known survey methods. In several developing countries my observation is that available trained personnel are not used for this important work and that there are too many poorly done, non-comparable local surveys.

I believe that any significant national program should have in its central evaluation and research unit a strong survey research unit which could do regular KAP[9] surveys, surveys of IUD users, and also spot studies of the places and problems which turn up as administrative difficulties. Such special studies will be most useful if they have regular cross-section surveys as points of comparison. The work of such units should also include surveys of health personnel and the administrative staff of the programs. An essential part of the work of such a unit should be to help the administrator know what is actually going on. In such large and complex programs as those of India and Pakistan, for example, even the vigorous administrators will have difficulty in knowing from month to month what is really happening without some independent information source of this sort. Precisely when administration is vigorous, the lower levels of the administration may find themselves constrained by the system to tell the higher administrators what they want to hear rather than what is really happening.

Much important research, both basic and applied evaluation, can be done through the records of the ongoing action program. The coupon

9 This abbreviation is used commonly now to stand for surveys of knowledge, attitudes, and practice.

system adopted in a number of countries in the IUD programs, for example, provides very significant and useful data. In these and other instances serious consideration should be given to having reports go directly to a central unit to bypass the delays and errors of a step-by-step march up the administrative ladder.

At various points in the Conference, there was a recognition that in many places basic fertility trends will be affected by actions and trends outside the program as important as the influence of the formal programs themselves. For example, the Korean plan projects a substantial adoption of family planning outside the formal program. This suggests the need in research for placing the formal program and its effects in the context of more general data on marriage, family planning, and reproductive patterns. For this purpose it was recognized that general field studies rather than analysis of clinical or program records alone will be required. Even for studies of the formal programs routine administrative records will have to be supplemented by field studies. For example, since many people accepting the IUD mass programs will not return to the clinics for checkups, sampling of the acceptors in the field will be required to estimate the rates of expulsion, removal, pregnancy, and so on.

In a conference involving both persons primarily oriented to action and those primarily oriented to research, it was inevitable that there should be some disagreement about the kinds and amounts of research that should be done. There was also discussion of whether "basic" research would impede or help the action programs in the near or longer future. I have expressed my own view, as a researcher, earlier in the Conference: that basic research could often best be done in an action setting, that it was likely to yield unforeseen practical benefits if located close to central administrative institutions, and that there is no evidence that avoiding "basic" research makes for more effective or vigorous programs. Those interested in basic research can earn the respect and the co-operation of the administrators for their work if they will provide the administrator simultaneously with the related operational and evaluational data he needs in the short run and if they give priority in analysis to the data the administrator needs to guide his program. As family planning programs assume a massive character, they become one of the natural phenomena which the demographer or the social scientist will want to include in his plan for studying the basic forces affecting fertility change.

12. The more successful programs probably are distinguished less by their content than by the systematic and persistent and thorough implementation of whatever the program is. Moye Freymann has given us in the Conference a significant and insightful classification of

important organizational principles. Given an initial elimination of absurd lines of action, vigorous implementaton of any of a number of reasonable alternatives is likely to give rather similar results.[10] I agree with Leona Baumgartner's assessment that organization and administration may be the key problem in family planning programs today. While further research on administration is needed and desirable, I agree with her that enough is known now to organize and administer the programs effectively for at least those large population groups ready for the first or second initial rounds.

My impression is that significant parts of the populations have been ready for some time, and that the leadership finally is recognizing and catching up with the readiness of the population. There are many signs in field reports and in the discussions of this Conference of a robust spirit of "do it now," "do it vigorously," and "do it thoroughly."

[10] This idea is very well stated in the paper by Bernard Berelson, "National Family Planning Programs: A Guide," *Studies in Family Planning*, No. 5 (supplement), December, 1964. Many of the ideas in the present summary are drawn from this excellent paper.

CLOSING REMARKS

FRANK W. NOTESTEIN
President, The Population Council

It is my pleasant duty, on behalf of the Ford Foundation, the Rocke-feller Foundation, and the Population Council, to thank all of the participants.

To me, this Conference is particularly important as evidence that we have passed the stage of haranguing one another about the need for action in the regulation of fertility. Instead, we discussed, on the basis of actual experience, the ways in which the practice of family planning can be most efficiently spread. Our field is thus coming of age. We have explored many aspects of the subject and the quality of the work has been high. I am sure, however, that I express the general hopes and expectations in suggesting that ten years from now our work here will seem to have been both amateurish and shallow. We are at the early stages of systematic efforts to reduce birth rates. The significant fact is that in so many places throughout the world we have passed the stage of policy formation and moved on to that of action. You are the pioneers in that endeavor, and the record of these meetings shows that you are very effective pioneers indeed.

I would like to give my personal impression of three points that seem to me to have a bearing on the future of our work. One refers to the events that have fostered the formulation of population policies, one to the motivation for family planning, and one to my personal estimate about the future.

Political leaders, whatever their personal convictions, need the sup-port of the articulate public for their innovative programs everywhere in the world. One of the most fruitful ways of attaining such support for family planning is to involve a broad spectrum of the intellectual life of the community in the actual study of population problems and

827

their solution. Study by respected leaders in demography, biology, medicine, economics, sociology, and religion of the implications of the developing situation for their special fields has done much to dissipate earlier misunderstanding, to foster the early appreciation of emerging trends, and to create solid backing for the regulation of fertility.

It is, of course, true that so far as objective science is concerned, much research does not need to be duplicated in country after country. But, politically at least, much duplication is essential. Particularly where the modification of ancient values is concerned, there is a very high tariff on imported ideas. Research is important for the new knowledge it uncovers, for testing the local validity of imported knowledge, and for involving the interest and political support of major sectors of the intellectual community.

It is my personal opinion that concern about questions of population in the emerging nations has not been aroused mainly by hortatory speeches about "The Population Problem." It has come mainly, I think, from two sources: (1) the economic planning boards, where technical people with slide rules face the task of planning for schools, jobs, savings, investment, urbanization, and the whole range of practical problems faced by nations making the effort to modernize in the face of population growth; and (2) the medical profession, which has had to deal with the sufferings of the mother whose health and life have been endangered by excessive childbearing, or jeopardized by crude abortions. The interest of both groups is essential if strong support for national family planning programs is to be obtained.

Turning now to the problem of motivation for family planning, I would urge that we move rather carefully. A good many speakers have emphasized the fact that it is important to strengthen the parental interest in family planning. Clearly, the problem is one of both means and motives. At present three facts impress me: (1) the motivation to practice birth control is shown to be present in substantial parts of many populations; (2) it is constantly being strengthened by the whole process of modernization; and (3) it seems likely that the motivation to practice birth control will be further strengthened by the example of those who practice birth control successfully.

In the present state of affairs, then, it seems to me more important to provide service to those already interested than to strive hard for new converts. It is my belief that in the securing of new converts, moreover, low-pressure informational services will be more effective than exhortation.

I also hope that we will study the problem of motivation carefully before launching programs with strong positive or negative inducements to parents. There is real danger that sanctions, for example through taxation, would affect adversely the welfare of the children. There is also danger that incentives through bonuses will put the whole matter of family planning in a grossly commercial light. It is quite possible that to poor and harassed people financial inducements will amount to coercion and not to an enlargement of their freedom of choice. Family planning must be, and must seem to be, an extension of personal and familial freedom of choice and thereby an enrichment of life, not coercion toward its restriction. I hope that work in the field of motivation will go forward carefully, bearing in mind the importance of strengthening parental awareness of the freedom to choose.

Finally, I should like to join those who have been making predictions about the future course of events. Such predictions are nothing more than guesses, but I should like to enter mine along with the others we have had. Mine, too, are optimistic.

I should like to hazard the guess that in two decades the major problems of overriding population growth may well be on the way to solution. Consider how far we have come. Ten years ago, in most of the developing countries, the field was so sensitive that the subject of family planning could be discussed, if at all, only with the greatest care. Who then would have guessed that in a single decade the governments of the majority of the people in the newly developing world would have decided to try to reduce the birth rate as a matter of national policy? Who would have dreamed that the technology of birth control would have been so dramatically advanced? Most remarkable of all, who would have thought that the people themselves would be so alert and interested, as they have shown themselves to be, in country after country?

But the events of the past decade represent the beginning, not the end. They are only the beginning of governmental concern, of public interest, and of technological development. We have every reason to expect at least equally dramatic developments in the next decade. Indeed, the trend will almost certainly accelerate. We are not working in a vacuum of social-economic change. The world is now aroused to problems of poverty, and the world's governmental, international, and religious institutions now recognize the bearing of population growth on these problems. We have the policies, the interest, and the technology, and we are in process of getting the organization. Against this background it seems reasonable to expect an acceleration in the spread of family planning.

Under these circumstances, I think that within two decades the rate of population growth may well be brought to 1% or 1.5% throughout major sectors of the newly developing world. If so, we are entitled to hope that population growth will not remain the almost insuperable obstacle to economic development that it appeared to be only a few short years ago. I am not suggesting that the task is done—it is scarcely started. But we know now what to do, and in the first approximation how to go about the job. If we have learned in the past, it is reasonable to assume that we can learn even more in the future. Whether or not my guess is justified will depend considerably on the people attending this Conference and their colleagues at home. The situation is one of unparalleled responsibility and opportunity for us all, whether in private foundations, planned parenthood organizations, or in governmental and international service. I am not in the least worried about duplication. All our efforts are urgently needed. As the Foreword points out, we as a group are fortunate in being in the right place at the right time.

All who have attended this Conference and have seen the high caliber of leadership and professional skill can gain new hope that our present problems will be well on their way to solution in a much shorter time than we have thought.

If so, a generation that is chiefly conspicuous for conducting the most brutal wars in the world's history may yet redeem itself by creating for the first time in man's history a world in which health, education, and opportunity for individual fulfillment can be secured for all the world's people.

PARTICIPANTS IN THE CONFERENCE

ADIL, ENVER, *Commissioner of Family Planning, Pakistan*

ADRIASOLA, GUILLERMO, M.D., *School of Public Health, University of Chile*

ALLEN, LeROY R., M.D., *The Rockefeller Foundation, India*

ANDERSON, LEWIS S., M.B., CH.B., *Technical Assistance Division, The Population Council*

ANDERSON, RICHMOND K., M.D., *Director, Technical Assistance Program, The Population Council*

ANGULO ARVELO, L. A., M.D., *Division of Population, Ministry of Public Health, Venezuela*

ARIFFIN BIN MARZUKI, M.B.B.S., *Maternity Hospital, Kuala Lumpur, Malaysia*

ASAVASENA, WINICH, M.D., *Chief, Division of Maternal and Child Health, Ministry of Health, Bangkok, Thailand*

ASNA, ALAEDDIN, *Family Planning Program, Turkey*

AVENDANO, ONOFRE, M.D., *Chief, Obstetrical and Gynecological Service, Hospital Ramón Barros Luco, Santiago, Chile*

BALFOUR, MARSHALL C., M.D., *Medical Adviser to the President, The Population Council*

BAUMGARTNER, LEONA, M.D., *Assistant Administrator for Technical Cooperation and Research, Agency for International Development, Department of State, Washington*

BERELSON, BERNARD, *Vice-President, The Population Council*

BERMAN, EDGAR, M.D., *Chief Health Consultant for Latin America, Agency for International Development, Department of State, Washington*

BLAKE, ROBERT R., *The Ford Foundation, India*

BLAND, FRANCIS E., *Ministry of Overseas Development, London*

BOGUE, DONALD J., *Director, Community and Family Study Center, University of Chicago*

BOWERS, JOHN Z., M.D., *President, The Josiah Macy Jr. Foundation, New York*

831

BRONNENKANT, PAUL H., *President, Hallmark Plastics, Inc., Buffalo, New York*

BROWN, GEORGE F., M.D., *The Population Council, Tunisia*

BURLESON, DAVID, *Associate Director, The Pathfinder Fund, Milton, Massachusetts*

CALDWELL, JOHN C., *The Australian National University, Canberra*

CHANDRASEKARAN, C., *United Nations Regional Demographic Adviser, Economic Commission for Asia and the Far East, Bangkok*

CHINNATAMBY, SIVA, F.R.C.O.G., *Family Planning Association, Colombo, Ceylon*

CHOLDIN, HARVEY M., *The Population Council, Academy for Rural Development, Comilla, East Pakistan*

CHOW, LIEN-PING, M.D., *Taiwan Population Studies Center, Taichung*

CHUN, DAPHNE, M.D., *President, Family Planning Association, Hong Kong*

CORFMAN, PHILIP, M.D., *Consultant in Obstetrics and Gynecology, National Institute of Child Health and Human Development, Bethesda, Maryland*

CORSA, LESLIE, JR., M.D., *Director, Center for Population Planning, University of Michigan, Ann Arbor*

CUMMINS, G. T. M., M.R.C.O.G., *Chief, Obstetrics and Gynaecology, Queen Elizabeth General Hospital, Barbados*

DALY, AMOR, M.D., *Le Sous-Directeur Medical, Ministry of Public Health and Social Affairs, Tunisia*

DAVIS, RUSSELL H., JR., *The Population Council, Turkey*

DELGADO GARCÍA, RAMIRO, M.D., *Faculty of Medicine, Universidad del Valle, Cali, Colombia*

DEVERELL, SIR COLVILLE, *Secretary-General, International Planned Parenthood Federation, London*

DEVINNEY, LELAND, *Deputy Director, Humanities and Social Sciences, The Rockefeller Foundation, New York*

DILL-RUSSELL, P. W., M.R.C.S., *Deputy Medical Adviser, Ministry of Overseas Development, London*

DIXON, MORRIS S., JR., M.D., *The Population Council, Pakistan*

DOOLEY, SAMUEL W., M.D., *School of Public Health, University of California, Berkeley*

DURAND, JOHN, *Assistant Director, Bureau of Social Affairs, Population Branch, United Nations, New York*

ENGEL, HERMAN J., *Herman J. Engel Film Productions, New York City*

ERENUS, NEÇDET, M.D., *Ankara, Turkey*

FAWCETT, JAMES, *Demographic Division, The Population Council*

FIŞEK, NUSRET H., M.D., *Undersecretary of State, Ministry of Health and Social Assistance, Turkey*

FLORENDO, PURIFICACIÓN T., M.D., *Silliman University Medical Center, The Philippines*

FLORIO, LLOYD, M.D., *Chief, Health Services, United States Operations Mission, The Philippines*

FREEDMAN, RONALD, *Director, Population Studies Center, University of Michigan, Ann Arbor*

FREYMANN, MOYE W., M.D., *The Ford Foundation, India*

AF GEIJERSTAM, GUNNAR, M.D., *Department of Obstetrics and Gynecology, Karolinska Sjukhuset, Sweden*

GEISENDORF, WILLIAM, M.D., *Department of Obstetrics and Gynecology, Hôpital Cantonal, Geneva, Switzerland*

GENTRY, JOHN T., M.D., *Assistant Dean, School of Public Health, University of North Carolina, Chapel Hill*

GIDEON, HELEN, M.B.B.S., *The Rockefeller Foundation, India*

GILLE, HALVOR, *Deputy Chief, Office of Social Affairs, The United Nations, Geneva*

GILLESPIE, ROBERT W., *The Population Council, Taiwan*

GLASS, DAVID V., *The London School of Economics and Political Science*

GOLDENSTEIN, ADOLPHO, M.D., *Clinical Director, Family Planning Service, São Paulo, Brazil*

GRIFFITHS, WILLIAM, *School of Public Health, University of California, Berkeley*

GUAL, CARLOS, M.D., *Presidente, Sociedad Mexicana de Nutrición y Endocrinologia, Mexico City*

GUNAWAN, KARTONO, *Chief, Perspective Planning Bureau, National Development Planning Authority, Djakarta, Indonesia*

GUSTAFSON, HAROLD, *School of Public Health, University of California, Berkeley*

GUTTMACHER, ALAN F., M.D., *President, Planned Parenthood–World Population, New York City*

HANSON, HALDORE, *The Ford Foundation, Pakistan*

HARKAVY, OSCAR, *Director, Population Program, The Ford Foundation*

HARPER, PAUL A., M.D., *School of Hygiene and Public Health, The Johns Hopkins University, Baltimore, Maryland*

HARTMAN, PAUL, *The Population Council, Korea*

HAUSER, PHILIP M., *Director, Population Research and Training Center, University of Chicago*

HAWLEY, AMOS H., *The Population Council, Thailand*

HAYES, GUY S., M.D., *The Rockefeller Foundation, Colombia*

EL HEFNAWI, FOUAD, M.CH., *Department of Obstetrics and Gynecology, University of Cairo*

HELLMAN, LOUIS, M.D., *Downstate Medical Center, State University of New York, Brooklyn, New York*

HILL, R. T., M.D., *Division of Public Health Services, World Health Organization, Geneva*

HILL, REUBEN, *Program Associate, The Ford Foundation*

HIMES, JAMES, *The Ford Foundation, Argentina*

HSU, SHIN-CHU, M.D., *Chief, Rural Health Division, Joint Commission on Rural Reconstruction, Taipei, Taiwan*

HUSEIN, HASAN M., *Vice-Chairman, Egyptian Association for Population Studies, Cairo*

KANGAS, LENNI, *The Ford Foundation, Cairo*

KAPRIO, L., M.D., *Director, Division of Public Health Services, World Health Organization, Geneva*

KATAGIRI, TAMEYOSHI, *Regional Secretary, Western Pacific Region, International Planned Parenthood Federation, Tokyo*

KEENY, S. M., *The Population Council, Taiwan*

KIANOURI, ROBABEH, M.D., *Director of Family Planning, Public Health, Teheran, Iran*

KIM, TAEK IL, M.D., *Chief, Maternal and Child Health Section, Ministry of Health and Social Affairs, Seoul*

KINCH, ARNE, M.D., *Sweden-Ceylon Family Planning Pilot Project, Colombo*

KIRK, DUDLEY, *Director, Demographic Division, The Population Council*

KISER, CLYDE V., *Milbank Memorial Fund, New York City*

KLINGER, ANDRAS, *Hungarian Central Office of Statistics, Budapest*

KOIDE, SAMUEL S., M.D., *Bio-Medical Division, The Population Council*

LAMONTAGNE, RAYMOND, *Associate to Mr. John D. Rockefeller 3rd, New York City*

LAURENCE, KENNETH A., *Bio-Medical Division, The Population Council*

LEAVITT, HAROLD J., *School of Industrial Administration, Carnegie Institute of Technology, Pittsburgh, Pennsylvania*

LEVIN, HARRY L., *Consultant for Distribution Channels, The Population Council*

LIKIMANI, J. C., M.B., CH.B., *Chief Medical Officer, Ministry of Health and Housing, Kenya*

LIM, MAGGIE, M.R.C.S., *Medical Representative, Southeast Asia and Oceania Region, International Planned Parenthood Federation, Singapore*

LIPPES, JACK, M.D., *Department of Obstetrics and Gynecology, University of Buffalo, New York*

LUBIN, DONALD, *Director, Western Hemisphere Region, International Planned Parenthood Federation, New York City*

MCALLAN, JAMES W., M.B., CH.B., *Medical Officer of Health, Kenya*

MAIER, JOHN, M.D., *Associate Director for Medical and Natural Sciences, The Rockefeller Foundation*

MARTÍN PINTO, ROBERTO, M.D., *Head Professor of Obstetrics, University of Buenos Aires, Argentina*

MASLOWSKI, JAMES, *Office of Technical Cooperation and Research, Agency for International Development, Department of State, Washington*

MATHEWS, BETTY, *The Ford Foundation, India*

MAULDIN, W. PARKER, *Associate Director, Demographic Division, The Population Council*

MEHLAN, K.-H., M.D., *Director, Institute of Hygiene, and Dean of the Medical Faculty, University of Rostock, East Germany*

MENDOZA, OFELIA, *Field Director, Western Hemisphere Region, International Planned Parenthood Federation, New York City*

MENDOZA HOYOS, HERNÁN, M.D., *Chief, Division of Population Studies, Colombia Association of Medical Faculties, Bogotá*

MERRILL, MALCOLM, M.D., *Director, Health Service, Office of Technical Cooperation and Research, Agency for International Development, Department of State, Washington*

METINER, TURGUT, M.D., *Director of Population Planning, Turkey*

MEYLAN, JACQUES, M.D., *University Obstetrics and Gynecological Clinic, Cantonal Maternity Hospital, Geneva*

MIRO, CARMEN A., *Director, Latin American Demographic Center, Santiago, Chile*

MORSA, JEAN, *Institute of Sociology, Free University of Brussels, Belgium*

MOTT, STEWART R., *The Mott Foundation, Flint, Michigan*

MUÑOZ TORCELLO, CARLOS, M.D., *Center of Population Studies, Ministry of Labor and Indian Affairs, Lima, Peru*

MURAMATSU, MINORU, M.D., *Department of Public Health Demography, Institute of Public Health, Tokyo*

NORTHROP, EUGENE P., *The Ford Foundation, Turkey*

NORTMAN, DOROTHY, *Statistician, The Population Council*

NOTESTEIN, FRANK W., *President, The Population Council*

NOZARI, A., M.D., *Director General, Public Health Services, Iran*

PEASE, CLIFFORD A., M.D., *Technical Assistance Division, The Population Council*

PEERS, ROTHA, *Secretary, Medical Committee, International Planned Parenthood Federation, London*

PENG, JUI-YUN, M.D., *The Population Council, Thailand*

PHON, SANGSINGKEO, M.D., *Undersecretary of State for Public Health, Thailand*

POFFENBERGER, THOMAS, *The Ford Foundation, India*

POOL, D. IAN, *Department of Sociology, University of Ghana, Accra*

PRACHUABMOH, VISID, *Faculty of Political Science, Chulalongkorn University, Bangkok, Thailand*

PRICE, DAVID, M.D., *Deputy Surgeon General, Department of Health, Education, and Welfare, Washington*

PUGA, JUAN, M.D., *Clinica Obstetrica Universitaria, Hospital José Joaquín Aguirre, Santiago, Chile*

RADEL, DAVID, *Research Assistant, The Ford Foundation*

RAHMAN, SHAFIQUR, M.B.B.S., *Family Planning Officer, East Pakistan*

RAINA, LIEUT.-COL. B. L., *Director, Central Family Planning Research Institute, India*

RAMACHANDRAN, SOUNDARAM, *Deputy Minister of Education, India*

RAO, K. N., M.D., *Additional Director General of Health Services, Ministry of Health, India*

RETTIE, JOAN, *Regional Director, Europe, Near East and Africa, International Planned Parenthood Federation, London*

REVELLE, ROGER, *Director, Center for Population Studies, Harvard University, Cambridge, Massachusetts*

RIDER, ROWLAND, *School of Hygiene and Public Health, The Johns Hopkins University, Baltimore, Maryland*

RIVERA NIEVES, PEDRO, M.D., *Department of Obstetrics and Gynecology, University Hospital, San Juan, Puerto Rico*

RODRIGUEZ, ANIBAL, M.D., *Universidad Católica de Chile, Santiago*

ROMERO, HERNÁN, M.D., *Catedra de Higiene y Medicina, Escuela de Medicina, Universidad de Chile, Santiago*

ROSALES, VINCENT J. A., M.D., *Department of Medicine, Santo Tomas University, The Philippines*

DEL ROSARIO, APOLONIO, M.D., *City Health Officer, Manila, The Philippines*

ROSS, JOHN A., *Demographic Division, The Population Council*

SATTERTHWAITE, ADALINE P., M.D., *The Population Council, Puerto Rico*

SAUNDERS, LYLE, *Program Associate, The Ford Foundation*

SEGAL, SHELDON J., *Director, Bio-Medical Division, The Population Council*

SEHGAL, B. S., *Specialist (Rural Health), Planning Research and Action Institute, Lucknow, India*

SELTZER, WILLIAM, *The Population Council, Pakistan*

SEN, MUKTHA, M.B.B.S., *Director, All-India Institute of Hygiene and Public Health, Calcutta*

EL SHAFEI, A. M. N., *Director, North African Demographic Center, Cairo*

SOBRERO, AQUILES J., M.D., *Director, Margaret Sanger Research Bureau, New York City*

SOUTHAM, ANNA L., M.D., *Department of Obstetrics and Gynecology, Columbia College of Physicians and Surgeons, New York City, and Medical Consultant, The Population Council*

STEPHAN, FREDERICK F., *Senior Consultant, Demographic Division, The Population Council*

STYCOS, J. MAYONE, *Director, International Population Program, Cornell University, Ithaca, New York, and Consultant on Latin America, Demographic Division, The Population Council*

SWINGLER, JOAN, *Executive Secretary, International Planned Parenthood Federation, London*

TAEUBER, IRENE B. *Office of Population Research, Princeton University, Princeton, New Jersey*

TAKESHITA, JOHN Y., *Population Studies Center, University of Michigan, Ann Arbor*

TATUM, HOWARD L., M.D., *Department of Obstetrics and Gynecology, University of Oregon School of Medicine, Portland, and Medical Consultant on Latin America, The Population Council*

TAYLOR, HOWARD C., JR., M.D., *Chairman Emeritus, Department of Obstetrics and Gynecology, Columbia College of Physicians and Surgeons, New York City, and Medical Consultant, The Population Council*

TEN HAVE, RALPH, M.D., *Research Associate, Center for Population Planning, School of Public Health, University of Michigan, Ann Arbor*

THAKOR, V. H., M.B.B.S., *Deputy Director of Public Health Services, Gujarat State, India*

TIETZE, CHRISTOPHER, M.D., *Director of Research, National Committee on Maternal Health, Inc., New York City*

TOTTIE, MALCOLM, M.D., *Swedish Committee on International Health Relations, Stockholm*

TROWBRIDGE, JAMES W., *The Ford Foundation, Mexico*

TURABI, BATUL, M.B.B.S., *Senior Medical Officer, National Research Institute of Family Planning, Pakistan*

VAILLANT, HENRY W., M.D., *Cytology Laboratory, Queen Elizabeth General Hospital, Barbados*

VALAORAS, VASILIOS G., *Director, Department and Museum of Hygiene, University of Athens, Greece*

VELÁSQUEZ PALAU, GABRIEL, M.D., *Dean, Faculty of Medicine, Universidad del Valle, Cali, Colombia*

VIEL VICUNA, BENJAMIN, M.D., *Department of Preventive Medicine, University of Chile Medical School, Santiago*

WAYLAND, SLOAN, *Teachers College, Columbia University, New York City*

WELLS, BRADLEY, *The Ford Foundation, India*

WHITNEY, VINCENT H., *Representative for Asia, Demographic Division, The Population Council*

WIKNJOSASTRO, HANIFA, M.D., *Department of Obstetrics and Gynecology, School of Medicine, University of Indonesia, Djakarta*

WILLIAMS, L. L., F.R.C.S., *Senior Medical Officer, Victoria Jubilee Hospital, Kingston, Jamaica*

WINNICKA, WIKTORIA, M.D., *Chief Medical Officer, Maternal and Child Health, World Health Organization, Geneva*

WISHIK, SAMUEL S., M.D., *Graduate School of Public Health, University of Pittsburgh, Pittsburgh, Pennsylvania*

WITSCHI, EMIL, M.D., *University of Basel, Switzerland*

WRAY, JOE, M.D., *The Rockefeller Foundation, Colombia*

WRIGHT, R. D., *Department of Community Health, University of Lagos Medical School, Nigeria*

YANG, JAE MO, M.D., *College of Medicine, Yonsei University, Seoul*

YPSILANTIS, JAMES N., *International Labour Office, Geneva, Switzerland*

ZSCHOCK, DIETER, *The Ford Foundation, Colombia*

INDEX

Jacobs, Aletta, 184
Jamaica: contraceptives in, 444, 448–49; Family Planning Association, 444, 449; IUD in, 444–49; Lippes loop in, 444–49; Papanicolaou smear in 445; Population Council in, 444; sterilization in, 444, 448
Japan: abortion, induced, in 7–9, 13, 16–17, 19, 194, 811; charges to patients in, 12–13, 17; contraceptives in, 8–13, 16, 17, 19, 194; contraceptives, oral, in, 488; Eugenic Protection Law, 8, 9; Family Planning Federation, 15; government role in, 8–17, 775; industry, private, role of, in, 14–15, 17; information and education in, 9–18; IUD in, 18, 19; Japanese Medical Association, 8; literacy in, 15; MCH in, 11; midwives in, 10–11, 12, 16; National Eugenic Law of 1940, 8; Population Association, 8; Population Problem Council, 8; religion, attitude of, in, 7; volunteer organizations in, 15
Java: government role in, 503; literacy in, 507–8; MCH in, 504; Population Council in, 504
Johns Hopkins Hospital, 459–60
Johns Hopkins University: in Pakistan, 127
Johnson, Lyndon B., 261, 269, 795

KAP (knowledge, attitudes, practices) studies, 579, 655–68
Kennedy, John F., 269
Kenya: budget and cost of program in, 773; government role in, 172, 773
Knowlton, Charles (*Fruits of Philosophy*), 184
Konikow, A. F., 377

Lactational amenorrhea as contraceptive method, 379–80
Latin America: abortion, induced, in, 255, 256, 618; Center for Population and Development Studies of Peru, 250; contraceptives in, 628–32; contraceptives, oral, in, 423, 631–32; Cornell University in, 615–18; Demographic Association of El Salvador, 250; Family Growth in Metropolitan America Study, 631; Family Welfare Society of Guatemala, 250; government role in, 249–50; information and education in, 624–26, 633, 634; IPPF in, 794; Latin American Demographic Center (CELADE) in, 250, 252, 615–18; Population Council in, 615; Program of Comparative Fertility Surveys, 615–34; religion, attitude of, in, 257, 627–34; Roman Catholic Church in, 249; United Nations in, 250; United

Nations Population Branch in, 615–18. *See also* individual countries
Lippes loop, 425–32; problems of manufacture of, 495–99; widespread use of, 488–89; in Barbados, 451–54; in Chile, 241, 242, 243; in India, 120; in Jamaica, 444–49; in South Korea, 22–25, 26, 28, 425–26; in Taiwan, 57, 61–67, 69, 675–88, 692–93, 699; in Thailand, 103; in Tunisia, 155, 157, 158. *See also* Intra-uterine device
Literacy: in Hong Kong, 79; in Japan, 15; in Java, 507–8; in Pakistan, 124, 127–29, 478, 479; in South Korea, 26; in Thailand, 96, 526; in Tunisia, 152; in Turkey, 298; in USSR, 215. *See also* Information and education; KAP studies
Los Angeles County Grand Jurors Association: and induced abortion, 456–57

Malaysia: budget and cost of program in, 86–88; contraceptives in, 87; contraceptives, oral, in, 87; Federation of Family Planning Associations, 86–89; Ford Foundation in, 89; government role in, 85–89; information and education in, 86–87; IPPF in, 86–87, 88; IUD in, 87; MCH in, 86–87, 88; National Family Planning Board, 88; Pathfinder Fund in, 86; religion, attitude of, in, 87; Sarawak Family Planning Association, 88; Singapore Family Planning (SFPA), 86; Social Welfare Lotteries Board, 86, 87; sub-fertility in, 87
Malthus, Thomas R., 184, 186–87
Malthusian League: Germany, influence of, in, 188; Great Britain, 184, 187
Margulies coil: in Barbados, 451; in Chile, 242, 243; in Taiwan, 57; in Tunisia, 155, 158. *See also* Intra-uterine device
Maternal and child health service (MCH), 433–41, 768; in Ceylon, 109; in Chile, 230, 246; in Hong Kong, 72, 75, 76, 80; in Japan, 11; in Java, 504; in Malaysia, 86–88; in Puerto Rico, 230–32; in Singapore, 89–90, 93; in South Korea, 22, 28, 309, 315; in Sweden, 198; in Taiwan, 56, 68; in Thailand, 96–97; in Tunisia, 153, 155; in Turkey, 302; in UAR, 145, 146, 150; in Yugoslavia, 220–21
Mauritius: budget and cost of program in, 773; government role in, 773
Mendoza, Ofelia, 237
Mensinga pessary, 184
Michigan Population Studies Center (MPSC): in Taiwan, 57
Midwives, 324, 408; as agents for materials,